TECHNOLOGY OF RUBBER AND RUBBER GOODS INDUSTRIES

TECHNOLOGY OF RUBBER AND RUBBER GOODS INDUSTRIES

Written By

EIRI BOARD OF CONSULTANTS & ENGINEERS

ENGINEERS INDIA RESEARCH INSTITUTE

4449, Nai Sarak, Main Road, Delhi - 110006 (India)

Ph: 91-11-23918117, 23916431, 23840361

Fax: 91-11- 2391 6431, 2391 8117

*** E-Mail: eirisidi@bol.net.in**

***Website: www.eiriindia.org**

Sole Distributor :

INDIAN INSTITUTE OF CONSULTANTS, 4/27 ROOP NAGAR, DELHI -110007

PRINTED & PUBLISHED BY

ENGINEERS INDIA RESEARCH INSTITUTE

4449, Nai Sarak, Main Road, Delhi - 110006 (India)
Ph: 91-11-23918117, 23916431, 23840361
Fax: 91-11- 2391 6431, 2391 8117
* E-Mail: eirisidi@bol.net.in
*Website: www.eiriindia.org

DISTRIBUTED BY

SMALL INDUSTRY RESEARCH INSTITUTE
INDIAN INSTITUTE OF CONSULTANTS

ISBN: 81-86732-59-4
Printed in New Delhi (INDIA)

Rs. 900/-

Printed & Published by Sudhir Gupta for "Engineers India Research Institute" 4499 Nai Sarak, Main Road, New Delhi -110006

Preface

*The book **Technology of Rubber and Rubber Goods Industries** covers almost all the basic and advanced details to setup own Rubber Goods Industries. The new edition of the book is covering latest technology including Natural Rubber, Classification, Properties, Uses and Manufacture; Latex Processing and Applications; Chemical Aspects of Rubber Technology; Physical Aspects of Rubber Technology; Styrene Butadiene Rubber (SBR); Butyl and Halobutyl Rubbers; Nitrile and Polyacrylic Rubber; Neoprene (Polychloroprene) and Hypalon Rubber; Silicone Rubber; Reclaimed Rubber; Elastomeric composites with Reference to Tyre Technology; Latex and Foam Rubber; Vulcanisation; Manufacturing Techniques of Rubber Products; Recycling of Wastes from Rubbers and Plastics; Useful Information; Quality Control in Rubber Industry; Suppliers of Plant and Equipment; Suppliers of Raw Materials.*

The book has been written for the benefit and to prove an asset and a handy reference guide in the hands of new entrepreneurs and well established industrialists.

Director
ENGINEERS INDIA RESEARCH INSTITUTE
Nai Sarak, New Delhi (INDIA)
E-Mail: eirisidi@bol.net.in

Contents

1

Natural Rubber, Classification, Properties, Uses and Manufacture

INTRODUCTION

Any of a number of natural or synthetic high polymer shave unique properties of deformation (elongation or yield under stress) and elastic recovery after vulcanisation with sulphur or other cross-linked agent, which in effect change the polymer from thermoplastic to thermosetting. The yield or stretch of the vulcanised material ranges from a few 100 to over 1000%. The deformation after the break, called permanent set, is usually taken as the index of recovery. It ranges from 5-10% of natural rubber to 50% or more for some synthetic elastomers, and varies considerably with the state of vulcanisation and the pigment loading.

NATURAL RUBBER

The structural formula of natural rubber polyisoprene (C_5H_8) is given below:

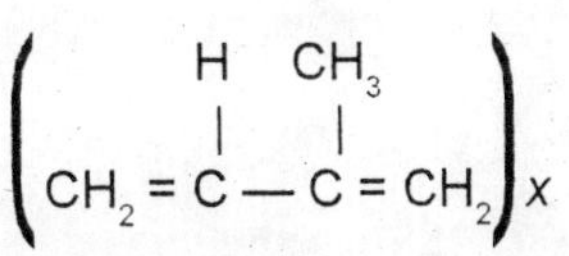

Crude (Unvulcanised)

Properties - Crude rubber has a specific gravity of 0.92. It is chemically unstaturated and amorphous when unstretched, but has oriented crystal structure on stretching. Not stable to temperature changes (thermoplastic); readily oxidisable by mastication. Soluble in acetone, carbon tetrachloride and most organic solvents. Refractive index 1.52; dielectric constant about 2.5. Combustible, Nontoxic. Processed by calenders and extruders; can be injection-moulded with low sulphur and high accelerator. Cured by hotmoulding or in open steam, at temperatures from 120 to 150°C after addition of about 3% sulphur, 1% organic accelerator, 3% zinc oxide, plus fillers or reinforcing agents. The only factors of significance in vulcanisation are the time of exposure to heat and the temperature used.

Derivation - From latex (q.v.) obtained from hevea trees; coagulated with acetic or formic acid. Also made synthetically.

Occurrence - Brazil, Malaysia, Indonesia.

Grades - Ribbed smoked sheets; pale (yellow) creep; brown creep.

Containers - Burlap or polyethylene-warapped bales; wooden boxes.

Uses - Cements, adhesives, electrical Insulating tapes and cable warpping.

Cured (Vulcanised, i.e., Sulphur Cross-linkages)

Properties - High tensile strength; relatively low permanent set; insensitives to temperature changes; attacked by heat, atmospheric oxygen, ozone, hydrocarbons and unsaturated fats and oils; insoluble in acetone; permeable to gases; supports combustion; abrasion resistance poor unless compounded with carbon black; dissipates vibration shock; high electrical resistivity.

Uses - Vehicle tyres, hose, conveyor belt covers, footwear, speciallsed mechanical products, drug sundries, foam rubber, electric insulation, etc.

Note - Gutta-percha and balata have similar chemical composition (isomeric) but have different properties and few commercial uses. Neither can be vulcanised.

SPECIAL GRADES OF NATURAL RUBBER

Special grades of natural rubber are mentioned below-

i. Air dried sheet (pale amber unsmoked sheet)
ii. Anti-crystalline rubber
iii. Cyclised rubber masterbatch
iv. Heaveaplus MG Rubber
v. Partially purified creep (pp creep)
vi. Rubber powder
vii. Skim Rubber
viii. Softened or peptised rubber
ix. Superior processing rubber
x. Technically classified rubber.

Methods have also been laid down for testing for conformance or nonconformance, e.t., milling test, test for powder, clay whiting, gypsum, starch, and glue. At the end a glossary of terms used in connection with the classification of rubber has also been added.

As stated earlier, all the above classifications are based on visual methods only and mode of manufacture and not based on physical or chemical properties. There is in fact no discernible difference even in chemical properties between first quality smoked sheet and pale creep in spite of the fact that considerable effort goes in for the preparation of the latter. Unwanted non-rubber constituents such as dirk, sand, etc., should be eliminated as much as possible and exposure to oxidative breakdown should be avolded. There is no way to find out from the classification, the cure characteristics or oxidative degradation of the product marketed.

For purposes where colour and purlty are important as in this case of surgical goods, cut thread and for making rubber derivatives (transparent films) the finest grade of pale creep is used, For purposes where traces of mechanical impurities are not likely to be harmful, where colour is obtained in association with the addition of substantial quantities of compounding ingredients as in the case of play balls, extruded mechanical rubber goods and flooring, lighter grades of brown creeps are satisfactory, For purposes where strength and toughtness are far more important then colour (tyre treads) smoked sheet with Carbon Black is the first choice. Ultimately, it is the competitive price of the various grades which will decide the issue without jeopardising the properties of the finished product.

TECHNICALLY CLASSIFIED RUBBER

The main purpose of technical classification is to supply to consumers a reliable raw material which can be used without blending and without testing. A test compound (ACS-1) is vulcanised for 40 minutes at 140°C and tested for strain under a load of 5 kg/cm^2, other conditicns being kept constant. The tests are carried out by the producer and rate of vulcanisation is marked on the bale in addition to making regular market grade. Slow curing rubbers are marked with a red circle, rubbers with a medium rate of cure, yellow circle and fast curing rubber, a blue circle. Rubber which vulcanises very slowly or very quickly, or which display excessive variation from bale to bale is not classified. Technically classified rubber is a forward step in improving the grading of rubber; however, it has not been widely used; perhaps, it costs more than unclassified rubber. Its proportion in the total production of natural rubber is below 5%.

STANDARD MALAYSIAN RUBBER OR SMR

This represents new developments in production and grading of rubbers. With up-to-date methods of preparing packing and grading of natural rubber. The preparation envisages streamlining of methods of manufacture. Packing is being done similar to that of synthetic rubber, viz., small compressed and neatly wrapped bales on the basis of technical specifications of few grades.

The Rubber Research Institute, Malaya, has introduced a simplified scheme based on technical quality. Rubber produced under this scheme is called 'Standard Malaysian Rubber, (SMR). All rubber, whether produced by the conventional methods or new methods can be adopted to this scheme. These specifications are largely based on dirt content, freedom from harmful contaminants (Cu, Mn), low volatile matter, etc. Colour forms no part of the scheme but light coloured rubber may be obtained by specifying SMR 5L where 5L means the colour on Livibond scale-amber unit. It also specifies the weight of the packing as 112 lbs and is wrapped in poyethylene sheets, etc. Gradually more and more rubber is being produced as per these specifications.

The details of some of the features of 'Standard Malaysian Rubber' (SMR) are given as under

Latex grades—Rubber

The four latex grades are designated as SMR CV, SMR LV, (both are viscosity stabilised), SMR L (colour specified), and SMR WF (whole field latex). The rubbers are being graded according to their improved over all quality.

Viscosity stabilisation is brought about by treating the latex with NH_4OH which combines with the aldehyde group of the rubber molecule thus preventing the hardening of the stock during storage which is an irreversible phenomenon as opposed to hardening due to temperature variations which is a reversible phenomenon.

SMR LV is obtained by adding 4 parts phr of light non-staining mineral oil.

To test for the correct amount of oil in SMR LV, the material is extracted with acetone. Natural rubber contains 2-4% of acetone extractable material. SMR LV will have acetone extract between 6-8%.

SMR GP Latex Grade Rubber

A new general purpose GP grade is introduced to meet the demands of a large volume grade of rubber having consistent processing characteristics. This GP grade is viscosity stabilised and is a blend of latex grade rubber/ sheet material and field coagula. Its specification is similar to SMR 10.

Specification of general purpose rubber

Dirt content on 44 aperture (max. % wt.)	0.10
Ash (max % wt.)	0.75
Nitrogen (max % wt.)	0.60
Volatile matter (max. % wt.)	0.80

P.R.I. (min.)	50.00
Cure	Rheograph
Viscosity (Mooney) ML 1+4, 100°V.	Between 58 and 72 units

Composition of the blend for SMR GP

Raw material	% wt.
SMR Factory/GPC processed latex/and or sheet material)	60
Field coagulum	40

A typical flow-sheet for manufacture of SMR GP is given below:

Selected latex → Bulking → Coagulation → Creeping → Size reduction → Drying → Chemicals

Selected cup lump (CL) → Pre-cleaning and size reduction → Creeping → Size reduction → Drying → Chemicals

Selected unsmoked sheet (USS) → Creeping → Size reduction → Drying → Chemicals

Chemicals → Blending on pre-breaker → Packing

Viscosity OFS SMS CV/LV

The viscosity range of sub-grades of SMR CV and SMR LV are given below:

Grades	Mooney viscosity ML 1+, 100°C
CV 50	45-55
CV 60	55-65
CV 70	65-75
LV 50	45-55

Cure Testing

The basis of cure testing has been a single point test using MOD cureindicator system. The test determines the relaxed modulus at 100% extension using ACS I maix. The rubbers are then classified as MOD 5, MOD 6 and MOD 7.

Formulation of ACS I mix is as follow:

Ingredients	Parts by Wt.
Rubber	100.0
Zinc oxide	6.0
Steric acid	0.5
Sulphur	3.5
MBT	0.5

Cured for 40 min at 140°C.

MOD categories and modulus ranges

Category	*MR 100 range (kgf/cm²)*	*Typical classification for SMR grades*
MOD 5	4.5-5.49	Viscosity stabilised rubbers.
MOD 6	5.5-6.49	Viscosity stabilised rubbers, acid coagulated rubbers; SMR 5 and SMR 5L.
MOD 7	6.5-7.49	Biologically coagulated rubber and matured acid coagulated rubber cup lump rubber (SMR 10).

10.2 kgf/cm^2 = MN/m^2

Main features of the new scheme of SMR are as follows:

i. Improved designation of grade types
ii. Restriction of types and quality of raw materials which are allowed in producing the various grades
iii. Termination of SMR EQ grade
iv. Introduction of SMR GP grade of viscosity stabilised rubber
v. Rationalisation of the number of sub-grades in SMR 5 CV and SMR 5 LV.

Basically the specifications have been modified as under

i. Reduction in dirt and ash limits for the latex grade
ii. Reduction in volatile matter and nitrogen limits for all 5 SMR grades.

Cure testing is carried out with the help of a Rheometer for all grades of rubber obtained from latex including SMR GP.

SPECIALITY RUBBERS

Superior Processing of S.P. Rubber

This is the name given to sheet and creep which has been prepared by coagulating a mixture of fresh and vulcanised latex. Though apparently identical with sheet and creep prepared wholly from fresh latex and differing from natural rubber only slightly in respect of its physical, mechanical and vulcanising properties, the outstanding feature is reduced tendency to recover from deformation when the masticated and mixed material is passed through a calender or extruder. For example, where masticated smoked sheet shrinks about 40% in length, with a corresponding increase in thickness, S.P. smoked sheet shrinks about 20%.

The vulcanising system used in the preparation of vulcanised latex is as follows:

Rubber (ammoniated field latex)	100.00
Sulphur	2.00
Zinc oxide	0.75
Zinc diethyl dithiocarbamate	0.20
Mercapto benzothiazole	0.40

The vulcanising agents are added as a finely ground suspension with a dispersing agent in water and the latex heated by injection of live steam so that the temperature reaches slowly 82-85°C where it is held for 2 hours. The vulcanised latex is then blended with diluted field latex, the mixture coagulated and the coagulant dried and packed in the usual manner.

For the preparation of a product which is to be marked as superior processing brown creep, the master batch is in the form of undried crumb containing 80% vulcanised particles.

Hevea Graft Polymer

These are made by polymerising vinyl monomers in latex under suitable conditions. The socalled Heva-plus family includes both, the true graft polymers and mixture of already polymerised monomer with rubber by mutual coagulation. Methyl methacrylate is generally used as the modifying polymer. In the preparation of hevea plus M-G from latex, preferred initiator for graft polymerisation is a polyamine activated hydroperoxide. The rubber chain contains a methylenic hydrogen which is liable and acts as a transfer agent for the termination of the growing polymethyl methacrylate chain, with the formation of free radical centres on the rubber molecule from which are formed polymethyl methacrylate side chains attached to the rubber.

With low ratios of polymethyl methacrylate to rubber, the coagulum is sufficiently rubber.

Polystyrene is used as the modifying polymer, the product is known as Heva plus S.G.

Below 40% of modifying polymer, the M-G or S-G product resembles a fairly hard sheet, which is softened at 70°C.

Arctic Rubber

All organic rubbers, both natural and synthetic become hard and brittle when exposed to low temperature, a partial transformation of the cis bond to the trans variety leads to a hundred fold retardation of crystallisation and thus retention of flexibility under conditions of extreme cold. Such modified rubbers are useful in aircraft operations at high altitudes or in polar regions. Particularly useful types of rubbers are obtained by treatment of natural rubber either in solid or latex form with small quantities of acids.

Rubber Powder

It is prepared by spray-drying of preserved and concentrated latex in the presence of about 40% infusorial earth. The main use of this type of rubber is for dissolving in hot bitumen for road surfacing and similar applications. Small quantities of rubbers known as skim rubbers and cyclised rubber are produced.

PRODUCTION OF DRY RUBBER

Preparation of Ribbed Smoked Sheet (RSS)

The latex received from the tapper is sieved through a 60 mesh sieve made of monel metal into a bulking tank to remove leaves, pices of coagulum, particles of sand, etc. The whole day's supply of latex is diluted to about 15% DRC. This allows the remaining dirt to settle out easily. The latex is run into coagulation tanks once again through monel metal sieves to remove particles of coagulum. The coagulating tank is an aluminium lined wooden rectangular container, 16" deep holding about 250 gallons of latex. The sides of the tank are provided with vertical slots at an interval of 1-1/4" to receive removable aluminium partitions. Before the partitions are fitted into position, the coagulation solution is added evenly over the surface of the latex and mixed into its bulk avoiding trapping of air (which would lead to bubbly sheets). A little foam formed on the surface is skimmed off. The partitions are placed in position. The latex thickens and eventually forms a soft coagulum.

The usual coagulants are acetic acid and formic acid. The dilution of latex and the amount added to, determine the speed of coagulation. For 15% latex which has to be coagulated overnight, it is usual to add 100 parts of 1% acetic acid solution to 1000 parts of latex. If the coagulant is formic acid the amount required is about 50% higher. The amount of anticoagulant added in the field also effects the amount of acid required. Sulphuric acid also is sometimes used as coagulant. The advantages of acetic acid as a coagulant is that it is a weak acid and variations in the amount used will have relatively small effects on the pH of the latex coagulant dispersion.

When the latex is coagulated, the partitions are removed and the coagulum is fed as separate pieces to a series of even speed rolls provided with water sprays and adjusted to give progressively tighter grip and corresponding faster speeds. There are usually 5 pairs of rolls, the last pair being marking rolls which impress the grooved pattern of the rolls on the sheets. During the passage through the 5 pairs of rolls, the thickness of the coagulum is reduced form 1-1/4"-1-1/8", the serum is squeezed out and washed away.

The coagulum thus obtained is tougher. It is hung on racks to drip in open for about 2 hours shaded from the sun. During this time, the moisture content of the sheet is reduced partly by superficial drying and partly by synerising from 60% to 40%. The sheets are finally dired in an atmosphere of smoke suspended for about 4 days. During this process, the sheets absorb smoke constituents, lose their white colour and take on a dark shade. This method of drying has the advantage that it can be done very cheaply with little or no capital expenditure.

The smoking is done in smoke houses; these are rectangular tunnels with dimensions suitable for 4 days output. The furnace which provides heat and smoke by the burning of wood is built on the side towards the end of smoke house, the products of combustion being carried into the smoke house by means of a flue which passes along the length of the smoke house a floor level and has openings for smoke under the centre of each day's output. Adjustable flue apertures and roof ventilators are provided so that heat and smoke can be varied to the extent required to each part of the house.

During the first day, the rubber is kept at the cooler end (110°F); the removal surface water is rapid but must be done at a lower temperature as this would avoid formation of blisters due to expansion of internal moisture. Further drying involves the slow diffusion of water from within the sheets; when water content is reduced, the rubber can safely be subjected to higher temperature which may progressively reach 140°F at the furnace end. Higher temperatures would tend to produce tackiness which would reduce the market value. The sheets are thus inspected and packed into bales. The bales are approximately cubical, occupying 8 cu. ft. of shipping space. The weight of such a bale ranges from 225 lbs. to 250 lbs. The normal procedure is to pile the sheets in layers to the prescribed weight and compress in a box to required dimensions. The compressed bales are wrapped in sheets of rubber. Massing in transit is prevented by painting the exterior of the bales with surface lubricants such as talc, clay or whiting dispersed in a rubber solution.

Pale Creep

All latices contain yellow colouring matter (β-carotene) and in the absence of special precautions yield yellowish creep has a tendency to become dark during drying. The market requires that the best quality should be as white as possible. This is achieved by (i) addition of sodium bisulphite; (ii) fractional coagulation of latex to remove yellow colouring matter first; and (iii) by the addition of chemical bleaching agents. The most effective bleaching agent is xylyl mercaptan.

The field latex is strained and diluted to 20-25% DRC. (The dilution is less as the though coagulum is to be macerated by cropping machine.) About 0.5% sodium bisulphite on the weight of rubber and in the form of 20% solution is added to the latex and well stirred. This is then fractionally coagulated by adding limited quantity of 2.5% acetic acid (0.15% on weight of rubber). After a few hours, a yellow clot is formed which is skimmed off. The residual latex is strained through a 60 mesh sieve to remove small pieces of yellow coagulum. The bleaching agent is then added in the form of an aqueous emulsion (0.1% on the weight of rubber).

The latex is then coagulated by acetic or formic acid. The coagulum is then made into creep. These differ only in the thickness. The creeping is done on 4 pairs of rolls revolving at differential speeds under sprays of water. The sequence is a macerator with heavily grooved rolls, a creeping machine with lighter grooving and lower gear ratio followed by the finishing machines which consists of plain rolls operating at higher gear ratio than the creeping machines. The macerator rolls bite into the coagulum, squeeze out the serum and produce rough and highly crinkled thick blanket full of holes. The creeping machine produce a thinner sheet of more even texture. This creep is ready for marketing when dry, but for thick creep, the dry thin creep is further machined by passing through smooth rolls 3 times. The drying of creep is done by suspending long sheets over horizontal wooden bars in large drying sheds with adequate ventilation at a temperature of 95°F, drying temperature above 100°F has an adverse effect on colour. The heating is done by hot water radiators. The drying takes about a week. These are packed in hessian cloth or rubber.

Sole Creep

The creep is built up to the required thickness by superimposing a number of plies of thin creep of selected colour. The plies are pressed together by hard rolling and compressed a little further by passing several times between even speed smooth rolls. The slabs are cut to the required length and width.

Brown and Blanket Creeps

Considerable amount of rubber is obtained from naturally coagulated or dired, rubber in the course of regular plantation operations. The 'earth scrap' 'cup lump' bark scrap (recovered from bark after tapping), 'earth scrap' (recovered from spilled latex on ground at the base of the tree) are each standard graded in the international grading system. Other sources of scrap are lumps of coagulum from premature coagulation, forth skimmed off the surface of dilute latex after the addition of coagulants. Processing these various types of scrap is done in fewer number of remilling factories situated near ports. The scrap is first sorted out into grades dependent on cleanliness and colour. Each lot is soaked overnight in a solution of sodium sulphite to loosen the dirt and to improve the colour. It is then macerated with water in a universal washer consisting of paddles. Rubber emerges out of this in from of lumps. The partly cleaned scrap is subjected to creeping. The rubber is dried in air sheds.

OTHER FORMS OF NATURAL RUBBER

Many other forms and types of natural rubber have been produced to meet the specific requirements of on summers. These have usually involved chemical modification of the polymer chains or simple changes in the production process. Some of the commercially more important ones are described below.

Oil-Extended Natural Rubber (OENR)

OENR is a rubber containing 20-30% of an aromatic or naphthenic process oil.

Tyre Rubber

This is made from a mixture of 30 parts rubber (as latex), 30 parts sheet rubber, 40 parts cuplumps and 10 parts of an aromatic process oil. It is viscosity stabilised and requires no premastication. It is similar to SMR except for the oil.

Deproteinised Natural Rubber (DPNR)

DPNR is prepared by diluting latex and reacting it with an enzyme that removes most of the proteins from natural rubber. DPNR's properties of low creep and stress relaxation and highly reproducible modulus make it suitable for use in engineering components.

Peptised Rubber

This is a low-viscosity rubber prepared by adding a peptiser to latex before coagulation or to the dry rubber itself.

Skim Rubber

Skim latex is the by-product of latex centrifugation. It is coagulated (usually with sulphuric acid) and made into sheet, thick-creep or granulated rubber. It contains a higher proportion of non-rubbers, especially of proteins, than the average grades and fast-curing.

Superior Processing Rubbers (SP)

These are made by blending normal latex and prevulcanised latex before coagulation, and drying by conventional methods. Prevulcanised latex is made by adding a curative dispersion containing sulphur, zinc oxide and accelerator to natural-rubber latex and heating to 82-85°C for a few hours. PA 80 contains 80% prevulcanised rubber and 20% unvulcanised rubber.

Hevea-plus MG Rubbers (MG)

These are made by polymerising methyl methacrylate monomer in the presence of natural-rubber latex. The polymethyl-methacrylate (PMMA) chains are thereby grafted to the rubber molecules. The resultant latex is coagulated and made into creep.

Epoxidised Natural Rubber (ENR)

This is perhaps the most important modification of natural rubber ever made. It is produced by epoxidising natural rubber in the latex stage by reaction with formic acid and hydrogen peroxide. The introduction of epoxide groups progressively increases the glass-transition temperature of natural rubber and changes some of its properties markedly.

Thermoplastic Natural Rubbers (TPNR)

These are physical blends of natural rubber and poypropylene, mixed in different proportions to impart rubbers the different stiffness properties. Mixing is done at 180°C or higher. TPNR may also contain a third polymer, viz. polyethylene. They are suitable for injection moulding into products for automotive applications such as flexible sight shields and bumper components.

Many other chemically modified forms of natural rubber were available in the past. These included cyclised rubber, chlorinated rubber, hydrochlorinated rubber, is omerised or anticrystallising rubber, and depolymerised rubber. These are now not commercially significant since sysnthetic equivalents are available at cheaper prices.

PROPERTIES OF RAW NATURAL RUBBER

Natural-rubber latex consists of particles of rubber hydrocarbon and non-rubbers suspended in an aqueous serum phase. The average dry-rubber content of latex may range between 30% and 45%. A typical composition of firesh latex is shown in Table 1.

Table 1: Typical composition of fresh latex and dry rubber

Composition	Latex, %	Dry rubber, %
Rubber hydrocarbon	36.0	93.7
Protein	1.4	2.2
Carbohydrates	1.6	0.4
Neutral lipids	1.0	2.4
Glycolipids + phospholipids	0.6	1.0
Inorganic constituents	0.5	0.2
Others	0.4	0.1
Water	58.5	

Non-rubber Substances

During the preparation of dry rubber, much of the water-soluble non-rubber substances are lost, but most of the lipids are retained together with more than half the proteins and small quantities of inorganic salts and other substances. Each of these classes of non-rubber consists of many individual substances. The lipids, for example, consist of mono-, di- and tri-glycerides, sterol and sterol esters, tocortrienols and their esters, free fatty acids, glycolipids and phospholipids. Natural rubber easily contains more than 100 individual chemical compounds. Some of these non-rubber substances greatly influence the properties of natural rubber, in both the raw and vulcanised states.

The properties affected by the non-rubber substances are summarised in Table 2.

Physical Properties

The rubber hydrocarbon in freshly tapped latex is almost completely soluble (more than 95%) in common solvents such as toluene and tetrahydrofuran. It has a chemical structure of almost 100% cis-1, 4-polyisoprene units.

Storage Hardening

The Mooney viscosity (V_R) of freshly prepared rubber ranges from 50 to 90 units (ML 1+4 at 100°C) depending on the mixture of clonal latices used in the preparation. On storage, the rubber hardens or stiffens spontaneously and the viscosity increases. The storage hardening reaction is increased by conditions of higher temperature and lower humidity. This reaction is believed to be due to abnormal groups, probably aldehydic, present in the rubber molecules. These groups react with the amino groups of free amino acids and proteins to give crosslinks. The concentration of these groups is only about 5-10 × 10^{-6} moles per gm rubber, equivalent to only 1 or 2 groups per molecule. These groups can be deactivated and the storage hardening action inhibited by reacting rubber with 0.15% of hydroxylamine salt. Such viscosity stabilised CV grades show an average increase in V_R of only 4-8 units after 4-5 years of storage at ambient temperature.

Table 2: Properties of natural rubber influenced by non-rubber substances

Property	Influence of non-rubbers
Latex stability	Carbohydrates act as substrates for bacterial growth—lead to increased volatile acid formation and lower stability.
Colour	Yellow—caused by B-carotenes. Dark-enzymic reaction of polyphenol oxidase.
Cure	Phospholipids and some proteins are natural accelerators; fatty acids are activators.
Storage hardening	Proeins and free amino acids react with abnormal groups in rubber.
Crystallisation	Unstrained crystallisation rate increased by stearic acid, some water-soluble substances retard rate.
Creep and stress relaxation	High contents of proteins and ash lead to moisture absorption, which results in high creep and stress relaxation in vulcanisates.
Modulus	Increased by proteins.
Filler effect	Proteins act as fillers. One part of protein is equivalent to 3 parts of HAF black.
Heat build-up	Heat build-up in the Goodrich flexometer test is decreased by fatty acids and increased by proteins.
Tear strength	Increased by proteins.
Dynamic crack growth	Resistance increased by proteins.

Gel Content

Freshly prepared natural rubber has a low gel content, about 5-10%. On storage, the gel content increases and may reach 50%, or even higher on long storage. The increase in gel content mainly involves storage hardening but may also partly be due to free radical reactions. The gel is not a true network and the gel content depends on the solvent used, being lower in good solvents. It is a loosely crosslinked structure with a very high M_c value.

Gel in rubber easily breaks down on mstication. Masticated rubber is completely soluble in common aliphatic and aromatic solvents, chlorinated hydrocarbons, tetrahydrofuran and carbon disulphide. Lower ketones, and lower esters are non-solvents.

Molecular Weight

The molecular weight distribution of the rubber hydrocarbon in freshly prepared rubber is a bimodal or a skwed unimodal distribution, depending on the clone. A random blend of the common clonal rubbers would have a weight-average molecular weight of 1-1.5 × 10^6 and a number average of 3-5 × 10^5. The molecular weight of commercial grades of rubber is a little uncertain because of the presence of gel. The average molecular weights and typical distributions of the soluble portion of some commercial grades of rubber are shown in Table 3 and Figure 1, respectively. Old samples of rubber except the CV grades usually have a skewed unimodal distribution.

Table 3: Molecular weights of soluble natural rubber

Grade	Mw × 10^{-6} from GPC	Mn × 10^{-5} from GPC
RSS 1	1.00-2.3	2.3-4.5
SMR 5	0.95-2.7	2.2-5.6
SMR CV	0.80-2.0	1.8-3.7
SMR 20	0.92-2.2	2.1-4.0

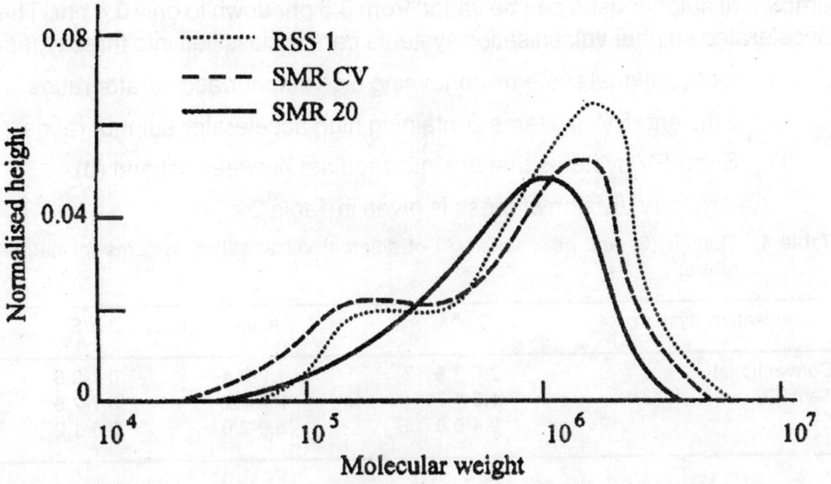

Fig. 1: Molecular-weight distribution curves for commercial grades of natural rubber

Crystallisation

Due to its high stereoregularity, natural rubber crystallises spontaneously when stored at low temperatures or when it is stretched.

Unstrained rubber has a maximum rate of crystallisation at about -26°C. But even at 0°C, natural rubber can crystallise in a few weeks. The maximum degree of crystallinity reached is only about 25-30%.

Crystallised unstretched rubber melts within a range of a few degrees. The melting point depends on the crystallisation temperature. An equilibrium melting temperature of over 40°C is estimated for unstretched rubber. Crystallisation leads to a stiffening of the rubber. This is different from storage hardening and is reversible by heating the rubber. Natural-rubber samples stored in warehouses at ambient temperatures in temperate climates crystallise and must be melted in a hot room before they can be mixed and compounded. Crystallisation can be inhibited by isomerising a few of the cis-groups to trans-groups by treating the rubber with sulphur dioxide.

Rapid crystallisation on stretching gives natural rubber its unique high tensile strength and tear resistance impure gum or in non-reinforced vulcanisates. Crystallisation occurring on extrusion through a die, even at temperatures above 100°C, may sometimes lead to processing problems.

VULCANISATION OF NATURAL RUBBER

Sulphur Vulcanisation

Sulphur vulcanisation is still the most widely used method of cross-linking natural rubber. In natural-rubber compounds, except ebonite, the amount of sulphur used can be varied from 3.5 phr down to only 0.4 phr. The accelerated sulphur vulcanisation systems can be classified into three types-

i. Conventional systems containing high sulphur/accelerator ratios
ii. Efficient (EV) systems containing high accelerator/sulphur ratios
iii. Semi-EV systems that are intermediate between (a) and (b).

An arbitrary division of these is given in Table 2.4.

Table 4: Sulphur (S) and accelerator (A) of different vulcanisation systems for natural rubber

Vulcanisation system	S phr	A phr	A/S
Conventional	2.0-3.5	1.2-0.4	0.1-0.6
Semi-EV	1.0-1.7	2.5-1.2	0.7-2.5
EV	0.4-0.8	5.0-2.0	2.5-1.2

The structural features of the network obtained in the accelerated sulphur vulcanisation of natural rubber are shown in Figure 2. Typical vulcanisate structures at optimum cure times and some properties are shown in Table 5.

Conventional systems give vulcanisates which posses excellent initial properties like strength, resilience and resistance to fatigue and abrasion, and are satisfactory for many applications. However, their heat-ageing resistance, creep and stress-relaxation properties are less satisfactory. For good heat-ageing resistance and low compression set, an EV system is essential; or a semi-EV system may be chosen as a compormise between cost/performance. EV systems can also be vulcanised at higher temperatures (18-200°C) and are less antagonistic to antioxidants than conventional systems.

Table 5: Vulcanisate structures and properties

Vulcanisate structure	Conventional	Semi-EV	EV
Poly- and disulphidic cross-links, %	95	50	20
Monosulphidic cross-links, %	5	50	80
Low-temperature crystallisaton resistance	High	Medium	Low
Heat-ageing resistance	Low	Medium	High
Reversion resistance	Low	Medium	High
Compression set, 22 hrs at 70°C, %	30	20	10

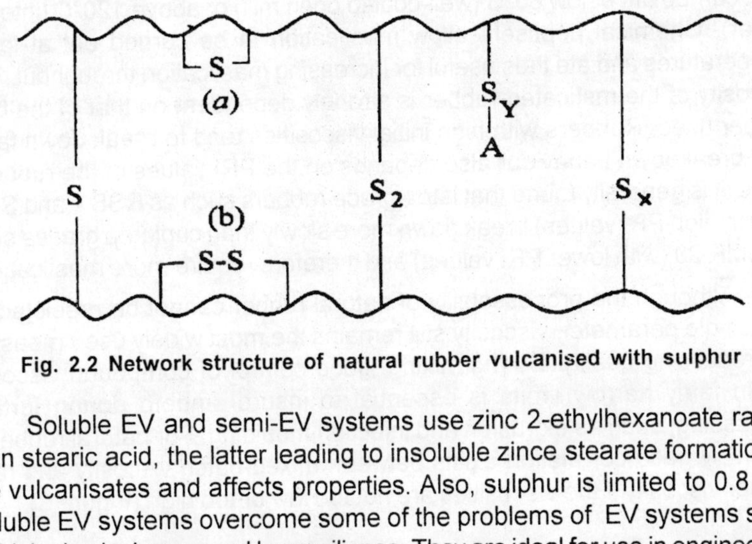

Fig. 2.2 Network structure of natural rubber vulcanised with sulphur

Soluble EV and semi-EV systems use zinc 2-ethylhexanoate rather than stearic acid, the latter leading to insoluble zince stearate formation in the vulcanisates and affects properties. Also, sulphur is limited to 0.8 phr. Soluble EV systems overcome some of the problems of EV systems such as high physical creep and low resilience. They are ideal for use in engineering components that require low compression set, low creep, low stress relaxation, and high reproducibility in modulus and strength.

Urethane Vulcanisation

Vulcanisation of natural rubber can be carried out by a new class of reagents. They are basically direthanes that are stable at processing temperatures, but which diissociate into their components species of nitrosophenols and disocyanates at the vulcanisation temperatures. The free nitrosophenols react with rubber molecules to give pendant aminophenol groups that are than cross-linked by the diisocyanate.

Urethane-cross-linked, natural-rubber networks show a marked increase in fatigue resistance on ageing compared to most sulphur systems. Vulcanisation can be carried out at 200°C without loss of modulus and tensile properties. However, these systems are expensive and may also have scorch problems. In practice, they are used as covulcanisation agents with sulphur systems.

PROCESSING OF NATURAL RUBBER

Natural rubber is usually considered to have good processing properties. Although it is tough and "nervy" at temperatures well below 100°C, it breaks down easily to a usable plasticity. Generally, it can be adapted to any fabrication technique of the rubber factory. The viscosity-stabilised grades of natural rubber to not generally require premastication before the incorporation of fillers and other compounding ingerdients. For the non-stabilised grades, a short mastication time before compounding is common practice.

The efficiency of mastication is lowest at around 100°C. Mastication is best carried out below 80°C (well-cooled open mill) or above 120°C (internal mixer). Chemical peptisers allow mastication to be carried out at lower temperatures and ate thus useful for increasing mastication throughout. The viscosity of the msticated rubber is strongly dependent on that of the bale rubber used. Rubbers with high initial viscosities tend to break down fater. The breakdown behaviour also depends on the PRI values of the rubbers. Thus, it is generally found that latex-grade rubbers such as RSS 1 and SMR L (with high PRI values) break down more slowly than cuplump grades such as SMR 20 (with lower PRI values) and therefore require more mastication.

Although the processability of natural rubber cannot be predicted by any single parameter, viscosity still remains the most widely used measure of processing quality. During mixing, good control of compound viscosity within fairly narrow limits is essential to insure smooth during further processing, such as extrusion and injection moulding. For natural rubber, a relatively good correlation exists between mixed-batch viscosity and raw-rubber viscosity if the viscosities are not too low or too high (Figure 3).

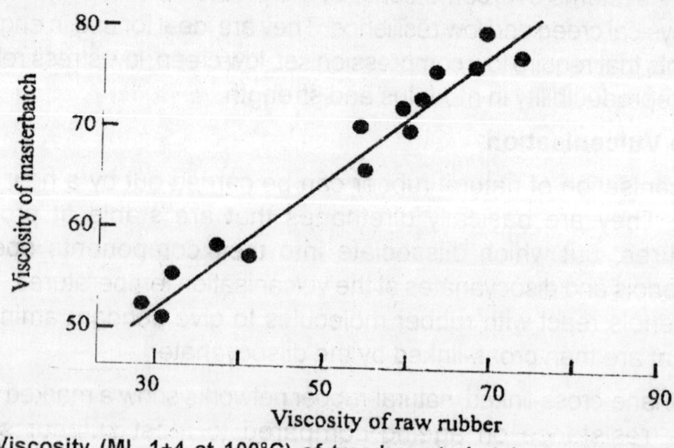

Fig. 3 Viscosity (ML 1+4 at 100°C) of tread masterbatch as a function of raw rubber viscosity

In extrusion of a fully mixed batch, the batch viscosity is the main factor controlling the die swell and the stress developed. The grade of rubber has a lesser influence. Thus viscosity is a useful guide to processing behaviour for masticated rubbers at intermediate viscosity levels. However, this is not so for the viscosity-stabilised grades. A masticated rubber has better extrusion properties than a non-masticated rubber of the same viscosity.

Unvulcanised compounds of natural rubber have superior green strength and building tack compared to other elastomers.

VULCANISATE PROPERTIES

The physical properties of natural rubber vulcanisates are dependent, like other elastomers, on several variables such as compound viscosity, type, and amount of fillers, degree of filler dispersion, degree and type of cross-linking, and so forth.

Strength

Natural rubber is well-known for the strength properties of its vulcanisates. The tesile strength of gum vulcanisates range from 17 to 24 PMa while those of black filled vulcanisates range from 24 to 32 PMa. Strength can also be characterised as tear resistance (i.e., the force needed to induce tear) or as cutgrowth resistance, in both of which natural rubber is excellent. This high strength of natural rubber is certainly due to its ability to undergo strain-induced crystallisation. The strength drops rapidly with increase in temperature but is still better than in other elastomers.

Abrasion and Wear

Natural rubber has excellent abrasion resistance, especially under mild abrasive conditions. The abrasion resistance of natural-rubber compounds is improved by blending with a small proportion of polybutadiene. The wear resistance of tyre treads depends on the tyre-surface temperature. Below about 35°C, natural rubber shows better wear than SBR, while above 35°C, SBR is better.

Skid Resistance

The skid resistance of tread compounds of the same hardness depends on their viscoelastic properties. Thus the highly resilient natural rubber compounds show lower skid resistance than SBR at temperatures above 0°C. The wet-skid resistance of natural rubber above 0°C can be improved by extending with oil during mixing or by use of OENR. Treads from OENR are as good as OESBR on wet roads and are superior on icy roads. Thus OENR blended with polybutadiene is suitable for treads of winter tyres.

Dynamic Properties

Natural rubber has high resilience, with values exceeding 90% in well-cured gum vulcanisates. However, except for DPNR, the values are 1-2%

lower than those of synthetic *cis*-1, 4-polyisoprene. In black-filled vulcanisates, the differences are smaller.

At large strains, the fatigue life of natural rubber is superior to that of SBR; the reverse is true for small strains. Good resistance to flexing and fatigue together with high resilience makes natural rubber useful lin applications where cyclic stressing is involved.

Compression Set

Compression set and related processes, such as creep, are poorer in natural rubber than in synthetic polyisoprene. This advantage for the latter is due to the effect of the non-rubber substances, and DPNR shows much improved properties. Compression set is reduced by a good cure.

Ageing

Natural-rubber vulcanisates can be given adequate heat-ageing resistance by a suitable choice of vulcanisation systems and by use of amine or phenolic antioxidants. Similarly, the poor ozone resistance under both static and dynamic conditions can be improved with waxes and antiozonants of the p-phenylendiamine type.

PRODUCT APPLICATIONS

With its wide range of useful properties, natural rubber can be used in a large variety of applications. The increase in the share of natural rubber in the last few years is due to the large switch to radial tyres.

Tyres

Almost no natural rubber is used in the treads of passenger car tyres in the USA, Western Europe, and Japan due to the better wet-skid resistance and wear characteristics of OESBR/BR blends. There is a small use of OENR in winter-tyre treads. In passener-car bias-ply tyres; natural rubber is used only in the carcass where the hot tear resistance, adhesion, and tack of natural rubber are used to advantage. In passenger-car radial-play tyres, natural rubber is used in the carcass as well as the sidewall, the latter due to the superior fatigue resistance and low heat build-up of natural rubber.

In commercial vehicles, the amount of natural rubber used increases with the size of the tyre. In large earthmove tyres, for example, almost 100% natural rubber is used due to the requirements of low heat generation and high cutting resistance.

Natural rubber is used in blends with halobutyl rubbers in the inner liner of tubeless tyres.

Mechanical Goods (Industrial Products)

These include a large variety of products such as hose, conveyor belts, rubber linings, gaskets, seals, rubber rolls, rubberised fabrics, etc. In these products, the choice of elastomer is made on the best compromise between price and performance. Natural rubber is used in some products only because it has certain properties that cannot be matched by any other rubber.

Engineering Products

Engineering products deserve special mention as a special class of industrial products. Rubber is a unique engineering material because, unlike other engineering solids, it has high elastic deformability and an almost theoretical value for Poission's ratio (0.5). The stiffness of a natural-rubber component in different directions may be varied independently by the judicious use of shape effects. In dynamic applications such as springs, antivibration mountings, bushings, and so forth, high fatigue resistance, good strength, and durability are additional points in favour of natural rubber. However, natural rubber is not suitable if it has to come in contact with oil. In other applications such as bridge bearings, factors such as weathering, ozone resistance, and low-temperature flexibility are also important. Natural rubber is now accepted as suitable for use in bridge bearings, in place of, for example, neoprene.

Latex Goods

Natural-rubber latex has now been largely replaced by polyurethane in form for upholstery and bedding. The main uses of latex are in dipped goods, foam, carpet backing, thread and adhesives.

Footwear

Natural rubber is extremely suitable for rubber footwear manufacturing. Its use is limited only by cost.

WHY RUBBER HOLDS ITS PLACE

A consideration of the many uses of rubber shows that it is used principally as a structural material and that its use depends on certain mechanical or physical properties.

Electricity is one of the most important property. A rubber band can be stretched to 9 or 10 times its original length. As soon as the load is released, it retracts almost immediately to its original length. Similarly, a block of rubber can be compressed, and as soon as the load is relased the block will assume its original shape and dimensions. In the extent to which it can be distorted, in the rapidity of recovery, and in the degree to which it recovers its original shape and dimension, rubber is unique. Hence, these are the prime requirements of "rubberiness".

Of almost equal importance with elasticity are strength and toughness. The high strength and great toughness of rubber permit the use of its elastic qualities under conditions in which most other elastic materials would fail. It is relatively impermeable to both water and air. Hence, it can be used to hold water, as in hose and water bottles, or to keep water out, as in rain coats. It can also be used either to contain air and other gases or to provide protection from them.

Along these properties, and probably because of them, rubber shows excellent resistance to cutting, tearing and abrasion.

Furthermore, this combination of useful physical properties is well maintained over a rather wide range of temperatures, from -40° or -50° F to 200 or 250° F, which covers the usual range of climatic conditions.

Also, rubber is relatively inert to the deteriorating effects of the atmosphere and of many chemicals. Hence, it has a relatively long, useful life under a wide variety of conditions. This long life is adversely affected by exposure to coal tar and petroleum solvents, high temperature, direct sunlight (especially when stretched), and certain chemicals such as ozone, chlorine, some strong acids, and strong oxidising agents. The special purpose synthetic rubbers have gained their positions primarily because they are resistant to one or more of these deteriorating influences.

Another quality of great importance is the ease with which such properties as hardness, strength, and abrasion resistance can be modified.

A very important and almost unique quality of uncred rubber is "building tack". When two fresh surfaces of milled rubber are pressed together, they coalesce to form a single piece. This tack makes relatively simple the building of acomposite article, such as a tyre, from many separate pieces. The separate components of the green tyre are held together by the building tack, and during cure they fuse together to make a single piece.

Thuse, we see that the importance of rubber is based on three factors. The crude rubber is easily processed. It can be vulcanised. The vulcanisate has a remarkable combination of useful mechanical properties. A fourth factor should not be overlooked. Rubber is relatively low in cost both for the raw material and for its manufacturing process.

TRENDS IN THE USAGE OF RUBBERY MATERIALS

In order to try and predict trends in the usage of a particular material, it is necessary to consider a variety of underlying trends. Some of these underlying trends may be very long-term and others very short. It is clearly most sensible to determine the primary long-term trends and then to superimpose on them the secondary trends of shorter duration.

In the specific case of the consideration of trends in the usage of rubbery materials, the following global underlying trends may be identified.

i. Changes in standards of living.
ii. Changes in patterns of transportation.
iii. Changes in the design of automotive equipment.

iv. Changes in tyre design and the use of rubber in other automotive applications.

v. Changes in non-automotive uses for rubber.

vi. Changes in raw material supplies.

vii. Trends in legislation, for example in areas associated with health, safety and toxicity.

THE PLACE OF RUBBER IN THE MODERN WORLD

In the crises of war, the need for rubber was soon evident to all. The success of the Allied blockade in keeping rubber out of Germany during World War I was a major factor in winning the war. It was for this reason that the Germans and Russians were so active in the synthesis of rubber between wars. In USA it was the conquest of the Far East by the Japanese that brought there to the public the vital and widespread importance of rubber.

Rubber is used in such widely varying items as washers, gaskets, shoe soles, raincoats, hose, belting, tyres, milking machines and surgical goods. One company in USA alone has advertised the production of some 30,000 different items. The motorist of 1910 was much more conscious of his tyres than was his son 30 years later. The cost per tyre went down and at the same time the mileage was increasing from 2000 to 20,000 miles and the demands on tyres became more severe.

RUBBER TECHNOLOGY FROM THE COMPOUNDERS' VIEW POINT

Development of Rubber Compounding

Rubber compounding is a term covering a wide scope including the art and procedures that are necessary to produce useful products from natural or synthetic elastomers. A competent rubber compounder must be able to use the proper elastomers and additives available to meet the conditions required for the finished product. This requires a through understanding of the following factors.

i. Properties of the elastomers available.

ii. Vulcanising or curing systems to give the potential properties needed.

iii. Modifying materials which give required physical properties and ageing resistance.

iv. Compounds must be able to process properly depending on processing equipment.

v. Commercial compound design.

vi. How to test and evaluate raw materials and finished products.

Commercial compounds of elastomeric materials described in the following articles are designed to be practical and result in overall properties that meet requirements for the end use.

A discussion to trace the development, a natural base compound will show the importance of the various ingredients the compounds contain. The use of rubber in its uncured state is very limited. Nearly every rubber compound contains at least an antioxidant and usually a vulcanising system.

Rubber and Sulphur

Goodyear's discovery of vulcanisation produced articles such as water proof clothing and allied products. These were made by heating rubber in the presence of sulphur and led the way to our present day compounding.

i. Natural rubber	100
Sulphur	8
Total	108

This compound developed a tensile strength of 3,200 lbs. per square inch and an elongation of 950% after being heated for 5 hours at 287°F. This vulcanised product was more stable over a wider temperature range and was more resistant to swelling in gasoline or toluene but is not suitable for today's use since it takes too long to produce (cure) and ages badly.

Rubber-Sulphur-Zinc Oxide

The next development in compounding is the addition of various metallic oxides to the rubber-sulphur base. These are found to shorten the curing time.

ii. Natural rubber	100
Sulphur	8
Zinc oxide	5
Total	113

This compound develops its maximum physical strength in 3 hours at 287°F as compared to 5 hours for the rubber-sulphur mix. This activating effect of zince oxide continues to be an important part of present-day compounding.

Organic Acceleration

The original accelerator of vulcanisation was aniline which first used by Oenslager in 1906. This material was objectionable because of its toxicity. A reaction product of aniline with carbon disulphide, thiocarbanilide, was found to be more effective and less toxic, and became the first widely used organic accelerator.

iii.	Natural	100
	Sulphur	6
	Zinc oxide	5
	Thiocarbanilide	2
	Total	113

Introduction of the organic accelerator in the base compound reduced the required vulcanisation time by 50% or more. Following the discovery of the favourable effects obtained with aniline and thiocarbanilide, a large number of nitrogenbearing organic compounds were investiaged as organic acceleratiors for rubber vulcanisation. In 1921, MBT (Mercapto benzothiozole) was introduced as the first truly commercial accelerator that offered the following advantages in compounding.

i. Reduction of sulphur to improve ageing.
ii. Shorter curing cycle
iii. Reduced tendency to bin-cure (scorch)
iv. Improved physical properties invulcanised compounds.

During the period of investigation and rubber compounding research that produced MBT, it was found that fatty acids present in the non-hydrocarbon constituents of natural rubbers contributed to the efficiency of the accelerators of vulcanisation. It became standard practice to add stearic or some similar fatty acid to compounds as precaution against possible deficiencies of this material in the raw rubber.

iv.	Natural rubber	100
	Zinc oxide	5
	Sulphur	3
	Stearic acid	1
	MBT	1
	Total	110

This compound can be cured in 20 minutes at 142°C/287°F.

Antioxidants

Despite better ageing properties of rubber compounds that came with the wide use of organic accelerators, early failure in many applications suggested the need for further improvements. A number of organic materials now referred to as antioxidants were investigated and adapted for compounding to impart better ageing, thus adding one more ingredient to the most suitable rubber compound.

v.		
v.	Natural rubber	100
	Zinc oxide	5
	Sulphur	3
	Stearic acid	1
	MBT	1
	Antioxidant	1
	Total	111

To combine the materials in Formula 5 the rubber is masticated on a rubber mill or in a Banbury type internal mixer, usually with the addition of a "processing aid" to speed the operation, and the other ingredients are mixed into the masticated rubber.

ROLE OF COMPOUNDER IN THE RUBBER INDUSTRY

In considering the technology of the rubber industry, compounders are interested in materials and ideas and their relations.

Materials

The flow of materials from the forests, plantations, mines, etc., to the tyres, belts, girdles, golf balls, and thousands of rubber products which are essential to modern civilisation is shown in Figure 4.

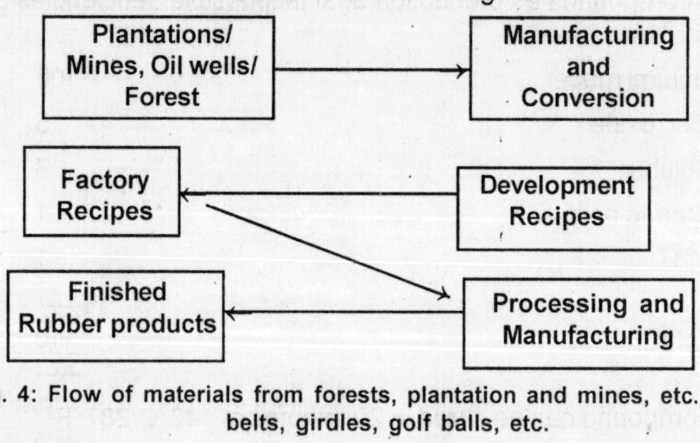

Fig. 4: Flow of materials from forests, plantation and mines, etc., to tyres, belts, girdles, golf balls, etc.

All the raw materials from A, for accelerators, to z, for zinc oxide, flow into the stream of rubber manufacturing through the medium of the factory recipe. Besides the knowledge of all raw materials by the compounders as to its quality and effect on rubber compound, all organised rubber industries have specifications which are acceptable for each raw material and before it is released for production the compounder must ensure review laboratory data.

Ideas

Technical structure in the rubber industry and the flow of ideas are in Figure 5. Here the role of compounder in relation to other functions in the factory is furnished.

PRINCIPLES OF RUBBER PRODUCT DESIGN

Specifications or service conditions of rubber product are the basis for design of rubber compound formulation. The problem of deciding the compound to be used for a particular application is often difficult. Generally, there are conflicting requirements which means that a decision has to be made on the relative importance of the original specifications. Even when this has been done it may not be possible to find a rubber compound which meets all the revised requirements and a compromise may have to be made.

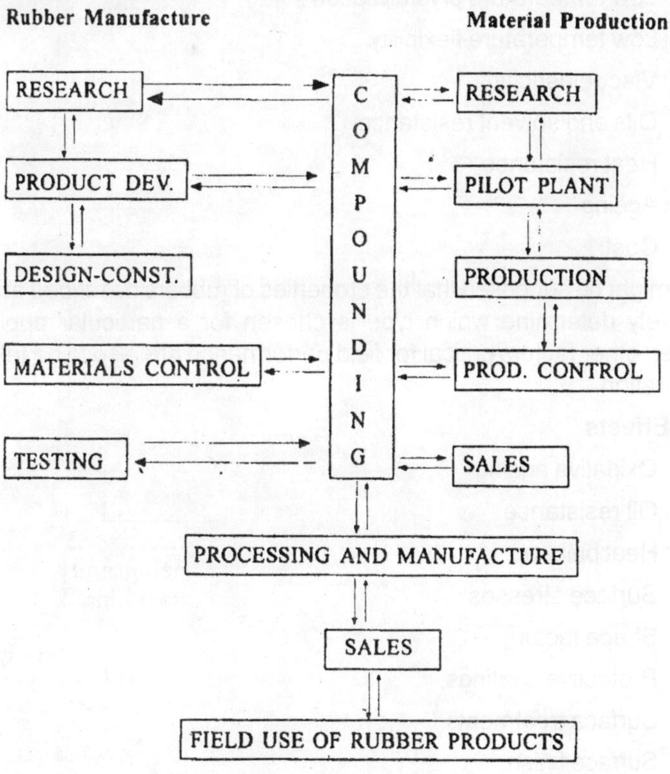

Fig. 5: Flow diagram showing the role of compounder in factory

Ideally product design calls for a detailed knowledge of the physical properties of the commonly available rubbers together with expertise in manufacturing process and a sound knowledge of engineering principles. It is perhaps not too surprising that designers of rubber products are not always as familiar with the properties of rubbers as they should be for optimum performance at minimum cost. The object is to survey the general properties of rubbers from the designer's point of view and then to show how other factors, such s shape, can often permit the use of a rubber which does not appear to meet the original requirements in terms of general physical properties.

Initially compound formulation is developed in laboratory in order to ensure all possible properties are met by the compound as specified by initial lat testing. Depending on specification requirement following factors after satisfactory evaluation must be reviewed.

i. Vulcanisation
ii. Low temperature crystallisation
iii. Low temperature flexibility
iv. Viscoelasticity
v. Oils and solvent resistance
vi. Heat resistance
vii. Ageing
viii. Cost.

It might be supposed that the properties of rubbers described above will exclusively determine which type is chosen for a particular application. However, other factors critical for field performance are also to be taken into consideration.

Shape Effects

i. Oxidative ageing
ii. Oil resistance
iii. Heat build-up
iv. Surface stresses
v. Shape factor
vi. Protective coatings
vii. Surface treatments
viii. Surface finish
ix. Type of deformation
x. Fatigue life.

Often for critical products, simulated tests are designed in order assess satisfactory filed performance of the rubber products. Interpretation of such results is very important to the compounder in order to ensure compliance of specification as laid down by the purchaser.

LABORATORY TO FACTORY

The best of the preliminary recipes, as judged by laboratory evaluation, are then subjected to factory trials, which show how the compound works on production equipments and which give finished items for service tests. On the basis of these factory trials, the most satisfactory receipts are selected for production use.

The extremes in this general scheme of operation are, first, the case where one recipe is written and then put into production the next day and at the other end, the case where a groups of compounders work year after year to maintain and improve the quality of compounds for specific products, such as tyres.

The central line is the work of the factory compounders in the rubber manufacturing plants. The research and development compounders operate in the research laboratories and in the plants of both the rubber manufactures and the suppliers of raw materials, and also in academic institutions. The control compounders work in the factories of the rubber manufacturers and of the suppliers. In every case, the essence of the job is the writing of recipes for a definite purpose. The immediate objective avaries with the work of the individual compounder, but the final objective is always a production compound.

In brief, what the compounder does is to write recipes and to evaluate compounds. How this work permeates the technology of the industry is illustrated in Figure 6.

DIE SWELL AND WALL SLIP BEHAVIOUR OF NATURAL RUBBER

Die Swell

The study and knowledge of die swell is of considerable importance in the spinning of fibres, control of extruded sheet thickness, in blow moulding and in surface finish of the products. When polymer melt emerges out of an extruder die it undergoes relaxation in stresses which acts as restraining forces inside the capillary or extruder. As a result of this the jet expands in its cross-section area. This effect is represented as die swell (ratio of extrudate diameter to capillary diameter).

Investigations have been carried out on the die seell behaviour of different polymer melts. It has been reported that the die swell depends on various factors like:

i. Shear rate
ii. Pre-shearing time and rate of preshearing
iii. Length of the dimeter ratio of capillary
iv. Residence time of polymer inside the capillary
v. Temperature of operation
vi. Molecular weight of polymer
vii. The ratio of M_w/M_n
viii. Long chain branching
ix. Type of die
x. Presence of fillers in the polymers.

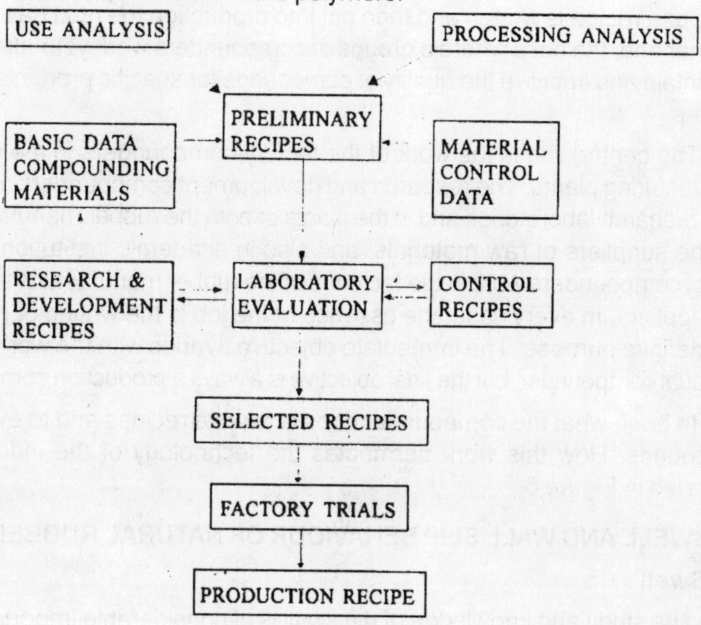

Fig. 6: Flow diagram showing the steps involved in formulating recipe by a compounder

Wall Slip

The force balancé for fluid flow through the pipe pre-assumes that the fluid in contact with the pipe surface completely wets it and that the velocity of the fluid at the interface is zero. This assumption is found to be quite valid for normal incompressible Newtonian fluids, but for polymer melts it does not seem to be true. It has been pointed out by Mooney that non-zero velocity may exist at the wall of the pipes and also a relationship between wall shear stress and shear rate for such situations is derived. Further research work has also reported the existence of wall slip during the flow of polymer melts.

The studies on die swell and wall slip as indicated by the literature review has been confined mostly to the synthetic polymers, and no work has been reported with respect to natural rubber melt flow.

Procedure

Materials required-

i. Standard Malaysian Rubber - SMR-L.

ii. SMR-Cr (70) (viscosity stabilised rubber)

Temperature - 120°C

Apparatus - Davenport Extrusion Rheometer.

The rubber samples are masiticated in a two roll mill at 50°C for different interval of times. The extent of mastication is indicated by the change in plasticity number which is measured with Wallace Rapid plasticity meter. The die swell and wall slip measurements for different samples are done with extrusion reheometer using different capillaries. For die swell measurement care is taken to avoid any drawdown effect, and for this purpose the extrudate is first cut as close to the capillary exist as possible and then a small piece is cut again for the measurement of diameter. The extrudate diameter measurements are taken after keeping the sample overnight for complete relaxation. As the extrudate was distorted on the surface, the average diameter can be calculated from the knowledge of weight of known length of sample and its density.

GRAFTING OF VINYL MONOMERS ONTO NATURAL RUBBER

The growth of polymer chemistry has led to the development of new materials in direct competition with natural materials, many of which have been in use since earlier times. This has encouraged the chemists to look more critically at natural macromolecules, to learn more of the underlying structure and the relation to the properties exhibited by the macromolecules. Hence, chemical modifications have been devised to give natural macromolecules more desirable properties and the application of synthetic macromolecules forms an important area of such chemical modification. The literature abounds with the examples of successful formation of copolymers from natural and synthetic macromolecules. The molecular architecture of the natural substrate is not affected by the presence of polymer, but the nature of the polymer formed in the environment of a natural substrate may be quite different from the homoplymers formed under similar polymeristion conditions.

FORMATION OF GRAFT POLYMER

A graft copolymer results from the chemical interaction of a polymer chain with a different polymeric substrate. Polyerisation may be induced within a substrate without chemical bonding and because of its size and conformation, the new molecule is firmly anchored in the substrate. Extraction of the copolymer with a suitable solvent for the homopolymer has been used as a criterion for the presence of grafting.

Rubber occupies a dominant position among natural macromolecules being modified for chimerical use by compolymerisation with synthetic polymers. Copolymers of natural rubber are prepared and characterised by techniques applicable to wholly synthetic copolymers and their properties can be duplicated by the characteristics of an appropriate synthetic rubber.

Styrene and methyl methacrylate are the monomers most commonly used commercially to produce natural rubber copolymers. High grafting yields may be obtained with these monomers. Many copolymer properties, such as torsional modulus are identical with the properties of simple mixtures and are not affected by grafting. On the other hand, the copolymer is insoluble in normal solvents for the rubber and polymer components. The low brittleness of rubber copolymer as compared with that of the unmodified synthetic polymers enables them to find commercial use as a reinforced vinyl resins. This is the principle underlying the manufacture of high impact polystyrene, although the product is usually prepared by copolymerisation of styrene and a synthetic rubber.

The successful grafting of vinyl monomers onto natural rubber involves the creation of free radical on the backbone of rubber. This can be achieved by several methods, such as chemical and irradiation. Out of all these methods, chemical method has attracted attention in recent years.

Research has been carried on graft copolymerisation of vinyl monomers onto natural rubber using a multitude of metal and non-metal ions such as $Cr^{6}+$, $V^{5}+$, $Ce^{4}+$, $Mn^{3}+$, $KMnO_4$/oxalic acid, $Fe^{3}+$, $Cu^{2}+$, metal chelates, peroxydisulphate, peroxydiphosphate and postassium bromate-thiorea as the initiators. Effects of monomer, initiator, temperature, solvents, acids, substrates and surfactants on the rate of grafting have been studied.

Procedure

Effect of Monomer Concentration

In case of all the above initiating systems, the effect of momomer concentration on the extent of grafting is investigated by changing the monomer concentration from very low to very high. It is observed that there is an increase in the percentage of grafting in the lower concentration range and at very high monomer concentration, the graft yield decreases. At higher monomer concentration, reactions that are competitive to grafting probably take place in solution, i.e., homopolymerisation is much faster than grafting at higher monimer concentration.

Effect of Initiator Concentration

The rate of grafting was investigated by varying the concentration of the initiators i.e.,

$Cr^{6}+$, $V^{5}+$, $Ce^{4}+$, $Mn^{3}+$, permanganate/oxalic acid, etc., from very low to very high concentration. In case of all the initiating systems, the rate of grafting increases with increase of initiator concentration at the lower range, but at very high concentration of the initiatiors, the rate of grafting decreases with increase of initiator concentration. This could be ascribed to the faster rate of termination of the chain at higher initiator concentrations.

Effect of Temperature

The graft copolymerisation is carried out by varying temperature within the range of 40-70°C keeping the concentration of all the other reagents constant. The perusal of the result indicates that with increasing temperature, the percentage graft-on increases. From the Arrhenius plot of log Rp versus 1/T, the values of the overall activation energy are computed in case of all the initiating systems.

Effect of Reaction Medium

Reaction medium plays an imporat role in grafting vinyl monomers onto natural rubber. The variation of grafting upon using different solvents could be associated with difference in their following properties:

i. Capability of swelling of natural rubber
ii. Miscibility with monomers
iii. Formation of solvent radicals from the primary radical species of the initiating system
iv. Contribution of the solvent radical in the activation of natural rubber
v. Termination of the graft chain radical and the natural rubber macroradical via chain transfer.

While the first four factors favour grafting by simplifying access and diffusion of the monomer, the last factor adversely affects grafting by lowering the molecular size of the graft.

Mechanism

In a system consisting of initiator, monomer and natural rubber, the following mechanism for grafging vinyl monomers is suggested.

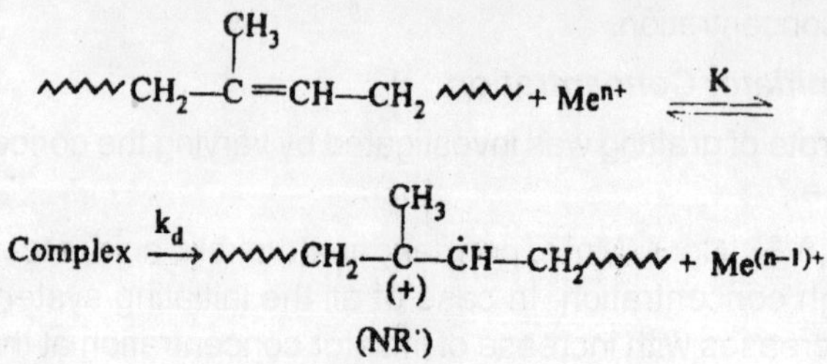

Initiation

$$NR^{\cdot} + M \xrightarrow{K_i} NRM^{\cdot}$$

Propagation

$$NRM^{\cdot} + M \xrightarrow{K_p} NRM_1^{\cdot}$$

$$NRM^{\cdot}_{n-1} + M \xrightarrow{K_p} NRM_n^{\cdot}$$

Termination

$$NRM^{\cdot}_n + Me^{n+} \xrightarrow{K_t} NRM + Me^{(n-1)+}$$

$$NR^{\cdot} + Me^{n+} \xrightarrow{K_t} \text{Oxidation products} + Me^{(n-1)+}$$

Applying steady state conditions to the concentrations of [NR*] and [NRM_n*], the overall rate of polymerisation was derived as-

$$R_p = \left(\frac{k_p}{k_t}\right)[M]^2 \frac{K\,k_d[NR]}{[M] + (k_o/k_i)\,[Me^{n+}]}$$

The above rate expression was verified by plotting R_p versus $[M]^2$ and R_p versus $1/[Me^{n+}]$ which were linear.

2

Latex Processing and Applications

INTRODUCTION

Natural rubber, on which the technology of the industry is built, is obtained by the coagulation of the milky aqueous dispersion of rubber called latex. It is synthesised by the tree Hevea brasiliensis and is an important bye-product. Originally an inhabitant or native of Brazil in South America, it is now widely cultivated in Southern regions of Asia. The height of the tree is more than 40 metres if untrapped and the economic life of tree is about 30-35 years. The levels are trifoliate and are shed once a year in the process called wintering. Latex is found in the latex vessels contained in the cortex, especially in the layer 2-3 mm thick nearest to cambium. They have internal diameters of about 20 mm. They turn spirally up the tree at an angle of about 4° to the vertical, thus forming a right handed spiral. The trees produce latex all the year round, but the yield usually drops during winter season.

Latex is obtained from the latex vessels without damaging the trees by the process called tapping. A slice of bark is shaved off with a special knife to a depth just short of cambium layer. The cut is made at an angle of 25-30° to the horizontal to sever the maximum number of latex vessels. Tapping is done before sunrise, when the turgor pressure in the tree is maximum and the yield of latex is highest. The latex flows from the cut along a metal spout and into a cup made of the glass or glazed earthenware. Tapping is continued at regular intervals by reopening the cut down the tree. Many variations have been used in the size and shape of the cuts and in the frequency of tapping. A very common method is to tap each tree halfway round the circumference every other day.

Immediately after tapping, the latex flows rapidly, then decline to a steady rate, then slows down and finally stops. The stoppage of the flow is due to plugging of latex vessels by the coagulum formed at the opening of the cuts.

PROCESSING OF LATEX

The latex is collected from the tree after 3-4 hours after tapping. It is then treated to prevent premature coagulation and brought to the factory.

Ammonia (about 0.05-0.06%), the most common stabiliser is added to the latex, though others like sodium sulphite and formaldehyde can also be used. Mixed stabilisers such as boric acid-ammonia and hydroxylamine ammonia are used to make certain special grades of rubber. When latex itself has to travel a long distance, higher concentration of ammonia are used. In the initial collection (3-4 hours), about 80-85% of the latex produced by tree is collected as latex (field latex).

The latex continues to exude very slowly for several hours after the initial collection. This latex is left to coagulate spontaneously in the cup to form field coagulation or cuplump, a small amount of latex also coagulates as a thin sheet on the tapping cut to form tree lace. These are collected on the next tapping and constitute about 15-20% of the total yield.

On arrival at the factory, the latex is sieved and blended. Field latex is either concentrated by removing part of the water to give latex concentrate, or it is deliberately coagulated and processed into solid dry rubber. All cuplumps are processed into dry rubber. A wide range of polymer latices is available commercially. The principal varieties contain the following polymeric materials:

Natural rubber

Styrene-butadiene copolymers

Acrylo-butadiene (nitrile) rubbers

Chloroprene rubbers

Acrylic copolymers

Vinyl acetate copolymers

Vinyl chloride copolymers

Synthetic cis polyisoprene

Butyl rubber.

Natural rubber latices are concentrated and purified forms of the latex obtained from botanical species *Heva brasiliensis*. The second group is produced by emulsion polymerisation and the third group is produced by solution polymerisation and converted into latex.

To recapitulate, natural rubber latex, obtrained from the tree which contains approximately 35% rubber hydrocarbon, is further preserved and concentrated by three well known methods, viz. centrifuging, creaming and evaporation. The approximate rubber content and the proportion of the preservatives of various categories of latices are given below:

	Type of latex				
	Centrifuged			*Creamed*	
Constituents	*HA*	*LA*	*XA*	*HA*	*LA*
Dry rubber content % minimum	60.0	60.0	60.0	64.0	64.0
Non-rubber solids, % maximum	2.0	2.0	2.0	2.0	2.0
Ammonia, % water content	1.6 (min.)	0.8 (max.)	< 0.3	1.6 (min.)	1.0 (max.)
	Evaporated				
		HA	KHS	KLS	
Total solids, % min.		61.5	72.0	67.0	
Non-rubber sokids, % max.		05.5	08.0	07.5	
Ammonia, % water content		1.5 (min.)			
KOH (moles/kg water)			0.5 (min.)	0.45 (min.)	

An international condification scheme is available for synthetic latices and includes nominal total solids and bound styrene content.

APPLICATIONS OF LATEX

Like solid rubbers, latices also find many applications, principal amongst them being latex backing of carpets, foam products, binders for non-woven fabrics, latex adhesives, products obtained by dipping, e.t. balloons and gloves, or those obtained by moluding, e.g., latex thread, rubberised hair, microporous ebonite for battery containers, etc. For obtaining any of these products, a whole range of compounding ingredients used in latex technology may be divided into the following categories-

a. Stabilisers, including surfactants
b. Vulcanising agents
c. Antioxidants
d. Vulcanising accelerators
e. Fillers
f. Viscosity modifiers (thickeners)
g. Gel sensitisers.

Latex stabilisers comprise alkalis, protective colloids and numerous surface active agents. The most common vulcanising agent is elemental sulphur or sulphur donors like fetramethyl thiuram disulphide. The latter confers enhanced heat resistance. Metal oxides including zince oxide are used as cross-linking agents with carboxylic latices.

The most important vulcanising accelerators for latex are zinc diethyl dithiocrabamate (ZDEC) with zinc salt of mercaptobenzothiazole (ZMBT) as the common secondary accelerator. Latex antioxidants fall into three main classes viz. amine derivatives, hindered phenols and styrenated phenols. Wax is included in latex formulation to serve as antiozonant.

Main types of fillers used in latex technology are the clays, e.g. hydrated aluminium silicate, aluminium trihydrate and calcium carbonate. As thickeners, polyacrylate, cellulose derviatives and aliginates are the most important. Gel sensitisers may be, those which are effective t ordinary temperatures but with delayed action and those that are activated at higher temperatures. The best known delyaed action gelling agent is sodium sillicofluoride. A common heat sensitiser is polyvinyl methyl ether.

MANUFACTURING TECHNIQUES OF RUBBER GOODS FROM LATEX

Manufacturing of rubber goods from latex would require techniques which are peculiar to the nature of latex itself. Latex is a colloidal solution, the rubber particles being suspended in a serum and carry a negative charge. Any compounding ingredinents to be incorporated in latex should be so processed that these do not destablilise the resulting mix. After a suitable mix has been prepared, the next step is to get the shape of the article and then cure of vulcanise. The different techniques that are applied to the fabrication of materials from compounded latex can be classified as under-

a. Dipping
b. Casting and moulding
c. Spreading
d. Spraying
e. Extrusion
f. Electrodeposition.

Vulcanisation of the resulting matrix is carried out a comparatively low temperatures, i.e., of the order of 100°C. It is for this reason that ultra-fast accelerators are used in the compounding of latex.

Stabilisation of Latex

The stability of rubber latex is due to the presence of adsorbed layers of proteins and phospholipids on rubber globules. Left exposed to the atmosphere, acids are developed on account of bacterial action which destabilise the latex. Ammonia is used as a preservative and stabiliser. It acts through a series of complex reactions generating fatty acid soap. Further degree of stabilisation is sought through the addition of proteins like casein which has the disadvantage of subject to putrifaction. Synthetic stabilisers have been increasingly employed. In the following paragraphs is a brief description of two typical compounds-

a. *Anionic surface active agent* - Sodium salt of acetylolyl sulphate. A 20% solution is added to the latex. Heavily loaded spreading compounds require as much as 5% on the filler content; in case of spray mix, 1.5% on the filler content; in case of spray mix, 1.5% on dry rubber content, and in dipping compounds, the dosage is 1% on the rubber content.

b. *Non-ionic surface-active agent* - A condensation product of ethylene oxide, it confers stability in latex against mechanical action, acid and poly-valent salts. It prevents zinc oxide thickening and are employed when highly active accelerator systems are employed. It loses its activity at elevatd temperatures and is used in heat sensitive compounds.

Softeners and Fillers

Solid rubber is subject to breakdown through mastication; such a treatment is not meted out to rubber in the latex form. Therefore, articles prepared from latex are much tougher. To overcome this defect, softeining agents are added to the latex. Following are some of the important softeners-

a. *Liquid paraffin* - It is a good softener and is incorporated to the extent of 20% on the dry rubber content.

b. *Paraffin wax* - It is incorporated in concentration above 2%.

c. *Stearic acid* - Upto 10% may be used in proofings, the addition of stearic acid is essential when MBT is the sole accelerator present.

Fillers

Addition of fillers to latex confers the following advantages-

a. Reduces the cost

b. Increase the viscosity of the compound

c. Prevent the spreading mixes in fabric processing from striking through.

Fillers do not have the same effect in latex as in dry rubber compounding. For example, carbon black serves as a pigment and does not confer any reinforcing action.

Following are some of the important fillers found suitable for incorporating in a latex formulation:

i. China clay is added in concentration as high as 400% on the rubber content of the latex. Being lightly aggregated, these can be easily dispersed by ball milling or with the help of colloid mill. Suitalbe grades of China clay can be used to produce latex mixes having a wide range of viscosity. Colloidal clays of the bentonite type are used for producing tough latex rubber but they cause considerable thickening.

ii. Mica powder.

iii. Whiting (clacium carbonate) are available either as ground limestone or precipitated chalk.

iv. Lithopone may be added upto 200% in the rubber content of latex.

v. Blance fixe (barium sulphate) gives a smooth product.

Vulcanising Agents and Accelerators

Sulphur, zinc oxide and accelerators collectively form the vulcanising system. Vulcanisation of the rubber may be effected by either of the two ways:

a. Rubber maybe vulcanised after it has been shaped into the desired form and dried.

b. The latex may be completely vulcanised while in the fluid state so that it deposits elastic films of vulcanised rubber on drying.

The doses of vulcanising agents are adjusted according to the requirements of the end product:

i. Sulphur (rubber grade) free from acid. A 50% dispersion is prepared by ball milling.

ii. Zinc oxide is an important vulcanising aid and is incorporated as dispersion. By itself it has very low solubility but in the presenice of ammonia and its salt, it dissolves to give zinc ammonium complexes which are soluble. The latter leads to progressive thickening and destabilisation. The zinc oxide thickening may be overcome by the following methods:

- Addition of stabilisers
- Reduction of ammonia content
- Addition of fixed alkali such as sodium or potassium hydroxide.

Accelerators

In latex compounding fast accelerators are used. Dithiocrabamates are the most commonly used accelerators for latex products. Thiazoles and thiurams also find some application, the former mainly as secondary accelerators for the dithiocrabamates.

a. Zinc diethyl diethyl dithiocarbamate (ZDC) is used for normal heat cures and yields vulcanisates of excellent physical properties. A satisfactory formulation, comprising 1% ZDC, 1.5% ZnO, and 1% sulphur on dry rubber content will give a satisfactory cure in 30 minutes at 100°C in air. The cure is flat.

b. Zinc salt of mercaptozobenzothiazole (ZMBT) by itself is slow accelerator under the conditions in which latex is cured. It is mainly used in combination with ZDC giving vulcanisate of higher modulus and load bearing capacity.

c. Tetramethyl thiuram disulphide (TMT) is a good accelerator of satisfactory cure. Rubber from a latex mix containing 0.5% TMT, 1.5% sulphur, and 1.0% zinc oxide can be cured in 30 minutes at 115°C.

A very important use of TMT is in sulphurless cure. Incorporation of sulphur donor like thiourea is necessary to obtain a satisfactory cure at 100°C.

Antioxidants

It is of interest of note that rubber product obtained directly from latex show ageing properties superior to those of identically formulated compound from raw solid rubber which has to be milled before compounding. However, it is useful to incorporate antioxidant in the latex mix. Following is the range of antioxidants usually employed.

a. *Ketone-amine condensation product* affords very good protection against normal ageing and confers flex-cracking resistance. It is not recommended for white or light coloured goods. Dosage, 1% on dry rubber content.

b. *Phenyl β-naphthylamine (PBNA)* is similar to above in B properties but causes more discolouration on exposure to light. On account of its limited solubility, it tends to bloom when added more than 1.5%.

c. *Styrenated phenol* is non-staining antioxidant and recommended for white or light coloured articles. It offers a very good protection against the effect of sunlight. Proportions between 1 and 2% on the weight of rubber are recommended.

Preparation of Aqueous Dispersions and Emulsions

Water insoluble solids which have to be incorporated in the latex are suitably dispersed in water, and the dispersion is stabilised suitably. This is done with the help of a ball mill or a colloidal mill. The ball mill consists essentially of a cylindrical container half to two-thirds filled with a grinding charge capable of being securely sealed. The container is roated about its cylindrical axis in a horizontal plane at such s speed that the charge is tumbled. The grinding charge consists of unglazed porcelain or glass balls. Depending upon the size of the mill, the diameter of the balls varies from 1.2-1.5 to 2.5 cm. A variation uses flint gravel.

The mill should be charged with the solid to be disperesed, water, wetting, and dispersing agent until the ball and the gravel are just covered. The ratio of water and solid matter in the paste should be such as to render the contents sufficiently fluid to tumble as the mill rotates. The rate of grinding in the mill is related to the diameter of the container. If the mill rotates too rapidly, centrifugal force will cause of charge to adhere to the container walls and there will be no grinding Larger mills must roate more slowly than the smaller ones. Time of grinding will depend upon the nature of the material.

Selection and amount of dispersing agent are determined by the physical properties of the material to be dispersed. The function of these agents are to wet the powder, to prevent and reduce frothing and to obviate reaggregation of the particles. The concentration of the dispersing agent should be maintained at the minimum required to produce the desired effect. Ordinarily 2% of the total charge are used.

Of the non-proprietary dispersing agents, soaps are the best. Ammonium oleate is commonly used soap. It may be prepared by agitating 19 parts by weight to oleic acid with a slight excess of concentrated ammonia solution, and water to make upto 100 parts by weight. Proteins such as casein and gums have also been recommended for preparing dispersions. The former have a marked tendency to putrefy but a more stable solution may be prepared with 10 parts of casein, 1.5 parts of borax and 88.5 parts of water. Gums possess inferior wetting power but have the advantage of increasing the viscosity.

In all these operations, dispersions or solutions which are to be added to latex should be prepared with distilled or soft water.

The following table gives broadly the suggested speed of rotation of ball mill in relation to the diameter of the container.

Internal diameter of the container: cm	inch	R.P.M.
10	4	93
15	6	76
20	8	66
25	10	59
30	12	53
38	15	48
46	18	44
53	21	41
61	24	38

Preparation of Aqueous Dispersions

The following basic formulae and methods are suggested for the preparation of the aqueous dispersions of the common compounding ingredients used in the processing of latex:

		Parts by weight
i.	Sulphur (50% dispersion)	
	Sulphur	100
	Dispersing agent	4
	Distilled water	96
	Ball mill 48 hrs.	
ii.	Zinc diethyl dithiocarbamate (50% dispersion)	
	ZDC	100
	Dispersing agent	2
	Distilled water	98
	Ball mill 24 hrs.	
iii.	Zinc oxide (40% dispersion)	
	Zinc oxide	100
	Dispersing agent	3
	Distilled water	147
	Bill mill 24 hrs.	
iv.	Antioxidant (20% dispersion)	
	China clay	50
	General purpose heat resistant antioxidant (Acetone-diphenylamine condensate)	50
	Dispersing agent	3
	Distilled water	147
	Ball mill 24 hrs.	

Alternate to ball milling, colloid mill may be used for the dispersion of solid materials. The machine consists essentially of two circular plates, one of which is stationary and the other rotates at a very high speed, 1000-20,000 revolutions per minute. The clearance between the two plates is generally adjustes do withing very narrow limits (0.25-0.2 mm). The slurry is fed into the clearance; on account of the very high revolution of the plate, a tearing action for the material fed takes place which helps in dispersing the solid material.

Preparation of Liquid Compounding Ingredients

Liquid compounding ingredinents which are water immiscible, can be emulsified in water with the aid of an emulsifying agent such as potassium oleate. The emulsion for use in latex should be O-in-W (oil in water) types in which water is the continuous phase and the suspended droplets carry a negative charge. A simple equipment for the preparation of emulsion consists of a tank and a high speed stirrer. Very fine and stable emulsions can be prepared by a device which imparts a shearing action e.g. a colloid mill and or a homogeniser. The emulsifying agent may be prepared in situ. In this method, the cationic part of the soap (ammonia, KOH or amine) is dissolved in water and the anionic part (oleic, stearic or resin acid) is dissolved in the liquid to be emulsified. Often the technique is modified in that the water solution is added in small amounts to the non-aqueous phase producing first water-in-oil emulsion which undergoes an inversion to an oil-in-water emulsion on further addition of the aqueous phase. Recipes for the preparation of typical emulsions are given as under:

i. Liquid paraffin (50% emulsion)	Parts by weight
Liquid paraffin	50
Oleic acid	2.5/A
Conc. ammonia soln.	2.5/B
Water	45/B

Oleic acid is mixed with the liquid paraffin and the mixture added to the water containing concentrated ammonia solution. The two phases are mixed by agitation and the emulsion is improved by passing through a homogeniser.

ii. Styrenated phenol (50% emulsion)	
Styrenated phenol	50/Part A
Oleic acid	2/Part A
Triethanolamine	1.5/Part B
Water	46.5/Part B

Part A is heated to about 60°C and then added with high speed stirring to Part B also at the same temperature. The stirring is till the emulsion attins the room temperature.

iii. Stearic acid (16% emulsion)	100.0
Oleic acid	2.5
KOH	2.5
Conc. ammonia soln.	2.5
Water	490.0

Stearic acid, 100 parts, is melted with 2.5 parts of oleic acid and poured with vigorous stirring into 490 parts of water at 70°C containing 2.5 parts of KOH. Ammonia (2.5 parts of 0.880 sp. gravity) or an equivalent amount of amore dilute solution is then added and the mixture cooled while continuing the stirring.

Calculation of Latex Formulation

Compounding of latex should be performed in a vessel that is chemically resistant to the latex and compounding ingredients. Preferably the vessel should be equipped with a mechanical stirrer, the blades of which are located low in the vessel and have a shape that indeces agitation without foaming. The compounding ingredient is best added to the continually stirred latex in a slow steady stream with minimum of splashing.

Latex formulations are usually calculated on dry rubber content (DRC) in case of natural rubber latx and on total solids coutent with synthetic latices.

An illustration of a latex compound in parts by mass is given below:

Ingredient	parts of the principal constituent (dry)	Wet parts
Natural rubber latex (60% DRC)	100	167.5
20% Potassium hydroxide soln.	0.5	2.5
50% Sulphur dispersion	0.5	1.0
50% Antioxidant dispersion	1.0	2.0
50% ZDC dispersion	0.5	1
50% Zinc oxide dispersion	1.0	2.0

Forming of Products from the Compounded Latex

For the production of useful articles from the latex compound, it is necessary to convert the rubber into the desired form. A wide range of methods are available, of which the important one straight dip method is described below.

Straight Dip Method

Articles like toy balloons, teats, globes, contraceptive can be prepared from the compounded latex by dipping process. The prcess consists essentially of dipping a former in the shape of the article to be made in the compounded latex. The deposited film is dried, vulcanised and then stripped from the former.

A dipping mix of general utility suitable for the above is given below:

Ingredients	Parts by Wt
60% Centrifuged latex	167.0
20% Stabilising solution (Cetyl oleyl sulphate)	3.5
50% Sulphur dispersion	3.0
50% ZDC dispersion	2.0
50% zinc oxide dispersion	2.0
Cure 30 min. at 100°C.	

Since zinc oxide has a thickening action on the latex compound in the presence of ammonia, it is preferable to reduce the ammonia content to about 0.1% by blowing air or reacting with formaldehyde.

In case of balloons, softenrers may be incorporated to reduce the modulus and thus render them easier to inflate.

For articles such as gloves, a filler such as China clay may be added in the form of 50% dispersion. Antioxidants can also be incorported.

When fabric lined gloves are prepared by dipping, a wetting agent and a thickening agent may be included to control the penetration and better keying of the rubber to the fabric.

Products like teats, contraceptives, surgeon's gloves and electician's gloves are to be made from extra purified latex. Surgeon's gloves must be thin yet strong and stand repeated sterilisations. A combination of good tensile strength and high elongation is required so that the choice of curing conditions is quite critical. A proper non-staining antioxidant is also necessary.

Electrician's gloves are much thicker and must be as free as possible from non-rubber constituents which would affect electrical resistance.

Following are the essentials of equipment of flow-

Former

These may be made from metal, glass, lacquered wood, porecelain (both glazed and unglazed).

Dipping Tanks

The containers for the latex may be made from stone, enamelled iron, stainless steel, or wood lined with pitch, rubber, gutta percha or the like. The temperature should be thermostatically controlled and the vessel should be equipped with a mechanical stirrer. Slow stirring of the latex mix assists in the removal of bubbles and constantly changing the surface minimises the formation of a skin. If a skin is formed, it can be removed by skinning the surface.

Coagulant

There are two types of coagulants, viz.

a. Salt coagulant

b. Acid coagulant.

Following are the compositions of these coagulants-

	Ingredients	Parts by Wt.
i.	Calcium chloride	20.0
	Ethanol	60.0
	Water	20.0
ii.	Calcium nitrate (hydrated)	20.0
	Ethanol	20.0
	Water	60.0
iii.	Cyclohexyl amine	12.4
	Accetic acid	7.6
	Ethanol	80.0

Dipping Process

The formers are held in racks which may be lowered mechanically either into the coagulant or the latex bath.

The process itself consists of dipping the former into the coagulant and after withdrawing, solvent is allowed to evaporate. This is followed by dipping into latex. For balloons, one such dipping cycle is sufficient. If no coagulant is used, several latex dips may be required and the coating dried or partially dired between each dip.

After dip in the latex, rate of withdrawal should be such as to allow adequate drainage of fluid from the former. Inversion and possible rotation of the former, as soon as it has been withdrawn from the bath serves to eliminate the drop of latex which tends to collect at the lowest part.

Given below are some typical formulations:

Industrial gloves	Parts by Wt.
60% Centrifuged latex	167.0
20% Stabilising solution	5.0
Sulphur dispersion	4.0

50% ZDC dispersion	2.0
40% Zinc oxide dispersion	4.0
50% China clay dispersion	50.0
20% Antioxidant dispersion	5.0
25% Carbon black dispersion	As required
Cure 30 min. at 105-110°C	

Surgical gloves	Parts by Wt.
60% N.R. latex	167.0
Thickening agent	1.0
50% Sulphur dispersion	1.5
50% ZDC dispersion	1.5
40% zinc oxide dispersion	2.0
20% Ketone amine antioxidant	2.5
50% Styrenated phenol antioxidant	2.0
50% Liquid paraffin emulsion	5.0
Cure 30 min. at 100°C	

Prevulcanised latex	Parts by wt.
60% Centrifuged latex	167.0
10% Dispersing agent	5.0
50% sulphur dispersion	2.0
50% ZDC dispersion	2.0

The mixture is heated for 2-2 1/2 hrs at 80°C. To the vulcanised latex may be added dispersion of fillers, mineral oil, pigments as desired.

Casting and Moulding

Casting as the name implies, involves the using of a mould on the inside of which the rubber article is formed. The moulds are of two types.

i. Plaster of Paris

ii. Metal.

The compounded latex is poured inside the mould and the same is roated in all the directions so that the latex is evenly distributed. Gelation in the plaster mould is brought about by partial absorption of water by the material of the mould. In the metal mould, gelation is brought about using a heat sensitising compound in the latex mix.

In case of casting with plaster mould, the same is filled with the compound. As the water is taken up by the absorbent plaster, the level of latex will fall; further quantities of latex are added to fill the mould. After the desired thickness has been built up, the excess latex is poured out and the same may be used again.

The plaster mould together with the deposite of latex is placed in an oven at 40-60° For several hours for consolidation and partial drying. At the end, the moulded article is carefully taken out, dired and finally cured at 100°C.

A typical formulation is as under-

Ingredients	Parts by Wt.
60% NR latex	167.0
20% Stabilising solution	3.0
50% Sulphur dispersion	3.0
50% ZDC dispersion	2.0
40% Zinc oxide dispersion	4.0
50% Filler dispersion	As required
20% Pigment dispersion	5.0
Cure 30 min. at 100°C.	

Moulding with Metal Moulds

The case moulds of light alloys, e.g., of aluminium or stainless steel are available. Copper, brass, iron or alloys containing copper or manganese should be avoided.

The mould is heated in an oven or water bath to about 85°C and filled with the latex compound. Gelation of the compound takes place starting at the hot walls of the mould. After two to three minutes, the excess ungelled latex is taken out for subsequent use taking some precautions like not mixing with fresh compound without a prior cooling.

The mould is then returned to the oven for 1-15 minutes to ensure complete setting of the rubber deposit, after which it is opened and the moulding removed. It is then partially dried at 40-50°C washed for several hours in cold running water for several hours, dired off at 50°C and finally vulcanised for 30 minutes at 100°C. In the formulation, heat sensitising agent, e.g. ammonium acetate and delayed action gelling agent, e.g., sodium silicofluoride can be used.

A typical formula is as under:

Ingredients	Parts by Wt.
60% Ammonia preserved latex	167.0
Stabilising agent	0.5
20% Ammonium acetate solution	7.5
50% sulphur dispersion	4.0
50% ZDC dispersion	2.0
40% Zinc oxide dispersion	4.0
50% Antioxidant emulsion	2.0
20% Pigment dispersion	As required
50% Filler dispersion	As required

In this case the stabilising agent should be so selected that it loses its activity above 70°C, when ammonium acetate brings about gelation.

Preparation of Latex Foam

A very major proportion of latex is used for the manufacture of foam articles, e.g., cushioning material for bedding, automotive seating, etc. The process consists of the following stages:

a. Preparation of the compound
b. Foaming
c. Addition of gelling agent
d. Pouring of the sensitised foam into a mould
e. Foam gelling
f. Foam curing
g. De-molding of the foam
h. Washing and drying.

Preparation of the Compounds

Compounds for latex foam production are based on natural rubber latex, SBR latex, could polymerised, reinforced or blends of natural and SBR latices. Zinc oxide is an essential ingredient in the preparation of foam, but in the case of high ammonia latices, zinc oxide will lead to thickening and final destabilisation, which is highly undesirable. Hence, the latex is de-ammoniated and brought down to 0.1-0. 15% by the addition of formaldehyde or by blowing moist air across the surface of the latex while stirring it.

The latex is allowed to mature and during the course of maturing, sulphur, acceleratiors, and other compounding ingredients except zinc oxide are added. A control on temperature is required.

Foaming and Gelling

Foaming is done by continuous or batch process. It is done by whipping, the extent of beating time being determined by the desired volume increase. After the desired volume increase has taken place, zince oxide with secondary gelling agent if the latter is required and followed by gelling agent, is added. The speed of beating is reduced. The beating is continued till the chemicals have been finally added. The foam is then poured into the mould.

The sequence of operations requires a very delicate balancing of time. The gelling action should start before there is a collapse of the forth and yet should enable the frothed material to be poured into the mould.

Vulcanisation

Steam at atmospheric pressure should be used for curing moulded foam product. In normal cases, a period of 30-40 minutes is adequate.

Washing and Drying

After vulcanisation, the foam product is stripped from the mould and trimmed. It is then thoroughly washed to remove salts, soaps, and eliminate any odoriferous residues. Excess water after washing is removed by squeezing and dried in hotair at 60-80°C.

The mechanism of gel formation in this case is as under-

The latex compound contains, in addition to the curing ingredients, ammonia and additional soap. After the forth has been made by mechanical agitation, zinc oxide and sodium silicofluoride are added. The pH at this stage is in the range of 10.0 to 10.5.

The hydrolysis brings about gelation of the latex foam in three ways-

i. The fall of pH due to the presence of hydrofluoric acid

ii. The adsorptive effect of silicic acid

iii. The destabilisation effect of zinc amines formed from the reaction of zinc oxide with ammonium fluoride.

By suitable choice of levels of zinc oxide and sodium silicofluoride, and in some cases, the use of secondary gelling agents such as diphenyl guanidine the reactions lead to the formation of open call. Following is a typical recipe:

Ingredients	Parts by Wt.
60% N.R. latex	167.00
20% Potassium oleate soln.	5.00
50% Sulphur dispersion	4.00
50% ZDC dispersion	2.00
50% ZMBT dispersion	2.00
20% PBNA dispersion	2.50
50% Styrenated phenol emulsion	2.00
50% China clay slurry	0.30
Fast Colour	As required
40% Zinc oxide dispersion	10.00
Secondary gelling agent	0.5-1.00
20% Sodium silicifluoride dispersion	5.0-7.50

SBR Latices - Compared with natural rubber, SBR latces yield foam of lower tensile strength and a poor hot tear strength. For these reasons, a bland of 50/50 NR - SBR is used. Following is a typical recipe:

Ingredients	Parts by Wt.	
	Wet	Dry
60% NR latex (ammonia 0.1%)	83.00	50.00
69% SBR latex	73.00	50.00
20% Potassium oleate soln.	1.25	0.25
50% Sulphur dispersion	4.00	2.00
50% ZDC dispersion	2.00	1.00
50% ZMBT dispersion	2.00	1.00
Antioxidant dispersion/emulsion		1.00
Foamed and then add		
Thickening agent 50% dispersion	1.50	0.75
50% Zinc oxide dispersion	8.00	4.00
20% Sodium silicofluoride dispersion	9.00	1.80
Cure - 45 min. at 100°C water or steam		

Polychloroprene Latex Foam - These latices posses superior flame, oil, chemical and ageing resistance. A typical formulation based on Neoprene 601A is given below:

Ingredients	Parts by Wt. (dry)
Neoprene 601A	100.0
40% Petrolatum emulsion	3.0
Stabiliser	2.0
50% Sulphur dispersion	2.0
50% ZDC dispersion 2.0	
Foam and then add -	
Secondary agents	2.0.
50% Zinc oxide dispersion	7.5
200%-Sodium silicofluoride disperssion	2.0
preferably equal proportions of sodium and potassium salts	
Cure initial 30 min. at 120°C in steam	
Post cure drying 16 hrs. at 80°C	

Manufacture of Latex Thread

Rubber thread from late is manufactured by a process of extrusion. A suitably compouded latex is allowed to pass through glass nozzles under pressure into a bath of cagulant. The extruded latex gel is in the form of a round thread which is drawn out of the bath and subjected to washing, drying and vulcanising operations.

The process for the manufacture of latex thread can be divided into the following operations-

a. Preparation of the latex compound

b. Extusion into the coagulant bath

c. Washing

d. Drying and curing.

Preparation of the Latex Compound

Following is typical recip:

Ingredients	Parts by Wt.
60% NR latex, deammoniated	167.0
10% Potasium hydroxide solution	3.5
20% Potassium oleate solution	5.0
50% Sulphur dispersion	2.0
50% ZDC dispersion	2.0

40% zinc oxide dispersion	2.5
50% Styrenated phenol emulsion	2.0
Colouring matter	As required

The ammonia content of the ammonia preserved latex is reduced to 0.1-0.2%. Deammoniation of the latex is essential since the presence of too much ammonia would lead toexcessive variation in viscosity during storage.

Dispersion of the compounding ingredients should be good and free from coarse particles and air bubbles.

Extrusion Process

The latex compound described above is transferred to the feed tank when it flows to a manifold leading to capillaries for extrusion into a coagulant bath. The coagulant normally used is acetic acid of 20-40% concentration.

Washing

The gelled threads are drawn out of the acid bath and conveyed through one or two washing tanks 6-9 ft. long to remove any surplus acid and water soluble impurities. The temperature is approximately 80°C.

Drying and Vulcanising

From the washing bath, the threads are carried by a conveyor belt into a heated tunnel in which air is circulated. A gradation of temperature 70°C to about 130°C is maintained. After leaving the heated tunnel, the threads pass through a bank of talc and then wound on to bobbins or drums.

Latex Application in Carpet Industry

Of the many techniques for the manufacture of carpets, largest volume is of the tufted type. Carpet, direct from the tufting machine, is limp and without any further processing is virtually unusable as a floor covering. It is essential to apply some sort of coating at the back for stabilisation. Latex (natural or synthetic) suitably compounded is applied on the underside as a backing. Three techniques for application are available-

i. Precoating, lick or froth
ii. Secondary backing, lick or high solids froth technique
iii. Foam backing, using a gelling agent like sodium silicofluoride, zinc-amine or non-gel.

The essential requirements of high density foamed carpet backing include:

i. Limits for wt. g/m^2

ii. Density
iii. Thickness
iv. Compression set
v. Compression resistance
vi. De-lamination
vii. Accelerated ageing
viii. Ash content.

In the formulation for various compositions for use inlatex or their compounding, following are the specifications/requirements of some of the ingredients used.

Polymer

Carboxylic SBR latex (50-60% styrene); (60-70% styrene) - The carboxyl functional group confers important advantages, such as ability to use sulphurless cross-linking system with other functional monomers and a high adhesive strength. The increased polarity of the polymer increases its compatibility with and affinity for polar substances such as fibres or inorganic fillers.

Under the international codification scheme, such latices are given the code XSBR with a number designation for the styrene content.

Styrene-butadiene latex - N.R. latex 60%, LA-SPP type (low ammonia, santobrite preserved) preferred on account of its conferring high mechanical stability.

Heaveaplus MG 49 - It is a copolymer latex made by grafting methyl methacrylate monomer on natural rubber latex. It is used inconjunction with NR LA-SPP latex to confer sitffening and improved bound strength.

Stabiliser

Sulphonated alkyl - ethylene oxide condensate.

Sequesterant

Polyphosphate e.g. sodium hexametaphosphate in order to sequester any free calcium ions and maintain long-term viscosity stability.

Defoamers

These are used to reduce tendency for frothing.

Fillers

Such as calcite, dolomite or clay moderately fine particle size. For meeting flammability requirements, alumina trihydrate (ATH) is used for replacing some or the entire quantity of calcium carbonate.

Thickeners

Used to minimise filler settling out of suspension and to control penetration into tufts. Polyacrylates, cellutostics, etc.

Antioxidant

Quinoline based or hindered phenolic typ, i.e., N.N'-dicyclohexyl phenylene diamine designated for heat protection and not light.

Gel Stabilisers

Sodium silicofluoride (NSR) or ammonium acetate.

Vulcanising System

Vulcanising include - Zno - ZDEC - ZMBT.

Forthing Compound

Sodium lauryl sulphate.

Following is a brief description of various techniques adopted as undercoating in carpet.

Precoating

The tufted carpet is carried over rollers which revolve in a lick bath containing the prepared latex mix. The compound is thus forced into the back of the carpet and excess is removed by the scraper baldes. Degree of peetration of the latex depends among other factors on compound viscosity. After passing over stentors, the heating is done by infrared heaters directed at the precoat side only.

Following are some typical formulations:

Using XSBR latex

Ingredients	Parts by mass (dry basis)	
	Lick coating	Forth coating
Carboxylic SBR latex (50-60% styrene)	100.00	-
Carboxylic SBR latex (60-70% styrene)	-	100.00
Sodium lauryl sulphate	-	0.75
Sodium hexametaphosphate	0.50	0.50
Defoamer	0.50	-
Calcium carbonate filler	600.00	500.00
Polyacrylate thickener	To viscosity	5-10 Pa.
Water	To 78% TSC.	

Using NR latex

Ingredients	Wet Wt.
60% NR latex, LA-SPP type	167.0
50% Heveaplus MG 49 latex	60.0
25% Surfactant solution	3.0
Tetrasodium pyrophosphate	1.0
Water	To 72-75% total solid content
Filler	400
10% Thiourea dispersion	10.0
50% Antioxidant dispersion	2.0
Anti-foam agent	As requied
10% Thickener solution	4.0 or as required

Secondary Backing

The process, also termed as jute backing, involves latex coating on the back side of the carpet in the same manner as for precoats and laminating to the secondary jute followed by drying in an air-circulating oven. To produce a satisfactory end product, the adhesive qualities of the compound must be good.

The following are typical formulations for secondary backing of tufted carpets:

SBR latex formulation

Ingredients	Lick coating	High solid froth technique
Carboxylic SBR latex (50-60% styrene)	100	
Carboxylic SBR latex (specially dsigned)	-	
Water	To 78% TSC	To 82-84% TSC
Sodium hexametaphosphate	0.25	0.5
Calcium carbonate filler	300	400
Sodium lauryl sulphate	-	0.5
Thickener (polyacrylate)	To 10 Pa.	To 20 Pa.

N.R. latex formulation

Ingredients	Wet. wt.
60% N R latex LA-SPP type	167
50% Heveaplus MG 49 latex	60
Surfactant solution	3
Tetrasodium pyrophosphate	1
Water	To 68-75% total solids
Filler	100
10% Thiourea solution	10
50% Antioxidant dispersion	2
10% Thickener solution	5 or as required

The above solution gives a maximum delamination strenath of 3.5 kg/g^2

Foam Backing

Three systems are in use:

a. Zinc-amine,
b. Sodium silicofluoride and
c. Non-gel process.

Wherever foam is used, a precoat is applied first. After the precoat is substantially dry, the foam then can be applied. Mechanical devices are used to deposit the foam evenly. After foam application, the carpet is carried on to a pin stentor which carries the carpet through the even and prevents carpet shrinkage during drying and vulcanisation.

Zinc-amine Gelation System

The above, also known as ammonium acetate system, is based on chemical reactions involving zinc ions, ammonium salts, ammonia and fatty acid soaps.

Gelation of latex involves a phase inversion from rubber-in-water (O-in W) to water in rubber (W-in-O). Following is a typical recipe:

Ingredients	Parts by mass (dry)
Styrenebutadiene latex	50.00
Potassium oleate	3.00
Water	To 70% TSC.
natural rubber latex	50.00
Sulphur	2.25
ZDEC	1.25
ZMBT	1.00
Antioxidant	1.00
Zinc oxide	3.00
Calcium carbonate filler	100.00
Polysiloxane system	0.15
Polyacrylate thickener	0.10
Ammonium acetate	2.00

Sodium Sillicofluoride System

Gelation is brogught about by the hydrolysis of NSF in water to liberate hydrofluoric acid. In combination with zinc ions, the HF reacts with the stabilising fatty acid soap to cause a controlled colescence a room temperature.

But in the carpet industry, there is insufficient time to allow a room temperature gelation and it is treated like all other foams in carpet industry to pass through the infra-red zone to accelerate gelation. Following is typical recipe:

Ingredients	Parts by mass (dry)
Styrenebutadiene latex	100.00
potassium oleate	1.75
sulphur	2.00
ZDEC	1.0
ZMBT	0.75
DPG	0.75
Antioxidant	0.75
Zinc oxide	3.00
Calcium carbonate filler	50.00
Polyacrylate thickener	To viscosity 3 Pa.s
Sodium silicofluoride (NSF)	3.50

Non-gel Prcess

Several systems were developed. Dow Co. put up a specially designed SBR latex. There were no gelling agent or complicated sulphur cure paste. Instead, the cross-linking was via a melamine-formaldehyde resin.

Another process was developed by using succinate surfactant which gives a high degree of stability. Lauryl sulphate is used which acts as a foam booster. Following is a typical recipe:

Ingredients	Parts by mass (dry)
Styrene-butadiene latex	1.00.00
Disodium octyl sulphosuccinate	4.50
Sodium lauryl sulphate	0.50
Sodium hexametaphosphate	0.50
Water	To 78% TSC
Sulphur	2.00
ZDEC	2.00
ZMBT	0.75
Antioxidant quinoline type	1.00
Zinc oxide	2.00
Calcium carbonate filler	2.00.00
Polyacrylate thickener	To 3 Pas.s.

In the following table are given the comparisions of physical properties of various foams:

Characteristics	Non-gel	Zinc-amine	NSF
Filler-level (phr)	200.0	120.0	50.0
Tensile strength (kPa)	42.0	77.0	190.0
Elongation at break (%)	160.0	150.0	290.0
25% Compression modulus (kPa)	28.0	30.0	35.0
Delamination (kg/5 cm)	0.7	1.3	2.3
Surface abrasion (no. of strokes)	4.0	14.0	30.0
Raw material cost, ratio	1.0	1.33	1.90

Rubberised Hair Products

This is the name given to high quality upholstery packaging material made by bonding together of a mass of curled animal hair with latex. Today most rubberised hair products are made from a mixture of animal hair and vegetable fibre, e.g., coir (cocont fibre).

In general, the use of animal hair gives a more resilient product than the use of vegetable fibre.

The process consists essentially of the following steps-

i. Preparation of the latex compound

ii. Curling the fibres

iii. Pre-arrangement of the fibres for spraying

iv. Spraying the latex compound

v. Drying

vi. Compressing and curing the article.

The latex compound is sprayed in the loosely arranged curled fibres in such a way that a sufficient quantity is sprayed throughout the mass. The sprayed mass is dried at 70-80°C, in such a manner that there is no apparent vulcanisation. The dried material is compressed in a mould to attain the desired shape and the mould heated for 30-60 minutes in hot air at about 100°C. The product thus obtained possesses good resilience and compression modulus.

For some applications, rubberised hair products are required to have a measure of fire resistance. This is achieved by incorporating in the latex mix chlorinated wax, hydrated alumina and antimony troxide dispersions.

A typical recipe is as under:

Ingredients	Aimal hair	Parts by wt. Coir or other vegetable fibre
60% NR latex (NH_3 content reduced to 0.1%)	167.0	167.0
25% Surfactant solution	4.0	4.0
20% Potassium hydroxide soln.	2.0	2.0
50% Antioxidant dispersion	3.0	3.0
50% ZDEC dispersion	2.0	2.0
50% ZMBT dispersion	3.0	3.0
50% Sulphur dispersion	8.0	5.0
50% Zinc oxide dispersion	10.0	6.0
Water distilled	To 50% total solids content.	

Tyre Cord Dips

The reinforcing cords used in the construction of pneumatic tyres are frequently precoated with a rubber composition designed to ensure good adhesion between the cord and tyre carcass. Originally, natural rubber latex based compounds were used for the purpose but inrecent years these have largely been replaced by synthetic latices which exhibit better adhesion with the cord materials like nylon, polyester, steel, etc.

The cord mixes are based on three components, viz., resorcinol-formaldeyde resin, vinyl-pyridine-butadiene terpolymer latex and styrene-butadiene latex.

In the coating of tyre cords, the cords are drawn over a roller immersed in the latex mix, then through a squeeze roller to remove excess latex and then into a drying oven where water is evaporated and the condensation of latex is complete. A final temperature of 130°C is necessary to complete the resin condensation and ensure adequate bond strength.

Following is a typical formulation for type dip composition:

Ingredients	Nylon cord	Polyester cord
	(Parts by mass)	
Vinyl-pyridine terpolymer latex (41% TSC)	285	428
Styrene butadiene latex (40% TSC)	145	-
Resorcinol formaldehyde resin soln*	465	500
Distilled water	105	72

* Prepared as follows-resorcinol 11.0; 40% formaldehyde 15.0; sodium hydroxide 0.3; water 240.

Miscellaneous Applications

Latices have been used extensively as binder particularly in the footwear and flooring industries and manufacture of reconstituted leather board. PVA latices have been used as wood adhesives and in paints. With a proper compounding and processing techniques latices offer a great versatility in their applications.

3

Chemical Aspects of Rubber Technology

INTRODUCTION

Molecular Formula - This indicates the kind of atoms present and their number in a chemical compound, e.g., C_2H_4 for ethylene. However, there may be compounds having same molecular formula but different physical and chemical properties, e.g., C_4H_{10} is the formula for seven different compounds. They are called *isomers* and the phenomenon, i.e., compounds having same molecular formula but differing in properties is called as *isomerism*.

Isomerism may be of various kinds. The most common one is known as *structural isomerism*. In this, the atoms in the molecule are arranged differently in the isomers, i.e., the isomers differ in structure or constitution. Thus, the compound, having molecular formula, C_2H_6OH can have two isomers.

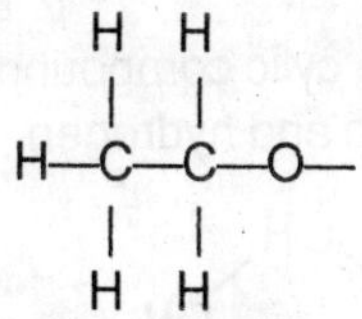

C_2H_5OH Ethyl alcohol or ethanol

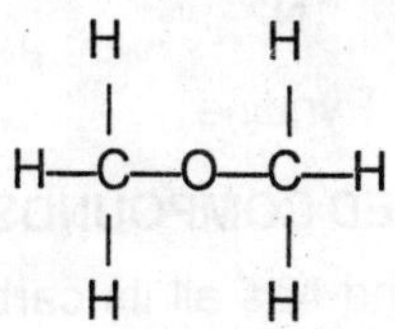

$CH_3—O—CH_3$ Dimethyl ether

CLASSIFICATION OF CARBON COMPOUNDS

Carbon compounds can be divided into four major groups.

i. **Aliphatic** - Open chain compound, e.g.,

$$CH_3—CH_3$$

C_2H_6 Ethane

ii. **Alicyclic** - Carbocyclic or saturated ring compound, e.g.,

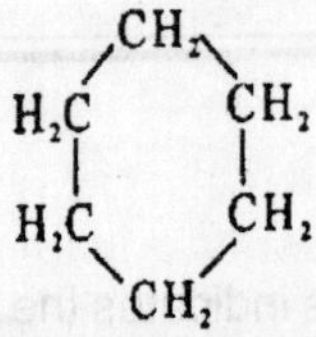

Cyclohexane

iii. **Aromatic** - These are cyclic compounds, contain alternate double and single bonds in the structure and usually derivatives of benzene (benzenoid compounds), e.g.,

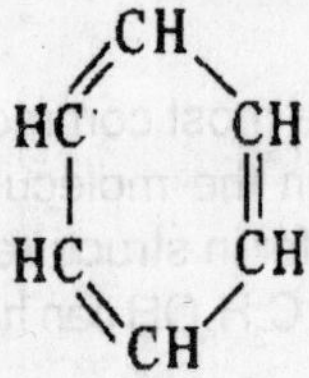

C_6H_6 Benzene

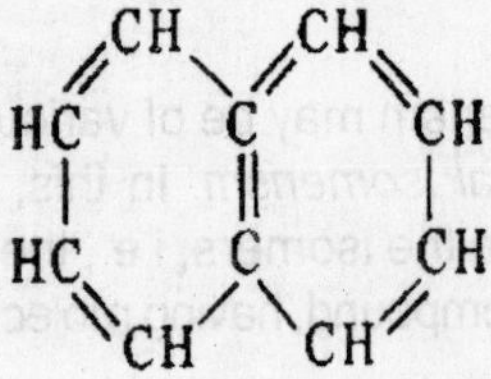

$C_{10}H_8$ Naphthalene

iv. **Heterocyclic** - These are cylic compounds containing at least one element other than carbon and hydrogen, e.g.,

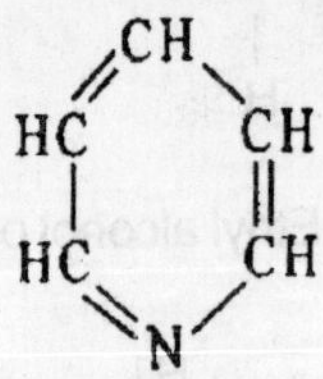

Pyridine

SATURATED AND UNSATURATED COMPOUNDS

When an organic compound has all its carbon atoms joined to any other carbon atom with a single (sigma) bond then it is called a saturated compound, e.g., ethane, cyclohexane.

When in organic compound there are at least two carbon atoms joined together by two (double) or three (triple) bonds then it is called an unsaturated compound, e.g.,

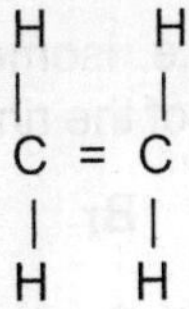

H—C ≡ C—H

$CH_2 = CH_2$

C_2H_4 Ethylene

CH ≡ CH

C_2H_2 Acetylene

The unsaturation can be of single or multiple type. The nature of double bond in multiple type may vary.

i. When there is alternate double and single bond in a compound, then the bonds are known as conjugated double bonds.

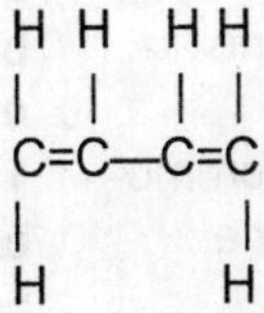

CH_2=CH—CH=CH_2

C_4H_6 1,3-Butadiene

ii. When the double bond occurs consecutively, these are called as cumulated double bonds.

CH_2=C=CH_2

Allene or propadiene.

Structural isomerism can also be possible as the number of carbon atoms increases in an aliphatic compound. Thus -

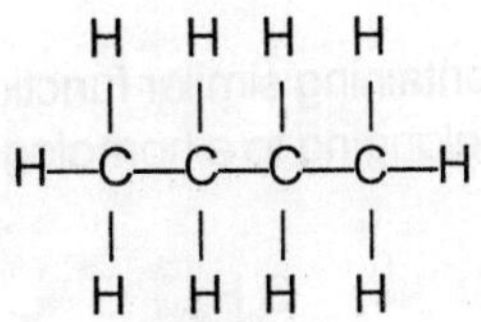

C_4H_{10}

CH_3—CH_2—CH_2—CH_3

Straight chain
normal compound
n-butane

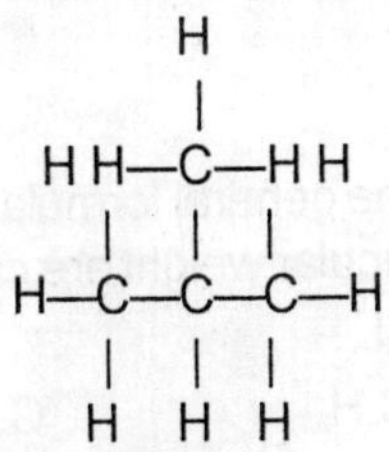

C_4H_{10}

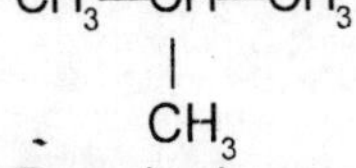

Branched compound
iso-butane
2-methyl propane

In cyclic compounds positional isomerism, i.e. isomerism occurring due to the presence of a group at different position of the ring occur.

C_6H_6
Benzene

C_6H_5Br
Bromo-benzene

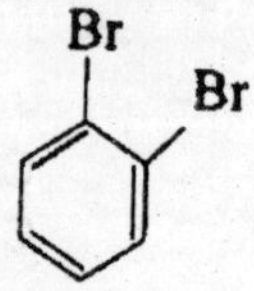

$C_6H_4Br_2$
Orth-di-bromo-benzene
0-
1, 2-dibromo-benzene

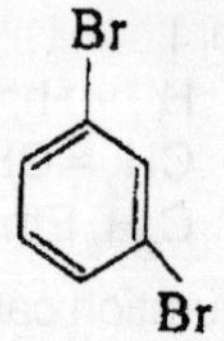

$C_6H_4Br_2$
Meta-di-brome benzene
m-
1,3-di bromo benzene

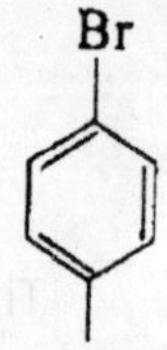

$C_6H_4Br_2$
Para-di-bromo benzene
p-
1,4-di-bromo benzene

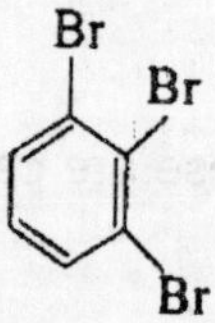

1, 2, 3-tribromo benzene

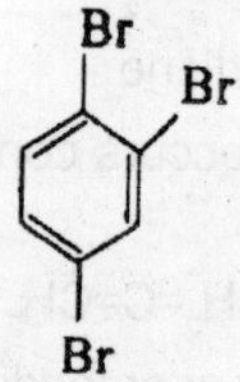

1,2,4-tri-bromobenzene

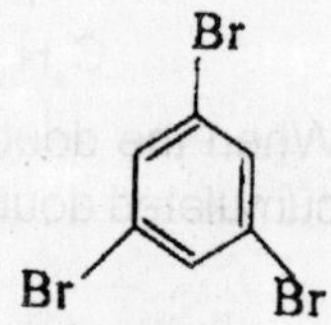

1,3,5 - tribromo benzene or sym-tribro-mo benezne

HOMOLOGOUS SERIES

Members having same general formula and containing similar functional groups but differing in molecular weight are called belonging to a homologous series. Thus,

CH_4	C_2H_6	C_3H_8	C_4H_{10}
Methane	Ethane	Propane	Butane

Genral Formula Paraffin Series - C_nH_{2n+2}

TYPE OF COMPOUNDS

Paraffins

Paraffins have the general formula, C_nH_{2n+2} and contain only C and H having single bonds between C atoms. The bonds are covalent, and non-polar. The paraffins have names ending with *ane*, e.g., *propane*, *butane*. They are inert and unreactive, from C_1 to C_4 they are colourless gases, C_5 to C_{17}

colourless liquids and C_{18} onwards colourless solids. The melting and boiling points, etc., increase regularly with the increase in chain length. They are isoluble in polar (e.g., water) solvents, but soluble in non-polar (e.g., benzene) solvents. They are not usually attacked by acids, alkalis, oxidising or reducing agents. The radical generated from a paraffin is called an alkyl group, ending with *yl*. Thus,

Ethane	Ethyl
C_2H_6	C_2H_5—
CH_3—CH_3	CH_3—CH_2—

Olefins

Their general formula is C_nH_{2n}. The simplest compound is ethylene and such compounds are also called as ethylenic compounds. They contain only C and H and have one or more double bond in the structure. Depending upon their structure they may be either polar or non-polar. If the structure is symmetric, e.g., C_2H_4, it is non-polar, otherwise it is polar. The name ends with *ene* and they may be named usually by three systems.

i. Lowest number is given to the double bond, and the number indicates the first of the two carbon atoms that are joined together by the double bond.

—C—C—C—C—C—C
6 5 4 3 2 1

CH_3—CH_2—CH=CH_2
α - butylene or 1-butylene or 1-butene

CH_3—CH=CH—CH_3
β - butylene or 2-butylene or 2-butene

Due to the presence of double bonds, olefins are reactive and undergo addition reactions.

$$CH_2{=}CH_2 + Br_2 \rightarrow \underset{Br}{\underset{|}{CH_2}}{-}\underset{Br}{\underset{|}{CH_2}}$$

Ethylene dibromide or 1,2-dibromo ethane

They also can undergo substitution reaction.

$$CH_3{-}CH{=}CH_2 + Cl_2 \rightarrow \underset{Cl}{\underset{|}{CH_2}}{-}CH{=}CH_2 + CHI$$

Allyl chloride

The most important radical derived from ethylene is vinyl group.

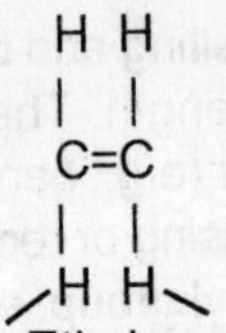
Ethylene

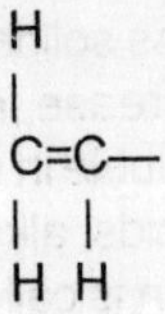
Vinyl

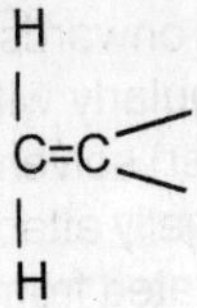
Vinylidene

Table 1 shows the name of various compounds alongwith functional groups.

Table 1 Classes and characteristics of organic compounds

Class of compound	Name of functional group	Formula of func. group.	Simple example	Name ending at
Paraffin (Alkane)	Single bond	-	$CH_3—CH_3$ Ethane	-ane
Olefin (Alkene)	Double bond	C = C	$CH_2=CH_2$ Ethylene	-ene
Alkyne	Triple bond	—C≡C—	CH≡CH Ethyne	-yne
Halogen derivatives of paraffin	Contains one or more halogen atoms	—Cl	$CH_3—CH_2Cl$ Ethyl chloride	
Monohydric-alcohols	Hydroxyl	-OH	$CH_3—CH_2—OH$ Ethyl alcohol or ethanol	—ol
Dihydric alcohol	Hydroxyl	—OH	HO-CH_2—CH_2—OH Ethylene glycol	—ol
Polyhydric alcohol	Hydroxyl	—OH	HO—CH_2—CH(OH)—CH_2—OH Glycerol	—ol
Ether	Ether	—O—	$CH_3—O—CH_3$ Dimethyl ether	ether
Aldehyde	Carbonyl	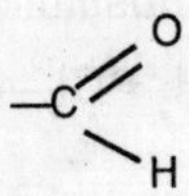	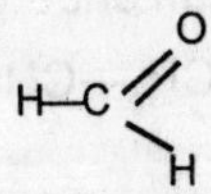 Formaldehyde or Formal	—al

Class of compound	Name of functional group	Formula of func. group.	Simple example	Name ending at
Ketone	Carbonyl	$>C{=}O$	$(CH_3)_2C{=}O$ Acetone	—one
Carboxylic acid	Carboxyl	$-C(=O)OH$	$H-C(=O)OH$ Formic acid	Acid
Cyanides or nitriles	Nitrile or cyanide	$-C\equiv N$	$CH_3-C\equiv N$ Methyl cyanide or acetonitrile	
Isocyanides or corbylamines	-	$-N\equiv C$	$CH_3-N\equiv C$ Methyl isocyanide	
Nitro compounds	Nitro	$-NO_2$	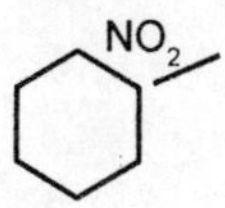 Nitrobenzene	
Amine (primary)	p-amino	$-NH_2$	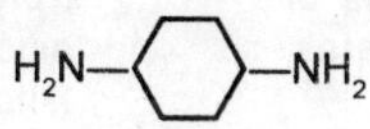 P-phenylene diamine	
Amine (secondary)	s-amino	$>N-H$	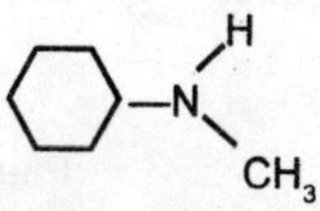 Mono methylaniline	
Amine (tertiary)	t-amino	$>N-$	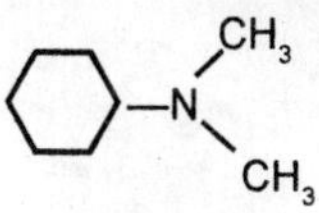 Dimethyl aniline	
Amide		$-C(=O)NH_2$	$CH_3-C(=O)NH_2$ Acetamide	
Amino acid	Amine and acid	$-NH_2$ and $-COOH$	H_2N-CH_2-COOH Glycine	-ine

Class of compound	Name of functional group	Formula of func. group.	Simple example	Name ending at
Diazo compound	Azo	$—N\equiv N$	$CH2—N\equiv N$ Diazomethane	
Mercaptan or thioalcohol	Mercaptan	$—S—H$	$CH_3—SH$ Methyl mercaptan	
Thioether or alkyl sulphide	Thioether	$—S—$	$Cl—CH_2CH_2—S—CH_2CH_2—Cl$ 2, 2'-dichorodi-ethyl sulphide or Mustard gas	
Sulphenamide	-	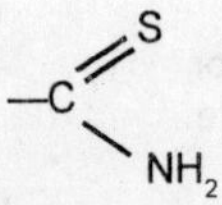	Accelerators	
Grignard reagent or organementallic compound	-	$—M—X$	$CH_3—Mg—Br$ Methyl magnesium bromide	
Dicarboxylic Acid	-	$—COOH$	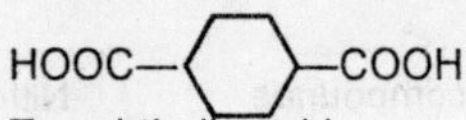 Terephthalic acid	
Saccharides or carbohydrates	Polyhydroxy aldehyde or ketone	—OH and C=O	Glucose $C_6H_{12}O_6$	
Phenyl compounds	Phenyl	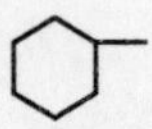 $—C_6H_5$	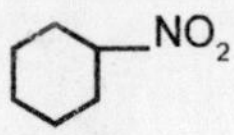 Nitrobenzene	
	Phenylene	 C_6H_4	 m-dinitrobenzene	
Naphthalene derivatives		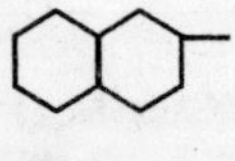	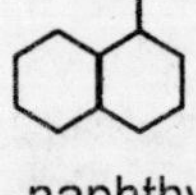 a - naphthylamine	

Class of compound	Name of functional group	Formula of func. group.	Simple example	Name ending at
Anthracene		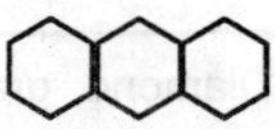	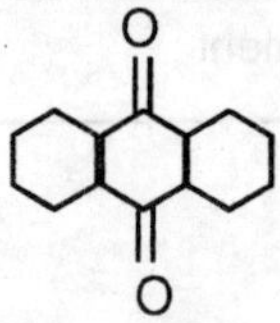 9-10-anthraquinone	

ALLOTROPY

When an element exists in various forms it is said to exhibit allotropy and the different forms are called as allotropic forms. Groups IV, V and VI elements of periodic table exhibit allotropic forms which are shown in Table 2.

Carbon

Of the various carbon forms, amorphous carbon which comes as channel or furnace black is used considerably in rubber industry as filler. The particle size is of great importance and usually varies between 10-300 mμ having a surface area of 8-250 sq. m/g.

The C-black can adsorb (dissolve by Vander Waal forces) gas. In channel black there is a layer of O and moisture is adsorbed onto the outside surface of the article. The surface of furnace black is different. Due to this, the furnace black can give rise to scorching. However, this can be prevented by some treatment (Cl_2 at room temperature).

Silica

Of the various forms, amorphous (fumed) silica, obtained by burning $SiCl_4$ in H, has a very low density and particle size giving rise to large surface area per weight. This is used as a very good non-black reinforcing filler.

Oxygen

Attacks rubber degrading it chemically (ageing). This is aggravated at high temperature and in humid conditions. During running, due to friction, the non-conducting tyre generates static electricity which, in turn, causes transformation of O_2 into O_3 which is a more powerful oxidising agent than O_2 and degrades rubber more quickly. Due to these reasons, antioxidants and antiozonants are incorporated in rubber formulations.

Sulphur

Rhombic sulphur is usually used for vulcanizing rubber. The reaction converts thermoplastic rubber into thermoset product by incorporating S cross-links between rubber molecular chains. The rubber changes from a plastic to an elastic material.

Table 2. Allotropic form of some elements found in nature

Group	Element		Allotropic forms	
IV	Carbon		Diamond, graphite and amorphous	
		[i.	charcoal from wood and sugars	
		ii.	lamp black from soot, acetylene black and c-black	
		iii.	animal charcoal as bone charcoal, ivory black	
		iv.	coke from coal, anthracite	
		v.	gas carbon and	
		vi.	electrode c from arc c)]	
IV.	Silicon as silica	a.	Crystalline	
			i.	quartz
			ii.	tridymite
			iii.	cristobalite and
			iv.	lechitelierite
		b.	Amorphous	
V.	Phosphorous	a.	White	
		b.	Red	
VI.	Oxygen	a.	Oxygen	
		b.	Ozone	
VI.	Sulphur	a.	Rhombic or α - S	
		b.	Monoclinic, prismatic or β - S and	
		c.	Amorphous S	
			i.	plastic S
			ii.	white S
			iii.	colloidal S

The rhombic sulphur has a chain of eight atoms.

$$\underbrace{\text{S-S-S-S-S-S-S-S}}_{S_8}$$

Under heat, it can break up into different chain lengths, e.g.,

$$S_8 \xrightarrow{\text{Heat}} S_4 + S_4 \text{ or } S_2 + S_6 \text{ or } S_4 + S_7,$$

i.e., in general, $S_x + S_{8-x}$

Of all these possibilities, the disulphide -S-S- bond is most stable and hence found mostly in vulcanized rubber. However, other types are also present.

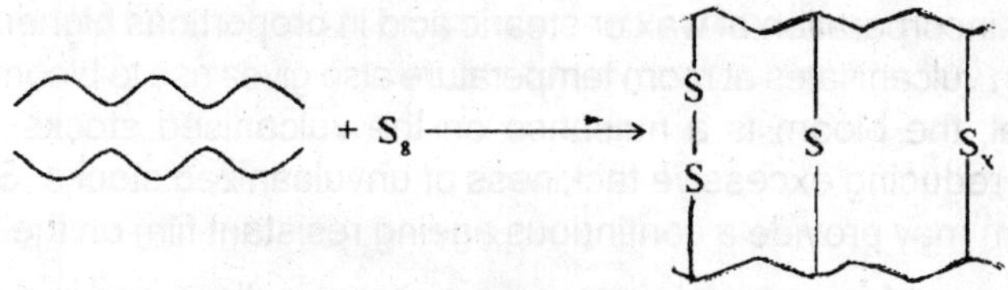

The disadvantage of ground rhombic sulphur is that it may cause bloom if it precipitates out from the vulcanised sample.

The problem of bloom can be avoided by the use of amorphous S as it does not recrystallise - due to the fact that it is insoluble in rubber. This application is useful for camel-back and repair gums manufacture where the uncured stocks are to be stored for a considerable time.

SOLUBILITY AND SOLUTION

Solubility is defined as the maximum weight of a substance (solute) that can dissolve in 100 g of a solvent at a particular temperature. Usually solubility increases with the increase in temperature. If the temperature is decreased, the solubility decreases. As a result the solute crystallises (precipitates) out from the saturated solution. However, if the temperature is brought down slowly without disturbing the solution, then no precipitation occurs and a supersaturated solution results.

If there are more than one immiscible solvents and one solute is present, then the solute is distributed according to its partiton coefficient (K) in the two liquids, where:

$$K = \frac{\text{Concentration of solute in solvent B}}{\text{Concentration of solute in solvent A}}$$

During compounding of rubber, a very large number of ingredients, such as, vulcanising agent, accelerator, activator, filler, antioxidant, etc., are mixed. The solubility of each such material in rubber or in each other is usually different. Also, the solubility may vary in vulcanised and unvulcanised stock.

Blooming is caused when any ingredient used in rubber formulation precipitates out on cooling to room temperature after vulcanising or processing. Hence, the amount of an ingredient chosen must be well below its maximum solubility in rubber.

Thus, antioxidant phenyl-alpha-naphthyl amine has a solubility of 5% and phenyl-beta-naphthyl amine has a solubility of 1.5% in rubber. Hence, the former can be used to a greater extent without the fear of bloom. However, many antioxidants are soluble in process oil and only a judicious use of oil can lead to greater incorporation of antioxidant in the stock.

The incorporation of wax or stearic acid in proportions higher than their solubility in vulcanisates at room temperature also gives rise to bloom. Though, in general, the bloom is a nuisance on the vulcanised stocks, it can be helpful in reducing excessive tackiness of unvulcanized stocks. Similarly, a wax bloom may provide a continuous ageing resistant film on the surface.

A colour bloom can take place if a pigment is dispersed in a plasticiser that have the tendency to bloom.

4

Physical Aspects of Rubber Technology

INTRODUCTION

The understanding of the fundamental laws of physics is necessary for a rubber technologist to play vital role in the following fields of the industry:

i. Measurement of various factors in manufacturing process.
ii. Design and maintenance of suitable instruments for controlling process.
iii. Operation, understanding, interpretation and improvements in laboratory test techniques.
iv. Development of new application areas for rubber goods.
v. The analysis, understanding and rectification of service failures so as to improve product and/or design.
vi. To help in assimilation of newer technology in other areas by rubber industry.

The following are the different branches of physics:

Mechanics → Statics
Mechanics → Dynamics

Properties of Matter → Solid state
Properties of Matter → Liquid state
Properties of Matter → Gaseous state

Heat, Light, Sound, Electricity and Magnetism

Nuclear physics → Cathode rays
Nuclear physics → X-rays
Nuclear physics → Structure of the atom

Only the topics relevant to rubber area will be discussed.

MECHANICS

Newton's first law states that a body at rest or in motion will remain at rest or in motion unless some external force is applied to it. *Inertia* is defined as that property of a body which tends to resist a change in the state of its motion.

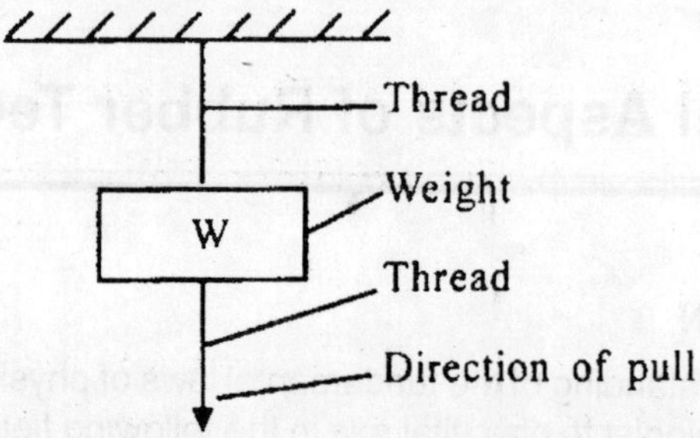

A weight of mass W is suspended from a fixed position by a thread and a piece of the same thread is attached to the lower side of the weight.

If a force F, is applied slowly and steadily to the weight (pull), the thread above W breaks and, on the other hand, if a sudden pull is given, the thread below W breaks.

This happens because in the first case the tension in the upper thread is equivalent to F and W, whereas in the second case the inertia of the weight retards its movement and F is applied to the lower thread only.

Rubber belts, V belts, etc., are used extensively to transmit motive power from one location to another. As soon as the system is energised, the sudden pull may break the belt due to inertia. Hence, the belts must be made of sufficient strength so that they can withstand the momentarily high forces produced when setting the equipment in motion.

Newton's second law states that the rate of change of momentum of a body is equal to the force acting and takes place in the direction of the straight line in which the force acts.

$$P = mf \qquad \text{....1}$$

where P is force, m is mass of the body and f is the acceleration.

The third law states that to every action there is an equal and opposite reaction.

Similarly, the *law of conservation of momentum* (mass × velocity) and *law of conservation of energy* are of great importance in rubber technology.

Simple lever and spring are used extensively in making various instruments for measurement of rubber properties.

The application of tension or compression to a coiled spring is used in:

a. Tensile machines

b. Tension set equipment

c. Compression plastometers

d. Creep and compression set equipment.

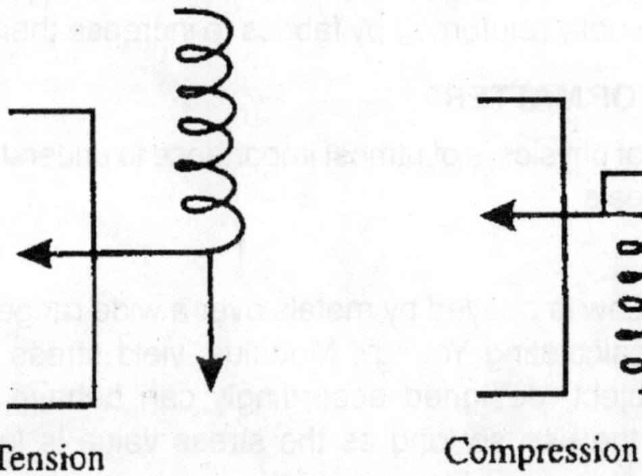

Hooke's law states that stress α strain

$$\text{or,} \quad \frac{\text{Stress}}{\text{Strain}} = \text{Constant} = K$$

Hence, the deflection of the spring (strain) in figure above is proportional to the magnitude of the forces (stress) applied. By fixing a scale to one end of the spring and a pointer to the other end it is possible to construct spring balances that will operate in tension and compression.

Friction is an interesting phenomenon which helps in finding several applications for rubber products. In certain cases, e.g., in releasing a product from the mould, the frictional force is to be reduced and a mould lubricant might be necessary. Similarly, a moving rubber wheel must be as smooth as possible so that the development of frictional forces are kept at a minimum. This will help in reducing heat build up in the wheel and the wear and tear can be kept at a minimum.

On the other hand, in making products like brake drums and brake shoes, design should be such that maximum use of the frictional forces can be made. The outer design on the tyre tread helps a tyre to maintain a strong grip on the road surface thus reducing the chance of skid.

Air friction is of great importance and the wind resistance increases with approximately the square of the wind velocity. Thus a car travelling at 60 kmph meets a wind resistance 16 times greater than that met when travelling at 15 kmph or 4 times that a 40 kmph. Similarly, a jetplane cruising at 600 kmph will meet a wind resistance 400 times that of a car moving at 30 kmph. These factors are to be taken into consideration during design of the car, jetplane or the tyres fitted on them.

Impact is another important property. An aeroplane tyre must have sufficient impact resistance so as to withstand the sudden compressive forces acting on it during touchdown by the aircraft.

Tear resistance, similarly, is important in products which are continuously subjected to tensile forces. V-belts, conveyor belts and similar products are usually reinforced by fabrics to increase their tear resistance.

PROPERTIES OF MATTER

This part of physics is of utmost importance to understand the behaviour of rubber materials.

Solid State

Hooke's Law is obeyed by metals over a wide range of stress values. This helps in calculating Young's Modulus, yield stress, etc., for a metal object. The object, designed accordingly can behave consistently and constantly for the use so long as the stress value is less than the yield stress over a wide range of temperature.

Unfortunately, rubber obeys Hooke's law within a very small limit of stress. In practical use, however, the stress is higher. Hence, design of rubber component is much more complex.

The *law of conservation of momentum* states that the total momentum before impact is equal to the total momentum after impact. This law does not predict the velocities of the two bodies individually after impact. The coefficient of restitution (K) or resilience is defined as follows-

$$K = \frac{\text{Velocity of separation}}{\text{Velocity of approach}} = \frac{V_2}{V_1} \qquad \text{....2}$$

In rubber industry the resilience is calculated in percentage by the use of the law of falling bodies and calculating the velocities (V) from the height (h) of fall and the rebound height.

$$\text{Resilience (\%)} = 100\, K_2 = 100 \frac{V_2^2}{V_1^2} = 100 \frac{h_2}{h_1} \qquad \text{....3}$$

Thus, resilience values for different materials when dropped on a steel plate are glass 95%, steel 90%, rubber 90%, and wood 60%.

Rubber under deformation load extends and when the load is removed the rubber tries to come back to the original shape. However, a very little permanent deformation remains. This is known as *creep*. Creep decreases with time. If a second load is applied again an additional residual deformation remains. This shows that rubber has a memory. Therefore, behaviour of a rubber sample will be dependent on the previous history of the sample.

The *viscoelasticity* property of rubber, (or polymer) is of great importance. Simply saying, rubber properties are greatly influenced by the temperature and time period of action of external force.

Liquid State

The various properties of liquid, such as density, specific gravity, cohesion, adhesion, surface tension, viscosity, etc., are of importance in understanding the behaviour of rubber.

Density is defined as mass per unit volume, e.g., gm/c.c

Specific gravity is defined as follows -

$$\text{S.G.} = \frac{\text{Weight of a given substance}}{\text{Weight of an equal volume of water}}$$

It is a ratio and hence has no unit (dimensionless).

The S.G. of a rubber compound is of importance as the production takes place on volume basis. Thus, at comparable price, if compound A has a lower S.G. than compound B, then for the same weight (say 1 kg) A will produce larger volume of product than B, making the product cost less. Let us suppose two rubber compounds, A and B, are available for cable insulation. The relevant data for economic compound can be found out as follows -

	A	B
Cost, Rs/kg	25.00	22.00
S.G.	1.15	1.50
Relative volume	25×1.15	22×1.50
cost index	= 28.75	= 33.00

So, though the cost on weight basis of compound B is lower, actually it is much costly than compound A for cable application.

The attractive forces between similar molecules is known as *cohesive force* and between different kinds of molecules as *adhesive force*. '*Tack*' of a rubber compound is a manifestation of cohesion. Similarly, the sticking of a rubber compound on the metal surface of the mould is due to adhesion. As the temperature is increased (as in melting or moulding) the cohesive forces decrease and adhesive forces increase. Now, if the adhesive forces have become stronger than the cohesive forces, during removal of the moulded article (in hot condition) from the moulded part of it may get term and stick to the mould. Due to this reason, it is always advisable to reduce the mould temperature before release of the article from the mould. Use of mould lubricants also help. Similarly, highly polished surface reduces the force of adhesion and hence the need for very good finish of the mould. As latex goods have low cohesion it is better to use non-adhering surface as mould, such as, made of glass or glazed procelain.

Surface tension is a liquid property due to cohesion and defined as the force of contraction across a line of unit length, the line and the force being perpendicular to each other, both lying in the plane of the liquid surface. Due to this property, surface of a liquid always tries to contract. Surface tension is partly responsible for the rise of sap in trees and it governs the flow of latex (or a rubber tree) in the cut and the rate of collection in the tapping cup.

Wetting agent reduces surface tension and is used frequently in latex process.

Viscosity is a measure of frictional force between two liquid layers. Its knowledge is essential as all rubber processing involve flow of the rubber compound and viscosity governs the nature and rate of flow.

Bernoulli's principle predicts that during a fluid flow, the pressure varies inversely to the velocity of the fluid. This is of great importance in understanding operation of several rubber processing machines. The following is an example with an extruder.

Suppose zone A represents the heat and barrel of an extruder, zone B the die and zone C the extruded article.

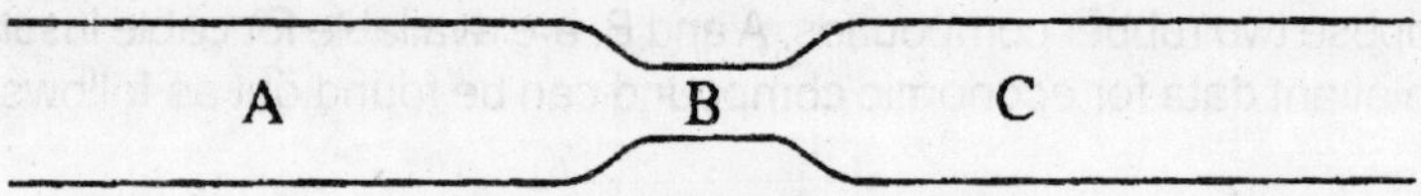

Hence, in

Zone A	velocity low	pressure	high
Zone B	velocity high	pressure	low
Zone C	velocity low	pressure	high

During operation, if scorching occurs at any point on the screw inside the barrel of the extruder, velocity decreases and pressure increases. As a consequence, the head or barrel may burst but not the die.

Gaseous State

One of the important properties demanded from rubber articles, such as, tyre tubes, hot water bags, etc., is impermeability to gases. It has to be remembered that rubber has generally low permeability to gas. Butyl rubber is superior in this respect and hence finds application as tyre tubes.

Heat

Heat is used in considerable extent during most of the stages of rubber processing. The behaviour of rubber, either in vulcanised or unvulcanised state, towards heat is different from those of metals.

Some fundamental concepts of terms are necessary to understand the effect of heat.

The unit quantify of heat, *calorie*, is defined as the amount of heat necessary to raise one g of water through one degree centigrade.

The *specific heat* of a substance is the quantity of heat (in calories) required to raise one gm of the substance through one degree centigrade.

The *heat capacity* of any body is the quantity of heat necessary to raise the temperature of the body by one degree centigrade.

Heat capacity = Specific heat × Mass

The *coefficient of volume expansion* of rubber (661×10^{-6} per °C) is many times greater than metals (steel 33×10^{-6} per °C, brass 57×10^{-6} per °C). Thus, rubber increases in volume during moulding and undergoes considerable shrinkage after cooling. This poses difficulty in the maintenance of close dimensional tolerances in moulded rubber artifacts.

Thermal conductivity is defined as the amount of heat flow required per second through a material of one unit length in thickness so as to raise its temperature by one °C. Its unit is cal/cm. sec. °C.

The thermal conductivity of rubber is 50×10^{-5} cal/cm. sec. °C and specific heat 0.5. These values are considerably higher than those for metals. Due to these reasons, heating of rubber is difficult, especially in thick sections. Special formulations of rubber compounds are to be used to solve this tendency of overcure at the face and undercure at the centre of thick articles.

In order to obtain uniform heating and also to shorten moulding cycle time, it is customary to preheat mould. However, heating of rubber compound is much more difficult than heating the metal mould. For example-

Quantity of heat required to raise the temperature of an iron mould (2000 g) from 40° to 140°C

= Mass × specific heat × temperature range

= 2,000 × 0.107 × 100

= 21,400 cals.

Quantity of heat required to raise the temperature of rubber (500 g) from 40° to 140°C.

= 500 × 0.510 × 100

= 25,500 cals.

Hence, the design of the mould is to be done to ensure quick and even heating of the rubber. In injection moulding, as the rubber is preheated, obviously the cycle time can be reduced drastically.

Light

The effect of light is deeply associated with colour. It is very difficult to say what is colour. But it is known that white light is a composite colour and can be resolved into seven different colours. In rubber technology, besides black, several colours can be developed by judicious blending of different colour pigments or dyes. Also, the brightness of colour can be increased by incorporating white pigments, such as, titanium dioxide.

The reason for colour development in organic compounds are assigned to chromophoric groups. Some of the important chromophoric groups are -

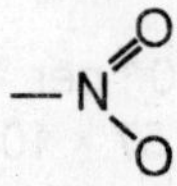

Nitro

—N = O

Nitroso

—N = N—

Azo

— N = N → O

Azoxy

— N = N—NH—

Azoamine

C = O

Carbonyl

C = S

Thiocarbonyl

As most of the antioxidants contain chromophoric and colour enhancing (auxochrome) groups, they are highly coloured.

Conjugated double bond compounds are usually coloured and the colour deepens with the increase in number of conjugation. If double bond is present, but either the conjugation is low or the number of double bond is less, then the compound is yellow. Due to this reason, most of the diene rubbers (NR, SBR, PBR, etc.) are yellowish.

On the other hand, vinyl rubbers having no unsaturation in the structure are white in colour. This EPR, Butyl, hypalon, etc., are white in colour.

Sound

Sound, a form of wave, is transmitted through gas, liquid or solid and the velocity (v) of sound in the medium-

$$v = \sqrt{\frac{E}{\rho}} \qquad .....5$$

where ρ is the density of the medium and E the bulk modulus of the system. The velocity of sound in various media in cm/sec is as follows -

Air	0.33×10^5
Rubber	0.50×10^5

Water	1.43×10^5
Iron	5.60×10^5

As the velocity of sound in rubber and density of the rubber are known, by passing sound wave, the dynamic modulus of the rubber can be determined. This method is a good one for determining this property of rubber.

Sound waves pass continuously through a medium. A discontinuity in the medium then leads to reduction in the transmission of sound. Thus, sound in a water piping system can be reduced by putting short lengths of rubber tubing inserted at intervals along the system.

When a sound wave reaches a boundary between two media (say air/rubber or air/iron) part of the sound wave is reflected and part transmitted.

The amount of reflection

= density of the medium × velocity of sound in the medium 6

Hence, air will be a very good absorber (amount of reflection lowest), but rubber will be much better than iron. This is the reason why rubber is used in making sound absorbing systems.

When frequency of vibration of sound wave exceeds 16 K cycles/sec, human ear cannot hear that sound. This type of sound waves is called ultrasonics. They can be used to detect faults in large rubber articles, e.g., tyres or belts. Porosity in rubber articles is very difficult to detect and ultrasonics have been very useful in detecting the fault. Each small area of the article is examined and wherever there is a small air gap, there is a reduction in the reflected energy and amplitude of the reflected sound wave when compared with the reflections from the surrounding rubber medium.

Electricity

This is a well-known fact that rubber is an insulator (non-conductor) and metals are conductor of electricity. It has to be noted here covalent compounds (rubber, plastic, ceramic, glass, etc.) cannot transmit electronics and hence behave as non-conductors.

There are three important measuring indices of electrical properties for rubber.

Ohm's law states that current (I) passing through a conductor is proportional to the potential difference (V), hence

$$V \propto I$$

$$\text{or} \quad V = IR \qquad ....7$$

The equality constant R is called as resistance. It can be shown that

$$R = \rho \frac{l}{s} \qquad ....8$$

where R is the resistance, l is the length of the wire and s is the cross-section ρ is called as *specific resistance or resistivity* of the wire. Hence, resistivity is the resistance of a material of 1 cm in length and 1 cm^2 in cross-section. It is usually expressed in ohm-cm.

Some resistivity values are given below (Table 1) -

Table 1: Resistivity values of some substances

Material	Resistivity (ohm-cm)
Copper	1.724×10^{-6}
Aluminium	2.828×10^{-6}
Graphite	8×10^{2}
Glass	9×10^{13}
Natural rubber	1×10^{16}

With increase in temperature, resistivity decreases.

To make a rubber article, specially for cables and other insulation application, compounding ingredients are to be carefully chosen so that there is no unnecessary reduction in the insulation property of rubber. Thus, resistivity of acceleartor MBT is 3300×10^{13} ohm-cm and that of DPG is 35×10^{13} ohm-cm. So MBT should be preferred.

Insulating property of rubber can create problems by generating static electricity (which may cause explosion or fire) on the surface in such products as rubber flooring or tyres. Conducting carbon black or metallic powder fillers can be incorporated in the compound thus producing semi-conducting or conductiong rubber product.

Inverse square law of electrical forces states that the magnitude of the force (F) exerted between two electrical bodies is proportional to the product of the two charges (q_1 and q_2) and inversely proportional to the square of the distance between them, i.e.,

$$F = C\frac{q_1 \times q_2}{r^2} \quad \text{....9}$$

where C is the constant dependent on the units in which the quantities are expressed and the nature of the medium in which the charged bodies are placed. In C.G.S. unit and when the medium is air, C = 1, so that

$$F = \frac{q_1 q_2}{r^2} \quad \text{...10}$$

The practical unit of charge is a *coulomb* and is equal to 3×10^9 C.G.S. unit of charge.

When the medium is not air, equation (10) takes the form,

$$F = \frac{1}{K} \cdot \frac{q_1 q_2}{r^2} \qquad \ldots.11$$

where,

$$K = \frac{\text{The magnitude of the force in air}}{\text{The magnitude of the force in that medium}} \qquad \ldots.12$$

This factor K is known as the dielectric constant or the *specific inductive capacity* or simply S.I.C. of that medium.

Some dielectic constant values are given below in Table 2.

Table 2 Dielectric values

Dielectric	Dielectric constant
Air	1.0006
Paraffin	2.0 - 2.3
Dry paper	2.0 - 2.4
Rubber	2.1 - 2.3
Shellac	3.1
Mica	5.7 - 7.0

Power factor or *power loss* is a measure of amount of power loss (dissipated) in a circuit (transmission) through which alternating current is passing.

In choosing a rubber for electrical application are has to keep in mind all these three properties which are given below in Table 3.

Table 3 Some physical properties of rubbers

Properties	NR	SBR	Neoprene	NBR	Butyl
Resistivity (ohm-cm)	10^{17}	10^{15}	10^{10}	10^{10}	10^{16}
Dielectric constant (50 cycles, 20°C, 75% RH)	2.8	2.85	8.0	13.4	2.6
Power loss (50 cycles, 20°C, 75% RH)	0.0090	0.0022	0.04	0.454	0.0026

NUCLEAR PHYSICS

This advanced branch of science is extremely helpful in analysis, structural studies and research and development work in the rubber field.

Light is a kind of wave and visible light forms a very small part of the whole wave spectrum.

Gamma rays	X-rays	U-V light	Visible light	Heat rays and infra-red rays

→ Wavelength

Arrangement of wave spectrum

The visible light spectra have a frequency range of 7,000-3,500Å. Below 3,500Å is U-V range, followed by still smaller X-rays and gamma rays. Above 7000Å is the infra-red spectrum.

A rubber, rubber chemical or for that matter any chemical has its characteristics spectra in infra and/or U-V range. These spectroscopic techniques can be used to detect or quantitatively estimate presence of, say, particular antioxidant in a rubber compound or vinyl content in a rubber, I-R and U-V spectra are invaluable as analytical tool.

The wavelength of X-ray being in the range of bond distance between two atoms this method can be used to know the length of the repeating unit of polymer (or rubber).

Rubber is an amorphous material and an X-ray picture produce a diffused halo. On the other hand, Some rubber when stretched crystallises and in that stretched condition if an X-ray picture is taken it shows some bright spots (due to crystalline areas) interspersed with halo space (amorphous zone). Development of crystallinity leads to increase in strength characteristics.

Natural rubber shows a high tensile strength in gum stocks when stretched. This is due to the reason that it crystallises on stretching (as evidenced by X-ray picture). Neoprene similarly shows a reasonable gum strength for the same reason. On the other hand, X-ray picture does not show development of any crystallinity in the case of stretched styrene-butadiene rubber. Consequently it shows poor gum strength.

Besides these, X-ray is also invaluable in the research field.

5

Styrene Butadiene Rubber (SBR)

COMPOUNDING AND PROCESSING OF SBR

The compounding of styrene butadiene rubber is similar to that of natural rubber and other unsaturated hydrocarbon rubbers. The most convenient and effective compounds in large scale usage, such as tyres, are all based on fillers, such as carbon black, extending oils; zinc oxide; sulphur; accelerators, such as mercaptobenzothiazole; and protective agents, such as antioxidants, antiozonants, and waxes. Processing these complex mixture into smooth compounds that can be quickly pressed, sheeted, calendered, or extruded is a most important step for manufacture. Emulsion SBR is the prototype of a "general-purpose" rubber because of its ability to be blended with any other such rubber into compounds that process and cure homogeneously. Thus, it is said to have "cure-compatibility" and excellent "processing" or "processability". Besides T_g, and possible chemical attributes that may be important but are poorly understood, the good processing of SBR results from its favourable combination of molecular weight and molecular weight distribution and the considerable proportion of long branches in its molecules. The main advantage of solution SBR is that it can be constructed so as to have just enough branching and molecular weight distribution for adequate processing, while at the same time providing maximised molecular weight for rolling resistance and wear.

Compounding recipes with low sulphur or with only organically bound sulphur, as in thiazoles, lead to vulcanisates with better ageing but slower curing. Zinc stearate, or zinc oxide plus stearic acid, is the most common activator for SBR. There are many accelerators that speed up slow-curing stocks and retarders that slow down "scorchy" ones. Recipes may also contain plasticisers, softeners, tackifiers, and other ingredients that have given evidence of solving some compounding problem or other.

Preparation of SBR compounds is similar to that of the rubbers. The ingredients are mixed in internal mixers or on mills and may then be extruded, calendered, moulded, and cured in conventional equipment. Mixing procedures vary with the compound. In general, the rubber, zinc oxide, antioxidants, and stearic acid are mixed, then the carbon black is added in portions with the oil. This "non-productive" mix may be considered a black masterbatch. It may be desirable at this point to dump, sheet out, and cool the batch. The next phase involves mixing in all the other ingredients, with the accelerator and sulphur being added last. The mix is now considered "productive", since it will "cure" – i.e., cross-link irreversibly – when held for a carefully regulated time at a selected temperature, such as 150°C.

Mixing procedures for rubber stocks vary with different companies. Some plasticise the rubber in a separate operation before blacks and other ingredients are added. Some make a masterbatch first, without a preliminary plasticising step. If additional plasticising is required, the masterbatch is remilled, and self-plasticisation of the rubber is avoided. Excessive remilling of SBR compounds may lead to gel formation and poorer extrusions.

Not only does modern styrene-butadiene rubber have extrusion properties superior to those of natural rubber, but its stocks have less tendency to scorch in processing. Although cold SBR is often preferable to hot for optimum physical properties, hot SBR can be better for both processing and product properties. Hot SBR breaks down more rapidly to a desirable molecular weight on the mill, develops less heat, and accepts more filler in processing. All types of SBR require less sulphur than natural rubber does for curing. The usual range is about 1.5 to 2.0 parts per hundred rubber. On the other hand, SBR requires more accelerator because of the lower unsaturation to achieve the same rate of cure.

Tyre tread-wear and ageing properties are superior to those of natural rubber, resistance to abrasion and resistance to crack initiation are better. Building tack is still poor and dynamic properties are such that heavy-duty tyres become too hot in use. Without reinforcing fillers such as carbon black or silica, the physical properties of SBR are much inferior to those of natural rubber. Similarly, its green strength properties, for example, the tensile strength of the fully mixed compound before cure, are distinctly inferior to those of natural rubber. This is the principal reason it was necessary to go back to a higher proportion of natural rubber in radial tyres, which would otherwise deform in transit from the tyre-building machines to the curing presses.

Applications of SBR

Of all the SBR made, about 75% goes into tyres. The rest goes into shoes and other footwear, mechanical goods, sponge and foamed products, waterproofed materials, hose, belting, adhesives, and other miscellaneous uses. Styrene-butadiene lateces constitute a more or less independent 10% of the market, mostly non-tyre. SB lateces typically have much more styrene than SBR and are supplied in latex form to customers, who use them principally in carpet-back coatings. The construction industry is the next largest user.

PROCESSING AND CURING OF POLYBUTADIENE AND POLYISOPRENE

The processing characteristics of polybutadiene are influenced by the polymer microstructure, molecular weight, molecular-weight distribution, and degree of branching. The polymer undergoes mastication, mixing, moulding, and curing. A Banbury mixer and a roll-mill are employed for mastication and mixing; a calender and extruder, for moluding.

Most polybutadienes are highly resistant to breakdown and have poor mill-banding characteristics and rough extrusion appearance compared to SBR elastomers. The solution polybutadienes process satisfactorily when blended with other elastomers such as SBR. Emulsion polybutadiene

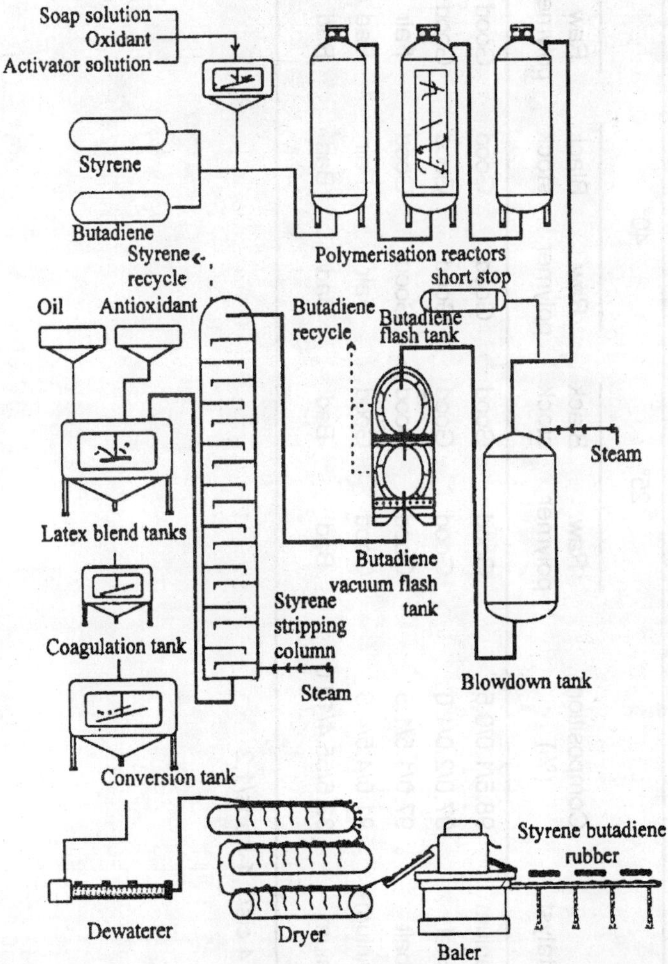

Fig.1: Manufacture of emulsion styrene-butadiene rubber (SBR)

Table 2: Processability of polybutadiene(s)

Catalyst	Composition* (%)	25° Raw polymer	25° Black stock	40° Raw polymer	40° Black stock	60° Raw polymer	60° Black stock	75° Raw polymer	75° Black stock
Uranium	98.5/1.0/0.5	Good	Good	Good	Good	Good	Good	Good	Fair
Nickel	97.0/2.0/1.0	Good	Good	Good	Good	Good	Fair	Fair	Fair
Cobalt	97.0/1.5/1.5	Good	Good	Good	Good	Fair	Fair	Bad	Bad
Titanium	91.0/4.5/4.5	Good	Good	Fair	Fair	Bad	Bad	Bad	Bad
Lithium	32.6/55.4/12.0	Bad	Bad	Bad	Bad	Bad	Bad	Bad	Bad

*1,4 cis/1,4-trans/1,2

processes better than solution polymer but not as well as SBR; it is commonly blended with other elastomers for enhanced processing.

Certain chemical peptisers slightly increase breakdown and improve processing. A lower Mooney viscosity also improves processing but may lead to cold-flow problems. In addition, a broad molecular-weight distribution and branching both improve milling and extrusion behaviour as compared to a linear polymer. Excessively high-molecular-weight polybutadiene tends to crumb on the roll mill.

Very-high-*cis*-polybutadiene prepared with a uranium catalyst is reported to have greatly improved millability, calenderability, tack, green strength, and adhesion to fabric. Such processability would eliminate the need for blending with other elastomers. The mill processabilities of polybutadienes comprise of variable microstructures and catalysts are presented in Table 2. The processability improves with increasing cis-content.

Curing and compounding recipes depend upon the choice of the individual manufacturer. Polybutadienes are cured employing conventional sulphur recipes or peroxide systems. Normally, the polymer is blended with another elastomer, then mixed with filler (HAF, ISAF blacks, for example); typically an aromatic processing oil, wax, antioxidant, antiozonant; and curing ingredients at a later stage. For curing, thiazoles and sulphenamides are generally employed alone or in combination with secondary accelerators. Cure rates are close to SBR using similar loads of sulphur.

Typical vulcanisate properties are given in Table 3.

Table 3: Poly(butadiene) vulcanisate properties

300% modulus, kg/cm^2	70.0
Tensile strength, kg/cm^2	165.0
Elongation, %	540.0
Shore A hardness	59.0
Tear strength, die C, kg/cm^2	50.3

SBR blended with *cis*-polybutadiene has significantly improved abrasion resistance and tear resistance, but the skid resistance is slightly decreased. The SBR/medium vinyl polybutadiene blend has enhanced blow-out resistance, improved abrasion and decreased skid resistance. Elastomers with high mobility and low glass-transition temperatures have high elasticity, very good abrasion, and poor skid, and vice versa.

Modium vinyl polybutadiene is a potential partial or full replacement for SBR and has only recently become commercially important to the rubber industry. Use of medium vinyl polybutadiene would compensate for styrene, should a shortage of this monomer occur in the petrochemical industry. This would cnevitably result in a price increase for butadiene monomer, since it would be in demand for both the existing conventional, as well as the new general-purpose medium vinyl polybutadiene rubbers.

Synthetic polyisoprenes containing gel are generally characterised by high initial Mooney viscosities, but they break down rapidly upon mastication. There is no premastication requirement for Al-Ti polyisoprenes, and the compounding ingredients can be readily incorporated with proper mixing. Li polyisprenes often require premastication in the presence of peptisers for better incorporation of compounding ingredients. Green strength (cohesive strength) is a prime requirement in fabrication applications involving stress (e.g., tyre building). Natural rubber possesses the highest green strength. Al-Ti synthetic polyisoprenes have low green strength, and Li polyisoprenes have little to no green strength after processing. Chemical additives, however, can be used to improve the green strength of Al-Ti; polyisoprenes, thus allowing it to be used as a replacement for natural rubber in tyres.

The cured properties of *cis*-1, 4-polyisoprene vulcanisate are in general similar to those for natural rubber. Both show high gum tensile strength, good mechanical strength in filled compounds, high resilience and low heat build-up in related applications.

MANUFACTURE AND PROCESSING OF EPDM

Manufacture

Unlike the development of SBR, EPDM was developed independently by different manufacturers. Not only the process of manufacture (solution vs slurry) but also the termonomer and catalyst systems employed can vary considerably. These factors, as has already been mentioned, can affect molecular weight distribution, branching, and cure rate. As a consequence, EPDMs from various suppliers possessing similar composition (E/P) and Mooney viscosity may possess considerably different rheological and curing properties.

EPDM's polymers are employed in a wide of applications and processes. In order to maintain competitiveness, each of the suppliers has developed polymers employing their own technical expertise. As a consequence, the number of varieties of EPM and EPDM has grown considerably. Before employing a particular EPDM, it would be advantageous to become familiar with the literature from the various suppliers.

Processing

Conventional rubber equipment is used for the processing of EPDM compounds. Selection of the polymer or blend of polymers is an essential consideration in order to obtain optium processability.

Mixing

Mixing usually is accomplished with an internal mixer, such as a Banbury mixer. In some instances, it may be desirable or necessary to use the mill mixing process. For practical mill mixing, the low-viscosity and higher-ethylene polymers are considered too difficult. Furthermore, compounds based on these polymers typically contain such high amounts of filler and oil that mill mixing is usually impractical from this standpoint alone.

Although all types of EPDM are suitable for the internal mixer, no single mixing procedure is satisfactory for all compounds. The variety of polymers, the range of compound qualities (which affect choice of filler type), and the condition of the particular mixer are some of the factors that influence the mixing technique.

The most procedure is to load the ingredients in "one shot", and so forth. Depending upon the particular machine (its mechanical condition, speed, etc.) mixing cycles can range from 3 to 7 minutes. Using this kind of procedure, the batch is usually dumped when the temperature reaches 115°C to 130°C. This procedure may be limited to compounds that are based on medium and low-ethylene polymers loaded with mineral fillers and/or semi-reinforcing types of carbon black (SRF, GPF, FEF).

For compounds utilising high-ethylene or very-high-molecular-weight EPDM polymers and for compounds containing reinforcing carbon blacks (HAF, ISAF), the "one-shot" or "upside-down" loading procedure often results in poor dispersion of black or rubber or both. These polymers and blacks will usually not disperse well if processing oil is added early in the mixing cycle. Better dispersion is attained by an incremental procedure in which rubber and part of the black are loaded into the mixer with little or no oil. The withheld black and oil may then be added in one, two, or more increments.

If allowable form the standpoint of providing required properties, an easy-to-disperse softer black or higher-structure black, should be used in combination with the more difficult-to-disperse, highly reinforcing black. Then the easy-to-diverse black can be added with the plasticiser as the second increment in the mixing procedure. The high ethylene EPDMs should be stored under warm warehouse conditions to minimise dispersion problems.

Other variations in mixing procedures are also successful. For example, a modified "upside-down" technique in which part of the EPDM polymer is added on top of fillers and platicisers provides rapid mixing and good dispersion. This procedure may also be further modified by withholding part of the oil, which is then added incrementally. In addition, two-stage mixing is frequently employed when better dispersion or batch-to-batch consistency is needed.

Extrusion

The selection of polymer is a prime consideration if the EPDM compound is to be used for extrusion processing. The high-ethylene types are most useful for this process because they provide good green strength for shape retention. In addition, some green strength seems necessary for good feeding into the extruder; in fact, lack of green strength in the uncured compound is usually associated with poor feeding characteristics. If compounds do not easily, and if feed is erratic, surging of the extrudate results in its size varying. Hence a well-designed extrusion compound should contain enough high-ethylene polymer to provide the desired processing behaviour. Since excessive green strength (tough compound) is a possibility, one of the lower ethylene types of EPDM should be part of the polymer blend to avoid it.

A wide variety of extrusion equipment is to be found. Most of the older extruders still in use are the short-barrel, hot-feed type, and for these the stock must usually be "warmed" on a mill and then fed to the extruder. This process, therefore, requires a compound that is reasonably easy to band on the warm-up mill. Excessive green strength and/or high compound viscosity will cause difficulty in banding and may also cause bagging. Thee results may be avoided by using a lower-ethylene and/or lower-viscositv polymer blended with the high-ethylene type in the compound.

In general, the newer cold feed extruder is preferred. Not only does it obviate the need for a warm-up mill, it also provides better control of processing conditions so that more uniform extrudates are obtained. For most compounds, the extruder screw should be operated at a higher temperature than the barrel. Conditions should be adjusted to provide a smooth surface and optimum rate of extrusion. In general, extrusion temperature conditions are somewhat higher for EPDM compounds than for other types of rubber compounds.

Moulding

Moulded rubber parts are made by either a compression, transfer, or injection process, for all of which polymers having medium to high propylene are usually preferred. In applications involving highly extended compounds, however, it may be desirable to use a high-ethylene polymer, either exclusively or in part, to take advantage of its greater extendability. The prime consideration is good flow characteristics, and polymer selection should be made accordingly.

EPDM compounds have proved to be particularly suitable for injection moulding. When properly compounded, EPDM provides a fast cure rate and good flow and is not prone to reversion at the high curing temperatures common to this process. Commounding considerations for injection moulding are not appreciably different from those for compression or transfer moulding. The curing system is usually the point of most concern and the plasticiser should be selected for low volatility at the processing temperature.

Calendering

The EPDM polymer selected for calendering should be in the medium-to-high propylene range. If the compound is to be lightly loaded, the lowest-viscosity, highest-propylene type is most suitable. Also, a polymer with broad molecular-weight distribution and medium-to-high propylene content is a better choice. For medium to highly loaded compounds, the higher-viscosity types are required. The desirable processing is also often attained by a proper selection of two types of EPDM polymers.

ELEMENTS OF COMPOUNDING EPDM

Curing System for EPDM

Substitution of one EPDM with another in an existing formulation without changing the cure system, the rate of cure and the properties will almost certainly not be the same, particularly if the two polymers utilise different third monomers. The properties also can be affected by differences in molecular weight and other variations in polymer composition. In general, polymers with DCPD or 1,4 HD will require somewhat more active accelerators and/or higher levels to provide satisfactory cure rates.

As already mentioned, EPDM has pendant unsaturation that allows sulphur vulcanisation. Like most other synthetic rubbers, common accelerators may be used. Since the particular combination selected depends upon many considerations - such as processing methods, the properties desired, cost, and compatibility - few generalisations are possible. Usually, however, the cure system will contain a thiazole accelerator (MBT, MBTS, or the like) in combination with a thiuram and/or a dithiocarbamate. Sulphur donor-type accelerators may replace elemental sulphur, if heat resistance and/or compression set requirements are severe. For some moulded-goods applications, accelerator bloom may be unacceptable. To assure a non-blooming compound, it is necessary to maintain the levels of the various chemicals below their solubility limits.

MBT, MBTS, CBS, ZMBT, ZDBDP	3.0 phr
ZDBDC, DTDM	2.0 phr
ZDEDC, ZDMDC, TDEDC, TMTD	0.8 phr
DPTT, TMTM, TETD, FDMDC	0.8 phr

It has long been known that low sulphur or sulphur donor cure systems give good heat resistance and improved compression set. By using a cure system with 3 to 4 phr of a thiazole (MBT, MBTS, or CBS) in combination with a thiuram and a dithiocarbamate and a level of sulphur below one part, it is possible to obtain outstanding heat resistance. For exposure temperatures above 150°C, a selected antioxidant should be added to enhance the heat resistance of this system. Another sulphur-donor, low-sulphur system that provides good heat resistance but better compression set than that obtained with a "high thiazole" system entails using 2- to 3-phr levels of a thiuram, of two different dithiocarbamates, of a dithiomorpholine, and a low level of sulphur.

In black, steam-cured extrusions, bloom is usually not a problem. Some cure systems that bloom when press cured may not bloom when cured in steam. Since steam curing cycles are typically longer and take place at lower temperatures than moulding cycles, the cure system may be quite simple, for example 1 phr MBTS (or MBT), 1.5-phr TMTD, and 1.5-phr sulphur. A dithiocarbamate may be added if an increased cure rate is desired.

Reinforcement

Like other non-crystallising polyers, EPDM requires reinforcement to be of practical value since the mechanical properties of the unfilled rubber are quite poor. Carbon black is the most useful material for this reinforcement, but silica, clay, talc and some other mineral fillers may also be used. To attain their full effectiveness as reinforcing agents in EPDM rubbers, carbon black and other fillers must be well dispersed. High tensile strength, good tear resistance, and improved abrasion resistance are usually associated with good reinforcement. Well-mixed batches also provide better and more uniform processing for extrusion, calendering, moulding, and so forth.

Plasticisers and Processing Aids

Naphthenic oils have been the most widely used plasticisers for EPDM compounds because they provide the best compatibility at reasonable cost. For applications at higher temperatures or in coloured compounds, paraffinic oils are usually chosen because of their lower volatility and improved UV stability. Some paraffinic oils tend to bleed from cured, high-ethylene EPDM compounds. If such oils are to be used, it is usually advisable to replace part (20-25-phr) of the high-ethylene rubber with one having somewhat lower ethylene content.

Aromatic oils have an adverse effect on some compound properties and, of course, must not be used in conjunction with peroxide curing systems.

Stearic acid, zinc stearate, or other internal lubricants are often included in a compound to aid processing.

EPDM compounds are inherently not tacky. Should there be a need for building tacks, it would be necessary to add a tackifier to the compound. Some care must be taken in making the selection because of compatibility problems and the effects on cure rate of tackifiers with excessive unsaturates. Some tackifiers have been developed specifically for EPDM.

COMPOUNDING EPDM FOR VARIOUS APPLICATIONS

The inherent properties of EPDM polymers have led to their use in a considerable variety of applications. Some of the more significant uses and formulations to illustrate concepts in compound development for specific applications are discussed below.

Sheeting

Rubber sheeting has been used for some years inroofing, but in rather limited quantities because of its cost compared to that of cheap asphalt. The situation has changed dramatically, and the economics for EPDM sheeting are now much more favourable. The formulation suggested for this application is based on a polymer that offers good physical properties at fairly high extension, good green strength, and good calendering. The filler loading is designed to provide good processability and reinforcement to meet the required tensile and tear strength properties. Because of long-term ageing conditions, a less volatile, paraffinic oil and a sulphur donor, low-sulphur cure systems are employed. Since the application involves making lap-seam splices in the field, the cured compound, to facilitate adhesion, is non-blooming. Test data show the characteristics of green strength, cured physical properties, and heat, water and ozone resistance that are required for good performance in roof sheeting applications. For a typical sheeting recipe see Table 2.

Automotive Hose

Generally EPDM polymers are used in the manufacture of automotive hoses because they offer good physical properties. Typical recipe of hose radiator is given in Table 3.

Wire and Cable

EPDM has found wide acceptance in wire and cable applications because of its inherently excellent electrical properties, combined with resistance to ozone, heat, could, and moisture. Apart from these advantages, the polymer chosen in Table 3 provides good extrusion processing with a relatively low level of oil and clay filler. Red lead is used to impart stable, long-term, wet electrical properties. A peroxide-coagent cure system is needed for best ageing.

Sponge Rubber Products

The sponge products are used in carpet industry, industrial sheet mouldings automotive extruded products and sealing strips. Typical recipe for continuous extruded closed cell automotive sponge is listed in Table 4.

MISCELLANEOUS EPM/EPDM APPLICATIONS

EPM/EPDM was originally considered as speciality rubber. However, it has found extensive usefulness in a wide variety of applications. The only major rubber application area it has not fully penetrated is automotive tyres. The wide usage of this elastomer is connected to its multifunctional nature.

Table 2: Typical recipe for sheeting

Ingredients	
EPDM A	100.00
N-347 black	120.00
Talc	30.00
Paraffinic oil type 104B	95.00
Zinc oxide	5.00
Stearic acid	1.00
MBTS	2.20
TMTD	0.65
TETD	0.65
Sulphur	0.75
	355.25
Mooney viscosity, ML-4 @ 100°C	53.0
Mooney scorch MSR-135°C, min	16.0
Rheometer 150°C, 1° arc, 1.7 Hz, micro-die	
Torque, min.	0.6
(N.m) max.	2.6
Time, ts^1	5.0
(min) tc_{50}	10.3
tc_{90}	27.0

Some areas outside typical rubber applications in which EPM/EPDM has found usefulness in significant quantities are viscosity index impoves for lubricating oils, impact modifiers for polyolefins, and thermoplastic elastomers. The latter materials are primarily blends with polyolefins where the elastomer is the major constituent.

Table 3: Radiator hose compound

Ingredients	
EPDM B	105.0
EPDM A	25.0
Zinc oxide	3.0
N-650 black	130.0
N-762 black	95.0
Ground whiting	40.0
High-viscosity, paraffinic oil type 104B	130.0
Stearic acid	1.0
TMTD	3.0
DTDM	2.0
ZDBDC	2.0
ZDMDC	2.0
Sulphur	0.5
	538.5

Table 4: Recipe for continuous extruded closed-cell automotive sponge

Ingredients	
EPDM E	100.0
Catalpo clay	50.0
N-762 black	75.0
N-550 black	15.00
York whiting	30.0
Zinc oxide	3.0
Stearic acid	1.0
Circosol 4240	65.0
BIK	1.0
CELOGEN AZ-130	8.0

Ingredients	
MBT	2.0
TDEDC	1.0
ZDBDC	2.0
DPTT	2.0
Sulphur	2.0
	367.0

Recommended continuous curing conditions

Precure-3 min. @ 310°F	
3 min @ 390°F	
Expanded density: lb/cu ft	19.6
kg/m³	313.9
Water absorption, % change in weight	0.3
25% compression deflection - psi	10.7
KPa	73

As with most polymers, EPM/EPDM polymers also lend themselves to chemical modification. Significant work has been done with halogenation; however, no commercialisation has yet resulted. A significant new application now developing involves the production of various grafts on the polymer, opening the way for the modification of many other plastics such as polystyrene, poly (acrylonitrile-costyrene), nylon, etc., where improved ageing and weathering are desired.

Table 5 Typical formulation for an EPDM insulation compound (90°C)

The EPDM insulation compound has excellent physical, ageing, and electrical properties and meets the requirements of UL 44-RHW and RHH. IPCEA 3.13 and 3.16 and ASTM D 1523 and D 1679 specifications. Data is from a No. 14 solid tineed copper conductor with 0.047-in, insulation cured 60 sec at 250 psi steam in a CV unit.

EPDM F	100	Burgess KE	60
zinc oxide	5	Sunpar 2280	15
NAUGARD@ Q	1	Sartomer SR 350	2

Red lead	5	Di cup 40%	7

Unaged	
Tensile strength, psi	1430
Elongation, %	295
M200%, psi	940
UL set, %	5
14 days air oven, 121°C-% retained	
Tensile strength	106%
Elongation	95
21 days air oven, 121°C-% retained	
Tensile strength	96%
Elongation	91

Electrical properties

	75°C Water Power factor			90°C Water Power factor		
	Sic	40V/M	80V/M	Sic	40V/M	80V/M
1 day	2.68	1.28	1.36	2.67	1.58	1.64
7 days	2.69	0.97	1.08	2.69	0.94	1.04
14 days	2.71	0.83	0.93	2.71	0.82	0.89
1 month	2.72	0.68	0.77	2.74	0.82	0.91
2 months	2.76	0.67	0.74	2.80	1.05	1.12
3 months	2.79	0.73	0.81	2.87	1.15	1.23
4 months	2.81	0.67	0.80	2.92	1.15	1.22
5 months	2.84	0.61	0.78	2.96	1.14	1.23
6 months	2.87	0.72	0.81	2.98	1.10	1.19
7 months	2.89	0.76	0.78	3.00	1.06	1.13
8 months	2.90	0.79	0.85	2.98	0.96	1.03

6

Butyl and Halobutyl Rubbers

INTRODUCTION

Butyl rubber is commercialy produced by cationically copolymerising isobutylene with small amounts of isoprene. The halogen derivatives, chloro- and bromo-, have been commercially available since then. The concept of halogenation to provide more active functionality to the butyl molecule. Their work emphasised the attributes of the brominated derivative. Goodrich commercialised a brominated butyl and prepared from a bulk-bath halogenation, but withdrew later. In this same period, Exxon Researchers originated the chlorobutyl product concept. The halogenated derivatives of butyl rubber provide greater vulcanisation-flexibility and enhanced cure compatibility with other, more unsaturated general-purpose elastomers. Butyl polymers are among the most widely used synthetic elastomers in the world, ranking third in total synthetic elastomers consumed.

Butyl rubber is a copolymer of isobutylene (97%) and isoprene (3%), polymerised below -95°C, with aluminium chloride catalyst. It has good abrasion resistance, excellent impermeability of gases, resistance to oil and greases. It is used in tyre car cases and linings, electrical wire, steam hose and other mechanical rubber goods.

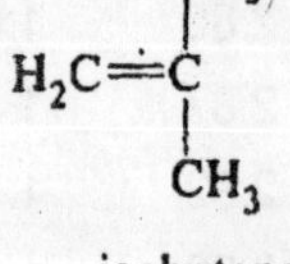

isobutene

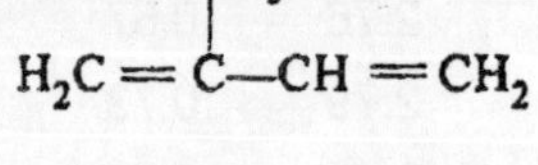

2-methyl prop-l-ene

The monomers are polymerised in solvents such as methyl chloride and at low temperature (-80°C) using Friedel Crafts catalysts such as aluminium chloride or barium chloride as mentioned above.

MANUFACTURE OF BUTYL RUBBER

A schematic diagram of a typical butyl plant is shown in Figure 1. The feed, which is a 25% solution of isobutylene (97-98%) and isoprene (2-3%)

in methyl chloride, which is the diluent, is cooled to -100°C in a feed tank. At the same time, aluminium chloride is also being dissolved in methyl chloride. Both of these streams are then continuously injected into the reactor, Because the reaction is exothermic and is practically instantaneous, cooling is very important. To remove the heat of reaction, liquid ethylene is boiled continuously through the reactor cooling coils, keeping the reaction at –100°C. As the polymerisation proceeds, a slurry of very small particles is formed in the reactor. This slurry overflows into a flash drum that contains copious quantities of hot water. Here the mixuture is vigorously agitated, during which time the diluent and unreacted hydrocarbons are flashed off overhead.

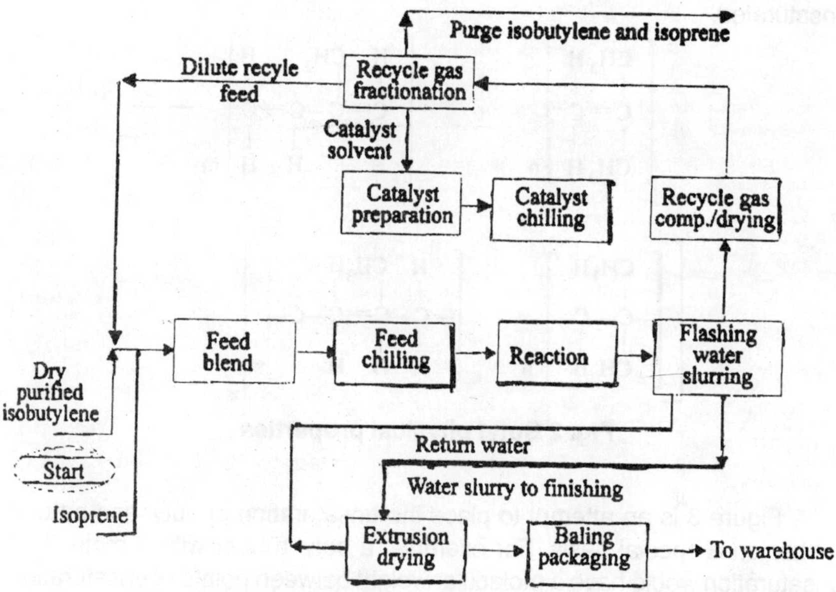

Fig. 1: Basic components of butyl-rubber process

At this point, an antioxidant and zinc stearate are introduced into the polymer. The antioxidant is added to prevent breakdown of the polymer in the subsequent finishing section. Zinc stearate is added to prevent the agglomeration or sticking together, of the wet crumb. The slurry is then vacuum-stripped of residual hydrocarbons.

In the finishing operation, the butyl-rubber slurry is dewatered in a series of extruders to bring the water content to 5-10% in the rubber. Final drying is accomplished in a third extruder by allowing the compressed polymer melt to expand through a die to form an exploded crumb. The crumb is air conveyed to an enclosed fluidised bed conveyor, where water vapour is removed and the crumb is cooled and baled.

PROPERTIES OF BUTYL RUBBER

Physical Properties

The most widely used butyl rubbers are copolymers of isobutylene and isoprene. Grdes are distinguished by molecular weight (Mooney viscosity) and mole % unsaturation. The mole % unsatruation is the number of moles of isoprene per 100 moles of isobulylene. This is illustrated in Figure 2, in which *n* represents the moles of isobutylene that are combined with *m* moles of isoprene. Thus in our case, *n* would equal 98, and *m* would equal 2. In comparison, natural rubber would have *n* equal to 0 and *m* equal to 100, since this molecule is 100% polyisoprene. It could be called 100-mole % unsaturated.

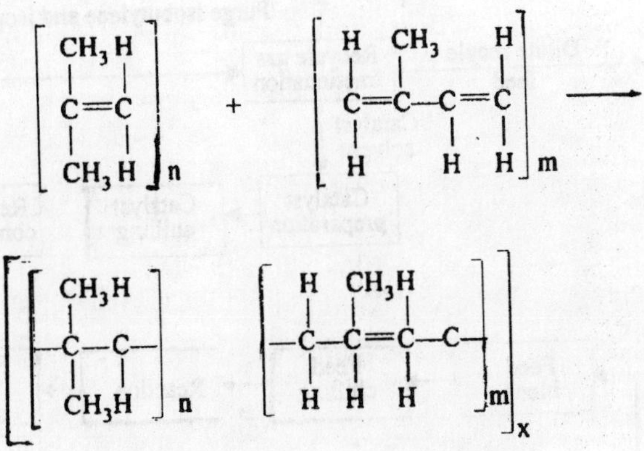

Fig. 2 Butyl physical properties

Figure 3 is an attempt to place the unsaturation of butyl and natural rubber on a special basis. For example, a butyl rubber with 1 mole % of unsaturation would have a molecular weight between points of unsaturation of well over 5000. Natural rubber, on the other hand, has a molecular weight between points of unsaturation of only 68. This is the molecular weight of an isoprene molecule.

Unsaturation is determined by an iodine absorption tenchique or by ozone degradation of the polymer followed by subsequent viscosity measurements of the degraded fragments, or, more recently, by nuclear magnetic resonance (NMR).

The isoprene unit enters the chain randomly in a *trans*-1,4 configuration, since chemical analysis shows little evidence for 1,2 and 3,4 modes of entry at the unsaturation levels present incommercial grades of butyl. The above three isomer forms for the isoprene unit in the polymer are given in Figure 4.

The discovery and development of butyl rubber not only furnished rubber technology with a new elastomer, but, as mentioned earlier, it also provided a new principle. This the concept of low functionality. A low functionality elastomer has sufficient chemical unsaturation so that flexible low-modulus vulcanised networks can be produced, but the larger inert portions of the chain constribute towards oxidation and ozone resistance. Today the concept of low functionality is well-established. For example, vulcanisable ethylene-propylene terpolymers (EPDM) now extends the family of low-functionality elastomers.

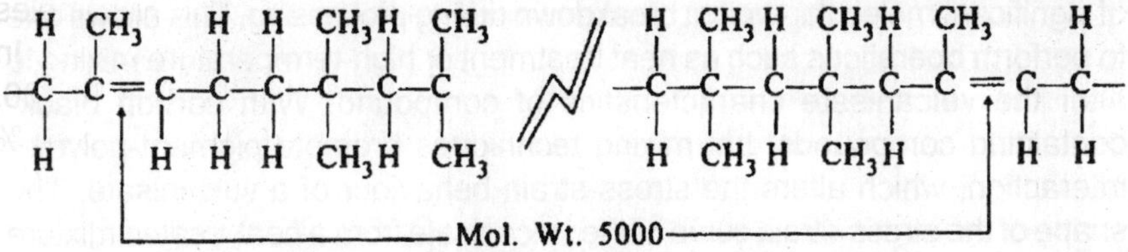

Butyl rubber

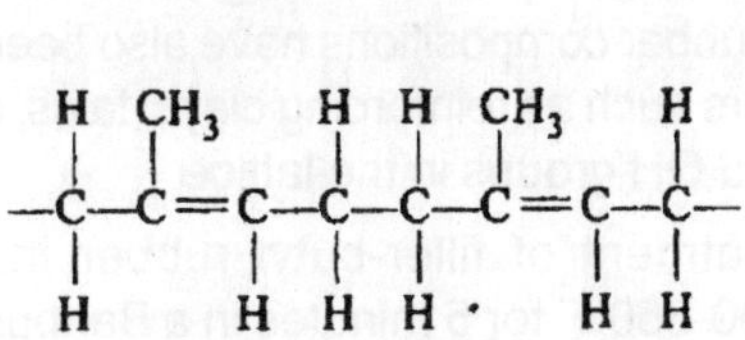

Natural rubber

Fig. 3: Unsaturation of butyl and natural rubber on special basis

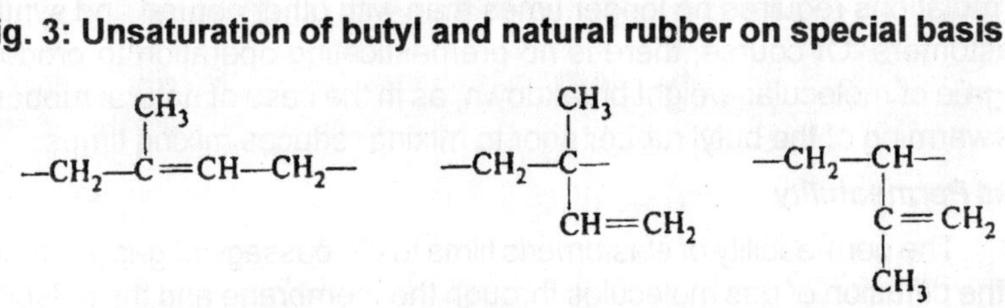

trans-1,4 1,2 3,4

Fig. 4 Three isomer forms of isoprene

This polymer is used primarily in coatings and sealants applications. A aqueous dispersion of butyl (55-65% solids) utilising an anionic emulsifier is also available. The latex is also used in adhesives and coatings.

Butyl-rubber Properties, Vulcanisastion, and Applications

The molecular charactristics of low levels of unsaturation between long segments of polyisobutylene produce unique elastomeric qualities that find application in a wide variety of finished rubber articles. These special properties can be listed as -

i. Low rates of gas permeability
ii. Thermal stability
iii. Ozone and weathering resistance
iv. Vibration damping and higher coefficients of friction
v. Chemical and moisture resistance.

The more chemically inert nature of butyl rubber is reflected in the lack of significant molecular-weight breakdown during processing. This allows one to perform operations such as heat treatment or high-termperature mixing to alter the vulcanisate characteristics of compound. With carbon black-containing compounds, hot mixing techniques promote pigment-polymer interaction, which alters the stress-strain behaviour of a vulcanisate. The shape of the stress-strain curve of the vulcanisate from a heat-treated mixture is a reflection of a more elastic network, and heat treatment has resulted in more flexible vulcanised compounds for a given level of a carbon black type. More flexible butyl-rubber compositions have also been prepared with certain types of mineral fillers such as reinforcing clays, talcs, and silicas that contain appropriately placed OH groups in the lattice.

The heat treatment of filler-butyl rubber masterbatches can be accomplished at 300-350°F for 5 minutes in a Banbury mixer with the aid of promoters (for example *p*-quinone dioxime). In genral, the processing of butyl rubber follows accepted factory operations. Banbury mixing in conventional formulations requires no longer times than with other natural and synthetic elastomers. Of course, there is no premasticating operation to produce a degree of molecular-weight breakdown, as in the case of natural rubber, but prewarming of the butyl rubber prior to mixing reduces mixing times.

Gas Permeability

The permeability of elastomeric films to the passage of gas is a function of the diffusion of gas molecules through the membrane and the solubility of the gas in the elastomer. The polyisobutylene portion of the butyl molecule provides a low degree of permeability to gases and is a familiar property, leading to an almost exclusive use in inner tubes. For example, the air permeability, at 65°C, of SBR is about 80% that of natural rubber, while butyl shows only 10% permeability on the same scale. The difference in air retention between a natural-rubber and a butyl inner tube can be demonstrated by data from controlled road tests on cars driven 60 mph for 100 miles per day. Under these conditions, it is shown (Table 1) that butyl is at least 8 times better than natural rubber in air retention. Other gases such as helium, hydrogen, nitrogen, and carbon dioxide are also well retained by a butyl bladder membrane. While the significance of these properties in inner tubes is waning, it is of importance in air barriers for tubeless tyres, air cushions, pneumatic springs, accumulator bags, air bellows, and the like. A typical formulation for a butyl-rubber passenger-tyre inner tube is given in Table 2.

Table 1 : Air loss of inner tubes during driving tests

Inner tube	Original Pressure (pusi)	Air pressure loss (psi) 1 Week	2 Weeks	1 Month
Natural rubber	28	4.0	8.0	16:5
Butyl	28	0.5	1.0	2.0

Thermal Stability

Butyl-rubber sulphur vulcanisates tend to soften during prolonged exposure to elevated temperatures of 300-400°F. This deficiency is largely the result of the sulphur cross-link, coupled with low polymeric unsaturation which allows no compensating oxidative (cross-linking) hardening. However, certain cross-linking systems, and specifically the resin cure of butyl, provide vulcanised networks of outstanding heat resistance. The has found widespread use in the expandable bladders of automatic tyre-curing presses.

Table 2 : Composition, butyul inner tube

Exxon butyl 268	100.0
GPF carbon black	70.0
Paraffinic process oil	25.0
Zinc oxide	5.0
Sulphur	2.0
TMTDS[a]	1.0
MBT[b]	0.5
Cure range 5' at 350°F—8' 330°F	

a TMTDS = Tetramethyl thiuram disulphide.

b MBT = Mercaptobenzothiazole.

Two tyre-curing bladder fomulations are given in Table 3. In compound 1, the neoprene serves as a halogen-containing activator, while compound 2 uses a partially brominated resin that does not require an external source of halogen. Butyl-rubber tyre-curing bladders have a life of 300-700 curing at steam temperatures of 350°F or higher for approximately 20 minutes per cycle. Other applications would be conveyor belting for hot-materials handling, and high-temperature service hoses.

Table 3 : Compounds, tyre-curing bladers

	1	2
Exxon butyl 268	100	100
Neoprene GN	5	-
HAF carbon black	50	50
Process oil	5	5
Zinc oxide	5	5
Reacitve phenol formaldehyde resin	10	-
Brominated phenol formaldehyde resin		10

Ozone and Wathering Resistance

The low level of chemical unsaturation in the polymer chain produces an elastomer with greatly improved resistance to ozone when compared to polydiene rubbers. Butyl with the lowest level of unsaturation produces high levels of ozone resistances, which are also influenced by the type and concentration of vulcanisate cross-links. For maximum ozone resistance, as in electrical insulation, and for weather resistance, as in rubber sheeting for roofs and water management application, the least unsaturated butyl is advantageously used. A typical butyl-rubber sheeting compound is given in Table 4.

The ozone resistance of butyl rubber coupled with the moisture resistance of its essentially saturated hydrocarbon structure finds utility as a high quality electrical insulation. A cable-insulation formulation for use upto 50 KV employs the lowest unsaturated butyl and the *p*-quinone dioxime (GMF) cure systems, as shown in Table 5.

Vibration Damping

The viscoelastic properties of butyl rubber are a reflection of the molecular structure of the polyisobutylene chain. This molecular chain with two methyl side groups on every other chain carbon atom possesses greater delayed elastic response to deformation. The damping and absorption of shock have found wide application in automotive suspension bumpers. An elastomer with higher damping characteristics also restricts vibrational force transmission in the region of resonant frequencies. Transmissibility is the ratio of output force to input force under impressed oscillatory motion.

Table 4 : Butyl sheeting compound

Exxon butyl 065	100.0
HAF carbon black	48.0
SRF carbon black	24.0
Zinc oxide	5.0
Petrolatum	3.0
Wax	4.0
Sulphur	1.0
TDEDC[a]	0.5
MBT[c]	0.5
ZDMDC[b]	1.5

[a]TDEDC = Tellurium diethyldithiocarbamate.

[b]ZDMDC = Zinc dimethyldithiocarbamate.

[c]MBT = Mercaptobenzothiazole.

Table 5 : Cble-insulation formulation

Exxon butyl 065	100	
Zinc oxide	5	
Calcined clay	100	
Pb_3O_4	5	Masterbatch-mixed
130°C m.p. wax	5	at 300°F
Low density polyethylene	5	
SRF carbon black	10	
MBTS[a]	4	Added as a separate
P-quinone dioxime	1.5	cooler mix

[a]MBTS = Mercaptobenzothiazyl disulphide.

In the region of resonance where the impressed frequency of vibration is equal to natural frequency of the system, the more highly damped butyl compositions more effectively control vibrational forces. These frequencies are in the region of vehicular-body vibration, and as a result butyl compositions are employed in the fabrication of automotive body mounts. In theory, more highly damped systems will less effectively isolate vibration at very high frequencies. However, the damping coefficients of viscoelastic polymers decrease with increasing frequencies in actual practice. This effect partially alleviates higher-frequency defficiencies of butyl systems. In addition at higher frequencies, dynamic stiffness becomes a controlling factor governing transmissibility, and this dynamic behaviour can be greatly influenced by compounding variations as well as by the size and the shape of the moulded part. For this reason, it is difficult to provide a typical butyl body-mount compound, but the one listed in Table 6 can be considered representative of a 50 Shore A hardness vulcanisate.

Higher damping behaviour of an elastomer can be associated with higher coefficients of friction between a rubber and a surface with a measurable degree of roughness or undulations. This property of butyl has potential for improving the coefficient of friction of tyre-tread mterials against a variety of road surfaces.

Chemical and Moisture Resistance

The essentially saturated hydrocarbon nature of butyl obviously imparts moisture resistance to compounded articles. This capability is utilised in applications such as electrical insulation and rubber sheeting for external use. This same hydrocarbon nature provides useful solubility characteristics that can be applied to a variety of protective and sealant applications. These useful solubility characteristics are again based upon the hydrocarbon nature of the elastomer back-bone that is expressed as a solubility parameter of 7.8. This value is similar to the solubility parameters of aliphatic and some cyclic hydrocarbons (7 to 8), but very different from the solubility parameters of more polar oxygenated solvents, ester-type plasticisers, vegetable oils, and synthetic hydraulic fluids (8.5 to 11.0).

Table 6 : Butyl body-mount compound

Butyl	100.0
HAF carbon black	45.0
MT carbon black	15.0
Paraffinic oil	20.0
Zinc oxide	5.0
CdDEDC[a]	2.0
MBTS	0.5
Sulphur	1.0

[a]CdDEDC - Cadmium diethyldithiocarbamate

Thus while butyl vulcanisates will be highly swollen by hydrocarbon solvents and oils, they are only slightly affected by oxygenated solvents and other polar liquids. This behaviour is utilised in elastomeric seals for hydraulic systems using synthetic fluids, as Figure 5 demonstrates.

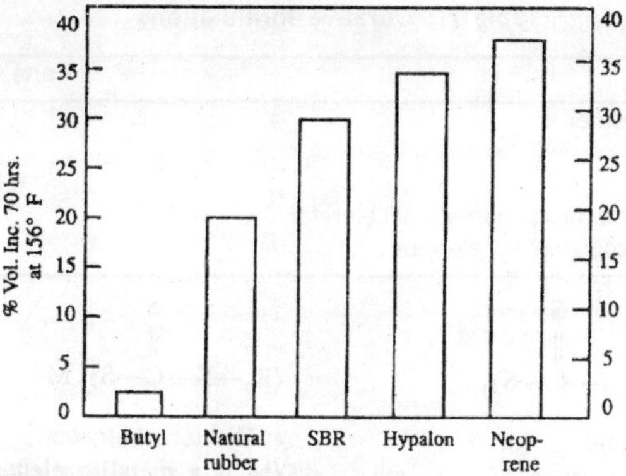

Fig. 5 : Swelling of butyl and other elastomeric vulcanisates in phosphate ester fluids

The low degree of olefinic unsaturation in the saturated hydrocarbon back-bone also imparts mineral acid resistance to butyl-rubber compositions. After 13 weeks immersion in 70% sulphuric acid, a butyl compound experiences little loss in tensile strength or elongation while a natural rubber or SBR will highly degraded.

BUTYL VULCANISATION

Regular butyl rubber is commercially vulcanised by three basic methods. These are -

i. Accelerated sulphur vulcanisation
ii. Cross-linking with dioxime and related dinitroso compounds
iii. The polymethylol-phenol resin cure.

The three methods are described as under.

Accelerated Sulphur Vulcanisation

In common with more highly unsaturated rubbers, butyl may be cross-linked with sulphur, and activated by zinc oxide and organic accelerators. In contrast to the higher unsaturated varieties, however, adequate states of vulcanisation can be obtained only with the very active thiuram and dithiocarbamate accelerators. Other less-active accelerators such as thiazole derivatives may be used as modifying agents to improve the safety of processing scorch. Most curative formulations include the range of ingredients shown in Table 7.

Thiurams and dithiocarbamates provide the primary accelerating activity which promotes the most efficient use of sulphur. Thiazoles, generally mercaptobenzothiazoles, reduce scorch during processing. High levels of dithiocarbamates and low levels of sulphur favour the formation of more stable monosulphidic cross-links. The use of sulphur donors in place of elemental sulphur also promotes simpler monosulphidic bonds.

Table 7 : Curative formulations

	Parts by wt.
Butyl elastomer	100
Zinc oxide	5
Sulphur	0.5 - 2.0
Thiuram or dithiocarbamate accelerator	1-3
Modifying thiazole accelerator	0.5 -1

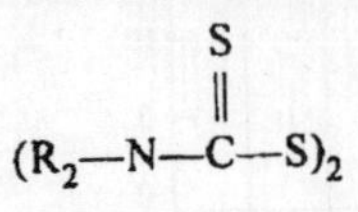

Thiuram

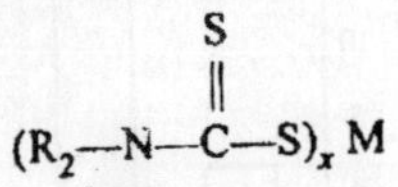

Dithiocarbamates
(M is a metallic element)

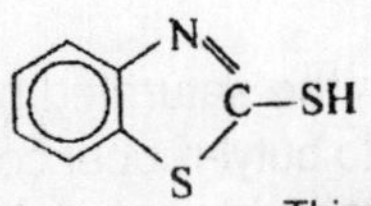

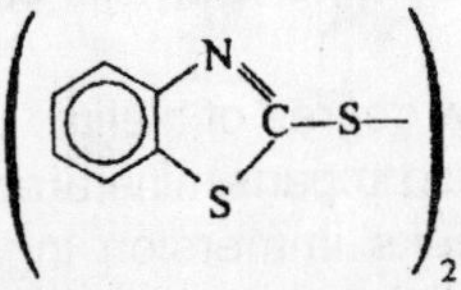

Thiazole

Vulcanisation temperatures may range from 275-375°F, with temperature coefficients of vulcanisation of 1.4 per 10°F for carbon black containing compounds. This means that the vulcanisation time, to a given state of cure, is multiplied by 1.4 for every 10°F decrease in temperature. Conversely, for every 10°F rise in temperature, the vulcanisation time is divided by 1.4.

Dioxime Cure

The cross-linking of butyl with *p*-quinone dioxime or *p*-quinone dioxime dibenzoate proceeds through an oxidation step that forms the active cross-linking agent, *p*-dinitrose-benzene, as shown in Figure 6.

The use of PbO_2 as the oxidising agent results in very rapid vulcanisations, which can produce room-temperature cures for cement applications. In dry rubber processing, the dioxime cure is largely used in butyl-rubber electrical insulation formulations as outlined in a preceding section, to provide a maximum of ozone resistance and moisture impermeability to the vulcanisate.

Resin Cure

The cross-linking of butyl rubber (and other elastomers containing olefinic unsaturation) by this method is dependent upon the reactivity of the phenolmethylol groups of reactive phenol-formaldehyde resins -

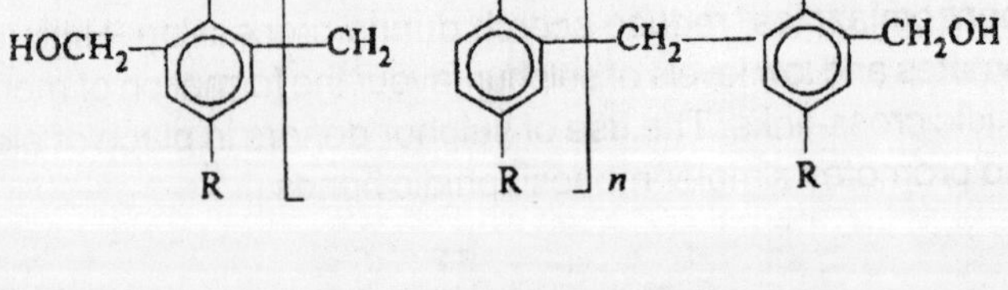

Two mechanisms involving the isoprenoid unit have been postulated. One involves reaction with allylic hydrogen through a methylene quinone intermediate, and the other an actual bridging of the double bond. The low levels of unsaturation of butyl require resin cure activation by halogen-containing materials such as $SnCl_2$ or halogen-containing elastomers such as neoprene. A series of curves in Figure 7 illustrates the activating effect of stannous chloride and the stability of the resultant cross-link to reversion upon prolonged heating. This feature of the resin cure is utilised in the fabrication of tyre-curing bladders.

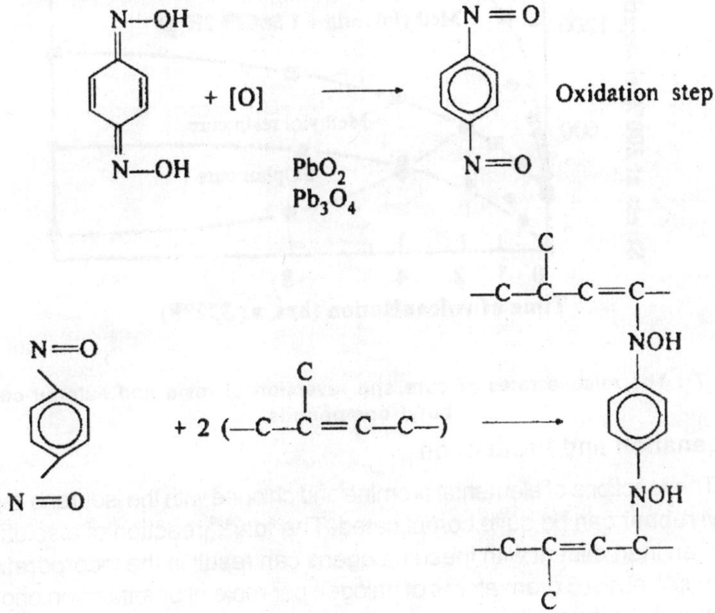

Fig. 6 : Dioxime cure of butyl rubber

A more reactive resin cure system requiring no external activator is obtained if some of the hydroxyl groups of the methylol group are replaced by bromine.

HALOGENATED BUTYL

The introduction of chlorine to the butyl molecule, in approximately 1/1 molar ratio of chloride to double bond, achieved a broadening of vulcanisation latitude and rate, and enhanced covulcanisation with general purpose, high-unsaturation elastomers, while preserving the many unique attributes of the basic butyl molecule. Bromination in the same approximate molar ratio further enhanced cure properties and provided greater opportunity for increased covulcanisation or adhesion, or both, to general purpose elastomers. These property enhancements are vital to the major applications for halobutyl tubeless tyre innerliners. Thus halogenated butyls contributed the required level of covulcanisability and adhesion to the highly unsaturated tyre elastomers to carry the advantages of butyl inner tubes forward through the development of the radial tubeless tyre.

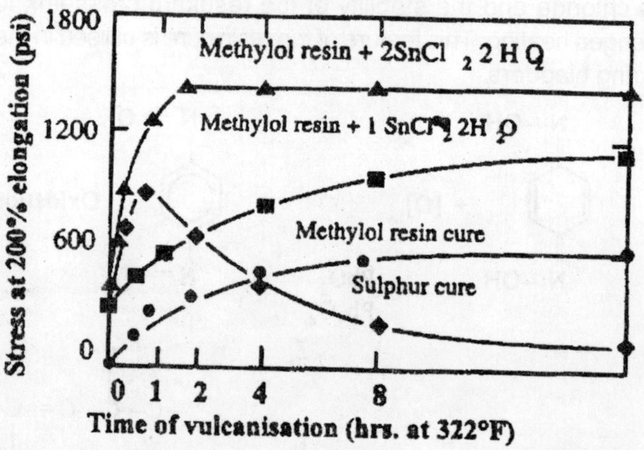

Fig. 7 : The relative rates of cure and reversion of resin and sulphur-cured butyl compounds

Halogenation and Production

The reactions of elemental bromine and chlorine with the isoprene residue in butyl rubber can be quite complicated. The "dark" reaction of a solution of butyl in an inert diluent with these halogens can result in the incorporation of butyl in upto about 3 gram atoms of halogen per mole of unsaturation originally present in the polymer. It has been found that the overall halogenation occurs substantially as a series of consecutive reactions, each being slower than the preceding one.

Synthesis in the halogenated-butyls production facilities involves the "dark" reaction of a solution of butyl in hexane with elemental halogens at conventional process temperatures (40-60°C). The target is to produce a product in which no more than 1 halogen atom is introduced into the polymer per unsaturated site initially present, within the constraints of a final product weight per cent halogen specification range.

Under the above conditions, the reaction with chlorine is very fast, probably completed in 15 seconds or less, even at the low molar concentration of reactants employed. The bromine reaction is considerably slower, perhaps about 5 times that of chlorination. In both cases, through mixing is a prerequisite to meet the synthesis targets (i.e., to avoid multiple halogenation at a particular site). That these actions lead primarily to substituted products has been well documented.

These fast reactions are presumed to occur via an ionic mechanism. The halogen molecules are polarised at the olefinic sites, and undergo heterolytic scission and consequent reaction. This ionic reaction can be depicted as follows -

i. Heterolysis and addition of halogen (X)

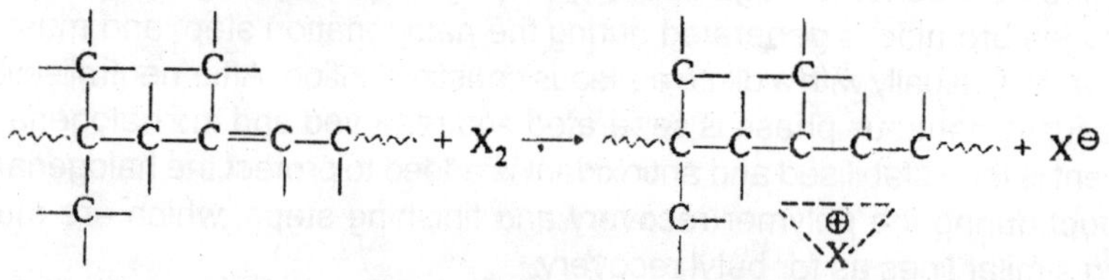

There is interaction between positively charged carbon and added X up until.

ii. Proton abstraction by Xq

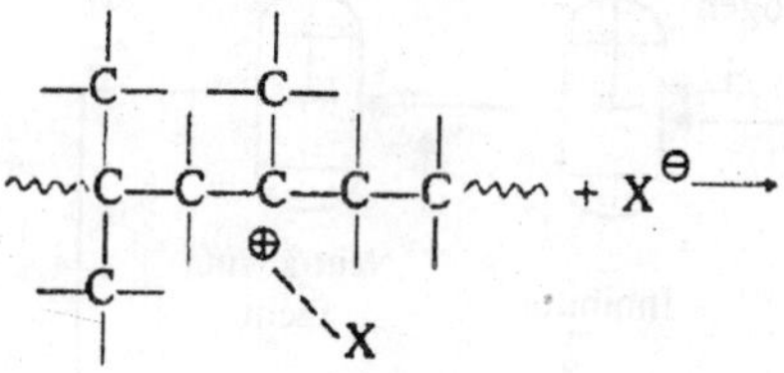

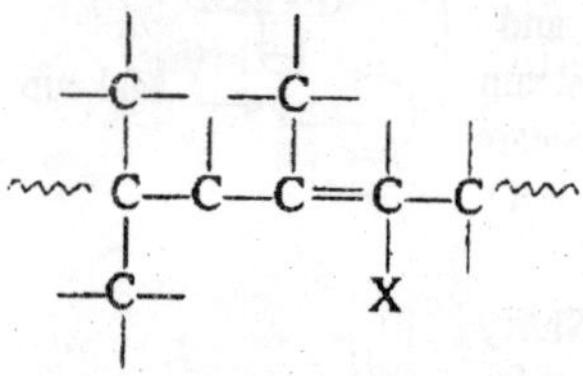

(II) Thmodynamically most favoured structure

+ HX

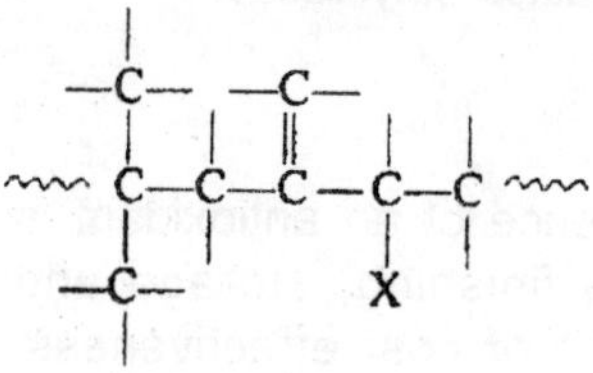

(III) Product found in highest concentration

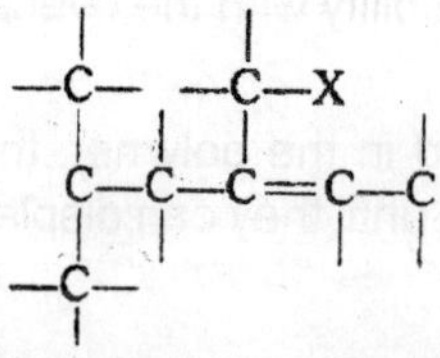

(IV) Isomerised form of III

Apparently the steric constraints imposed by the dimethyl-substituted carbon alpha to the in-chain charged carbon render III the kinetically favoured structure by far. The structural features of commercial products can be accounted for to a level ≥ 95% by the summations of the concentrations of structures I-IV with III dominant.

Actual production is conducted in hexane solvent and the process flow chart is shown in Figure 8. Butyl rubber in solution is treated with chlorine or bromine in a series of high-intensity mixing steps. Hydrogen chloride or hydrogen bromide is generated during the halogenation step, and must be neutralised, usually with a dilute aqueous caustic solution. After neutralisation, the caustic aqueous phase is separated and removed and the halogenated cement is then stabilised and antioxidant is added to protect the halogenated product during the polymer recovery and finishing steps, which are much along similar lines as for butyl recovery.

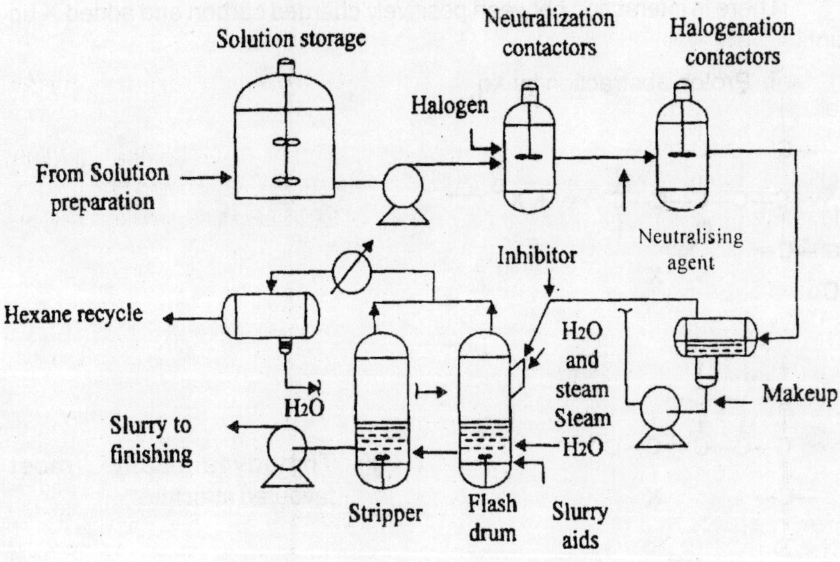

Fig. 8 : Process of manufacture for halogenated butyl-rubber

Stabilisation

As in all hydrocarbon polymers, the presence of an antioxidant is required to protect those elastomers during finishing, storage and compounding. These are chosen on the basis of cost effectiveness, discolouration tendencies, FDA approval, and compatibility with the overall process.

These reactive halogens having been implanted in the polymer, the principal stabilisation problem is how to preserve them until they can display their main utility in cross-linking reactions. Unstabilised, both elastomers will undergo thermal dehydrohalogenation and simultaneous cross-linking, the brominated product more readily than the chlorinated. The dehydrohalogenation is catalysed by the evolved acid.

Useful stabilisation must meet numerous criteria. The stabiliser or package thereof must -

i. Prevent the accumulation of evolving HX and yield harmless by-products.

ii. Not be itself highly reactive with allylic halogens.

iii. Have process compatibility.

iv. Interact favourably, or at least not unfavourably, with cross-linking systems to be employed.

v. Not introduce a health hazard.

vi. Be economical within the foregoing constraints.

Many materials will satisfy one or more of these demands, but very few all of them.

Experiment and experience have combined to teach that calcium stearate fulfils these objectives for chlorinated butyl. Brominated butyl, being less stable and more reactive, requires a combination of calcium stearate and an epoxidised vegetable oil.

Compounding Halobutyl

The following summarises the influence of compounding ingredients on processing and vulcanisate properties of halobutyls.

a. *Carbon Black* - Carbon blacks affect the compound properties of halobutyl in a similar way as they affect the compound properties of their rubbers: particle size and structure determine the reinforcing power of the carbon black and hence the final properties of the halobutyl compounds.

   i. Increasing reinforcing strength, for example, raises the compound viscosity, hardness, and cured modulus.

   ii. Cured modulus increases with the carbon black level up to 80 phr. Tensile strength goes through a maximum at 50-60 phr carbon black level.

b. *Mineral Fillers* - Mineral fillers vary not only in particle size but also in chemical composition. As a result, both cure behaviour and physical properties of a bromobutyl compound are affected by the mineral filler used, although to a lesser extent than chlorobutyl compounds.

   Generally the common mineral fillers may be used with halobutyl but highly alkaline ingredients and hygroscopic fillers should be avoided.

i. *Clays are semireinforcing* - acidic clays give very fast cures, therefore extra scorch retarders may be needed. Calcined clay in the preferred filler for pharmaceutical stopper compounds based on halobutyl.

ii. *Talc* is semireinforcing in halobutyl without a major effect on cure.

iii. *Hyerated silicas* even at moderate levels cause compound stiffiness and slower cure rate, so their use should be restricted.

iv. *Silane-treated mineral fillers* so one way to enhance the interaction between polymer and silicates, and hence to improve compound properties, is to add small (1 phr) amounts of silanes. Particularly useful silanes are the mercapto- and amino-derivatives.

c. *Plasticisers* - Petroleum-based process oils are the most commonly used plasticisers for halobutyl. They improve mixing and processing, soften stocks, improve flexibility at low temperatures and reduce cost.

Parffinic/naphthenic oils are preferred for compatibility reasons. Other useful plasticisers are paraffin waxes and low-molecular-weight polyethylene. Adipates and sebacates improve flexibility at very low temperatures.

d. *Process Aids* -

i. *Mineral rubber* not only improve the processing characteristics of halobutyl compounds by improving fillers dispersion, but they also enhance compatibility between halobutyl and highly unsaturated rubbers.

ii. *Tackifying resins* should be selected with care. Phenol-formaldehyde resins, even those where the reactive methylol groups have been deactivated, react with halobutyl especially bromobutyl, causing a decrease in scorch time.

iii. *Stearates, stearic acid* should be noted that zinc stearate (which can also be formed via the zinc oxide and stearic acid reaction) is a strong dehydrohalogenation agent and a cure catalyst for halobutyl. Similar effects will be observed with other organic acids such as oleic acid or naphhthenic acid. Alkaline stearates, on the other hand such as calcium stearate, have a retarding action on the halobutyl cure.

Anti-degradants - amine-type antioxidants/antiozonants such as Flectol H, mercaptobenzimidazole and especially *p*-phenylene-diamines will react with halobutyl. They should preferably be added with the curatives, not in the masterbatch. Phenol derivative antioxidants are generally preferred.

Processing Halobutyl

The following recommended processing conditions are applicable to both chloro-and-bromo-butyl.

a. *Mixing* - The mixing is done in two stages. The first stage contains all the ingredients except for zinc oxide and accelerators. The batch weight should be 10-20% higher than that used for a comparable compound based on general purpose rubbers. A typical mixing cycle and processing for a halobutyl innerliner compound are as follows -

First stage	0 min	Halobutyl, carbon black, retarder.
	1.5 min	Process aids, plasticisers, fillers, stearic aid.....
	3.5 min	Dump at 120-140°C

Higher dump temperatures could result in scorching -

Second stage	0 min	Masterbatch + curatives.
	2 min	Dump at 100°C.

Mill-mixing on two-roll mill is best accomplished with a roll-speed ratio of 1.25/1 and roll temperatures of 40°C on the slow roll and 55°C on the fast roll.

The following sequence of addition is recommended part of the rubber together with a small amount of a previous mix as a seed; 1/4 fillers plus retarder; remainder of polymer; rest of filler in small increments; plasticisers at the end; acceleration below 150°C.

b. *Calendering* - Feed preparation can be done either by mill or by extruder. Halobutyl follows the cooler roll; therefore, a temperature differential of 10°C between calender rolls is reommended. Starting roll temperatures should be -

Cool roll	75-80°C
Warm roll	85-90°C

Normal calendering speeds for halobutyl compounds are between 25 and 30 metres/minute.

Rapid cooling of the calendered sheet is beneficial for optimal processability (handling) and maximum tack retention.

c. *Extrusion* - Feed temperature should be 75-80°C while the temperature of the extrudate is around 100°C. During calendering and extrusion of halobutyl compounds, the most important problem is blister formation. The reason for this phenomenon is the low permeability of these polymers, which tend to retain entrapped air or moisture. Preventive action should be taken at all stages of the process, for example -

i. Ensure the stock is well mixed in full mixer to prevent porosity.

ii. Avoid moisture at all stages.

iii. Keep all rolling banks on mills and calender nips to a minimum.

d. *Moulding* - Halobutyl can be formulated to have a fast-cure rate, good mould flow and mould release characteristics, and can, therefore, be moulded into highly intricate designs with conventional moulding equipment. Entrapped air can be removed by bumping of the press during the early part of the moulding cycle.

Halobutyl is also very well-suited for injection moulding because of its easy flow and fast, reversion-resistant cures. Low-molecular-weight polymer grades may be required for optimum flow and good scorch safety.

7

Nitrile and Polyacrylic Rubber

INTRODUCTION

A synthetic rubber can be made by random polymerisation of acrylonitrile with butadiene by free radical catalyst. Alternating polymers using Natta-Zeglier catalyst can be used. The main raw materials required are the monomers, butadiene and acrynitrile.

Its repeating structure can be represented as -

$$—CH_2—CH{=}CH—CH_2—CH_2—\underset{\substack{|\\ CN}}{CH}—$$

In theory, the polymerisation reaction can be written as -

$$CH_2{=}CH—CH{=}CH_2 + CH_2{=}\underset{\substack{|\\ CN}}{CH}$$

$$\longrightarrow \left[(—CH_2—CH{=}CH—CH_2)_m—\left(CH_2—\underset{\substack{|\\ CN}}{CH}\right)_y\right]_n$$

The values of *n* and *y* depend on the precise polymerisation recipe and the temperature of polymerisation. It is important to bear in mind that, except under azeotropic conditions, the ratio of the two monomer units in the final polymer will not normally be same as the ratio in which the monomers were charged in the reaction vessel. As the ratio of butadiene to acrylonitrile in the polymer largely controls its properties, the design of the polymerisation recipe and the temperature at which this is carried out are important features of nitrile rubber production. The properties of the product may be influenced by other details of the recipe, such as the nature and the amount of modifiers and emulsifier. Thus, nitrile rubber is defined as copolymer of a diene and an unsaturated nitrile.

Nitrile butadiene and polyacrylic elastomers fall into the class of special-purpose, oil-resistant rubbers. Nitrile elastomers offer a broad balance of low temperature, oil, fuel and solvent resistance as related to *acrylonitrile* content.

These characteristics, combined with their good abrasion and water-resistant qualities, make them suitable for use in a wide variety of applications with heat-resistant requirements to 149°C (300°F).

Conventional unsaturated diene-type nitrile rubbers tend to embrittle (or case-harden) when exposed to temperatures above 149°C due to -

a. Oxidative cross-linking or

b. Cross-linking by oils containing sulphur-bearing additives.

Acrylic elastomers contain little or no residual unsaturation and therefore are more resistant to these effects. In general, the acrylics exhibit 55°C (100°F) higher service-temperature capability than the nitriles and are specifically recommended for those applications requiring heat and oil resistance in the 149°C-204°C (400°F) temperature range.

MANUFACTURE OF NITRILE RUBBER

In addition to the monomers, a basic polymerisation recipe would contain water, emulsifier, modifier, electrolytes, catalyst, activator, shortstop, and stabilisers. The basic steps involved in the manufacture of nitrile rubber are as follows -

The monomers are emulsified in water, a free radical-generating catalyst is added and the mixture is agitated while a constant temperature is maintained. After the desired degree of polymerisaiton is reached, a shortstop and stabilisers are added; residual monomers are removed; the latex is concentrated, coagulated, washed, dewatered; and the resulting crumbs are dried and compacted to form bales. Both batch and continuous methods of manufacture are in use today.

Nitrile rubbers are available in several forms such as sheets, crumb, powders and liquid.

PROPERTIES OF NITRILE RUBBER

Oil resistance is the most important property of nitrile rubber. Nitrile rubber is available in several grades of oil resistance based on the acrylonitrile content of the polymer. Available grades range from 15-50% acrylonitrile content.

Many of the properties of nitrile rubber are directly related to the proportion of acrylonitrile in the rubber. The most important property trends related to the acrylonitrile content are shown in Table 1.

Table 2 illustrates some of the properties one can expect of a typical nitrile rubber compound when only the ratio of acrylonitrile to butadiene content of the polymer is varied. Other important characteristics which can affect the properties of nitrile rubber, more particularly the processing properties are Mooney plasticity and gel content. Typical Mooney viscosity ranges of nitrile rubbers are 30 to 95.

Table 1 : Property trends influenced by the per cent of acrylonitrile in nitrile rubber

Characteristics	% Acrylonitrile 15 → 50
Oil resistance improves	→
Fuel resistance increases	→
Tensile strength increases	→
Hardness increases	→
Abrasion resistance improves	→
Gas impermeability increases	→
Heat resistance increases	←
Low-temperature flexibility improves	←
Resilience improves	←
Plasticiser compatibility increases	←
Compression set decreases	←

Gel content generally ranges from 0% to over 80%. The type of gel present also affects the properties. Permanent gel or cross-linking generally results in lower tensile strength and lower per cent elongation and abrasion resistance in cured compounds, but in calendered or extruded goods, lack of nerve or reduced shrinkage is valuable. Non-permanenet gel, which generally can be temporarily milled out of a compound, results in increased green strength and reduced cold flow of uncured compounds, but also results in reduced surface tack and poor mould flow characteristics.

A modification of the nitrile rubber molecule, i.e., the addition of carboxyl groups, results in a rubber with the usual oil resistant characterisitics of nitrile rubber, but with much improved abrasion resistance. Blends of poly (vinyl chloride) and nitrile rubber also are produced either by blending the two latices or by physically blending the polymers. The resulting products have much improved ozone resistance and improved flame-retardant properties.

Uses of Nitrile Rubber

Because of its oil- and fuel-resistant characteristics, nitrile rubber finds its greatest market in applications where these characteristics are necessary.

There are many applications in the hose industry where oil, fuel, chemicals and solutions are transported. Typical hose constructions requiring a nitrile-rubber tube or liner are automotive, marine, aircraft fuel lines, and bulk-fuel transfer hose; oil-tanker, barge-loading and unloading hose; chemical transfer hose, industrial air hose and food handling, dairy and creamery hose. Other automotive applications include emission hose and tubing, shaft seals, bushings, gaskets carburetor parts, fuel-pump diaphragms and oil-filter gaskets.

Table 2 : Typicla properties of nitrile rubber related to acrylonitrile content

% Acrylonitrile	41	33	29	21
Original properties ASTM D412				
100% modulus, MPa (psi)	2.0 (300)	2.3 (340)	2.3 (340)	2.4 (355)
300% moldulus, Mpa (psi)	12.0 (1750)	12.0 (1750)	11.7 (1710)	14.6 (2130)
Tensile strength, MPa (psi)	22.0 (3200)	20.9 (3040)	20.8 (3030)	21.0 (3055)
Elongation, %	380	500	490	390
Hardness, points	66	64	62	62
Compression set, plied discs, ASTM D395, method B				
70 hrs @ 125°C	34	34	39	38
Low-temp. brittleness, ASTM D2137				
°C	-20	-36	-40	-45
Oil-resistance, volume-change per cent, 70 hrs @ 100°C				
ASTM No. 1	-1	+1	+3	+4
ASTM No. 3	-10	+17	+32	+49
Fuel-resistance, volume-change per cent, 70 hrs @ 23°C				
ASTM Reference Fuel B	+29	+39	+54	+76
ASTM Reference Fuel C	+48	+66	+88	+133
Distilled-H_2O-resistance, volume-change per cent, 70 hrs @ 23°C				
% change	+11	+10	+8	+5

Another large user of nitrile rubber is the oil-drilling industry in such items as blowout preventors, down-hole packers, drill-pipe protectors, pump-piston elements and rotary drilling hose. Powder and particulate forms of nitrile rubber are especially useful in cements, adhesives, binders for cork gaskets and break linings. Another interesting application for nitrile rubber is in plastics modification to improve impact strength and flexibility.

COMPOUNDING

Nitrile rubber can be compounded to obtain a broad range of properties. Basically nitrile rubbers are compounded in much the same fashion as natural rubber or the styrene-butadiene rubbers. Polymer selection is important to obtain the best balance of oil resistance and of low-temperature flexibility. The higher acrylonitrile content polymers have the highest oil and fuel resistance, but poorer low temperature properties. The lower acrylonitrile content polymers have good low temperature properties at some sacrifice in oil and fuel resistance.

As with natural rubber and styrene-butadiene rubber, zinc oxide at 3-5 phr level and stearic acid at a 1-2 part level are added for proper activation. A good antioxidant is usually added in all nitrile compounds to improve stability. Proper choice of antioxidant depends on the requirements such as high-heat resistance, extraction resistance, or staining characteristics.

Nitrile rubber is not inherently ozone-resistant; therefore protection must be added to the compound to achieve a desired degree of ozone-resistance. Protective waxes, usually at the 1-2 part level, are generally added to the compound in addition to the ozone inhibitors. Ozone resistance can also be obtained through blending techniques with other materials such as poly (vinly chloride), chlorosulphonated polyethylene, chlorinated polyethylene, epichlorohydrin and ethylene-propylene terpolymers.

Reinforcing fillers are necessary in order to achieve optimum properties with nitrile rubbers. Carbon black is the most widely used filler and the nitrile rubbers respond to the full range of available carbon blacks from the largest to the smallest particle sizes and range of structures. Non-black applications will require the use of reinforcing silicas of various types, calcium crbonates, hard clays, talc and other pigments.

Plasticisers are generally used in nitrile-rubber compounds to improve processing and low-temperature properties. Typically they are ester types, aromatic oils, and polar derivatives and can be extractable or non-extractable depending upon the end-use requirements.

Vulcanisation can be achieved with sulphur, su!phur-donor, or peroxide systems. Table 3 illustrates some typical vulcanisation systems in general use. Tables 4 and 5 represent typical compounds designed for automotive-hose tubes, oil-well-packer elements, and general-purpose moulded goods.

Mixing and Processing

All of the commercially available nitrile rubbers can be mixed either on a two-roll mill or with internal mixing equipment. Compounds can be designed to be easily extruded, calendered, or moulded with injection, compression, or transfer techniques.

Table 3 : Typical vulcanisation systems

System	Level	Characteristics
Sulphur MBTS	1.5 parts 1.5 parts	Low cost, general purpose, slow curing
Sulphur TMTD	0.3 parts 3.0 parts	Fast-curing, low compression set, blooms
Sulphur TETD TMTD CBTS	0.5 parts 1.0 parts 1.0 parts 1.0 parts	Faster curing, lower compression set, non-blooming
DTDM OTOS TMTM	1.0 parts 2.0 parts 1.5 parts	EV system, excellent heat ageing
Dicumyl perioxide (40%)	4.0 parts	General-purpose peroxide system, low compression set

The proper choice of polymer Mooney viscosity determines how well a compound will process. The low-Mooney-viscosity polymers lend themselves to injection moulding and calendered friction compounds. The medium-Mooney-viscosity polymers will generally transfer- and compression-mould and provide good calendering characteristics. The high-Mooney-viscosity polymers provide excellent extruded compounds, particularly when high "green" strength is required. Blends of polymers with different Mooney-viscosity ranges often provide the solution to many processing difficulties.

Latest Developments

i. Nitrile rubbers containing "bound" antioxidants, i.e., antioxidants attached to the polymer chain are less fugitive and are less likely to be soluble in fuels or oils and are less volatile, thereby improving dry-heat resistance.

ii. Hydrogenated nitrile rubbers containing little or no unsaturation show promise of better heat resistance and resistance to oxidised gasoline as well as improved resistance to the harsh environments found indeed, sour wells.

POLYACRYLIC RUBBERS

Polyacrylic rubbers are usually copolymers of ethyl acrylate and a minor proportion of a second monomer containing chlorine, e.g., 2-chloroethyl vinyl ether.

$CH_2{=}CH{-}COOC_2H_5$ — Ethyl acrylate

$CH_2{=}CH{-}O{-}CH_2{-}CH_2{-}CL$ — 2-chloroethyl vinyl ether

Table 4 : Oil-well-packer element

Ingredients	
Hycar 1051[a]	100.0
Zinc oxide	5.0
Stearic acid	1.0
N550 black	70.0
Antioxidant	2.0
Plasticiser	5.0
Sulphur	0.4
MBTS	3.0
ZDMC	1.5
	187.9

[a]Typically, 75 Mooney, 41% acrylonitrile

Expected properties

Tensile strength, psi	2940
Elongation, %	370
Hardness, points	78

Table 5 : General-purpose moulding compound

Ingredients	
Hycar 1052[a]	100.0
Zinc oxide	5.0
Stearic acid	1.0
Antioxidant	1.5
N774 black	65.0
Plasticiser	15.0
Sulphur	1.5
MBTS	1.5
	190.5

[a]Typically 50 Mooney, 33% acrylonitrile.

Expected Properties

Tensile strength, psi	2700
Elongation, %	550
Hardness points	65

Vulcanisates of polyacrylic rubbers are superior to those of nitrile rubbers in resistance to swelling and deterioration by hot hydrocarbon oils, extreme pressure lubricants, and transmission and hydraulic fluids, and in resistance to heat, being suitable for intermittent use at a temperature upto 180-200°C.

Composition

Acrylic elastomers are copolymers based on two major components -

i. The back-bone (95-99%)

ii. The reactive cure site (1-5%)

These are shown in Figure 1. Reactivity of the cure site monomer governs the cure behaviour of the polymer.

MANUFACTURE OF POLYACRYLIC

Conventional acrylic elastomers are commonly emulsion-polymerised to form a latex, or are polymerised in suspension. The solid product is recovered by conventional coagulation, washing procedures, and dried by hot air, vacuum, or extrusion techniques. The ethylene/acrylic type is solution-polymerised under pressure.

Conventional ACM (Hycar cyanacryl)

Back-bone

(1) Alkyl

$(CH_2—CH)_x$
    |
  C=O
    |
  $O—C_nH_{2n+1}$

e.g., if $n = 2$: ethyl acrylate

e.g., if $n = 4$: butyl acrylate

(2) Alkoxy

$(CH_2—CH)_x$
    |
  C=O
    |
  $O—C_nH_{2n}O—C_mH_{2m+1}$

e.g., if $n = 2$ and $m = 1$: methoxy ethyl acrylate

e.g., if $n = 2$ and $m = 2$: ethoxy ethyl acrylate

Ethylene/acrylic (Vamac)

Back-bone

(1) Ethylene

$(—CH_2—CH_2—)_x$

(2) Methyl acrylate

$(—CH—CH_2—)_y$
  |
C=O
  |
OCH_3

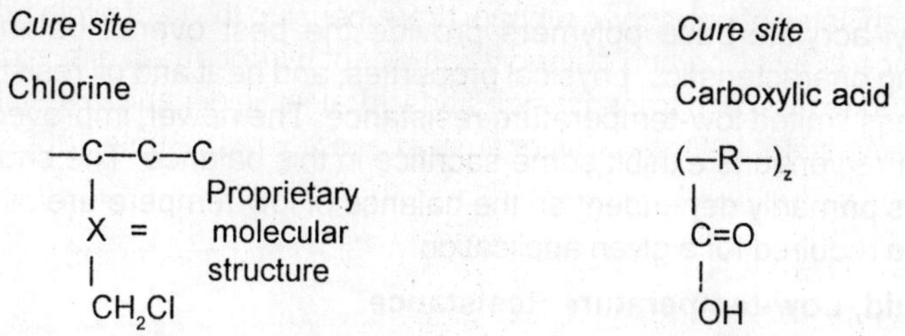

Fig. 1 : Major components, acrylic elastomers

Raw Polymer Characteristics

Conventional acrylic polymers have a specific gravity of 1.10 and are off-white in colour. Current commercial types are manufactured in a 25-55 Mooney (ML-1 +4'/100°C) viscosity range. All are normally supplied in solid, slab form. Some special solution grades are also available in both solid and crumb form. The ethylene/acrylic polymer has a specific gravity of 1.03, is pale-gray in colour; and supplied in a 16 ± 3 Mooney (ML -1 + 4/100°C) viscosity range. Black and non-black masterbatch versions are also available. All are supplied in slab form only. The shelf stability of acrylic rubbers is excellent (>12 months) when stored in their original package under normal room temperature, dry conditions.

Physical Characteristics

As a class, acrylic elastomers are inherently resistant to -

i. Temperature from -40 to 204°C (400°F)
ii. Oils at elevated temperatures.
iii. Oxidation.
iv. Ozone.
v. Alphatic hydrocarbons
vi. Sunlight (UV) discolouration.

Typical vulcanisate properties are as follows -

Tensile strength (MPa/psi)	5-17/700-2500
Elongation (%)	100-600
Hardness (Duro A)	40-90

In addition, the acrylics exhibit good damping qualities, are not highly corrosive to steel, and can be compounded to provide excellent flex life, fair electrical-insulation resistance and some degree of flame resistance. The more polar conventional acrylics can also be compounded to provide a high degree of electrical conductivity. The ethylene/acrylic type also provides improved abrasion resistance, but tends to lose this advantage after oil-ageing as a result of its high swell characteristics.

Ethyl-acrylate-base polymers provide the best overall balance of processing characteristics, physical properties, and heat and oil resistance, but possess limited low-temperature resistance. The newer, improved low-temperature versions exhibit some sacrifice in this balance. The choice of polymer is primarily dependent on the balance of low-temperature/oil-swell resistance required for a given application.

Heat, Fluid, Low-temperature Resistance

The high-temperature service capability of acrylic elastomers is rated at > 70 hr maximum/190-204°C short-term, intermittent; and > 1000 hr maximum/163-177°C long-term, continuous, in dry heat. Short-term exposure above 204°C is also possible. The ultimate mode of heat-ageing failure for all acrylic elastomers is embrittlement.

Acrylic elastomers are highly resistant to petroleum base lubricating oils, transmission fluids and greases, including the sulphur-bearing, extreme-pressure gear lubricants. In addition, they are also quite resistant to the newer, longer-service SF and synthetic ester-type lubricants. The use of butyl acrylate and ethylene/acrylic-based polymers is limited to applications that can tolerate high-oil-swell characteristics. Acrylic elastomers are not recommended for service in aromatic hydrocarbons, e.g., gasoline. Most conventional acrylic polymers are also not suitable for continuous use in hot water or steam, or in water-soluble materials such as methanol or ethylene glycol. However, the ethylene/acrylic type is recommended for service in hot water and in ethylene glycol media.

Current commercial types are supplied in a -14°C to -40°C low-temperature range as characterised by differential thermal analysis, glass-transition temperature (DTA T_g).

Applications

Conventional acrylic elastomers have been successfully utilised in a wide variety of critical automotive seal applications. These include automatic transmission seals, valve-stem seals, crankshaft seals, pinion seals and oil-pan seals. The newer, more versatile types are also gaining rapid acceptance in other mechanical-goods applications such as hose, tubing, electrical-cable jacketing, rolls, and belting.

GENERAL COMPOUNDING

Cure Systems

Because acrylic elastomers have a saturated back-bone, cross-linking is accomplished via incorporation of copolymerised reactive cure sites. The nature of this cure site varies in commercial products, and therefore different cure systems have been developed for specific types. Thus, acrylic elastomers from different suppliers are not generally directly interchangeable in a given recipe. Conventional domestic acrylics respond to soap/amine, activated thiol, soap/sulphur or sulphur donor, lead/thiourea, diamine and trithiocyanuric acid (TCY) cure systems. The ethylene/acrylic type responds to diamine and peroxide cures. Since the majority of acrylic cure systems are baisc in nature, they are retarded by acids and accelerated by bases. Specific cure-system recommendations should be obtained directly from the polymer suppliers.

Despite significant advancements in acrylic-cure technology, all current, state-of-the-art acrylic elastomers require a relatively long cure cycle or must be subsequently post-cured (tempered) in a circulating hot-air environment to realise optimum compression-set resistance.

Reinforcing Agents

Acrylic elastomers do not provide high gum strength when cured. Reinfocing agents are required to develop useful properties. Carbon black reinforcing agents provide the best overall balance of vulcanisate properties.

The use of mineral reinforcing agents is primarily limited to electrical resistant and colour-coded applications. Aluminium silicate or silica types are commonly utilised, either alone or in combination. Amino or vinyl silane coupling agents are also sometimes employed to gain improved vulcanisate properties. Organic colourants are generally recommended since inorganic metallic-oxide colour pigments tend to have an adverse effect on the cure and heat-ageing characteristics of silica-reinforced compounds.

Synthetic graphite is also utilised in conjunction with carbon black and/or mineral reinforcing agents to promote improved surface lubricitycharacteristics in, for example, rotary-shaft-seal applications. Neutral-to-high-pH-alkaline pigments are recommended since acidic types will tend to retard the basic cure mechanism of most acrylic elastomers.

Plasticisers

Plasticisers are used inacrylic-rubber compounds as process aids or to gain improved low-temperature resistance. However, type and amount is limited by their volatility and extraction characteristics, as related to post-cure conditions and service requirements. Low-volatility ester and polyester plasticisers are generally utilised.

Process Aids

Lubricating agents are essential to promote the release characteristics of acrylic compounds. Stearic acid is commonly used, usually in combination with commercial process aids, which provide both external (release) and internal (viscosity-reducing) lubricating qualities. However, it is cautioned that high lubricant levels can interfere with mould knitting and metal-bonding properties.

Antioxidants

Although acrylic elastomers are nighly resistant to oxidation, certain antioxidants can promote marginally improved dry-heat resistance. Low-volatility diphenylamines have been found useful for conventional acrylics, while hindered phenols are suggested for the ethylene/acrylic type. The use of antioxidant is specifically recommended in the ethylene/acrylic gum polymer and for all non-black reinforced compounds.

GENERAL PROCESSING

Mixing

Acrylic compounds can be Banbury- or mill-mixed. However, internal Ban-bury mixing is preferred and generally utilised by the industry. Typical Banbury- and mill-mixing procedures are as shown in Table 6.

A two-pass Banbury-mix procedure is most common, but a one-pass mix is also possible on relatively non-scorchy compounds. An "upside-down" mixing procedure is sometimes desirable for use with highly loaded, dry compounds. Because acrylic elastomers are somewhat thermoplastic in nature and tend to lose shear resistance fairly rapidly on mixing, it is recommended that reinforcing agents be incorporated very early in the mixing cycle to obtain good dispersion. Maximum cooling is also essential, to maintain polymer integrity during the initial phase of mixing.

Extrusion/Calendering

Most acrylic compounds extrude well enough for standard mould-preparation. However, for finish goods, special compounding may be required to obtain satisfactory green strength, size, and finish characteristics. In general, the use of high-structure reinforcing agents along with increased process aid is usually effective. Compound extension through the use of softener is also sometimes necessary. The range of die temperatures is 65-107°C.

Calendering compounds are designed much the same as for finished extrusions. However, additional lubricant may be required to promote good release characteristics. The range of calender-roll temperatures is 27-107°C.

Compound Storage Stability

Typical finished acrylic compounds provide reasonably good shelf-stability characteristics in the range of one week to several weeks when stored under normal room-temperature, dry conditions. Shelf life is primarily dependent on the activity of the cure system employed. Storage under refrigerated (4°C), low-humidity conditions is also an effective means of extending shelf life. In practice, aged compounds are usually mill-freshened prior to subsequent processing.

Table 6 : Banbury vs. mill-mixing

Banbury	Mill
Start: slow speed, full-cooling water	Start: room-temperature rolls, full-cooling water.
Master	
1. Charge polymer	1. Band polymer.
2. Add filler, lubricant, antioxidant.	2. Adjust nip to provide rolling bank.
3. Add process aid, plasticiser.	3. Add lubricant, filler, antioxidant. Open nip as required to retain rolling bank.
4. Bump and sweep.	4. Add process aid.
5. Dump time 3-6. Dump temp 100-105°C. Dip cool.	5. Add process aid. Dip cool (optional)
Finish	
6. Charge 1/2 master, curatives 1/2 master. Dump at 100-121°C Dip cool.	6. Add curatives. Dip cool.

On completion of mixing, the stocks should be given 6 cuts from each side plus 6 refining passes on the mill before stripping.

Vulcanisation

Acrylic elastomers lend themselves to all common cure processes. They are commonly compression-, transfer- and injection-mould, but can be steam-cured as well. Typical cure cycles (in minutes) are as follows -

Compression-mould	3'/190°C to 1'/204°C
Transfer-mould	12'/163°C to 4'/177°C
Injection-mould	3'/90°C to 1'/204°C
Open-steam cure	30-90'/163°C

In addition, acrylic elastomers respond to most continuous vulcanisation (CV) cure techniques. Special compounding may be required for the low viscosity types to gain adequate back pressure in compression moulding operations.

As indicated previously, a post-cure is usually necessary to develop optimum compression-set resistance. Oven post-cure cycles in the range of 4-8 hr/177°C are commonly utilised.

Bonding Characteristics

A variety of commercially available solvent-base, curing-type adhesives have been found to provide excellent bonds of acrylic compounds to metals and other substrates. Bonding is carried out during the vulcanisation process. Recommended substrate preparation and application procedures are provided by the manufacturer.

Solution Characteristics

Certain acrylic elastomers also lend themselves to solvent-solution coatings and adhesive applications. These dissolve readily in common industrial solvents such as methyl ethyl ketone, acetone, ethyl acetate, and toluene. Polymer concentrations in the 30-40% total solids range are possible.

Blends

The blend capability of acrylic elastomers is limited. However, certain conventional types can be utilised to reduce the cost of diamine curable fluorocarbon (FKM) compounds or to improve the heart-resistance of epichlorohydrin (CO/ECO) compounds. In addition, modified low-T_g versions are believed to have potential as high-temperature resistant-impact improvers for poly (vinyl chloride), polycarbonate, and poly (phenylene oxide) plastic materials. Although not reported, the ethylene/acrylic type may also have interesting blend possibilities.

Future Developments

Although significant advances have been made in acrylic-cure technology, continued research is aimed at the development of more highly reactive polymers and/or cure systems to completely eliminate the necessity of post-cure for short-cycle moulded-goods applications.

8

Neoprene (Polychloroprene) and Hypalon Rubber

INTRODUCTION

Neoprene or polychloroprene is a synthetic elastomer available in solid form, as a latex, or as a flexible from. It is vulcanised with metallic oxides rather than with sulphur. With a specific gravity of 1.23, it is resistant to oils, oxygen, ozone, corona discharge and electric current. It is combustible but less so than natural rubber and an isocyante modified form has high flame resistance.

Its chief uses are as follows -

Solid-Mechanical rubber products, lining oil loading hose and reaction equipment; adhesive cement; binder for rocket fuels; coatings for electric wiring, gaskets and seals.

Liquid - Speciality items made by dipping or electrophoresi from the latex.

Foam - Adhesive tape to replace metal fasteners for automotive accessories; seat cushions; carpet backing sealant.

COMMERCIAL NEOPRENE (POLYCHLOROPRENE)

Emulsion polymerisation is used to make a number of variations of the product. Varieties are marketed both as solid polymers and as latices, but not all of them are readily available in all trading areas. The solid types vary over a wide viscosity range. In some instances, either non-staining or staining antioxidants are included at the time of manufacture. The characteristics of the new polymer and the vulcanisation of family are listed in Table 1.

Properties of Neoprene

Most neoprene compositions are made by selecting the base elastomer, adding a variety of ingredients, and then processing and vulcanising. The choice of the ingredients used affects the physical properties of the finished product. Because of the abundance of applicable ingredients, a wide variety of compounds of different compositions and properties are available. The introduction of new synthetic rubbers has vastly increased the number of possible permutations and added to the complexity of designing with an elastomer.

Consider the property called *oil resistance*. When an elastomeric product is exposed to a liquid hydrocarbon, several reactions take place. The most obvious, and readily documented, is a change in dimensions. Less apparent, but frequently of much greater importance than swelling, is a deterioration of the original physical properties. If dimensional stability is functionally necessary, as in O-rings or tubing, swelling would spell failure. In many applications, however, retention of original mechanical characteristics such as high tensile strength, resilience, and abrasion resistance in the swollen state is vital to long service life. For practical purposes, then, oil resistance is the ability of an elastomeric part to retain its utility in spite of contact with oil.

Properly compounded, neoprene resists sun, ozone, and weathering while remaining tough and durable. It is practical in cold environments to -25°C (-13°F) and in heat to 93°C (199°F). Specifically formulated compositions permit service at temperatures as low as -55°C (-67°F). The flame resistance of neoprene products can be enhanced by special compounding.

Table 1 : Family characteristics of the neoprenes

G types	W types	T types
	Raw polymers	
Limited storage stability	Excellent storage stability	Excellent storage stability
Peptisable to varying degrees	Not peptisable	Least nerve
Fast curing but safe processing		Best extrusion calendering performance
No acceleratiors necessary		
	Vulcanisates	
Best tear strength	Best compression-set resistance	Properties similar to W types
Best flex	Best heat-ageing	
Best resilience		

Crystallisation

Crystallinity is an inherent property of all polychloroprene rubbers but some of the neoprenes crystallise more readily and to a greater extent than others. An understanding of this predilection is essential to the understanding of polychloroprene technology.

Neoprene, as well as natural rubber, butyl, and other linear elastomers, becomes highly oriented upon being stretched and shows X-ray diffraction patterns that indicate varying degrees of crystallinity. The crystalline structure of neoprene is indicated by a sharp peak in diffraction intensity at the Bragg angle of 19°30'. As crystallisation develops, a small decrease in volume occurs, and stressed specimens tend to relax and elongate in the direction of the stress. Crystallisation does not take place at high temperatures because these forces (orientation) are overcome by vigorous molecular motion. Crystallisation rate and the incidence of favourable alignment is reduced. Anything that aids mobility of molecules at low temperatures actually encourages crystallisation at those temperatures. Crystallisation is a completely reversible phenomenon. Warming a crystallised specimen to a temperature above that at which the crystallites are formed destroys them, for example, an increasing molecular motion by vibrating or flexing causes decrystallisation. When neoprene is decrystallised, it returns to its original softness and flexibility and recovers from any relaxed condition that may have developed as a result of crystallisation under stress.

Crystallisation, which is time-dependent, should not be confused with thermal stiffening and embrittlement effects, which occur at very low temperatures and are a function of temperature only. Neoprene, as do all elastomers, becomes progressively stiffer as it is cooled. This type of stiffening becomes evident just as soon as thermal equilibrium is established. An unplasticised neoprene compound, for example, will have an ASTM D-749 brittleness temperature of about -40°C for both crystallised and uncrystallised vulcanisates.

The practical aspects of crystallisation are seen in the hardness of the raw polymer in the bag and the "quick grab" and high cohesive strength of a neoprene adhesive. Other evidences are the stiffening of an unvulcanised compound that has been in shelf storage for a week or two and the hardening of a vulcanised part with time at moderately low temperatures.

It would be a good idea to show a comparison of the relative crystallisation rates of the various neoprenes. Dry neoprenes are produced with widely different crystallisation rates so that crystallisation can be avoided if it might be a liability in a product or exploited if it might be an advantage. Uncompounded polymer crystallises faster than its vulcanisate. The relative crystallisation rates of the neoprenes are presented in Table 2. This table is based upon room-temperature observations important to adhesives. It should be noted, however, that maximum crystallisation occurs at -10°C.

Special-purpose Solid Types

The special-purpose types of neoprene — AC, AD, AF, AG, and AB - are designed primarily for a particular application (e.g., adhesives, coatings, sealants). Neoprene AC, AD, and ADG have a high degree of crystallinity, whereas Neoprene AF has a low degree of crystallinity. None contains a staining type of stabiliser.

Table 2 : Room-temperature crystallisation rates (measurements made on freshly-milled polymer)

Rlative time	Neoprene
Hocrs	AD, AC, ADG
Upto 3 days	W, TW
Uuto 7 days	FB. GN, GNA, WX
One or two weeks	AF
More than two weeks	GW, GRT, WRT, WD, AG, WB, WK, TRT

Toluene is a satisfactory solvent for dissolving AC or AD. With AF, some polar sovlent should be used with toluene to increase polymer-solution stability.

Neoprene AC is a sol polymer that crystallises rapidly. The viscosities of AC and its solutions change very little during storage. Low-viscosity grades readily go into solution without milling.

Neoprene AD is a readily crystallising sol polymer with solubility characteristics similar to those of AC. Colour stability and solution stability are superior to those of AC, even when stored in metal containers.

Neoprene AF, which contains small amounts of carboxyl functionality, is essentially a non-crystallising polymer designed for one-part adhesives. Films from AF adhesives rapidly develop high room temperature or elevated bond strengths. Adhesive solutions made with AF are resistant to phasing.

Neoprene AG, a chloroprene polymer of high gel content, exhibits thixotoropy when dissolved or dispersed insolvents. It is very suited for high solids and high-viscosity mastics, which require easy extrudability and resistance to slump. Low-viscosity adhesives prepared from AG not only spray more easily than those based on other neoprene polymers but offer the performance properties required for many contact adhesive applications. Generally speaking, AG can be formulated in the same fashion as AC and AD.

Neoprene FB is a soft, partly crystalline solid at room temperature, but its viscosity drops rapidly as temperature is increased and it becomes fluid at 50°C. It is used in adhesives and caulks and as a non-volatile, vulcanisable plasticiser for other neoprenes. It dissolves readily in aromatic hydrocarbons, chlorinated hydrocarbons, or low-moleculer-weight ketones and esters.

COMPOUNDING DRY NEOPRENES

As indicated earlier the key to the all-around performance of neoprene products in a variety of services lies in the words "properly compounded". Once the service requirements have been documented, the compounder is free to take over, but with his freedom of choice subject to the limitations of process requirements and economics, of course.

Compound development logically begins with the selection of the type of neoprene that best provides the required physical properties within the applicable cost and processing limits. The response of all general-purpose types to compounding ingredients is similar. Compounding of the G types, however, differs from that of the W and T types in three ways.

i. They can be softened by the addition of chemical peptisers.
ii. They soften under mechanical shear and may, therefore, need less plasticiser to prepare compounds in a workable viscosity range.
iii. They can be used with metal oxides alone; organic accelerators are not required.

By peptising, the compounder can achieve workable compound viscosity at high filler loading without the reduction in vulcanisate hardness and strength that usually occurs when additional plasticisers are used to lower compound viscosity.

Minimum requirements for a practical compound include antioxidant, metallic oxide, filler or reinforcing agent, processing aid, and vulcanising system. Optional ingredients may include antiozonants, retarders, extenders, plastics or resins, other elastomers, and blowing agents.

Curing Systems

Curatives for neoprene are limited by the ingenuity of the compounders, the processing and end user requirements, and economics.

Metal oxides are an essential part of the curing system. They regulate scorch, cure rate, and cure state; in addition, they serve as acid acceptors for trace amounts of hydrogen chloride that are released from the polymer during processing, curing, and vulcanisate ageing. Combinations of magnesiu oxide and zinc oxide produce the best balance of processability, cure rate, and vulcanisate performance. With the G types, the relationship between these properties is markedly affected by the amounts of MgO and ZnO used. Similar effects are noted in the W and T types, but to a much lesser degree because of the pronounced influence of the accelerator.

For improved resistance to swell and deterioration by water, an oxide of lead may be used in place of the magnesia/zinc oxide combination. Red led

(Pb_3O_4) is the preferred oxide. Using lead oxide results in a sacrifice in colourability, tensile strength, compression set resistance, and heat resistance compared to the strength, compression set resistance, and heat resistance compared to the characteristics offered by MgO/ZnO combination. It is more expensive usually.

The oxides of other metals are either impractical to use or exert no appreciable influence on the curing characteristics. Calcium oxide is sometimes used as a desiccant to facilitate vacuum-extrusion and, with Permalux accelaration, to control scorch. Iron oxide (Fe_2O_3) and titanium dioxide (TiO_2) are often used for their tinctorial properties in coloured stocks.

The grade of magnesia used in neoprene compounds is important to the processing and properties of the finished product. The grade of magnesia used has two characteristics.

i. It is precipitated (not ground) and calcined after precipitation.

ii. It is very active, having a high ratio of surface to volume.

Types of zinc oxide that have fine particle size and high surface area are preferred. This ingredient should be added late in the mix cycle to avoid scorch, with appropriate care exercised to insure good dispersion. Incomplete dispersion results in localised overcure and inferior physical properties. Because of the importance of good dispersion, of the protection of magnesia from the effect of moisture contamination, and of the economics of reduced mixing cycles, predispersed forms of the various metallic oxides are available from many suppliers.

For practical cure rate and vulcanisate properties, an organic accelerator is required in addition to metal oxides for the W and T types of neoprene. Amines, phenols, sulphenamides, thiazoles, thiurams, thioureas, guanidines, and sulphur are the common accelerators and/or curing agents. The curing mechanism for organic curing agents other than thioureas has been reviewed. Sulphur vulcanisation is probably similar to that of natural rubber or of copolymers containing butadiene. Thiourea accelerators, particularly ethylene thiourea, have for many years been the accelerators of choice for a broad range of applications. Characteristics of thiourea acceleration, information on the potential toxicity of ethylene thiourea, and suggested handling precautions for it, as well as alternatives to ETU, are covered in detail in the literature elsewhere. Today, ETU is the single most popular accelerator.

Antioxidants

Antioxidants are essential in all neoprene compounds for good ageing vulcanisates. Those commonly used in other elastomers usually behave similarly in neoprene.

Processing Aids

Processing aids include lubricants, tackifers, and agents for controlling viscosity and nerve. Stearic acid, microcrystalline waxes, and low-molecular-weight polyethylenes make good lubricants. Hydrogenated rosin esters and coumarone-indene resins are preferred as tackifiers. Viscosity modification may be achieved in either direction. Dithiocarbamates and guanidines peptise (soften) the G types. Increased viscosity is best obtained by blending the neoprene with a high-molecular-weight neoprene WHV. Decreased viscosity is achieved by using plasticisers or blending with the low-molecular-weight neoprene FB. Nerve may be reduced for smooth extrusion and calendering by blending with neoprene WB, employing high structure carbon black or hard clay as fillers.

Fillers

The effects of carbon blacks and mineral fillers on the processing and vulcanisate properties of neoprene are generally similar to their effects on other elastomers, with the possible exception that reinforcing fillers are of less importance. Like natural rubber and other polymers with pronounced crystallisation tendencies, neoprene gum vulcanisates have high tensile strength. The need for reinforcement, therefore, is less for such elastomers as SBR, butyl rubber, and nitrile rubber. Practical vulcanisates are obtained for the majority of uses by filling ("loading") with the soft, relatively non-reinforcing thermal type of carbon blacks (MT and FT) or with clays and fine-particle calcium carbonate. These fillers are not only relatively inexpensive but afford extra economy because they may be added in greater amounts than more reinforcing fillers for a given hardness. If the superior physical properties ordinarily associated with higher tensile strength are required, SRF blacks are usually used. Carbon blacks of finer particle size - either furnace or channel black - are used as a rule only when the ultimte in certain properties such as abrasion and tear resistance is required.

Of the fillers other than carbon black, clays are usually preferred for good processing and overall vulcanisate quality. Whitings, especially coarse ones, provide poor vulcanisates that weather badly. Whitings of finer particle size, however, are used to provide vulcanisates with superior resistance to heat ageing. Hydrated calcium silicate and precipitated silicon-dioxide fillers of fine particle size give neoprene vulcanisates remarkably high tensile strength, hot tear resistance, and abrasion resistance, but impaired dynamic properties.

Plasticisers

The plasticisers and softeners most often used in neoprene are low-cost petroleum derivatives. Amount ranging from 10 to 20% by weight of the filler loading are usually required for processing reasons alone. The W types require more than the G types. When the total amount of petroleum plasticiser fails to exceed 20-25 parts per 100 of neoprene, naphthenic oils may be used. These have the advantage over aromatic oils of not darkening light-coloured vulcanisates of staining contacting surfaces. When platicising oils are used in greater amounts in order to produce very soft vulcanisates or to accommodate the high amounts of filler used in low-cost compounds, aromatic oils are recommended to insure compatibility.

Petroleum plasticisers seldom improve the flexibility of a vulcanisate at low temperature. Dioctyl sebacate is excellent for this purpose, although many other organic chemicals, mostly high-molecular-weight esters, are widely used.

PROCESSING DRY NEOPERENES

The methods for processing neoprene reflect the principles common to the processing of most elastomers, but some peculiarities bear mention.

Mixing

With few exceptions, neoprene compounds should be mixed at as low a temperature and with as short a cycle as possible. This handling minimises the danger of scorch and is especially important with the G types, which are likely to give soft and sticky stocks on over-mastication. Omission of both zinc oxide and accelerators until late in the mixing cycle is also necessary to avoid scorching. Magnesia should be added early, if possible, with the neoprene.

Calendering and Extrusion

Calendering of neoprene stocks demands more critical control than other processing operations, particularly of the G types, which are very temperature sensitive and perform best below 70°C. The W types are usually calendered with slightly hotter rolls because they release more easily and require a higher temperature to avoid shrinkage. The three states of neoprene (elastic, granular, and plastic) are most apparent in calendering, especially with stocks of low loading. In the elastic phase, the sheet will shrink and become rough on release but may be fairly smooth on the roll. The granular phase is self-descriptive, and the sheet is relatively free from nerve. In the plastic phase, it is glossy smooth, weak, and nerve-free. The temperature at which phase changes occur varies with the type of neoprene, the phase change from elastic to granular ranging from 60°C in the case of type WRT to 70°C for type GN. The plastic phase exists at about 93°C for all neoprenes.

For frictioning, the plasticisable, crystallisation-resistant neoprene GRT is recommended. Best results are obtained using prewarmed fabric, a top roll temperature of 93°C or above, a centre roll at 65°C-82°C, and a bottom roll at room temperature to 65°C, depending on the weave.

Most neoprene compounds extrude best with a cool barrel and screw, a warm head, and a hot die.

These are the major variations in the processing of neoprene that differ from the normal routines followed with other elastomers.

APPLICATIONS OF NEOPRENE

Some of the most important uses are in adhesives, the transportation industry, the energy industry, the construction industry, wire and cable, hose, belting, and consumer products.

Adhesives

Neoprene-based adhesives are available both in fluid and dry-film form. The fluid types are classed as -

i. Solvent

ii. Latex

iii. 100%-solids compositions.

Solvent adhesives consist of the neoprene polymer and suitable compounding ingredients dissolved in an organic solvent or combination of solvents (toluene, ethyl acetate, naphtha, methyl ethyl ketone). Latex adhesives are composed of particles of neoprene and compounding ingredients dispersed in water. Both solvent and latex types are normally supplied in ready-to-use "one-part" adhesive systems. When specified, "two-parts" adhesive systems can also be produced to meet specific end-use requirements. Solvent and latex neoprene adhesives achieve their bonds through evaporation of the fluid and subsequent *crystallisation and curing* of the elastomeric residue.

Solid adhesives, on the other hand, are based on fluid neoprene polymers and contain neither solvent nor water. Adhesives of this type are normally the choice in speciality applications where fluidity is required, yet where volatile loss or shrinkage cannot be tolerated. They possess little "green" strength and usually require application of either heat or catalytic agent to develop an adhesive bond.

Dry-film adhesives based on neoprene are 100%-solids materials normally supplied in the form of a tape or sheeting. This type of adhesive is compounded so that it softens when heated. Cooling then resolidifies the material and forms the adhesive bond.

Neoprene adhesives are made in a range of consistencies, i.e., from very thin liquids through heavy-bodied "putties" to dry films. These adhesives can be controlled to offer a wide range of properties, for example, tack, "open tack time", storage stability, bond-development, flexibility and strength, heat and cold resistance, and all of the basic characteristics of polychloroprene polymers. The most significant ingredient in a neoprene adhesive, apart from the polymer, is the resin. Various types of resin are used in order to enhance specific adhesion, improve cohesive strength and hot bond strength, or to impart better tack retention. Resins are usually compounded at a level of 25-60 phr and are rarely added above 100 phr. The most commonly used resin types are alkyl phenolic resins, terpene phenolic resins, hydrogenated resin and rosin esters, coumaroneindene resins, and hydrocarbon resins such as poly (x-methyl styrene).

Trasportation

In the automotive field, neoprene is the base elastomer for a variety of components such as V-belts; timing belts; blown sponge gaskets for door, deck, and trunk; spark plug boots; power brake bellows; radiator hoses; steering and suspension joint seals; type sidewalls; ignition wire jackets; and many other items. In aviation, neoprene is used in mountings, wire and cable jackets, gaskets, seals, deicers, etc. In railroading, it is used in track mountings, car body mountings, air brake hoses, flexible car connectors, freight-car interior linings, journal box lubricators, and so forth. All of these uses require physical strength, compression set, resilience, fluid, weather, and temperature degradation resistance.

Energy Industry

A durble oil-resistant neoprene rubber has a multitude of uses in the exploration, production, and distribution of petroleum, such as packers, pipeline "pigs", seals, gaskets, hose, coated fabrics, wire and cable, and so forth.

Construction Industry

This application arena, while not new, is now gaining in popularity. Outstanding items are extruded window-wall sealing gaskets, calendered sheeting for membrane waterproofing, flashing and roof covering, highway joint seals, bridge mounting pads, soil pipe gaskets, sound and vibration isolation pads, etc. Neoprene-modified asphalt is gaining acceptance in roads, parking lots, and airport runways. Proven serviceability and economic acceptability account for this growth.

Wire and Cable

Practically the oldest use of neoprene is as a jacket for electrical conductors (low and high voltages). Its superior resistance to abrasion, oil, flame, weather, and ageing over natural rubber accounts for its broad acceptance.

Hose

Neoprene hose has been made almost continuously for a long time and is used in the cover, cushion, and tube compounds. All types of hose are involved.

Belts

Maximum durability in service climates requiring a range of temperature and flex resistance makes neoprene the polymer of choice for belting. Applications include V-belts, power-transmission belts, conveyor belts, and escalator hand rails.

Consumer Products

Sponge shoe soles made of closed-cell neoprene combine cushioned comfort with long wear. Neoprene latex foam has played a critical role in matterss and cushioning fire safety, offering an added margin of improved flame-protection and low smoke institutional furnishings.

NEOPRENE LATEX

Neoprene latices are aqueous, colloidal dispersions of polychloroprene or of copolymers of chloroprene and other monomers such as methacrylic acid or 2,3 dichloro-1, 3-butadiene. They are available in both anionic and non-ionic surfactant systems.

A variety of articles, particularly those that are relatively thin or of complicated shape, are more easily made from latex than from dry neoprene. An example would be neoprene household and industrial gloves, which are readily made from latex. Also, the production of neoprene balloons from dry neoprene would be difficult. Other major applications include latex-based adhesives, protective coatings, binder for cellulose and other fibres, and elasticising additive for concrete, mortar, and asphalt.

As with dry neoprene, the neoprene latex must be compounded with other materials to be converted into useful products. Some of these materials are mandatory for optimum performance, whereas others are optional. In some cases, a more expensive type of neoprene latex may actually provide greater value-in-use to the user because it can accommodate more additives or because its inherent strength eliminates the need for curing. The characteristics of many neoprene latices are given in Table 3.

End-use performance, processing, and economics usually dictate the choice of neoprene latex type. Included in processing are the cost of storage and handling, coagulation and drying rates, curing time, and production yield. Usually cost can be minimised by maintaining low compound viscosity at the highest practical solids content.

COMPOUNDING NEOPRENE LATICES

All neoprene latex compounds must contain a metal oxide and an effective antioxidant. Metal oxides function in several ways. They serve to vulcanise the polymer; they make it more resistant to ageing, heat, and weathering; and they act as acid acceptors. Zinc oxide has proven to be the

Table 3 : Comparison chart for the neoprene latices

Neoprene latex type	Co-monomer	Emulsifier	Emulsifier class	Chlorine content %	pH at 25°C [77°F] (Typical values)	Standard solids (%)	Distinguishing features	Major applications
1	2	3	4	5	6	7	8	9
60	Sulphur	Sodium salts of disproportionated rosin acids	Anionic	37.5	11.0	59	Develops high wet gel strength	Foam
115	Methacrylic acid	Poly (vinyl alcohol)	Non-ionic	36.0	7.0	47	Carboxylated polymer with outstanding mechanical and chemical stability	Adhesives
400	2,3-dichloro-1,3 butadiene	Potassium salts of disproportionated rosin acids	Anionic	48.0	12.5	50	Maximum chlorine content; rapid crystallising; outstanding ozone and weather resistance	Coatings
571	Sulphur	Principally sodium salts of rosin acids	Anionic	37.5	12.0	50	High-strength cured films combined with low permanent set	Adhesives, Coatings, Dipped goods
622	-	Potassium salts of disproportionated rosin acids	Anionic	38.0	12.5	61	High solids, low viscosity, high gel polymer	Foam
654	-	Potassium salts of proportionated rosin acids.	Anionic	38.0	12.0	59	High solids, low viscosity, low gel polymer	Adhesives Binders, Coatings
671A	-	Potassium salts of disporoportionated acids	Anionic	38.0	12.5	59	High solids, low viscosity, medium-high gel polymer	Adhesives Binders Coatings

1	2	3	4	5	6	7	8	9
								Dipped goods Elasticised asphalt Elasticised concrete Foam
735 A	-	Sodium salts of disproportionated rosin acids	Anionic	38.5	12.0	45	Designed for wet-end addition to fibrous slurries	Binders Elasticised asphlt
750	2,3-dichloro-1,3 butadiene	Potassium salts of disproportionated rosin acids	Anionic	40.0	12.5	50	High wet gel strength; low-modulus films having a very slow crystallisation rate.	Adhesives Dipped goods
842 A	-	Principally sodium salts of rosin acids	Anionic	37.5	12.0	50	Medium-strength cured films having a slow crystallisation rate	Adhesives Binders Coatings Dipped goods

most desirable of these oxides from both processing and film-property standpoints. The presence of a good antioxidant in neoprene is as important as a metal oxide. Both are necessary to bring out the inherently good ageing properties of the neoprene and, as a general rule, it is recommended that neoprene latex compounds contain at least 5 phr of zinc oxide and 2 phr of an antioxidant.

Accelerators are used to increase the rate of cure and to enhance the physical properties of neoprene. The addition of thiocarbanilide to neoprene latex produces polymers with high modulus. Where tensile strength is of primary importance, the use of both tetraethylthiuram disulphide and a water solution of sodium dibutyldithiocarbamate is recommended. This combination imparts outstndingly high tensile strength with little increase in modulus. Other accelerators commonly used in neoprene latices are zinc dibutyldithiocarbamate and di-o-tolyguanidine.

Mineral oils and light process oils are used as plasticisers and to improve the "hand" in neoprene latex. Petroleum-based plasticisers have been found most effective as crystallisation inhibitors, and ester-type plasticisers are employed to improve the low-temperature serviceability of the product. Three to ten phr are usually used.

Fillers such as clay, whiting, titanium dioxide, carbon black, hydrated alumina, and fine silicas can be used to impart specific properties to the neoprene or to act as low-cost diluents. Loadings vary from as little as 10 phr in dipped goods to several hundred parts in adhesives and coatings.

Anionic, non-ionic, and amphoteric surfactants are used as both shear and chemical stabilisers in the preparation of neoprene latex compounds. Usually 0.1-1 phr is sufficient in most applications to produce the necessary processing stability.

Thickeners are more often needed with neoprene latex compounds than with natural-rubber latex because the viscosity of neoprene latex at a given solids content is less than that of natural rubber latex. Both natural and synthetic gums are excellent thickeners for neoprene latex. If it is necessary to decrease the viscosity of neoprene latex compositions, they can be diluted with de-ionised or distilled water.

Processing Neoprene Latices

The manufacture of articles from both neoprene and natural rubber latex is similar, and the processes used with natural rubber are adaptable in most instances for use with neoprene. Exceptions exist, however, the most important being that of cure. Neoprene has the advantage of not procuring or aftercuring, but in order to obtain the optimum physical properties, neoprene films must be cured at temperatures above 100°C and preferably in the range of 120-140°C.

The general techniques suggested for good rubber latex compounding procedures also hold for neoprene latex. Fine-particle-size dispersions and emulsions, compounding pH above 10.5, and the use of de-ionised or distilled water in preparing all ingredients are all recommended for processing uniformity.

Product Safety

For all the solid polymers, however, routine industrial hygiene practices are recommended during handling and processing to avoid such conditions as dust build-up or static charges.

Neoprene latices similarly have a very low order of oral toxicity. Since most are strongly alkaline, however, they may cause burns if they come in contact with eyes or skin. Volatile organic materials in neoprene latices include chloroprene monomers, toluene and butadiene.

Compounding ingredients used with neoprene to prepare finished products may present hazards in handling and use. Before proceeding with any compounding work, consult and follow label directions and handling precautions from suppliers of all ingredients.

HYPALON (CHLOROSULPHONATED POLYETHYLENE)

These are olefin based rubbers in the form of white chips, having specific gravity 1.10-1.28. These are resistant to ozone, as well as the weather, being better than neoprene and butyl rubber in this respect. These are also resistant to oil, solvents, chemicals and abrasion.

When polyethylene is treated with a mixture of chlorine and sulphur dioxide, some chlorine atoms are substituted on the chains and some sulphonyl chloride group (—SO_2Cl) are formed. A typical polymer contains 25-30% chlorine (one chlorine for every seven carbon atoms) and about 1.5% sulphur (one—SO_2Cl for every 90 carbon atoms). This elastomer can be cross-linked by a large variety of compounds including many rubber accelerators.

The material is poor in snap and rebound and has low elongation and some permanent set. Its abrasion resistance, flex life, low temperature brittleness, and resistance to crack growth are good.

This elastomer is widely used in insulation for wire and cables, shoe soles and neels, automotive components, building products, coatings, flexible tubes, and hose seals, gaskets, diaphragms. 'Hypalon' 45 can accept large amount of fillers and is used as a binder for powdered metal to produce magnetic gaskets for doors, and sheet goods for X-ray burners.

PROCESS OF MANUFACTURE

The process for its manufacture involves the simultaneous chlorination and chlorosulphonation of polyethylene in solution. HYPALON, as a chlorosulphonated polyethylene, is described as a CSM rubber, according to ASTM D1418. A simplified form of its chemical structure is shown below -

$$\text{—CH}_2\text{—CH—CH}_2\text{—CH}_2\text{—CH}_2\text{—CH—}$$

½ ½

Cl SO_2Cl

The rubberiness of HYPALON is derived from the natural flexibility of the polyethylene chain in the absence of crystallinity; the introduction of the chlorine atoms along the polyethylene chains provides sufficient molecular irregularity to prevent crystallisation in the relaxed state.

The crystallinity of the polyethylene chain can also be eliminated by an alternative method of introducing molecular irregularity - by copolymerising the ethylene with propylene. The process is used in the manufacture of EPDM polyolefin elastomers.

Gum vulcanisates of non-crystalline grades of EPDM and CSM are compared in Table 4 CMS vulcanisates are seen to have better oil and flame resistance; and, as indicated by the substantial difference in their tensile strengths, better all around mechanical toughness. The chlorine atoms on the polyethylene back-bone not only provide elastomeric properties, but also give useful improvement in oil resistance and flame resistance. The sulphonyl chloride groups provide crosslinking sites for the non-peroxide curing processes.

Table 4 : S-cured elastomers with a saturated hydrocarbon backbone

	EPDM	CSM
O_2, O_3 resistance	Excellent	Excellent
colour stability	Excellent	Excellent
Gum strength, psi	500	5000
oil resistance	Poor	Fair-good
Heat resistance	Very good	Very good
Flame resistance	Poor	Good
Low-temperature properties	Excellent	Fair-excellent

The sulphur content of most grades of HYPALON is maintained at 1% by weight on the polymer. The chlorine content varies between the different grades and has a significant effect on the oil resistance of the polymer.

Many other properties of compounds and vulcanisates of HYPALON are affected by chlorine content, besides oil resistance. At low-chlorine levels, the polymers retain some polyethylene-link characteristics - they are harder and stiffer because they are partially crystalline; they also show good electrical properties, good heat resistance, and good low-temperature flexibility. With increasing chlorine, the compounds and vulcanisates get increasingly rubbery but then at higher chlorine levels again become stiffer, because of increasing glass transition temperature. The high-chlorine grades are characterised by their excellent oil resistance and good flame resistance.

Grades of Hypalon

All grades are produced in the form of irregular creamy-white chips with excellent storage stability and no odour. All grades show certain properties that are characteristic of CSM elastomers in general. Their vulcanisates are tough, colourable, weather-resistant, and show excellent resistance to attack by oxygen and ozone.

HYPALON 20, formerly used for the manufacture of moulded and extruded goods, is now used mainly in coatings applications to give curable rubbery films with good low-temperature flexibility. Its principal coatings applications are for roof coatings and the manufacture of tarpaulins, but it is also used in caulks and adhesives.

HYPALON 30 is also used mostly for coatings. It gives solutions of much lower viscosity than HYPALON 20. Its higher chlorine content gives its coatings a dryer, slicker feel than ones from HYPALON 20, and a better oil and flame resistance. Low-temperature properties are not as good as those for HYPALON 20, however.

LD-999 can be considered a low-viscosity analogue of HYPALON 40 and is used mostly in the extrusion of wire and cable jackets. It is also used as blending elastomer to reduce the viscosity of hose compounds from HYPALON 48 and 48S.

HAPALON 40 AND 40S are 35% chlorine, medium-viscosity elastomers having good heat and oil resistance. Compounds from these grades have good extrusion characteristics. Major applications are in hose construction, wire and cable coverings, industrial rolls, and automotive spark-plug boots.

HAPALON 4085 is similar to HYPALON 40, but is useful where higher green strength or better vulcanisate properties are required.

HYPALON 45 and its low-viscosity analogue HYPALON 623 are semicrystalline polymers that have useful physical properties in the uncured state. Their main uses are in pond liners and in roofing membranes. A smaller but growing application is in vulcanised wire covering with very good electrical properties, excellent heat-ageing resistance, and good low-temperature flexibility.

HYPALON 48 and its lower-viscosity analogue HYPALON 48S have a high-chlorine content and show excellent oil resistance, including a very low permeability to refrigerants. Their principal use is in the manufacture of automotive air-conditioner hose. HYPALON 48S is also used as a coatings polymer. It gives a higher viscosity solution than HYPALON 30, but it has better resistance to low-temperature brittleness while providing the same low-friction property to the dry film.

Compounding Ingredients

A typical vulcanisable compound is made up of the components listed in Table 5. Components of the curing systems are considered to be both the acid acceptor and is activator as well as the vulcanising agent and its accelerator. These will be described first because the curing of HYPALON involves substantially different chemistry from other elastomers.

Table 5 : A typical CSM compound

	Ingredient	Function	phr
1.	HYPALON 40 (35% Cl)	Polymer	100
2.	Magnesia	Acid acceptor	4
3.	Pentaerythritol	Activator for 2	3
4.	Hard clay	Filler	80
5.	Aromatic oil	Plasticiser	25
6.	Paraffin wax	Process aid	3
7.	Sulphur	Vulcanising agent	1
8.	Tetramethylthiuram disulphide	Accelerator for 7	2

Acid Acceptor/Activator

The choice of acid acceptor will depend on the vulcanising agent used and the functional requirements of the vulcanisate. The main functions of an acid acceptor are to act as a heat stabiliser, to absorb acid by-products of the curing reaction, and to maintain sufficient alkalinity to allow effective curing reactions to proceed.

Note that zinc oxide is excluded from this list because its reaction product, zinc chloride, causes polymer degradation on heat-ageing or natural weathering. For the same reason, other zinc-containing additives should also be excluded.

The activator increases the effectiveness of the acid acceptor apparently by solubilising it in the polymer. Adding an activator allows a substantial reduction in the amount of acid acceptor needed and this, in addition to a cost saving leads to lower-viscosity, safer processing stocks.

Fillers

Carbon black is the preferred filler for CSM vulcanisates because it gives best reinforcement of physical properties and best resistance to chemical degradation, to compression set, and to water absorption. SRF carbon black gives a good balance of properties and is widely used as a general-purpose filler. Weathering of CSM with as little as three parts of carbon black as a protective pigments is outstanding.

Mineral fillers are often used to take advantage of CSM's non-discolouring characteristics. Best heat resistance is obtained with whiting or black fixe; best electrical properties and very good water resistance are obtained with calcined clay; and hydrated silicas and alumina are preferred for improved flammability performance. When compounded with suitable protective pigments, non-black CSM compositions show excellent long-term weathering performance.

Plasticisers

Aromatic petroleum oils are widely used as plasticisers primarlily because of their low cost. Ester plasticisers give compounds that are light in colour, with good low-temperature properties, while liquid chlorinated paraffins give vulcanisates with good flammability performance and weatherability. Polymeric plasticisers are less volatile than the other types and are preferred for heat-resistant compounds.

Processing Aids

Stearic acid and stearates are effective release agents but should not be used in litharge-containing compound in which they reduce scorch safety. Zinc stearate should be avoided in compounds designed for heat resistance or weatherability. Stearic acid should also be avoided in maleimide cure because of cure retardation.

Paraffin wax, poly (ethylene glycol) and low-molecular-weight polyethylene, separately or in combination, are all effective process aids for CSM that do not affect scorch safety in litharge-containing compounds, or the effectiveness of maleimide cures.

Curatives

Many types of curing processes are available with CSM elastomers and some are effective regardless of the level of chlorine in the elastomer and are discussed hereunder.

Ionic Cures

Ionic cures of CSM are possible when the acid acceptor is a divalent metal oxide. Ionic cures are characterised by their ability to proceed at low temperatures, by the fact that they are accelerated by moisture, and by the development of a high modulus. Ionic cross-linking is responsible for the limited bin stability of CSM compounds when they contain divalent metal oxide acid acceptors and are stored under humid conditions.

The ability of HYPALON to cure under mild ambient conditions is useful for both pond liners and roofing membranes. It allows a sheeting that is readily bondable to itself, by means of solvent – or heat-welding, to be put in place and then to slowly cure as a result of exposure to ambient conditions.

Covalent Cures

CSM is also capable of undergoing covalent cross-linking, and most applications for CSM make use of this type of curing. Three different systems are commonly used – sulphur cures, which give the widest choice of compounding ingredients; peroxide cures, which are non-discolouring and give good heat and compression-set resistance; and maleimide cures, which also give good heat and compression-set resistance, but which are less sensitive to the type of compounding ingredient. Covalent curing systems rely on a cross-linking agent and one or more accelerators for their curing action.

Sulphur Cures

A recipe for a typical sulphur cure is shown in Table 5. Sulphur-based cures are very versatile and are practical for all types of moulding and extrusion processes. They allow high states of cure to be achieved even in low-cost, highly extended compounds.

Vulcanisates with properties of both covalent and ionic cross-linking result from the low-temperature moisture curing of a compound such as shown in Table 6. Practical cures can also be achieved in hot water. Although the cure rate is slow, it is very convenient since it allows wire insulation to cure while the wire is on the reel. Typically, insulation is cured in this way by standing the reels in a steam room or immersing them in a tank of hot water. For a comparison, it would take about 20 hours in a press at 100°C to achieve the state of cure obtained with 2 hours in steam at 100°C.

Peroxide Cures

CSM is readily cured with a peroxide. Frequently, a cure promotor such as triallyl cyanurate is added to improve the effectiveness of the peroxide. An acid acceptor must also be added. Compounds to be cured with peroxides can contain low levels (e.g., upto 40 phr) of fully-staturated plasticisers; higher levels will cause progressive cure retardation. Chlorinated paraffins are best and ester plasticisers are less satisfactory, but adequate. Aromatic process oils will drastically retard the cure.

Maleimide Cures

(N, N'-*m*-phenylenedimaleimide) is a primary curing agent for HYPALON, Maleimide cures also require the presence of calcium hydroxide as an acid acceptor and the antioxidant VANOX AT (a butyraldehyde-amine condensation product) as an accelerator. Maleimide cures are very safe and characteristically produce good water resistance and excellent resistance to compression set and to heat ageing. Unlike peroxide cures, maleimide cures are relatively insensitive to type and proportion of plasticiser. Although the maleimide cure system is deactivated by moisture, it is effective in high-pressure steam; some cure retardation may be seen in low-pressure steam cures, however.

Table 6 : Low-temperature moisture cure of CSM

HYPALON 40		100
Magnesia		10
Pentaerythritol		3
Mineral fillers		100
Plasticisers		35
TETRONE A		2
Stress/strain properties[a] of 0.64 mm (.025 in) slabs		
	Cured in steam, 2 hrs/100°C (212°F)	
100% modulus	MPa (psi)	8.2 (1190)
Tensile strength	MPa (psi)	16.7 (2420)
Elongation at break	%	400

[a]Samples tested after drying in a desiccator.

Special Additives

Nickel dibutyl dithiocarbamate (NBC), a drak-green powder, is widely used with CSM to improve the heat resistance of black or dark-coloured compounds. Upto 3 parts of NBC are added in sulphur-cured compounds based on mixed metal oxides. The addition of NBC reduces scorch safety. Also, NBC is not effective in peroxide cures.

Other additives include low-melting thermoplastic polymers such as PVC copolymers and high styrene resins, which may be added to CSM to prevent contact-sticking and distortion of wire covering while it is being cured on the reel in steam or hot water.

Mixing

All elastomers will soften as their temperature rises while being worked on processing equipment. This softening effect is somewhat greater for CSM than for most other elastomers. However, it is entirely thermal and reversible so that a CSM stock that is warmed up on a mill and then allowed to cool back to room temperature will regain its former stiffnerss. This means that CSM compounds can be reworked without significant change in processing behaviour, as long as scorch is not a factor.

Mill-Mixing

CSM compounds are easily mixed on conventional mills. Because of longer heat exposure, mill-mixed compounds are likely to be scorchier than those mixed in internal mixers. Cold water should be used on the mill except when processing the more thermoplastic grades, such as HYPALON 45 and 623, which require a mill temperature of around 70°C. A typical mill-mixing time for a normal CSM batch would be about 25 minutes, depending on the type and amount of fillers and plasticisers used.

Internal Mixing

Internal mixing is the most cost-efficient volume system for producing well mixed CSM compounds. Short mix cycles are preferable due to the need to minimise the heat history of the batch.

The preferred mix procedures generally use upside-down mixing without premastication of the polymer, and as high a ram pressure as practical. Load factors varying from 0.55-0.80 are normal, with the higher load factor being used for the lower-viscosity stocks. Typical ram-down times will be 1-1/2 to 3-1/2 minutes.

Production compounds can generally be made on a single-pass mix cycle, but if processing safety is marginal, a tow-pass mix procedure may be needed. Dump temperature should be around 121°C (250°F) if no sulphur curatives are included, and around 107°C (225°F) when sulphur curatives are added.

PROCESSING

Moulding

CSM compounds are successfully processed by compression, transfer, or injection moulding. In these processes, where reproducibility of flow of the compound is important, steps should be taken to compound for good bin stability, to mix so as to minimise scorch, to store the mixed compound under cool, dry conditions, and to rotate the inventory so that compounds to be moulded have a similar storage history.

Due to the marked thermoplasticity of CSM compounds, multicavity transfer and injection moulds require carefully balanced runner systems and similar flow restrictions for the gates, so that uniform filing of all cavities is achieved.

Extrusion

CSM compounds can be processed in standard hot- or cold-feed rubber extruders. The compounds are normally fed in strip form. In general, CSM compounds require little work to attain physical uniformity and very-low-compression-ratio screws are usually adequate. Die L/D ratios of 1/1 are common, with stock temperatures of around 120°C at the die.

Exruded parts can be cured in zero-pressure steam, hot-air ovens, LCM, fluidised bed, CV, and by microwave. Curing with ionising radiation is also effective for CSM.

Calendering

Substantial amounts of CSM are used in calendering operations. Compounds from the intermediate chlorine grades, for example, HYPALON 40, are calendered at 60-100°C (140-212°F) onto a fabric with, normally, uneven roll speeds on the calender and usually with the top roll slightly hotter than the middle roll. The maximum practical gauge for these sheets is about 40 mills (1.02 mm) for a single pass. The calendered sheets are normally cured in an autoclave while wrapped on a drum with a curing liner. Adhesion between the plies is usually excellent.

Compounds from the low-chlorine CSM grades, as represented by HYPALON and the lower-viscosity HYPALON, are calendered without curatives for use in pond liners and roofing membranes. Because of their crystallinity and scorch safety, these compounds are calendered at higher temperatures, 100-150°C (212-302°F), with the easier-processing compounds from HYPALON 623 being calendered at the lower end of this temperature range.

PROPERTIES AND PERFORMANCE

CSM is classified as a specialty synthetic rubber, with a "DE" rating in the "heat-resistance/oil-resistance" classification of ASTM D2000 and SAE J200. The applications for CSM depend only in part on its combination of oil and heat resistance. CSM is much more resistant to corrosive or oxidising chemicals including ozone, than are neoprene and nitrile rubbers; it is tougher than silicones and EPDM rubbers; and it has electrical properties that are not as good as EDPM's but exceed those of many other elastomers. CSM has excellent radiation resistance, making it well-suited for wire and cable coverings in nuclear applications. Further, it is colour-stable and highly weather-resistant.

Oil-resistance and Low-temperature Properties

The oil-resistance and low-temperature properties of CSM vulcanisates depend mainly on the chlorine content of the CSM used. Low-temperature properties can additionally be controlled by the choice of plasticiser in the compound.

Heat Resistance

CSM elastomers, as a class, have good-to-excellent heat resistance, depending mainly on the choice of compounding ingredients, although within this class of elastomer the low-chlorine grades tend to have slightly better heat resistance than the high-chlorine grades. The thermal limits of typical CSM vulcanisates are shown in Figure 1.

Flame Resistance

Best flame resistance is obtained with the high-chlorine grades of CSM. Chlorinated plasticisers, brominated resins, and antimony trioxide synergist are commonly used additives. Mineral fillers, excluding carbonates, are preferred. Hydrated alumina is frequently used as the major filler where smoke suppersion is important.

Water Resistance

The use of magnesia acid acceptor is the major cause of water sensitivity in CSM vulcanisates. Replacing magnesia with litharge in black stocks with a sulphur cure, or with dibasic lead phthalate in all other systems, will result in improved water resistance. Where the presence of lead is undersirable, synthetic hydrotalcite will provide significantly better water resistance than magnesia. Water resistance is also affected by the choice of filler - carbon black is the best, followed by non-black fillers with calcined clay preferred.

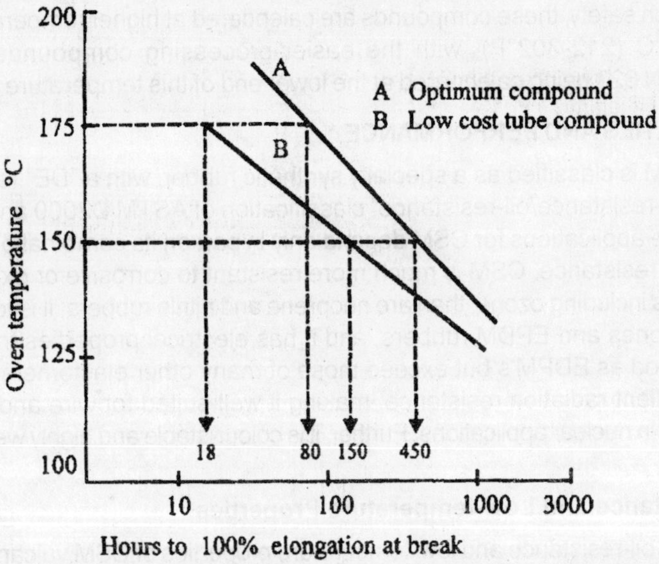

Fig. 1 : The thermal limits for practical performance of CSM vulcanisates

Weather Resistance

When suitably compounded with protective pigments, CSM vulcanisates and the unvulcanised crystalline grades are highly weather-resistant. They are also colourable with good colour stability. CSM compounds, provided they are free of nutritive compounding ingredients, are also resistant to mildew growth.

Oxygen/Ozone Resistance

CSM vulcanisates are highly resistant to attack by ozone and do not need the addition of antiozonants in their compounds. They also are very resistant to oxidation; however, the addition of an antioxidant will improve performance under severe heat-ageing conditions.

Electrical Properties

Best insulation resistance is obtained with the low-chlorine grades of CSM. Good electrical properties may also require formulating for good water resistance in compounds containing little or no carbon black. Compounds can be formulated so that combustion products are low in both smoke and corrosive gases.

Chemical Resistance

CSM vulcanisates are very resistant to degradation caused by exposure to corrosive chemicals. Litharge is the preferred acid acceptor for vulcanisates for generally good chemical resistance although for certain highly concentrated chemicals such as Baume sulphuric acid, or concentrated nitric acid, manesia will give better service. The best general-purpose filler for chemical-resistant stocks is blanc fixe or barytes.

Resistance to solvents is limited by the resistance of the vulcanisates to swelling in those solvents rather than to any chemical degradation caused by the solvents. Table 7 shows a guide that will indicate the likely performance of vulcanisates based on HYPALON 40 in a variety of chemical media. The guide refers to room-temperature exposure; higher temperatures of exposure may cause worse deterioration.

Dynamic Properties

The resilience of CSM vulcanisates is generally in the 55-75% range for grades having medium- and low-chlorine content. High-chlorine grades are more highly damped and the resilience of their vulcanisates are generally too low at room temperature to measure on a Yerzley Oscillograph.

Applications

Industrial Uses

Two areas in which CSM has proven advantages are in hose and in electrical applications. In the hose industry, CSM is particularly useful because of its oil and chemical resistance, its outstanding ozone and weather resistance, and because of the frequent need for bright colours.

CSM is used in the electrical industry as a protective jacketing or sheathing on top of other elastomers with superior insulating properties. CSM also finds considerable usage as an integral or "one-shot" insulation/jacket for wiring carrying upto 600 volts. The combination of insulation resistance and long-term resistance to the deteriorating effects of ozone, weather, oil, and heat make CSM a clear choice for high-quality wire applications.

Table 7 : CSM chemical resistance guide

Chemicals	Rating[a]
Acids, mineral	A
Acids, organic	A
Alcohols	A
Aldehydes	C
40% formaldehyde	A
Alkalis, caustic	A
Aniline	B
Aromatic solvents	C
ASTM Oil No. 1	A
ASTM Oil No. 3	B
ASTM Reference fuel A	A
ASTM Reference fuel C	C
Asphalt	B
Chlorinated solvents	C
Esters	C
Ethers	B-C
Gasoline	B
Hydrogen peroxide	A
Inorganic salts	A
Ketones	B-C
Triethanolamine	A
Wear	A

[a]For room temperature exposure, using vulcanisates based on HYPALON 40 -

A - little or no effect

B - minor to moderate effect

C - severe effect.

Automotive Uses

In the auto industry, high-volume CSM usage includes hose, tubing, and electrical applications. In addition, low permeability to moisture and refrigerants make high-chlorine CSM an ideal polymer for air-conditioning hoses.

Construction Uses

Considerable usage of CSM in reservior-liner construction has resulted from a combination of excellent weather resistance and the ease of fabrication of uncured liners made of CSM. Over 500 million square feet of CSM liners have been installed, with an exceptionally low rate of failure due to the liner's easy and reliable seaming characteristics.

For many of the same reasons, CSM use is also well-established in single-ply roofing memberanes. Here, the flame resistance and moisture resistance of CSM is very desirable and the fact that weather-resistant membranes can be made in heat-reflective light colours helps reduce the cost of air-conditioning.

In an alterative construction method, colourable weather resistant roof surfaces of HYPALON are prepared by roller coating HYPALON paint over a neoprene base.

Miscellaneous Applications

Other applications for CSM include roll covers for use in strong acids, and in applications where corona discharge produces ozone and electrical stress; CSM is also used for tank linings, industrial maintenance coatings, and extruded sponge. CSM compositons are binder for cork in automotive gaskets, and for magnetic fillers in refrigerator gaskets.

Product Safety

When recommended handling procedures are followed, HYPALON synthetic rubber polymers and the products derived from them present no health hazards. HYPALON synthetic rubber may contain a small amount of carbon tetrachloride (CCl_4) and a lesser amount of chloroform ($CHCl_4$) as residues from its manufacturing process. Both are regulated as air contaminants. When large quantities of raw polymer are stored or processed, it is advisable for the protection of personnel to provide adequate ventilation to keep employee exposure below the regulated levels.

9

Silicone Rubber

INTRODUCTION

Natural rubber, tapped from tress, finds a great variety of uses in the form of tyres, footwear, sponges, cushions, mattresses, surgical articles, sports goods, electrical insulation, corrosion-resisting lining for chemical equipment, balloons and toys, to mention a few. During the two world wars, when the normal supply sources of this essential commodity were cut off to their major consumers, efforts to develop synthetic rubbers had started almost overnight. As a result, a number of organic and inorganic materials, which resemble rubber, have come into existence. In fact any chemical structure which forms long, flexible coil-like chains, when cross-linked to a specific degree, can exhibit rubbery properties. Some synthetic rubbers even overcome the deficiencies of natural rubber and hence are called speciality rubbers. For example, acrylonitrile rubber has much better oil resistance, butyl rubber is much less permeable to air and silicone rubbers withstand much higher temperatures. None of the synthetic rubbers, it should be stressed, has all the characteristics of natural rubber and hence are called "elastomers".

Silicone rubber, with which we are concerned, is different from the other rubbers in one important respect. It has an inorganic back-bone made of silicon and oxygen atoms, and belongs to the family of compounds known as 'silicones'. Natural rubber is a hydrocarbon material with a back-bone of carbon-carbon chain.

Akin to other members of the silicone family, namely, fluids and resins, the silicone rubbers (elastomers) possess unique properties not shared by any other type. The most outstanding of these is the retention of flexibility (a measure of elongation), resilience (a measure of rebound) and tensile strength (a measure of stiffness) to an amazing degree in the wide temperature range of -150°F to +600°F. All other rubbers get hardened and turn brittle at low temperatures and become soft and lose their elasticity at high temperatures. The useful life of a rubber, considered as the time of retention of elongation of at least 50%, for the best organic rubber is of the order of days in the temperature range 250-300°F while for the silicone rubbers it is upto 20 years at 250°F and 5 years at 300°F, Silicone rubber is the best available flexible electrical insulation as it retains its dielectric strength, power factor and insulation resistance over a wide temperature range when other insulations become useless. Moreover, it has an excellent resistance to ozone and its corona resistance approaches that of mica. The other notable features which make it an ideal material for electrical insulation are its ability to bond into a continuous, homogeneous insulation jacket, imperviousness to water, oil and conductive contaminants, resistance to noise and vibration damage even at sub-zero temperatures and a lack of attraction to rodents, unlike their organic counterparts. Some other important properties of silicone rubber include its release characteristics, chemical, fuel and oil resistance, inertness, non-toxicity, high permeability to gases and resistance to weathering. Silicone rubber is as superior ablative material. Mechanical parts of rockets and re-entry vehicles which are exposed to very high temperatures can be protected with shields made of such materials.

TYPES OF SILICONE RUBBER

Chemically, silicone rubber is a specially prepared polymer of dimethylsiloxane. The chemical reaction is controlled to get linear chains of several thousand units of silicon-oxygen with two methyl radicals having molecular weights of the order of 500,000. This elastomeric polymer in the form of a gum is mixed with suitable inorganic fillers to give mechanical strength. To make it elastic, it is heated with a suitable chemical, for a specified time (vulcanisation). This brings about elasticity through intramolecular cross-linking. The unique properties of silicone rubber are partially accounted for by the bond energy of the silicon-oxygen linkage which is about 1.5 times as strong as the carbon-carbon linkge present in organic polymers. Special rubbers are produced by modifying the dimethyl polysiloxane gum. Rubber gums with 0.1 mole per cent methyl-vinylsiloxane give low compression-set rubbers. By incorporating one boron atom per 300-400 silicon atoms, fusible rubbers have been prepared. Solvent-resistant rubbers are made by incorporating polar groups such as fluorinated alkyl and cyanoalkyl into the polymer molecule. Replacement of 5-15% of the methyl groups by phenyl groups yields rubbers which retain their elasticity even at -150°C. 'Bonding pastes' or rubbers with paste-like consistency are formulated from an elastomeric gum, calcium carbonate and benzoyl peroxide.

A spectacular growth area for silicone rubber has been the liquid compounds known as RTV (Room Temperature Vulcanising). Although originally these compounds were cured (curing means that the rubber mix in the form of a paste, to which all desired chemicals have been added, is heated to make it elastic; when it is set, it also takes on the required form) almost exclusively at room temperature, they are now available in a range of viscosities as thin fluids or thixotropic pastes (whose viscosities can be lowered by mechanical shear), whose curing times can be varied over a wide range. In many applications curing, is accomplished at elevated temperatures in a matter of seconds. The principal difference between the polymer used in heat-cured silicone rubber and RTV is the length of the polymer chain. The average polymer for heat-cured rubber has around 7000 silicon units in the chain while the average RTV polymer has around 1000 units.

Silicone rubber can be bonded to many materials, including metals. The surface phenomena of silicones not being fully understood, the science of binding silicone to a substrate is mixed with a good deal of empirical art.

Though the raw material, silica, from which silicone rubber is made, is cheap and plentiful, the manufacturing process is difficult and expensive. In spite of its high cost, silicone rubber is preferred in many applications as they need less maintenance and prove economical in the long run. A major consumer of this speciality rubber is the aircraft and aerospace industry. It is used for gaskets and sealing rings for jet engines, in ducting for circulating hot air to the cabins and to surfaces requiring deicing, as sealing strip for doors, windows, turrets, switch boot covers, vibration dampers, for sealing cavities and junctions for environmental protection, for bonding and sealing aircraft components exposed to fuels and oils and as groove injection sealants for aircraft fuel tanks. Silicone rubber can withstand temperatures upto 9000°F (5000°C) for several minutes while still retaining good insulation properties. The superior ablation characteristics thus enable its use in the coating of rocket fuel valves, supply cables and silo doors for protection from rocket blast.

The automotive field is currently showing the maximum growth for the use of silicone rubber. A critical application of silicone rubber bonded to metal is in the shaft seals used in automatic transmissions. The silicone rubber not only resists the action of the hot transmission fluid and the frictional heat of the shaft on the seal lip but also prevents the corrosive pitting of the shaft during extended periods of engine idleness, which generally occurs with sulphur-containing rubbers. Silicone rubber hoses which have superior resistance to hot ethylene glycol, diesel fumes and engine-cleaning solvents, last as long as the engine itself. High ignition voltages and higher under-the-hood temperatures necessitate the use of extruded silicone rubber ignition wire insulation and moulded silicone rubber spark plug boots. Moulded flourosilicone rubber check seals are used in carburettors to replace metal components. RTV sealants are used for formed-in-place engine gaskets, repair and installation of wind shields and light covers. It is estimated that 3 to 3.5 kg of silicone rubber is used per car at present.

Electronics and Electrical Industries

In the electronics industry, silicone rubber is used for semi-conductor junction passivation, protection of electronic components, general potting and encapsulation for modules, relays, power supplies, amplifiers, etc., as a-particle barrier. For calculators and adding machine keyboards it eliminates corrosion and makes bounceless contact possible, minimising electrical noise and double signals. In the electrical industry, silicone rubber is used for wire and cable insulation, encapsulation of transformers and motors, class H electrical connectors for industrial and household requirements, in insulating tapes for transformers, heating pads and several electrical parts. Effective microwave oven gasketing is made from conductive silicone rubber. It also helps to reduce RF (radio frequency) interference and is used in oven sealing. Special silicone rubbers which are high-loss dielectrics are used in microwave transmission lines. The largest growth area in the coming years will be for wire and cable insulation with emphasis on fire safety in nuclear plants.

Silicone Rubbers to Mimic Flesh

Silicone rubber is largely used in biomedical and prosthetic devices to replace a missing ear, to restore movement to arthritic hands and for many other body parts. Their chracteristic inertness, resistance to geing, flexibility, softness, dependability, sterilisability and biocompatibility make them ideal for this purpose. As a biomaterial in extracorporal devices, polymethylsiloxane tubing is used with heart-lung machines, dialysers and related devices, after incorporating heparin as an anti-coagulant for the blood. By reacting polyurethane with polyorganosiloxanes having reactive end groups, a tough material called Avcothane has been developed by AVCO Everett Reserach Laboratory in the USA. This tough elastomer is able to withstand millions of flexings without failure and as such is used widely in heart assist devices like interaortic balloons, artificial hearts and artificial blood vessels. Other uses of silicone rubber are in surgical tubings, heart valves, catheters, hydrocephalus, shunts, nerve cuffs, replacement of bladders, contact lenses and prosthetic parts to correct deformation due to heredity, disease of accident. In the prosthetic applications, it is used widely for reconstructing breast, ear, eye, bone, finger joint, limb, tendon and ligament. The most popular of silicone implants is the mammary implant which consists of a strong, thin but very stretchy silicone rubber envelope filled with a clear silicone gel of the same general weight and texture as the breast tissue. Other gel or liquid-filled silicone rubber devices include testicle implants for cosmetic replacement, vaginal forms for the reconstruction of vagina, penile implants for males who have erectile incompetence. Kneecaps and hernia defects have also been corrected by the use of silicone rubber. In dentistry, RTV is increasingly used as replica for moulding the jaw in the manufacture of dentures. The combination of low levels of haemolysis (loss of haemoglobin for red blood cells) with the high rate of gas permeability makes silicone rubber membrane an ideal gas transfer material in blood oxygenators.

Silicone rubber is also used for many other applications. Flexible mould materials of silicone rubber allow excellent reproduction of details of casting of metals, plastics, waxes and plaster. The non-stick characteristic leads to its, use in rolls for handling hot plastics in the production of films, embossing, laminating and smoothing of hot tin over tin plate steel. Its release properties find application in coatings on release paper and parts of machinery or rolls handling sticky materials such as hot polyethylene, candy and adhesives. Constancy in transmissibility or resonant frequency in the temperature range -65-300°F and the retention of dynamic absorption characteristics in spite of ageing makes it an ideal material for effective noise and vibration control. Thin films of silicone rubber are selectively permeable to different gases and as such may be used for separating gases to obtain relative enrichment of one gaseous component over another. Its outstanding weatherability in the hottest and flexibility in the coldest of climates makes it ideal for the building industry to caulk joints of masonry, metal, wood or plastics, to seal windows, as protective coatings for plywood, metal or masonry building materials indoors as well as outdoors.

Silicones in general and silicone rubber in particular, have proved versatile materials meeting the challenges of technology and have not only extended the life of capital equipment but also of life in general.

The estimated service life of silicone rubber at various temperatures is given in Table 1.

Table 1 : Estimated service life of silicone rubber

Temperature	Lifespan
90°C (194°F)	40 years
121°C (250°F)	10-20 years
150°C (300°F)	5-10 years
200°C (392°F)	2-5 years
250°C (481°F)	3 months
315°C (600°F)	2 weeks

Synthesis of Silicone Polymers

The silicon used in the synthesis of silicone polymers is obtained by the reduction of SiO_2 which, in the free or combined form, makes up about

60% of the earth's crust. The abundance of SiO_2 is one reason for the favouarble trend in the cost of silicone rubber relative to the organics. The direct process involves the reaction of methyl chloride with silicon in the presence of a copper catalyst. Dimethyldichlorosilane is the major product, but many other products are produced, some of which are listed in Table 2. These are seprated by large distillation towers.

Table 2 : Major products of the director process

Compound	BP (°C/760 mm)
Dimethyldichlorosilane	70
Methyltrichlorosilane	66
Trimethylchlorosilane	57
Methyldichlorosilane	40
Dimethylchlorosilane	35
Trichlorosilane	32

Both the methyltrichlorosilane and trimethyl monochlorosilane must be reduced from per cent levels to low ppm levels either by distillation or subsequent purification steps. The trimethylchlorosilane is a chain-stopper and affects the molecular weight of the silicone polymer. The methyltrichlorosilane causes branching or cross-linking of the desired linear silicone polymer, which affects processing. After purification, the dimethyldichlorosilane is then hydrolysed (as shown below) to a mixture of linear polymers and low molecular-weight cyclics.

$$Me_2\text{-}SiCl_2 + H_2O — HO(Me_2SiO)_nH + (Me_2SiO)_m + HCl$$

The hydrolysate was originally polymerised to high molecular-weight with acid catalyst. Today the cyclics are usually removed as an additional purification step. Recently it has been found that a superior silicone rubber polymer is produced when solid alkalis are added in small amounts to the cyclics. The polymer normally used in dimethylsilicone rubber varies from 300,000 to 800,000 in molecular-weight. This corresponds to a viscosity of 4×10^6 to 140×10^6 cps, or 4000-11,000 silicon atoms per molecule. There are also two monofunctional groups per molecule as chain-stopper, or 180-500 ppm chain-stopper. One can then see how relatively small variations in the level of chain-stopper can lead to large variations in molecular weight and even larger variations in viscosity.

Further, an impurity in dimethyldichlorosilane which increases the cross-linking is methylvinyldichlorosilane. Today most dimethylsilicone polymers and compounds contain this vinyl source. When the latter is present at less than 0.5%, the resulting polymers make more efficient use of peroxides and thus require less for cure. The cured rubber has less tendency to revert and thus has lower compression-set.

Dimethylsilicone rubber tends to become stiff below -60°F. However, the low temperature flexibility may be improved by substitution of phenyl ($-C_6H_5$) groups for some of the methyl groups attached to the silicon atoms in the polymer chain as shwon in Table 3. Replacement of only 5% of the methyl groups by phenyl groups will lower the crystallisation temperature and extend the useful service temperature range to below -130°F.

Table 3 : Types of silicone polymers

Classification	Uses	Basic Polymer Units
MQ	The first silicone polymer	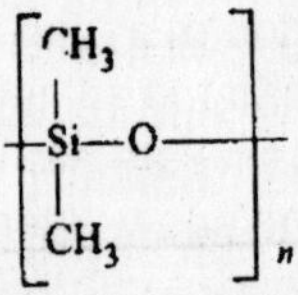
MPQ	The first low-temperature copolymer	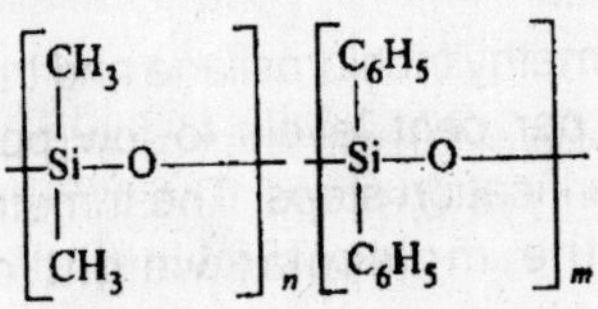
MVQ	Low-compression-set copolymer	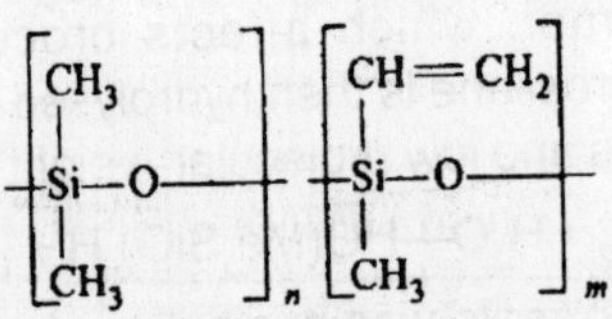
MPVQ	The first high-strength low temperature terpolymer	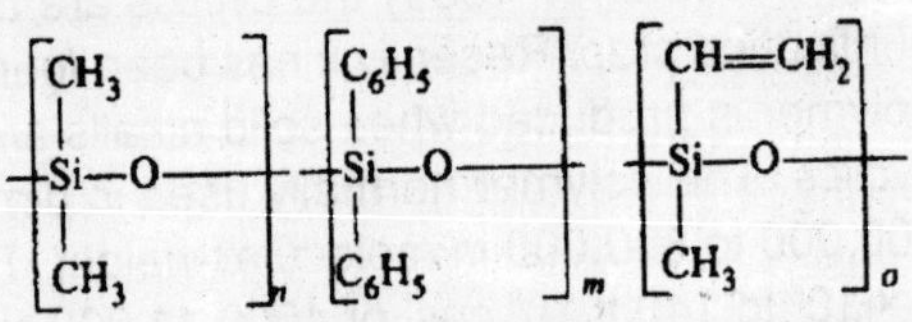
FVQ	Oil-resistant polymer	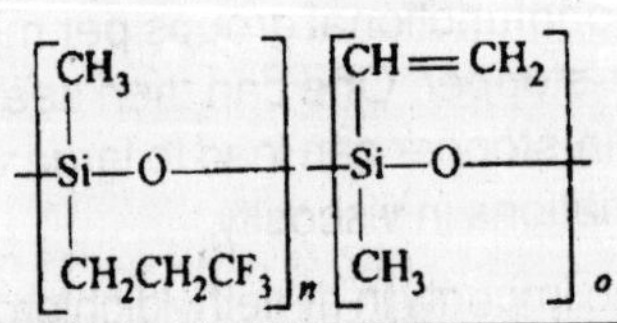

The dimethylsilicone rubbers show good performance in acetone and diesters but undergo up to 200% swell in aliphatic and aromatic hydrocarbons. The replacement of one methyl group on each silicon atom with a polar group such as trifluoropropyl (—$CH_2CH_2CH_3$), as shwon in Table 3, reduces the swelling in acetone and diesters. Figure 1 compares neoprene rubber, methyl silicone rubber and fluorocarbon rubber in various solvents. Fluorosilicone rubber behaves similarly to fluorocarbon rubber in these solvents. In solvents with a higher solubility parameter such as methanol or ethanol, the swelling of fluorosilicones drops down again to less than 25%.

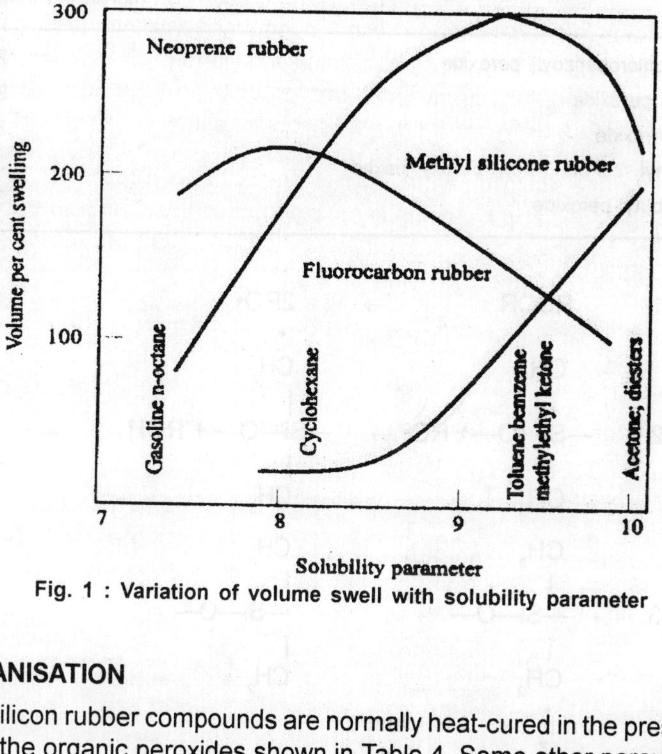

Fig. 1 : Variation of volume swell with solubility parameter

VULCANISATION

Silicon rubber compounds are normally heat-cured in the presence of one of the organic peroxides shown in Table 4. Some other peroxides are used to a limited extent; however, the first four in the table are the most important ones.

In the case of the cure of a dimethyl polymer with a diaroyl peroxide, the cure mechanism shown in Figure 2 has been fairly well established.

It is apparent that these reactions could produce no more than 1 mole of chemical cross-links per mole of peroxide. The hydrogen abstraction reaction has been estimated at 50% efficient, and the ethylene bridge formation at 40% efficient. And, indeed, independent work has shown that the actual cross-link yield in an unfilled polymer is 0.1-0.3 moles of chemical cross-links per mole of diaroyl peroxide. The above ratio decreases as the level of diaroyl peroxide is increased. This corresponds to a chemical cross-link density of 0.4-0.7 moles of cross-links per 1000 moles Si in the polymer. It is not practical to increase the cross-link concentration much further by raising the peroxide levels.

Table 4 : Organic peroxides used for silicone rubber vulcanisation

Peroxide	Temperature, °F for half-life = 1 minute
Bis (2,4-dichlorobenzoyl) peroxide	234
Di-bienzoyl peroxide	271
Di-cumyl peroxide	340
2, 5-dimethyl -2,5-bis (t-butyl peroxy) hexne	354
Di-tertiary butyl peroxide	379

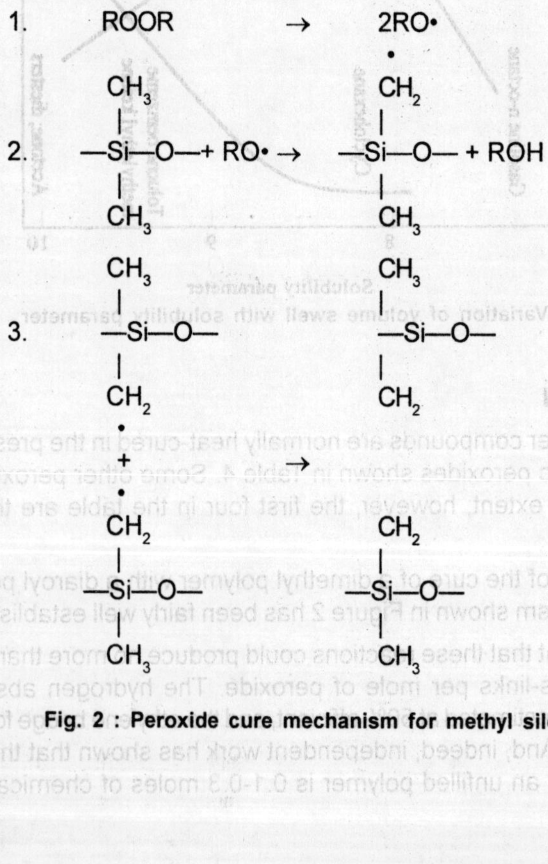

Fig. 2 : Peroxide cure mechanism for methyl siloxanes

The cure mechanism for the methyl vinyl siloxy containing copolymers shown in Figure. 3 seems to account for available experimental observations.

This mechanism predicts more than 1 mole of cross-links per mole of peroxide, and not more than 1 mole or cross-links per mole of vinyl groups.

In the case of unfilled methyl vinyl siloxy containing copolymers, actual cross-link yields have also been measrured. data on a polymer with Vi/Si = 0.0026 are shown in Table 5. Efficiencies are high, and these results are consistent with the "trimethylene bridge" cure mechanism.

Hexane, dicumyl peroxide, di-t-butyl peroxide and 2,5-*dimethyl*-2,5-*bis* (*t-butyl peroxy*) are usually considered to be "vinyl-specific" in that they will give good cures only with vinyl containing polymer. The two diaroyl peroxides, benzoyl and *bis* (2,4-dichlorobenzoyl), will cure both vinyl and non-vinyl containing gums. This difference is illustrated in Figure 4, again using the polymer with Vi/Si = 0.0026. Di-tertiary butyl peroxide seems to be truly "vinyl-specific" in that the chemical cross-link density is constant inthe range 0.2-6% peroxide. However, the cross-link density is dependent upon peroxide concentration in the case of the *bis* (2,4-dichlorobenzoyl) peroxide.

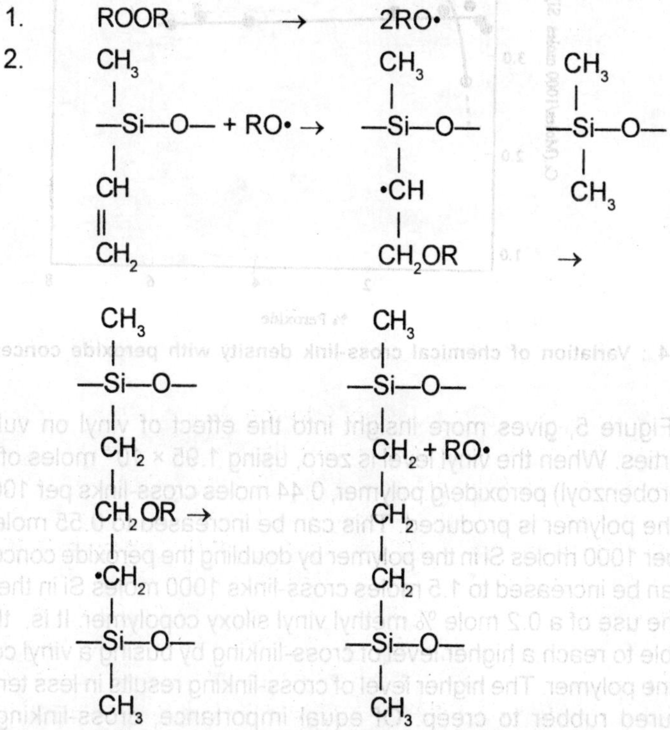

3. Repetition of Step 2 followed eventually by termination.

Fig. 3 : Peroxide cure mechanism for methyl vinyl siloxanes

Table 5 : Cross-linking efficiency–polydimethylcomethylvinylsiloxane (Vi/Si = 0.0026)

Peroxide	% Peroxide (optimum level)	Moles chemical cross-links/ 1000 moles Si	Moles chemical cross-links/ mole peroxide	Moles chemical cross-links/ mole vinyl
2,5-dimethyl -2,5-*bis* (t-butyl peroxy) hexane	0.315	2.4	3.2	0.9
Dicumyl peroxide	0.315	2.4	3.0	0.9
Di-t-butyl peroxide	0.21	3.3	2.4	0.9

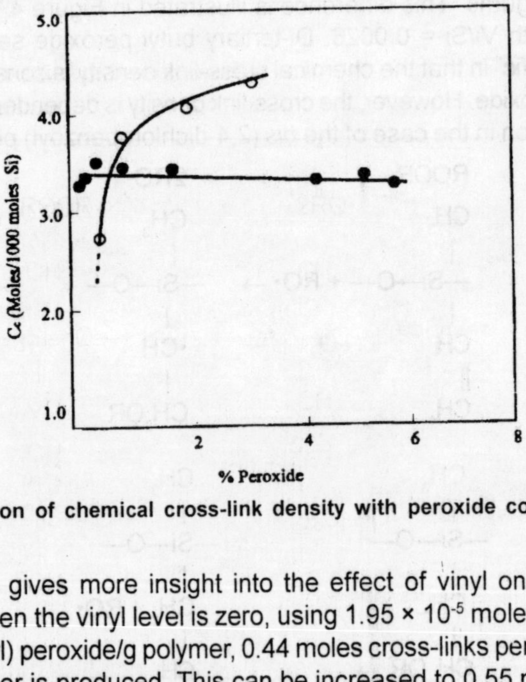

Fig. 4 : Variation of chemical cross-link density with peroxide concentration

Figure 5, gives more insight into the effect of vinyl on vulcanisate properties. When the vinyl level is zero, using 1.95 × 10^{-5} moles of *bis* (2,4-dichlorobenzoyl) peroxide/g polymer, 0.44 moles cross-links per 1000 moles Si in the polymer is produced. This can be increased to 0.55 moles cross-links per 1000 moles Si in the polymer by doubling the peroxide concentration, or it can be increased to 1.5 moles cross-links 1000 moles Si in the polymer with the use of a 0.2 mole % methyl vinyl siloxy copolymer. It is, therefore, possible to reach a higher level of cross-linking by busing a vinyl containing siloxane polymer. The higher level of cross-linking results in less tendency of the cured rubber to creep. Of equal importance, cross-linking can be accomplished with lower levels of acid-forming peroxides and peroxides that do not led to acidic decomposition products. This last process, in turn, leads to less tendency to revert in curing or during post-bake processing. By optimising the vinyl level and the type and level of peroxide catalyst, the compression set at elevated temperatures can be minimised.

Vulcanisation rate is conveniently studied by means of the Monsanto Rheometer and it provides a continuous measurement of complex dynamic shear modulus while a rubber is being cured in a mould under heat and pressure. This study is accomplished by measurement of the torque on a conical disk rotor that is embedded in the rubber, and is being sinusoidally oscillated through a small arc. The torque is a linear function of cross-link density as determined by swelling measurements, though the proportionality constant varies with the stock. The torque readings can, therefore, be considered as relative cross-link densities.

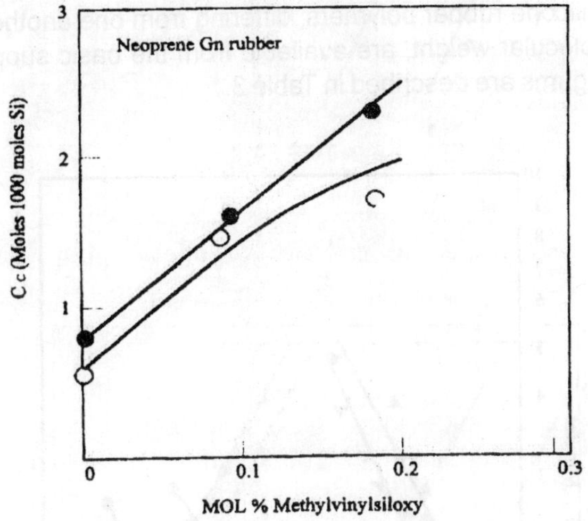

Fig. 5 : Variation of chemical cross-link density with vinyl level and concentration of *bis* (2,4-dichlorobenzoyl) peroxide.

From a rheograph, it is possible to get an idea of how the compound will flow in the mould before cure starts (mimimum viscosity and scorch time), cure rate (and consequently time to various degrees of cure), and a measure of the final cross-link density. If a series of these curves are run at different temperatures with the various peroxides, the data may be used to estimate hot-mould residence times required to effect a given degree of cure at a given temperature with a given peroxide. Figures 6, 7 and 8 may be used to make such estimates for the vulcanisation of a high-tear-strength methyl vinyl compound. For example, with *bis* (2,4-dichlorobenzoyl) peroxide at 0.65 phr, and at a temperature of 230°F, the induction period is 2 minutes. The hot-mould-residence time is 4 minutes for 90% cure and 8 minutes for full cure. A technically satisfactory cure (in terms of durometer, tensile, and elongation) is obtained by introduction of the cross-links; however, a full cure is required to obtain the lowest compression set. In order to obtain full cure in 8 minutes, the mould temperature should be 230°F for bis (2,4-dichlorobenzoyl) peroxide, 270°F for benzyl peroxide, 255°F for dicumyl peroxide, and 365°F for 2,5-dimethyl-2,5-*bis* (*t*-butyl peroxy) hexane.

COMPOUNDING INGREDIENTS

A typical silicone rubber formulation contains a silicone polymer, reinforcing and (or) extending fillers, process aids or softeners to platicise and retard creep-ageing special additives (e.g., heat-ageing and flame retardant additives), colour pigments, and one or more peroxide curing agents.

Silicone Polymers

Pure silicone rubber polymers, differing from one another in polymer type and molecular weight, are available from the basic suppliers. These polymers of gums are described in Table 3.

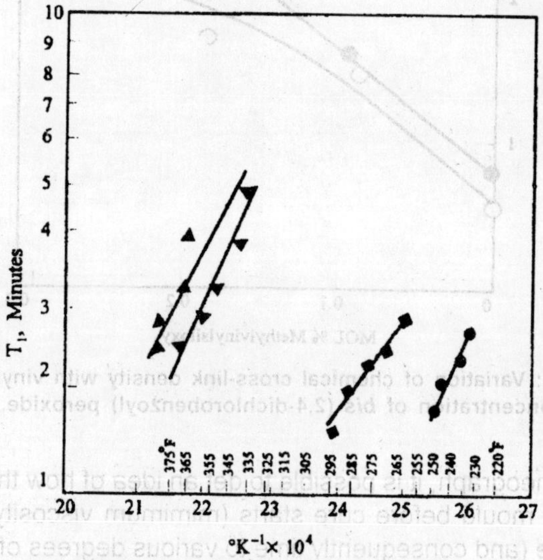

Fig. 6 : Induction times for cure with various peroxides

Silicone Rubber Elastomers

Although pure polymer may be used, it is generally easier and more economical for the rubber fabricator to compound from silicone-reinforced gums or bases. Over the years, silicone suppliers have developed a wide variety of silicone rubber compounds to meet special requirements and specifications. However, the most recent offerings have been in bases which are mixtures of pure polymer, of process aids, and of reinforcing silica fillers that have been specially processed. Both of these product lines are made up of blendable bases plus selected additives for enhanced properties such as heat-ageing, flame retardancy, and oil resistance as well as processing aids.

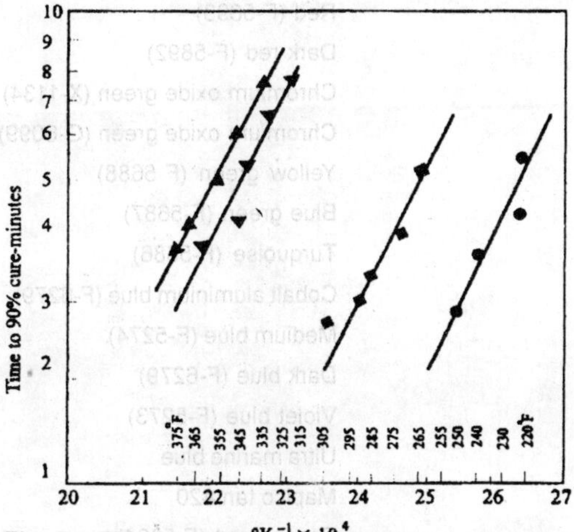

Fig. 7 : Time to 90% cure with various peroxides

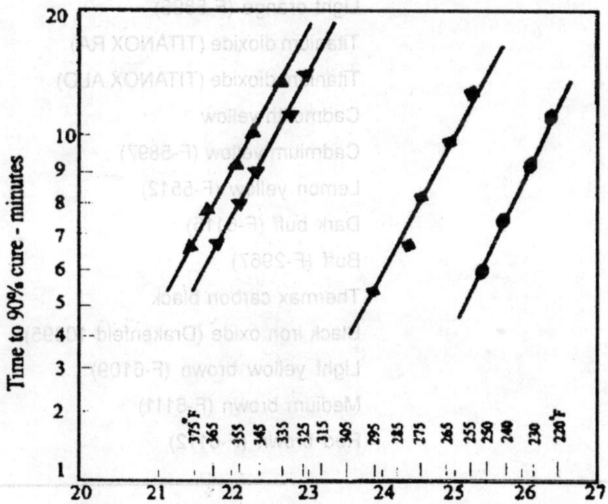

Fig. 8 : Time to full cure with various peroxides

Reinforcing Fillers

The fumed process silicas reinforce silicone polymer to a greater extent than any other filler. Due to the high purity of the filler, the rubbers containing it have excellent insulating properties, especially under wet conditions.

Table 6 : Colour pigments for silicone rubber

Reds	Red (RY-2196)
	Red (RO-3097)
	Red (F-5893)
	Dark red (F-5892)
Greens	Chromium oxide green (X-1134)
	Chromium oxide green (G-6099)
	Yellow green (F-5688)
	Blue green (F-5687)
	Turquoise (F-5686)
Blues	Cobalt aluminium blue (F-6279)
	Medium blue (F-5274)
	Dark blue (F-6279)
	Violet blue (F-5273)
	Ultra marine blue
Oranges	Mapico tan #20
	Orange red (F-5894)
	Orange (F-5895)
	Light orange (F-5896)
Whites	Titanium dioxide (TITANOX RA)
	Titanium dioxide (TITANOX ALO)
Yellows	Cadmolith yellow
	Cadmium yellow (F-5897)
	Lemon yellow (F-5512)
Buffs	Dark buff (F-6115)
	Buff (F-2967)
Blacks	Thermax carbon black
	Black iron oxide (Drakenfeld 10395)
Browns	Light yellow brown (F-6109)
	Medium brown (F-6111)
	Red brown (F-6112)

Precipitated silicas impart moderately high reinforcement, as shown in Table 7. Some precipitated filler may give high water absorption due to residual salts. If so, the wet electrical properties will not be very good. However, recently some precipitated silicas are available with very-low-salt content and provide better electrical properties.

Table 7 : Reinforcing fillers for silicone rubber

Filler	Type	Particle size, mean diameter (millimicrons)	Surface area (square metres per gram)	Specific gravity	Reinforcement produced in pure silicone gum: Tensile strength range, psi	Reinforcement produced in pure silicone gum: Elongation range, %
CAB-O-SIL HS-5	Fumed silica	10	300-350	2.20	1600-1800	200-1000
CAB-O-SIL MS-7	Fumed silica	15	175-200	2.20	600-1200	200-800
AEROSIL 300	Fumed silica	7	270-330	2.20	600-1800	200-1000
AEROSIL 200	Fumed silica	12	175-225	2.20	600-1200	200-800
FK 160	Precipitated silica	18	160	2.20	600-1100	200-800
HiSil	Precipitated silica	20	140-160	2.20	600-1100	200-800

Semi-reinforcing or Extending Fillers

The extenders (Table 8) are important for use in compounds containing reinforcing fillers in order to obtain an optimum balance of physical properties, cost, and processability.

Ground silica and calcined kaolin do not provide significant reinforcement. As a consequence, they can be added to a reinforced gum or compound in relatively large quantities in order to reduce pound-volume cost. These extenders are satisfactory in either mechanical or electrical-grade rubber.

The reinforcement obtained with calcined diatomaceous silica is greater, though quite modest, than that obtained with any other extender. Therefore, as an extender, it is not as useful as ground silica. However, it is used in electrical stocks, low-compression-set stocks, and in general mechanical stocks to reduce tack and modify handling properties.

Calcium carbonate and zirconium silicate are special-purpose extenders, used mainly in pastes that are coated on fabrics via solvent dispersion.

Zinc oxide is used as a colourant, and as a plasticiser. It imparts tack and adhesive properties to a compound.

Additives

Organic colours, and many inorganic colours, have adverse effects on the heat-ageing of silicone rubber. The inorganic pigments listed in Table 6 have been found suitable for use. Usually 0.5 to 2 parts per 100 parts of compound are sufficient for tinting purposes. It is often desirable to masterbatch colour pigments in order to get good dispersion and close colour matches.

Red iron oxide is used a colour pigment, and as a heat-ageing additive; 2 to 4 parts per 100 parts of gum will give improved heat stability at 600°F.

Process aids are used with highly reinforcing silica fillers. These have a softening or plasticising effect, and they retard the "crepe-ageing" or "structuring" or "pseudocure" of the raw compound that occurs due to the high reactivity of the reinforcing filler with silicone polymer.

Curing Agents

In commercial practice, it has been found that none of the six commonly used peroxides is a universal curing agent. The three aroyl peroxides (Table 9) may be considered general-purpose in that they will cure both non-vinyl and vinyl-containing polymers. However, none of them is suitable in all types of fabrication procedures. The three dialkyl peroxides (Table 10) are "vinyl-specific" since they will give good cures only with vinyl-containing polymers.

Bis (2,4-dicholorobenzoyl) peroxide normally requires a curing temperature of about 220-250°F. Its decomposition products (2,4-

Table 8 : Semi-reinforciing or extending fillers for silicone rubber

Filler	Type	Particle size, mean diameter (millimicrons)	Surface area (square metres per gram)	Specific gravity	Reinforcement produced in pure silicone gum: Tensile strength range, psi	Elongation range, %
Blance rough		1-5	5	2.65	100-400	200-300
Celite supper floss	Flux calcined diatomaceous silica	1-5	5	2.30	400-800	75-200
Celite 350	Calcined diato-maceous silica	1-5	5	2.15	400-800	75-200
Iron oxide RP-3097	iron oxide	1		4.80	200-500	100-300
Iron oxide RY-2196	Iron oxide	1		4.95	200-500	100-300
Min-u-sil	Ground silica				100-400	200-300
5		5	5	2.65		
10		10	5	2.65		
15		15	5	2.65		
SUPERPAX	Zirconium silicate			4.50	400-600	100-300
TITANOX RA	Titanium dioxide	3		4.20	200-500	300-400
WHITETEX CLAY	Calcined kaolin	1-5	5.0	2.55	400-800	75-200
WITCARB R	Precipitated carbonate	0.03-0.05	32.0	2.65	400-600	100-300
ALBACAR 5970	Precipitated calcium carbonate	1-4	8.0	2.71	400-600	100-300
ZINC OXIDE XX-78	Zinc oxide	0.3	3.0	5.60	200-500	100-300

Table 9 : Peroxide curing agents for silicone rubber – general purpose

Peroxide	Form	Assay (%)	Cure Temperature (°F)	Decomposition products	Uses
Bis (2,4-dichloro-benzoyl) peroxide	Paste	50	220-250	Non-volatile	Hot-air vulcanisation Continuous-steam vulcanisation Autocalve Thick-section moulding Low compression set
Benzoyl peroxide	Paste	50	240-270	Volatile	Continuous-steam vulcanisation Autoclave Tower coating Low compression set Thin-section moulding
Tertiary butyl perbenzoate	Liquid	95	290-310	Volatile	Usually with other peroxides; sponge; generally for high-temperature activation.

dichlorobenzoic acid and 2,4-dichlorobenzene) volatilise relatively slowly, at commercial curing temperatures; and, consequently, compounds containing it may be cured without external pressure, provided that air removal and forming have been done (e.g., by extrusion or calendering) prior to the application of heat. In fact, one of the main uses of this peroxide involves hot air vulcanisation of extrusions in a few seconds at temperature of 600-800°F.

Although this peroxide may be used for moulding, it has some undesirable features. Since it starts cross-linking at an appreciable rate as low as 200°F, thin sections may start to gel before flow and air removal are complete. In addition, a thick section must be carefully programmed through a post-vulcanisation oven bake cycle in order to remove acidic decomposition products without degrading the interior of the part. The peroxide may be used for steam cures in autoclaves and in continuous-steam vulcanisers. However, benzoyl peroxide is more desirable, particularly in the latter case, because of its higher cure temperature (240-270°F). With benzoyl peroxide, there is less tendency for the compound to scorch in the dies when extruding at high speed into a continuous-steam vulcaniser that is operating at 100-200 pounds of steam.

Due to the volatility of its decomposition products (benzoic acid and benzene), external pressure is required to prevent porosity when curing with benzoyl peroxide. The only exception is in the very thin sections involved in tower-coating fabrics from solvent dispersions of silicone rubber. In this case, benzoyl peroxide is nearly always used because it has long shelf life in the dip tanks, and because it is not volatilised from the rubber during the solvent-removal operation prior to cure.

Low-compression-set rubber may be produced with either of the diaroyl peroxides, provided that the polymer contains vinyl groups and that the acidic decomposition product are removed by an oven post-bake.

Unlike the aroyl peroxides, the so-called “vinyl-specific” peroxides (Table 10) may be employed to vulcanised stocks containing carbon black. If dicumyl peroxide is used, these stocks can be hot-air-vulcanised.

All there “vinyl-specific” peroxides are good for thick-section moulding, with dicumyl being less preferable due to a slight tendency to “air-inhibit” in the same manner as benzoyl peroxide. In addition, dicumyl peroxide has somewhat less volatile decomposition products (acetophenone and a, a,-dimethylbenzyl alcohol) than do the other two. This means that external pressure during cure is less important, but still required; and that longer oven post-bakes are needed for thick sections than in the case of the other two peroxides. Just as with the diaroyl peroxides, optimum physical properties require relatively close control of dicumyl peroxide concentration.

Table 10 : Peroxide curing agents for silicone rubber – vinyl-specifie

Peroxide	Form	Assay (%)	Cure Temperature (°F)	Decomposition products	Uses
Dicumyl peroxide	Solid	95	300-320	Fairly volatile	Thick-section moulding Low compression set Carobn black
2,5-dimethyl-2, 5-*bis* (*t*-butyl peroxy) Hexane	Powder	50	330-350	Volatile	Thick-section moulding Low compression set Carbon black.
D-tertiary butyl peroxide	Liquid	97	340-360	Volatile	Thick-section moulding Low compression set Carbon black

Due to their non-acidic decomposition products, the "vinyl-specific" peroxides require less oven post-bake after vulcanisation; and, in addition, close-stepped programme post-bakes are not necessary. Lower compression sets are obtained with these peroxides than with the general-purpose curing agents.

During vulcanisation with di-*t*-butyl peroxide, external pressure is especially important due to the extreme volatility of the peroxide and its decomposition products (acetone and methane). The state of cure is determined primarily by the vinyl content of the polymer, and not by peroxide concentration; air inhibition is absent; pre-vulcanisation or scorch is seldom a problem; and the innocuous decomposition products can be removed by short, high-temperature oven post-bakes. This peroxide also produces a rubber with the best overall balance of properties. Its main deficiency lies in its extreme volatility. A stock must be moulded with external pressure shortly after the peroxide has been added.

Although it does not produce rubber with quite as good a balance of properties, 2,5-dimethyl-2,5-*bis* (*t*-butyl peroxy) hexane is quite similar to di-*t*-butyl peroxide in its performance. It has the advantage of lower vapour prssure at room temperature. In fact, it can be added to a compound 1 to 2 months before vulcanisation. However, external pressure is still required during cure due to the volatility of the decomposition products.

COMPOUNDING

A very extensive body of compounding information that has resulted in compounds, bases and formulations with which the fabricator can meet well over a hundred industrial and military specifications for silicone rubber. The range of physical properties typically obtained are shown in Table 11

Mixing

Silicone rubber may be compounded in conventional equipment, such as Doughmixers, Banburys and two-roll mills. A Banbury works well with a dry, non-sticky stock, but is undesirable with compounds that require a relatively long heat cycle and become too tacky to unload easily.

While a two-roll mill is capable of compounding silicone rubbers, the nature of the silica fillers creates an undesirable work atomosphere. However, two-roll mills are excellent for colouring, catalysing, and preforming some of the firmer stocks.

FABRICATING

Freshening

Freshening has been the first fabrication step. This is a remilling operation, to reverse the "crepe-hardening" or "structuring" that has taken

Table 11 : Typical physical properties of selected formulations

Property	Low compression set	High-strength methyl	Addition cure	Extreme high tempe-rature	Extreme low tempe-rature	High strength extreme low temperature	Solvent resistant	Wire	Cable	Insulation
Hardness, Shore A	60	50	55	46	50	63	50	60	68	72
Tensile strength, psi	925	1300	1300	1000	900	1500	1000	900	900	1400
Elongation, %	200	650	700	430	400	700	220	300	500	220
Tear strength, Die B pi	70	200	250	95	95	200	75			
% compression set (22 hrs/350°F)	14	30	40	14	20	42	50			
Brittle pt (°F)	-85	-90	-90	-85	-150	-150	-90			
Oil resistance, % volume change -										
7 days @ 160°F Skydrol 500A				+10	+25		+30			
70 hr @ 300°F ASTM 1	+7			+6	+10	+10	+1			
ASTM3	+40				+90	+90	+5			
Heat-ageing (48 hr/600°F)										
Hardness, Shore A				56						
Tensile strength, psi				400						
Elongation, %				194						
Volume resistivity, ohm-cm								5×10^{15}		1×10^{15}
Electric strength, vpm								650		650
Dielectric constant, 60 cps								3.15		3.4
Power factor, 60 cps								0.001		0.005

place since the compound was made. "Structuring" occurs more quickly and proceeds farther if the compound has been aged at higher temperatures. It is caused by the formation of hydrogen bounds between the hydroxyl groups of the filler and the hydroxyl groups of oxygen atoms of the polymer. Two factors have reduced the amount of structuring that occurs in the current silicone compounds: first, the hydroxyls on the polymer are kept to a low level; second, the hydroxyls on the filler are reduced by treating the filler with silanes or siloxane process aids. However, freshening is still often carried out by the fabricator because the material has been in inventory at a high temperature or for a long time. It is also freshened when the fabricator catalyses it.

Before the mill is loaded, the roll clearance should be set fairly loose Usually the silicone compound will band on the slow roll first (crumbling and lacing can be, but usually are not, encountered). As the milling continues, the nip should be gradually tightened. In the case of a hard compound, the original roll setting will be somewhat tighter for a short time. Then the mill is set fairly loose and gradually tightened. This procedure, combined with the proper amount of stock on the mill (slight bank), minimises air entrapment during further milling and blending. After a smooth sheet has formed on the fast roll, compounding ingredients may be added if desired.

Milling is continued until the stock reaches the desired consistency. Under-freshened stock will flow poorly upon moulding, and will form parts with a rough surface upon extrusion. An over-freshened compound loses green strength, and becomes sticky and hard to handle. Stock must not be allowed to warm up above 100-130°F after a curing agent has been added.

At this point, the stock is freshened and ready for use in one of the following fabrication procedures.

Moulding

Compression and transfer moulding are the most widely used methods for moulding silicone rubber parts. However, large-volume applications, in the automotive industry for spark-plug boots and in the health-care industry for catheters, are resulting in a large growth for injection moulding. Compression and transfer mouldings are run at pressures of 800-3000 psi and temperatures of 220-370°F. Three mould variables that must be controlled are temperature, speed of mould closing, and pressure. Temperature is influenced mainly by the choice of a peroxide curing agent. If the temperature of the mould increases after repeated moulding, the temperature of platens has to be decreased to prevent scorching. The speed of mould closing has to be adjusted to allow complete filling of the mould and escape of all air, again without scorching. The pressure has to be sufficient to prevent thick flash but low enough to avoid excessive wear and tear on the mould. The moulded silicone piece will vary in size if the pressure is varied, because of the great compressibility of silicones. To optimise the use of material in compression moulding, the preform must be shaped and sized to minimise flash.

The mould shrinkage of silicone rubber is about 2-4% and is affected by a number of factors, but primarily that the linear thermal expansion of silicone rubber is 17-20 times that of steel and about 2 times that of organic rubber. The shrinkage is, therefore, largely dependent on the temperature of the moulding. It should be noted that silicone compounds with higher loadings of filler have lower shrinkage. Mould shrinkage is augmented by the release of volatiles during the cure and post-bake stages.

Injection moulding involves pressures of 5000-20,000 psi, and temperatures of 370-485°F. Injection times are approximately 3-10 seconds, while moulding time is in the range of 25-90 seconds. This method, relative to compression moulding gives less flash, better properties, and greater uniformity. Blow moulding has also been used on some simple parts. In this process, heavy-walled parts are usually made because of the variation in wall thickness.

Prehardened stainless steel is recommended for the moulds with chromium plating, also used where a high finish is desired and where the undercuts are minimal. Assistance in mould design is available from the basic silicone rubber suppliers. Silicone mould-release agents are unsuitable for use with silicone rubber. Household-detergent water solutions of 0.5-2.0% are recommended for spray or brush applications to the mould. A thin layer is preferred to avoid build up on the mould.

Extrusion

Gaskets, tubing, tape, wire and cable, seals, rods, channels, and hoses in a variety of shapes and sizes may be extruded. The equipment is similar to that used with organic rubber. When silicone rubber is extruded, however, the low green strength and decomposition temperature of the peroxide curing agent must be considered.

Typical extruders have screws with a length-to-diameter ratio of 10/1 to 12/1 although shorter screws are sometimes used. A single flight screw is usually used but sometimes a second flight is added near the discharge to minimise the pulsating of the extrusion. The screw has a compression ratio of 2/1 for harder stocks, and up to 4/1 for stickier stocks, or when less porosity or close tolerances are needed. The compression ratio is preferably provided by a variable-pitch screw, keeping the flight depths constant from feed to discharge. If the flight depth is reduced, there is a tendency in the longer barrels to build excessive heat. Because of the abrasive nature of silica fillers, especially the larger particle sizes, both the barrel and screws should be built of abrasion-resistant alloys. However, many of the organic rubber houses are successfully extruding tubing and wire and cable, using unhardened equipment. Both the barrel and screw should also be water-cooled to prevent scorch.

To prevent feeding problems, a roller feed is usually used. The roller is fed from a "hat" (coiled strips of compound) or from strips removed from an in-house mill. The roller should have a higher speed than the screw. The breaker plate should contain at least two screens (40-200 mesh) to ensure clean extrusions. A fine mesh is backed by a coarser backing screen. This assembly increases the back pressure that ensures air removal and better dimensional control. The finer screens will give cleaner extrusions, but will slow production and will have to be changed more often. Usually the screens are not cleaned but are discarded after removal.

A front flange assembly is used to hold and centre both the die and the mandrel (pin) when extruding tubing. Fine adjustments are made with adjusting screws on either the die or the pin. The die should be made from prehardened stainless steel and designed to produce smooth flow with no dead spaces to hold up material that may start to cure. The pin should be drilled so that low-pressure air can be used to support the tubing and keep it round. The die opening is often different from both the shape and size of the extrusion because of differential flow and die swell. These differences can be compensated for to some extent by reducing the thickness of the lasts where the die dimensions are smaller. Die swell is also greater if the silicone polymer is branched or if the extrusion is speeded up. More heavily loaded compounds have less die swell. The extrusion can be considerably reduced in size by stretching it before cure. Again, the shrinkage that takes place on curing and post-bake must be taken into account.

In forming wire and cable insulation, the extruder must be fitted with a cross-head. Reinforced hose may also be made by feeding tubing reinforced with high-temperature fibre or wire through a cross-head and extruding a second layer of silicone rubber over it.

Several methods of vulcanisation are available for extrusions. Hot-air vulcanisation is very common and the catalyst is *bis*-(2,4-dicholrobenzoyl) peroxide. Other catalysts are too volatile and cause bubbling in the extrudate and lead to undercure due to loss of catalyst. Two types of hot-air vulcanisation are possible – vertical and horizontal. In the horizontal type, the extrudate is laid on an endless belt and passes through an oven 10 to 30 feet long. The oven is usually at 600-800°F although the first zone may be cooler to minimise loss of the catalyst. Air turbulence should be present inside the oven to improve heat transfer and to drive off the volatile by-products. A vertical hot-air vulcaniser with a variable-speed drum at the top may also be used. Cure usually takes place only on the up-cycle, and speeds up to 60 feet per minute are obtained.

Although hot-air vulcanisation can be used to cure wire and cable insulation, continuous steam vulcanisation is usually used because it is much faster with speeds up to 1200 feet per minute. Benzoyl peroxide is preferred to 2,4-dichlorobenzoyl peroxide to avoid scorching. Continuous-steam vulcanisation is more expensive, longer, and more complicated. Other less common types of vulcanisation are steam autoclave vulcanisation, hot-liquid vulcanisation and fluidised-bed vulcanisation.

Calendering

Continuous thin sheets of unsupported silicone rubber are produced on a calender. One can also coat a reinforcing fabric on one side with a 3-roll calender or on both sides with a 4-roll calender. The resulting product gets its strength from the fabric and its flexibility, and good electrical properties and moisture resistance from the silicone rubber. Silicone rubber should be processed at slower speeds than organic rubber. The range of 0.2 to 2 feet per minute is best for the start-up until even release from the rolls is assured and running speeds are generally around 5 to 10 feet per minute.

Silicone rubber is often calendered onto fabrics such as glass,nylon, aromatic nylons, polyester, and cotton. A variety of waves are used. Woven fibre glass has the best combination of properties and is most commonly used with silicone rubber. The high-temperature properties of aromatic nylons are making them increasingly popular.

A typical 4-roll calendering set-up is shwon in Figure 9. An extruder or a ram feeds silicone rubber to the first and fourth rolls. These rolls are slower and warmer than the centre rolls. Since silicone rubber moves to the faster and cooler rolls, it is transferred to the centre rolls. The centre rolls then transfer the rubber to the fabric. While the outside rolls may be warmed to facilitate transfer, the temperature must be kept below 130°F in order to prevent scorching. If the silicone rubber is unsupported, the fabric is replaced with a liner. Poyester film, holland cloth, polyethylene and release-coated paper are commonly used. The liner is stripped off after cure or just before use if the sheet is to be used green. A major use for green sheet is to cut it into strips to build hoses or to manufacture electrical tape. A 3-roll calender is actually more common than a 4-roll calender. In that case, roll 4 in Figure 9 is eliminated.

Calendering sheet can be vulcanised in a steam autoclave, provided the roll is first pressure-taped. The thickness of the roll must be controlled and preferably heated inside and out to achieve complete cure. The sheet can also be cured or semi-cured by eliminating the liner feed, and bypassing the supported or unsupported sheet over a hot drum placed between the calender and the take-up roll.

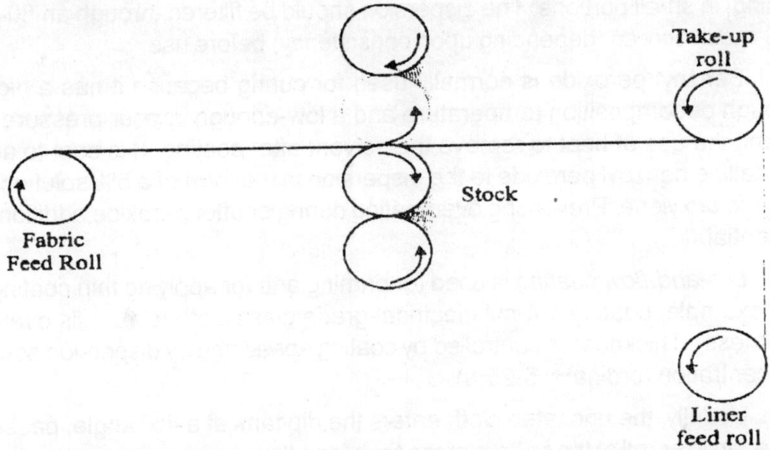

Fig. 9 : Schematic diagram of set-up for calendering supported sheet

Dispersion Coating of Fabric

This technique of fabric coating permits thinner coatings and provides more through penetration of the fabric than does calendering. A thin coat from a 5-15% silicone-rubber dispersion will improve the strength and flex life of glass cloth, and provide a good "anchor coat" for calendering. Excellent high-temperature electrical insulating materials, diaphragms, and gaskets can be made from glass cloth with thicker coatings. Silicone rubber can also be dispersion-coated on organic fabrics, and then used in many applications such as aircraft seals, radome covers, and general-purpose control diaphragms.

The silicone rubber is generally supplied by manufactures in dispersions of soft, readily dispersed pastes that have been especially designed for cloth coating. However, any silicone rubber compound can be dispersed in solvent and probably most dispersions are made at the fabricator's plant.

Xylene, toluene and mineral spirits are common solvents, except for the fluoroxilicones for which the solvent must be a ketone such as methyl ethyl or methyl isobutyl ketone. Chlorinated solvents and solvents containing antioxidants, rust inhibitors, and similar additives should be avoided since they interact with the peroxide vulcanising agent.

The coating pastes are readily dispersed with a propeller mixer. Compounds containing reinforcing fillers should be freshened, sheeted off thin, cut into small pieces, and soaked overnight in just enough solvent to cover the compound. The mixture should then be stirred with the propeller mixer until it becomes uniform. The remaining solvent is then added, with mixing, in small portions. The dispersion should be filtered through an 80- to 150-mesh screen (depending upon consistency) before use.

Benzoyl peroxide is normally used for curing because it has a high-enough decomposition temperature and a low-enough vapour pressure to permit the use of heat to remove the solvent after coating. It is best to add crystalline benzoyl peroxide to the dispersion in the form of a 5% solution in toluene or xylene. Preventing overheating during or after peroxide addition is essential.

Dip-and-flow coating is used for priming and for applying thin coatings (for example, coating a 4-mil electrical-grade glass cloth to 10 mils overall thickness). Thickness is controlled by coating speed and by dispersion solids concentration (ordinatily 5-25%).

Usually, the uncoated cloth enters the dip tank at a 45° angle, passes under an idler roll at the bottom of the tank, and then up into a vertical oven or coating tower. Excess dispersion flows off the cloth between the tank and the tower. The coating tower is heated by hot air, and, ideally, is divided into three zones. The solvent is removed in the first zone at 150-175°F. Vulcanisation takes place in the second zone at 300-400°F in the case of glass cloth, and at 250-300°F in the case of organic fabrics. When glass cloth is being coated, the third zone is maintained at 480-600°F. This last temeprature range removes final traces of volatiles, including peroxide decomposition products. Maximum bond to the cloth and optimum electrical properties are developed in the third zone.

Dispersion coating is somewhat faster than calendering, with speeds of 10-20 feet per minute common.

Dip-and-knife coating is similar to dip-and-flow. However, thicker dispersions (35% solids is typical) are used, and a knife or rod is placed between the dip tank and the tower. The coated fabric is pulled past the knife (a second knife can be placed on the opposite side of the fabric), which wipes off excess dispersion. Thickness is controlled by dispersion solids concentration and knife position relative to the fabrics. Heavier coatings can be obtained by this method than by dip-and-flow.

In *reverse-roll coating*, the knife is replaced by a roll which rotates in opposition to the direction of the cloth movement. This often improves penetration.

Heavy-duty Hose

The production of hose on a continuous basis was described earlier in the section on extrusions. Heavy-duty hose for autos, trucks, aircraft and industrial use requires different techniques. Uncured and semi-cured, unsupported and fabric-supported silicone rubber sheets and tape may be fabricated into ducts and heavy-duty hose. This is done by wrapping a hollow mandrel, a collapsible mandrel, a core made with a low-temperature-melging alloy or a foundry sand core. Aluminium mandrels are widely used, but release of the finished part is often a problem. The mandrel should be sprayed or brushed with a dilute aqueous solution of household detergent or dusted with mica or talc.

The aluminium mandrel works best for straight sections of hose. Silicone rubber sheets are wrapped around the mandrel to the desired thickness. It is easier to get a tight, wrinkle-free construction if the mandrel is turned on a lathe. Smooth liner for hose may be made by butt-wrapping uncured tape or sheet on the mandrel, or by using extruded and cured tubing.

For more complex shapes with curves, a core made from a low-tmperature-melting alloy or from foundry sand and resin is often used. The cores are spiral-wrapped with fabric-reinforced tape cut on a a 45° bias. Bias-cut tapes are more stretchy and give the hose maximum flexibility.

After the hose has been built, it should be pressure-taped with wet cotton or wet nylon. This is necessary to prevent sponging during cure, and to provide maximum ply adhesion.

Curing is usually accomplished by running steam into the hollow mandrel, or by placing the warpped core in a steam autoclave. Curing time and temperature depend upon the peroxide used, and the heat capacity of the hose assembly. Following cure, the pressure tape should be removed, and the mandrel stripped, while the assembly is still warm. The release agent should be washed off before the part is oven post-baked. If a core of a low-temperature-melting alloy has been used, the alloy is melted to free the cured hose. If a core of foundry sand has been used, the brittle core is broken up to release the cured hose.

Bonding

Silicone rubber can be bonded to many materials, including iron, nickel, copper, zinc, aluminium, titanium, various steels, ceramics, glass, masonry, many plastics, organic and inorganic fabrics, vulcanised and unvulcanised silicone rubber and other elastomers.

In all cases, it is essential to thoroughly clean the surface to be bonded. Metal surfaces containing loose scales, oxides, other salts, and embedded dirt should be sandblasted, sandpapered or acid-etched. Metal surfaces should be cleaned with a solvent such as methylene chloride or trichloroethylene. Some surfaces, such as plastics and vulcanised rubbers, should be roughened with abrasives. It helps to wash the surface with acetone before application of the primer. Primers are applied in dilute solution by brushing, dipping or spraying. If the bond is inadequate, the layer of primer may be too thick or the primer solution may be too concentrated. One may also try several primers to find the one best suited to the particular materials being bonded.

The typical primer for silicone ruober has two types of reactive sites. The first reactive site reacts with the surface hydroxyls of the metals, glass, or masonry. The reactive specie is usually an alkoxy silane (e.g., SiOMe) which hydrolyses to a hydroxy silane that can then form either a hydrogen bond or a covalent bond with the surface hydroxyls. A catalyst to speed this reaction may also be present. The second reactive site in the primer is some type of unsaturation to react with the silicone rubber. The hydrolysis of the alkoxysilanes usually takes place within 60 minutes of the time the primer is applied. The reaction with the surface hydroxyls takes place while the primer is drying and also during vulcanisation. The reaction of the primer unsaturation with the silicone rubber takes place during vulcanisation and is catalysed by peroxide.

Bonding Unvulcanised Silicone Rubber

A curing agent should be added to the freshened compound. After preforming, the stock should be carefully laid on the freshly primed surface. Vulcanisation must be done under heat and pressure at temperatures appropriate to the peroxide used. Approximately 15-30 minutes at 330-350°F is usually sufficient when using dicumyl peroxide or VAROX, and 15-30 minutes at 260-280°F, when using powered benzoyl peroxide. A stepped oven post-bake is usually required to develop optimum bond strength.

The self-bonding compounds may be bonded to many metals in the same manner, except that no primer is required. Unlike bonding to primed surfaces, this technique is insensitive to part geometry and to the degree of compound flow in the mould during bonding.

Bonding Vulcanised Silicone Rubber

Cured silicone rubber may be bonded to a primed surface with a 10-40 mil interlayer of heat-curing silicone rubber adhesive. Vulcanisation is conducted under heat and pressure. The pressure must not be so great as to squeeze out the adhesive. This bonding can also be accomplished under pressure at room temperature with a room-temperature-vulcanising silicone rubber adhesive. Both techniques can be used for splicing, or for bonding cured silicone rubber to itself.

The self-bonding compounds are excellent for bonding cured silicone rubber to itself, and are recommended for splicing. These bonds will usually be stronger than those obtained with adhesives.

Post-baking

With trimming or deflashing, oven post-baking is often the final step in the fabrication of silicone rubber parts. Post-baking removes volatile materials such as low-molecular-weight silicones and peroxide decomposition products. Removal of the low-molecular-weight silicones results in less shrinkage later and in low extractables. Removal of the peroxide decomposition products improves reversion resistance, compression set, electrical properties, chemical resistance, and the bond to other substrates.

Ovens should have forced-air circulation with no dead-air pockets. Air flow should be sufficient to keep the oven atmosphere outside the explosion limits of the volatiles from the rubber. Oven vents to the outside of the building should be checked periodically to ensure that they are not plugging up and reducing air flow. Temp erature control should be ± 10°F and the oven should go up to 500-600°F. The oven should be equipped with a temperature-limit switch, and a safety switch should be provided to turn off the heat if the blower stops.

The rubber charge should be on stainless steel trays designed to provide maximum contact with the circulating air. The parts must not be in contact with one another, as this would slow the removal of volatiles and lead to parts sticking together.

For some applications, no post-bake is necessary. However, it is generally desirable to post-bake at least a few hours at 300-400°F. Usually, longer cures to at least 50°F above the service temperature are required. Thicker sections should be step-cured, especially if the aroyl peroxides have been used. Also, 2,4-dichlorobenzoic acid and benzoic acid will cause internal reversion if the part containing them is not step-cured.

There are no set curing schedules that will cover every situation that a fabricator may encounter. In each case, the optimum curing schedule must be worked out. The size and shape of the part, number of parts in the oven, and the air flow through the oven, have major influences on the curing cycle. A possible schedule for a thicker part is 3 hours at 300°F followed by 4 hours at 350°F followed by 10 hours at 400°F.

LIQUID SILICONE RUBBER COMPOUNDS

The silicone rubber polymers we have dealt with up to now have a common formula with the polymers in liquid silicone rubbers, i.e..

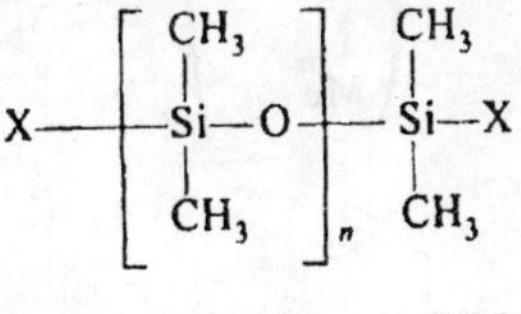

However, while n = 200-1500 for the liquid silicone rubbers, it equals 3000-11,000 for the conventional silicone rubbers. For liquid silicone rubber, the chain-stopper X depends on the cure system and is typically hydroxy, vinyl or methoxy. For the conventional silicone rubbers, the chain-stopper X is typically methyl or vinyl. The liquid silicone rubber compounds have historically been called *room-temperature-vulcanising* (RTV) rubber, but the group does contain some compounds which are vulcanised at high temperature. Indeed, the high-temperature-addition-cure liquid systems have a combination of easy processing, fast cure, and excellent physical properties. Good growth is anticipated in this area as experience is gained by the processors.

Liquid silicone rubber is not quite as old as the higher-consistency silicone rubber. The production of liquid silicone rubbers requires careful quality control if the material is not to cure prematurely or too slowly. Thus they are sold as "ready-to-use" products.

Suitable compounding ingredients include the silicone polymer, cross-linker, and catalyst as well as the usual reinforcing and extending fillers, colour pigments, heat age additives, adhesion promoters, stabilisers, thickeners, plasticisers, and other additives.

Liquid silicone rubbers come in both one- and two-component systems. Chemically they can be subdivided by cure type into the three categories below.

Condensation Cure – One-component

These are called one-component systems because both the catalyst and cross-linking agent are incorporated in the base compound at the time of manufacture.

These one-component systems are dependent on moisture for curing. They are generally made by compounding a silanol-stopped silicone polymer with an excess of cross-linker. A reaction takes place during compounding, end stopping the polymer with the cross-linker.

Upon exposure to atmospheric moisture, further reaction takes place, leading to cure of the rubber. Both steps are shown below -

i. Reactions during compounding

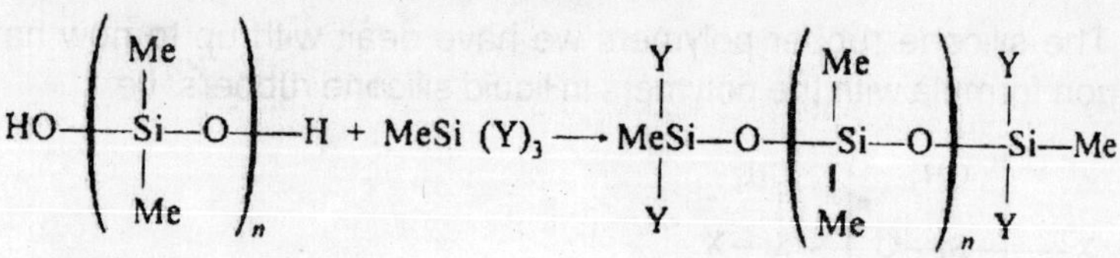

2. Reaction during cure

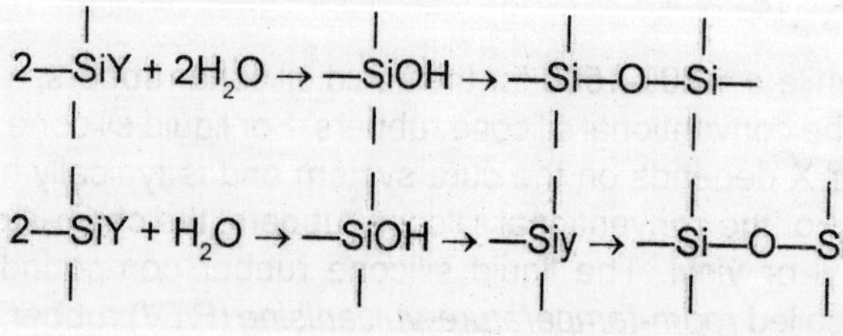

Vulcanisation occurs first at the surface, and then progresses inward with the diffusion of moisture into the rubber.

These rubbers are classified as acidic, basic, or natural, depending on the nature of the byproduct hydrolysed during the cure. Acids released are acetic and 2-ethylhexanoic. Bases released are cyclohexylamine and butylamine. Neutral groups used are aldoxime, ketoxime, alkoxy, enolate, aminoxy, and amido.

Organo-tin and organo-titanium catalysts are used in small amounts. These products make excellent adhesive sealants, formed-in-place gaskets and can be used to form films from solvent dispersion.

Condensation Cure – Two-component

These are called two-component systems because the cross-linker and (or) catalyst must be added to the base compound just before use. They are generally made by using a silanol chain-stopped polymer. The cross-linker is usually an alkoxy silane or oligomers thereof (e.g., ethyl o-silicate) and the catalyst is an organic tin compound such as dibutyl-tin-diacetate, dioctyl-tin-maleate or dibutyl-tin dilaurate. Theatalyst level is generally much higher in the two-component systems than in the one-component. Applications include moulds for plastic parts, coatings, adhesives, therapeutic gels, and encapsulants. This system is used where deep-section cures are needed although aeration to remove the ethanol byproduct is desirable for complete cure. The cure can be independent of moisture although moisture can accelerate the cure.

$$6\ \text{—SiOH} + (\text{EtO})_3\ \text{SiOSi}\ (\text{OEt})_3 \xrightarrow{\text{Sn}} (\text{—SiO})_3\ \text{SiOSi}\ (\text{OSi—})_3$$

Addition Cure

These are usually two-component systems although one-component is possible if the catalyst is inhibited sufficiently. In this case, the inhibitor must be volatilised, or decomposed by heat in order to start the cure. These systems are made by adding a polyfunctional silicon hydride cross-linker to a vinyl containing silicone polymer. Vinyl on the end of the polymer is more reactive than vinyl on the chain. The catalyst is usually a complex of platinum although palladium, rhodium and ruthenium are also used -

$$\text{—Si—H} + \text{CH}_2 = \text{CH Si—} \xrightarrow{\text{pt}} \text{Si—CH}_2\text{—CH}_2\text{—Si—}$$

The reaction is exothermic, but the concentration of reactive groups is too low to cause much of a temperature rise. This system is used where deep section cures are needed in a confined space since there are no volatile by-products. They have excellent resistance to compression set and to reversion. Applications include flexible moulds, dip-coating, and the potting and encapsulation of electrical and electronic components.

The cure rate and physical properties of all the liquid silicone rubber compounds can be varied over a rather wide range by suitable choice of polymer type and molecular weight, reinforcing and extending fillers, pigment, cross-linker, and type and concentration of catalyst.

RELATION BETWEEN PROPERTIES OF CRUDE AND CURED SILICONE COMPOUNDS

In silica filled silicone rubber, a sharp increase in elastic modulus or conductivity appears when the silica loading exceeds a critical value (see the thin line on Figure 9). The experimental data are well-fitted by a power-law as in the case of a percolation mechanism.

The microscopic observations corroborate the connectivity of the silica particles after the critical threshold.

Microscopy also reveals that the filler particles in the established network are always separated by the bound which surrounds the particles.

When using different kinds of silica, it can be demonstrated that this threshold coincides with the optimum of elongation at break versus filler concentration (Figures 9 and 10).

Moreover, if one uses the elasticity law in the limit conditions, ultimate strength behaviour can be deduced from those of elongation at break and modulus (Figure 11). Other obviousness of the influence of the filler network can be found when studying the swelling of the vulcanisates.

So, it seems reasonable to attribute the ultimate properties behaviour of the vulcanisates to the organisation of the filler particles which is already established in the corresponding crude compound.

10

Reclaimed Rubber

INTRODUCTION

Reclaimed rubber is the product resulting when waste vulcanised scrap rubber is treated to produce a plastic material which can be easily processed, compounded and vulcanised without the addition of either natural or synthetic rubbers. It is recognised that the vulcanisation process is not truly reversible; however, an accepted definition for devulcanisation is that it is a change in vulcanised rubber which results in a decreased resistance to deformation at ordinary temperatures.

Reclaimed rubber is manufactured by suitable treatment to old and worn out tyres, tubes and other used rubber articles with certain chemical agents. A substantial devulcanisation or regeneration is effected to the rubber compound in this process whereby its original plasticity is regained. In short it may be stated that reclaiming is essentially a depolymerisation process where the combined sulphur is not removed. The reclaimed rubber is used in the manufacture of rubber goods, with or without admixuture of natural or synthetic rubber.

Recycled rubber can be more generally described as any sort of rubber waste that has been converted into an economically useful form such as reclaimed rubber, ground rubber, reprocessed synthetic rubber, and die-cut punched parts.

One method of recycling some scrap is to grind it as fine as possible and work it into new rubber as an elastomeric filler. This was the first method of reclaiming and is suitable only for compounding carriage springs, which were fairly large barrel-shaped moulded articles but not suitable for footwear products.

In order to make a high-quality reclaim, the fibre must be removed from the rubber scrap by soaking the rubber in water, and then taking a small knife and starting the rubber from the cloth and stripping it off. But this was not an effective way to produce large quantities of products.

TYPES OF RECLAIM

A variety of grades or reclaimed rubber is offered today, but mention is made here of only the important ones.

Whole Tyre Reclaim

Whole tyre reclaim is the one produced in the largest quantity. First-quality reclaim made from whole tyres contains about 45% rubber hydrocarbon by weight. The remaining 55% consists of valuable carbon black, a little mineral filler, and softeners, all of which are substantially unchanged by the reclaim manufacturing operation, and may be considered to function as virgin materials. The manufacturing process of tyre from reclaim rubber is shown in Figure 1.

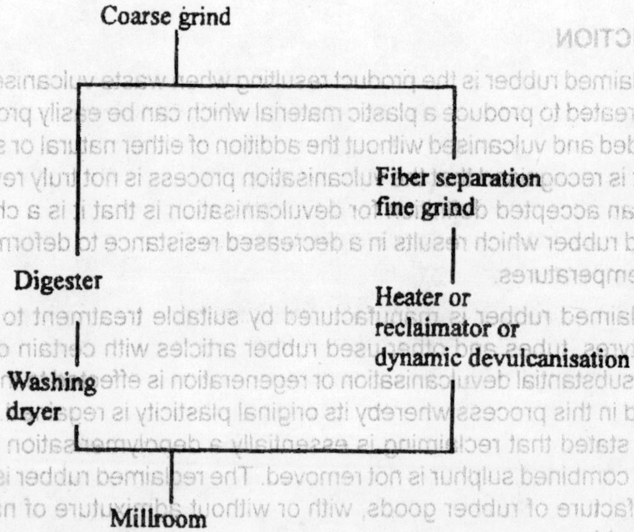

Fig. 1 : Flow diagram of manufacturing process for whole tyre reclaim

Minimum Staining Reclaim

Minimum staining reclaim can replace the conventional whole tyre material when occasion demands. As implied, it has a much lower tendency to stain, by either migration or contact, than conventional reclaim. The reduction in staining characteristics is acheived by the use of activated-carbon non-staining oils and by selecting tyres containing a higher proportion of natural to synthetic rubber.

Drab and Coloured Reclaims

As the names imply, drab and coloured reclaims are made from non-black scrap. The digester process is usually employed and, when fabric is present, a small addition of caustic is made in order to destroy it. The period of heat treatment is usually several hours at 195°C.

Butyl Reclaim

Whereas reclaimed rubbers have been successfully produced from scrap CR, NBR, SI, and other speciality rubbers, the only one of substantial commercial importance is butyl reclaim. The starting material for this is butyl inner tubes. A modified digester process is adopted, every precaution being taken to avoid contamination by NR or SBR, because of their adverse effect on the curing characteristics of the butyl. Extensive control tests are necessary to ensure that the curing properties are satisfactory. The nerve of butyl reclaim is much reduced compared with that of the original polymer. Because of this, compounds containing butyl reclaim will mix, calender, and extrude faster and more smoothly than similar compounds based on virgin rubber.

EVOLUTION OF RECLAIMING PROCESSES

It had been common knowledge for many years that acid has a degrading effect on fabric and that rubber is resistant to acid. In the acid process, the ground scrap was boiled for several hours in a farily strong solution of either sulphuric or muriatic acid to destroy the fabric; the rubber was washed and then devulcanised with high-pressure steam in the pan process. It was a two-step operation.

Although the acid process was used quite successfully for a period of time, there were problems with the method. If the acid was not thoroughly washed, it could cause poor ageing characteristics. More important, there were coming on the market many types of higher-sulphur scraps, such as bicylcle-tyre scrap, that could not be processed by the acid method. If the high quantities of free sulphur in such types of rubber scraps are not removed, they tend to cause further vulcanisation during the open steam heater process rather than devulcanisation. Something better was needed.

A breakthrough came with the invention that came to be known as the *alkali digester process*. The ground rubber, fibre, and a dilute solution of caustic soda were cooked at high pressure for about 20 hours. This system caused the defibring, desulphuring, and devulcanisation of the rubber scrap *all in one step*. This technique could be used to reclaim any type of rubber scrap available at that time. Later, on an improved method which involved steam-jacketing the vessel and agitation of the mass is developed. This is the cooking method used by most reclaimers.

In the devulcanisation of rubber two other important developments involved the introduction of new machines to greatly improve the quality of reclaimed rubber. One development was the *refiner*, which is a special type of mill used to produce a much more smooth and homogeneous product than would otherwise be possible. The other was *the strainer*, which is used to remove foreign matter from the rubber. With the exception of invention of the reclaimator.

RECLAIMING PROCESSES

Scrap-rubber Preparation

The first stage of any reclaiming process is size reduction of the scrap. This is most generally accomplished using corrugated two-roll cracker mills. Other types of equipment have been employed such as a rotating cutter to obtain a rip, tear, or shear action, while others have rotating-knife slitter actions. The capital cost for these types of equipment is less than for a standard two-roll cracker installation; however, in most cases they have not been proven to be heavy-duty enough to withstand 24-hour operation.

The tyre bead wire is either cut from the carcass before grinding or manually removed after the first pass through the cracker. At many points in the system, the ground rubber is passed over magnetic separation equipment to remove remaining bead wire and steel belt wire. Gyratory classifier screens return the oversize rubber particles to the cracker for further size reduction. There may be more than one stage of grinding before the desired size of approximately 3/8 inch is obtained. At this point, the coarse-ground rubber could be conveyed to the digester or processed further for one of the other devulcanisation methods.

The fibre from the coarse-ground tyres is removed by some sort of fluidised-bed, specific-gravity table. The action of controlled streams of air moving through a bed of ground rubber on an inclined gyrating table of special design causes the fibre to separate from the clean rubber. The size of the rubber particles may now be further reduced to perhaps 20 or 30 mesh by fine grinding. Fine-corrugated, high-friction mills are employed in this operation.

Reclaimed Rubber

By the application of heat and chemical agents to ground vulcanised waste rubber, a substantial regeneration of the rubber compound to its original plastic state is effected, yielding a product known as 'reclaim' or reclaimed rubber, capable of being processed, compounded, and revulcanised. The process is essentially one of depolymerisation. Reclaimed rubber has become weidely accepted as a raw material which possesses processing and economic characteristics that are of great value in the compounding of natural and synthetic rubber stocks.

There are four principal reclaiming processes in use today, of which the digester and reclaimator processes are important.

The raw material for reclaiming is scrap rubber in a wide variety of forms, but tyres, as is to be expected, form the major quantity.

The first stage, in all processes, are the cracking and grinding of the scrap rubber to reduce it to a crumb passing through a 20 to 30 mesh screen.

Digester Process

At one time, most reclaim was made using the digester process. A digester is essentially a steam-jacketed, agitator-equipped autoclave, mounted either horizontally or vertically. This is a wet process in which the coarsely ground scrap is submerged in a solution of water and reclaiming agents. These agents may include many types of light and/or heavy oils, naval stores, pine tar and coal tar pitches, and chemical peptisers.

Until the advent of synthetic rubber, the digesting solution also included caustic soda to remove free sulphur and to act as a defibring agent. In fact, the process was generally referred to as the *alkali digester method*.

The ground waste is loaded into a digester along with water, reclaiming okils, and other additives, such as activated black (for minimum staining grades). The digester is a cylindrical jacketed pressure vessel fitted with a horizontal agitator, and steam can be supplied to both interior and jacket, thus enabling a uniform temperature to be maintained throughout the mass. The contents of the digester are then heated to about 190°C and maintained at this temperature for some 4-10 hours with continuous agitation. The digester is then 'blown down', and the contents deposited on to a conveyor. Any necessary adjustments to the specific gravity and plasticity by addition of plasticiser, carbon black, or fillers are carried out in a ribbon blender, and stock is then automatically conveyed to extruders for straining, refining, and leafing on to a drum from which it is removed in slabs.

Reclaimator Process

The reclaimator process is the only commercially successful continuous technique for devulcanising tire scrap; all the others are batch processes. Tyres are ground, the metal and fibre are mechanically separated, then the rubber is further ground to a fine particle size. This fine-ground rubber and the various reclaiming agents are all metered into a blending system and conveyed to the reclaimator.

The reclaimator is a special type of screw-extrusion machine. It is jacketed to provide for several zones of contolled temperature using either hot oil or cooling water; in addition, the clearances between the screw and the chamber wall are close and adjustable. The object is to subject the rubber to a controlled amount of high heat and pressure in a continuously moving environment. The residence time of the rubber in the machine is less than 5 minutes. During this period, the rubber undergoes devulcanisation. After the softened rubber is discharged from the head of the machine, it is cooled and further processed in refining mills just as is done in other reclaiming methods.

It can be shown that ground vulcanised rubber heated in a temperture range of 120-200°C undergoes a rapid initial increase in plasticity, and, on continued heating, passes through an inversion point and rehardens unit, after prolonged heating, a further but slower increase in plasticity is attained. It follows, therefore, that three points of equal plasticity occur in this cycle (Figure 2)

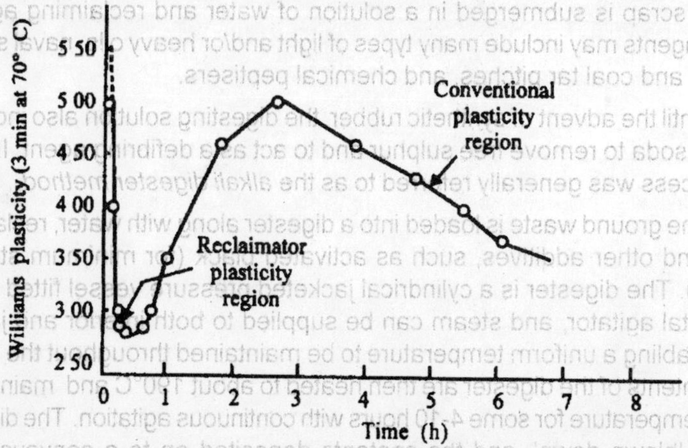

Fig. 2 : Plasticity time curve for rubber in steam at 170°C; note that the more plastic the material, the lower the Williams plasticity value because it is the pellet thickness after compression

Although this behaviour is characteristics for certain vulcanised rubbers, the resultant plasticity-time relationship will vary with the type of rubber, reclaiming agents, and physical conditions used. Synthetic rubbers behave in a similar manner, but the rehardening process tends to predominate, so the initial increase in plasticity is less marked and can only be achieved under special conditions.

Whereas some earlier processes completed the cycle mentioned above, the reclaimator process depends on arresting the reaction at the point where the initial rapid increase in plasticity is achieved in the presence of plasticisers, oxygen, and catalytic materials. The rapid heating of the rubber while it is being worked mechanically gives the desired plasticity in a matter of 3-6 minutes. The total cycle time is only 30 minutes, and the process is entirely dry.

The reclaimator machine, from which the process takes its name, is of the screw extrusion type with a hopper at one end into which the crumb previously mixed with oil and chemicals is automatically fed at a predetermined rate. It generates its own heat for depolymerisation by mechanically working the finely divided rubber crumb under pressure, and then discharges it as reclaimed rubber. Temperatures in the machine are controlled by alternating oil and water jackets.

The raw material for this process is whole tyres, and, in the preparation of the crumb, fabric is removed mechanically by a series of operations in which fractionating and sizing screens, harmer mills and reel beaters, air flotation, and gravity tables are used. The reclaimed rubber is compounded as necessary and refined and sheeted using conventional machines. The full sequence of the above operations is shown in the flow charts (Figures 3 and 4)

Pan Process

This is the simplest of all the reclaiming processes. A "heater" is a large, single-shell horizontal pressure vessel or autoclave. The ground rubber is mixed with reclaiming agents in an open ribbon mixer then placed into containers rolled into the vessel. The main consideration is to allow an even penetration of heat in the mass of rubber. To achieve this uniform steam penetration, shallow pans or boats equipped with hollow metal pipes or inverted "V" sections are used as the stock containers. Live steam at pressure of 100-250 psi with cycle times of 5 to 12 hours are typical.

The raw material, fabric free, is cracked on the same type of equipment as for whole tyre. The ground waste intimately mixed with the required oils is loaded into steam vulcanisers and subjected to steam heating at pressure of the order of 10 kg/cm^2. This is followed by straining and refining in the conventional manner. Not only NR and SBR scraps but also IIR, CR and NBR compounds are reclaimed by this method.

Engelke Process

This process is extremely simple as it requires no wetting of the stock or elimination of the fibre. Vulcanised scrap rubber containing fabric is subjected to very high temperatures for short periods of time, 10-20 minutes and upwards, in small autoclaves. Any fibre is completely carbonised *in situ* throughout the mass. The cracked stock, when necessary, can be premixed with plasticising oils and peptisers. The reclaim is strained and refined in the usual manner.

Testing and Evaluations of Reclaimed Rubber

The resting and evaluation of reclaimed rubber includes both chemical and physical testing. Although the list of tests given in Table 1 is very comprehensive, the decision as to which tests must be applied to a particular reclaimed will depend upon the end product and the specification agreed between the consumer and manufacturer. In general, the test methods are those laid down by the BSI for the testing of vulcanised rubber.

DYNAMIC DEVULCANISATION

The digester process has been used for decades, and millions of tons of excellent-quality reclaim have been produced. However, it became apparent

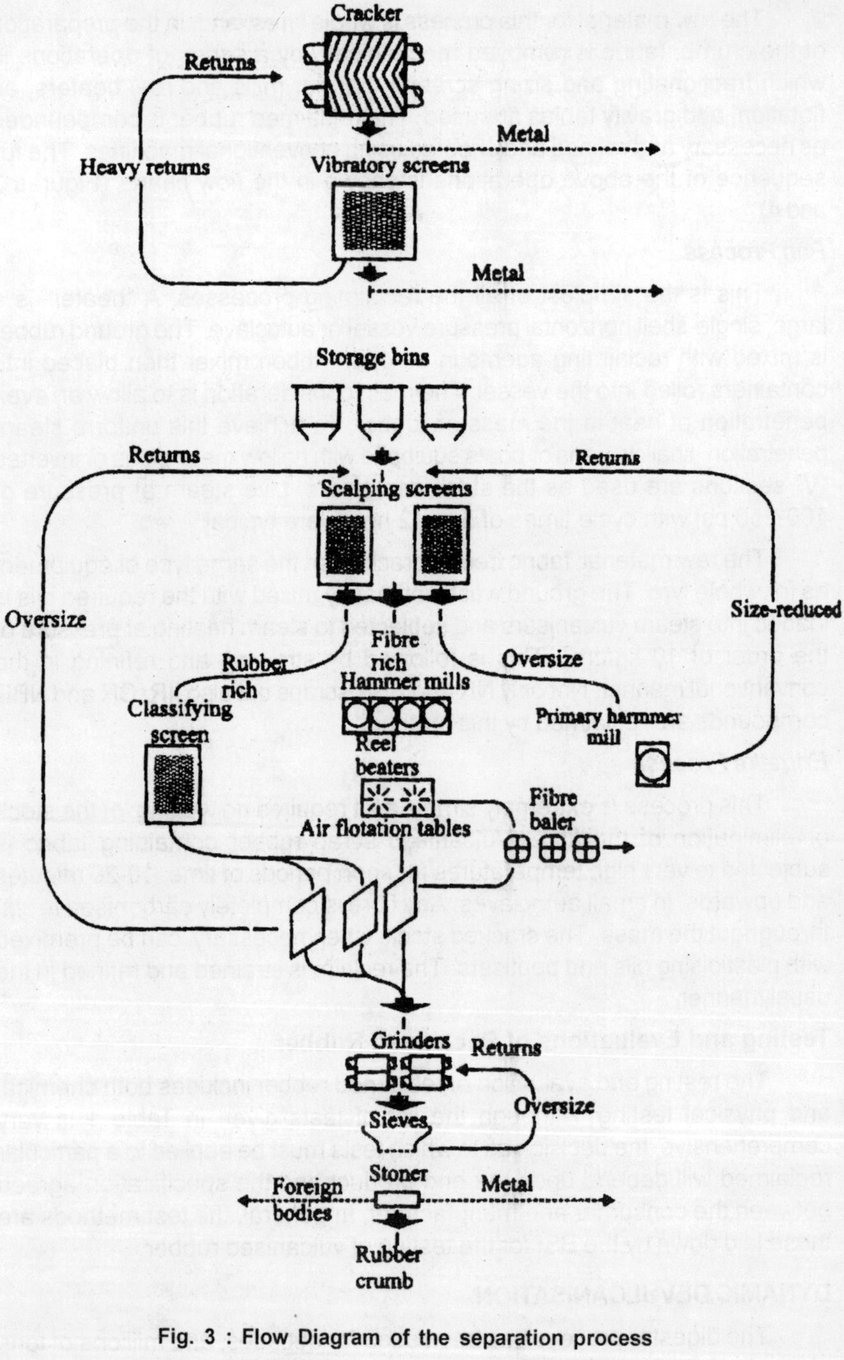

Fig. 3 : Flow Diagram of the separation process

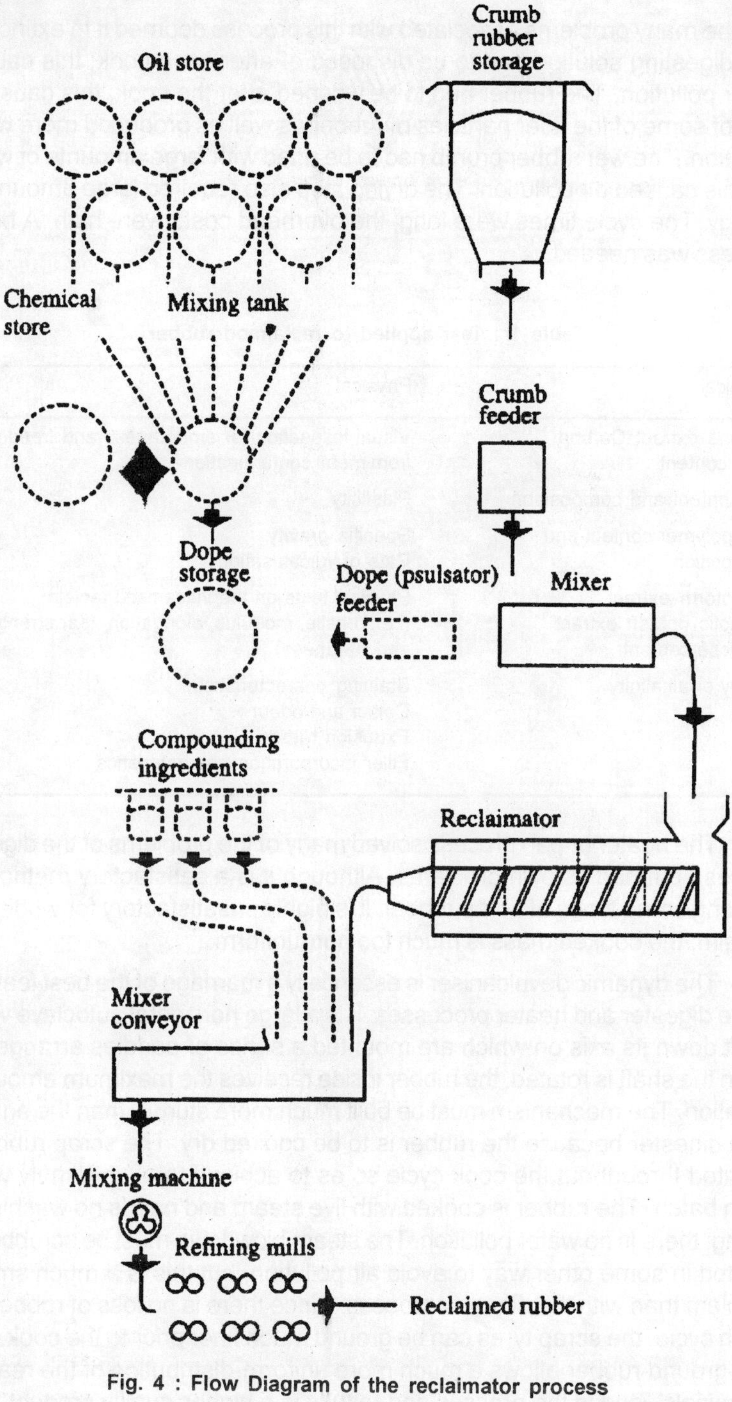

Fig. 4 : Flow Diagram of the reclaimator process

that the many problems associated with this process doomed it to extinction. The digesting solution had to be disposed of after each cook; this caused water pollution. The rubber had to be washed after the cook; this caused a loss of some of the finer particles of rubber as well as produced more water pollution. The wet rubber crumb had to be dried with large amounts of warm air; this caused air pollution. The drying step also required large amounts of energy. The cycle times were long; the overhead costs were high. A better process was needed.

Table 1 : Test applied to reclaimed rubber

Chemical	Physical
Acetone extract Carbon black content	Visual inspection for smoothness and freedom from metal contamination
Ash content and composition	Plasticity
Total polymer content and composition	Specific gravity Rate of vulcanisation
Chloroform extract Alcoholic potash extract Cellulose content	Physical tests on the vulcanised reclaim (i.e., tensile, modulus, elongation, tear strength, and hardness)
Acidity or alkalinity	Staining characteristics Colour and odour Extrusion rate Filler incorporation characteristics

The heater or pan process solved many of the problems of the digester process but had its own problems. Although it is a satisfactory method for cooking some types of scrap rubber, it is highly unsatisfactory for whole tyre reclaim; the cooked mass is much too non-uniform.

The dynamic devulcaniser is essentially a marriage of the best features of the digester and heater processes. It is a large horizontal autoclave with a shaft down its axis on which are mounted a series of paddles arranged so when the shaft is rotated, the rubber inside receives the maximum amount of agitation. The mechanism must be built much more sturdily than the agitator on a digester because the rubber is to be cooked dry. The scrap rubber is agitated throughout the cook cycle so as to achieve total uniformity within each batch. The rubber is cooked with live steam and needs no washing or drying; there is no water pollution. The steam blowdown must be scrubbed or treated in some other way to avoid air pollution, but this is a much smaller problem than with the digester process. Since there is no loss of rubber in a wash cycle, the scrap tyres can be ground much finer prior to the cook. This fine-ground rubber allows a much more uniform-distribution of the reactive chemicals used in the process and results in a higher-quality product.

The dynamic devulcaniser enables a higher-quality product and also a more economical one. The finer particles of rubber and its continuous agitation allows higher steam pressures and shorter cycles. The greater uniformity of the cooked stock allows higher production rates in the millroom. Both of these factors increase productivity and reduce costs in a very capital-intensive industry – necessary if reclaim is to compete against synthetic rubber in the market.

Millroom Operations

The rubber that has been softened by one of the methods described above is then converyed to the millroom for the final stage of the reclaiming process. The stock is generally first mixed with weighed amounts of pigments, carbon black, or other ingredients in a blender. Next, an extended barrel mixer strainer may be used to warm and plasticate the stock. It is then fed to a high-friction breaker mill and on to the strainer where tramp metal and other foreign particles are removed. The final milling step is the finishing refiner. A high friction ratio for the refiner mill is achieved with different-size rolls turning at considerably different speeds. The rolls are set quite tightly to obtain a thin sheet of rubber. The object is a product that is smooth, uniform, and free of grain or lumps.

In the past, the finished sheet from the refiner was pulled to a windup drum and allowed to build up to a thickness of perhaps an inch before being cut off by hand with a small knife. The resulting rubber slab was dusted and stacked. Today most reclaim manufacturers use balers to package their product.

THE ADVANTAGES OF USING RECLAIMED RUBBER

The primary, but not exclusive, advantage of using reclaimed rubber in the manufacture of tyres and other rubber goods is one of cost. There are, of course, the direct cost savings resulting from the lower cost of the reclaimed product as compared to natural rubber and virgin synthetic rubbers, but there are equally important indirect cost benefits resulting from the proper use of reclaim.

Special strengths Through Reclaiming

Whole-tyre reclaim is extremely uniform due to the extensive blending that occurs at every step of the manufactring process. What is produced is best considered as a unique new raw material rather than some sort of modified SBR/natural blend. Just like any other ingredient chosen by the compounder to be incorporated into a formula, the raw material – reclaimed rubber – has its specific purposes. The purpose of reducing formula compound cost is certainly a legitimate one; however, there are other reasons to include reclaim in a formula that will result in processing advantages and indirect, but real savings.

When the vulcanised tyre rubber is reclaimed, it is softened through a reduction by scission of the molecular weight of the cross-linked elastomeric chains. That is, carbon-carbon bonds in the synthetic and natural-rubber polymers are broken, not the sulphur cross-links that are formed when the tyre is vulcanised. The result is a system of cross-linked fragments that is much more "three-dimensional" in nature than the original polymers.

The three-dimensional character of the rubber fragments causes the reclaim to have properties different from the original tyre compound. The shorter length of the polymer chains that make up the fragments give a lower tensile strength than the original compound when the reclaim is revulcanised. However, the three-dimensional nature of the fragmented elastomers in reclaim also produces some very desirable properties. The most important of these is the dimensional stability and reduced nerve imparted to compounds that include reclaim, improving the rate and the gauge stability of calendered and extruded stocks. The improved calendering production rate and lower reject rate result in significant cost savings that should be considered in the calculation of formula costs.

Further Advantages of Reclaiming - Applications

The intense mechanical work and chemical treatment given to the rubber in the reclaiming process result in further properties very beneficial to the end user. Reclaim can be expected to break down in mixing much more quickly than virgin polymers. This means that the mixing cycle can be shortened or, in the case of a two-pass mix, the reclaim can be added in the second pass. The reduced mixing time equals more indirect savings in the form of greater productivity - more product using less labour and overhead cost per unit.

In addition to the reduced mixing time when using reclaim, studies have shown that there is a sizable reduction in power consumption during mixing. This is significant at today's power cost, and will become even more important as the cost of electric power continues to escalate.

Reclaim can be used in a great many different applications. Where cost is a primary consideration and tensile strength requirements are not particularly demanding, reclaim can be the sole source of polymer. Examples of such products are mats and semipneumatic tyres. In other cases, reclaim is blended with virgin synthetic and natural rubber. The virgin polymer adds strength and the reclaim contributes to improved processing, cooler mixing, and less sensitive, less scorchy cure systems. Such applications include most of the constituent parts of both passenger and truck tyres, bias and radial-ply.

Formulating with reclaim is not difficult, but the compounder must remember that reclaim, unlike most processing additives that do little to the cure except for dilution, enters into the cure system. The reclaim elastomers become part of the overall cross-linked system. However, it is unrealistic to expect that the optimum cure system used with synthetic and/or natural rubber polymers will remain the same when reclaim is added. The optimum cure system must be re-established when reclaim is added, just as it should be whenever changes are made to the types or proportions of virgin rubber.

The material, mixing, manpower, and energy-consumption savings associated with reclaimed rubber are but a part of the total benefit of its use. These savings are substantial and significant, but there are further positive aspects to the use of reclaim, which accrue to our society as a whole. They include the employment of hundreds of people in the reclaim industry and the alleviation of solid-waste-disposal problems. They also include the conservation of petrochemical raw materials, conservation of the energy required to convert the petrochemicals into synthetic rubber, and conservation of the foreign exchange needed to pay for imported oil, a large proportion of the petrochemicals' source.

Major Uses of Reclaimed Rubber

i. Carcass, sidewell and undertread or passenger, light-truck and off-road tyres
ii. Tubeless passenger-tyre innerliner
iii. Inner tubes
iv. Semipneumatic tyres
v. Automotive floor mats
vi. Mechanical goods
vii. Adhesive, sealing, and tape compounds
viii. Rubberised asphalt.

Typical formulations of reclaimed rubber as used in various applications are given below -

Automobile floor mat

Ingredients	Amount
Whole tyre premix	250.00
SBR 1712	70.00
Zinc oxide	2.00
Stearic acid	2.00
Benzothiazyl disulphide	2.30
Methyl zimate	0.56
Sulphur	5.00
Hard clay	70.00

Calcium carbonate	85.00
Austin black	95.00
Process oil	20.00
Cure at 316°F-6 min	

Semi-penumatic tyre

Whole-tyre premix	170.00
SBR 1849	98.00
Hard clay	150.00
Whiting	50.00
Mineral rubber	20.00
Tackifier	15.00
Zinc oxide	3.00
Stearic acid	3.00
Antioxidant	0.50
Sulphur	6.00
N-tert-butyl-2-benzothiazole sulphenamide	2.00
Tetramethylthiuram disulphide	0.40
30-mesh ground rubber	10.00
Aromatic process oil	20.00
Cure at 350°F-7 min	

Butyl inner tube

Butyl 218	81.00
Butyl reclaim	25.00
Paraffinic plasticiser	20.00
Zinc oxide	5.00
Tetramethylthiuram disulphide	1.00
Mercaptobenzothiazole	0.50
Sulphur	1.75
N-660 carbon black	60.00
Cure at 340°F-5 min	

Innerliner

Halobutyl	50.00
SBR 1500	35.00
Buty reclaim	30.00
Stearic acid	1.50
N-660 carbon black	30.00
Dixie clay	60.00
Piccopale 100	5.00
Austin black	10.00
Paraffinic process oil	16.00
Zinc oxide	3.00
Tetramethylthiuram disulphide	0.25
Sulphur	0.25
Cure at 350°F-15 min	

Carcass

No. 1 ribbed smoked sheet	40.00
SBR 1500	40.00
Whole-tyre reclaim	46.00
N-660 carbon black	45.00
Stearic acid	1.00
Naphthenic-process oil	14.00
Petroleum resin	3.00
Antioxidant	1.00
OBTS accelerator	1.00
Insoluble sulphur	3.00
Cure at 350°F-15 min	

RUBBERISED ASPHALT

The concept of using rubbers to modify asphalt can be traced back to the very early days of paved-highway construction, when asphalt became a basic construction material. Many different types and forms of rubber have been tried. In the earliest work, latices of natural rubber, SBR, and neoprene were evaluated along with dry forms of these polymers. The concept of using recycled rubber began to emerge as an economical and technically effective method for enhancing asphalt properties. Many combinations of asphalts and rubbers have been found to have utility in various paving applications.

The incentive for asphalt modification derives from the extreme temperature sensitivity of asphalt. The viscosity of asphalt will change greatly between 10° and 50°C. Moreover, at room temperature and above, most asphalts are only weakly viscoelastic. On the other hand, their brittle points lie fairly high, typically between 40 and 45°F (4 and 7°C). With these asphalt properties in mind, the objective of polymer modification of asphalt is to inhibit flow at elevated use temperatures while simultaneously improving low-temperature flexibility. In practical terms, addition of rubber to asphalt will typically increase its softening point and lower the brittle point.

During the past couple of decades as the use of recycled rubber in paving applications has increased, terminology defining the various types of recycled materials has also evolved. The majority of usage has concerned ground whole-tyre rubber and ground tread rubber. Use has also been made of devulcanised or reclaimed rubber.

Applications

Asphalt rubber in paving applications takes many forms, but the principal ones are as follows -

i. Asphaltic concrete hot mixes.

ii. Stress-absorbing membrane inner layer.

iii. Stress-absorbing membrane.

iv. Joint and crack sealers.

In the preparation of asphaltic concrete hot mixes, the rubber may be added directly to the pug mill used for mixing the asphalt and aggregate. For example, a powdered devulcanised reclaimed rubber can be added in an amount ranging from 0.7 to 1.0 weight-per cent on total aggregate. The resulting asphalt-concrete mix results in a pavement that exhibits less reflection cracking and reduced rutting, shoving, and bleeding.

In stress-absorbing membranes (SAM) or seal coat, the asphalt-rubber blend is prepared by preheating the asphalt, adding a diluent, if required, and then blendign in the rubber components at 350° to 425°F (175° to 220°C). The proportion of rubber is usually in the range of 20-25% by weight of the total blend. The resulting asphalt-rubber mixutre is then sprayed on the road surface using a pressure-type bituminous-distributor truck. The application rate is typically 0.60 gallons per square yard. After the asphalt rubber binder has been applied, rock chips are immediately laid into the asphalt rubber layer at a rate of 25-40 pounds per square yard.

In stress-absorbing membrane inner layers (SAMI) applications, the preparation and installation of the asphalt-rubber system is identical to the system used for stress-absorbing membranes (SAM). However, the application rate may be somewhat higher, e.g., up to 1.0 gallons per square yard. After the asphalt-rubber membrane has been applied, 1 to 1-1/2 inches of asphalt concrete is applied over the asphalt-rubber layer. Field-prepared joint sealers may be produced by dissolving powdered devulcanised rubber into asphalt cement at approximately 20 weight-per cent. Joint sealers may also be prepared at a factory and prepackaged for use in the field.

In summary, the use of recycled rubber in paving applications provides a means for utilising a material that is otherwise discared and, in addition, provides the following advantages -

i. Reduction in reflective cracking
ii. Waterproofing the paving structure and thus preventing water infiltration into the base of the paving structure
iii. Less tendency for rutting, shoving, and bleeding
iv. Reduction in spalling of asphaltic concrete around pot holes and large cracks
v. Loer paving-maintenance costs
vi. Lower total life-cycle costs.

RECLAMATION OF WASTE RUBBER FROM LATEX BASED RUBBER INDUSTRIES

The formation of a higher percentage of waste rubber in latex factories (WLR) is due to the unstable nature of latex compound and the strict specifications on the quality of latex products such as condoms and surgical globes. These waste materials contain about 90-95% rubber hydrocarbon.

Process

Waste condom is used as the starting material. The reclaiming agent used is activated pentachlorothiophenol.

The waste rubber is powdered by passing through a hot two roll mill (80-90°C) to a size of about 40 mesh. The powdered material is admixed with 10 parts by weight of naphthenic oil and different dosages of reclaiming agent in a cold mill. The resulting compound is heated in an air oven at different temperatures (80-140°C) for different periods of time. The extent of degradation is assessed by measuring the Wallace plasticity of the treated material. The results are given in Table 2.

Characterisation of Reclaimed Waste Latex Rubber (WLR)

Characteristics like volatile matter, ash content, acetone extract and rubber hydrocarbon of the reclaimed WLR are determined as per IS 6306-1971. Results are given in Table 3. For comparison, the values for the above parameters for Whole Tyre Reclaim (WTR) are determined and are given in the same table.

Table 2 : Effect of dosage of reclaiming agent, temperature and time of heating on plasticity

Sl. No.	Dosage of reclaiming agent (%)	Tempe-rature (°C)	Heating time 30 minutes Po	Heating time 60 minutes Po
1.	0.00	80	98	98
2.	0.25	80	61	57
3.	0.50	80	60	55
4.	1.00	80	61	50
5.	0.00	100	96	94
6.	0.25	100	57	58
7.	0.50	100	58	54
8.	1.00	100	49	53
9.	0.00	120	96	90
10.	0.25	120	66	60
11.	0.50	120	60	58
12.	1.00	120	53	57
13.	0.00	130	95	95
14.	0.25	130	57	63
15.	0.50	130	58	55
16.	1.00	130	49	45
17.	0.00	140	80	64
18.	0.25	140	44	26
19.	0.50	140	41	19
20.	1.00	140	24	12

Table 3 : Characterisation of reclaim

Parameters	Reclaimed WLR	Whole tyre reclaim (WTR)
Volatile matter (%)	0.01	0.60
Acetone extract (%)	15.54	12.97
Ash content (%)	2.40	7.93
Carbon black (%)	-	30.49
Rubber hydrocarbon (%)	82.05	48.01

The processing and technological properties of compound containing reclaimed WLR is evaluated in comparison with compound containing equivalent loadings of WTR. For this 3 tread compounds are prepared as per formula given in Table 4. The properties of these compounds are evaluated as per relevant IS/ASTM test methods. The test results are given in Table 5. based on the laboratory evaluation, 3 tread compounds as described earlier are prepared again and used for retreading car tyres for assessing the service performance.

Table 4 : Compounding recipe

Ingredients	Parts by weight		
	I	II	III
Natural rubbers (RSS.I)	100	80.0	80.0
Reclaimed WLR	-	24.4	-
Whole tyre reclaim (WTR)	-	-	41.6
Zinc oxide	5	5.0	5.0
Stearic acid	2	2.0	2.0
Phenyl-β-naphthylamine	1	1.0	1.0
N- (1, 3 dimethyl butyl) -N' Phenyl p-phenylene diamine	1	1.0	1.0
HAF black (N 330)	50	50.0	50.0
Aromatic oil	5	5.0	5.0
N-cyclohexyl-2-benzothiazyl sulphonamide	0.6	0.6	0.6
Sulphur	2.5	2.5	2.5

The effect of dosage of activated pentachlorothiophenol, temperature and time of heating on the extent of degradation as indicated by plasticity, are shown in Table 2. Results show that the extent of degradation increases with increase in the dosage of reclaiming agent, temperature and time of heating. The reclaimed material is found to form a smooth band on the mill when the Po value is in the range of 25-30. So in this study, the conditions which resulted in reclaimed rubbers having plasticity in the range 25-30, are selected as the optimum conditions for reclaiming. From the results in Table 2, it is seen that the following conditions are suitable for reclaiming WLR.

i. Reclaiming agent 1% and heating at 140°C for 30 minutes.

ii. Reclaiming agent 0.25% and heating at 140°C for 60 minutes.

In the present studies, the first set of conditions was selected for further trails.

The composition of reclaimed WLR as shown in Table 3 reveals that it contains 82% rubber hydrocarbon whereas the WTR contains only 48% rubber hydrocarbon. It is observed from physical properties of vulcanisates (Table 5) that addition of reclaimed rubber causes a decrease in tensile strength, elongation, resilience, tear strength, flex resitance and abrasion resistance. Compression set is not much affected by the addition of reclaimed WLR. An increse in heat build up and hardness is also observed. But the compound containing reclaimed WLR shows better processing characteristics and physical properties when compared with that containing WTR. The same trend is also observed from the service performance of the retreads (Table 6). The tread prepared with the incorporation of reclaimed WLR gave higher mileage than the one prepared with equivalent amount of WTR.

Table 5 : Properties of tread compounds

Properties		I	II	III
1.	Modulus at 300 % elongation (kg/cm²)	93	97	95
2.	Tensile strength (kg/cm²)	273	233	198
3.	Elongation at break (%)	660	604	540
4.	After ageing at 70°C for 96 hours			
	a. Retention of modulus at 300% elongation (%)	129	123	127
	b. Retention of tensile strength (%)	95	93	95
	c. Retention of elongation at break (%)	85	81	81
5.	Tear strength (kg/cm)	106	86	79
6.	Abrasion resistance (loss in volume, cc/hr)	0.64	0.69	0.78
7.	Hardness (Shore A)	61	65	60
8.	Heat build up at 50°C (DT, °C)	23	25	32
9.	Compression set (%)	34	34	40
10.	Rebound resilience (%)	51	45	43
11.	Flexing (Kilocycles)			
	Crack initiation	71	42	31
	Crack failure	229	179	94
Cure time at 150°C (minutes)		10	9	9.5
Scorch time at 120°C (minutes)		25	17	14

Table 6 : Service performance of retreads

Compound No.	Original non-skid depth (1/32")	Distance covered (km)	Present non-skid depth (1/32")	Projected mileage (km)
I	12	3674	8.25	11,756
II	12	3674	7.75	10,373
III	12	3674	7.50	9,797

11

Elastomeric composites with Reference to Tyre Technology

TEXTILE REINFORCEMENT IN RUBBER

Fibres play a dominant role in rubber reinforcement and without which it is impossible to think about major rubber products such as pneumatic tyres, conveyor belting, transmission and V-belts, hose etc. which undergo service conditions.

Initially needs of rubber industry for reinforcement materials were met with Cotton which of course is still widely used.

As the progressively the stringent performance requirements came up, various reinforcing materials such as high tenacity rayon, nylon 6 and 66, polyester, steel, fibre glass, and more recently Aramid (Kevlar) has come into existence and each being used to meet the specific requirements of various rubber composite products.

TYRE CORD FABRIC

Tyre is a composite material consisting of cords embedded in the rubber matrix. The overall strength, and ability to bear load by the tyre depend strongly upon the nature of cord. At the early stage of pneumatic tyre development cotton was used for this purpose but due to the stringent performance requirement various other materials such as rayon, nylon, polyester, glass fibre, steel cord and Aramid (Kevlar) have come into existence (Table 1).

In the early days, the cotton fabric was square woven. Around 1920 cotton cord fabric replaced square woven. The use of plies of cord added tremendous durability and resilience to the tyre. Around 1938 rayon was introduced followed by nylon in 1947 in commercial production. In 1955, wire made appearance for speciality applications. In 1962 polyester was introduced and fibre glass sin 1967. Aramid came into picture in 1970's.

In India mainly rayon and nylon tyre cords are used. To a very limited extent glass fibre and steel cord have been introduced in belt.

Table 1 : Mechanical properties of fibres used in tyre cord

Fibre	Density (g/cm³)	Stength (kgf/mm²)	Specific strength (g/den)	Modulus (kgf/mm²)	Specific modulus (g/den)
Rayon (dry)	1.52	70	5	1900	140
Nylon	1.14	90	9	500	40
Polyester	1.40	110	9	1100	90
Glass	2.56	350	15	7500	320
Steel	7.8	280	4	21000	300

A tyre cord should have following properties to meet the demand of a good reinforcing material.

- High tensile strength
- Dimensional stability
- Fatique resistance
- Thermal stability
- Adhesion

In general, tyre cords are as simple in construction as possible, consistent with performance requirements, e.g.

Rayon 1100d × 2
160d × 2 and
Nylon 840d × 2
1260d × 2 or 3
1680d × 2
Polyester 1000d × 3 or 4

] Z & S twist per Meter about 470-500

Tyre cord is usually woven into a fabric for convenience of processing. Large number of cords are laid parallel to each other depending upon the number of cords per dm required to achieve the desired carcass strength; this array being known as warp. Light weight weft threads are interlaced alternatively over two or three cords and under the next at right angles to the warp direction, to form a woven fabric. The spacing of these weft (mostly cotton) are also specified. Since weft percentage is very less, this is known as warp sheet. The warp sheet after weaving is wound into roll form.

TYRE CORD PROCESSING

Tyre cord processing is the critical stage in preparing a cord fabric for use in a tyre. During processing a dip solution is applied and fabric is treated under controlled conditions of time, temperature and tension. This is commonly known as 3T processing. This processing, besides applying dip solution (essential for adhesion to rubber), optimises physical properties of the cord, stabilises the fabric for further processing and in service of the tyre (minimising of growth) and equalises differences due to fabric source.

DIPPING

A dip unit is the largest and most expensive equipment in the tyre manufacturing process. The dip solution (adhesion system) comprises only 1.0-1.5% of tyre weight but has large effect on tyre performance. Besides providing excellent adhesion, the dip solution must also conform to different requirement (a) rapid rate of adhesive formation (b) high fatique resistance (c) compatibility with many types of rubber compounds (d) no adverse effect on cord properties (e) heat resistance (f) ageing resistance in tyre service (g) mechanical stability and (h) preferably be water based.

Adhesion between rubber and tyre cord fibre is an important parameter related to tyre performance and strong adhesion between the two must be attained. The adhesive coating is selected on the basis of (1) closest possible match in fibre and adhesive surface energies (2) chemical stability of the adhesive and (3) mechanical properties of the adhesive.

The most popular adhesives are based on resorcinolformaldehyde resin/ latex (RFL) combinations. A single coat system of above adhesive gives required adhesion with rayon and nylon. For polyester a sub coat is given followed by RFL treatment. With high modulus aramid satisfactory adhesion has been obtained with one epoxy subcoat and a modified RFL formulation.

The processed fabric from dip unit is coated on both sides with rubber compound by passing the tyre cord fabric through calender rolls under controlled pressure, tension and temperature. The compound gauge on the fabric is controlled, by the gap between the rolls and is automatically monitored by beta gauges or manually be measuring coated fabric gauge or determining weight per unit area.

TYRE TECHNOLOGY

A tyre is an integral component of a vehicle and is the intermediary between the vehicle and the road. Its major functions are : (1) to carry load (vehicle + goods). (2) To provide grip with the road for traction and safety during vehicle movement (braking effect), (3) To provide cushioned ride (shock absorbing), (4) To give directions control to the vehicle (steering).

Further one would expect from a tyre - high milage, resistance to cuts and damages, no failure and constant performance, number of retreading, saving in fuel consumption etc.

Tyre technology is a vast complex combination of science, technology/ engineering and art; bringing together a variety of disciplines. The science of tyres involves knowledge in the area of composite structures and geometry. These concepts have been used to derive mathematical models of tyre mechanics.

The chemistry and technology of component materials involves areas of speciality such as tyre reinforcing systems, adhesive theories and applications and rubber and matrix technology. The properties of these materials and their relationship determine the integrity of tyre. The construction and composite configurations must be designed to fulfil dynamic tyre behaviour requirements.

Fundamentally a tyre along with stipulated rim fitment forms a toroidal pressure vessel (carcass) capable of supporting load at a quantified degree of deformation. The deflection or degree of deformation of the tyre complements the vehicle suspension.

Mechanics of a pneumatic tyre and tyre design are apparently seem to be dealing same aspects of tyre technology. But, infact, they are entirely different subjects. Mechanics deals with answering questions what makes tyre to fulfil its functions whereas design deals with how to manufacture such a tyre.

What is a tyre? Geometrically, a tyre is a torus. Mechanically, a tyre is a flexible membrane pressure container. Structurally, a tyre is a high performance composite. Chemically, a tyre consists of materials composed of long chain macromolecules.

FUNCTIONS OF A PNEUMATIC TYRE

Basic functions of a penumatic tyre are : (a) Load carrying capacity, (b) Cushioning and enveloping, (c) Transmit driving and braking torque, (d) Produce cornering force, (e) Provide lateral stability/dimensional stability, (f) Provide cushioning and flotation, (g) Resist abrasion, (h) Provide steering force/response, (i) Low rolling resistance, (j) minimum noise and road vibration, (k) Durable and safe.

These functions of a tyre can be generally grouped into three areas : (1) Vehicle control/mobility (lateral/vertical/forward), (2) Performance (structure integrity) (forward), (3) Aesthetics and comfort (vertical).

Mobility including cornering, steering response and abrasion act in the lateral direction where as the forces in vertical direction deal with aesthetics and comfort aspects and the forward direction deals with performance. The vehicle mobility requirement is also based on types of application and the performance level required.

COMPONENT OF TYRE TECHNOLOGY

The different disciplines essential for satisfying the expectations and function of tyre can be grouped as below :

1. Technologies related to materials : (a) Rubber - its compounding and vulcanisation (b) Textiles (c) Other raw materials (e.g. Chemicals, Fillers, bead wire etc.) (d) Bonding rubber/rubber, rubber/textiles, rubber/steel, rubber/glass fibre etc.
2. Tyre Design : (Pattern design, Tyre geometry, Structural design).
3. Manufacturing Technology : (Mixing, Textile processing, Calendering, Extrusion, tyre building, vulcanization, inspection etc.).
4. Quality Control : (Raw material, Intermediate steps, Process, Components, Finished products).
5. Product evaluation methods/controls.
6. Application Engineering.

TYRE DESIGNATION

A tyre is designated by its size, "ply rating", pattern and code besides the manufacture's name, serial nos, load place etc. These are marked on the side wall of the tyre.

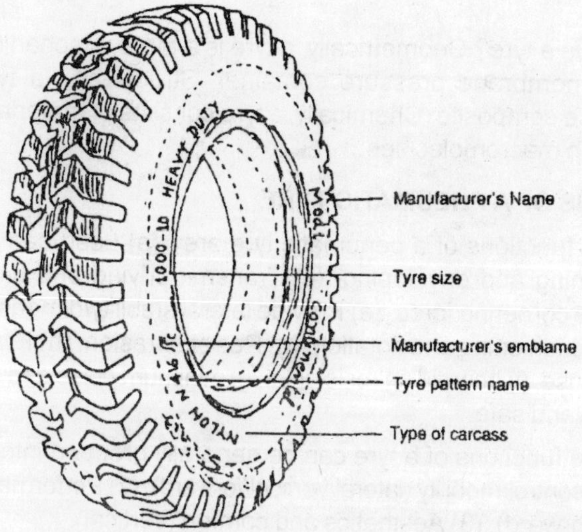

Fig. 1

Here 10.00 denotes approx 10" nominal sectional width and "20" as nominal diameter of the desired rim in inches.

BASIC TYRE TYPES

There are three basic types (construction) of tyres in use today.

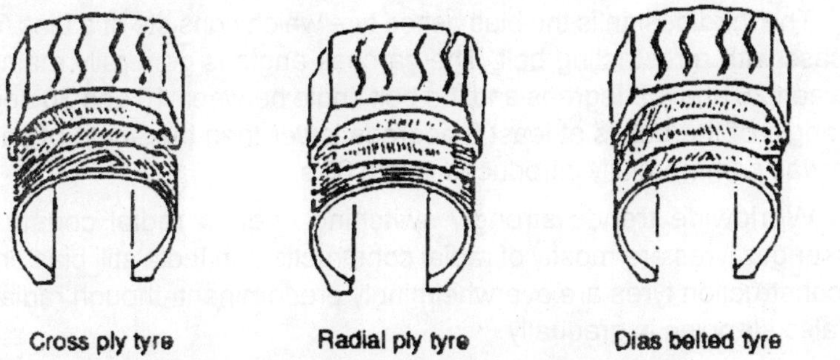

Fig.11.2: Types of Tyres

First is the bias or cross ply tyre. In this construction, the reinforcing cords extend diagonally across the tyre from bead to bead. The angle of the cord path to the centre line of the tyre is generally in the range of 30-40 degrees. The cords run in opposite directions in each successive layer (ply) of reinforcing material. This has been a standard tyre construction for many years.

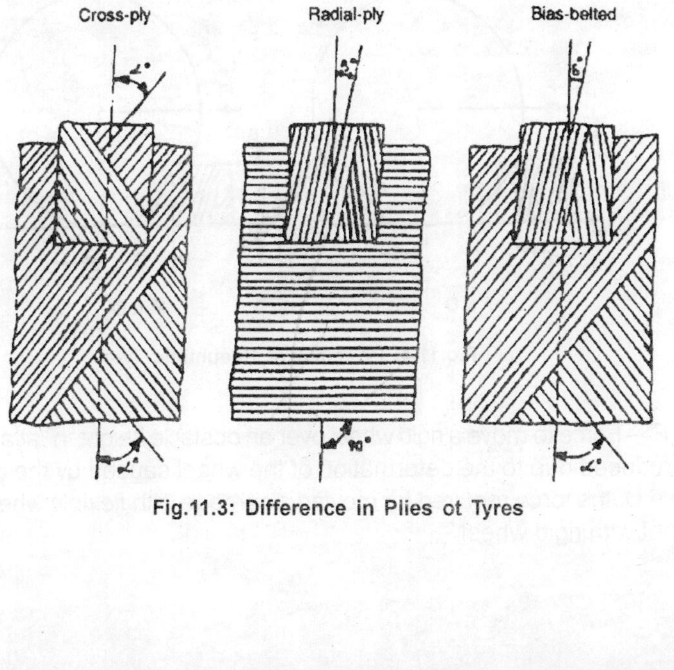

Fig.11.3: Difference in Plies ot Tyres

Second is the radial ply tyre. In this tyre, the plies of reinforcing cords extend transversely from bead to bead. On top of the plies (under the tread) is an inextensible belt composed of several layers of cords. The belt cords are low angle (10-20') and act to restrict the carcass plies. This construction was introduced at later stage.

The third design is the bias belted tyre which consists of a bias (angle) carcass with a restricting belt. The carcass angle is generally maintained between 25 and 45 degrees and the belt angle between 10 and 30 degrees, the angle of the belt is at least 5 degrees lower than the angle of carcass. This was commercially introduced in late 60's.

Worldwide trends strongly switching over to radial construction. Passenger tyres are mostly of radial construction. In India still bias or cross ply construction tyres are overwhelmingly predominant, though radial tyres are also stepping in gradually.

PRINCIPLE OF PNEUMATIC TYRE

In 1845 R.W. Thomson developed a wheel of the carriage by using an inflated tube and observed that the carriage could move with much ease and power needed to move the carriage was minimised. The basic principle for moving the carriage can be described as below :

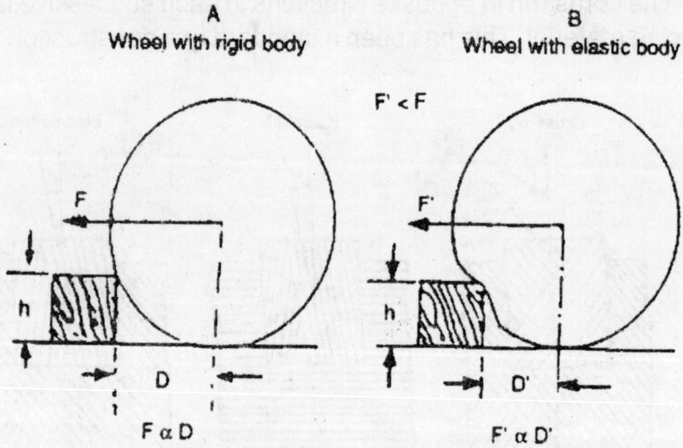

Fig.11.4: Principle of Pneumatic Tyre

"F" – Force to move a rigid wheel over an obstacle height "h" at a distance "D" is reduced due to the deformation of the wheel caused by the obstacle. As the F D, the force required for moving a carriage with flexible wheel is less than that with rigid wheel.

TYRE DESIGN

A tyre is a cord/rubber composite. The tyre composite is in the form of a network of cord structures arranged in a parallel configuration and embedded in a rubber matrix.

The composite materials approach to the analysis of pneumatic tyre is based on the finite element technique. A finite, three dimentional element is considered as a laminated composite structure. Each of the laminates are considered separately in terms of the cord and matrix (rubber) components. The properties of the lamina is combined with the geometry of the laminate structure to describe the character of the finite element.

The stress-strain characteristics of cord and rubber are more dissimilar than most composite components. The cord component is high in strength with relatively low elongation; the rubber matrix is relatively low in strength with high elongation. The ratio of ultimate cord stress to ultimate rubber (matrix) stress is approx, 50. Therefore, in the case of tyre composite, the reinforcing cords carry the major share of the structural load. The rubber contribution to strength can be neglected.

DESIGN

Like any other design and construction work, tyre design also starts with the understanding of certain parameters.

1. Types of service : This refers to requirements expected of the tyre in service.
2. Tyre size required : For most conventional tyre sizes, the basic dimensions of section width and height, skid depth, rim width and profile have been established for load capacity by industry experience with various service conditions (ITTAC, T and RA, ETRTO etc.).

Like any other design work, tyre design also starts with the understanding of limitations. The limitations are the dimensional mainly governed by vehicles parameters.

DESIGNING OF MOULD CAVITY

Based on the selected tyre size, standards and vehicle parameters, tyre dimension are decided. Then the growth of the reinforcing material e.g. rayon, nylon, steel, etc. is taken into consideration. Table 2 gives guidelines in this respect.

On settling the above basic parameters, the designer has to finalise tread pattern, under and side wall areas.

Table .2 : Flexaton of Mould to Tyre Dimension

Reinforcing material	Overall Diameter	Sectional width
Rayon	-1 to 0%	Msc 10%
Nylon	0 to 2%	Max 15%
Steel	0%	0%

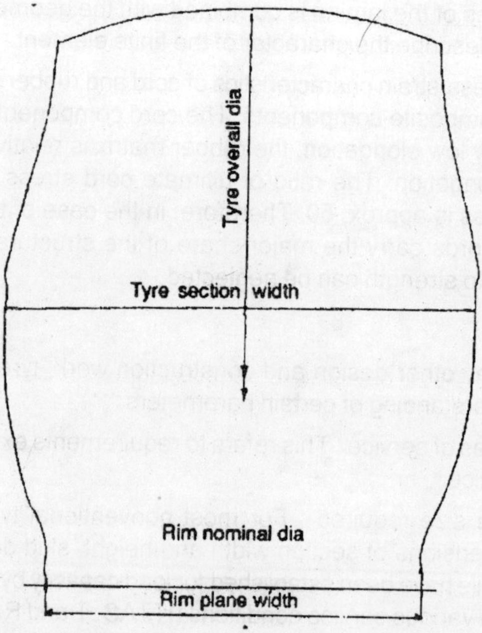

Fig.11.5: Limiting Dimensions of Tyre

Tread pattern : A tyre operates best in service for which its tread pattern has been designed. These are generally classified as :

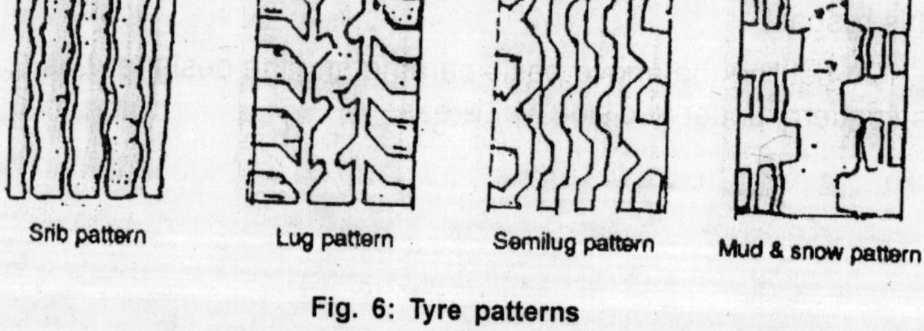

Fig. 6: Tyre patterns

Rib Pattern	:	Used mainly on front/driven axle because of steering response.
Lug Pattern	:	Used mostly on rear/driven axle for heavy haulage and long distance operation.
Semi lug pattern	:	Generally used on front axle, but as well on rear axle.
M and S Pattern	:	Known as Mud and snow pattern and used on rough roads.

Other terminologies like Hiway, Crosslug, Cross country etc., are also frequently used for tread pattern.

Other design parameters like stability, smooth ride, appearance, noise, traction, long life etc., are explored to achieve these desired properties.

Tread width controls the foot print width of the tyre, whereas length is controlled by the tyre diameter and deflection. With wider tread, shoulder thickness increases which leads to higher heat build up. Preferably shoulder to shoulder dimension should not exceed 75-80% of the total tyre width. Tread width also influences traction characteristics.

Tread life is proportional to its depth upto an optimum limit. Beyond this increasing of tread depth brings life to a plateau level.

CARCASS DESIGN

Carcass or casing is the backbone of the tyre. A tyre is fabric rubber composite and its strength entirely depends upon this composite matrix of rubber and reinforcing material extended from bead to bead and turned around them. Reinforcing materials are selected for each components of carcass (Plies, breakers, chafer etc.) to achieve optimum reinforcement for the intended service performance.

Commonly used reinforcing materials are rayon, nylon, polyester and steel. In India tyres are based mainly on rayon and nylon for the manufacture of crossply tyre. Due to prevalent service condition in our country, nylon as reinforcing material is predominant and preferred for bigger size tyres because of its advantages over rayon.

Strength of the casing or carcass depends on the material, number of cords in unit area (per 10 cm or per inch) and number of plies. Higher number of cord per unit area results in higher tyre plunger impact values/strength whereas lower number of cords give better separation resistance because of sufficient compound insulation. Breakers are also of lower cord number to improve adhesion to tread. Maximum number of cords per unit area is restricted by heat build up and minimum number is by fatique and strength failure. Also, cord construction plays an important role in the design of carcass.

Table 3: Comparative Advantages of Nylon Tyre Cord over Rayon Tyre Cord (Per cent Comparison)

	Rayon (16500 × 2)	Nylon (12600 × 2)
Cord Strength (Breaking Load) : Raw	100	152
: Cured	100	148-156
Retention on Heat ageing (one month at 100°C)	30%	72%
Strength retention (Saturated in moisture)	60%	90%
Cord extendability (Elongation at 4.5 kp load)	100	182
Resistance to impact (Plunger energy value)	100	167
Flex Fatigue resistance	100	200

BEAD

Bead is the part of the tyre which holds the tyre on the rim under high inflation pressure and dynamic flexing. It is important to calculate the bead strength critically as any failure can be hazardous. Bead is composite of rubber and high tensile steel wires which applied together to form a bundle.

TYRE CONTROL STANDARD

After calculating and deciding all design parameters, finally a control standard for a particular design has to be laid down. A control standard contains all details like rubber gauges, pattern depth, crown angle, ply turn up heights, material under bead, bead core construction etc. Figure. 7 shows a typical tyre control standard. It is necessary to check these parameters under routine check to maintain quality and uniformity of a tyre.

TYRE TESTING

As an all fields of technology, methods of measuring performance is essential for development. Major areas of tyre testing system are :

1. Laboratory testing of compounds, cords, bed etc.
2. Indoor (Resilometer) endurance testing.
3. Outdoor or field testing.

After designing and manufacturing, a tyre is then subject to rigorous indoor (endurance) and field test evaluation.

Performance evaluation of a tyre is carried out by mainly (a) Plunger Strength, (b) Wheel endurance or Resilometer test and (c) Wheel high speed performance tests.

MANUFACTURE OF TYRE

A brief description of tyre manufacture is illustrated in Fig. 7. The production sequence is briefly described below :

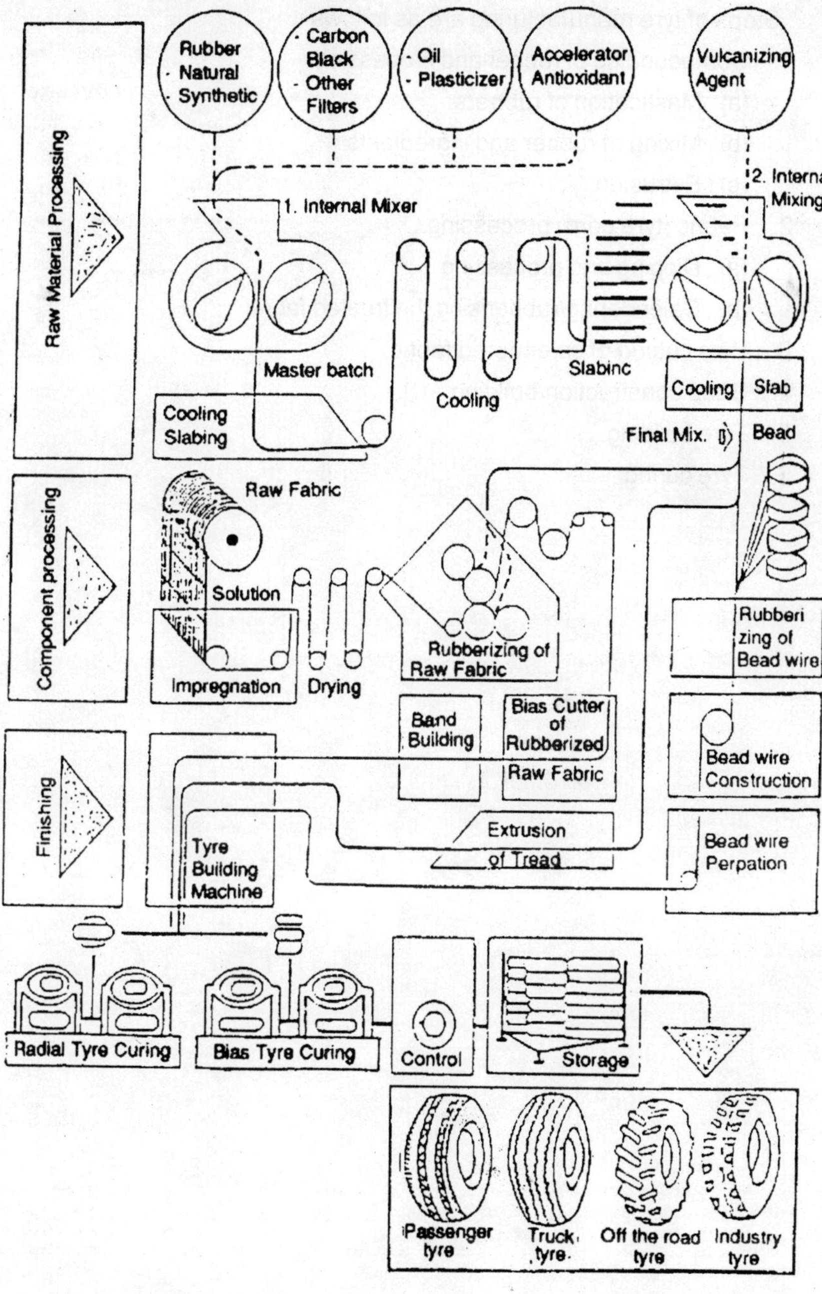

Fig.11.7: Tyre Manufacturing process

Steps of tyre manufacturing are as follows :

1. Compounding of rubber and processing.
   (a) Mastication of rubbers.
   (b) Mixing of rubber and ingredients.
   (c) Extrusion.
2. Fabric (tyre cord) processing.
   (a) Dipping and processing
   (b) Calendering/rubberising the treated fabric.
3. Bias cutting of calendered fabric.
4. Bead construction/building.
5. Tyre building.
6. Tyre curing.

12

Latex and Foam Rubber

INTRODUCTION

Rubber latex is a term used to cover a range of colloids having macro molecular substances as the dispersed phase and water as the dispersion medium. Most important latex used in the rubber industry is natural (NR) latex. This is an aqueous dispersion of *cis* 1,4 polyisoprene in water containing dissolved serum substances. NR latex is harvested from *Hevea brasilienesis* trees by inflicting controlled wounds on the bark of the trunk of the tree. This process is called tapping. Composition of fresh latex is as follows -

Rubber	30-40%
Water	60-70%
Protein (on fresh latex)	Upto 1.0%
Lipids (on fresh latex)	Upto 0.9%
Carbohydrates (on fresh latex)	Upto 1.0%
Inorganic salts (on fresh latex)	0.5%

Under inorganic salts seven different types of ions are identified. Similarly, under each of the organic ingredients a number of compounds belonging to that group are characterised. In synthetic lattices also, a number of ingredients other than the polymer and water are present.

PRODUCTS FROM LATEX

There are eight important steps in the manufacture of products from latex -

i. Selection and quality control of raw materials

ii. Preparation of raw materials

iii. Compounding and design of the mix

iv. Maturation

v. Processing/shaping

vi. Vulcanisation

vii. Testing for grading

viii. Packing and marketing

There are different types of products manufactured from latex. Some of the steps are common in all products but differences exist in others. The similarities and differences in the various steps for different types of products are discussed below briefly.

Selection of Raw materials

Following are the raw materials used in the latex industry -

Latex containing the polymer

Stabilisers and viscosity modifiers

Activator

Accelerator

Curing agent

Antioxidant

Special additives, if any

Gelling/coagulation system.

The raw material selected for product manufacture must be good quality and conforming to specifications prescribed for this by reputed institutions like the BIS (ISI). In the case of natural rubber latex, there are few processors who can supply high ammonia-preserved concentrated neutral rubber latex conforming to IS 5430 (1981). It may be noted that the specifications for this HA latex have been formulated by the combined effort of experts from rubber plantations and the goods manufacturing industry. It is desirable for the industry to insist that the suppliers should deliver of HA latices conforming to IS 5430 (1981). The requirements under this are given in Table 1.

The procurement of certified quality raw material, gives the manufacturer both commercial and technical advantages. It is preferable to use certified quality raw materials wherever such items are available. But many rubber chemicals are now not marketed with ISI Certification. Even in such the consumers should check the quality of chemicals occasionally for conformity to set national standards. Assessment of raw material quality is helpful in minimising percentage rejection of end products. It will also help in saving inventory for raw materials.

Preparation of Raw Materials

The ingredients to be used in latex product manufacture have to be pre-treated before product manufacture. The type of pre-treatment of latex varies, depending on its nature. When ammonia preserved field latex is taken by consumers, they may concentrate it by creaming. When centrifuged latex with high ammonia is the starting material, de-ammoniation of it is a preliminary step. For those who procure low ammonia-preserved latices, expenses on de-ammoniation can be avoided. In some countries, the premium is paid for low ammonia-preserved latices.

Table 1 : Requirements for concentrated and preserved natural rubber latices IS: 5430-1981

Characteristic	Requirement			Method of Test Ref. to	
	Type HA	Type MA	Type LA		
Dry rubber content, % by mass, minimum	60.0	60.0	60.0	NRL :	1 of IS: 3708 (part I)-1966
Non-rubber solids, % by mass, maximum	2.0	2.0	2.0		-
Coagulum content, percent by mass of latex, maximum	0.05	0.05	0.05	IS : 9316 (Part III)-1979	
Sludge content, % by mass, maximum	0.10	0.10	0.10	NRL :	5 of IS : 3708 (Part I)-1966
Alkalinity as ammonia, % by mass of latex	0.6 Min	Above 0.3 but below 0.6	0.3 Max	NRL :	7 of IS : 3708 (Part I)-1966
KOH number, maximum	1.0	1.0	1.0	NRL :	8 of IS: 3708 (Part I) - 1966
Mechanical stability, *s, minimum*	475	475	475	NRL :	9 of IS: 3708 (Part I) - 1966
Volatile fatty acid number, maximum	0.15	0.15	0.15	NRL :	10 of IS: 3708 (Part I)-1966
Copper content, ppm of total solids, maximum	8	8	8	NRL :	13 of IS: 3708 (Part I) - 1966
Manganese content, ppm of total solids, maximum	8	8	8	NRL :	15 of IS : 3708 (Part I)-1966

The compounding ingredinets used in latex product manufacture are either solids or liquids. The solid ingredients are added to latex as dispersions and the liquid ingredients added as emulsions. Ball mills are used in producing dispersion from solid ingredients. Suitable emulsifiers are added to liquid for emulsifying it with water.

The important general principles regarding solutions, dispersions and emulsions for addition to lattices are given under -

i. The particle size of dispersions and the droplet size of the emulsions should, as far as possible, be comparable with that of the latex to which they are to be added.

ii. The stability of dispersion and emulsions should be comparable with that of latex to which they are to be added.

iii. pH of latex and dispersions/emulsions added to it should, as far as possible, be the same.

Compounding and Design

This is a very important step in product manufacture. Two general principles are to be remembered by technologists in the selection of ingredients for the product mix.

i. The product manufactured, using the selected items, should not be costlier when compared to those already in the market.

ii. The product manufactured should meet the service requirements for which it is designed.

Products falling under general categories like dipped goods, foam rubber, cast toys, proofed fabrics, etc., will be considered here for discussion. Raw materials used in rubber latex industry are referred to earlier. In this section the doses and the purpose of their addition is disucssed.

Zinc oxide is an activator for vulcanisation. But in latex goods, if the concentration of zinc oxide exceeds 0.5 phr, it may cause thickening of the latex. This is due to the formation of zinc amine salts which will destabilise latex, partly by an insoluble soap formation and partly by an ionic reaction. ZDC is an accelerator which is a fast curing. But the thermal stability of products prepared with it is not good, this accelerator is preferable in products liek balloons or rubber bands. For articles which need high heat stability, accelerators like TMT or zinc salt of MBT are used. Thus in surgical gloves, or rubber threads use of ZDC as accelerator is not desirable. There are certain combinations of chemicals that can provide high heat resistance and good ageing properties for thé vulcanisates. One such is TMT/thiourea (3:1 parts by weight) system. This system is good for producing heat resistant type rubber threads. Similarly, in surgical gloves or balloons the formula used should be such that the effective modulus of the vulcanisate at low elongation should be low. This requires reduction in level of sulphur used for vulcanisation. For dipped goods production prevulcanised latex can also be used. This will reduce cost of production. There are some reduction in properties for the pre-vulcanised latex films. But these will not affect the end product properties.

A typical formula for dipped goods product is given in Table 2.

Table 2 : Recipe for dipped goods products

Ingredients	Dry Wt.	Wet Wt.
Rubber at latex (60% HA NR latex)	100.0	167.0
Zinc oxide (50% dispersion)	0.5	1.0
Sulphur (50% dispersion)	1.2	2.4
ZDC (50% dispersion)	0.6	1.2
Antioxidant SP (50% emulsion)	1.0	2.0
Spindle oil	3.0	6.0
China clay (50% dispersion)	6.0	12.0

In the production of cast toys an important consideration is the rigidity of the shaped products. The formulation used contain a high level of fillers. This is also helpful in bringing down the cost of the products.

In proofed fabrics the viscosity of the compound used in important. There should be proper additives for ensuring proper penetration and bonding of the polymer with the fibres of the fabric.

In foam rubber production, additives should be used to ensure proper expansion of the latex to the desired level and also for its gelaation at the expanded stage. These are special additives. Foam rubber also contains fillers for giving it proper rigidity and physical properties. There are additives which can help in extending or reducing gelation time. A typical formulation for production of foam rubber is given in Table 3 -

Table 3 : Typical formulation for production of foam rubber

Ingredients	Dry Wt.	Wet Wt.
Natural rubber as 60% latex	100.0	167.0
Ammonium casinate solution 10%	0.2	2.0
Potassium oleate solution 20%	0.5	2.5
Sulphur 50% dispersion	2.5	5.0
Zinc diethyl dithriocarbonate 50% dispersion	0.75	1.5
Zinc mercapto benzothiazole 50% dispersion	0.75	1.5
Zinc oxide 50% dispersion	3.0	6.0
Sodium silicofluoride 20% slurry	1.0	5.0

Potassium chloride can be added to conrol the gelation time to desired levels. If SBR latex is used along with NR latex for foam rubber production, the quantity of the gelling agent to be used will be more. By addition of soluble potassium salt the rate of hydrolysis of sodium silicofluoride is retarded. Soluble fluorides can also bring about the same effect. The latter have a commun ion effect. The former reduce the effective concentration of silicofluoride anions because of the lower solubility of potassium silicofluoride.

Maturation

Maturation is an important step in product manufacture. In latex compounding, three or more colloids are mixed together and physically homogenised. It is necessary to give some time for the particles in these different colloidal systems to adjust and co-exist in the new environment. Maturation period is given for this. During maturation some chemical reactions also take place to a limited extent. Maturation gives processing advantages such as uniform viscosity, stronger gel and uniform vulcanisation of the product. In dipping operations maturation period given is usually 10-20 hours. But in foam rubber production 2-3 days maturation is given to latex for getting best results.

Processing and shaping

Different processes are adopted in the manufacture of different products. Even in same type of products there exist differences as in the case of dipped goods produced by different methods of dipping. The processes adopted in important products are described below briefly.

Dipped Goods

Products like gloves, balloons, rubber bands, nipples, condoms, etc., are produced by dipping formers in latex. Thin walled products are produced by straight dipping. Coagulant dipping is employed when thicker articles are to be produced. Heat sensitised dipping procedure is also used for the production of some thicker products.

In coagulant dipping process, it is advisable to immerse the former first in latex before being immersed in coagulant. This will ensure formation of a more uniform film deposit on the former. Formers may be given a "dwell time" while they are immersed in latex. This will help in obtaining desired thickness with minimum number of dips. Dwell times of the order of 1-5 minutes are common for the production of some latex goods.

The formers used for dipping should be absolutely clean. The speed of immersion should be sufficiently slow to prevent air being drawn to the bath with the former. Immersion speed of the order 3-6 feet per minute are usually found to be acceptable. Withdrawal speed recommended in coagulant dipping process is of the order of 1-2 feet per minute. Leaching is an important step in dipped goods production. This is done to remove water soluble serum ingredients, residual coagulant and surface active substances. Warm water or hot water is recommended for leaching. If water soluble accelerators are used in compounding this step may be avoided. Dusting is done on unvulcanised films to prevent sticking of surfaces.

In case toys, the important processing step is production of moulds for casting. Plaster of Paris is used for mould making in most small industrial units. Light alloys of metals are also used in mould making. When latex is poured into the Plaster of Paris mould the following changes are believed to occur.

i. Plaster is porous and so it absorbs water.

ii. The Ca^{++} iones of plaster de-stabilise latex and hasten film formulation. In casting conditions of rotation of moulds, temperature of the moulds during casting, etc., are important. When heat sensitised latex is used for casting, the excess latex poured out of moulds may be cooled before being mixed with the bulk of the compound.

In foam rubber their are two important processes in vogue commercially. One is called the Dunlop process and the other called Tullalay process. In India most factories use the Dunlop process. In Dunlop process, foaming is carried out in two stages. In the first stage latex is whipped up with foam promoters and stabilisers till the desired expansion is obtained. Thereafter the whipping rate is reduced and the foam is clarified or refined. Gelling agents are added at the end of the foam clarifying stage. The density of foam rubber produced depends on froath height. The level in which latex is whipped should be calibrated properly for specific gravity for various froath heights.

The materials selected for mould construction for foam production must be light, cheap, should have high thermal capacity and good thermal conductivity. A mould designed from copper free cast aluminum meets these requirements. It is generally reported that in the cost of production of foam rubber around 5% of the cost is on account of contribution from mould cost. The tensile and cure properties of the hot we gel are appreciably lower than those of the dry finished products. So if care is not exercised in stripping the foam from mould, it may as well be damaged. For enabling easy and quick stripping, the mould surface should be kept clean and polished. Mould release agent has to be applied on surface of mould after each operation. Examples of mould release agents are aqueous or alcoholic solution of poly ethylene glycol of fairly high molecular weight such as carbo wax-4000, carboxymethyl cellulose or silicone fluids.

In Tullalay process, the expansion of latex compound is achieved by liberation of gases like oxygen liberated by catalytic decomposition of hydrogen peroxide.

Latex Thread

In the production of latex rubber thread the matured latex has to be carefully processed to avoid defects. The compounded matured latex is de-aerated and filtered before it is allowed to pass through capillaries for injection into an acid bath. The nozzle of the capillary is immersed in coagulant. The nozzle depth in coagulant bath has relation to the thread diameter. The rate of extrusion is 30-40 feet per minute. The orifice of the nozzle is usually round and the size of the bore varies from 0.5 to 1mm. Coagulant normally used is 15-40% acetic acid. Generally, weaker solutions of acid are used for large diameter thread and strong solutions for higher count threads. For the production of high count thread alcohol is the most suitable coagulant. Between extruding nozzle and winding, the thread is usually subjected to some degree of stretching which may be upto 200%. Stretching is necessary to facilitate washing, to reduce permanent set and to increase modulus of the thread.

Vulcanisation

Latex products are generally vulcanised at low temepratures and pressure when compared to dry rubber products. It is desirable to wash, leach and dry the latex products before subjecting them to vulcanisation temperature. Vulcanisation of some products is carried out in hot air. Some others are vulcanised in open steam in autoclaves.

Hot Air Cure

The equipment used for vulcanisation is an oven. Ovens used for drying the rubber film should be kept at a temeprature of 55-65°C. But the oven for vulcanisation may be kept at 100°C. The heating ovens should not be placed near the dipping tanks. Vulcanisation may be carried out after thorough drying to avoid formation of bubbles/blisters on the surface of products. The advantages of hot air vulcanisation are its simplicity, low cost of equipment, and the ease with which it can be adopted for continuous operation. The process is clean and free from the dangers of rusting/corrosion associated with hot water vulcanisation.

Hot Water Vulcanisation

This process consists in immersing rubber articles in hot water or boiling water. Aluminium is a suitable material for constructing tanks for vulcanisation. Water used in the tank may be changed at intervals to avoid problems due to materials leached out to water.

Autoclave Vulcanisation

Foam rubber is generally vulcanised in open steam in autoclaves. The product while still in closed mould is subjected to moderate steam pressure in autoclave to bring about vulcanisation. Steam curing of smaller articles can be carried out in a device like big size pressure cookers.

Radiation Vulcanisation

Infra red heating is successfully applied to vulcanisation of certain products. The temeprature of the product is rapidly increased and vulcanisation is effected very efficiently. Uniform heating of the product can be obtained by rotating the formers during vulcanisation or by subjecting them to radiation from emitters mounted at different angles, so that each part of the surface receives approximately the same amount of radiation.

Microwave curing devices are now available for use in manufacture of certain type of products. *Radiation from g source and electron beams* are also used in vulcanisation of latex and thin products. Radiation pre-vulcanised latex is available from a plant set up in Jakarta. Indonesia by the International Atomic Energy Agency.

Ultrasonic Wave Curing

Unlike microwaves, ultrasonic waves are not electromagnetic, but are essentially mechanical waves which while proceeding through a medium, create alternate regions of compression and ratification at high frequency. In rubber, some of the energy will be converted to heat by the frictional and relaxation process. It is proved that uniform heating and vulcanisation of products is possibie by this method.

Testing of Rubber Products

Testing of end products is an important step in product manufacture. The product has to be examined for conformity to set standards before being released to the market. The products listed in Table 4 above have ISI standards. For those products which have no ISI standards conformity to other reputed national standards have to be examined. If a small unit has no facility for testing its products this may be done in common facility centres established for this purpose.

Table 4 : Latex based rubber products with ISI specifications

1.	IS 1741-1960	Latex foam rubber products
2.	IS 3701-1966	Rubber protective sheaths (Condoms)
3.	IS 4148-1967	Surgical rubber gloves
4.	IS 4149-1967	Post mortem rubber gloves.
5.	IS 4770-1968	Rubber gloves for electrical purposes
6.	IS 5915-1970	Single texture rebberised waterproof fabrics.
7.	IS 6110-1983	Double texture rubberised waterproof fabrics
8.	IS 8391-1977	Rubberised coir sheets for cushioning
9.	IS 9827-1981	shoe adhesive, natural rubber latex base
10.	IS 11060-1984	Moulded rubberised coir cushioning.

Packing and Marketing

A modern manufacturer has to pay adequate attention to the packing and presentation his products. Latex products manufactured in this country are labour intensive and so there is chance for export of these products to developed countries, where labour is expensive. Many of these countries give considerable importance to packing and presentation of goods procured. Some importers of surgical gloves want packed radiation sterilised gloves.

Conclusion and Recommendations

i. Manufacturers may try to use cost saving raw latices like low ammonia-preserved latices and pre-vulcanised latices.

ii. It is preferable to use raw materials of certified quality in product manufacture.

iii. Modernisation in process and machinery has to be made in latex products like gloves and rubber threads.

iv. Modern methods for vulcanising has to be popularised among small industries to reduce cost of production and to improve quality.

v. Finished products may be examined for conformity to set standards and may be marketed with ISI mark.

vi. Large marketing organisations should come up for undertaking organised marketing or produce from small scale latex goods manufacturing units.

vii. Common facility centres for testing and technical guidance to small scale rubber industries may be established in regions where there are concentration of rubber industries.

LATEX FOAM

Cellular rubber obtained from rubber latex is defined as a mass of cells in which the matrix is rubber. These are broadly classified into two types -

i. Sponge rubber in which the cells are open and interconnected

ii. Expanded rubber in which the cells are closed and non-intercommunicating.

'Expanded' and 'Sponge' rubbers normally denote cellular products made from dry rubber. Hence latex foam, a cellular rubber made from rubber latex, is described as such. However, since its cells are open and interconnecting, it may be classified as a sponge rubber.

Manufacture of Latex Foam

The process for the manufacture of latex foam essentially consists of expanding (foaming) a suitably compounded latex to a desired volume, setting (gelling) the rubber particles and then vulcanising the product.

There are two main processes for latex foam manufacture, viz. (i) Dunlop process and (ii) Tullalay process which differ mainly in the foaming and gelling methods.

Dunlop Process

In the Dunlop process, sodium silicofluoride is used as the gelling agent. The latex compound is mechanically beaten up to a foam and then the requisite amount of a dispersion of sodium silicofluoride is added, which, in the presence of zinc oxide, will set the foam to a 'gel' within a few minutes. The "gelled" product is then vulcanised in steam.

Mechanism of Gelling

Sodium silico-fluoride is sparingly soluble in water but hydrolyses in it as shown below into hydrofluoric acid and silicic acids. Liberation of hydrofluoric acid alone is not the cause of gelling as gelling is found to occur at an alkaline pH (about 8.2-8.5). The powerful absorptive effect of silicic acid formed also plays an important role and a combined effect of hydrofluoric and silicic acids bring about gelling. Now this gel is paste - like and lacks in strength. Zinc oxide in presence of ammonia and ammonium salt (in this case, ammonium fluoride) forms zinc diamines at the pH conditions available (i.e., around 8.3) which remove the protective soap layer on the layer on the latex particles and bring about gelling.

There is also another technique of gelling known as heat sensitising gelling process. In this process, gelling is brought about by the formation of insoluble zinc soaps. Zinc oxide is sparingly soluble in ammonia, but its solubility is increased with the addition of an ammonium salt forming zinc ammonia complex, as shown by the following reaction.

$$ZnO + H_2O + (NH_4)_2 SO_4 = [ZnO (NH_3)_4] SO_4 . 4H_2O$$

The tetrammonium complex dissociates on heating into the lower amines (diamines) which form the insoluble zinc soaps, thus removing the soap layer on the latex particles which leads to gelling of the foamed latex. Latex compounds using such gelling systems are generally stabilised by a non-ionic stabiliser (e.g., ethylene oxide/fatty alcohol condensate) which stabilises the latex against gelling at room temperature but on raising the temperature to above 70°C, it loses activity and consequently gelling takes place.

The production of a good foam ćushionrequires that the latex should gel before the dispersed air system is destroyed. But at a later stage there should be a gradual breakdown of the system so that the air bubbles become interconnected. In the heat sensitising gelling system, gelling takes place at a higher pH (9-10) at which the surface-activity of the soap is still high so that the air bubbles tend to persists and on rapid heating, internal pressure builds up which ruptures the cell walls (foam splitting) giving rise to what is known as a "feathery" structure. This effect is quite prominent in thick articles and hence is limited to thin sections only, e.g., carpet underlays.

In the gelling system based on sodium silicofluoride, liberation of hydrofluoric acid continues even after gelling is completed thus lowering the pH of the foam. When an acidic pH is attained, the foam, i.e. air dispersed system, breaks. This breaking of the air-dispersed system after gelling gives the interconnecting cellulr structure of the vulcanised foam product. This is the main reason for the widespread use of sodium silicofluoride gelling system in latex foam manufacture.

A typical formulation of latex foam based on NR latex suitable for Dunlop process is shown below -

Ingredinets	Parts by wt.
60% NR latex (de-ammoniated)	167.0
20% Potassium oleate soap solution[a]	5.0
50% Sulphur dispersion	4.0
50% ZDC dispersion[b]	2.0
50% ZMBT dispersion[b]	2.0
50% Antioxidant dispersion/emulsion[c]	2.0-3.0
50% Filler dispersion	Upto 40.0
50% Zinc oxide dispersion	8.0
Secondary gelling agent[d]	0.5 to as required
20% Sodium silicofluoride dispersion[e]	5.0-7.5 or as required
Cure in open steam (100°C)	30-45 Minutes

a. For higher density foams, a mixture of potassium oleate and potassium castor oil soaps is recommended.

b. ZDC-Zinc diethyl dithiocarbamate

ZMBT - zinc salt of mercaptobenzothiazole.

c. Styrenated phenol, condensation product of acetone/diphenylamine, acetone/aniline, di-b-naphthyl-p-phenylene diamine are commonly used as antioxidants for latex foam

d. Secondary gelling agent - The function of a secondary gelling agent is to prevent foam collapse. Foam collapse is specially exhibited by those latices whose gelling pH is low (acidic) and also which require excessively prolonged time for gelling. In such cases, the air, dispersed system (i.e., foam) may be largely destroyed before the latex gels properly. This results in what is known as foam collapse. The minute bubbles coalesce before gelling giving a coarse and irregular cellular structure. Steps should therefore, be taken to destabilise the rubber particles thus causing gelling before the air-dispersed system starts breaking. Various secondary gelling agents, e.g., a triamine base (e.g., triethyl, trimethylene triamine), diphenyl guanidine and a cationic soap like cetyl trimethyl ammonium bromide have been successfully used to relevant foam collapse. All of them function by raising the gelling pH and cutting down the gelling time.

A 20% dispersion of sodium silicofluoride is conveniently prepred by the following method-

Ingredients	Parts by weight
Sodium silicofluoride	80
Bentonite clay	16
Water	304
Ball mill for 24 hours	

Dosages of the secondary gelling agent and the primary gelling agent, i.e., sodium silicofluoride need to be adjusted by experiment, depending on the gelling time required for the latex used. Neither too prolonged a gelling time nor a very short gelling time is advisable. In the former case, there may be setting of the chemicals in the mould, leading to non-uniform density and curing of the product and in the latter case, handling of the foam after addition of the gealling agents will be difficult and mould flow may be restricted. Optimum gelling time to be decided depends on the type of process used, e.g., in a batch foaming process a gelling time of 4-6 minutes in generally suitable.

The process for the production of latex foam by the Dunlop process can be divided into the following steps -

i. Compounding
ii. Foaming and gelling
iii. Vulcanisation
iv. Washing, drying and finishing

Compounding

High ammonia latex, if used, should be de-ammoniated (reducing ammonia content to 0.3-0.15%) either by blowing air or by adding formaldehyde solution, the former method being generally preferred in the industry. A small amount of casein may be added during de-ammoniation as a stabiliser. De-ammoniation may require 8-24 hours, according to the quantity of latex and efficiency of the de-ammoniation plant.

Sulphur, accelerator, antioxidant and fillers (in the form of dispersion or emulsion) are then added to the de-ammoniated latex taken in the mixing tank fitted with a slow speed stirrer. The compound is then allowed to mature by keeping it slowly stirred for several hours; the period of maturing should be decided by the ambient temperature. Maturing has been shown to improve upon the properties of the final product. Over-maturing, however, should be avoided as it gives poor strength of the vulcanised foam and handling of the product before drying may be difficult. Maturing also reduces the stability of the latex, making the gelling to take place faster.

Foaming and Gelling

Foaming may be done either by the batch or continuous process.

Batch Process - In the batch process, a planetary mixer is used for foaming. The mixer is provided with a wire cage (cage beater) which rotates in a planetary motion (hence the name of the equipment) at about 200 rpm. The latex compound is weighed out into the mixer bowl, soap solution added and the mix mechanically whipped into a foam by the rotating cage beater. The beating time normally varies between 15 and 20 minutes and the volume increase of the compounded latex is generally from 4-6 times for cushions upto about ten time for soft products.

After the desired volume increase has taken place, zinc oxide with the secondary gelling agent, if required, is added, followed by sodium silicofluoride. The speed of beating is usually reduced at this stage in order to 'refine' the foam, i.e., to reduce the bubble size and this beating is continued till the chemicals finally added are uniformly distributed. The foamed compound is then poured into the mould and the lid placed in position. The gelling is allowed to be completed and then the mould is placed in the vulcaniser.

Continuous process - The most popular frothing machine used in the continuous process is what is known as the Cakes mixer. The mixing head of the Cakes machine consists essentially of a rotor which is totally enclosed within two stator members, Both the rotor and stator halves carry teeth enmeshing with each other. Latex compound and air are metered accurately in the right proportion to this head and broken into a fine form. The foam flows into a second chamber in which zinc oxide, secondary gelling agent and sodium silicofluoride are metered in and mixed into the foam. The foam is then charged into moulds with the help of a flexible plastic hose.

Construction of Moulds

The moulds for foam rubber are usually made from cast aluminium because of the lightness, durability and good heat conductivity of the metal. When cushions and mattresses are made, cylindrical cores are attached to the lids which give the characteristic cavity structure of the back side of the foam. These cavities help to minimise the actual thickness of the product to about 1 inch to ensure uniform curing throughout the mass of the product. The cavities also assist in great saving of the latex compound (of the order of 40%) without affecting the comfort. In designing moulds, allowance should be given to shrinkage of the product which amounts to roughly 8-10% linear.

Mould lubricants like polyethylene glycol and alkyl sulphate solutions are applied to the mould surface to facilitate easy stripping of the product after vulcanisation.

Curing

Mould foam products are normally cured by open steam (at 100°C) which is more efficient and quicker than hot air curing. Thin sections of foam, e.g., as used in carpet underlays, can be suitably cured by hot air.

Washing

After vulcanisation, the product is stripped from the mould and washed in water to remove water solubles like soap, etc., which may produce a foul odour during use. Washing is best carried out by passing the product between rollers under the surface of the water bath. The excess water absorbed during washing is removed by passing the product through squeeze rollers.

Drying

Drying of the product is best carried out in hot air ovens at 60-80°C. There must be a good circulation of air to ensure efficient drying. Complete drying is very important and takes about 4-8 hours.

Finishing

The foam products are trimmed to remove flash before packing. Foam products are invariably used under cover (cotton or leather-cloth) to protect it from the deleterious effect of sunlight.

Common Defects in Foam Making

The following are the common defects encountered during foam manufacture -

i. Shrinkage
ii. Foam collapse
iii. Setting
iv. Complete distortion of the foam.

Shrinkage

Under normal working conditions, there is about 10-20% shrinkage of latex foam on drying and allowance for this should be made while designing the moulds. It has been experienced that maturing the latex compound before use considerably improves the shrinkage. If an excessive dose of the gelling agent is used, very quick setting may take place leading to enormous shrinkage. The dosage of the gelling agent should, therefore, be correctly adjusted by preliminary trials. Often suitable modification of the gelling agent, e.g., adjusting the pH to 7.0 or adding a potassium salt which reduces the rate of hydrolytic decomposition of sodium silicofluoride helps considerably in conrolling the gelling rate and the consequent shrinkage.

Foam Collapse

In certain cases, specially with those latices which show too low a gelling pH, gelling may take too long a time which means that the dispersed air system may be largely destroyed before the latex gel is properly formed. The result is a collapse of the foam structure. Various secondary gelling agents, e.g., Vulcastab TM, Vulcastab EFA, and Vulcafor DPG have been recommended to 'sensitise' the gel formation so that the rubber particles are destabilised before the dispersed air system is affected. All these secondary gelling agents cut down the gelling time by raising the gelling pH.

Setting

If the dose of the gelling agent is not sufficient to gel the latex in the desired time, there may be settling of the gelling agent, resulting in a non-uniform density of the foam.

Complete Distortion of the Foam

Complete distortion of the latex foam may take place either by foam collapse or by incomplete vulcanisation. The Dosages of the gelling and curing agents should, therefore, be properly adjusted and adequate curing time in open steam should be given.

ESTIMATION OF PROTEIN CONTAMINATION IN LATEX

Latex contains a significant amount of water soluble proteins. Latex products such as gloves, condoms and surgical blooms come into contact with humans, and contaminating proteins pose health risks. Latex protein is easily absorbed through skin and can trigger allergic responses. Fortunately, most of the soluble protein in latex can be easily removed by simply washing the latex products in water.

Because of the health risk associated with latex protein, latex-based products that are likely to come into contact with humans require removal of the protein and careful monitoring of the protein content in the finished products. Estimation of protein concentration in latex is complicated, time consuming and requires specialised skills and instruments. Most protein assays are based on colorimetric methods. Colorimetric assays require a large sample volume, running of known standards, use of colorimeters, plotting of standard curves and so forth. The most widely used method for estimation of protein in latex is based on the method of Lowry. The Lowry method is complicated to perform and has low sensitivity.

A simple and reliable method for estimation of protein content in latex called the Latex dotMetric protein assay has been developed. Protein estimation can be performed anywhere and with a minimum of skill and instrumentation. The test takes 10-15 minutes to perform after protein has been extracted from the test samples. The test detects protein in latex in amounts as small as 5 mg/ml latex protein.

A proprietary test strip and reagent solutions have been developed such that when am ml protein solution is applied onto the test strip, it produces compact and symmetrical protein spots (Figure 1). The diameters of the protein spots are proportional to protein concentration (Figure 2). Thus, by measuring the diameter of protein spots with the dotMetric card (supplied with each kit), protein concentration can be reliably determined. Figure 2 shows the linear relationship of protein concentration (bovine serum albumin, BSA) with the diameters of protein spots.

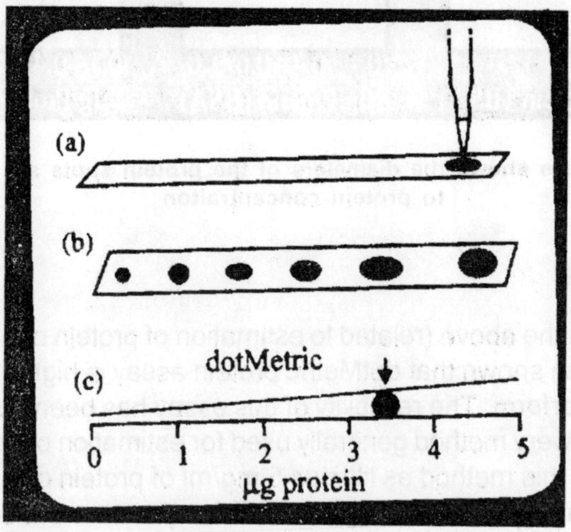

Fig. 1 : Latex dot Metric protein assay

A protein spot measuring scale, the dotMetric card, has been prepared using these plots (Figure 2) for measurement of protein concentration in test samples. The proteinassay kit consists protein extraction solution, test strips, reagent solutions for developing protein spots on the test strips, a card for protein spot diameter and a simple-to-follow protocol.

Protein estimation protocol

The protein estimation protocol involves a simple step for extracting soluble protein from latex. Simply take a piece of latex and weigh it, shake it for 20-30 minutes in the extraction solution supplied with each kit, and within 20-30 minutes most of the extraction solution. After the protein extraction, prepare a serial dilution with the extracted protein by diluting the protein extract two-fold with each successive dilution into a series of additional five tubes. Apply 1-3 ml of the solution from each tube onto the test strip. Develop the test strip for 8-10 minutes, and read the protein concentration in the latex extract with the dotMetric card.

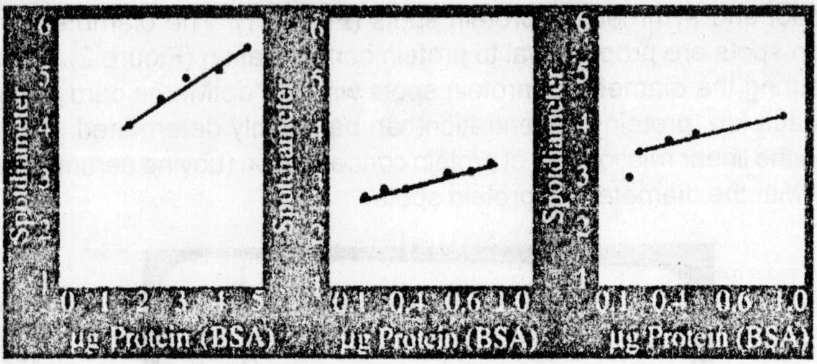

Fig. 2 : The figure shows the diameters of the protein spots are proportional to protein concentraiton

CONCLUSION

Thus from the above (related to estimation of protein contamination in latex) it has been shown that dotMetric protein assay is highly reproducible and simple to perform. The reliability of this assay has been compared with the standard Lowery method generally used for estimation of protein in latex products. From this method as little as 5 mg/ml of protein can be detected. The dotMetric assay does not require use of any instrument or specialised skills, making it a particularly useful tool for rapid estimation of the range of protein concentration in an industrial production setting. The test can be performed on the factor floor.

13

Vulcanisation

INTRODUCTION

After rubber compounds have been properly mixed and snapped into blanks for moulding, or calendered, extruded, or fabricatied into a composite item (as a tyre), they must be vulcanised by one of many processes. During vulcanisation, the following changes occur:

i. The long chains of the rubber molecules become cross-linked by reactions with the vulcanisation agent to form three-dimensional structures. This reaction transforms the soft weak plastic-like material into a strong elastic product.

ii. The rubber loses its tackiness and become insoluble in solvents and is more resistant to deterioration normally caused by heat, light, and ageing processes.

These changes generally occur with the use of vulcanisation systems discussed in this chapter.

VULCANISATION SYSTEMS

Sulphur Vulcanisation

With general purpose rubbers containing unsaturation, vulcanisation with sulphur is possible, and it is in general the most common vulcanising agent used. With sulphur, cross-links and cyclic structures of the following type are formed as shown below -

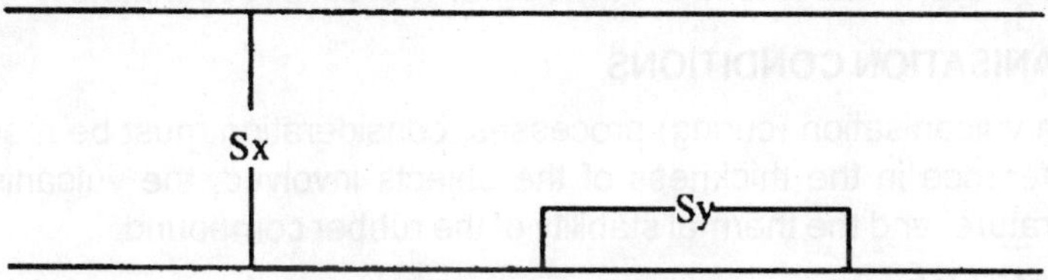

Generally, x in an efficient accelerated curing system is about 1 or 2, with little or no cyclic structures formed. In inefficient systems x equals upto 8 and many cyclic structures are formed. The total amount of sulphur combined in these networks is usually called the "coefficient of vulcanisation" and is defined as the parts of sulphur combined per one hundred parts of rubber. For most rubbers, one cross-link for about each 200 monomer units in the chain is sufficient to produce a suitable vulcanised product (molecular weight between cross-links equal ca. 8,000 to 10,000). It is these amounts of cyclic sulphur (y) and the excessive sulphur in the cross-links (x) which contribute to the poor ageing properties of the vulcanisates.

Sulphurless Vulcanisation

Vulcanisation effected without elemental sulphur, by the use of thiuram disulphide compounds (accelerators) or with selenium or tellurium produces products which are more resistant to heat ageing. Whit the thiuram disulphides, efficient cross-links containing only 1 or 2 sulphur atoms are found, and in addition the accelerator fragments act as antioxidants.

Peroxide Vulcanisation

The saturated rubbers cannot be cross-linked by sulphur and accelerators. Organic peroxides are necessary for the vulcanisation of these rubbers. When the peroxides decompose, free radicals are formed on the polymer chains, and these chains can then combines to form cross-links, as shown below -

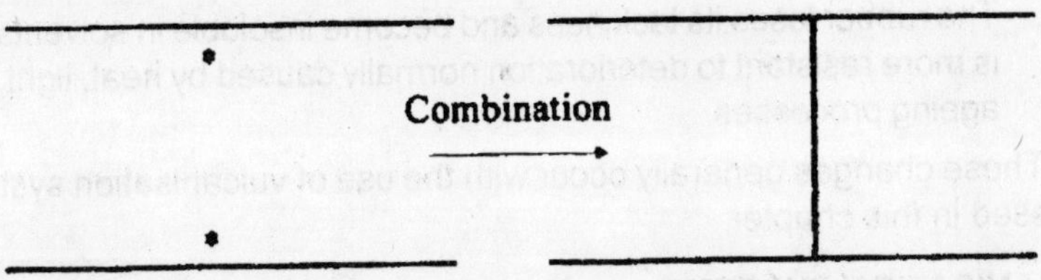

Cross-links of this type only involves carbon-to-carbon bonds and are quite stable, they are also formed by gamma radiation and X-radiation.

Other Systems

Some elastomers can be vulcanised by the use of certain non-sulphur bifunctional compounds which form bridge type cross-links, for example, neoprene with metal oxides or butyl rubber with dinitrosobenzene.

VULCANISATION CONDITIONS

In vulcanisation (curing) processes, consideration must be made for the difference in the thickness of the objects involved, the vulcanisation temperature, and the thermal stability of the rubber compound.

Effect of Thickness

Rubbers are poor heat conductors, thus it is necessary to consider the heat conduction, heat capacity, geometry of the mould, heat exchange system, and the curing characteristics of a particular compound when articles thicker than about one-quarter of an inch are being vulcanised. Since these defects are complicated, generally an estimate of the time required can be determined by adding an additional five minutes to the cure time for every one-quarter of thickness. In exceptionally thick or complicated articles, the item may be built up using sections with different curing characteristics, or by controlling the rate at which the mould is heated or cooled.

Effect of Temperature

The vulcanisation temperature must be chosen in order to produce a properly cured product having uniform physical properties in the shortest possible moulding time. The "temperature coefficient of vulcanisation" is a term used to identify the relationship that exists between different cure time at different temperatures. With information of this type, optimum cure times as higher or lower temperatures can be estimated for many rubber compounds with known coefficients of vulcanisation. For example, most rubber compounds have a coefficient of approximately 2. This indicates that the cure time must be reduced by a factor of 2 for each 18°F (10°C) increase in cure temperature, or, if the temperature is reduced 18°F, the cure time must be doubled.

Effect of Thermal Stability

Each type of rubber has a definite range of temperatures which may be used for vulcanisation. These temperatures may vary somewhat but it is quite important not to exceed the maximum for each, as some form of deterioration will occur. This effect is either shown by the appearance of the finished product or by its physical proeprties.

VULCANISATION TECHNIQUES

Finished articles can be prepared by numerous vulcanisation techniques. However, the specific methods used in most industries are usually based on producing suitable commercial goods utilising standard techniques. These methods are briefly outlined as follows.

Compression Moulding

This method, or modification of it, probably utilises the most common type of mould used in the rubber industry. Essentially, it consists of placing a precut or shaped "slug" (or black), or a composite item, into a two-piece mould which is closed. The pressure applied by the press forces the material to fit the shape of the mould, and the slight excess present flows out of the material of the mould or through special vents. This excess is known as "mould flash".

Transfer Moulding

Transfer mouding involves the distribution of the uncured stock from one part of the mould (the pot) into the actual mould cavity. This process permits the moulding of complicated shapes or the imbedding of inserts in many porducts, these procedures are difficult with the usual compression moulds. Although the moulds are relatively more expensive than compression moulds, the actual process permits shorter cure times through the use of higher temperatures and better heat transfer which is obtained due to the higher pressure applied to force the compound into the mould.

Injection Moulding

In recent years, injection moulding processes which are normally used for the production of plastics, have been developed so that small rubber compounds can be moulded and vulcanised by this method. By careful temperature control of the feed stock, items can be vulcanised in less than several minutes (cure times are generally reported in seconds).

Open Cures

i. Hot air ovens can be used to vulcanise thin articles (balloons, etc.), items which have been preshaped (by extrusion) or by a combination of precuring in a mould, followed by post-vulcanisaton in an oven. The last process is used to remove peroxide decomposition products from items cured with peroxides. The system is not too efficient due to the poor heat transfer of hot air, and longer cure time at lower tempearatures are necessary to prevent the formation of porosity or deformation of the unvulcanised products.

ii. Open steam can be used in closed containers called "Autoclaves" (which resemble home pressure cookers). The process involves the use of saturated steam under pressure. The saturated steam act as an inert gas, better heat transfer is obtained, thus higher temperatures can be used and shorter cure times are possible, making this process more desirable than the air oven. Hose, cables, built-up footwear, tyres in pot-heat moulds are cured by this method.

iii. Water cures can be used for articles that are not affected by immersion. The method is useful for large items (for example, large containers or rubber-lined containers) and is especially useful for hard rubber compositions. Direct contact with water produces better heat transfer than with air or open steam, consequently, with this system, less deformation and faster cures are obtained.

iv. Lead sheathing can be used to cover soft, large extrued sections with a protective cover for vulcanisation in steam. The process is used for garden and other hose, the lead sheath is usually applied by hydraulic pressure or extrusion immediately as the hose emerges from its extruder.

v. Continuous vulcanisation process - Continuous vulcanisation generally involves the use of some form of heating in a manner such that the vulcanisation step usually occurs immediately after the rubber article is formed. The process is normally used for extruded goods, coated wiring, conveyor belts and flooring.

a. *Liquid curing methods* - These involve the use of suitable hot liquid baths in which extrusions may be vulcanised in a continuous process. Items can be cured rapidly at temperatures from 200-300°C, however, the compounds must be modified to prevent porosity, as this is always a problem with any extrudate. Suitable materials for the curing medium includes bismuth-tin alloys, a eutectic mixtures of potassium nitrate, sodium nitrite and sodium nitrate, poly-glycols and certain silicone fluids.

b. *Fluidised beds* - These consist of small particles (glass beads) suspended in a stream of heated air are efficient vulcanisation systems. They are normally used for continuous vulcanisation of extrusions. The heat transfer is approximately 50 times greater than with hot air alone.

c. *Continuous hot air tunnels* - These can be used in the same manner as hot air ovens are used. Thin articles, for example, dipped goods, can be vulcanised after dipping by passing an endless conveyor carrying the items through a series of heated tunnels (ovens) at a rate that will complete vulcanisation by the time articles are stripped from the forms.

d. *Steam tubes* - These are used for the continuous vulcanisation of sheathing. After extrusion of the rubber cover into the wire, the cable passes into a jacketed steam tube containing steam under pressure. Depending on the thickness of the cover, the period of time in the tube can be controlled to complete the vulcanisation, or conversely, the length of the steam tube can be extended.

e. *The rotacure process* - It can be used to vulcanise large conveyor belts and continuous flooring strips. The process involves the use of and edless steel band which presses the article against a large heated drum. Slow rotation of the drum permits the vulcanisation to occur after approximately ten minutes contact time. Belt curing presses are also used; however, this system is not completeley continuous, although long lengths of belting are made by this method.

vi. Cold vulcanisation - These articles may be vulcanised by treatment with sulphur monochloride (S_2Cl_2) by dipping in a solution or exposure to its vapours. The process has been essentially replaced by using ultra accelerators which are capable of curing at room temperatures.

vii. High energy radiation - Systems using either gamma radiation from cobalt 60 or electron beams have been used for vulcanisation. The electron beam method has been used to cure both polyethylene and silicone rubbers. This is generally accomplished by passing the materials through the beam on a conveyor.

viii Microwave vulcanisation - Ultra high frequency fields (HMF) developed by alternating electromagnetic circuits can be used to warm up or vulcanise articles with large or uneven cross sections. The process required polar rubber mixtures since nonpolar materials will not absorb the energy produced. It is possible to warm articles upto 200°C within 30 seconds with some UHF systems. Continuous process utilising extruders and microwave heaters are available.

DYNAMIC VULCANISATION OF A MIXTURE OF NATURAL RUBBER WITH POLYPROPYLENE

Dynamic vulcanisation is based on a procedure, in which the rubber is vulcanised while homogenised with melted thermoplastics. The mixture is plastic above the melting temperature of thermoplastics and it shows the properties of a vulcanisate below this temperature. Several combinations of thermoplastics with elastomers have been described recently. They form mixtures capable of dynamic vulcanisation with good resulting properties. Physical and mechanical properties of the mixtures depend on the vulcanisation system used as well on the morphological state of the blend in molten state which, in turn, depends variables associated with the preparation of blends, such as the intensity and duration of mixing.

The possibilities of dynamic vulcanisation of a mixture of natural rubber with polypropylene have been described using two different vulcanisation systems. The properties of final products have been examined also from the point of view of the mixing conditions.

Procedure

Unstabilised isotactic polypropylene Tatren HPF with the melting flow index 8.4/g/10 minutes is used. Rubber white crepe is used as elastomer. Dicumyl peroxide is purified by recrystallisation from ethanol. The components of the sulphur vulcanisation system are used in quality as usually supplied for rubber industry.

The samples are prepared by mixing in a chamber of Plastoraf Brabender at 175°C. After taking the samples out, they are rolled into a foil on a cold roll-mill then pressed at 175°C for 2 minutes and cooled to 100°C in the press.

Tensile strength and elongation at break are determined on a tensile tester schopper. Hardness is measured by a durometer Shore. The content of insoluble portion is determined by weight after sample extraction with boiling xylene for 14 hours.

Figure 1 shows the gel content after dynamic vulcanisation as a function of the composition of a mixture NR/PP for vulcanisation initiated by tetramethyl thiuram disulphide (TMTD) and by dicumyl peroxide (DCP). It is known that TMTD does not react with polypropylene. Formation of the gel after vulcanisation of TMTD decreases with the increasing polypropylene content as expected. If dicumyl peroxide is used as initiator of vulcanisation, the decomposition products of which react with both components of the mixture, higher yield of gel is obtained. Dicumyl peroxide initiates vulcanisation so that the amount of the gel when the content of PP is 30% and 40% respectively, exceeds the amount of rubber present in the mixture (Figure 2). Part of polypropylene is built into the formed network in this case. The formation of hybrid branched structures is also assumed. These are part of the sol. Their presence in the mixture will affect the compatibility of components and contribute to the improvement of the properties of vulcanisates.

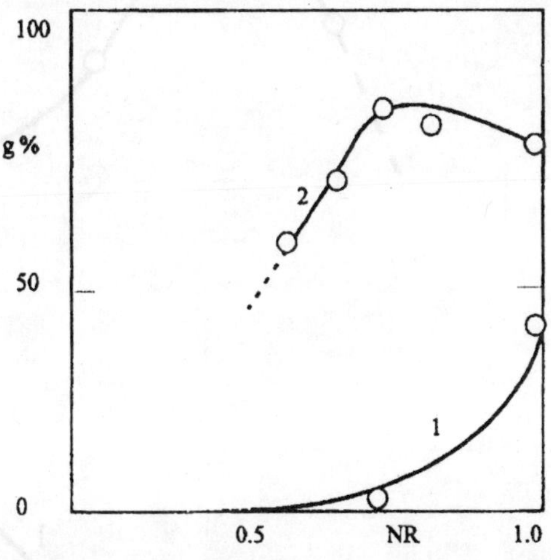

Fig. 1 : Dependence of gel amount (g) vs. portion of rubber (NR) in a mixture NR/PP vulcanised by TMTD (1) or DCP (2)

The mechanical properties of the mixtures prepared in this way are shown in Table 1. The properties of the mixtures vulcanised by peroxide are compared with unvulcanised mixtures prepared under the same conditions and with mixtures vulcanised by sulphur in the presence of accelerators of curing. Under these conditions, some defects occurred in uncured mixture containing 30% of PP. The defects are caused by separation of the components so that the probes could not be prepared. With mixtures vulcanised by sulphur at PP content of 50% and more, the vulcanising system does not cause the vulcanisation. The Table 1 shows that with the increasing portion of PP in uncured mixtures the tensile strength increases. A similar effect is observed for mixtures vulcanised by peroxides; when compared with unvulcanised mixture the tensile strength is higher at the PP content of 40%, but appreciably lower at 60% of PP. This trend corresponds to the assumption that radicals formed by the decomposition of dicumyl peroxide react with both components in a mixture NR/PP. As long as the rubber predominates in the mixture, the polypropylene macroradicals react mostly with rubber giving *in situ* block copolymers. These copolymers improve the compatibility of the components and tensile strength is higher. On the other hand, as the proportion of PP increases, more and more polypropylene macroradicals decay via fragmentation and by the reaction with the present oxygen. This leads to the destruction of PP matrix and to deterioration of the tensile properties.

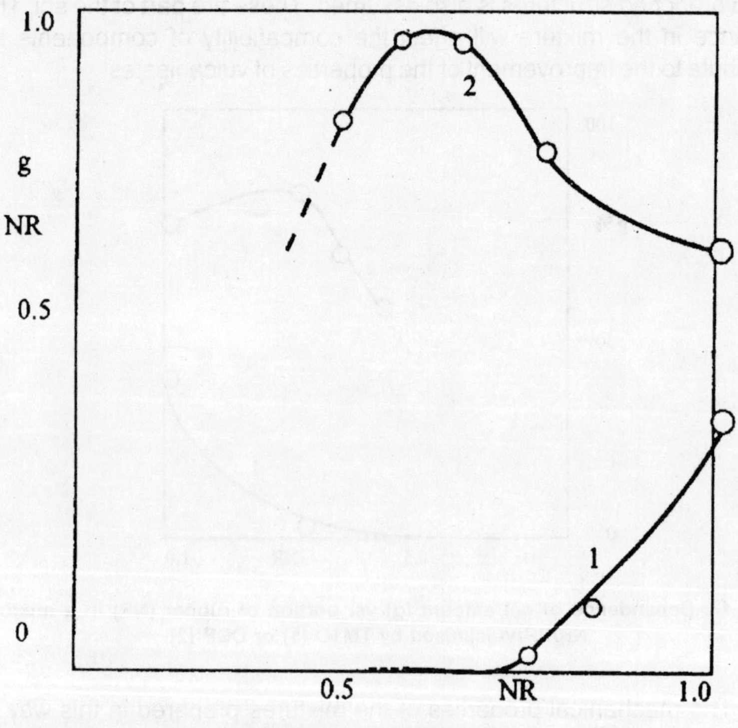

Fig. 2 : The data from Figure 1 calculated as ratio of gel to weight unity of elastomer (g/NR)

Vulcanisation by sulphur gives a material with similar properties at the ratio NR/ PP 70 : 30 as the cross-linking by peroxide. The increase of the PP content causes worsening of the properties on the contrary to the initiation by peroxide. This is explained by the decrease of the cross-linking degree of

Table 1 : Properties of the mixture NR/PP vulcanised by various systems

NR	Tensile strength MPa				Elongation at break %				Hardness Sh			
%	uncur.	DCP	Sulphur		Uncur.	DCP	sulphur		uncur.	DCP	sulphur	
			1%	1.7%			1%	1.7%			1%	1.7%
70		7.2	8.8	7.4	-	200	200	270	-	82	81	81
60	7.7	9.0	6.0	5.9	100	180	160	110	92	95	87	91
50	13.5	-	-	-	130	-	-	-	97	-	-	-
40	16.8	10.8	-	-	30	25	-	-	98	96	-	-

elastomer and by lowering the probability of the formation of hybrid rubber-polypropylene chains. These considerations are supported by the data on hardness since the mixtures NR/PP 60 : 40 vulcanised by sulphur show lower hardness than similar unvulcanised mixtures. The hardness of the mixtrue 40 : 60 vulcanised by peroxide is also lower, which probably reflects the degradation of polypropylene matrix.

The whole system is sensitive to the conditions of mixing. Its influence on the properties is seen in Table 2 on an example of the mixture NR/PP 70 : 30 vulcanised by dicumyl peroxide at the concentration of 1%. The properties of vulcanisate depend on the rate and time of mixing. At low (30 rpm) and medium (75 rpm) rate, 1 minute is not enough for obtaining samples with good mechanical properties. The enhanced mixing rate (150 rpm) leads to an increase in the strength by 60% and in the elongation at break by 160%. If the time of mixing is prolonged to 8 minutes, good properties of the mixture are found at low and medium mixing rate. At the highest rate, the longer time of mixing leads to deterioration of the properties. There is an optimum degree of mixing given by a proper combination of mixing rate and time. Insufficient homogeneity of the mixture is achieved below the optimum value. On the other hand the mechanical and thermo-oxidative degradation of the original polymer and products of the reaction takes place at higher than optimal degree of mixing. Thus, the resulting properties of the mixture are worse for various reasons.

Table 2 : The influence of the conditions of mixing on the properties of the mixture NR/PP 70 : 30 vulcanised by 1% DCP

Speed rpm	Time min	Tensile stress MPa	Elongation %	hardness Sh
30	1	3.4	70	78
75	1	3.6	50	82
150	1	5.6	160	80
30	8	6.6	180	82
75	8	7.1	210	82
150	8	4.5	140	80

VULCANISTION OF HYDRAULIC WIRE BRAIDED HOSE

Perhaps the most important property required of a wire reinforced hydraulic hose is that it should be well bonded together, with good consolidation and compaction and low compression set. This is a very necessary property of the cured hose in order to obtain satisfactory impluse field and user performance. It is usually achieved by applying pressure to the hose just prior to and during vulcanisation, and over the years has consisted of straight steam pressure in open pans, cloth wrappings, underlead sheaths, applied after the cover rubber has been extruded into positon or indeed more recently by well established electric cable industry continuous systems, such as steam pressure tube or molten salt in pressurised tubes (PLCV).

Here, the performance of underlead cured hydraulic hose is comparable with the newer PLCV system. Additionally, hose made with braid insulations of liquid rubber in place of conventional calendered sheet rubber are also examined.

Presently, the ultimate hose performance is measured by the so-called "secant square wave" pressure impulse test (ISO, 1436), but this has not been considered 100% satisfactory, because of a large scatter of test results even on the same piece of hose, the testing time is too long, and the test does not include flexing, and in this connection does not truly reflect operating conditions. Therefore, an alternative to the straight impluse test is also examined - the new half omega flexing test (ISD DIS 8032).

Impulse Performance

Figure 3 shows an increased pattern of straight impulse performance in favour of PLCV. This is considered to follow automatically from improved adhesion properties and brought about by the greater consolidation pressures of the PLCV system.

Impulse-flex (Half Omega)

By using the parameters of the half omega impluse-flex test, and as has been shown (Figure 3), the fall-off in impluse performance under flexing conditions is consistent in the three sizes of hoses tested, as are the consolidation trends between lead covered and PLCV systems together with calendered and liquid rubber insulations.

Energy Usage

It has been clearly shown that by the use of liquid rubber insulation, the calendering operation can be eliminated. The liquid may either be in solvent based form or the more desirable true liquid form, as solvents do not then need to be used.

Thus, both the higher capital cost and energy usages of a conventional rubber calender can be eliminated by the use of low energy and comparatively low capital cost drought mixing equipment for the application of the insulation rubbers used in wire braided, hydraulic hose.

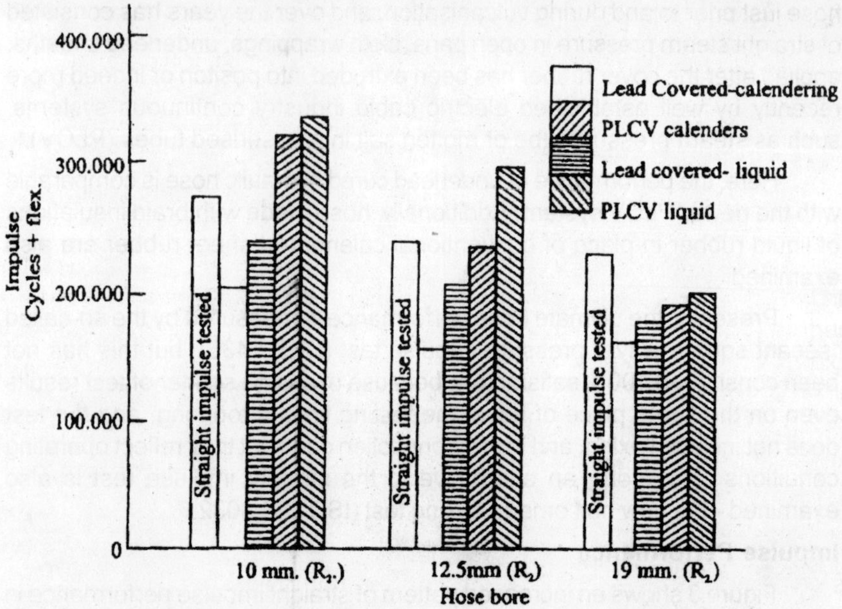

Fig. 3 : Lead PICV V Calenders/Liquid in solution (under impulse + flex pressure)

Procedure

Hose in bore sizes 10, 12.5 and 19 mm are made using calendered sheet and liquid rubber insulations and are vulcanised under lead or by PLCV systems.

Straight impluse (ISO 1436) and impluse + half omega flex (ISO 8032), are carried out. Impluse rests are determined which form the basis for the ISO Draft 8032.

The results are shown in Figure 3. Adhesion is improved in all hose when manufactured by the PLCV system because of the higher pressures on the hose during vulcanisation in PLCV than on the conventional lead system. This is more marked when using liquid rubber insulation because the liquid rubber flows into and between the wire braided interstices during casting and is then further subjected to even higher pressures during the PLCV processing.

Taking F Ratio's derived from the results in Figure 3 it can be seen that -

a. The size of hose is very significant with regard to level of impluse.

b. There is a very significant difference by the use of liquid rubber as an insulant in the hose rather than by the use of calendered rubber.

c. There is a very significant improvement by the use of PLCV cure over the underlead system.

d. There is a very important fall-off of impulse properties, under flexural conditions.

e. There appears to be significant interaction between bore size/cure system/insulation but none of these observations are considered of practical field value.

Because of the hose improvements brought about by the use of PLCV and liquid rubbers, the fall-off in impluse/flex performance for straight impluse performance is perhaps not quite as great as might have originally been expected, but it does nevertheless show the importance of such as test, when considered in the light of service operating conditions, and the length of time required to carry out the test. To give further reduction investing time a full scale omega test could be used.

KINETICS OF CURING

The rate of cure is traditionally obtained from a rheometer/curemeter. It is considered that a useful adjunct to reheometry would be the study of curing using differential thermal analysis. It is, therefore, decided to investigate the standard NA 22 and S Donor curing systems. Additionally, Denka M40 C.R. is used as an alternative to Baypren C.R.

Procedure

Three compounds (Table 3) are used in the experiment, and are examined using a Stanton Redpath differential thermal analyser, Model DTA 673-4.

This equipment consists of the following modules -

i. The lead assembly module with furnace

ii. The temperature programme

iii. The amplifier module

iv. The recorder.

The base module consists of the furnace mounting assembly and is fitted with connections for water cooling, gas, and vacuum, and flowmeter for atmosphere control around the sample. A twin specimen holder is positioned within the assembly, so that the temperature monitor is adjacent to the sepecimen under examination. The furnance has capability at temperature upto and over 100°C, although for this investigation the temperature limit is upto 200°C.

Table 3 : Compounds and equipments used in experiment

Test		Current recipe	NA22 base	Pyrogallol/s donor
Rheometer	T Max.	96.0	94.0	94.0
@ 177°C	T Min.	12.0	12.0	12.0
	Search	1.7	1.7	1.7
	T 90	4.6	4.6	4.6
ASTM oil No.3 (70 Hrs. @ 100°C)		+ 43.0	+ 45.0	+ 45.0
IRHD hardness		83.0	81	83.0
T/S (MPa)		11.4	11.0	10.9
E/B (%)		210.0	210.0	220.0
Compression set (24 hours @ 70°c)		36	35.0	33.0

The specimen holders within the head assembly consist of small platinum crucibles, which locate into wells in a ceramic block.

The other components of the analyser are connected in series to the recorder which, in turn, produces a graphical recording of the reaction as it takes place.

Results of the data obtained from the DTA traces (Table 4) as proposed by Borchardt and Daniels and derived from their equation, also confirms that the pyrogallol/S Donor system has a rate of reaction at least equal to or faster than that of NA 22 in compounds based on either Baypren or Denka C.R. rubbers, and also has excellent compression set (Table 3).

Table 4 : Comparative energy of activation for accelerators in neoprene compounds

	E_{comp} KJ/cml	
Accelerator	Baypren	Denka
NA 22	25.52	31.75
S/Donor pyrogallol	24.77	26.60

Equation

$$K = \left[\frac{KAV}{n_0}\right]^{x-1} \left\{\frac{C_p \frac{d\Delta T}{dt} + K\Delta T}{[K(A-a) - C_p \Delta T]^x}\right\}$$

For first order reactions (x = 1) since $C_p T$ is relatively small, this simplifies to -

$$K = \frac{\Delta T}{A - a}$$

(This method can only be used for comparative studies).

CONTINUOUS VULCANISATION METHOD

Continuous vulcanisation generally involves the use of some form of heating in a manner such that the vulcanisation step usually occurs immediately after the rubber article is formed. The process is normally used for extruded goods, coated wiring, conveyor belts, and flooring. These methods are described briefly as under.

LCM (LIQUID CURE METHOD)

The vulcanisation medium may be -

i. An eutectic mixture of three inorganic salts: KNO_3, $NaNO_2$ and $NaNO_3$, etc., composition being 53-40-7% and eutectic point 143°C

ii. A mixture of 50% KNO_3 and 50% $NaNO_3$ has an eutectic point of 219°C

iii. A commonly applied vulcanisation temperature is 240°C, the dwell time for thin-walled sections in ten-metre bath being 1 minute as shown in Figure 4.

The specific energy consumption of a ten-metre salt bath (including bath and belt heating, motors, fans, etc.), measured at a batch temperature of 240°C, is on an average 0.25 KW per kilogram of section. About 30% of this energy is effectively used for vulcanisation.

The specific vulcanisation costs are, on an average, DF1. 0.44 per kilogram of rubber section, for a production capacity of 200 kg/hr. In this figure all factors have been taken into account (labour, energy, depreciation, salt losses, overheat, etc.).

Microwave Pre-heating Plus Hot Air Vulcanisation

With this method one or more magnetrons are used for generating an electromagnetic field with a frequency of (usually) 2450 Mega Hertz. A rubber profile transported through this field is very quickly heated; depending on the polarity of the compound, it will take 30-40 seconds, for example, to heat it from 90-190°C. Vulcanisation proper takes longer, and is usually done in a hot air tunnel arranged immediately behind the microwave of UHF equipment. Typical vulcanisation conditions, for automotive and building profiles, are a temperature of 300°C and a dwell time of 5 minutes in the Hot Air tunnel. The microwave plus Hot Air method is often used for thick or thick-walled rubber sections. The compound to be vulcanised must be polar; if it is not, some polarity can be obtained by using fine, especially low-structure carbon blacks, diethylene glycol (DEG) or triethanolamine.

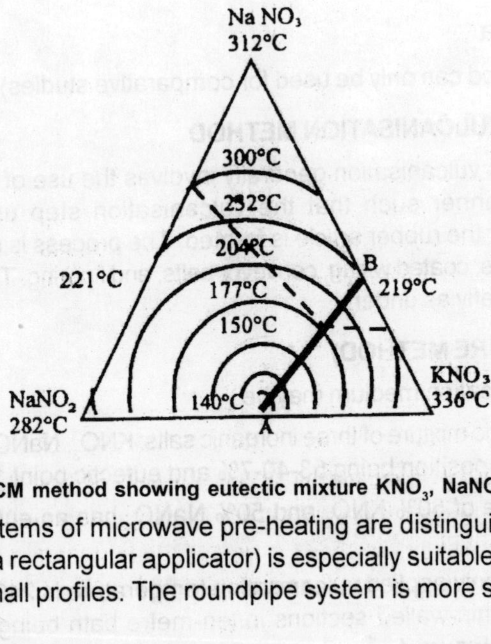

Fig. 4 : LCM method showing eutectic mixture KNO_3, $NaNO_2$ and $NaNO_3$

Two systems of microwave pre-heating are distinguished. The cavity system (with a rectangular applicator) is especially suitable for large profiles or multiple small profiles. The roundpipe system is more suitable for single small profiles.

The specific energy consumption of a 2× 6 KW microwave unit for a capacity of 200 kg/hr and a temperature increase of 100°C, is 0, 17 KW per kilogram of rubber profile. For an assembly including a hot air tunnel this figure is 0.3 KW/kg. The power efficiency of a microwave unit is slightly more than 50%.

Hot Air Vulcanisation

Modern Hot Air vulcanisation tunnels have a number of features ensuring good heat transfer.

i. The vulcanisation temperature is high 300-350°C.

ii. The air velocity in the tunnel has been increased to about 300m/min.

iii. By applying three tiered conveyor belts instead of a single belt, the dwell time has been increased by a factor three without an increase in floor space or energy.

The method is suitable only for thin-walled sections, which may be white or black.

Some tunnels use fresh air only, while in others the Hot Air is recycled. In practically all tunnels, a heat exchanger has been incorporated.

The energy consumed in vulcanisation of 300 kg of rubber sections per hour in an 18-metre tunnel which is traversed three times by the sections (giving a total vulcanisation length of 54 metres) is about 60 KW/hr. (i.e. 0.28 KW/kg), when the vulcanisation temperature is 300°C and the two final segments (of 3 metres each) are not provided with air heaters.

SSK (Scher-SpritzKopf) Pre-heating Plus Hot Air Vulcanisation

This method involves conversion of mechanical energy into heat with the aid of the SSK, which is mounted on the extruder head. The extruder forces the rubber compound into the gap between the thermostated mandrel and the surrounding jacket. Heat-up takes place by fast rotation on the mandrel (e.g. 160 rpm). With a capacity of, for example, 200 kg/hr, heat-up from 90 to 170°C will take about 8 seconds. This is five times as fast as heat-up by microwave equipment. After heat-up, vulcanisation takes place in the Hot Air tunnel.

This means that the SSK has exactly the same function as a microwave unit, but there are a number of typical differences.

i. Microwave heat-up an electromagnetic field is used, whereas the SSK-unit uses mechanical energy.

ii. The microwave method is suitable for polar compounds only, while the SSK method is also suitable for non-polar compounds.

iii. The floor space needed for the SSK-unit is six or seven times less than for a microwave unit.

iv. The SSK unit is considerably cheaper than microwave equipment, though on the other hand a more expensive extruder is required, 24D instead of 16D, because a higher pressure must be delivered.

v. The power efficiency of the microwave is just above 50%, but that of the SSK is 80%.

For a capacity of 300 kg/hr, with $\Delta T = 70°C$, the energy consumption of an SSK is 14 KW/hr, which is 0.05 KW/kg of rubber profile, The combination of SSK + Hot Air tunnel requires a total of 50 KW/hr., which is 0.22 KW/kg of rubber profile produced.

Fluidised-bed Vulcanisation

The vulcanisation medium is in effect a mixture of air and very small glass beads (0.1-0.2 mm), the so-called ballotinis. The continuous rubber section which is to be vulcanised is transported through the bed of ballotinis, and is kept fluidised by hot air. On account of the excellent heat transfer in this system (the medium behaves like a liquid) vulcanisaiton takes only a short time. Maximum temperature is 250°C. Fluidised beds are about as long is LCM baths, that is, 10-12 metres. The main problem with this vulcanisation method is that the glass beads tend to stick to the rubber profile. The fluidised bed method is more common in Britain. A striking feature of rubber sections or hoses produced by this method is their velvet-like surface.

Electron Beam Vulcanisation

This vulcanisation method is based on irradiation of rubber surfaces with β rays. β radiation, i.e., an electron beam, is preferred to other types of radiation because of its higher penetrating and ionising power. The radiation equipmnt can also be used for preservation treatment of fruits and potatoes and for sterilising medical instruments. The electrons cause C-C bonds via radical formation. Sulphur of peroxide vulcanisation systems is not needed. The method is very quick, and practically no heat is generated. However, the depth of penetration is only a few millimetres and even irradiation from both sides will fail with compounds thicker than 6 mm. It is not surprising that the method is frequently used for the thin cables or flat articles. Speeds of 400-500 m/min. air feasible (for cable).

PLCV (Pressurised Liquid Continuous Vulcanisation)

The vulcanisation medium is an LCM salt mixture, but this time the mixture is under pressure ca.2 atm. The method is used for cables only, pressurisation helps to decrese porposity. An advantage of this method over the steam-pipe method is that the vulcanisation temperature is independent of the pressure and the vulcanisation medium is dry.

HVGC (High Velocity Gas Cure)

In this system vulcanisation takes place in high-speed, recirculating N_2 gas. The maximum vulcanisation temperature is 350°C, the maximum gas velocity 1800 m/minute and the maximum pressure 10 atm. The method is used for cables only. The curing unit includes apparatus for monitoring the concentration of O_2 and CH_4 (by products of the decomposition of vulcanising agents).

Steam-pipe Vulcanisation

The steam pipe method is used for cables only, because components that lack a metal core cannot be transported through the pipe. The length of pipe where vulcanisation takes place is 50-80 metres, and the subsequent cooling section is 10-25 metres. Steam pressure may reach 25 atmospheres gauge pressure, which corresponds to a temperature of about 223°C.

The steam pipe is horizontal (HCV for cable diameters upto 15 mm), catenary (CCV) or, for heavier cables, vertical (VCV). Depending on factors such as steam-pipe length, steam pressure, cable diameter etc., vulcanisation speeds of 200 to even 500 metres per minute can be achieved.

Rotocure Vulcanisation

This method is highly suitable for vulcanisation of broad rubber belting, conveyor belts and V-belts. By means of a steel belt the sheeting is pressed against an internally steam-heated drum. The reversing rolls may be steam heated. If steam is not available the drum(s) may be heated with oil or with electric quartz radiators.

Helicure

Helicure vulcanisation involves passing the profile to be vulcanised through a hose (length 50-150 mm) containing a fast-flowing heating medium. The heating medium, e.g., PEG or glycerol, is kept at ca. 160°C by recirculation over a heater.

Pressureless vulcanisation	Pressurised vulcanisation
1. LCM	1. PLCV
2. UHF + Hot Air	2. HVGC
3. Hot Air	3. Steam Pipe
4. SSK + Hot Air	4. Rotocure
5. Fluid Bed	5. Helicure
6. Radiation curing (β-radiation)	

14

Manufacturing Techniques of Rubber Products

INTRODUCTION

Manufacturing techniques pose a few of the key problems which are common to the industry and are worthy of note. These arise mainly from the intrinsic properties of textiles and rubber stocks and from the semi-plastic condition of materials in the unvulcanised state.

Although the rubber coating applied to textiles provides protection from moisture absorption, it is important to limit exposure time to a practical minimum. A high moisture regain in rayon, for example, can result in separations within the casing structure when internal pressure is released at the conclusion of the vulcanisation process. For this reason, and also to prevent self-adhesion, 'in process' stocks must be interleaved at all stages in dry low-moisture absorbent textile linings.

The instability of rubbered materials and compounds creates handling problems. For example, relatively minor distortion to cut ply materials will alter the bias angle and regularity of cord spacing. This can affect ultimate casing tension and uniformity of the tyre. In critical areas, like radial ply tyres, the plant is designed with festoon appliances and air flotation systems to minimise this danger.

Care is necessary to ensure that compounds are free from incipient scorching and that the desired surface condition is retained at the time of tyre building. Clearly, over-tacky or over-dry materials present handling difficulties and due attention has to be paid to maturing times and shelf life. It is imperative that interface bonding, during assembly, is good, and cleanliness is a key requirement at all stages of manufacture. The development of surface blooming, with some compounds, can be counteracted by light application of a solvent-soaked textile pad during the tyre casing assembly operations.

One of the anathemas of tyre manufacture is included air. Even after all precautions have been taken in the fitting and progressive consolidation of individual components, it is inevitable that minute channels of air will persist at the stepped edges within the structure. During the power stitching operations, this air may collect in the form of small blisters which require to be released by manual pricking.

Regularity of the outside contour of the raw tyre is important in the avoidance of vulcanised tyre surface defects. Considerable movement or flow of stock can take place in the initial of vulcanisation owing to its thermoplastic properties and to the influence of the high internal pressure applied to the casing. Any surface irregularities induce flow which can result in moulding defects in the form of splits or blisters.

Apart from the normal laboratory checking of incoming raw materials, it is essential to apply quality controls, on a statistical basis, throughout the manufacturing process and to the finished product.

The mixed compounds are subject to specific gravity checking and to curemeter testing for scorch, plasticity, and modulus. Water hardness, viscosity, alkalinity, and total solids of impregnants, used for textile treatment, must be controlled, and a routine check of static rubber-to-cord adhesion is desirable with certain critical materials before release of processed rolls for use in manufacture. Rubbered ply and belt materials must be examined for extensibility, regularity of cord spacing, and, in some instances, percentage moisture regain. The continuous auditing of all key operations in component preparation and tyre building is essential, including the dimensional accuracy of components and machine settings. Finally, tyre uniformity and grading machines are used to check stiatic or dynamic balance, radial and lateral run-out, etc., of the finished product.

PNEUMATIC TYRES

Recent emphasis has been placed on safety, which has brought about the development of more complex tread patterns to assist water displacement and thereby to minimise the tendency to aqua-plane. The 'wet grip' requirement has also led to the introduction of special rubber compounds. These features have tended to complicate factory processing of the tread elements, including the steps of vulcanisation and extraction of the finished tyre from the mould.

Improvements to road networks and, in particular, the construction of motorways, have led to higher sustained operating speeds. Concurrently, suspension systems and chassis designs have altered significantly, resulting in more sensitive structures. The combined effect of these developments has tended to highlight the ill effects of vibrations and resonances excited by forces generated by lack of uniformity within the tyre structure. As a direct result, vehicle manufacturers insist upon rigid specifications for tyre uniformity, particularly in the passenger car field and, to a growing extent, for the truck ranges. This requirement has become more critical with the adoption of the radial ply tyre and the increasing use of high-modulus materials in the carcass.

Variables that require to be controlled include radial and lateral force variations, static unbalance, and radial and lateral run-out. It should be appreciated that the force or unbalance actually measured on the tyre is a vectorial summation of an infinite number of small forces or moments about the central axis. A complete reappraisal of previously accepted manufacturing practices and operating tolerances has been made, leading to the raising of quality acceptance standards for raw materials, inprocess components, tyre manufacture, and finished tyre grading.

CONSTRUCTION OF TYRE

Tyre manufacture has also been complicated, particularly in the passenger car range, by a trend towards the adopteion of squat section tyres. Whereas a few years ago the section height-width ratio was approximtely 100%, in present-day tyres, it is nearer 80% and the trend is still downwards. From the car manufacturer's point of view, this results in vehicles with a lower centre of gravity and consequently, improved control characteristics. Often the opportunity is taken to increase wheel diameters to permit the fitting of more efficient brakes while still maintaining the low vehicle line. Such changes tax the designer's art in producing mould shapes and manufacturing processes to ensure that the inflated raw tyre shape, immediately prior to mould closure in the vulcanising press, is reasonably in keeping with the tyre mould profile. Failure to achieve this condition can create undesirable rubber flow, which affects dimensional accuracy in the vulcanised product and also promotes moulding defects.

During past few years there has been a progressive swing from diagonal ply or cross ply tyre construction to radial ply in the passenger car and truck ranges. This is likely to continue and may extend to earth-mover and other specialised tyre types. Types. This revolutionary concept demanded a complete change in manufacturing methods and factory control practices. Not only did it involve the introduction of entirely new tyre building plants and far more sophisticated tyre moulding techniques, but also created the need for a much tighter overall quality control system. By virutue of its basic construction, this type of tyre is far more sensitive to in-built variables than the conventional diagonal ply tyre. The alternative belted bias construction, counter to the radial tyre, has the virtue that the carcass can be assembled using the standard type of tyre building and vulcanising plant. Economic considerations undoubtedly promoted this development, which only goes part of the way towards the advantage in tread life which the radial holds over the conventional cross ply tyre. Furthermore, the improved vehicle handling imparted by the radial tyre is not realised with belted bias constructions.

Materials

For a long period, high-extensible cotton cord was the universally used textile. Steam stretching techniques were introduced to achieve lower extensibilities, improved strength, and a lower cord denier, thereby yielding cord of higher tenacity. This development was quickly outmoded by the general adoption of rayon, with nylon coming into use for specialised applications. Both these latter fibres required the use of adhesives to achieve adequate bonding to rubber compounds. Recently, polyester, glass fibre, and steel have been added to the carcass materials available to the designer; in the future, carbon fibre may find applications in this field.

The physical properties of materials used in tyre structures influence, to a marked degree, the initial rubbering techniques, handling and storage of the processed sheet, and tyre building and vulcanising procedures. Features which are of importance include moisture regain, extensibility, thermal stability, flexibility, and acceptability of adhesives.

The scorch rate, plasticity, modulus, shrinkage factor, ease of processing, tack, and shelf life of rubber compounds likewise affect manufacturing procedures. Equally, such properties as heat build-up, abrasion resistance, flex cracking and cut resistance, and gas permeability determine the selection of compounds for the various components of the tyre. The raw polymers used are NR, SBR, IIR, BR, IR, and most recent, EPDM. The differences in their properties in relation to their use in tyres are shown in Table 14.1.

Table 14.1: Features of general purpose elastomers for use in tyres

Property	NR	IR	SBR	BR	IIR	EPM/EPDM
Wear resistance	2	2	3	4	2	3
Road holding	2	2	3	2	4	2
Low heat build-up	3	4	1	1	1	1
Tear resistance	4	3	1	1	2	1
Gas and vapour impermeability	1	1	1	1	4	1
Ageing resistance	1	1	2	2	3	4
Ozone resistance	1	1	1	1	3	4

Tyre Design

The tyre designer is faced with an impossible task in trying to satisfy all the needs of the vehicle manufacturer and the user, and is, therefore, forced to seek a compromise with emphasis on the important factors of safety and tread life.

In determining the tyre size and type, the vehicle and tyre designers give prime consideration to the following aspects.

i. Vehicle weight distribution, which will determine the load-carrying capacity of the tyre and the operating inflation pressure.

ii. Axle height and clearance for the chassis, suspension, and braking system; these decide the overall diameter, section width, and bead diameter of the tyre.

iii. The vehicle suspension system, which will influence the basic tyre construction, including the selection of either radial or diagonal ply construction.

iv. The speed capability and operating conditions, both of which will have to be considered in relation to construction, compounds, and tread pattern design.

Having established the basic tyre dimensions, which must conform to agreed industry standards, the tyre designer is in a position to decide on the tyre mould dimensions, tread pattern details, rubber mixes, textile reinforcement, and the form of the structure. From the vehicle weight and speed requirements, mathematical calculation of the casing and bead wire strengths can be made; the materials can then be selected and their make-up settled.

When formulating a tyre design it is essential, from a manufacturing stand-point, to pay due regard to the cost and availability of materials, factory plant, and production methods, so that a viable product is produced at an economic price and meets the need of the consumer.

Tyre Sizing

The generally accepted system for indicating tyre dimensions is to quote the approximate cross-sectional width of the tyre, followed by the nominal diameter of the bead seat of the wheel to which the tyre must be fitted. These dimensions are either expressed in inches or millimetres but dual imperial and metric unit markings are sometimes employed.

The load-carrying capacity of a tyre is dependent on its internal volume and its inflation pressure. It therefore follows that, for a fixed section height-width ratio, the load-carrying capability will increase with increasing wheel diameters. This arrangement has been applied in the past for standard passenger car and truck tyre ranges, but recently, in the car group, there has been a trend towards designing tyres of common load-carrying capacity for all wheel diameters. This means that the cross-sectional area reduces as the nominal bead diameter increases, i.e., the internal volume remains constant regardless of the normal bead diameter. In this latter circumstance, the convention is to identify a tyre by a letter of the alphabet indicating the load-carrying capacity, followed by the percentage height-width rario, and finally the wheel diameter.

Although the basic principles of tyre manufacture are similar for all tyre ranges, it will be appreciated that the method and plant used to produce a simple motor cycle tyre made up of approximately 10 components, will differ radically from that necessary to handle an extra large earthmover tyre embodying around 175 individual units. A typical tyre of this type will contain as many as 40 laryers of textile in the carcass plies and a composite tread weighing 600 kg, giving in overall tyre weight of 1.25 Mg. Although semi-automatic building machinery is employed, much of the assembly is a skilled manual operation requiring more than 24 hours to complete and followed by a vulcanising time of 8 hours. Other specialised ranges include tyres for aircraft and racing cars.

Tyre construction

Standard Diagonal Ply Tyre Construction

It will be seen (Figure 14.1) that the internal structure comprises layers of cords, normally two or four in number which run diagonally from bead, with adjacent layers assembled at opposite bias. Each layer or rubbered cord is known as a ply. It will be noted that the outer edges of the plies are interlocked around the steel wire bead coils in order that reorientation of the casing angles, during the vulcanisation process, will take place in a controlled manner. It is imperative that individual cords are evenly tensioned in the finished product, in order to contain tyre growth, obtain the optimum structural performance, and achieve an acceptable level of uniformity.

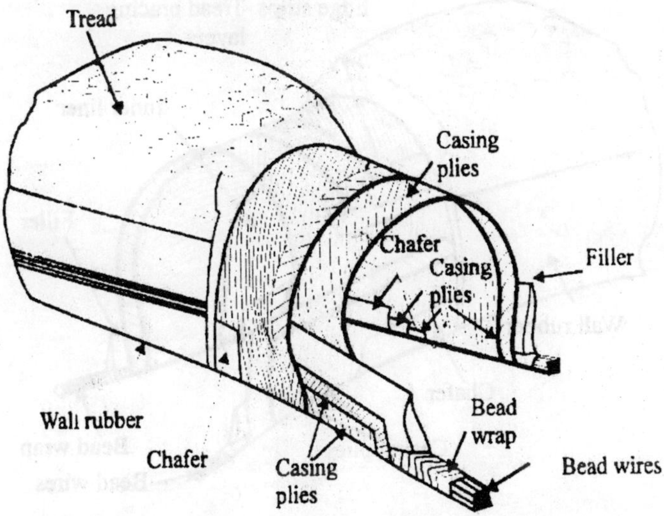

Fig. 14.1: Diagonal ply tyre (four-ply construction) tubeless

Belted Bias Tyre Construction

Again the casing plies are cut at an angle approximately to that used for standard diagonal ply tyres and are assembled together in a similar manner to producea balanced and uniformly tensioned structure (Figure 14.2).

The fundamental difference in the construction is that the plies are surmounted by two or more layers of rubbered cord material, cut at a lower angle than the carcass plies. These are in the form of circumferential strips extending across the full width of the crown area of the tyre, and fitted with an opposed bias relationship to the casing plies, and to each other. These form a restraining belt which raises the modulus of the tread area, thereby controlling the inflated tread profile and also reducing tread pattern movement.

Radial Ply Tyre Construction

As the terminology implies, the essential difference between the radial ply tyre and the two alternative constructions just described lies in the disposition of the casing ply cords (Figure 14.3). In the radial ply tyre, the cords lie at approximately 90° to the circumference. This results in an extremely flexible sidewall which acts independently of the tread bracing belt, thus fruther reducing the distortion which takes place in the belt and the tread block as the tyre passes through the road contact zone. Advantages include increased tread life, improved comfort at high speed, and improved security on cornering.

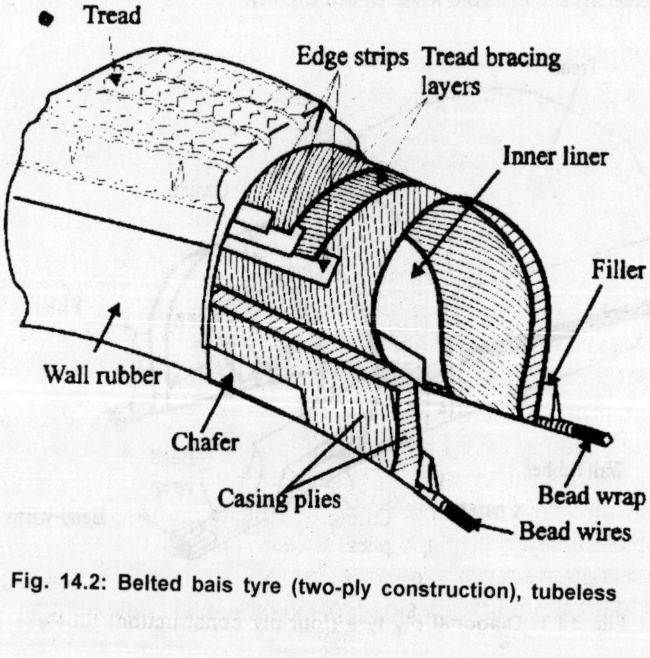

Fig. 14.2: Belted bais tyre (two-ply construction), tubeless

The belt construction, in general use, comprises four low-angle plies of textile cord; some manufacturers have adopted steel or glass fibre cors for the belt. The choice depends upon performance requirements, practical manufacturing facilities, and economic considerations.

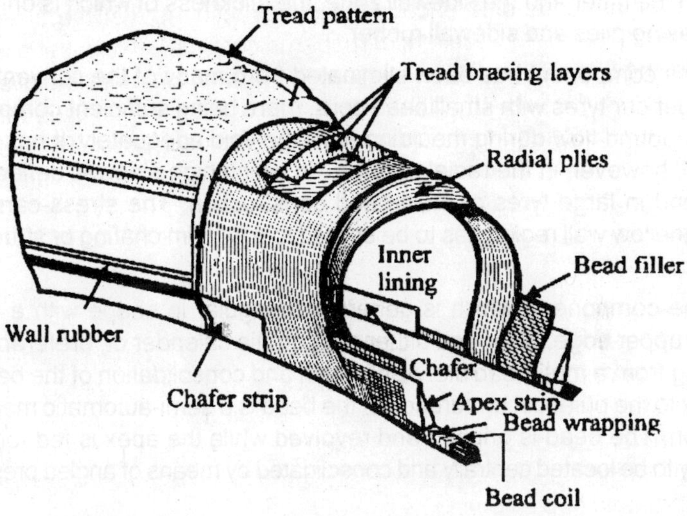

Fig. 14.3: Radial ply tyre (two-ply construction), tubeless

Tyre Components

Before dealing with the detailed operation of raw tyre assembly and ancillary operations, prior to tyre vulcanisation, it is necessary to outline the basic components forming a tyre structure and to indicate their function and method of preparation.

Beads

The bead coils are a combination of multi-strand copper-coated high-tensile steel wires. They have the function of providing rigid, practically inextensible units, which retain the inflated tyre on the rim under all conditions of lading.

The appropriate number of wires, formed into a flat layer and uniformly separated, are coated with rubber compound by means of a T-head extruder. The layer of wires is coiled to form a ring, and the free wire ends are taped or stapled. The wire treatment and use of fast-curing compound ensure good bonding and a regular bead shape in the finished product. For some purposes, the bead coil is covered with a light cross-woven rubberised textile to contain the wires and preclude any possibility of looseness in service.

Bead Apex

The bead apex is a fibrous or rubber compound strip located on the top face of the bead; its primary function is to pack out the area of the structure immediately above the bead coil and so provide a steady gradation of thickness between the latter and the sidewall zone, the thickness of which is only that of the casing plies and sidewall rubber.

This component has been eliminated from many of the conventional passenger car tyres with small bead coils, there being sufficient compound and compound flow during moulding to fill the void adequately. It has to be retained, however, in the radial ply tyres, in which high sidewall deflections occur, and in large tyres of multi-bead construction. The stress-carrrying zone in the low wall region has to be spread to avoid rim chafing or structural break-up.

The component, which is generally triangular in shape with a finely tapered upper edge, is formed either on a profile calender or, preferably, by extruding from a muti-head die. Application and consolidation of the base of the apex to the outer circumference of the bead is a semi-automatic machine operation. The bead is gripped and revolved while the apex is fed forward manually to be located centrally and consolidated by means of angled pressure rollers.

Bead Fillers (Flippers)

In those instances where further reinforcement of the tyre bead area is required, the already wrapped and apexed bead may be enclosed by a strip of rubberised textile or, in some applications, by steel cords. Emphasis is on the avoidance of localised circumferential stress lines which could promote looseness or cord break-up under constant flex conditions. High-grade flexible heat-resistant compounds are essential for this region of the tyre.

Carcass Plies

It is the carcass plies that give the tyre its strength. These consist of cords of cotton, rayon, nylon, or polyester, woven as the warp of a fabric with only very light yarns, widely spaced, as the weft. These weft strands serve to maintain the uniformity of cord spacing during handling but play no part in the performance of the product. The fabric is treated with adhesive, rubberised to a thickness of approximately 1.0 mm, and interleaved with a low moisture regain textile lining. Steel is produced in weftless from a creel feeding directly through a rubber calender. The large rolls of rubbered textile, approximately 1.5 m wide and 300 m long are cut into strips, termed plies, on a horizontal Banner machine. This ply-cutting plant has facilities for mechanically unwinding large rolls of fabric and simultaneously rewinding the interleaving lining. The fabric sheet is fed forward, through a festoon unit to allow for continuous operation, and then guided along a horizontal multi-belt conveyor to a cross-beam rotary cutting knife. This knife is complete with its own drive motor, and the entire unit traverses across the support beam when cutting the material to predetermined width and bias angle: the latter is variable between 45° and 90°, and the operation is controlled by photoelectric cells.

Cut plies are placed manually on adjacent batching tables, where they are joined, end to end, into a continuous length and batched into roll form, interleaved with a textile lining to prevent self-adhesion. Suitable devices are provided at all stages to prevent distortion of the material.

Tread Bracing Components (Breakers or Belts) for Radial or Belted Bias Tyres

Tread bracing components raise the modulus of in tread area, thereby maintaining the inflated tyre tread profile and reducing tread pattern movement as it contacts the road.

The method of strip cutting the rubbered textile is identical with that used for cutting plies, but, in this case, the travelling beam on the bias cutting machine is adjustable for angles of 15°-25°.

The method of converting the single-layer low-angle cut strips into the form of the final belt varies. The most widely used construction, for radial ply tyres, employs four layers, made from folded strips, adjacent layers being of opposite bias angle. In practice, the two strips are slightly offset to achieve a graduated step-down in thickness at the belt edges, thereby reducing stress concentration and minimising the development of losseness in service.

Insulating Components (Undertread, Breaker Cushion Insulations)

These insulating components are calendered strips of rubber compounds usually of 1 mm gauge or less. They are located in positions within the structure where additional insulation is required between components to prevent chafing. The compounds are similar to those used for coating the carcass plies.

Tread

The tread is the wearing surface of the tyre. It is applied in the raw state as an extruded slab of rubber compound. In cross-section it is substantially rectangular across the centre protion, tapering down to very fine edges. The thickness must be calculated to accommodate the pattern fragmentation in the tyre mould and to allow an adequate residual thickness beneath the pattern grooves. The tread width is such that the tapered edges extend to a position slightly above the maximum flex zone in the upper sidewall region.

The extruding operation is continuous, and the extrudate is either batched as a continuous length into a band dispenser, for subsequent cutting to length at the tyre building machine, or pre-cut into individual lengths and stored on flat metal trays in multi-leaf stillages. The former method is preferred; length variation of pre-cut treads often occurs as in-built stresses in the compound are released.

Sidewall

The sidewall is an extruded rubber compound layer which serves to protect the carcass structure from weathering and chafing damage. Together with the tread, which it overlpas in the buttress region, it forms the outermost layer of the tyre.

As with the tread, the extruding operation is continuous, and sidewalls are normally batched into spools interleaved with a textile or polyethylene lining material.

For conventional diagonal ply and belted bias tyres, built on relatively flat drums, frequently a common formulation permits extrusion of tread and sidewalls as one piece. Two separate compounds are used either to achieve performance or for reasons of economy. Modern dual extruders, feeding through a common Y-box head, produce a combined tread-sidewall unit; by joining the two stocks under high pressure and at high temperature, interface failures are eliminated.

Chafer

The chafer is a narrow circumferential strip of material which encloses the completed bead area. Its supper edge is located slightly above the rim flange height and extends downwards and around the bead base. This arrangement provides some protection from rim chafing and, in the case of tubeless tyres, serves to prevent air leakage either into the tyre or through the tyre in the bead area. To meet these conditions, the material used is either a rubber-coated wick-proof cross-woven textile cut at 45° bias or a strip of calendered compound. In the latter case, the strip, of approximately 1 mm gauge, is generally fully cured, buffed, and solutioned, prior to assembly into the raw tyre. In this way, stock flow during vulcanisation is avoided and the retention of an adequate rubber covering over the casing ply edges is assured.

Processing of cured rubber strips is a continuous operation of multi-strip calendering and vulcanising by drum cure. After surface buffing and solutioning, individually on an ancillary unit, the strips are spooled in continuous lengths suitably interleaved with polyethylene.

Inner Lining

For tubed tyres, the inner lining is a thin layer of compound usually calendered direct onto the underside of the first ply after the latter has been joined and batched in continuous lengths. The component serves to insulate fully the tyre cords from the inner tube and thereby prevent tube chafing damage. It also protects the cords from possible degradation due to atmospheric moisture absorption.

In tubeless tyres, the inner lining is the air-retaining member and is usually calendered as a two-layer laminate having stepped edges. The overall gauge may be as high as 2.5 mm, and the width must ensure that the edges are overlapped by the inner edges of the chafer. This provides a low permeability layer bead to bead.

Clinch Strip

The clinch strip may be considered as an extension to the lower edge of the sidewall, introduced as a further anti-abrasion measure on radial ply tyres, which are more subject to rim chafing than the cross ply tyre. It is a narrow extruded strip, about 25 mm wide and tapered a both edges, which is normally hot-assembled to the sidewalls by operating extruders in train.

Truck tyres and allied ranges are far more complex, involving many additional components, inserts, and compounds. Also, it will be obvious that preparation and handling techniques have to be adjusted to deal with the sheer dimensional size and weight of components used in these products. Steel ply radial giant, earth-mover, and aircraft tyres are particular examples.

Tyre Building

The Building Drum

Throughout the conventional diagonal ply and belted bias tyre ranges, including passenger car, truck, and earthmover tyres, the tyre building drum in general use is a plain segmental open-ended metal drum which is mounted on a driven shaft. The internal mechanism is designed so that the segments can be collapsed radially to permit the removal of the completed tyre carcass. The ends of the drum are flanged to suit the bead configuration of the tyre to be built. In all cases, the drum overall diameter exceeds the nominal tyre bead diameter. This difference, known as the drum crown height, varies from 25 mm for single bead tyres to 300 mm for large truck and earthmover tyres. Furthermore, in the latter cases, the flange profile has an appropriate undercut to achieve a balanced ply-to-ply tensioning in the finished product. The raw tyre can be completed on the building drum and is transformed from the cylindrical to a toroidal shape during the mould closing operation, the circumferential stretch being of the order of 60%.

The fact that the tread bracing components or 'belt' of radial ply tyres from a relatively inextensible unit and must be fitted at a diameter within 5% of its final diameter in the moulded tyre, means that for this type the partly built casing has to be inflated into a toroidal shape. Radial ply tyres necessitated, therefore, new complex and costly machinery incorporating inflatable textile-reinforced diaphragms, overlying a skeletal metal drum shell, to shape the carcass plies and other foundation components up to the diameter for belt fitting. It will be understood that, to achieve this, the shoulders of the drum move inwardly in a controlled manner so that the correct tension is maintained in the carcass plies.

Because it can still be accommodated on standard tyre building machinery, the batted bias tyre has come into being.

Diagonal Ply Tyres

A modern building plant, for passenger car tyres, is highly mechanised and constructed for maximum accuracy and productivity. For diagonal ply tyres, including the belted bias version, the standard form of building machine is designed specifically for operation with low-crown building drums; the uncured raw tyre is completed in a one-stage operation.

Belted Bias Tyre

The procedure outlined for the building of a conventional diagonal ply tyre is applicable to a belted bias construction but with the addition of the breaker belt layers. These strips are assembled centrally to the top prior to fitting the tread unit.

Radial Ply Tyres

No standardised type of building machine has yet emerged for radial ply tyres, but two general methods of tyre building are currently employed.

First Method

Plies, beads, and chaffers are assembled in the manner already described on the same machine as used for diagonal ply and belted bias tyres. The partly built carcass is then transferred to another machine, which comprises a driven shaft carrying a shaping drum. The first operation on this machine is to inflate the flexible drum sleeve and shape the casing (Figure 14.4). During the operation the drum flanges and bell-shaped housings traverse inwardly in a controlled sequence, partly to enclose and also to contain the tyre casing.

A pre-folded breaker length is applied manually to the exposed top carcass ply, the recessed inner edges of the bell surfacesserving as guides. A marginal overlap joint is made, and a second breaker lengths is applied with the fold on the side opposite to that of the first length. The assembled belt is then consolidated by roller pressure. A pre-cut tread length is run on by drum rotation, joined, and hand consolidated.

At this stage the shaping bells are withdrawn to allow pivoting disc rollers to traverse and consolidate the tread. Sidewall rubbers, extending from the tyre hands to overlap the centre tread tapered edges, are fitted, cut to length, joined, and consolidated, first manually and then by rollers. In some variants of the machine, inflatable rolling bags automatically apply sidewalls to the otherwise completed tyre. Vacuum is applied to collapse the flexible durm centre and permit removal of the finished tyre.

In the above method, the initial partly built casing is in a very unstable condition and precautions have to be taken to avoid contamination and distortion.

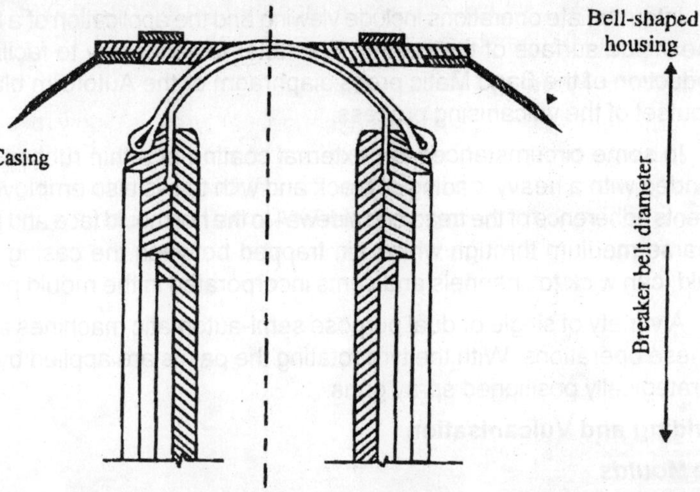

Fig. 14.4: Shaping of tyre casing - the casing is shaped and the belts are positioned for belt assembly

Second Method

One of the most modern building machines carries out the building and shaping operations automaticially. All components are prepared on an ancillary plant designed to place material accurately in rechargeable cartridges so that no operator intervention to correct for misalignment is necessary.

The central inflatable drum portion is used in its collapsed state for the flat building operation and serves to shape the casing when inflated. Lateral diaphragms, on either side, turn up the ply material edges around the bead and also apply the pre-assembled sidewalls and chafers to the casing. Bell-shaped housings control the shape of the inflated casing and incorporate bead setting rings, ply turn-down fingers, and in-built diaphragms for consolidation of the outer ply edges.

The breakers and tread are assembled on a separate machine and are transferred to the building operation supported internally by a narrow split metal ring and externally by an inflatable transfer ring. The operator's function is confined to fitting beads, joining components, fitting the transfer ring, initiating the automatic sequences, and removing the finished tyre. Inevitably a high degree of skill is required forsetting up and maintaining this equipment.

Preparation of Raw Tyres for Vulcanisation

Tyres from the building machine lines are generally transferred by line conveyors, either to a holding stock area or direct to the vulcanising department.

Intermediate operations include viewing and the application of a lubricant to the inside surface of the casing. The latter is necessary to facilitate the introduction of the Bago Matic press diaphragm or the Autoform bladder at the outset of the vulcanising process.

In some circumstances, an external coating of a thin rubber solution extended with a heavy loading of black and with talc is also employed. This prevents adherence of the tread and sidewall to the hot mould face and provides a coarse medium through which air, trapped between the casing and the mould, can wick to channels and vents incorporated in the mould profile.

A variety of single or dual purpose semi-automatic machines are used for these operations. With the tyre rotating the paints are applied by means of strategically positioned spray guns.

Moulding and Vulcanisation

Tyre Moulds

For most applications, tyre moulds are basically of two-piece construction, in steel or aluminium, with the split being circumferential sand either central or slightyl off centre, dependent upon tread pattern complications. The use of male and female registers and dowels ensure both circumferential and radial location during mould closure. Each mould half is recessed just above the bead diameter to accommodate rings, termed 'slip rings', which incorporate the tyre bead profile.

The tread pattern in each mould half may be either cut from the solid, produced in the form of a ring which is then bolted to the mould shell, or built up from a series of aluminium die cast segments. The latter method is advantageous for complex pattern designs, incoprorating sipes, tunnels, buffer, bars, and variable-pitch arrangements, because segments from a few master dies, in the requisite number of pitches, can be utilised for a range of tyre diameters and section by making small machining adjustments. Larger truck tyres, and tractor and earthomver tread patterns are either sand cast (simple bar designs) or produced as tread rings.

For the vulcanisation process, heat is applied externally to the tyre within the mould either (i) by locating the mould in a suitable form of pressure vessel with direct circulation of steam around it, or (ii) by mounting the mould between two steam-heated chests or platens.

Curing Bags, Bladders, and Diaphragms

To avoid porosity, to consolidate the components, and to force the uncured tyre into contact with the mould profile, internal pressure must be applied. Advantage is taken of this requirement to introduce a secondary source of heating. The media are normally contained withing a pre-cured form of tube, termed a curing bag, made from a resin-cured butyl rubber; this component is introduced into the uncured tyre as an ancillary operation prior to loading the combined unit into the mould. In the modern vulcanising plant, the curing bag has been largely replaced by a curing diaphragm or bladder which remains permanently *in situ* in the vulcanising unit. For internal inflation, either high-pressure steam, within the range from 12.6 kgf/cm^2 (193°C) to 19.7 kgf/cm^2 (213°C), or circulating hot water is used; use of the latter enables pressure and temperature to be varied independently. High internal pressures up to 24 kgf/cm^2 are generally employed for steel casing tyres, and for aircraft, earthmover, and large truck tyres, having thick cross-sections.

Thus heat is applied externally to the tyre mould to cure the outer layers of the tyre (tread, sidewalls, etc.), whilst the secondary source of internal hearing cures the inner layers of the structure. The internal heating is less direct than the external because the fortmer is transmitted by conduction through the thickness of the containing curing bag or diaphragm.

Cure Temperatures and Times

The thickness of the tyre to be vulcanised determines the highest temperature that can be used.

At one end of the range, cycle tyres, having a thickness of 5 mm, are cured for 4 minutes at 170°C mould temperature, whereas very large earthmover tyres, at the opposite extreme, with a thickness of, may be, 150 require 8 hours with a mould temperature of 120°C.

The cure requirements are derived from laboratory tests on slab mouldings, but it is not always practicable to set the ideal cure in tyre manufacture. From a technical aspect a long cure at a low temperature is preferable, but for productivity reasons maximum temperatures must be employed to reduce curing cycles to minimum. Where bonding of metal to rubber is involved, cure setting requires to be precise for consistent high fatigue performance and bond strength.

Vulcanisation Plant

Autoclaves and Pans

Originally the general purpose curing plant, for conventional diagonal ply tyres, was in the form of a deep circular pan or autoclave, having a hydraulically operated centre ram and capable of containing a vertical stack of up to 20 individual moulds, dependent upon their cross-section depth.

The curing bag, painted with lubricant to facilitate centralistation and prevent adhesion, is inserted in the raw tyre by a machine, and the tyre is transformed to an approximation of the toroidal shape of the vulcanised product. Bagged-up tyres are placed manually in the lower mould half, the bag valve is located, and the top mould half is positioned; the assembly is gravity fed along the track, via the mould closing press to the autoclave, into which it is hoist loaded. The steam inlet supply is connected to each curing bag. After the lid of the fully loaded autoclave has been locked, hydraulic pressure is applied to the central ram, closing the moulds tightly against the lid. External stream services are admitted through the side of the autoclave, with the steam circulating around the moulds during the curing sequence. Some cooling of moulds, prior to unloading, is effected by a short cold-water flood introduced after exhausting the steam. After disconnection of inflation fittings, moulds are transferred, by hoist, to the roller track and opened; the vulcanised tyre with bag *in situ* is ejected. Condensate is syphoned from the bag, which is extracted from the tyre and put back into circulation.

Autoclave moulding is a flexible but inefficient system in curing time, because moulds require a lengthy warming up period at the commencement of each cure, and is now considered obsolescent. For very large tyres, the principle is retained and a relatively shallow 'pan' or 'kettle' accommodating two or three moulds is used, the hydraulic ram often being replaced by an inflatable rubber diaphragm located beneath the base plate on which the moulds rest. To obtain the higher internal pressures, hot water rather than steam is used, and cold water is circulated prior to pressure release at the end of the cure to provide some degree of cooling.

Presses

Various forms of press, generally accommodating a pair of moulds, have replaced the autoclave or kettle. The mould halves are bolted to the lid and base of the press and remain *in situ*. At the end of the curing cycle, the press opens automatically.

For supplying external heat, in the case of small tyres, e.g., cycle tyres, a stem chest may be an integral part of the tyre mould. For passenger car tyres, use is made of steam chests or 'cavities' which remain permanently in the press and into which the mould halves are fixed in intimate contact. In other circumstances, mould halves may be fixed directly to flat upper and lower platens. For press operation with relatively deep section truck tyre moulds, steam circulates directly around the moulds, using the sealed press dome as a pressure vessel. As with autoclave curing, these early press processes used inflatable solid-base curing bags previously inserted into the uncured tyre.

The other forms of press are the Bago Matric Press (MBP) and Autoform Press (AP). In the BMP the diaphragm is of an open-ended barrel shape with a bead formation at either extremity for attachment to ring assemblies carried at the head of a central sheaved piston rod, projecting from the press base. In the AP, the bladder is again barrel-shaped but the upper end is closed. It has merit because it eliminates hydraulic and vacuum services and the bladder can be replaced quickly.

Instrumentation and Control Systems

The toral cure time, and the sequence of service requirements during this time, are controlled by a cycle timer, having a series of manually adjustable cams. According to their setting, these cams produce a pneumatic servomechanism to open or close the appropriate diaphragm-actuated valve, and so permit or terminate the flow of the inflation media.

Press platen temperatures are individually controlled and recorded for each press by means of a complex instrument using solid state electrical circuits.

Where high-pressure circulating hot and cold water is used as the curing medium, instrumentation requires to be more elaborate, e.g., flow rates need to be known, and also the differential tempertures between internal inlet and outlet.

After-Treatments

When employing textile casing materials which are thermally unstable, e.g., nylon or polyester, it is frequently necessary to prevent heat retraction and tyre distortion by cooling the tyre to below the critical temperature while still inflated. Two alternative methods are as follows:

i. At the conclusion of the curing cycle, the internal steam or hot water is replaced by cold water under pressure. This method is somewhat inefficient and may increase cure cycles appreciably.

ii. Immediately after extraction from the mould, the tyre is mounted on a rim and allowed to cool under an air inflation pressure of approximately 2 kgf/cm^2. A fully automatic plant for this purpose is located immediately behind modern presses. Some units have dual mountings which rotate in order that each pair of tyres from a twin press can be held for the duration of two curing time cycles.

BELTING

The main type of belting manufactured is for the conveyance of materials. Belting is also produced for power transmission purposes in the form of flat transmission belting and V-belting.

Conveyor Belting

Conveyor belts are constructed of a reinforcement, either textile or steel cord, which is protected from mechanical damage, arising from impact or the ingress of moisture, by a rubber or plastic cover. The rubber conveyor belt is usually manufactured by laminating a number of plies of a rubberised textile reinforcement, and consolidating and vulcanising them in a special press or rotary curing machine.

The emphasis, in recent years, has been to design conveyor belting for a given application or purpose. As examples of different constructions, mention may be made of heat-resistant belting for carrying hot sinter and coke, oil-resistant types, and others specially designed to be non-toxic for food carrying. Belts are also made with a moulded rough or chevron surface for incline conveying.

Materials

The main synthetic fibres used are continuous filament fibres of rayon, of polyester, and of nylon (Table 14.2 gives their physical properties in comparison with cotton). Rayon and polyester are both high-modulus materials, being paricularly suitable for use in the warp or longitudinal direction for long-haul high-tensile belting which requires to undergo the minimum amount of stretch in service. Rayon is lower in strength than polyester and has the great disadvantage of losing strength when wet.

Table 14.2: Physical properties of textile fibres

Physical properties	Polyester	Nylon	Rayon	Cotton
Tenacity (g/den.)	8.0	8.5	5.0	1.5-2.0
Elongation at break (%)	8.5	13.5	11.0	3-10
Initial modulus (g/den.)	110-130	40-50	90	12-70
Moisture regain (%)	0.4	4.2	13.0	8.0
Specific gravity of fibre	1.38	1.14	1.5	1.54

Nylon is the most widely used synthetic fibre in belting today. It has the highest tenacity or strength of the three fibres, a comparatively low modulus, and a high elongation at break compared with rayon or polyester. The principal application is in low to medium strength belting, where its high strength and extensibility give very good energy absorption characteristics and, therefore, excellent resistance to impact damage. However, when used as a warp member for high-tensile long-haul conveyor belt installations, problems arise owing to its extensibility.

The physical properties of the synthetic fibres can be modified during manufacture by heat stretching and heat relaxing processes. The former process increases the modulus and gives lower stretch characteristics for use as a warp member, the yarn losing some tenacity. Heat relaxing the yarn gives a lower thermal free shrinkage, which is particularly advantageous for a weft member, to give maximum stability to the fabrics during processing.

Continuous filament fibres such as nylon and polyester are more difficult than staple cotton to bond to rubber and have a far lower weight for equivalent strength this factor can lead to load support problems of the belt in service. In the low to medium strength type of belting, a proportion of cotton or staple fibre rayon may be woven with continuous filament yarn to aid adhesion of the laminated belting by normal frictioning methods and to provide the bulk required. However, with the development of improved bonding techniques for synthetic fibre, a significant growth has taken place in the use of 100% synthetic fibres, e.g., nylon, in belting. For the lower strength products, the bulk is maintained by introducising additional rubber between the plies.

High-tensile very long-haul belts are manufactured from fabrics with a nylonweft and a polyester warp, as mentioned above, a steel cord reinforcement, which gives the required very small stretch in service, is employed.

Fabric Designs

Sample interlacings, such as plain or oxford weaves, are normally used for fabrics for plied belting. Special weaves are used to enhance such physical properties as fastener holding, stretch characteristics, edge wear, and tear resistance. Slid woven or compound weaves are also used, whereby two-or three-layer fabrics are combined together during weaving to produce a monopoly construction.

Rubber Formulations for Carcass and Cover

Choice of rubber mixes will depend on the type of belt being manufactured, i.e., general purpose, heat resistant, oil resistant, or food quality.

The carcass compound for the general purpose belt is usually a high-quality natural rubber with low-modulus fillers and a high-scorch-time vulcanising system.

For underground mining, conveyor belting is mainly based on PVC to provide flame resistance, which will prevent the danger of the spread of fire, and has antistatic properties to minimise the risk of the explosion of mine gases due to static discharge.

Manufacture

Drying

Drying of the fabrics is essential to avoid blowing of the laminate occurring during the vulcanising operation. The fabric is dried by passage over a multiple steam-heated drum drier or hot plate at speed of 15 m/min at a surface temperature of 115°C. A moisture level of 1.0% for cotton-containing fabrics is required. It is desirable to carry out the frictioning operation as soon as possible after drying; alternatively, temporary storage boxes must be available at a temperature of 70°C.

Frictioning and Topping

To ensure good frictioning, a hot fabric is essential. Frictioning on each side is carried out on a three- or four-bowl rubber calender. The lighter-weight fabrics are friction coated, and the heavier fabrics are also topped or skim coated to give additional rubber between plies and between the outer plies and covers.

To obtain good adhesion, synthetic fibre fabrics are either pre-spread with isocyanate-based solutions or RFL-dipped prior to calendering. A topped skim coating of rubber only is then required; with a four-blow calender, this can be carried out on both sides in one operation. The rubberised fabrics are stored in cotton liners to prevent sticking.

Recently, techniques have been developed whereby no pre-treatment of the fabric is required, the bonding being achieved by special bonding agents added to the fricition or topping compounds.

Belt Building

Usually full-width fabrics to the optimum width of the calender are used for the calendering operation. Fabrics are then cut accurately to the width required on a cam-cutting machine which has multiple circular cutting knives. The actual cutting widths will depend on the construction required; typical constructions used are shown in Figure 14.5.

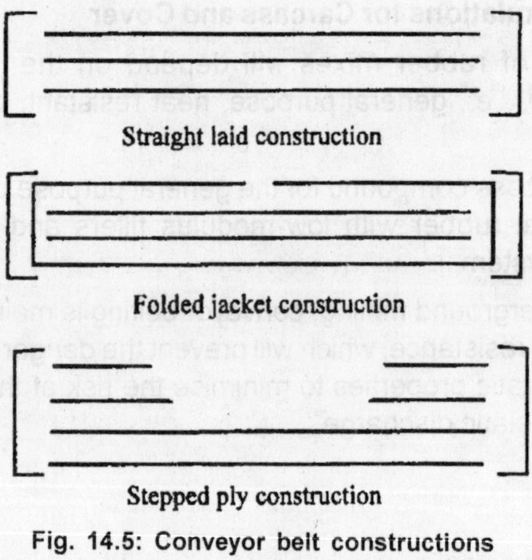

Fig. 14.5: Conveyor belt constructions

The cut plies are generally plied together on long building tables equipped with two-bowl consolidating rolls. Semi-automatic tables, letting off a multiple number of plies in one operation with individual liner rewind for each roll and tension control, are also used.

Transverse and longitudinal joints are allowable within certain prescribed limitations, the joints in adjacent plies being staggered to avoid any weakness occurring in the belt.

The separate face and back rubber sheeting calendered to the required thickness are applied to the carcass on the building table to provide the rubber cover. The completely built belt is then consolidated and passed through pricking rollers to remove any trapped air. Alternatively, the covers may be calendered directly on to the belt carcass using a three or four-roll calender. The finished raw belt is stored in a cotton or polyethylene lining, or chalked to prevent sticking prior to the vulcanising operation.

Vulcanisation

Vulcanisation of conveyor belting is carried out in either a press or a continuous drum-curing machine.

Pre-heating by Microwave Techniques

The latest development is the introduction of pre-heating, by means of microwaves, into the production press and continuous vulcanising operations, with upto 50% saving in vulcanising time.

Because materials, such as rubber, are difficult to heat uniformly without degrading their structure, many attempts in the past to reduce vulcanising cycles by pre-heating through conduction, convection, or radiation methods have met with little success. The development of microwave heating has opened up new possibilities. Rubber has high dielectric characteristics and thus can absorb energy of very high frequency, generating heat uniformly within the material structure. Microwave heating is basically similar to dielectric heating but, with the frequency increased from 100 MHz to 2000 MHz, the disadvantages and difficulties of the latter are overcome.

The microwave heating systems consists essentially of power supply to raise the main voltage to approximately 7KV, which is then fed to a magnetron oscillator. The magnetron oscillator contains within its vacuum envelope a tuned circuit and delivers the energy via an aerial and waveguide to the applicator.

One form of applicator is a metal chamber so designed that, for the frequency generated, the chamber becomes a resonant cavity. The laminate is placed inside the cavity: no direct contact with metal is required as in dielectric heating, and the material can be heated irrespective of the product shape. Even distribution of energy is obtained through cavity design and the provision of a specially designed rotary deflector system mounted at each entry point.

The pre-heaters is kept in series with a 10 m press, a system of approximately 20 multiple 1-1/2 kW power units and magnetrons being used to generate the microwave energy. This makes it possible to distribute energy evenly over the wide face of the belt and so eliminate non-uniformities.

The pre-heater is worked in conjunction with the press by automatic electronic controls; pre-heat times, power input, and press conditions are carefully selected. The reduction in overall cure time depends on the particular type of belt but reductions of up to 50% are achievable.

In addition to reduced cure time, the reduction in strain during vulcanising and the more consistent vulcanising conditions lead to a better-quality product.

Press Operations

Various types of large flat multi-ram presses are used, frame or column construction, both single and double daylight.

The raw belt is unreeled from a braked let-off station to the press, and a section is vulcanised. The presses have cool areas at the ends to prevent overcure between successive sections of the belt. Each press is equipped with stretching gear, usually consisting of flat hydraulically operated clamps, the belts being stretched a given amount prior to closing the press. This stretching process is essential to prevent excessive lengthening of the belt occurring in service. A moulding frame is made from flat 50-75 mm wide metal irons placed along each side of the belt. Lateral pressure to form the belt edges is usually applied by hydraulically operated cams which move the metal irons in a fixed amount after the press has been closed on low pressure. The thickness of the metal irons is selected to give 10-12% compression on the raw belt thickness. A specific pressure of the order of 21 kgf/cm^2 is used.

The length of cure depends upon the thickness of the belt, and a average cure time world be 17 minutes at 145°C. On completion of the cured of a section, the next length is indexed into the press, the small semi-cured end section being brought to the exit end of the press and its cure completed on the next press operation.

Because synthetic fibres, such as nylon, are not affected by the ingress of moisture or by microbiological attack and also have good edge wear, belting is now being manufactured from these materials to the full width of the press without a moulded rubber edge. The slab of belting produced is slit to the required width after vulcanising, two or three belts being obtained from one making and one pressing operation.

Continuous Vulcanisation of Belting

The belt is passed between a rotating steel drum and an endless high-tensile-steel band, pressure being applied by tensioning the latter hydraulically; heat is applied to both sides of the product, from the internally heated drum and also through the steel band by contact with steam-heated shoes. Typical dimensions of one such machine (the Show-Boston 80 inch Rotocure) are as follows: width of steel band, 2 m; width of main drum, 2.3 m; approximate maximum product width, 1.9 m; drum diameter, 1.5 m; maximum pressure, 4.8 kgf/cm^2. The maximum product thickness is 32 mm, but the maximum product width varies with the application. The curing speeds are variable between 65 m/h and 4 m/h, giving a cure times from 3.5 minutes to 53 minutes, which adequately covers the range normally required for rubber belting. The belt being fed through the vulcaniser is subjected to an initial tension accurately set and maintained, and also to a predetermined stretch.

Passenger Conveyor Belting

Belts for passenger carrying have been used for some time. However, the problems associated with handling large numbers of people at airports, railway stations, and coach terminals have led to considerable developments recently.

The most widely used type of belt today is designed to run short (50 mm) edge-support rollers so that the area on which the passengers stand is completely free from hard and uncomfortable supports and a smooth ride is obtained. To achieve this result, the belt is designed to have high lateral rigidity supporting the load 'bridge wise', coupled with good longitudinal flexibility enabling it readily to negotiate small terminal pulleys.

Essentially, the belt consists of a rubber-textile reinforcement sandwiched between two outer layers of transverse steel cords which are at opposite sides of the sandwich, the whole being enclosed in a rubber casing. The textile reinforcement provides longitudinal strength to take the drive tension, and the combined action of the upper and lower steel cords creates lateral rigidity across the belt to limit deflection. Such a belt 1.1 m wide, supported on 50 mm edge rollers and loaded at the centre with 68 kgf, will deflect no more than 9.5 mm at the centre.

Travelling speeds are dictated by the ease and safety with which passengers can center and leave the belt. It has been found in practice that a maximum speed of 36 m/minutes suits the variety of passengers travelling.

The surface of the belt is ribbed along its length, the ribs approximately 6 mm wide and 6 mm apart, meshing in and out of a comb-like platform at the entry and exit points. The ribs are moulded to very close tolerances in order to ensure that they move smoothly through the teeth of the combs without wear or damage. The ribbed surface sliding into a comb, removes the danger of clothing being trapped between the moving belt and the stationary platform at the exit point. If any obstruction is encountered, the comb plate is designed to trip out the conveyor drive. Moving handrails are an integrate part of the passenger conveyor installation.

Transmission Belting

Flat Transmission Belting

Flat transmission belting is still mainly manufactured from plain weave 1.05 kg/m^2 and 1.15 kgm/m^2 cotton fabrics, known as hard driven types, giving the required high modulus characteristics combined with good edge wear and fastener holding efficiency. Belts are also manufactured from polyester- or rayon-containing fabrics.

The fabrics are friction and skim coated with natural rubber compounds, or, in case of belts operating in contact with excessive oil, with chloroprene or nitrile compounds, formulated to have low heat build-up, high strength, and good adhesion to fabric. The finished belts can range from 3 to 10 plies, and in manufacture, widths of calendered fabric are plied together to form a slab. The slab is then vulcanised in a press or drum-curing machine, a high percentage stretch being applied during vulcanising to ensure that the minimum amount of stretch occurs in service.

The slabs are usually from 200-400 metres long and 2 metres wide and are slit on a multi-slitting machine to the widths and lengths required for stocking. This type of flat transmission belting, known as 'cut edge', is the main type manufactured today. Folded-edge type belts which are made in the narrow finished widths, with the outer plies folded round a centre core to form a jacket, show better edge wear but their production is slow.

Transmission belting is also manufactured from single ply or compound weave fabrics, usually made from specially latex-impregnated and coated yarns.

V-Belts

Endless V-belts are manufactured in various types, including fan belts for automobile use, fractional horse power drives for domestic and light industrial applications, and larger industrial belts.

The standard industrial belts are manufactured in five section sizes, usually from rayon cord material. More recently, premium industrial belts, known as 3 V, 5 V, and 8 V belts, or wedge-type belts, are used. In these, the ratio of depth to the top width is greater than in the standard sections, which results in a more compact drive. These constructions are made possible by the use of high-tenacity materials such as polyester cord.

V-belts are generally constructed of a top filler layer of rubber, a cord section situated at the neutral axis, and a base or cushion rubber, the whole assembly being surrounded by a fabric jacket. The shorter belts are manufactured on rotatable collapsible drum formers. The required number of layers of rubber are applied to the drum, and the cord is wound on at touch pitch. The individual belts are then parted off by means of circular knives and transferred to a skiving machine, which roughly forms the V shape. Finally, according to the size of the belt, one or two jackets are applied by machine. The belts are subsequently vulcanised in multi-ring moulds in open steam.

The long-length belts are made similarly, except that they are built on twin-drum building machines using weftless cord fabric instead of an individually wound cord. The belts are vulcanised endlessly by moulding in a press under controlled stretch conditions. After manufacture, the belts are checked for length and made up into matching sets.

A link form of V-belting is also manufactured, with the advantage that any endless length required can readily be made up. The links are stamped out of slabs of transmission-type material and joined together with metal components.

Positive Drive Belts

Positive drive belts, for precision drive and timing equipment applications, are moulded with a toothed inner surface which meshes with mating axial grooves in the pulley to give positive non-slip engagement. The belts are required to have very low stretch characteristics. Steel or glass fibre cord is, therefore, used and is continuously helically wound at a set pitch onto a backing of suitable compound which encases the load-carrying members. The teeth are moulded integrally with the belt, and a tough nylon fabric is also moulded onto the wearing surface to protect the teeth. The nature of the backing compound and teeth can be varied according to the application, to be resistant to oil, heat, or fire.

HOSE

Within the rubber industry it is generally accepted that, as distinct from a plain tube, which is solid-walled throughout and contains no reinforcement, a rubber hose consists of the lining or tube, the reinforcement or carcass, and the cover for outer protection.

The lining, which is the innermost section, has to be specially compounded to meet the conditions and resist the action, either chemically or physically, of the material passing through. This may be in any form (solid, liquid, or gaseous) and either acid, alkaline, or neutral. A solid may be extremely abrasive and flow at a fairly high velocity, as in the case of sand or shot blasting operations. Furtheromre, certain liquids also have active solvent properties, and operating temperatures may vary from as low as - 65°C to +200°C and higher, added to which there may be a requirement for some flame or fire resistance.

Very fortunately, not all of these properties are required simultaneously; nevertheless, on occasion, the ingenutiy of the compounders and hose designers is stretched, to say the least!

Materials

Nearly all of the extremely wide range of available rubbers are used by the hose industry, either singly or in various blends.

All the following fibrous materials have applications as the reinforcement or carcass in current and future hose manufacture, and are selected according to properties for each service requirement.

Asbestos fibre	Linen	Polyester
Carbon fibre	Rayon	Polypropylene

Cotton	Nylon	Steel wire
Flax		Glass fibre

The reinforcement is applied to the lining in yarn form by knitting, braiding, spiralling, or circular loom weaving, or as cut woven fabric wrapped straight or on the bias. If more than one ply of textile is applied, it is usual to include a layer of insulating rubber between them to prevent chafing in service.

Generally speaking, the operating pressure of the hose is the deciding factor in the selection of material. For a low-pressure application, such as a garden hose, steel wire would not be used, but rather a weaker material such as cotton or flax. Nylon has little use as a reinforcing material, mainly because of its low modulus and high extensibility, but it is these very properties that make it eminently suitable for the expanding hose portion of the power steering system of an automobile or truck.

The cover, generally speaking, is the outer protective layer of the hose, and has to be compounded to resist environmental conditions such as weathering (including ozone in certain circumstances), temperature extremes, oil and chemical contamination, as well as cutting and abrasion when the hose is dragged around.

It is essential for optimum service performance that the lining, reinforcement, and cover of the hose are fully consolidated and bonded together.

Manufacture

The method and machine used in the production of a particular hose, as a general rule, depend upon the type of reinforcement necessary for the service conditions to be met and upon such practical considerations as the bore size and length required. The manufacture of hose will be described under five headings which form a convenient breakdown by type, use, process, and production method.

Moulder Hose

In the manufacture of moulded hose, as the name implies, the hose is formed during the vulcanisation stage by being moulded against a lead sheath.

The lining (tube) is normally extruded in lengths of upto 500 metres, depending on bore size. The extrusion may be carried out on conventional equipment, either cold or hot fed or a combination of the two, and in either strip or pellet form. To meet the subsequent processing requirements, the compound has to be fairly hard and firm in the green uncured state.

After cooling and maturing, the linings are reinforced by either braiding or spiralling the textile around them. The braid is mainly of cotton for the general purpose hose (air, water, garden) or it is of rayon. Alternate left and right-hand laid textile reinforcement is also used.

A braider is a machine which applies the textile yarn to the hose lining in a manner very similar to a maypole dance. In fact they are often called maypole machines, and in this instance are usually installed in a vertical position.

The outer-cover coat of rubber is next applied to the reinforced hose by means of a cross-head extruder. After covering, the hose is passed through either a lead press or a lead extruder.

After lead covering and winding onto drums, the lining is filled with water (in some instances, air is used also), pressure is applied, and the ends of the hose and lead are clamped. The drum and contents are placed in large pans for vulcanising. The water inside the hose, infact, expands and becomes super-heated, and the hose in pressed against the lead, which acts as a mould (hence the name of the process). If the inside of the lead is fluted, then such a finish is imparted to the hose. If smooth dies are used to form the lead, then, of course, a smooth finish is produced.

After vulcanisation and cooling, the clamps are cut from the hose, and then the lead is removed by slitting along its length in a stripping machine. The cured hose is coiled up, tested, and inspected, and the scrap lead is returned to the melting pot for re-use.

Generally speaking, moulded hose in used for comparatively low-pressure applications and is manufactured in lengths of upto 500 metres, depending on size, of which the range is inclusive to 38 mm bore.

Hydraulic Hose

Another interesting process is that used for the manufacture of hydratulic hoses. Basically, hydraulic hoses, depending on pressure ratings, are reinforced with either textile (usually rayon) or steel wire, applied by either braiding or spiralling techinques; in this process, the braiders and spiralling machines are usually mounted horizontally.

The process consists basically of extruding the lining tube (which must be hard and firm uncured, and must also have good compression-set characteristics when cured), blowing it onto a steel mandrel with compressed air, and then braiding and/or spiralling with reinforcement. Covering, usually with CR, and cloth wrapping is then carried out. After vulcanisation, the finished hose is stripped from the mandrel.

In this method, the production length of the hose is limited to 40 metres by the steel mandrel length. The introduction of the flexible mandrel process has made lengths upto, and even longer than, 300 metres possible, depending on bore size. The limiting factor in this case becomes the handling weights and the wire capacity of the trading machine carriers and bobbins.

Vulcanisation under lead is often used instead of cloth wrapping, particularly in the flexible-mandrel long-length process. In this process, the steel mandrels are replaced by long lengths of flexible cores of suitable polymetic materia, on which the lining is applied. Braiding is carried out conventionally, and then the cover is extruded into position. After the tubing has stood for some time for maturing purposes, the lead is applied through either a lead ram press or a lead extrüder, the who is vulcanised, and then the lead and mandrel are removed from the hose. In modern hose plants, the curing may be carried out in steam pans, continuous cateneries, fluidised beds, or salt baths, or by high-frequency methods.

Flexible hydraulic hoses are used in almost every industry, the main ones being aircraft, automobiles, earthomoving, materials handling, and mining.

In the majority of hydraulic hoses, the linings consists of either NBR- or CR-based compounds, which are suitable for most of the hydraulic fluids in common everyday use. Because of the extremely low temperatures encountered, hose made for outside use in some latitudes are specially compounded for temperatures below the normal specification limits of -35°C to -40°C. Special liquids, such as the phosphate ester type, require other materials, e.g., IIR of EPM, to be used.

Over the years, service reqirements and conditions have increased in severity, particularly for burst pressures and for impulse performance. Considerable research and development in the field of metallurgy has been directed to discovering the best type of steel alloy and wire finish to be used, the correct tensile strength of wire, the pressure of application during braiding, and the angle of braids and/or spirals, to ensure that all layers of wire are working together in harness and unison.

As a general guide, the universally recognised operating factor for burst pressure to working pressure is 3:1 for static conditions and 4:1 for pulsating conditions.

Considerable progress in design has been made over the past few years and wire-reinforced braided hoses capable of well over 500,000 impulse cycles are now commonplace, whereas such performance was only possible in the past with hose of all-spiral-wire contruction. Under certain conditions, with attention to the operating and safety factors, cycles of well over 1000 000 impulses can be achieved with braided constructions.

Machine-Made Wrapped Hose

As the name implies, this type of hose is made on machines, consisting of three rollers whose centres are on the corners on an equilateral triangle, the base being formed by two of these rollers.

The process consists of extruding the lining tube in the straight position, and, after cooling, blowing it onto a circular-section mandrel treated to prevent sticking. The mandrel, the outside diameter of which is the nominal bore size of the hoses, may be made either of steel for the smaller-diameter hoses or of light alloy for the larger sizes to facilitate ease of handling and movement; its length is that of the available three-roll making machine, which can be as much as 40 metres. The mandrel, together with its blown-on lining tube, sits nicely on and between the two bottom rollers, the third top roller applying pressure as the fabric reinforcement is applied lengthways in strip form into the revolving rollers. The woven fabric (or duck, as it is sometimes called), previously frictioned on a calender or spread-coated on a spreading machine, is supplied cut to the required width, at a bias angle of 45° to give the hose flexibility.

The cover rubber is now applied lengthways and is pulled into position and consolidated by the rollers, after which a wrapping cloth, usually of nylon, is applied by spiralling it through the rollers. After vulcanisation, the hose is stripped of the nylon cloth wrapping (which is used for future cures) and removed from the mandrel.

A new concept is the development of a machine which laps the lining reinforcement and cover around the mandrel; the textile fabric is usually straight cut and may be applied at any angle as required. There is, therefore, greater flexibility in angle control than with the normal 45°C bias cut and joined fabrics. Furthermore, weftless cords can be laid in position by this machine and if so desired, armouring wires can also be incorporated in one operation and on the run during manufacture. The hose is completed by applying a wrapping cloth in line with the other taping heads, and thus all the hose manufacturing stages are completed, ready for cure, in simultaneous operations.

Hoses made by either of these methods are used, for example, for water, compressed air, and steam delivery, for welding and shot blasting equipment, and for conveying beer, wine, and food.

Hand-Made Hose

Many special large-size hoses required in the oil industry are made by hand on large lathes or making tables which rotate as necessary, each layer of lining, carcass, and cover being hand applied and rollered into position. Steelwire helices are incorporated by spiralling them into position when it is required to prevent collapse of the hoses under suction conditions.

Oil suction and discharge (OS & D) hoses are currently produced with bore sizes up to a nominal 600 mm (24 inch), and development work in active on even larger sizes to keep pace with the requirements of the oil companies.

Furthermore, with the advent of the super oil tankers, and the need for loading and discharging on the open sea to avoid the cost of very expensive port and docking facilities, buoy mooring systems have been introduced. In addition to conventional OS & D hoses used in the system, there is a need for some of the hoses (those between the buoy and the ship) to be capable of flotation. This is achieved by one of the two methods. The first is to place flotation beads around the hose. While this is very effective, it has the disadvantages that assembly is difficult and time consuming and the outfit is prone to damage. The other method is to build into the hose an intergral flotation system by the use of expanded rubber, with a closed-cell structure, introduced into the carcass of the hose.

Circular Woven Hose

The carcass of this type of hose consists of long lengths of fabric woven on circular looms. The warp threads run in the longitudinal or lengthways direction, and the weft threads are woven into the warps to produce a seamless circular weave.

One type of kerbside petrol-pump hose is produced by weaving around an oil-resistant lining tube, with wire helices included in the weft. The largest volume user of this form of reinforcement is, however, fire hose, and briefly, such hoses are made by weaving the jacket (which also serves as the cover), as a separate operation, on vertical looms.

The lining tube is extruded or hand-built from calendered material, and either in an uncured or in semi-cured state (backed with an uncured compound) inserted into the woven jacket. Consolidation and vulcanisation of the hose are completed by admitting live steam to each length, the ends of which have been suitably closed. The fabric is usually treated to prevent mildew, etc.

Other Processes

The five processes (just described) cover the vast majority of manufacturing methods, but, of course, there are others which are only in very small volume production by comparison. These include open steam and water curing methods, where the consolidation pressures necessary during vulcanisation are applied externally to the hoses in autoclaves by either steam or super-heated water.

Another interesting hose is that containing convolutions and which has applications as flexible connections in low-pressure systems, such as are encountered in the cooling systems of internal combustion engines. This type of hose is usually made in discreet short lengths by moulding as extruded tube (with or without fabric interplay) between shaped metal formers. Provision is sometimes made for the application of a low negative pressure during vulcanisation to assist the forming operation.

Hose Design

Apart from the general characteristics of the rubber mixes used in the linings and covers of the various hoses, the most important design feature of a hose is probably its carcass construction. Reference has been made to the various textiles which are used and to some of the safety factors. The angle of application of textile yarn cord or fabric to the hose lining (the braid angle) and the ultimate bursting pressure achieved are of paramount importance in hose design. With regard to the former, generally speaking, the designer aims at obtaining the so-called neutral angle, at which there is no change in length or diameter of the hose, under internal pressure, assuming no elongation of the reinforcement.

The effect of any departure from the neutral angle can be predicted. When the braid angle is greater than neutral, the hose will increase in length and is diameter will decrease. When the braid angle is less than neutral, the hose will shorten in length and its diameter will increase.

RUBBER FOOTWEAR

The many differing types of footwear which include rubber compounds in their make-up can be classified as heavy industrial boots, light protective Wellingtons and fashion boots, sports shoes and casuals with cavas uppers, slippers, and rubber-soled leather footwear.

Rubber has in the past been associated with utilitarian type footwear, but of late, it has become an established commodity in fashion footwear. Traditionally, rubber footwear was manufactured by hand-assembling pre-shaped component parts on a last or tree and vulcanising in an autoclave. During the post-war period there have been great advances in machinery equipments and automated processes, thereby reducing the high labour content of the hand-assembled product. The rubber footwear industry has also taken advantage of new developments in polymer science and technology to formulate compounds which meet the new process requirements and give products with practically any desired feature.

Materials

The rubber footwear industry has to meet a wide diversity of quality, depending on the end-use of he product, the method of manufacture, and the price, with the result that compounds vary considerably and there is no typical footwear formulation.

Compounds for hand-assembled products are normally based on natural rubber because good building tack is essential and excessive shrinkage can cause distortion of shaped component parts. Adhesives for hand-built products are also based on natural rubber. The grades of natural rubber selected depend on the end-use. For good quality thin upper compounds, where flexing is a factor, a rubber with minimum dirt content is necessary, but lower grade rubber can be used for soles and heels. In moulded products synthetic rubbers are used extensively, such as non-staining low-Mooney SBR, oil-extended SBR, IR and BR. Where heat- and oil-resistance properties are required, compounds are based on nitrile rubbers, blends of nitrile rubbers and PVC, or polychloroprene, the last of these being used mainly in hand-assembled products because of its superior tack. Whole tyre reclaim is used extensively in black solings and in some moulded black upper compounds. Finely ground vulcanised crump can be used for their cheapness and to help reduce porosity.

Carbon black is the reinforcing ingredient for black industrial boots, but, to meet the demand for non-black compounds, reinforcing siliceous fillers are used. A highquality non-black soling will have fine particle size silica as a reinforcing agent, and the medium grade solings either aluminium or calcium silicate. Goodquality clays or activated calcium carbonate will give reasonable reinforcement with natural rubber, but to obtain equal reinforcement with SBR and particularly with oil-extended SBR, the addition of some siliceous fillers is required. The main diluents are whiting and cheap clays, and for whiteness it is titanium dioxide.

The accelerator system is normally a thiazole with a guanidine, thiuram, or dithiocarbamate as a secondary, depending on the rate of cure required. For white and light-coloured products, an antioxidant must be selected which is non-staining.

Cotton is still the most commonly used fabric in the rubber footwear industry. Blends of cotton and man-made fibres are sometimes used where additional resistance to abrasion is required. The leg and foot lining of an industrial boot is normally a square-woven fabric of 0.30-0.40kg/m^2 in weight, rubberised by frictioning and topping, and with sufficient elongation to enable it to be lasted onto the shape of the boot tree. On moulded boots, knitted fabrics (either plain knit of ribbed) are also used, giving the bootleg a more flexible feel.

The upper material of canvas-topped footwear is prepared from a square-woven face fabric combined to a twill backing fabric by means of a thick rubber solution or compounded latex. For top quality sports shoes, the combined weight of the fabrics is approximately 0.50-0.60 kg/m^2. For slippers, which are very much a fashion article, a variety of fabrics are used such as cotton, wool, nylon, suede, and lurex.

Hand Assembled and Hot Air Vulcanised Product

Although this method is labour intensive, it still has its advantages in that it allows for greater flexibility in changing product design without the need for acquiring new and sometimes expensive equipment. Some all-rubber industrial and wellington boots, and canvas-topped sports shoes and plimsolls are still made by this method.

A pair of all-rubber industrial boots may consist of 40 rubber or rubberised fabric component parts, each prepared and cut to the required shape prior to assembly. These parts consist of the outer rubber leg, outer rubber vamp, fabric leg lining, fabric vamp lining, anklet, insole, fillings, toe and heel reinforcements, back strips and strengthening pieces, foxing strips, top binding, sole, and heel (Figure 14.6).

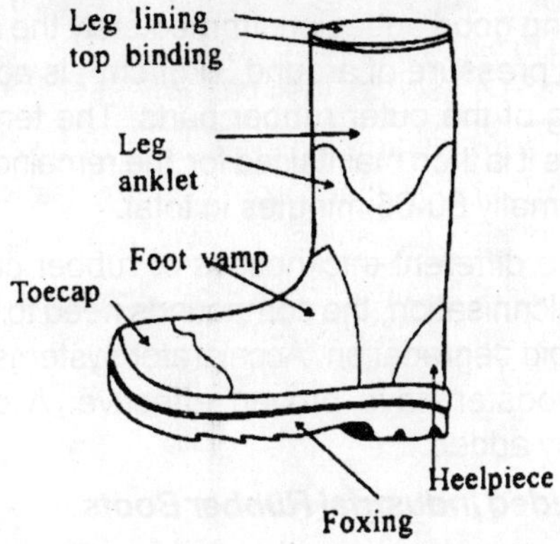

Fig. 14.6: Rubber boot components

The calendred sheet for the production of outsoles is produced on a four-roll calender where the fourth roll is engraved with the necessary sole pattern and profiled to give the variations in thickness. Any required sole design and thickness is obtained by changing the fourth roll.

The heel of an industrial or wellington boot which is hand-assembled, is usually pre-moulded to the required pattern, size, and shape. The insole, heel-piece, and fillings are made from unvulcanised rubberised fabric waste which has been ground on a tight mill and sheeted to the required thickness or topped onto fabric.

The components, freshened by a solvent wipe on this rubber solution, are assembled, in a specified sequence, tightly on the metal last and then thoroughly rolled to ensure good bonding.

Another method of manufacturing is to omit the outer rubber leg and vamp and to apply a coating of compounded latex by dipping and coagulating to provide the outer surface. After thoroughly washing and then drying off the moisture, the foxing strip, outsole, heel-piece, and top binding are attached. The latex forms a seamless, impermeable layer of rubber around the carcass.

For canvas-topped footwear, the fabric components are die cut and machined together to form the upper, onto which bindings have been sewn and eyelets or gussets and heel-pieces fitted. This is lasted onto the last, and the necessary rubber components attached.

Vulcanisation is carried out in large cylindrical autoclave heated internally by banks of steam coils fitted in the base and around the sides. The boots are loaded onto carriers and wheeled into the autoclave. In some factories, the carrier peg on which each boot is fixed is attached to a vacuum pump so that, as the boot is vulcanised, the component parts are drawn tightly around the last, thus ensuring good adhesion. Immediately the autoclave doors are closed, and air, at a pressure of around 3 kgf/cm^2, is admitted to offset any blistering or blowing of the outer rubber parts. The temperature gradually rises to 135°C, where it is then maintained for the remainder of the vulcanising period, which is normally 60-65 minutes in total.

Because of the different thicknesses of rubber components and the hot-air method of vulcnnisation, the compounds need to have a plateau-type curing system to avoid degradation. Accelerator systems based on thiazoles with TMTD as a booster have proved effective. A good heat-resisting antioxidant is usually added.

Compression Moulded Industrial Rubber Boots

A complete boot is moulded in one operation using vulcanising presses consisting basically of two lasts, two side moulds, suitably profiled to give the required pattern and thiknesses, and an engraved sole mould. Five components only are required by the moulder, a pre-formed fabric lining shaped to the last, a sole blank, a rubber leg, a rubber vamp, and a filler. A one-piece rubber leg and vamp is sometimes used. The lining fabric is first coated with rubber compound, and then pre-cured to avoid any strike-through of the outer rubber leg during moulding under high pressure. Correctly shaped legs, vamps, and insole socks, die cut from the pre-cured roll, are machined together to form the boot lining. This lining must have sufficient stretch to enable the moulder to fit it onto the last, and yet, when on, it must be a reasonably tight fit to avoid pinching during the moulding operation. Knitted fabric linings may also be used, suitably coated with rubber compound. The rubber leg and vamp compounds are calendered on a profiled roll and die cut to shape. The filler compound can be calendered or sheeted off a mill and die cut to shape. Correct distribution of the rubber in the mould is essential to give good mould definition. An economical method of preparing the sole blank is by the use of the Barwell Precision Performer, which can produce a pre-shaped sole and heel unit of accurate weight and dimensions.

The heel portion of the sole being the thickest in the boot, governs the vulcanisation time. Recently, a method has been incorporated whereby the sole and heel can be given double the vulcanising time set for the completed boot, reducing cure times by nearly half. While one boot is being vulcanised, a sole and heel blank is being moulded and semi-vulcanised in a second sole mould for the next boot. Overcuring the sole must be avoided, otherwise the bond of sole to the upper could be impaired. Two lasts, normally collapsible or split to ease the fitting of the lining, are provided so that, whilst one last is in the press vulcanising a boot, the other is having the lining and rubber parts assembled onto it. The press is fitted with automatic temperature controls and timing devices.

To obtain efficient economical operation, compounds have to be rapid curing yet with delayed action to give good mould flow and perfect definition of pattern. With sole plate and mould temperatures ranging from 150-155°C, a complete boot can be obtained every 4 minutes, the sole and heel having had two 4-minutes cures. Compounds with Mooney viscosity and scorch values at 120°C of 45-50 and 3-4 minutes (for a 10 points rise), respectively, are satisfactory for such conditions.

The vulcanised leg compound must be very flexible to avoid any discomfort in wear, have good flex cracking resistance, good atmospheric ageing resistance, and reasonable tear strength. The vulcanised sole and heel compounds must have adequate abrasion resistance and good cut growth resistance. Moreover the specific gravity of the compound should be no more than 1.2 to 1.25 to avoid excessive weight in the boot.

Direct Moulded Process for Shoe Bottoming

As the name implies, direct moulded footwear is produced by vulcanising rubber compounds directly to lasted uppers. More shoes are made in this way than by any other method. Moulding presses can be classified into types; for cellular rubber-soled footwear, internal pressure machines which rely on pressure created by the blowing agent in the compound; and external pressure machines, either pneumatically or hydraulically operated, for moulding solid compounds.

Cellular Rubber-Soled Footwear

By far the largest volume of cellular rubber footwear produced is the sponge-soled slipper.

There are several different types of internal pressure machines each consists essentially of (Figure 14.7) the following structures:

i. A base plate, having the contour of the sole and heel.

ii. A ring which sits on the base, split longitudinally, hinged at one end and forming the sole cavity.

iii. A last on which the upper is fitted and which acts as the top plate of the mould.

The sole plate and last are fitted with electrical elements, the sole plate being heated to 150-160°C, the last of 125-130°C.

This slipper upper, already prepared and shaped, is fitted onto the inverted metal last and held tightly to it by string or a sock lining which has been sewn to the base of the upper. A semi-vulcanised non-cellular outsole cover is placed centrally in the mould cavity, followed by a shaped blank of the unvulcanised sponge compound and a filling, usually a felt. The last is then lowered until it is clamped tightlyover the mould cavity. The total volume of material placed in the mould cavity is usually 60-70% of the volume of the cavity. The gas generated by the blowing agent expands the sponge compound, creating internal pressure sufficient to fill the cavity and form satisfactory bonds between the upper, cellular sole, and outsole cover. Vulcanisation time is from 6 minutes to 8 minutes.

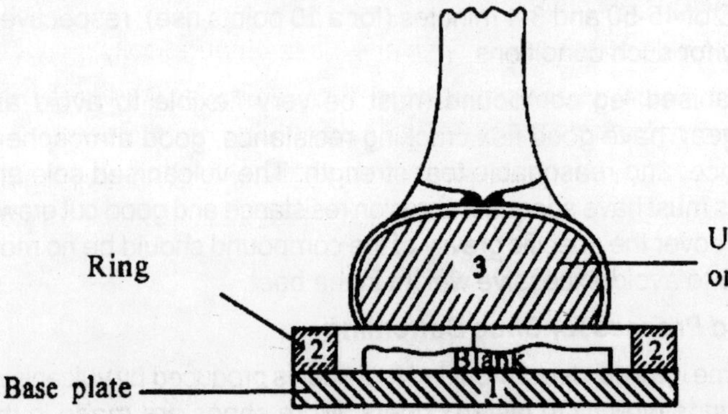

Fig. 14.7: Schematic diagram of internal pressure moulding machine

Both preparation and presentation of the sponge compound require exacting control. Inorganic blowing agents are used, with a small addition of an organic to give a finer overall cell structure. The polymers are given extended mastication with the addition of chemical plasticisers. The compound must be highly plasticised to allow for ease of expansion by the blowing agent, and vulcanisation must be delayed sufficiently to allow this expansion to take place. After mixing, several remills may be necessary to attain the required plasticity, and the finished batch is then calendered to the required thickness, well dusted to give ease of handling and die cut to the required shapes. The outsole cover compound is also calendered and pre-moulded into sheets 1.0-1.5 mm thick by approximately one meter square from which shapes are cut. This cover compound must have good ageing properties as the cut soles are to be given further vulcanisation in the slipper press.

Solid Rubber-Soled Footwear

The attachement of solid rubber soling to uppers of either canvas or leather by the direct moulded process has been a revolution in footwear manufacture. Essentially, it is a mass-production process and most efficient when allowed to operate as such. The operation is carried out by the shoe manufacturer in individual presses with electrically heated moulds.

External pressure machines operating at low pressures, between 10 kgf/cm^2 and 20 kgf/cm^2, on the sole area are used for canvas-topped footwear, leather bootees, and casuals. For walking shoes, work boots, and heavy footwear, high-pressure machines operating at 55-85 kgf/cm^2 on the sole area are used. The pressure is normally applied by the sole plate acting as a ram.

Machines consist essentially of (Figure 14.8) of the following structures:

i. A base plate, contoured to the shape of the sole and heel and carrying the required sole pattern.

ii. Movable side plates which open and close automatically.

iii. The last, which, when fitted with the prepared upper, fits exactly onto the cavity formed by the base and side moulds when closed.

The sole plate, side moulds, and lasts are fitted with electrical elements, and the machines include automatic temperature, pressure, and time controls.

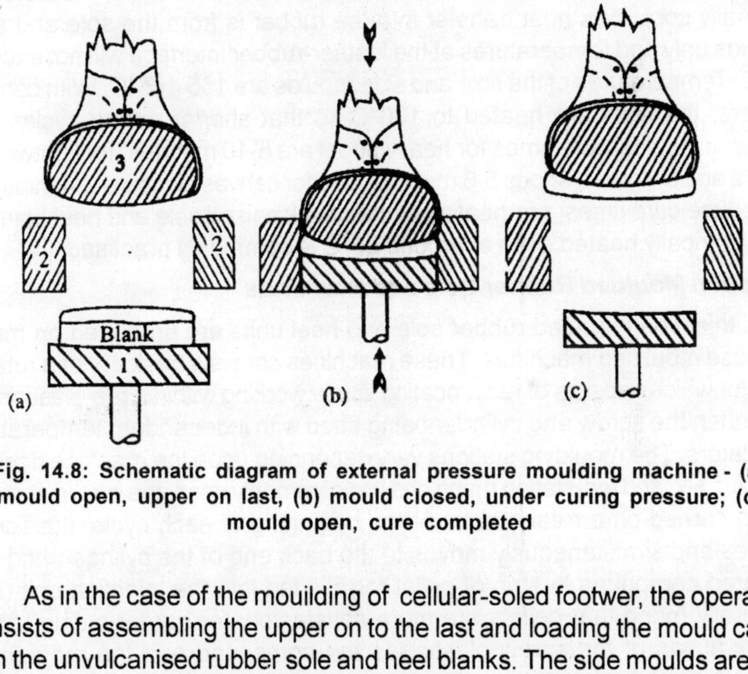

Fig. 14.8: Schematic diagram of external pressure moulding machine - (a) mould open, upper on last, (b) mould closed, under curing pressure; (c) mould open, cure completed

As in the case of the mouilding of cellular-soled footwer, the operation consists of assembling the upper on to the last and loading the mould cavity with the unvulcanised rubber sole and heel blanks. The side moulds are first closed tightly around the upper, and the sole plate is then forced up, acting as a ram, until it reaches a set position to give the required finished gauge of the outsole. The time control is set to the required cure time and when this is reached, the press automatically opens. The footwear is stripped of the last and allowed to cool, and the spew is trimmed off.

With fabric uppers, the pressure applied is sufficient to force the rubber compound into the interstices of the fabric to give is satisfactory bond of rubber to fabric. In the case of leather uppers, the bonding area is roughened to allow better penetration of adhesive into the leather fibres. Two coats of a fast-curing natural rubber cement, sometimes activated with an isocyanate, are applied to the roughened leather of the upper. A wooden or fibre-board heel filler is also included with the rubber blank. The lasted upper must fit correctly within the bite line of the side moulds so that a good edge seal is formed without cutting into the upper. This bite line follows the insole edge. A good bond of sole to upper is essential and on the toe-testing equipment, adhesion tests on finished shoes usually register figures of 32 kgf and over.

Accurate control is essential of the preparation and volume of the rubber blanks which are in cut shapes, strips, or granules, depending on the type of finished product and the sole pattern. The uncured rubber compounds must have fast-curing delayed-action characteristics and a shelf life of at least 3-4 weeks is essential. To utilise the equipment efficiently, the cycle times must be as short as possible. Where leather uppers are used, the lasts are normally cool, thus heat transfer into the rubber is from the sole and side moulds only and temperatures at the leather-rubber interface will not exceed 90°C. Temperatures of the sole and side moulds are 155-165°C. With canvas uppers, the lasts are heated to 130°C so that shorter curing cycles are possible. Typical cure times for heavy boots are 8-10 minutes, for lightweight men's and children's shoes 5-6 minutes, and for canvas plimsolls 3-4 minutes. To reduce cure times, pre-heating of the unvulcanised sole and heel blank in an electrically heated oven at around 95°C is commonly practised.

Injection Moulded Rubber Sole and Heel Units

Injection moulded rubber sole and heel units are produced on multi-purpose moulding machines. These machines consists basically of a rubber injector which consists of reciprocating screw working within a pre-plasticising cyclinder, the screw and cylinder being fitted with independent temperature regulators. The moulding stations vary depending upon the machine design, but four, six, and ten-station machines are commonly used, the mould stations being carried on a rotary table. At the beginning of each cycle, the screw rotates and simultaneously moves to the back end of the cylinder, and the uncured compound in strip of pellet form is fed into the injection unit (it is generally found that pellets are more satisfactory for harder stocks). The rotary action of the screw plasticises the compound and the movement backwards of the screw leaves hot plasticised material in front of the screw. The entire inejction unit then advances to form a tight seal between the nozzle and the mould sprue. The screw, acting as a ram, moves forward without rotating, forcing the compound through the nozzle into the closed mould. Pressure is maintanied for several seconds after the mould is filled, to allow the compound to set up. The injection unit then retracts, the rotary table moves the next station in front of the unit, and the cycle is repeated. At the same time, the station prior to the inejction point opens, allowing the moulded units to be removed from the mould cavities.

The number of mould cavities per station depends upon their volume and the maximum shot size of the machine. In addition, the total mould surface area must be such that the upward thrust is not in excess of the closing pressure of the presses themselves, which is in the region of 300-500 Mg, depending upon the machine.

Moulds of varying capacity may be used in any one run, since the volume of compound injected into each mould is determined by the back pressure developed in the mould. Effective flash-free mouldings are not produced from this type of machine, but by designing the moulds for tear trimming, minimum spew waste can be achieved.

Each station caries individual temperature controls, so that cure temperatures for mouldings of different sole and heel thicknesses can be achieved. The typical output from a six-station injection moulding machine would be -

Number of stations	6
Pairs per station	2
Mould temperature	177°C
Cycle time	35 secinds
Cure time	2-3/4 min
Output per hour	206 pairs

Whilst the process for bottoming footwear can be adapted as above, the manufacturing of full-length rubber boots presents difficulties in both engineering and rubber technology. Boots of this type are, however, being injection moulded by using PVC, which lends itself readily to this method and has proved to be a very satisfactory material for lightweight wellington boots.

Thermoplastic rubbers can be satisfasctorily injection moulded and are now used for some casual footwear.

Resin Rubber and Microcellular Soling

Rubber soling can be supplied to footwear manufacturers either in the form of soles cut from pre-moulded sheets or as pre-moulded sole and heel units. High-styrene resin rubber soling is light in weight, attractive in appearance, combines high hardness with good flexibility, and is 4-5 times as durable as leather. Because of these properties, it has practically replaced leather as a soling medium in fashion footwear. Microcellular soling containing minute discreet air cells and having a specific gravity as low as 0.3 is also used extensively. It is made by the addition of an organic nitrogen-generating blowing agent to a soling compound, usually based on NR-SBR blends, with the addition of high-styrene resin to obtain a satisfactory hardness and of siliceous-type fillers for good resistance to abrasion.

The manufacture of microcellular soling requires very careful control in mixing and moulding. Expansion occurs only after release from the press and therefore, the mould is loaded with a blank of volume slightly in excess of that of the mould. As soon as the press is opened, the sheet of vulcanised rubber immediately starts to expand and must not be restrained in any way, otherwise permanent distortion of the sheet occurs. The moulds are usually bevelled along the edges, and the press is made to open as rapidly as possible. The degree of vulcanisation affects the finished density, overcure resulting in near-solid sheets. Accurate control of vulcanising time and temperature is, therefore, essential. After initial expansion has occurred, some degree of shrinkage will continue indefinitely. Stabilisation is, however, achieved by heating the sheet in an autoclave at 120-130°C for approximately 30 minutes. Sheets can be moulded up to 20 mm thick and subsequently slit to any required thickness. Sole shapes are die cut from the finalised sheet.

Adhesive Attachement

The present-day method of attaching rubber soles and heel units is by the use of adhesives, based on CR or NBR. The adhesive is applied to the surfaces of both the upper and the sole, the sole is then accurately placed in position, and pressure applied. Where it is necessary to apply the adhesive some time in advance to meet production requirements, the adhesive-coated sole surface is reactivated by heat from infra-red lamps immediately before contact is made with the uppers.

Special Purpose Footwear

Safety Footwear

The need for added protection of the foot in the vulnerable areas has led to the manufacture of safety footwear, incorporating a steel toecap in the toe area and a spring steel midsole between the base of the foot and the outsole. The demand for this type of footwear in industry has increased recently. The inserts are fitted during the assembling of the product, which can be hand built, compression moulded, or direct moulded.

The steel toecap is shaped to fit over the toe area of the last and is fitted after the boot lining has been lasted. It is essential that the toecap is a tight fit so that no movement occurs during manufacture. The toecap must meet the impact test requirements as laid down in BS 1870. The steel midsole needs to cover as much of the sole area as possible, and BS 1870 specifices that the margin between the protective midsole and the edge of the insole must not exceed 6.35 mm. To ensure that no rusting occurs during service, the steel parts are given a chemical anti-rust treatment and enveloped between two thin layers of rubber compound. Depending on the service requirements of the product, safety footwer is manufactured with steel toecaps only, protective midsoles only, or incorporating both toecaps and midsoles.

Conductive and Antistatic Footwear

Where it is necessary to eliminate the build-up of static charges in the body to avoid sparking, as in factories handling explosives and in hospital theatres, conductive or antistatic footwear is used. Conductive footwear should only be used where there is no danger from electrical equipment. Where potential electrical defects can occur, it is essential to have a lower limit on resistivity to give adequate protection against dangerous electrical shock. This type of footwear is referred to as 'antistatic'.

In the manufacture of conductive and antistatic footwear, the upper parts are of standard materials but the base of the footwear is made of conductive materials. The insole, outsole, and any fillings required are prepared from compounds possessing the required resistivity.

For conductive footwear, BS 3825 specifies an upper resistance limit of $1.5 \times 10^5\ \Omega$, and for antistatic footwear, BS 2506 specifies a lower limit of $5 \times 10^4\ \Omega$ and an upper limit of $5 \times 10^7\ \Omega$.

GENERAL COMPOUNDING OF FOOTWEAR COMPOUNDS

The many different types of footwear which have rubber components common in their manufacture are *hawai* or beach slippers, canvas shoes, rubber-soled leather chappals or shoes, sports shoes, light protective or fashion boots and heavy duty industrial boots, etc. The primary function of any footwear is to protect the foot from external harmful factors such as rough ground surfaces, nails, thorns, stones, dampness and cold during walking or standing. Here we will discuss the manufacture of rubber compounds used in the manufacture of *hawai*/beach slippers, leather uppers, *chappals* and shoes and also manufacture of microcellular soling used for *hawai* slippers and leather chappals and shoes.

The advantages of microcellular expanded soling material are that they are light weight, comfortable to wear and usually have a high flex life. Besides, they are more economical than leather soles.

Types of Expanded Microcellular Soling

Microcellular soling is made in various qualities and can be generally classified into three categories -

i. Soft microcellular soling for *hawai* or beach slippers

ii. Medium hard microcellular for leather top *chappals*

iii. Hard microcellular soling for leather shoes.

Some characteristics of these soles are discussed below -

Category	Approx. specific gravity	Approx. shore A° hardness
Hawai/beach slippers	0.2 - 0.4	30 - 45°
Medium hard microsoling	0.5 - 0.6	55 - 65°
hard microsoling	0.7- 0.8	70 - 80°

a. Hawai Slippers

In western countries these slippers are known as beach sandals and are used on beaches or for indoor use. Because of their low cost, these slippers are within the reach of the poor population in India and hence have become very popular footwear. The hawai slippers consist of three components - expanded coloured sole, while upper topping and solid rubber strap.

b. Medium Hard Microcellular Soling

These solings are generally used for leather or resin upper chappals. This kind of footwear is in very high demand for fashion conscious urban people who need more elegant and light weight footwear rather than leather sole chappals. This soling has good resistance to wear and tear and has almost replaced leather soles.

c. Hard Microcellular Soling

This superior performance soling material is generally used for light wear and heavy duty industrial shoe soles because of its light weight and better wear resistance. It is more comfortable than crepe soles used for leather upper shoes.

Selection of Compounding Ingredients

Elastomers

The hawai and microcellular sheet compounds are normally based on natural rubber and high styrene resin rubber blend or natural rubber, SBR or polybutadiene and high styrene resin blend.

Natural rubber porvides good tack to the compound and high tear and resilience to the product. Because natural rubber gives very high tensile strength and elongation, it can take very high loading of fillers with comparatively less drop in physical properties, thus helping to reduce the cost of the rubber compound.

SBR rubber gives better ageing protection and abrasion resistance than natural rubber and is hence blended with natural rubber many times. High styrene resin polymer gives lower density and shrinkage and offers best flex and abrasion resistance. Its use, therefore, in microcellular products is essential. At higher loading it gives high hardness and a leather-like appearance to the product. Besides, high styrene resin rubber such as SBR-1958 gives higher thermoplasticity to the compound.

Polybutadiene rubber is also blended with natural rubber to give good abrasion resistance and resilience to microcellular products.

Nowadays, to manufacture low density microcellular products, a blend of nitrile/PVC resin is used. It also gives excellent abrasion resistance and resistance to oil.

Fillers

The function of a reinforcing filler is to improve the wear and tear properties of microcellular products. Reinforcing precipiated silica fillers and silicates give higher hardness which, to some extent, helps to reduce the use of high styrene resin rubber. Precipitated silica fillers such as ultrasil VN3 and Hisil-233 give high reinforcing characteristics and are generally used at 20-40 phr level. Silica fillers also help to improve their resistance, which is the most important property of the microcellular sheet.

The silica filler gives lower specific gravity of the product which, in turn, helps to reduce the volume cost of MC sheets. However, these silicas are very expensive and hence, many a time replaced with aluminium or calcium silicate, which are lower reinforcing than silica fillers. Along with silica and silicate, China clay, whiting or precipiated calcium carbonate are also used. Precipitated calcium carbonate is semi-reinforcing filler and gives better processing characteristics to the MC compounds. China clay and whiting are generally used as extenders to reduce the cost but they make the product heavier due to higher specific gravity and high bulk density.

Plasticisers such as processing oils and petroleum jelly, are used to improve the processing characteristics and reduce the hardness of solings. Cumarone indene Resin and Wood Rosin improve the dispersion of reinforcing silica and silicate and also help to improve expansion and reduce shrinkage of solings. Wood rosin and organic acidic materials also act as activators of DNPT type blowing agents, thus, giving higher expansion to the compound.

Zinc oxide is normally used at 4-5 phr as an activator for vulcanisation. Stearic acid is also an activator and due to its acidic nature helps to decompose blowing agents at a lower temperature and, hence, given better expansion to the compound. It is genrally used at 4-8 phr depending upon the filler loading of the compound.

Antioxidants are mainly used in MC soling to give a longer service life and to improve the flex resistance and storage life of the product. For white and coloured products. Montaclere SP at 1-2 phr is used. For dark coloured and black soling, Flectol Pastilles at 1-1.5 phr or Santoflex DPA at 0.5-0.75 phr are recommended.

The accelerator system for the MC sheet should be such that it should set the compound fast to seal the edges of the mould and should cure slowly to allow decomposition of the blowing agent first and then vulcanise the compound. This type of accelerator system gives higher expansion. The use of Thiotax (MBT) alone is more popular in the *hawai* sole compound at 1.2-1.5 phr level. For higher hardness micro sheets, use of Thiofide (MBTS) at 0.8-1.0 phr and Ureka White F at 1-1.4 phr of Santocure CBS at 0.8-1.0 phr with booster TMT at 0.2-0.3 phr is more common. Sulphur is generally used at 2-2.5 phr level. Higher levels of sulphur give poor tear resistance and higher shrinkage.

A DNPT type blowing agent properly stabilised with a sabiliser should be preferred because it gives good expansion to MC sheets. This material has a very high decomposition temperature -190-200°C. It decomposes at 120-140°C in an acidic medium and, therefore, in the MC compound, a higher dosage of stearic acid at 4-6 parts is used. During the vulcanisation, the blowing agent decomposes to give nitrogen gas and the fishy smelling amine is produced. The nitrogen gas under pressure dissolves into the rubber compound, which on releasing the press blows the compound, giving innumerous micro cells in the soiling. Use of blowing agent depends upon filler loading and hardness required for MC soling product. Generally 4 to 7 phr of blowing agent of DNPT type is used. It should be remembered that a higher dosage of blowing agent not only gives higher expansion but gives higher shrinkage due to higher internal pressure of nitrogen gas in microcell wall of the soling. It is essential to store MC compound for 8-24 hours after mixing of blowing agent in it, to get a uniform cell structure and expansion of sheets.

Organic or inorganic colours and pigments are used to give bright and pleasant colours. Care must be taken in using phthatocyanine blue or green colours, so that they do not contain free copper which poison the rubber, reducing the ageing resistance of the product.

Microcellular crumb is used to reduce the volume cost and it greatly helps to reduce specific gravity and shrinkage of MC soling. However, very high loading of crumb reduces split tear and wear of the product. At high loading of crumb, micro-cell wall strength reduces drastically, which results in the breakage, of micro cells ultimately resulting in coarse structure in MC soling.

Method of Manufacturing Microcellular Solings

Microcellular soling (MC) sheets are produced from rubber compound containing organic blowing agents of the dinitroso pentamethylene tetramine

(DNPT) type. The mould cavity is filled with the compound about 3% excess in volume which helps to seal off the edges of the mould. The moulding is done at high pressure in a hydraulic press normally at 140-150°C. The pre-cure is given in about 75 to 80% of its full cure.

During curing of the MC sheet, the blowing agent decomposes releasing nitrogen gas. The nitogen gas under the high moulding pressure diffuses into the sheet. On precuring the press is opened. On releasing the external pressure due to high internal nitrogen gas pressure, the compound expands and procured sheet props up from the mould cavity, giving innumerable micro cells within the body of the sheet. To facilitate easy release of the MC sheet, mould cavity has tapered edges, generally at 45°C. The C sheet on cooling shrinks to some extent. However, to stabilise its size and to optimise physical properties as well as to withstand wear and tear. It is then post-cured in hot air oven.

The quality of microcellular material can be judged from -

i. Specific gravity
ii. Hardness
iii. Split tear resistance
iv. Shrinkage control
v. Flex resistance.

If the basic formulation and curing system of the MC sheet compound is constant, the specific gravity and micro-cell structure of the product depends on -

i. The quantity of blowing agent used
ii. The volume loading of mould cavity
iii. The time and temperature of precure
iv. Moulding pressure applied during vbulcanisation of MC sheets.

It would be helpful to elaborate on the above factors in more detail.

i. *The quantity of blowing agent* - At constant condition of manufacture of MC sheets, higher the dosage of blowing agent, greater the expansion of MC soling and is lower its specific gravity.
ii. *The volume loading of mould cavity* - If the volume loading of MC compound in the mould is inadequate a coarse sponge irreguar cell structure is obtained. The mould is normally loaded 3% excess in volume of the mould. The small excess material forms a thin flash which seals the mould and prevents leakage of gas from the sheet. A large excess compound loading gives thick flash and causes leakage of nitrogen gas giving irregular shape soling sheets.

iii. *The time and temperature of pre-cure* - The curing of the MC sheet is carried out in press under high moulding pressure. The precure time and temperature are determined by the decomposition behaviour of blowing agent and cure system used in the compound. As cure time increases, modulus of the compound increases which increases the resistance to expansion of sheet. Thus, resulting size of the sheet is lower and consequently the internal pressure of decomposed gas becomes higher.

During storage and post-cure, when internal pressure of gas comes down due to diffusion of gas, the shrinkage of MC sheet becomes more. Hence to control the shrinkage of the product, it is necessary to give low degree of precure as possible. However, too low degree precure gives lower strength to the MC sheet and walls of microcells, the weaker microcells then burst due to high nitrogen gas pressure and big blow holes are developed in the sheets. Due to poor heat conduction properties of rubber, cure time of MC sheet depends upon the thickness of the sheet in the mould. Deeper mould cavity will need higher precure time. Generally, for medium speed curing system and normal filler loaded MC sheet compound, approximately 0.8 to 1 minute precure time should be given per mm depth of the cavity at 150°C curing temperature. In case of manufacture of MC sheet with uneven thickness or tapered sheets cure time for thickest section is considered. In such cases, thinner section of sheet gets higher degree of cure which obviusly gives slightly higher shrinkage. The temperature of 140-150°C is a good temperature.

iv. *Moulding pressure applied during vulcanisation* - In the case of microcellular compounds, the nitrogen gas liberated by decomposition of blowing agent generates internal pressure in the compound, which tends to open the mould. The external closing pressure on the mould, therefore, should be high enough to keep the mould closed and to keep liberated nitrogen gas dissolved in the microcellular sheet. The minimum specific pressure required will thus depend on the amount of blowing agent in the compound which is approximately 18 kg/cm^2 per phr of DNPT type of blowing agent in the compound.

The specific pressure on the mould area will depend on the area of hydraulic pressure × tonnage of gauge pressure.

Specific pressure = Total pressure/Mould area.

But total pressure = Maximum gauge pressure × Ram area.

$$\text{Specific pressure} = \frac{\text{Maximum gauge pressure} \times \text{TT } 4 \times (\text{Ram diametery})^2}{\text{Mould area}}$$

Since minimum specific pressure is dictated by the dosage of the blowing agent in the compound, the maximum area of the mould is given by -

$$\text{Max. mould area} = \frac{\text{Total pressure for moulding}}{\text{Min. specific pressure required for the compound}}$$

In case of specific pressure used is lower than minimum or the mould is of the larger area than indicated by above equation, all the liberated nitrogen gas does not dissolve into the compound.

As the part of nitrogen gas remains in the gaseous form in cells, coarser cell structure of MC sheet is obtained due to expansion of cells after precure. This gives poor appearance and lower abrasion resistance to the sheet.

Due to internal pressure of the blowing agent in the compound, it exerts a back pressure on the cylinder of the press. This sometimes excessively increases the pressure in the hydraulic system bursting pipeline. Hence, it is advisable to include safety valve in pipeline from the three-way valve to the hydraulic ram.

In a hand press though higher moulding pressure can be applied on the mould it becomes difficult to open the press against high internal pressure developed in the MC sheet due to the decomposition of blowing agent. Thus due to the slow opening of the press many a times MC sheet gets distorted.

In MC sheet moulding, the maximum moulding, area cannot be used as an opening of the mould expanded sheet. It may hit the guide post of the press and get warped, and edges may be cut.

In the MC sheet manufacture, tapered edges of the mould determine the relative expansion of sheet in the three directions. If angle is lower, it gives higher linear expanision while higher angle gives better thickness to the sheet.

Post-cure

After the precure, it is essential to give postcure to microcellular sheet. After postcure the MC sheet is completely cured and becomes permanently stabilised in the expanded size, whereby it achieves maximum physical and wear and tear properties. When the precured sheet, after moulding cools to room temperature, it shrinks due to lowering of internal gas pressure which lower down due to lower temperature. However, the nitrogen gas in each individual cell is still under pressure. The elastic microcell walls are still in a stretched condition due to interior nitrogen pressure. This gas under pressure slowly diffuses through the cell wall to the atmosphere during storage, which causes a fall in internal pressure and stretched cell wall shrink leading to further shrinkage during service life. Postcure accelerates the rate of diffusion of this gas at high postcure temperature which brings down internal pressure to atmospheric level and MC sheet stabilises.

Normally postcure is carried out at temperature of 100-120°C for 1-2 hours. The procured MC sheet from one or two shifts are collected and postcured in hot air oven having a circulating arrangement. As the heat transfer in hot air is very slow, the sheets take longer time to attain temperature around 100-110°C. After postcure sheets are cooled and stacked one above another for at least 24 hours, before final use, so the MC sheet gets stabilised after cooling.

QUALITY CONTROL OF RAW MATERIALS

a. ***Natural Rubber***

Natural rubber should be inspected for low dirt content, lighter colour and should be from fresh stock. Higher dirt or bark content will give poor flex and tear resistance, while dark coloured rubber may give variations in colour shades of the product and old rubber stock will give poor ageing and life to the product.

b. ***Synthetic Rubber***

Synthetic rubber should be checked for any foreign matter or contamination. It should also be tested for moisture content (less than 1%) and constant viscosity. Large variations in viscosity may result in uneven expansion and higher moisture content will give blow holes or blisters in the product.

c. ***Crumb***

Crumb should be properly sieved to get uniform mesh size and eliminate foreign matter. It should be checked for moisture content and suitably, the same coloured crumb should be used as of the compound to get uniform colour to the cut edges of MC sheets.

d. ***Fillers***

Fillers should be tested for presence of grit, moisture content (1% max.), pH, specific gravity, oil absorption, sedimentation value and solubility in dilute acids. Large variation in these properties will result in variations in the specific gravity of MC sheet, blistering, poor reinforcement, lower flex and tear resistance.

e. ***Processing Aids***

Liquids (oils) should be checked for colour, odour, viscosity, specific gravity (by hydrometer), flash point and aniline point.

Solid processing aids should be checked for consistent colour, odour, melting point/softening point, solubility, acid value and iodine value.

Variations in the properties will result in variations in the viscosity of the compound and finally, expansion and hardness of the MC sheet.

f. ***Blowing Agent***

Bolwing agent should be tested for grit and gas liberation which controls the expansion of the product. It should be properly stabilised.

g. ***Accelerator/Antioxidants***

Accelerator/Antioxidants should be tested for melting point/range and solubility in solvent to judge the purity of the material.

h. ***Sulphur***

To get good dispersion of sulphur it should be of finemesh. It should be tested for acidity, sieve analysis and solubility in carbon bi-sulphide to check its purity.

Trouble Shooting Guide

Table 14.3 given below shows the problems and their prossible solutions and Table 14.4 shows typical formulation for *hawai* sole (white upper).

Typical formulation for strap compound, micro compound, ISI specifications for microcellular rubber soles and heels and physical requirements for quality *hawai* sole are shown in Tables 14.5 to 14.8.

Testing of Finished Product

To ascertain the quality of the product it is essential to test the finished products.

Microcellular products should be tested for following properties -

i. Relative density or specific gravity

ii. Hardness of the sample

iii. Heat shrinkage at 100 ± 1°C for one hour

iv. Compression set

v. Split tear strength

vi. Ross Flex testing.

The *hawai* strap compound is also tested for stress-strain properties on tensile testing machine.

Table 14.3: Trouble shooting guide for footwear

Problem	Possibe cause	Possible solution
1. Coarse open cell structure	i. Too low viscosity	A. Reduce peptiser and/or plasticiser. B. Increase high Mooney polymer.
	ii. Excess blowing	A. Reduce blowing agent.
	iii. Low press cure time	A. Use faster cure system.
	iv. Low pressure on the mould	A. Incresed specific pressure per unit area.
2. Too dense cell structure	i. Too high viscosity	A. Increase peptiser and/or plasticiser. B. Increase blowing agent
	ii. Cure too fast or overcure.	A. Use slower curing system. B. Reduce booster level. C. Use blowing agent with low blow point temperature.
3. Uneven wavy sheet	i. Undercure	A. Increase press cure time/temperature.
	ii. Difference in the top and bottom platen temperatures or uneven temperature of platens	A. Faulty heater temperature control system. B. Water logging in steam lines. C. Insulate steam line.
	iii. Uneven pressure	A. Check for parallel alignment of platens.
4. Irregular shape	i. Leakage of gas from one side of a mould.	A. Check mould for parallel surfaces.
	ii. Due to thick flash from excess of loading.	A. Volume loading of the compound in the mould.
	iii. Inadequte comound.	
	iv. Low specific pressure per unit area.	A. Increase hydraulic pressure. B. Reduce blowing agent.

5. Blisters and pinholes on surface	i. Inadequate compound	A. Volume loading of compound - 103%.
	ii. Low cure time iii. Uneven temperature	A. Increase cure time/temperature.
6. Blow holes within the sheet	i. Under cure	A. Increase cure time/ temperature.
	ii. Air entrapment in the blank	A. Cut blank from calendered sheet. B. Or cut sheet out from faster roll of a mill. C. Remove trapped air while doubling. D. Increase resin level.
	iii. Poor dispersion of bolwing agent/resin/sulphur	A. Refine the compound through tight nip.
7. Blow holes in post-cure	i. Low cure time	A. Increase cure time/temperature.
	ii. Inadequate decompo-sition of blowing agent in press cure	A. Increase activation level and use faster cure system.
8. Cracks at edges	i. Cure system too fast.	A. Reduce booster/sulphur level. B. Reduce cure time/temperature.
9. High shrinkage	i. Low content of high styrene resin	A. Increase high styrene resin content.
	ii. Breakdown of nerve incomplete	A. Increase mastication time. B. Add Peptiser.
	iii. Poor dispersion of blowing agent	A. Pas through tight nip.
	iv. Excess blowing agent.	A. Reduce Blowing agent .
	iv. Inadequate reinforcement	A. Increase filler/crumb loading.
	vi. Undercure vii. Less postcure time	A. Increase curing time

Table 14.4: Typical formulation for *hawai* sole (white upper)

Ingredients	Hawai sole 1	Hawai sole 2	White upper
RMA	30.00	75.00	80.00
SBR 1958	10.00	25.00	20.00
RB 820	60.00	-	-
Zinc oxide	5.00	5.00	5.00
Stearic acid	5.00	5.00	4.00
Montaclere	1.00	1.00	1.00
Silica	15.00	-	-
Aluminium silicate	30.00	30.00	30.00
Ppted. calcium carbonate	30.00	-	30.00
Whiting	-	-	30.00
China clay	-	80.00	-
Hawai crumb	-	100.00	-
Petroleum jelly	5.00	5.00	5.00
Process oil	5.00	10.00	5.00
Wood rosin	3.00	4.00	4.00
DEG	2.00	2.00	-
Titanium dioxide	5.00	5.00	20.00
Sulphur	1.40	2.30	2.50
Ureka white F	-	1.20	1.00
Thiofide MBTS	1.40	-	-
Thiurad TMT	0.20	0.10	-
Blowing agent (DNPT)	8.00	7.00	5.00
Cured at 150°C for mins.	7.00	5.00	6.00
Specific gravity	0.23	0.40	0.55
Hardness shore A°	30	40.00	44
Split tear kg/inch	3.00	3.50	5.00
Shrinkage % (100°C/1 hr)	3.50	1.70	2.50
Ross flex test crack initiation kc	66.00	60.00	75.00
600% cut growth kc	140	140	140

Table 14.5: Typical Strap Compounds

Ingredients	Quantity
RMA	100.00
Zinc oxide	6.00
Stearic acid	1.50
Montaclere	1.00
Aluminium silicate	30.00
Pptd. calcium carbonate	30.00
China clay	30.00
Petroleum jelly	6.00
CI resin	2.00
DEG	1.00
Titanium dioxide	5.00
Thiofide MBTS	1.20
Thiurad TMT	0.20
Sulphur	1.80
Santogard PVI-50	0.25
Cured at 150°C (minutes)	4
Specific gravity	1.37
Tensile strength, kg/cm^2	170
Elongation at break, %	430
300% moduls, kg/cm^2	65
Angular tear strength, kg/cm^2	27
Hardness shore A°	54

Table 14.6: Typical formulation micro compound

Ingredients	Quantity	
RMA	20.0	20.0
SBR 1958	60.0	10.0
SBR 1502	20.0	-
RB 820	-	70.0
Zinc oxide	4.0	6.0
Stearic acid	5.0	5.0
Montaclere	1.0	1.0
Silica	20.0	20.0
Aluminium silicate	40.0	35.0
China clay	70.0	50.0

Ingredients	Quantity	
Micro crumb	50.0	-
Petroleum jelly	5.0	5.0
Process oil	10.0	5.0
Wood rosin	4.0	4.0
DEG	2.0	2.0
Titanium dioxide	5.0	5.0
Sulphur	2.2	1.5
Thiofide MBTS	-	1.4
Ureka white F	1.2	-
Thiurad TMT	0.1	-
Blowing agent (DNPT)	5.0	5.0
Cured at 150°C (minutes)	6.0	12.0
Specific gravity	0.5	0.4
Hardness shore A°	620.0	500.0
Split tear strength kg/cm^2	4.0	3.0
% shrinkage	1.50	2.0
Rose flex test	–	–
Crck initiation, kc	35.0	45.0
600% cut growth, kc	70.0	100.0

Table 14.7: ISI specifications for microcellular rubber soles and heels BIS/ISI : (6664-1972) Physical requirements for microcellular rubber sheets

		Type 1	Type 2
i.	Relative density	0.60-0.70	0.45-0.55
ii.	Hardness IRHD, min	65°	50°
iii.	Change in hardness after ageing at 100 ± 1°C for 24 hours.	+5 to -0	+5 to -0
iv.	Compression set at 27 ± 1°C for 24 hours, % max.	12	15
v.	Split tear strength, kg. min.	8.0	6.0
vi.	Heat shrinkage at 100°C ± 1°C for 1 hour in both directions, % max.	2	3
vii.	Water absorption, % by mass, max.	1.5	2.0

Table 14.8: Physical requirements for standaard quality *hawai* sople

i.	Relative Density	0.3-0.6
ii.	Hardness IRHD	45°-50°
iii.	Change in hardness after ageing at 100 ± 1°C for 24 hours.	+ 5 - 0
iv.	Compression set at 27 ± 1°C for 24 hours, % max.	15
v.	Split tear strength, kg.	4-5
vi.	Room temperature shrinkage at 27 ± 1°C for 4 weeks, % max.	1.0-2.0
vii.	Flex resistance, number of cycles - Roos Flex testing machine -	
	a. Initial crack, min.	40,000-60,000
	b. 600% cut growth	60,000-100,000

Table 14.9: Given below shows the physical requirements for standard *hawai* strap

i.	Relative density	1.3-1.4
ii.	Tensile strength, kg/cm^2	150-160
iii.	Elongation, %	400-500
iv.	Hardness IRHD	60 ± 5
v.	Change in initial hardness after accelerated ageing for 24 hours at 100 ± 1°C	+5 - -5
vi.	Flex resistance number of cycles on Ross Flex tester -	
	a. Initial cracks	60,000-85,000
	b. 600% cut growth	100,000-130,000
vii.	Tear strength, kg/cm^2	30-45

1. *Specific Gravity or Relative Density*

It helps to determine the volume cost of the compound, to keep check on a weighing of compounding ingredients and purity of raw materials. Specific gravity can be found by following formulations. For samples having specific gravity more than one -

Relative density

$$\text{or} = \frac{W_1}{W_1 - W_2}$$

Specific gravity

For MC sheet or *hawai* sole having specific gravity less than on -

$$\text{Specific gravity} = \frac{W_1}{W_1 + W_3 - W_4}$$

where W_1 = wt. of the sample in air

W_2 = wt. of the sample in water

W_3 = wt. of the sinker in water

W_4 = wt. of the sinker + sample in water

2. Hardness Test IRHD (International Rubber Hardness Tester)

This is a widely used hardness test for solid and cellular products other than ebonite to find out the hardness of the product.

3. Heat Shrinkage

Test piece of 125 × 5 × 5 mm after splitting all sides, is cut. After conditioning at a room temperature of 27 ± 2°C for 24 hours, length of tet piece is measured. It is then kept in air circulating oven at 100 ± 1°C for 1 hour. After removing the piece it is cooled for 2 hours at 27 ± 2°C and length is measured again. Shrinkage is calculated as -

$$\text{Heat shrinkage} = \frac{L_o - L_1}{L_o} \times 100$$

Where L_o = Length of the test piece in mm before heating

L_1 = Length of the test piece after heating.

4. Compression Set

Sample discs of diameter 30±0.2 mm and thickness of 9.5±0.2 mm or alternatively, two discs of same diameter and half of the thickness put one above other. The thickness of the samples after conditioning for 24 hours at 27±2°C, is measured as initial reading. The samples are placed in parallel plate compression apparatus to compression load of 140±1 kg for 24 hours. After releasing the load final thickness is measured after 1 hour.

$$\text{Compression set \%} = \frac{t_o - t_1}{t_o} \times 100$$

where t_o = Initial thickness in mm

t_1 = Final thickness in mm.

5. Split Tear Strength

Test piece of 25 × 100 × 7 ± 0.2 mm along and across the direction of sheet is cut. It is split in the centre between the top and bottom surfaces for a distance of 30 mm form one end, thus giving two tongues at the end. The tongues are fixed in a jaws of the tensile testing machine and allowed to separate at a constant rate of 75 mm per minute. The maximum load is recorded and the arithmetic mean of the four tests in kg is split tear strength.

6. Ross Flex Testing

Flex life of the sample is tested on the Ross Flex testing machine. A sample of 25 × 150 mm is cut and fixed in the machine. Visual inspection is done after every 500 cycles of flexing to check for initial crack. In another test, a 2 mm cut in the sample is made and sample is allowed to flex till it reaches 14 mm in width which gives 600% cut growth resistance in the sample. The number of cycles required to produce initial crack and 600% cut growth resistance is recorded.

Safety Measures

During the manufacture of the MC sheet, part of nitrogen gas and aldehyde/amines are evaporated on opening the press. This causes irritation of eyes and in extreme cases gives mild skin irritation. It is, therefore, essential that the moulding room should be properly ventilated and should be fitted with exhaust fan to drive away gas fumes. After working hours, operators should wash their hands and faces with plenty of water. In extreme cases of skin or eye irritation, a medical practitioner should be consulted.

Fire hazards due to improper storage of blowing agent have also been reported. It is essential that blowing agent should be properly stabilised with amino compounds. It should be stored away from heat source and at a cooler place.

RUBBER TO METAL BONDING

Rubber and metal are two materials differing greatly in their chemical structures and mechanical properties. Metals such as steel are hard, have a very regular structure and feature high tensile strength but poor elongation at break. In contrast, rubber is soft, considerably lower in tensile strength but higher in elongation at break and has a chemical structure similar to a long and inter wined chain.

Vulcanisation, the conversion from plastomer to elastomer, povides a certain fixation and the typical flexibility characteristics associated with rubber. Figures 14.9 and 14.10 elucidate the difference in stress-elongation behaviour and chemical structure of the two different materials.

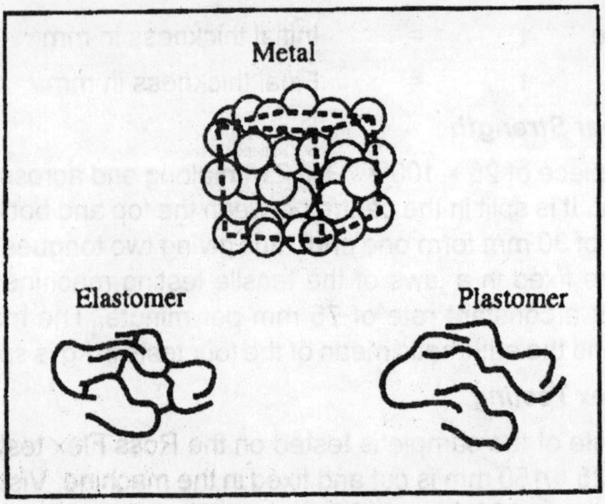

Fig. 14.9: Metal vs. rubber structure

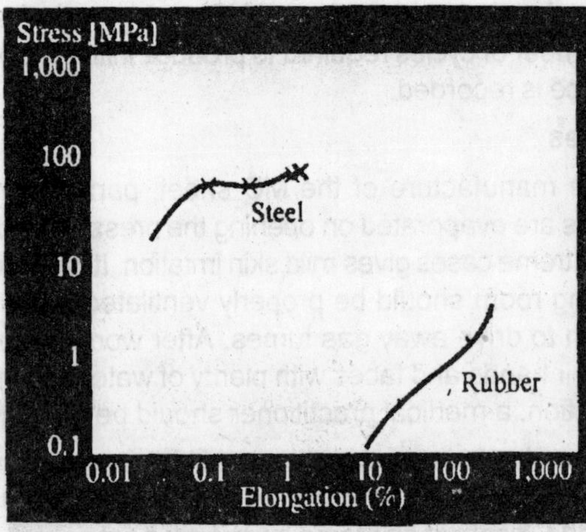

Fig. 14.10: Stress - Elongation behaviour of steel and rubber

By means of rubber-to-metal bonding agents, these two materials can be combined to form durable composites suitable for use as structural components without additional fasteners. This opens the door to new technologies for designers.

The main field of application for rubber-to-metal components is the automotive industry. Typical examples include -

i. Engine mounts
ii. Axle suspensions
iii. Shock absorbers

iv. Flexible couplings

v. Shaft seals

vi. Friction and torsion bearings

vii. Metal-reinforced profiles.

Rubber-to-metal components have also found broad application in other industries, for example in the manufacture of all kinds of suspension systems and bearings for the mechanical engineering and building industries. Typical examples are vibration damping elements, machine and bridge bearings or rubber-lined rollers for the paper, printing, paint, steel and food industries. Rubber-to-metal parts are also used for the manufacture of solid tyres and track pads for caterpiller vehicles as well as in the military industry. Further examples include rubber linings for tanks, piping, flexible tubing and cable manufacture.

The typical film thickness of the bonding system used is of approximately 20 μm (0.8 mil). Compared to the rubber layer to be bonded, this film thickness is relatively small.

In the manufacture of the above components, rubber-to-metal bonding agents only play a minor role from a quantitative point of view but they are essential in terms of function.

Unlike the adhesive technology, in rubber-to-metal bonding no prefabricated material but unvulcanised rubber is used. The bond is produced under conditions specific to rubber processing.

During vulcanisation of the elastomer, cross-linking also occurs in the adhesive film. This chemical reaction, together with the corresponding intermediate reactions, generate suitable reaction partners for the bonding process. As a result, this co-vulcanisation creates extraordinary strength properties. Rubber-to-metal components joined by adhesives typically have tear resistance values of 1 to 4 MPa. Vulcanised components, on the other hand, may well reach strengths of 10 to 12 MPa, depending on the type of elastomer used and other parameters.

Apart from the bond strength, there are of course, a number of other criteria that play a decisive role such as shelf life, range of application, processability and chemical resistance.

Against the ever more exacting demands of the automotive industry in terms of temperature and chemical resistance, adhesive technology as well as standard bonding agents soon reach their practical limits.

The manufacturing methods of the rubber-to-metal component producers have resulted in a drastic change in the requirement profile to be met by bonding agents, to mention only application methods such as hot or airless spraying.

The introduction of injection moulding processes has led to new requirements for bonding agents such as improved sweep resistance or higher reactivity.

The development of high-performance elastomers or improved cross-linking systems confront bonding agents' producers continuously with new challenges.

So the emission of solvents during the application of bonding agents increasingly poses problems.

Changing requirements make it necessary to develop more efficient and universal bonding systems. Thus, it comes as no wonder that rubber-to-metal bonding technology can look back on a long and eventful history that includes -

i. Ebonite

ii. Brass bonding

iii. RFL dip system

iv. Phenolic resins

v. Latex/albumin

vi. Isocyanates

vii. Chlorinated polymers/isocyanates

viii. Halogenated polymers/cross-linking agents

ix. Aqueous bonding agents.

Ebonite Process

The very beginning of rubber-to-metal bonding technology dates back to the middle of the last century. The ebonite process, patented around 1850 and still used today for tank linings, is the oldest bonding system. It uses vulcanisates with high sulphur contents (35-40%) which are almost thermoplastic in nature. Due to these thermoplastic properties, the ebonite technology is restricted to applications not requiring special temperature resistance.

When using suitable natural rubber qualities, ebonite coatings on steel reach bonding strengths of approximately 6 MPa. At temperatures above 60°C, the bond weakens noticeably and fails completely above 100°C.

Brass Method

Compared to the ebonite method, the brass method provides higher temperature resistance and also a stronger initial bonding strength (Figure 14.11.)

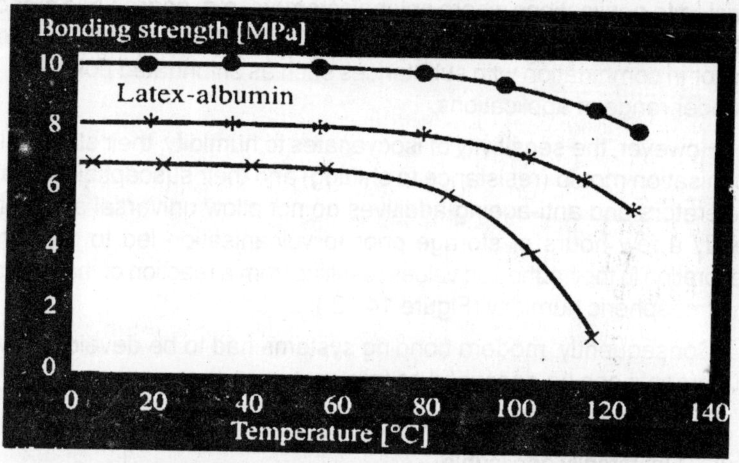

Fig. 14.11: Bonding strength as a function of the temperature

This technology dates back to 1862. However, it was not before 1911 that this method was used on a commercial scale in the production of rollers. In the tyre industry, this method is still employed today to produce steel cord-to-rubber bonds. The limitations of this technology are that it requires meticulously matched mix formulations to provide the desired bond. In addition, the brass layer, i.e., the copper concentration and the crystal structure, are of decisive importance to the quality of the bond.

Moreover, this bonding technology makes exacting demands on the preparation of the metal surface, from degreasing right through to the final deposition of the brass layer. Continuous bath monitoring is imperative, irrespective of the kind of bath used. Up to a temperature limit of 120°C, this method is superior to the ebonite technology in temperature resistance, but is still out-performed by latex-albumin bonding systems.

Latex-albumin Bonding Agents

Based on latices and haemoglobin, these adhesives feature the dual advantage of producing high-strength bonds while affording at the same time, improved temperature resistance. Their development dates back to the thirties. The product, Megum SK, as a trend-setting aqueous system for adhesives at that time, provided a standard for rubber-to-metal bonding agents for many years. However, the demands on chemical resistance, especially resistance to hot water, oil and fuel, soon showed the practical limits of this system.

Isocyanates, Resins, Chlorinated Polyomers

Apart from the systems descibed above, there are a number of other systems based on heat-reactive resins, halogenated polymers, isocyanates or mixes thereof. While resinous systems and chlorinated polymers are mainly restricted to applications where polar elastomers, e.g, acrylonitrile butadiene rubber (NBR), are bonded to metals or other substrates, isocyanates, either alone or in combination with substances such as chlorinated polymers, offer a broader range of applications.

However, the sensitivity of isocyanates to humidity, their slipping in the vulcanisation mould (resistance to shifting) and their susceptibility to amine accelerators and anti-ageing additives do not allow universal applications. Already a few hours of storage prior to vulcanisation led to a distinctive deterioration in their adhesion values resulting from a reaction of the isocyanate with atmospheric humidity (Figure 14.12.)

Consequently, modern bonding systems had to be developed whose requirements can be described as follows -

i. Simple, robust processes
ii. Universally applicable
iii. High quality of the finished part.

Modern Bonding Systems

Normally, modern bonding systems are used as two-coat systems. They can almost be said to be standard methods. The first coat, the so-called primer, is applied to a suitably treated surface. After drying, the second layer, also called cover cement, is applied. Once this coat has completely dired, vulcanisation can be started.

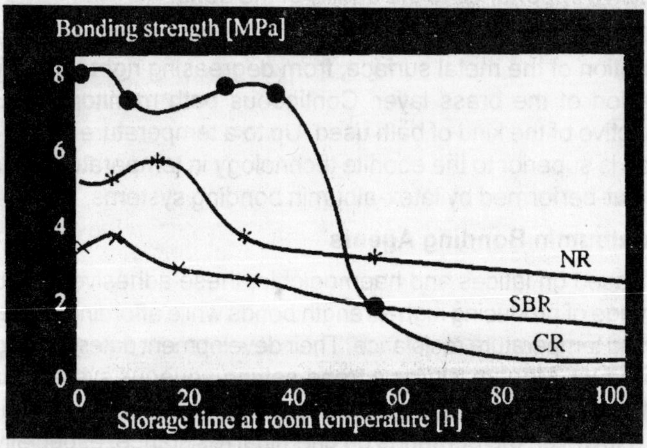

Fig. 14.12: Influence of the storage time on the adhesion of parts coated with isocyanate

Primers

The commercially available primers are combinations of halogenated polymers with heat-reactive resins and functional pigments, either dispersed or dissolved in organic solvents. The metal bond is achieved by physical actions (van der Waal's forces) and is decribed by the so-called adhesion theory. In the case of heat-reactive phenolic resins, a certain percentage of direct chemical bonds (free methylol groups) can be assumed.

Silane Bonding Agents

One special type of adhesives are those based on reactive silanes. Here, a chemical bond is supposed to form by reactions of the silane alcoxy groups with the hydroxyl groups on the metal surface. In addition, the reactive substituents of the silane react with the elastomer to be bonded to the metal (Figure 14.13).

However, the applicability of such systems is limited to such special elastomers as fluorocarbon elastomers or silicone rubber.

Cover Cements

The most commonly used rubber-to-metal bonding are neutral rubber, ethylene propylene diene rubber (EPDM) and styrene butadiene rubber (SBR). They require more complex bonding systems.

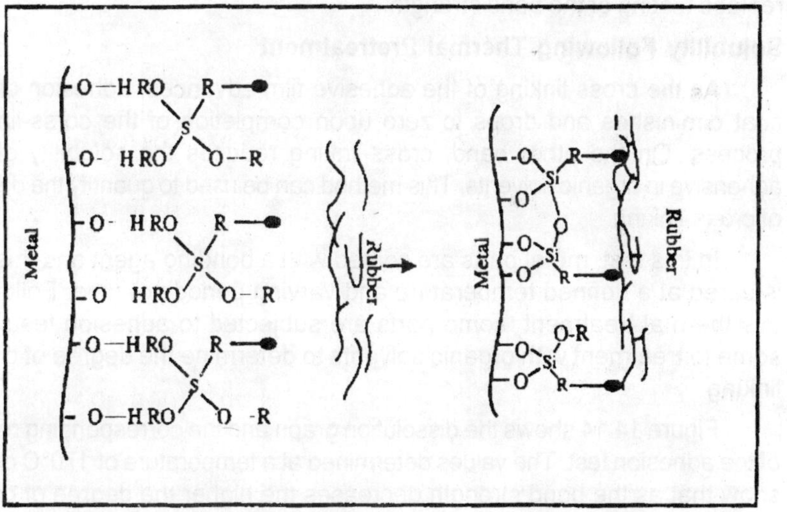

Fig. 14.13: Bonding mechanism of silanes

Such systems generally include chlorinated, brominated or chlorosulphonated polymers or mixes thereof. Given the varying structure of the polymer matrix of the bonding agent and the cross-linking system, the cover cements made from the above base materials differ greatly in terms of their mechanical properties.

Depending on the polymer system used, differences both in terms of tensile strength and resistance against external influences are found with a specific test mixture. A universally applicable system offering, the highest strength values as well as excellent chemical and thermal resistance, has not yet been found. This is why several different cover cement systems exist and are applied as a function of the type of application.

Combined with special cross-linking agents, e.g., polyfunctional nitrogen compounds or isocyanates, these polymers form the bonding agents whose properties are adjusted by adding functional pigments such as carbon black or lead compounds. In other words, the adhesive itself is already a cross-linking system which is activated prior to starting the vulcanisation process and which should remain active until the cross-linking process of the rubber matrix has been completed.

Analytical Methods

Methods to Characterise the Activity

Up to now, the activity or suitability of a bonding agent for a specific application can only be determined by practical tests on a specimen or finished part.

Different analytical methods may provide slight differences but cannot replace testing of the bond strength.

Solubility Following Thermal Pretreatment

As the cross-linking of the adhesive film advances, adhesion of this coat diminishes and drops to zero upon completion of the corss-linking process. On the other hand, cross-linking reduces the solubility of the adhensive in organic solvents. This method can be used to quantify the degree of cross-linking.

In this test, metal parts are coated with a bonding agent and this film is cured at a defined temperature and varying periods of time. Following this thermal treatment, some parts are subjected to adhesion tests and some to treatment with organic solvents to determine the degree of cross-linking.

Figure 14.14 shows the dissolution graph and the corresponding results of the adhesion test. The values determined at a temperature of 170°C clearly show that as the bond strength decreases the higher the degree of cross-linking of the film is, which is equal to a reduction in the amount of the soluble bonding agent.

The two graphs almost coincide at a vulcanisation temperature of 190°C (Figure 14.15). Compared of Figure 14.14, it also shows that the speed of the cross-linking reaction is dependent on the vulcanisation temperature.

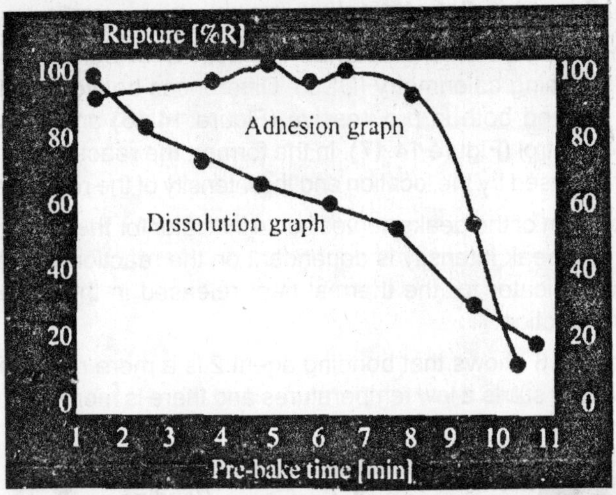

Fig. 14.14: Reactivity of the adhesive film following curing at 170°C

The resulting graphs somewhat give a picture of the cross-linking isotherm and are thus similar to rheometer graphs. They can be used to describe the reactivity of the adhesive film.

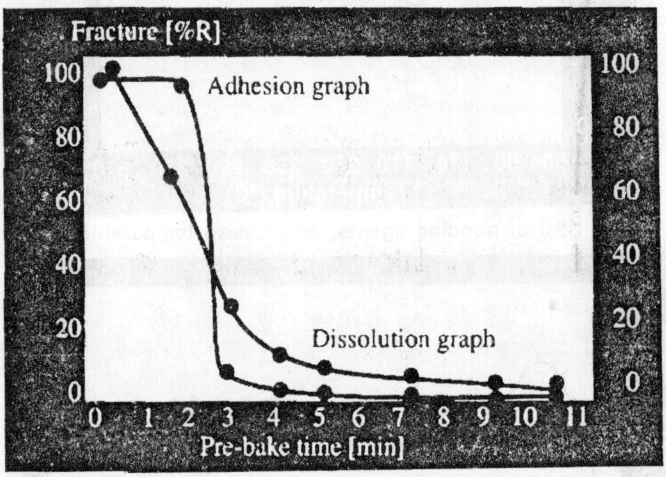

Fig. 14.15: Reactivity of the adhesive film following curing at 190°C

However, they are of only limited suitability to describe the interaction between the matrix of the elastomer and the bonding agent. The adhesion graphs may vary considerably as a function of the elastomer and cross-linking system used. The result of the bond adhesion test of a given compound cannot be predicted on the basis of the dissolution graph.

Differential Scanning Calorimetry

Another method to characterise the activity of bonding agents, is differential scanning calorimetry (DSC). Differences between the bonding systems are found both in progressive (Figure 14.16) and in isothermal temperature control (Figure 14.17). In the former, the reactivity of a system can be characterised by the location and the intensity of the registered peaks.

The location of the peaks serves as an indicator for the starting point of a reaction. The peak intensity is dependent on the reaction enthalpy, thus acting as an indicator for the thermal heat released in the course of the cross-linking reaction.

Figure 14.16 shows that bonding agent 2 is a more reactive system. Reaction already starts a low temperatures and there is more heat released during cross-linking.

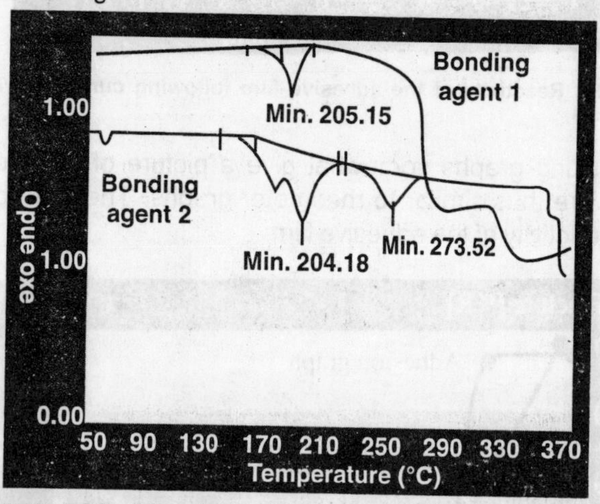

Fig. 14.16: DSC of bonding agents, progressive temperature control

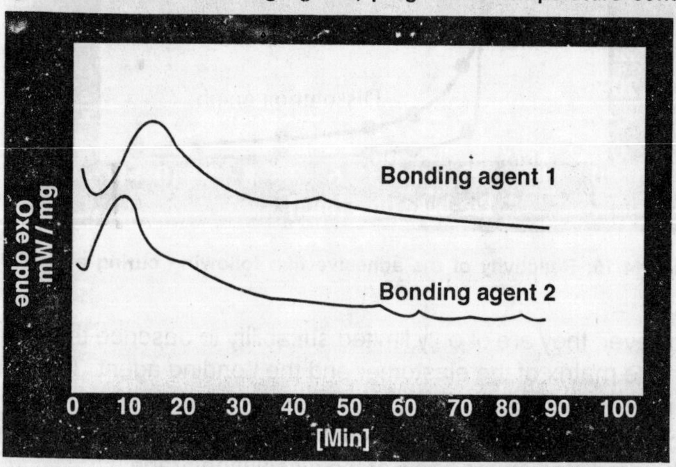

Figure 14.17: DSC of bonding agents, isothermal temperture control

The same applies to measurements at constant temperatures. During the test in question, the energy released during the cross-linking reaction is recorded as a function of time.

Figure 14.17 shows that the cross-linking reaction of bonding agent 2 starts at a much earlier point in time thus having an impact on process reliability. In addition, it proves that this type of adhesive is suited for quick-acting vulcanisation systems.

However, the two methods only describe the reaction within the adhesive film. Similar to what was stated for the dissolution curve, these measurements are of only limited indicative value for the corresponding bond strength.

Examination of the Phase Boundary Using X-ray Methods

Scanning electron microscopy (SEM) represents a method of analysis allowing for an insight into the interface which plays a decisive role in adhesion.

Combined with EDX (energy-dispersive-X-ray analysis) and microprobe analysis (analysis of the wave length dispersion of X-rays), SEM equally allows for an insight into complex systems such as the phase boundary between rubber and the bonding agent.

The topography is shown by means of secondary electrons. In addition, the element distribution within a defined sample section can be shown by X-ray distribution pictures which also allow for qantitative measurements. Hence, X-ray emission can be used to prepare concentration profiles for different elements by energy dispersion (EDX) and wave length dispersion (microprobe). In order to use these analytical methods for a description of the phase boundary between rubber, bonding agent and metal, this boundary first has to be set free.

Taking the examples discussed here, the boundary phase was set free by mechanically destroying the specimen at 180°C for subsequent analysis. To facilitate rupture and obtain an even fracture surface at the bonding agent/metal interface, a standard bonding agent is applied to a ground metal surface.

No primer is used because the objectives of the test is to analyse the interaction between the rubber and the bonding agent. Fractures are made after bonding a sulphur cured natural rubber compound to the metal substrate during vulcanisation.

Figure 14.18 shows the secondary electron picture of such a surface, focusing on, an enlarged section. For a quantitative analysis of the element concentration, element-specific X-ray emissions are recorded at different points of measurement (points 0-16; spacing between the points of measurement - 4 microns).

Figure 14.19 shows the result of this examination. The elements determined by analysis are typical components of a bonding agent, namely chloriné and bromine, as well as zinc and sulphur which are typical for the rubber matrix. As expected, the concentration of the halogens chlorine and bromine is highest within the bonding agent layer. These elements are also detected in the rubber matrix whereby their concentration continuously decreases as the greater the distance to the adhesive/rubber interface.

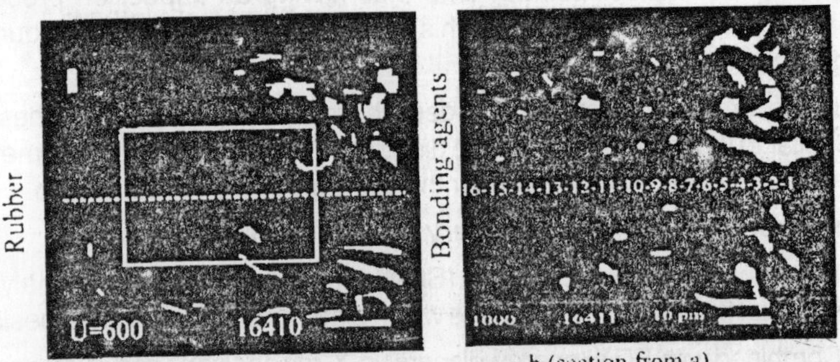

Fig. 14.18: SEM picture of a phase boundary between rubber and bonding agent

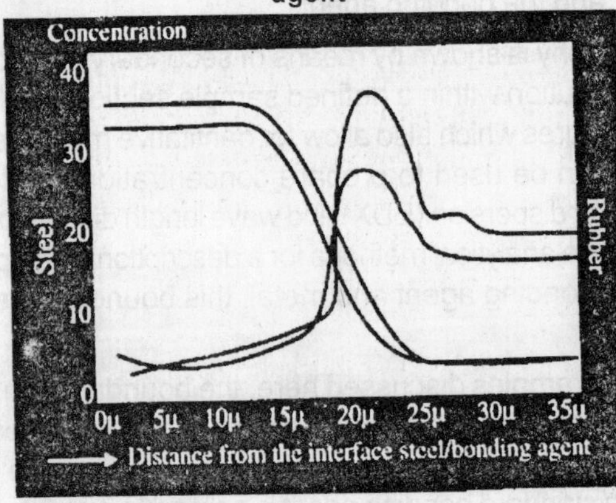

Fig. 14..19: Element distribution along a chain of measurement, EPX analysis

In the rubber layer, the elements sulphur and zinc, are found at rather constant concentrations. The concentration of these two elements is considerably higher at the interface between the bonding agent and rubber.

The X-ray emission picture showed the same results. Figures 14.20 and 14.21 shows the quantitative distributon of the elements zinc and sulphur. The white spots indicate that the element in question is detected. A significant concentration of zinc and sulphur is clearly visible around the interface between rubber and the bonding agent.

Polyfunctional nitrogen compounds play a decisive role in the cross-linkage of bonding agents. Hence, nitrogen is a typical element found in rubber-to-metal bondingagents. Microprobe analysis allows a quantitative determination of this element.

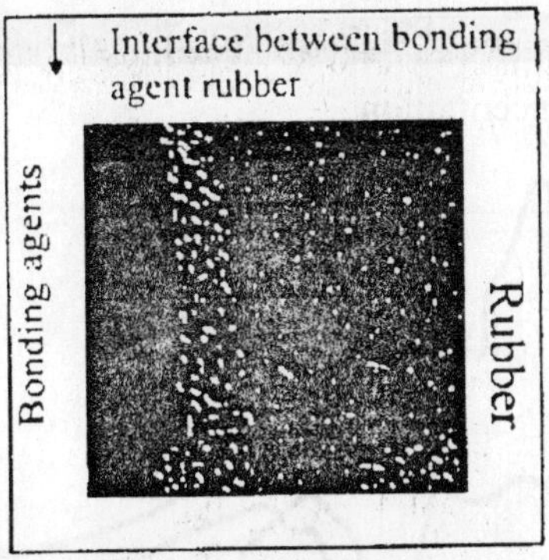

Fig. 14.20: Distribution of sulphur

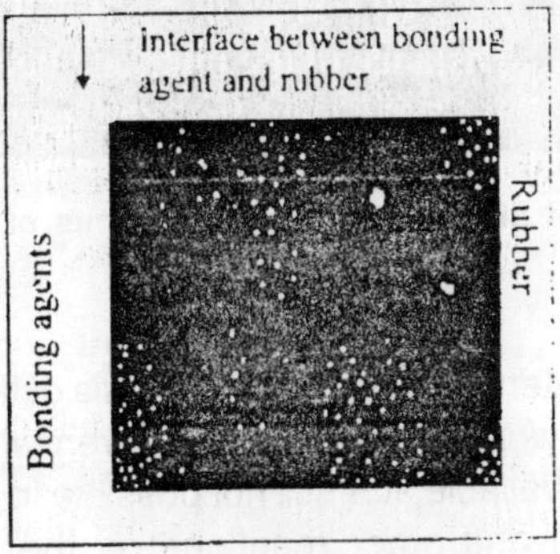

Fig. 14.21: Distribution of zinc

Figure 14.22 shows the concentration profile of nitrogen as well as those of zinc and sulphur. The accumulations of the latter two, determined by EDX analysis, is confirmed. In addition, an accumulation of nitrogen is detected at the interface adhesive/rubber.

The above-described effects indicate that diffusion from the rubber to the bounding agent occurs during vulcanisation (zinc and sulphur). Furthermore, componets of the adhesive diffuse towards the adhesive/rubber interface (nitrogen) and even into the rubber matrix (chlorine and bromine). Diffusion of zinc and sulphur explains a certain degree of hardening at the rubber boundary.

The mechanism is comparable to the bonding mechanism of the ebonite system. The compounds diffusing from the bonding agent may cause a local overcure at the interface and also in the rubber matrix next to the rubber.

But also the formation of chemical bonds by co-reaction of the polymer of the adhesive with the rubber matrix, or cross-linkage by polyfunctional nitrogen compounds, cannot be excluded.

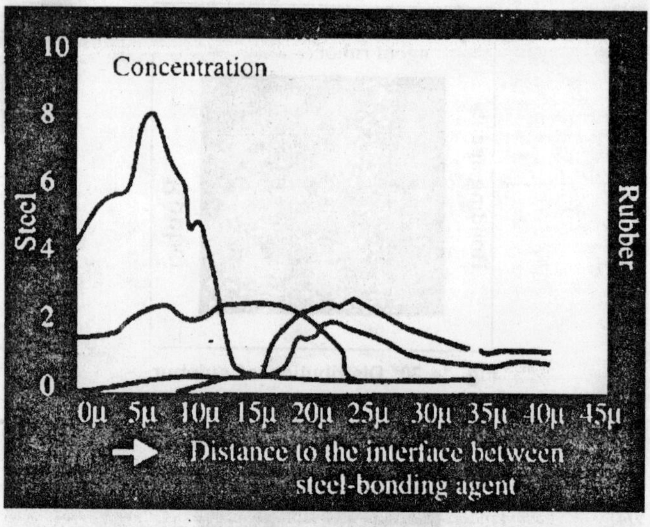

Figure 14.22: Element distribution along the points of measurement of the microprobe

However, the statements made on the basis of the above phenomena can only be used as working assumptions. Even with the highly efficient methods of analysis available, it is still not possible to determine the impact of physical, chemical and other reactions on the bonding strength by quantitative measurements. We are still very far from being able to give an exact account of the bonding mechanisms which occur in rubber-to-metal bonding.

CELLULAR RUBBER

Cellular rubber products are probably more varied than any other rubber product. In addition to the normal technological differences between one rubber formulation and another, the degree of expansion causes significant changes in the properties and these are further varied by the cellular structure, which may be open or closed. To help appreciate the differences between one cellular material and another, reference may be made to the glossary of terms in BS 3558.

Cellular rubber is defined as a mass of cells in which the matrix is rubber. The three main classes of cellular rubber are foam, sponge, and expanded rubber. Foam rubber is particularly defined as product made from liquid starting materials; the best example being latex foam, in which the cellular structure is intercommunicating.

On the other hand, both sponge and expanded rubber are made directly from solid starting materials; the essential difference is that the production method for sponge gives rise to an open or intercommunicating structure, whereas the term 'expanded rubber' is applied to those materials which have a substantially closed cellular structure. It is unfortunately common in the literature for the terms 'foam' and 'sponge' to be used to describe closed cell products. This confusion can only be resolved by studying the processing details or the properties of the end product.

Expansion Technology

To appreciate the refinements in technological formulations and the control of processing conditions in all types of cellular rubber production, it is imperative to have some understanding of the expansion process itself.

The expansion technology of cellular rubber is conveniently divided into two sections, covering foams on one hand and sponge and expanded rubbers on the other. The link between the two is the gas phase, which may be air, carbon dioxide, nitrogen, or ammonia, each of which has special functions in individual circumstances. Furthermore, they are not always interchangeable. It is essential, for example, in closed cell products, that the entrapped gas does not diffuse rapidly from the cells and allow collapse of the structure. The most suitable gas, next to air, is nitrogen. The gas phase may be introduced by beating in air, by dissolving nitrogen in the rubber under high pressure, or by the generation of various gases from the decomposition of inorganic or organic chemicals dissolved or dispersed in the mix. The timing of the expansion step is critical, and careful control has to be exercised over the rheological properties of the mix if high-quality products are to be achieved at an economic level or production.

Blowing Agents

The earliest chemicals employed as blowing agents were inorganic, such as sodium bicarbonte, which gave off carbon dioxide gas and was used to produce sponge rubber. Nowadays, particularly for expanded rubber production, organic substances are used, primarily because they are more readily dispersed in rubber and because the major gaseous decomposition product is nitrogen, which has a lower diffusion rate than carbon dioxide. The essential features of blowing agents are the yield of gas per unit cost, the decomposition temperature, the composition of the gases given off, and their effectiveness in producing uniformly fine cellular structures.

A number of gas-iiberating chemicals, including sodium carbonate, petrol, and metal hydrides and peroxides, have been tried in latex foam, but all commercial processes rely on mechanical air-foaming techniques.

Foam Rubber

The production of a foamed latex depends upon the inclusion, in a latex, of gas bubbles which are initially discrete and non-communicating, to enable an increase in volume to take place but which, in the end-product, are open and interconnecting and give the resulting foam its unique properties.

As foaming takes place, competing conditions exist between the formation of further bubbles, the breakdown of existing bubbles, and the densification of the rubber phase by flocculation. When conditions are optimised, it is necessary to gel the latex and, at the same time, control the breakdown of the air phase such that an interconnecting cellular system is produced. Finally, the gelled interconnecting foam is vulcanised.

The expansion technology of the competitive polyurethane foam closely resembles that of latex foam, but with the important differences that a highly regulated set of chemical reactions is used to produce the gelled polymer and that one of these reactions may be used to generate carbon dioxide as the pneumatogen. The high rate of diffusion of this gas through rubber makes it necessary that cell rupture is guaranteed; this is sometimes achieved by physically crushing the cell walls.

Sponge and Expanded Rubbers

The production of sponge and expanded rubbers indicate a requirement for a low-viscosity formulation. Figure 14.23 shows the qualitative relationship between the degree of expansion of a particular mix and its rheological properties as measured by Mooney viscosity. For the sake of simplicity, it has been assumed that the expanding gas is completely available for expansion at the appropriate level of viscosity. In practice, it is generated progressively over a period of time and the viscosity increases as the rubber is cross-linked by the vulcanisation reactions.

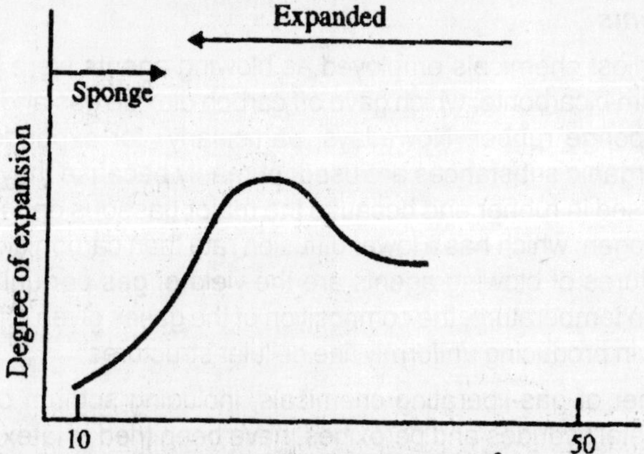

Fig. 14.23: Viscosity against degree of expansion for cellular rubber

At low levels of viscosity, the low strength of the rubber matrix allows the gas bubbles to coalesce and escape from the matrix, leaving a coarse open structure with a high density or low degree of expansion. If a more viscous compound is used, the matrix, first of all, withstands the expansion forces of the gases enough to increase the degree of expansion, but eventually the cells break down. At a higher level of viscosity, the forces with in the rubber are large enough to prevent sponge formation and a fine closed cell product results. In compounds with a still higher viscosity, the gas will be restrained and contained within the matrix at pressures higher than atmospheric, pressure leading to a reduction in the degree of expansion.

The non-quantitative character of Figure 14.23 is stressed, and it should be used only as a starting point in determining the specific parameters necessary to control a particular mix. Mooney viscosity has been used here as an illustration; other measurements such as Wallace or Williams plasticity may also be used but the important consideration is that the parameters must be determined and rigidly adhered to. A further point about Figure 14.23 is that it is representative of a formulation with one level of blowing agent, and the change in the degree of expansion is due entirely to viscosity change. If a second level of blowing agent were used, the basic character of the curve would be retained but its quantitative aspects would differ.

The choice of blowing agent is important. The use of bicarbonates for sponge rubber production has already been described, but nitrogen blowing agents may also be used. All closed cell products are expanded using nitrogen gas. In both sponge and expanded rubber production, the gas must be available at the viscosity level best suited to the product being expanded. A careful balance must be struck between the decomposition temperature of the blowing agent and the temperature reltionships of the vulcanising system adopted.

To summarise, it can be stated that the optimum rheological condition for a mix depends upon the polymer, its viscosity, the amount of softener used, the level of fillers, the curing system, and the blowing agent, not omitting to take account of the interaction of the latter with the curing system.

Density Variation

Cellular products are usually heterogeneous to a much higher degree than other materials, and it is not unusual to find variations in the degree of expansion throughout a moulded product, leading to a ± 2% spread in its properties. When a mass of cells are produced, the shaping of the cellular matrix within the mould is aided by the internally generated expansion forces. The gas pressure in the cells causes the matrix to move progressively to the surfaces of the mould, where gas diffusion and partial or complete collapse of the structure occur. This situation allows more matrix to move outwards from its centre to the surfaces until equilibrium is attained. The effect is more limited with sponge because of its open structure, but, nevertheless, the qualitative density variation represented in Figure 14.24 can be detected to a greater or lesser extent in all cellular products. A high-density structure with elliptical cells parallel to the moulded surface is produced at the surface, and a lower density with spherical cells exists in the centre. Complex mouldings obviously have very complicated density contours.

The density differential effect is not so important in whole mouldings because it is the integrated property which is under consideration. It assumes greater importance in slab stock which is sliced into thin sheets for later fabrication work; dimensional changes take place as the stresses due to the differential are relieved. These changes are not always instantaneous and are often aggravated over a period of time by a further dimensional change due to gas diffusion. The total change varies considerably with the product but can be upto 10%.

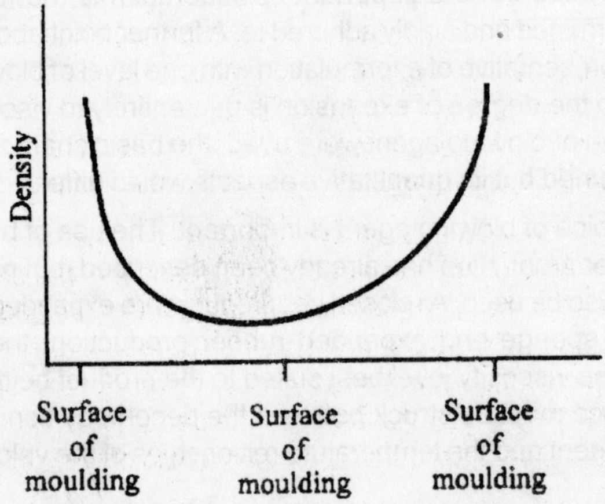

Fig. 14.24: Density against cross-section for cellular rubber

Manufacture

Sponge Rubber

Sponge rubber production follows normal mixing practices except that the highly plasticised formulations create sticking problems. Mixing in internal mixers is preferred to open mill mixing, and peptisation is commonly adopted to reduce cycles to an economic level. This procedure, however, creates some problems because of the difficulty of obtaining precise control over the level of viscosity required. Synthetic rubbers, particularly SBR, are widely used because they are supplied at low viscosity levels and are more consistent than natural rubber. To assist in achieving the low viscosity, it is common practice to incorporate high proportions of oil (50-100 pphr) of suitable compatibility with the rubber. The information on the formulation of compounds issued by the suppliers of rubbers and blowing agents will serve as a good starting point for the development of suitable production formulae.

Sponge products include carpet underlay, industrial sheet, mouldings, soling, and automobile sealing strips. The mixed batches are processed on extruders or calenders to give the required section or sheet stock from which the blank is prepared. In applications requiring a tough outer skin, such as door seals or dipper soling, a mix without blowing agents in calendered sheet form is applied to the sponge profile. This process has limitations because of the differential expansion behaviour of the two materials during the moulding process, but this is overcome, for example, in better quality soling, by first placing the solid compound in the mould, followed by the expansible blank.

The curing and blowing of the sponge is carried out either freely or in a mould which is only partially filled with the moulding compound. In the free blow method, the section is hot air or steam cured and the resultant product usually shows considerable dimensional variation. In the moulding operation, a trial and error procedure is adopted to determine the mould volume loading necessary to produce a product with the desired properties. Sponge compounds are not usually highly blown, and a volume loading of 40-60% is common. Adequate venting of the mould and liberal use of talc or other dusting agents enable air to escape freely from the surface of the matrix and so avoid the formation of surface blisters.

Expanded Rubber

Closed cell products are manufactured as sheets, profiles, and moudings, and in many ways follow the sponge manufacturing methods, except that the viscosity control values are higher; the fluid bed processes are used to manufacture profiles and moulding machines to produce footwear. A fuller description is given below of two methods of manufacturing industrial sheets by the nitrogen gassing and chemical blowing techniques.

Nitrogen Gassing

Normal processing methods are used to produce a calendered or extruded slab of rubber. Expansion of the slap is not usually isotropic, and careful control is exercised over the dimensions, residual strain in the slab, and its viscosity, to ensure that the dimensions of the finished expanded sheet are those required. The value of a typical linear expansion ratio for an industrial sheet of expanded rubber suitable for slicing and punching into gaskets is 2.0, giving a cubical (volume) expansion ratio of 8.0. In other words, a natural rubber formulation with a solid density of 1200 kg/m^3 is expanded eight-fold to a density of 150 kg/m^3.

The calendered or extruded slab is placed in a high-pressure vessel, and nitrogen gas at a pressure between 140 kgf/cm^2 and 700 kgf/cm^2 is introduced. The vessel is heated for upto 24 hours at temperatures between

100°C and 130°C to effect solution of the gas in the mix. After cooling, the gas pressure is released, causing the slab to expand partially. The expansion is completed by further heating of the slab in hot air or on a plate. The initial expansion of the slab takes place under relatively low temperature conditions and is an important difference from the chemical expansion procedure where expansion takes place hot. The fully expanded sheet is then cured either in hot or in a frame mould to obtain more accuracy in the final sheet dimensions

Gases other than nitrogen have been used in this process, but the products suffer from considerable shrinkage. Nitrogen is preferred because it is an environmental gas and there will be the minimum interchange between the enclosed gas and the external atmosphere.

Use of Chemical Blowing Agents

The processing also follows the normal methods, except that a blowing agent is added to the formulation. It is important that mix ingredients are adequately dispersed to prevent the production of coarse cellulary structures. For sheet production, the extruded or calendered slab is partially vulcanised in a pre-form mould; during the heating cycle, the blowing agent decomposes to give off nitrogen and other gases, which remain dissolved in the rubber because of the high specific pressures used in the pre-forming operation. The dimensions of the pre-form mould are as important as the extruded dimensions in the nitrogen gassing process. When the press is opened and the sheets 'explode' hot from the mould, the expanded dimensions relate to the original pre-form mould cavity dimensions. In some-pre-form mouldings, specific pressures as high as 350 kgf/cm^2 are used to prevent premature opening of the press. In formulating the compound, a balance has to be achieved between the rate of evolution of gases and the partial vulcanisation of the rubber which takes place in the pre-form operation. The expanded sheet is finally cured in a frame mould where the specific closing pressure is as low as 0.35 kgf/cm^2.

Reference has been made earlier to the dimensional stability of expanded rubber. The size of a fully expanded sheet is typically 1 m × 1 m × 30 mm and when this sheet is subdivided into thinner sheets by a splitting operation, the split sheets can shrink by as much as 10%. One of the methods used to minimise this problem is to heat mature the vulcanised sheet in an air oven at an elevated temperature. As a major part of the maturing treatment requires gas diffusion to take place, the cycle is necessarily a long one and can be upto 24 hours. In some cases, an alternative lengthy maturing cycle of 4-8 weeks at room temperature is used.

SPORTS GOODS

Many items of sports equipment incorporate rubber in some form; the grips on golf clubs and cricket bats, the bladders in footballs, and the pimpled surfaces of table tennis bats are examples. The largest quantities of rubber are, however, used in the manufacture of balls for the games of tennis and golf.

Tennis Balls

A tennis ball consists essentially of a hollow rubber core covered with a cloth usually composed of wool and nylon. The following specification is met at a temperature of 20°C and a relative humidity of 60% -

i. Diameter ('go-no-go' gauges), 2.575-2.700 in (65.4-68.6 mm)

ii. Weight, $2\text{-}2\frac{1}{16}$ oz (56.70-58.47 g)

iii. Rebound from 100 in (2.54 m) on to concrete, 53-58 in (1.35-1.47 m)

iv. a. Deformation under 18 lbf (8.2 kgf) load, 0.230-0.290 in (5.85-7.35 mm).

b. Deformation under 18 lbf (8.2 kgf) load on recovery after ball has been compressed through 1 in (25.4 mm), 0.355-0.425 in (9-10.8 mm).

The test in 4(a) measures the 'compression' or 'hardness' property of the ball, and that in 4(b) measures hysteresis after the ball has been compressed through 1 in (25.4 mm). The tests are carried out on a special 'Stevens' machine.

Two distinctly different types of tennis balls are now made. The type that is most common has a core pressurised with air or gas to about 0.7 kgf/cm^2 above atmospheric pressure. The second type has a non-pressurised or 'pressureless' core, having the advantage that its physical properties are retained over indefinite periods of storage. Permeation of the pressurising gas causes he pressurised type to become softer and less resilient in storage over periods of a few months, unless it is kept in pressurised containers.

The two types are made by similar methods, but different rubber compounds are used for the cores and the non-pressurised ball has a thicker-walled core. Compound formulations are given in Table 14.10. The high-styrene resin imparts the required stiffness to the core compound to achieve the necessary rebound and compression characstristics.

The compounds are normally formed into blanks of controlled size by an extrusion and pelletising process, and hemispherical shells are compression moulded and vulcanised at a temperature of 150°C. The edges of each shell are abraded and coated with a vulcanising rubber solution. Two shells are then joined together to form each core and are subjected to a further press moulding operation to vulcanise the joining solution. One of the two alternative methods is used for pressurisation of the pressurised type of core.

Table 14.10: Tennis ball mixes

Ingredients	Pressurised core	Non-pressurised core	
Natural rubber	100.0	Natural rubber	100.0
GPF black	30.0	High-styrene resin	30.0
Clay	32.0	Kaolin	20.0
Zinc oxide	9.0	Stearic acid	2.0
Sulphur	3.5	Sulphur	2.5
DPG	2.0	Accelerator	1.0
HBS	1.0		
Cure	2-1/2 min at 150°C	Cure	4 min at 150°C

i. Pellets of sodium nitrite and ammonium chloride are inserted inside the core before it is closed. During the subsequent press moulding operation, the chemicals are activated by heat to form nitrogen, which pressurises the core.

ii. The shells are mounted separately in the platens of a clamsheell press, and compressed air is introduced to each core by the following sequence of operations - the press closes until the pairs of shells are almost touching, when a rubber seal around the periphery of the platen area is actuated to isolate the platen area from the outside atmosphere. Compressed air is then introduced into this area, and the two halves of the mould are brought together so that the compressed air becomes sealed inside each core.

Cooling is necessary at the end of each cycle, as in the case of all inflated products.

These two methods of pressurisation offer different advantages. The 'chemical' method gives higher uniformity in practice, but, on occasion, the by-products of the chemical reaction crystallise and produce 'rattlers'. The compressed air method is somewhat cheaper, but cure times tend to be longer owing to the more complicated press arrangement and consequent greater mass of metal involved in the heat-cooling cycle. Tuypical cure times and temperatures are -

Chemical pressurisation	4 min at 150°C
Compressed air	16 min at 50°C

After this stage, the further processing is identical for both pressurised and non-pressurised balls. The moulded core is first subjected to surface abrasion in preparation for adhesion of the cloth, and the solution is then applied by a barrelling opertion.

Tennis ball cloth is made from weft yarns of blended wool and nylon woven into a cotton warp in such a manner that the weft appears predominantly on one side of the fabric. This side of the fabric is then given a teasling or 'raising' treatment so that a fluffy texture is produced on what is going to be the wearing surface of the cloth. The cloth is then subjected to a felting operation in which the raised surface is consolidated by the natural felting properties of the wool to give the cloth its final texture which is necessary for satisfactory flight and wearing properties. For adhesion to the core, the reverse side of the cloth is spread with a vulcanising solution and dumb-bell shaped blanks are then stamped out. These are arranged into packs and their cut edges coated with a vulcanising solution by a dipping process. It is this solution which subsequently forms the seam on the surface of the ball.

Two dumb-bell shaped pieces are applied to each ball, the first by a hand-operated jig and the second, purely by hand. This operation must be carried out with extreme precision if rejects are to be avoided in the subsequent press moulding operation, which iscarried out at 130°C for 12 minutes to vulcanise the cover to the core and form the seam. The moulded ball is steamed to raise the nap and to remove the mouding line. It is then tested for compression before applying the transfer marking and boxing.

It is interesting to note that the operation of making a tennis ball involves three separate moulding operations -

a. The hemispherical shells

b. The core

c. The covered ball.

Mouding conditions and compound formulations take recognition of this fact.

Golf Balls

Golf balls were originally made by stuffing feathers into spherical leather containers; they were first made from solid gutta percha in 1845. The present-day core-wound ball dates from the beginning of the century, from which time it has remained basically unchanged. During the last few years, solid balls have been reintroduced using modern materials, and these are now made alongside conventional wound balls. The latter are, however, still the only type acceptable to the majority of golfers.

Golf balls are made to meet specification laid down by two controlling bodies, that the ball must weight not more than 45.9 g (1.62 oz) but the specification for the diameter differs as follows -

Not less than 41.15 mm (1.62 in)

or

Not less than 42.67 mm (1.68 in)

Compared with a tennis ball, the specification for a golf ball is relatively simple and arises from the fact that, other things being equal, he smaller and heavier a ball, the further it will go. Manufacturers (in particular, those making 41.15 mm balls) are, therefore, encouraged to make balls as near as possible to the maximum weight and minimum size allowable so as to achieve the maximum flight length.

Certain properties cannot be adequately covered by specifications. Such properties are 'feel' and 'click' (which are subjective assessments of the club-ball contact), flight pattern (which depends upon the rotational inertia and aerodynamic qualities of the ball), and durability. Such qualities come into the category of 'know-how' perfected by individual manufacturers.

Conventional Wound Golf Balls

A 'wound' golf ball consists of four components -

i. The centre

ii. The windings of rubber thread

iii. The cover

iv. The paint and markings.

Each component has an important contribution to make to the properties of the finished ball and these will be considered in turn.

i. Centre

The centre must be the nucleus for the winding operation. It must be large enough for this purpose, but not so large that the resilience of the core is adversely affected. It must contribute a significant amount of mass to the ball because the overall ball weight and rotational inertia are largely dictated by those of the centre.

ii. Windings

Rubber thread used in the winding of a golf ball must produce the highes possible resilience in the ball core. The thread, normally based on natura rubber or a blend of natural rubber with *cis*-polyisoprene, is made by dry rubber or latex techniques on the cut thread principle.

The percentage of *cis*-polyisoprene is limited by the requirement of good chafe resistance necessary for the winding operation. A typical 'dry rubber' thread formation based on natural rubber is given in Table 14.11

Table 14.11: Golf ball thread formulation

Nature rubber	100.0
Sulphur	6.0
Aldehyde ammonia	0.5
Cure	150 min at 130°C

The thread is cut to dimensions of 0.5 mm × 1.5 mm for modern direct winding, in which one continuous thread is wound onto the centre. Older methods employed the use of thread of several different gauges, the thickest being applied nearest the centre. Such methods were particularly applicable to centres of the latex bag type.

iii. Cover

The cover of a golf ball provides protection for the core and carries the surface pattern necessary to produce aerodynamic lift. Covers have been traditionally made from natural gutta percha and balata, until recently the only materials having suitable properties - in particular, mouldability at 80-100°C, which is necessary to avoid degradation of the rubber core by heat. Synthetic gutta percha (*trans*-polyisoprene) is now also used for golf ball covers.

In conventional procedure, hemispherical shells are compression moulded by putting heated blanks into a cold mould. The sheels are then mounted on a core, and the assembly is subjected to a compression moulding process at 90°C, in which the shells are moulded to the core and to each other and the surface pattern is moulded in. The moulds are cooled by refrigerated water before extraction takes place. The spew lines are ground by rotating frozen balls against a revolving emery disc.

Vulcanisation of the cover is then carried out by exposing the moulded balls to carbon bisulphide vapour for several hours at a temperature of 32°C. The mechanism of the process is that of the Geer process, in which the carbon bisulphide reacts with a secondary amine and zinc oxide to form zinc diethyl dithiocarbamate. Vulcanisation is completed by putting the balls in ovens for 48 hours at a temperature of 32°C.

With other plastic materials, special moulding techniques must be used to avoid the problem of thread degradation.

iv. Painting and Marking

The balls are carefully graded for weight and compression, before being given a paint re-treatment. White polyurethane paint is then applied by rotating the balls, held by metal prongs, in the path of a spray gun which oscillates through the arc of a circle and covers the whole ball surface. The name and numerals are stamped on, and the ball is finished with a clear polyurethane coat, wrapped, and packaged.

Solid Golf Balls

Many attempts have been made in the past to produce acceptable golf balls by methods other than the complicated process of core winding. These have generally failed due to inadequate flight length and poor 'click'. The problem is to devise a compound which combines high resilience with extreme hardness and toughness. A material in a combination of certain monomers with an elastomer and a polymerisation initiator of the free radical type. The monomer is selected so that it is capable both of cross-linking the elastomer and of itself undergoing further polymerisation. Silica is used to adjust the gravity and to reinforce the compound. Typical formulations for a 42.67 mm ball are given in Table 14.12

Table 14.12: Typical mixes for solid golf balls

Cis-polybutadiene	100.00	*Cis*-polybutadiene	100.00
Butylene glycol dimethacrylate	56.20	Divinyi benzene	62.50
Silica	37.50	Silica	62.50
Dicumyl peroxide	3.13	Dicumyl peroxide	3.13
Cure	10 min at 150°C	Cure	10 min at 150°C

Although the performance of these balls is extremely good by the standards of earlier solid balls, their flight distance is about 10% inferior to that of top quality wound balls. However, being much more damage resistant, they appeal to the relatively inexpert golfer, and are now made in substantial quantities, particularly in the USA.

It is interesting to note that, because the solid ball is homogeneous in construction, its rotational inertia differs from that of a conventional core wound ball, which has much of its weight concentrated at its centre. For this reason, the solid ball accepts less spin from a lofted club and so has a flatter trajectory than a conventional ball.

CABLES

The modern elastomer-based electric cable consists generally of a metallic conductro covered with a cross-linked elastomeric compound formulated primarily with regard to its electrical properties, and a sheath or jacket formulated primarily with regard to its mechanical properties; in both formulations, the primary considerations are influenced by other environmental conditions.

In the period when natural rubber was the commonest alternative cable insulation to paper, its use developed in those areas where the smaller conductor sizes were appropriate - as in lighting and general low-power final distribution. These are areas where its greater manufacturing convenience in covering small wires and the greater flexibility of the resultant cable shows to the maximum advantage.

As the use of electrical power developed, the basic rubber cable construction extended into larger cables, particularly into areas where their flexibility was a salient advantage.

The availability of polychloroprene next brought improvement in cable sheaths since it provided outstanding technical advantage over natural rubber compounds under three main headings, namely flame retardance, weathering, and oil resistance. Consequently, it was adopted universally as the sheath material for mining cables, quarry cables, and ship cables, and to a major extent in, for instance, flexible cables in workshops and in farm wiring. Its inferior electrical properties were a deterrent to its use as an insulant, although it did see some use in this role in low-voltage cables, notably in aircraft, where size, weight, and flame retardance are primary considerations. Chlorosulphonated polyethylene (CSM) is now raplacing CR, particularly over EPM and IIR insulations.

In applications where flame retardance and electrical characterisitics are both primary factors and are equally important, as in ship cables and railway signalling cables, a layer of natural rubber isnulation compound is used immediately on the conductor, followed by a layer of polychloroprene compound bonded and covulcanised with it. This type of insulation system is now parallelled in the modern EPM-CSM and IIR-CSM combinations.

General Purpose Cables

The general purpose category is defined as that where the environment, or enduse, is typical of everyday modern life and such requirements as there are, can be met by most, if not all, elastomeric materials. In this group of applications, economics largely determine the choice of material.

In this field, natural rubber holds sway; only the cleanest grades are satisfactory for insulation, although less stringency is necessary for sheaths. The growth of bulk production methods, e.g., continuous vulcanisation has put emphasis on uniformity of quality and properties and reliable grading schemes such as the standard Malaysian rubbers have been of considerable assistance.

Illustrative of the general purpose cables are building wires and cables (BS 6007) and flexible cords for portable appliances (BS 6195). The wiring of domestic, commercial, and general industrial buildings is also an outstanding example of the dominance of economics in the selection of materials. It is in this area that the use of the thermoplastic PVC compounds has largely replaced that of elastomers.

Special Purpose Cables

The principal applications include shipping, mining, quarrying, Railway signalling, loco and rolling-stock wiring, Railway track feed, Naval ship wiring, lift wiring, welding electrode leads, medium voltage (15 kV) poor distribution,

X-ray tube supply, ignition (car, internal combustion engine, aircraft), coil leads, etc.

The salient design requirements for special purpose cables are as follows.

i. Heat resistance is defined as resistance to degradation and/or permanent deformation. Ageing is related to the life of the cable coverings at the maximum continuous operating temperature.

ii. Under the heading of electrical requirements are included dielectic strength, volume resistivity, permittivity, dielectric loss, and corona, resistance. Mechanical requirements cover tensile and compression stresses, abrasion, cut, tear, shearing, and flexing. Oil resistance also includes resistance to solvents.

iii. Fire resistance is meant to be the ability of an insulation system to operate for a limited time during, or after, a fire involving the cable, as distinct from flame retardance, which is the capability of a covering to prevent the propagation of flames.

iv. In the special purpose category, electrical, environmental, and mechanical performance requirements can limit the choice of polymer to a small number, leaving economics as the ultimate arbiter, or can narrow the choice to one polymer with very limited scope for compound variation, irrespective of price.

Ageing and Heat Resistance

The maximum continuous operating temperature of cable is the sum of the maximum continuous ambient temperature and the temperature rise in the conductor due to the maximum current rating of the cable. For general purpose cables, the maximum is approximately 60°C, and for the special purpose cables 85-90°C. NR, its alternatives, and CR are used for the former; EPM, IIR, CR, and NBR-PVC for the latter. A much smaller temperature category of the special purpose cables with operating temperatures in the range 100-150°C is satisfied by silicone rubber compounds. These temperature categories are generally understood to be associated with a life of at least 10 years, and usually 20-30 years.

The correlation between the accelerated ageing and natural ageing of NR has been obtained by experience. From this knowledge and the application of the Arrhenius reaction equation to data obtained from extended accelerated ageing programmes, it has been found possible to establish a logical basis for the minimum short-term accelerated ageing requirements of the new elastomers. Typical ageing curves for cable insulation and sheathing compounds are shown in Figure 14.25. Idealised Arrhenius plots are also given in Figure 14.26 for IIR and EPM insulation compounds in current use.

Mechanical criteria for the end of life are used, usually in terms of elongation at break, since electrical failure of a cable results from the mechanical consequence of ageing degradation. The different shapes of the ageing curves (Figure 14.25) render the old two-point test inadequate, and a three-point test to define the maximum slope, once the rate of ageing is stabilised, has been adopted (BS 2899, Part 4; BS 6899).

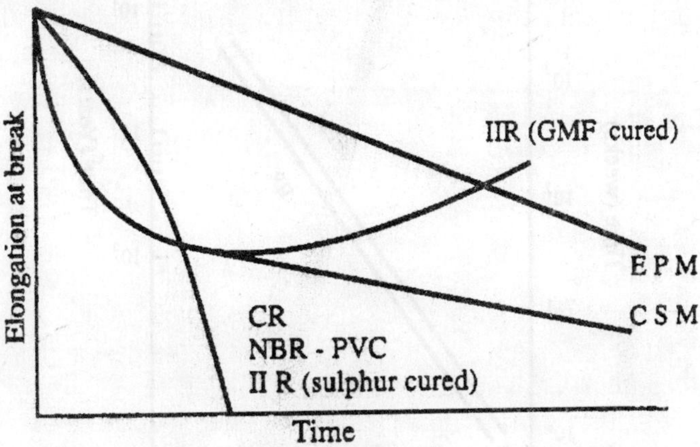

Figure 14.25: Characteristic ageing of various polymers

Because of the different mechanisms involved in the ageing behaviour of the different polymers and compounding systems, and because of their temperature sensitivity, the linear Arrhenius relationship (reciprocal of temperature proportional to the logarithm of time) holds reasonably well only over the lower part of the temperature range, representing continuous operating conditions. Hence, the results of short-term tests used to specify heat ageing behaviour at normal operating temperatures are inadequate; where heat resistance is a design factor, tests to simulate service conditions, consisting primarily of conventional ageing procedures carried out at temperatures considerably above the maximum continuous operating temperature, have been introduced. In ageing tests generally cable samples are usually included so that studies can be made of the catalytic interference of the conductor metal, shown to occur with some polymers, and the interaction between polymer compounding systems used in insulation and sheath. These tests are supplemented by, for example, current overload tests, the so-called 'threshold of damage' tests for power distribution cables, the varnish stoving test for coil leads (BS 6195; CSA C22.2, No. 116), or the heat endurance test for navy cables [MOD(N) Specification SES21, Part 1].

Electrical Properties

The electrical properties of polymers and their compounds and the factors affecting them have been reviewed as in low-voltage applications (upto 1 kV). Electrical parameters are not very critical and are usually limited to volume resistivity and dielectric strength. Adequate levels, where measured dry, are usually readily obtained with the hydrocarbon polymers.

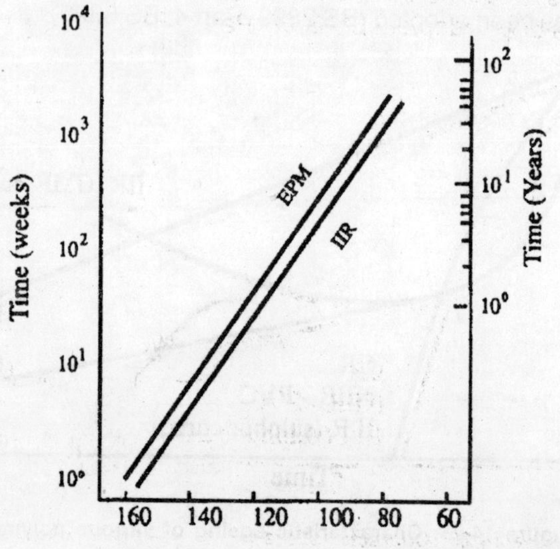

Fig. 14.26: Arrhenius plot of life against temperature for IIR and EPM insulation

Only barely adequate electrical properties are achievable with CR compounds, which are rarely used alone as insulants. With CSM, a balance can be struck with other design requirements so that 'single shot' coverings are feasible.

Electrical requirements, particularly in general purpose and low-voltage special applications, are often specified not as an indication of the performance necessary in service, but as a criterion of compound formulation or of manufacturing processes. For example, volume resistivity or insulation resistance can be used to dictate polymer-filler ratios in hydrocarbon polymer compounds.

Although the mechanisms involved in the ageing of elastomers result in molecular changes which can be traced by the changes in electrical properties, the changes in physical properties are much more significant.

Higher voltage cables are much more demanding with regard to compound design. Cables for power distribution have been manufactured for voltages of the order of 30-35 kV a.c., and X-ray cables operate up to 150 kV d.c. The normal criterion of performance of an elastomeric high-voltage cable insulant is the apparent dielectric strength against time characteristic, measured on cable samples. A typical example is given in Figure 14.27.

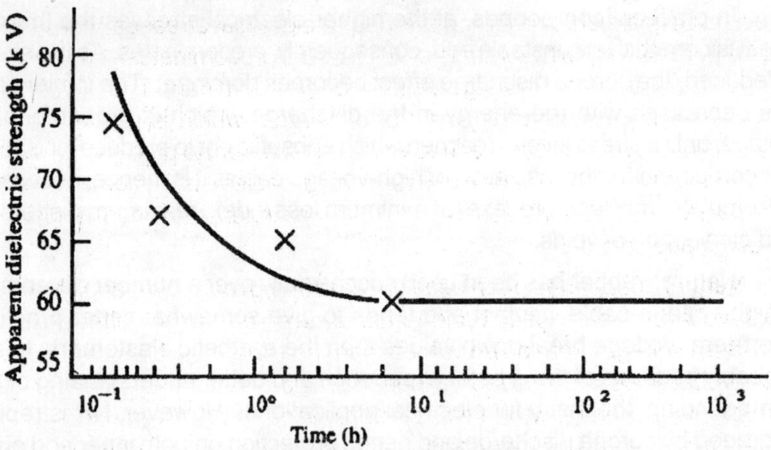

Fig. 14.27: Typical relationship between apparent dielectric strength and time, for 50 kV X-ray

It will be noted that the curve tends eventually to zero slope. It is the electrical stress represented by this part of the curve, corresponding to a time ≥ 1000 hours, which is used for cable design purposes. The early part of the curve, in which dielectric strength decreases rapidly with time, is indicative of the effect of degradation of the polymer due to corona discharge and thermal effects. Corona discharge is the result of the ionisation of a gaseous atmosphere and the acceleration of the ions in the electric field at the surface of the insulant, or in voids associated with filler agglomerates, or introduced accidentally within its body during manufacture. If the gas contains oxygen, one of the products of ionisation is ozone, which chemically attacks some polymers in addition to the erosion resulting from bombardment by other charged particles.

Within the insulant subjected to a high-voltage electric field, heat is generated owing to energy loss in the dielectric. This energy loss (loss index) is a function of volume resistivity, dielectric constant, and dissipation factor. Which of these parameters is dominant depends on whether the electrical field is unidirectional (d.c.) or alternating (a.c.) and on the frequency of the alternating field.

The degradation effects due to corona discharge and to thermal effects are highly temperature sensitive and interact: also, the intensity of the electric field at any particular point in the dielectric is affected by the dispersion of compound constituents and manufacturing flaws. Consequently, a considerable scatter is obtained in the determination of individual points and the shape of the early part of the curve is subject to considerable variation from compound to compound.

In practical compounds, at the higher electrical stresses the thermal effect is comulatively unstable and, consequently, predominates. As the stress is reduced, the corona discharge effect becomes dominant. The infulence of this decreases with the energy in the discharge, which is proportional to voltage, until a stress level is reached which is insufficient to produce ionisation. For compound for the insulation of high-voltage cables it is, hence, necessary to formulate, mix, and process for minimum loss index, maximum dispersion and elimination of voids.

Natural rubber has been used successfully over a number of years as a high-voltage cable insulant and tends to give somewhat better practical short-term voltage breakdown values than the synthetic elastomers; this is probably because of the greater experience and better understanding of the compounding chemistry for electrical applications. However, NR is rapidly degraded by corona discharge and needs protection on both inner and outer surfaces by a thin layer of a compound of a more resistant elastomer, such as CR. Such protective layers, based on the halogen-containing polymers, with high dielectic constants, modify favourably the electric stress distribution in the dielectric, particularly near to the conductor where the stress is highest and where discharge attack is most damaging.

IIR and EPM, with their low degree of molecular instruction, can be compounded to yield almost the same levels of practical dielectric strength and have the added advantage of considerably enhanced corona resistance and heat resistance. EPM has better corona resistance than IIR.

None of the hydrocarbon rubbers has yet been shown to be completely resistant to corona discharge, and hence cables are designed to be normally free from discharge at the working voltage. Corona resistance of a compound is, therefore, valuable as insurance against the accidental occurrence of discharge in service, or as the result of a minor manufacturing defect. Corona resistance is measured in terms of time to electrical failure by submitting a sample of cured compound, in either sheet or cable form, to an electrical stress such that an ionised air gap is included at the surface of the sample, between the electrodes. The compound is also usually submitted to mechanical stress during the test.

For the sake of flexibility, the conductors of cables often consist of a number of small wires, a formation which leads to local increases in electrical stress and the formation of air gaps at the inner surface of the insulant; corona discharge is thereby encouraged. To overcome this, a layer of conducting elastomer is commonly included immediately over the conductor and bonded to the insulating compound.

The mechanical properties required and, hence, the formulation of elastomeric compounds for cable sheathing, are similar to those of tyre compounds. The polymers are, for the general purpose cables where economics is important, natural rubber and, for the more special applications, the halogen-containing materials CR, CSM, and NBR-PVC. Many of these are inherently poor electrically and, being reinforced with carbon black, cannot be expected to have good electrical properties; nor are they necessary. However, if the volume resistivity, for instaisnce, is too low and the cable sheath contacts a terminal, current leakage can take place through and along the sheath. To avoid the risk of shock, a reasonable minimum value of volume restivity is 10^8 Ω cm. In most cases, the upper limit of volume resistivity is unimportant. An exception is the sheath on an X-ray cable, which may be used in an operating theatre; the value in this case should be low enough to discourage the accumulation of static charges.

Moisture Resistance

Perhaps of more concern than the initial electrical properties of compounds is the stability of electrical parameters which are most affected by the absorption and permeation of water. Access of an elastomeric insulant to free water leads fairly quickly to some deterioration in electrical properties and eventually to its electrical failure. The concept of 'life' with electrical failure as the criterion is thus suggested.

The mechanism of the absorption of water by componded rubber depends on the structure of the base polymer, the distribution of fillers and other components, the presence of water-soluble or hydrophilic constituents, and whether water is present in the liquid or vapour phase.

Elastomeric compound containing very little ionic material can absorb 2-3% of water without serious effect on electrical properites; in this case, an increase in dielectric constant can be detected without a corresponding deterioration in the dissipation factor, volume resistivity, or dielectric strength. Disturbing substances, such as cross-linking agents and antioxidants, can be introduced knowingly in designing the compound. Impurities, such as the residues of catalyst and initiatiors and regulators of polymerisation in synthetic polymers, impurities in fillers, and proteins and other water-soluble materials in natural rubber, also occur unitentionally. For this reasin, the more highly purified grades or rubbers are used for insulation compounds; the fillers are purified, or are treated to neutralise any polar impurities absorbed on their surfaces or to promote polyer-fillerbonding, e.g., coated calcium carbonates and the use of silane coupling agents. The less 'clean' grades are sometimes compounded with substances which combine with the polar residues from the polymeristion reaction to form non-polar substances, e.g., the use of metallic soaps with the corresponding oxide in EPM formulations.

During curing in steam, water in the vapour phase is forced into the compound and is released in a time dependent on the vapour pressure gradient, the temperature and the diffusion coefficient. The effect of the retained water, which may be in the liquid or vapour phase, is to cause a deterioration in electrical properties relative to those obtained with the dry cured compound by a factor of two or three. The volume resistivity of a steam cured sample can be several powers of 10, different from a press cured equivalent. In the case of insulated wire cured in high-pressure steam or in a continuous vulcanisation process, this effect can persist for several weeks after processing, during which a steady improvement in electrical properties occurs.

Polar sites in the molecular structure of polymers created by oxidation, contribute to the osmotic and diffusion effects. In the halogenated polymers, the products of degradation are particularly actively polar and hydrophilic. It has not been found practical, therefore, to apply physical laws even to a limited extent, as in the case of heat ageing.

With natural rubber compounds as a base, compound evaluation is by comparison of standard samples of insulated wire immersed in water, deterioration being traced by measuring insulation resistance with time. A typical plot is given in Figure 14.28. To accelerate degradation, the test temperature is of the order of the maximum service temperature and an electrical stress of about twice the working value is applied across the dielectric. Significant changes can be detected in about six weeks. No satisfactory short-term test is available, and a full evaluation of a compound's performance may take several years. Resistivity has been found to be a more sensitive criterion of performance than any other electrical parameter.

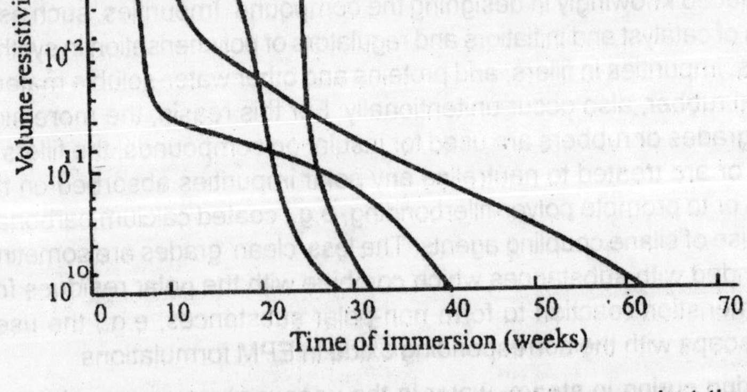

Fig. 14.28: Water stability test - insulation resistance against time of immersion for various IIR insulation compounds

Manufacture

Compound Production

The variety of polymers and corresponding compound constituents used in cable manufacture leads to some complication in maintaining segregation of non-compatible materials. The automation of the cable factory mill room and mechanical compound-handling arrangements are also influenced by this large complex range of materials. Mixing is commonly by internal mixer, with mill mixing being the exception. Because of the importance, electrically, of good dispersion, particular attention is paid to the particle size of fillers in respect of both level and range. Dispersions, in oil, of the components of curing systems (e.g., red lead) are generally úsed. In addition, insulation compounds are passed through a straining machine to minimise electrical failure due to power agglomerates or contamination.

Cable Covering

Application of rubber cable coverings is carried out with a plant designed for one of two basic methods, namely batch curing (discontinuous) or continuous curing. The older one involves the application of rubber as an operation separate from its cure. In the continuous process, the curing operation is integral with the application of the covering and thus labour cost is reduced.

Application of Insulation and Sheath

The three methods of fabricating the rubber coverings of cables are longitudinal, lapping, and extrusion. All three are used for insulating wire; only the latter two are appropriate to sheathing.

The two older methods - longitudinal and lapping - of rubber-covering wire have now been almost completely superseded by extrusion techniques. Both involve the application of calendered tapes of uncured compound; longitudinal covering consists of passing the wire, sandwiched between two rubber tapes, between grooved rollers so that a seam is formed on each side. A machine has three or four sets of rolls in tandem. The requisite thickness of covering is built up by applying the appropriate number of tapes of suitable thickness. Upto 36 wires are covered simultaneously, the covered wires being separated between each station by parting blades. Lapping consists of spirally wrapping tapes onto the wire with an overlap. Again, the appropriate thickness is obtained by using several tapes from heads in tandem.

The two methods require compounds capable of being handled in roll from with the conflicting properties of good building tack, good green strength, and low stretch. Bopth processes are very susceptible to ambient temperature variations and contamination.

Extrusion of insulation and sheath is carried out using conventional machines fitted with cross-heads. The conductor to be covered or the core or cabled cores to be sheathed, as the case may be, pass through a core tube supported coaxially within the head and located concentrically with the die by a tapered extension to the core tube - the 'cure point'. Cold feeding of the compound, either in chip or strip form, to machines with the length-diameter ratio of the scroll from 12:1 to 15:1 has been widely adopted.

The use of dual extruders (Figrue 14.29) permits the simultaneous application of the two components of composite insulation, e.g., EPM-CSM. NR-CR, is now common. Insulation and sheath, or stress control layer and in-sulation, are dealt with similarly. With appropriate combinations of compounds, the ensuing curing promotes bonding of the two layers. (It should be noted that, with such an arrangement, balancing of the cure characteristics and rheological properties of the two compounds is necessary).

Line equipment consists of a capstan, or capstans, either of the drum type of fitted with caterpillar tracks (caterpuller), together with pay-off and take-up stands. In modern extrusion lines, the two capstans, one behind the extruder, one in front, are interlinked - one with the other and with the extruder drive-and coordinated so that the line can be run at low speed for setting up and then run up to full production speeds with the minimum of extruder readjustment. Tension control is effected by adjusting the speed differential between the two capstan units.

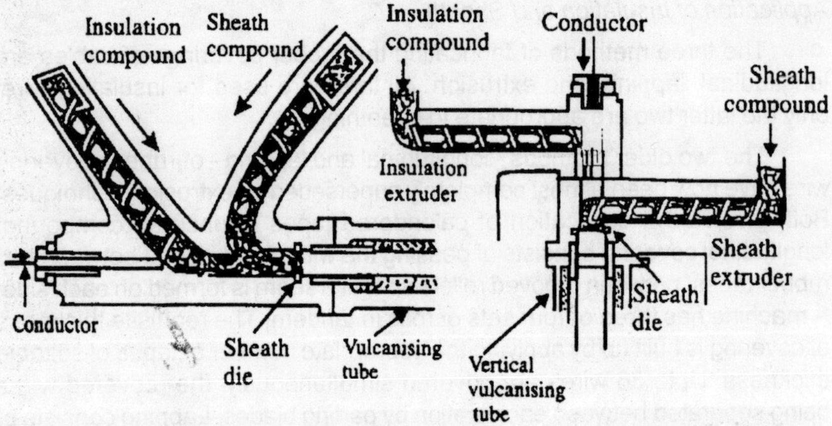

Fig. 14.29: Principle of synchronised dual extrusion machines

Curing Techniques

The choice of curing method, either discontinuous or continuous, is determined mainly by economics, dependent on the length and size of the cable to be produced. In some cases, technical requirements dictate the method to be used, e.g., the use of continuous vulcanisation for the insulation of high-voltage cables.

Batch Curing

In the batch, or discontinuous, method, the insulation or sheath applied by one of the processes outlined above is cured in an autoclave in steam at pressures corresponding to temperatures of 130-160°C; curing cycles vary between 15 and 90 minutes overall. Where a rubber sheath is applied over thermoplastic-insulated cores, the curing temperature is below the softening point of the insulant.

The cable or core, in its uncured state, is coiled in trays or reeled on drums, precautions being taken to avoid adhesion and deformation by dusting with talc, or other anti-tack agents. Cooling before take-up and some form of restraint during curing are also necessary. The smaller cables, particularly those covered by extrusion, are sometimes coiled spirally in a large-diameter shallow tray and packed in talc.

To provide support during handling and restraint during cure, spiral overlapped cotton tape is applied, in the case of the lapping or extrusion methods, as part of the rubber-covering operation; or separately, in longitudinal covering. The steam during the cure causes the tapes to absorb moisture, to shrink, and so to consolidate the covering. This is reinforced by the expansion forces within the rubber in the later stages of the curing cycle. Other low-stretch tapes, such as woven glass fibre and polyethylene terephthalate fibre (Terylene), or the latter in film form have been used under particular circumstances where cost is not the main concern. Choice of tape strength is dependent on the volume of rubber per unit length. In the case of core, the cotton tape is often 'proofed' with a coating of coloured rubber and left in place after cure is complete to serve as circulit identification. For sheath cures, however, the tape is dusted with dry talc and removed as a separate operation.

Where maximum consolidation is required, or to improve the transfer of heat from the curing medium, a metal sheath is applied either over a tape, as above, or directly onto the rubber.

The considerable length of cable required to fill a CV line and the consequent high scrap at each start-up, together with the high capital cost of the installation, make this method more appropriate to long production runs. Batch curing techniques have hence tended to be perpetuated for short-length manufacture and jobbing work.

The above circumstances relative to CV, encourage the highest practical line speeds, demanding the formulation of compounds with the shortest practical curing times. Table 14.13 gives examples of practical conditions.

Obviously, to achieve optimum cure times on a given CV line, the maximum practical steam pressures are used, subject to the thermal characteristics of the compound and the geometry of the covering, which determine the rate of flow of heat and, consequently, the radial cure gradient. Reversion must not occur on the outer surface of the covering before an acceptable state of cure is achieved at the inside.

Table 14.13: Practical conditions for the continuous vulcanisation of cables

Covering	Diameter under Covering (mm)	Covering thickness (mm)	Line speed (m/min)	Steam pressure (kgf/cm^2)	Steam length (m)	Cure time (s)
General purpose NR insulation	2.6	0.8	200.0	14.5	80.0	24.0
High-voltage EPM insulation (11 kV)	5.2	67.0	9.0	13.0	22.5	150.0
NR sheath	9.5	1.3	65.0	14.5	55.0	50.0
CSM sheath	9.5	1.3	30.0	14.5	55.0	110.0

Adequate cooling is also an important factor influencing optimum line speed since, otherwise, the high internal vapour pressure, resulting from CV conditions, results in 'blowing' of the covering.

Since equilibrium thermal conditions are not generally achieved during CV cures, the theoretical estimation of curing conditions is complex. Recently, electrical anlogue techniques have been developed which can be computerised to make it rapid and practical. It will be evident that compounds for CV must have a 'flat' cure characteristic at the curing temperature, and a compromise between minimum cure time and scorch time must be achieved.

Both horizontal and vertical fluidised beds, integrally coupled beads, integrally coupled with extrusion, are attractive for short-length jobbing cable production. Liquid salt baths also have considerable promise. The short individual lengtrhs require the use of shorter curing units than CV. Since these media are operated at, or near, atmospheric pressure, porosity of the extrudate from the occlusion of air and moisture in compounds has to be combated by the use of vented extruders and an hydrous lime in the compound, respectively.

Specialised Elastomeric Cable Components

Apart from the main elastomeric cable components of insulation and sheath, a number of other components are used which call for different compound formulations.

Cured conducting compounds of NR, IIR, and EPM, formulated to have resistivities of <10^3 Ω cm, are used for electrical stress control in high-voltage cables. NR and CR compounds with resistivites of <10Ω cm have been proposed for protective circuits in flexible mining cables and are now coming into general use, as defined in NCB specifications.

Radio frequency interference from petrol engines is suppressed by the use of CR compounds, with resistivities of the order of 1Ω cm, for the conductor instead of a metallic wire in cables for ignition circuits.

Paints based on CR and CSM are used to impart flame retardance and weather resistance to cable coverings, e.g., textile braids. They are also used for core identification, particularly CSM which gives better colours, and to add ozone resistances and oil resistance to insulants based on hydrocarbon elastomers.

MANUFACTURE OF MISCELLANEOUS PRODUCTS

Products Based on Spread Fabrics

Spreading of fabrics is carried out as a preliminary to their incorporation in the products. In addition, final products are made from fabrics, usually spread with natural or synthetic rubber on one side only, and used for their waterproof quality, e.g., machintoshes, groundsheets, and trapaulin-type covers.

The mechanical, electrical, automobile, and aircraft engineering industries have requirements for a great variety of gaskets and diaphragms which for strength and stiffness must have fabric reinforcement. These are frequently made by spreading fabrics of cotton, rayon, nylon, polyester, or glass fibre with rubber, all types of elastomer being used. The shape is punched from the fully cured sheet. Surface finish is important in many applications and determines the method of vulcanising the spread fabric. The finest, smoothest surface is obtained by moulding, but often an acceptable finish can be achieved by wrapping the fabric on itself on a large drum with an interleaf of fine textured cloth, special paper, or plastics film.

Flat punched diaphragms can be post-formed to simple convoluted forms by a short heat treatment when pressed between a metal and a rubber shaped jig.

Products Made by the Calendering Process

Unsupported Sheeting

For quantity production of unsupported sheet, i.e., without fabric insertion, the calendering operation is most economical, assuming that the vulcanisate requirements can be met by a mix which will calendef smoothly. Unsupported sheeting is required for hospital use, for sticky-back repair patches, for gaskets and diaphragms, and for cutting into thread for garment and golf ball manufacture. A calendered sheet is also required for built-up products, moulding, etc., e.g. the sheet may be wrapped on a mandrel to form a tube for subsequent parting off into washers.

Supported Sheeting

Many of the products can equally well be produced by means of the calender. The choice of method depends on many factors - the ability of the rubber mix to friction or calender smoothly, the degree of adhesion required and obtainable by the various methods, the thickness required, and the uniformity of thickness needed.

The vulcanising methods available for the cure of calender produced sheeting and fabric-reinforced sheeting are the same as for spread fabric.

Extrusions

Continuous or Long Lengths

It is hardly necessary to do more than mention the variety - tubing, sealing and trimming strips for automobiles and domestic appliances, shoe welting, etc., supplied in long lengths to other industries and users to cut up as required. The vulcanising methods are either back or continuous and both solid and cellular rubber sections are manufactured. Trade marks, names, sizes, and other details may be imprinted on the extrusion by allowing it to pass over an engraved or embossed roller as it leaves the machine.

Precision Extrusions

The compounder's and the diemaker's arts are usually adequate to ensure that extrusions meet the designer's requirements dimensionally and shapewise, at least in the smaller size range. There are, however, large sectionextrusions where collapse and distortion occurring during handling and cure, demand special treatment. Tubing may need to be blown onto a mandrel; other sections require support on specially made jigs. For fine dimensional tolerances or when the extruded surface is not perfect enough, grinding the outside of the tubing is commonly practised. In other instances, bends and other shapes are made by putting the uncured extrusion onto bent or shaped mandrels before cure.

Products Made from Cured Extrusion

Scarf-Joining

Vulcanised or semi-vulcanised solid or hollow extrusions are scarf- or butt-joined to produce rings for such items as seals and driving bands. The techniques vary. The freshly cut surfaces are coated with a solution of the same mix, with the addition of a bonding agent in the case of solvent-resistant polymers. A further aid to a satisfactory bonding is to insert a 0.1-0.2 mm calendered film between the two solutioned faces of the joint. After making the joint, it is clamped under light pressure in a sample two-piece mould, heated electrically or placed between heated platens. A short cure is given to the joint, followed frequently by an open steam or oven cure to complete the vulcanisation of the whole component.

Parted-off Components from Extrusions

Uncured tubing or any other extrusion is cut into suitable lengths for use as moulding blanks, by parting-off in a lathe, often by automatic mechanisms. The extrusion is supported on mandrels coated with rubber or other non-metallic material to protect the knife and avoid contamination of the blanks. Fully vulcanised tubing is similarly cut into washers and gaskets. If dimensional tolerances are tight on the internal and external diameters, the extrusion will need to have been cured on a mandrel of the correct size, allowing for shrinkage and the outside diameter ground before the parting-off operation. This is only one way of producing a rectangular section washer; punching or trepanning from calendered or moulded sheet and moulding arc alternatives. Stationers' bands are made from extruded tube allowed to flatten, and than vulcanised, and cut to the required width by guillotine.

Endless Shaped Seals from Extrusions

For automobile and aircraft window and domestic appliance door seals, accurately shaped corners may be required. A widely used technique, to save the cost of complicated and large moulds which would be needed to make them in one piece, is the corner moulding of extrusions. Semi-vulcanised extrusion is prepared and cut to length, the cut ends being coated with solution. Two lengths are placed accurately in a simple corner mould made to the shape of the corner with a section corresponding to that of the extrusion. The mould is clamped between the heated platens of a press, and rubber is transferred to the cavity to form a corner piece integral with the two lengths of extrusion. The operation is repeated with the necessary other lengths of extrusion to produce an endless seal shaped to fit the window or door. Alternative methods include the scarf-joining of the extrusion into an endless ring and then by means of suitable mandrels or formers (which may be of a meltable or soluble substance) setting the corners to shape by means of a heat treatment. In this case, the extrusion must be in such a state of cure that it will assume the required permanent set.

Solid Tyres

Rubber-tyred wheels, casters, and drive pulleys are manufactured in a variety of sizes and sections, and also solid rubber tyres for perambulators, punch-chairs, etc., as separate items for fixing to a grooved wheel.

The rubber-tyred product, in which the rubber is moulded and bonded to the metal or other rigid wheel, is made by applying an adhesive or ebonite layer to the metal surface followed by an extruded section or calendered strip; the assembled unit is then placed in a simple compression two- or three-piece mould and vulcanised under heat and pressure.

Solid rubber tyres for application to a wheel are moulded with an endless metal helix and/or fabric core on the inner diameter to give it the rigidity and stiffness to hold on the rim - sufficient stretch is present to permit assembly on a grooved wheel.

Hollow Articles

Inner tubes for tyres of all sizes are nowadays moulded. A pre-moulded rubber-based valve stem is cemented to an extruded tube, the ends of which are cut, usually with a hot knife, and butt-joined. The tube is then inflated and moulded in watchcase-type presses.

Under this heading are also included play balls, which may be moulded on the lines of tennis balls, and hand-built and open steam or oven cured products such as bladders, fuel tanks, liquid storage bags, and dinghies. In addition, there are the moulded hollow components and articles - boots and gaiters for engineering joints, cell sacks, handle grips, and hot water bottles - for which the mould contains a core rigidly positioned and located but separate, so that after cure the product can be removed. Careful blank sizing and shaping is necessary to ensure uniform and consistent wall thickness. If compression mouding is employed, the compound formulation and condition of the blank must be such that good knitting of the separate blanks occurs as they flow together. The vulcanisate; in the hot state as it leaves the mould, must have sufficient elongation to permit the extraction of the core, which, in the case of a hot water bottle, for example, is considerable. Transfer or injection moulding is necessary for many products of this type to eliminate uneven wall thickness, retracted spew (backrinding), air trapping, and other faults, and to save material.

Diaphragms

Reference has already been made to the production of simple flat or slightly convoluted diaphragms from unsupported and supported spread or calender proofed material. There are diaphragms with peripheral and/or centre beads and bosses for assembling and sealing purposes, and with deep convolutions which must be moulded. No special techniques are called for, apart from accurate blank preparation for the reinforced diaphragms to ensure that during moulding the fabric is neither distorted, strained, nor damaged by the flow of rubber. Simple two-plate compression moulds with accurate dowelling or taper location are commonly used.

Top hat diaphragms, which are designed to roll in use, giving long strokes with minimal resistance to movement, are the subject of patents. The majority of such products have a fabric reinforcement which may be square woven or knitted. The essential of the technique is the pre-forming of a top hat from the fabric and then moulding around it a rubber coating on one side of the fabric with the necessary beads or rims to provide sealing when assembled in the metal components.

It is common practice to produce diaphragms with the rubber on one side of the fabric only, the side which faces the pressure. This ensures that no separation of fabric and rubber takes place as is liable to occur if the fabric side faces the pressure.

Seals

Rubber seals are used to seal anything from a wristwatch to the freight door of an aircraft. The former may be an O-ring of bore 0.8 mm and cross-sectional diameter 0.5 mm; the latter may have a section more than 40 mm across and a circumferential length of 15 metre. Figure 14.30 is a chart of seal tyeps, not all of which are made wholly or partly of rubber. Some of these types have already been discussed as being manufactured by techniques other than moulding.

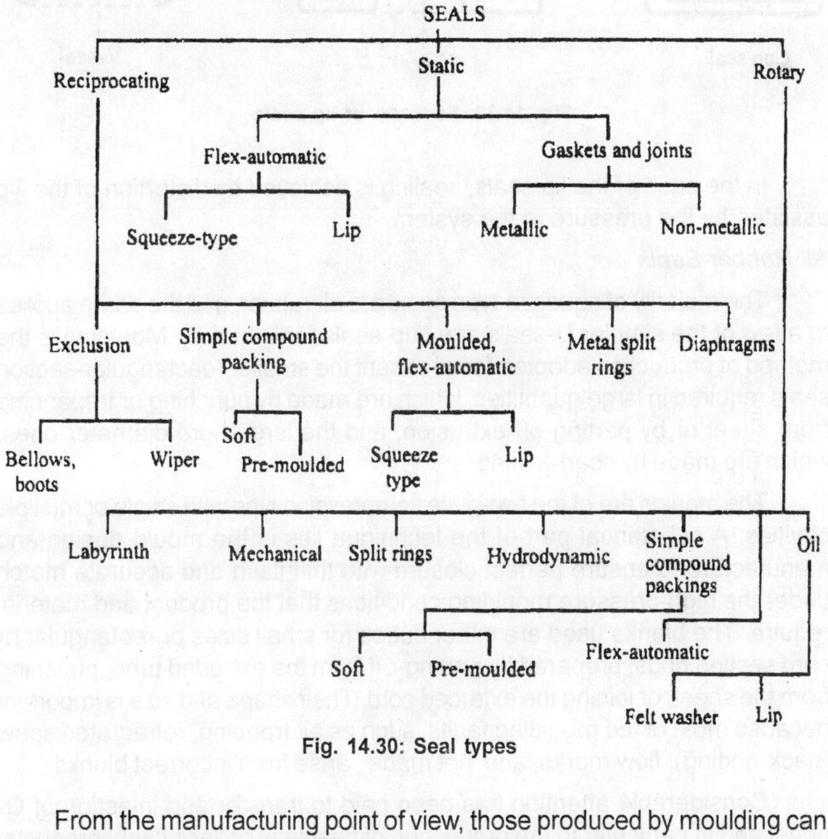

Fig. 14.30: Seal types

From the manufacturing point of view, those produced by moulding can be considered under three headings. Squeeze-tape seals and lip seals are in common use, and within each type there are several section shapes (Figures 14.31 and 14.32). The former operate by distortion under radial or axial compressive strain, as discussed below. The O-ring is very widely used, though some designers prefer the rectangular, D, or delta sections. The T-seal has the advantage that it can be clamped on assembly and does not, therefore, become easily displaced or twisted.

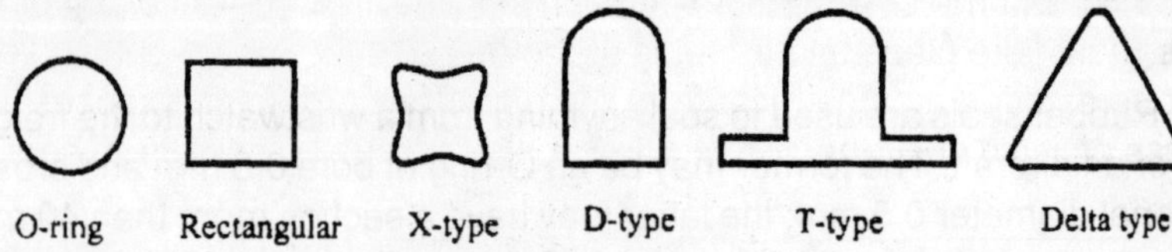

Fig. 14.31: Sections of squeeze-type seals

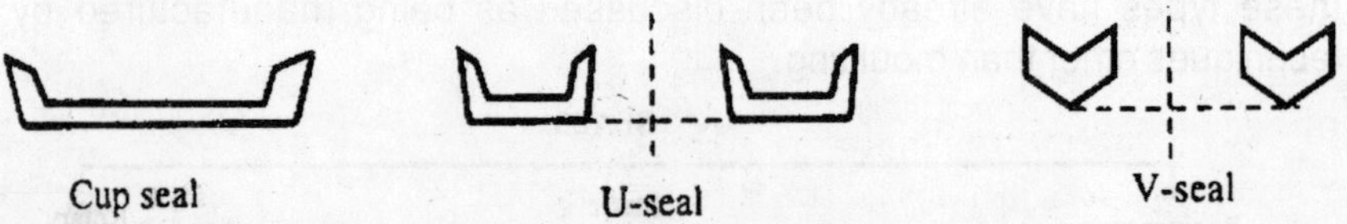

Fig. 14.32: Sections of lip seals

In the case of the lip seals, sealing is achieved by distortion of the lip assisted by the pressure in the system.

All-Rubber Seals

The majority of squeeze-type seals are all-rubber, and the same applies to a few of the simpler U-seals and cup-seals for light duty. Moulding is the method of production adopted for all except the smaller reactangular-section seals required in large quantities, which are made by punching or trepanning from sheet or by parting-off extrusion, and the large bore diameter ones, which are made by scarf-joining.

The moulds are of the two-plate compression type with single or multiple cavities. A substantial part of the technique lies in the mould design and manufacture to ensure perfect closure with thin flash and accurate match under the high-pressure moulding conditions that the product and material require. The blanks used are either cubes for small sizes or rectangular or cord section rings, prepared by parting-off from the extruded tube, punching from the sheet, or joining the extruded cord. Their shape and size is important because most of the moulding faults, such as air trapping, retracrated spew (back-rinding), flow marks, and 'not made', arise from incorrect blanks.

Considerable attention has been paid to transfer and injection of O-rings, and in particular to the production of flashless or 'less flash' products.

Fabric-Containing Seals

Fabrics are incorporated in seals to increase modulus and stiffness and to provide strength and wear and tear resistance. Fabrics of all available fibres are used depending on the service use, in particular, temperature. Manufacture involves the thorough impregnation of the textile fabric with the rubber compound, either by spreading or frictioning, and then a careful building upto, as near as possible, the shape of the finished product before planing in the mould. During the moulding operation, minimal flow and distortion of the fabric must take place and trapping of the fabric at the mould parting lines must be avoided as it detracts from the appearance of seal, exposes it to ingress of liquid and other foreign matter, and generally reduces its service life.

Metal-Containing Seals

Many seals for rotary shaft application contain metal stiffening, usually as a punched and formed cup to which the rubber is bonded (Figure 14.33). Attention needs to be paid to the location of the metal during the mouding operation and choice of blank shape to ensure satisfactory and consistent products.

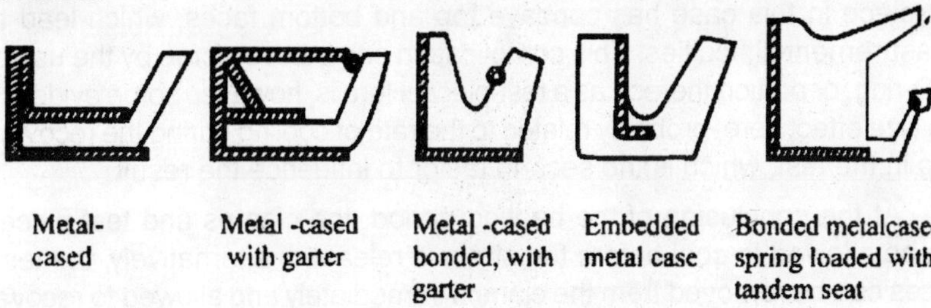

Fig. 14.33: Sections of rotary shaft seals

Finishing Seals

In lip seals, the sealing surface is the lip which must make uniform contact with the cylinder walls, against which it operates. Because it is not easy to mould this lip without a parting line near to its edge, it is a common practice to make the mould parting line at the lip, which is made longer than required and knifed off to the required dimension in a lathe as a subsequent finishing operation. Automatic machines are often used to do this.

Flash removal form O-rings and moulded rectangular and similar section seals is carried out by high-speed felt and cotton mops and abrasive wheels.

Seal Design and Material Selection

The development and selection of rubber mixes for seals is dictated usually by three factors. First, the fluid with which the seal will be in contact; secondly, the temperature range of the environment in which it will operate; and thirdly, the mechanical environment, including such factors as pressure, stressing, and abrasion. The fluid and temperture will restrict the choice of the base polymer, usually to one or two; compounding will be directed to achieving the correct hardness and abrasion resistance and to adjusting the swelling behaviour of the rubber in the liquid. The designer will want to know the likely dimensional changes in the seal material due to uptake of liquid and differential thermal expansion.

Important in seal applications is the elastic property of the rubber vulcanisate. The distorted rubber exerts a pressure on the contacting surface to maintain the seal. Unfortunately, no rubber is perfectly elastic, and the stress in the rubber decays or relaxes with time. This stress relaxation can be measured directly or more frequently, the degree of permanent compression set, the rubber has taken up on removal of the stress is determined.

There are two factors of importance in compression set testing. Firt, at the rubber-metal clamp interface, with the cylindrical test-piece of BS 903, there can be any degree of slippage, and the amount of slippage affects the result. It is probably easiest to achieve the no-slip condition, but the 'recovered' test-piece in this case has concave top and bottom faces, which lead to measurement difficulties. This complication can be overcome by the use of an O-ring, or portion thereof, as a test-piece. Here is, however, some evidence of a size effect here, probably related to the rate of cooling during the recovery step in the test, which is the second factor to influence the result.

At the conclusion of the heating period, the clamps and test-pieces can be allowed to cool before the strain is released; alternatively, the test-pieces can be removed from the clamps immediately and allowed to recover for the specified period of 30 minutes, either as the test temperature or at a room temperature. The spread of results obtained by such variations of procedure depends on the magnitude of the viscous component of the elastomer's viscoelasticity. If high, not only is the spread high but one arbitrarily chosen method may give misleading and unreliable indications of the elastomer's behaviour as a seal. It is in such circumstances that stress relaxation observations are valuable as giving a more complete picture of what is taking place.

Other factors related to those mentioned above are the change of hardness on heating the rubber and on immersion in the liquid which the rubber is sealing. Too great a softening may lead to extrusion of the seal between the clearances, with ultimate rapid failure. Strain in the rubber affects liquid uptake, and diffusion rates of various liquids in rubber of different types cover a wide range of values.

Nitrile rubber mixes are the workhorses of the seal industry, because of their resistance to mineral and ester-based lubricants and to hydraulic liquids. The mineral oils offered vary in composition and in the swelling they produce in nitrile rubbers. It is important that the rubber and oil are matched. The publication by the Association of Hydraulic Equipment Manufacturers (1968) of their proposed 'seal compatibility index' method is of interest. The idea is to categorise oils by the volume change they produce in a standard nitrile rubber, stated as the SCI. Oils with similar SCI, within a toleracnce, will be inerchangeable; additionally from the SCI of an oil, seal manufacturers will be able to provide suitable rubbers. This scheme is based on the observed liner relation between the SCI value and the swelling of commercial nitrile rubbers in a range of 52 mineral-based oils from a number of oil suppliers.

Hand-built Products

The broad principle of the manufacture of most important and typical products with a preference for natural rubber, if it meets the vulcanisate properties required because of its building tack have already been discussed. Butyl rubber has become established as a reservoir-lining rubber and also for other water-storage containers which involve handwork. Nitrile, polyurethane, and chloroprene rubbers are used for fuel cells and storage containers on a base of nylon fabric.

Moulded Rubber Goods

Moulded rubber goods find extensive use in railways, automobiles, bicycles and also in many industrial and domestic appliances. The product rang varies from small O-ring play balls, bushes, shock absorbers, rubber rollers, battery containers, etc. This industry can also work as an ancillary one to many large scale units. In fact, almost all the large scale manufacturers of automobiles, scooters, moped, cycles, machines depend and largely on small scale units for their entire range of rubber products.

Raw material Required

Raw rubber, reclaimed rubber, sulphur, MBT, MBTS, TMT, powder, carbon black, China clay, whiting powder, zinc oxide, stearate, lubricants, binding materials, etc.

Process of Manufacture

All the rubber chemicals are mixed with raw rubber after proper mastication in a two-roll mixing mill. Depending upon the nature of rubber used, it might be necessary sometimes to pass steam through the rollers. After compounding is over, it is the usual practice to extrude the same to form slabs and cut pieces; after weighing they are fed into moulds and cured either with steam or electricity in presses (hand-operated). These are then taken out, screened, tested and packed.

Composition of rubber compound

Raw rubber	4 kg
China clay	5-18 kg
Sulphur	100 gm

TMT powder	100 gm
MBTS	100 gm
Zinc oxide	300 gm
Stearate	150 gm
Carbon black	100 gm

Machinery and Equipments Required

i. Two-roll mixing mills, 12" × 30", chilled cast iron rolls, complete with 25 H.P. motor reduction gear and other accessories.
ii. Extruder 2" complete with electric motor (1)
iii. Mou!d - assorted L.S.
iv. Steam heated presses (hand operated) - 14" × 14" size (4)
v. Steam heated presses (hand operated 16" × 16" size (4)
vi. Baby boiler with 80 psi steam pressure (1)
vii. Weighing machine (1)
viii. Micellaneous equipments and tools, etc.

Dipped Rubber Goods DRG

Dipped goods from rubber latex like surgical gloves, finger stalls, catheters and veterinary appliances are finding increasing use. Some of these may be classified as -

Industrial gloves

Surgical gloves

Finger stalls

Transfusion tubes.

Raw materials required

Latex	60%
DRC, Vulcastab L.S.	20%

Other materials required are - zinc oxide, sulphur, casein, caustic soda, accelerators, antioxidant, calcium nitrate, distilled water, packing material, etc.

Process of Manufacture

Rubber chemicals like sulpur, zinc oxide, accelerators, antioxidants, etc., are dispersed with Dispersol L.N. in a pot mill in suitable proportion separately. The dispersed solution is mixed with 60% DRC centrifugal latex in a Hobart type mixer. This is taken in a tank and moulds of the required products made of either wood, aluminium, or porcelain are dipped in the tank. These are then vulcanised with the moulds in air ovens, removed from the moulds and dusted with talc. No solid material should be fed into the mixer to avoid coagulation.

Machinery and equipment

i. Hobart type mixer - 3 speed, 25 litres capacity, complete with 2 H.P. electric motor.
ii. Pot mill - 6 pots complete with 3 H.P. electric motor.
iii. Thermostatically controlled air oven 3" × 3" × 2" (2 KW).
iv. Coagulation tanks of plastics, 25 litres capacity (2)
v. Moulds L.S
vi. Small weighing machine.

Rubber Mattings

Rubber mattings mainly find applications in automobiles. These are made by coating rubber compound over Hessian cloth either by spreading or calendering technique. Due to constant use, these need early replacement. There is a substantial demand for rubber mattings of different types for cars, scooters and household requirements.

Raw materials required

Hessian cloth, raw rubber, sulphur, rubber chemicals, solvents, coal dyes and colours, etc.

Machinery and equipment

i. Two roll mixing mills, size 12" × 30" (1)
ii. Spreading machine, size 12" × 20" (1)
iii. Churner, 200 litres capacity (1)
iv. Vulcaniser 2" × 6" (1)
v. Baby boiler for 80 psi pressure steam (1)
vi. Miscellaneous equipments and tools, etc.

Process of Manufacsture

Raw rubber is masticated and is mixed with all other ingredients in a two-roll mixing mill. The rubber compound so obtained is sheeted out thinly and dropped into suitable solvent for 10-12 hours. The rubber absorbs the solvent and becomes soft and plastic. The mass is then taken into mixing churners where little more solvent is added and mixed well to get a dough like consistency. It is then spread on Hessian cloth in spreading machine by the Doctor Blade Technique. To get designs, the sheets are passed through embossed rolls before curing. It is then cured in a vulcaniser.

Rubber Bushes for Automobiles

Rubber bushes are the important auto ancillaries which play an important role. Rubber bushes are also known as resilient bushes.

The following is the composition for rubber bushes -

Raw material required

Natural rubber	77.0%
Zinc oxide	6.5 %
Stearic acid	2.0%
Carbon black	7.5%
Process oil	0.4%
PBN	0.75%
MBT	0.75%
Sulphur	1.5%

The rubber, with other ingredients is compounded in a mixing mill. After compounding, the next step is extrusion to form slabs and cut pieces. After weighing these are fed into mollds and cured in a hydraulic press. Now the bushes from the hydraulic press are ready for packing.

Plant and machinery

Rubber mixing mill	(1 No.)
Hydraulic press	(1 No.)
Extruder	(1 No.)
Baby boiler	(1 No.)
Moulds	(5 to 6 Nos.)
Weighing machine	(1 No.)
Testing apparatus	(1No.)

Rubber Tubing

Rubber tubings are flexible rubber pipes of low diameter and used in the transfer of fluids from one place to another. These are generally known as delivery tubes. They are characterised by inertness to corrosive chemicals and even gases for burners. Rubber tubings are most popular because of their low cost as well as inertness to most of the materials which are conveyed.

Manufacturing Process

Rubber is compounded in a mixing mill after the addition of various ingredients. The mixed mass is then extruded through a suitable extruder in the form of tube in length of 50' to 100' which largely depends upon the diameter of the tube. The extruded tubes are continuously cooled with talc on a pan stick and then transaferred to vertical vulcaniser or autoclave where vulcanisation is done in open steam under pressure of 48-59 lbs per square inch.

Compounding is as follows -

Material	Parts by Wt.
Rubber	100.00
Petroleum	5.00
Antioxidant	1.00
Zinc oxide	15.00
White clay	250.00
Dibenzothiazol disulphide	1.25
Sulphur	3.00

It is vulcanised by steam at 50 psi pressure.

Plant and machinery requried

		Quantity
1.	Mixing mill 12" × 30" with chilled rolls and reduction gear, 30 H.P. Motor etc.	1
2.	Extruder, 2-1/2" - 7.5 H.P.	1
3.	Vulcaniser, size 4" × 8"	2
4.	Boiler (oil fired) with evaporation capacity 250 kg/hr, 100 lb/psi working.	
5.	Tray tables, weighing machines etc.	1
6.	Testing equipments like, thickness gauge, hardness tester, ageing blocks.	1 each 4cm col.

15

Recycling of Wastes from Rubbers and Plastics

INTRODUCTION

Rubber and plastics are, to the general public, materials which evince a degree of wonder and surprise. Properties such as elasticity, creep and flexibility are exhibited at levels which are far beyond those found in traditional materials and minerals.

Very little of the discarded material from rubber and plastics manufacture is completely 'scrap'. Uses can be, and are, found for almost any and every type of off-cut, trimming, flash or other waste. Thermoplastics are shown as being the easiest to feedback into the process stream. Rubber is equally easy before vulcanisation but afterwards it must be regarded as a type of thermoset. Re-use of thermoset plastics is inhibited by the curing process which it undergoes. Economic necessity is usually the determining factor. Some processes are economical only if material is recycled, some products are only viable if recycled material is used. Some incur high costs in collection and segregation so as to preclude any attempt to recycle at present market conditions. These controls are described together with opportunities which exist for secondary use by other industries. Aslo considered are the means of economical final disposal.

Lack of understanding and appreciation tends to result in an oscillating response to the effects of waste. On the one hand, criticism is levelled at the waste of valuable fossil fuels in providing the basic synthetic polymers, whilst on the other hand, fears are expressed about the effects of discarding an undecaying material.

To appreciate the true situation, it is necessary to understand something of the nature of these materials, how they are evolved and how they are manufactured and used. It is then possible to evaluate the potential of the waste and the economics of its recovery and re-use.

THE MATERIALS

Rubbers and plastics are generic terms for a very wide and diverse range of products. The chemistry associated with these materials has developed to a stage when compounds may almost be tailor-made to suit the particular processing and service requirements. Variety, which is at the root of widening applications, becomes a hazard when attempts are made at the recovery of waste. It is then that the trace additions which are included to obain specific physical properties present difficulties when mixed with other ingredients. Fortunately, some families of materials exist and one is able to make generalisations.

Figure 15.1 shows the broad families into which rubbers and plastics may be separated when considering the ways in which they are processed.

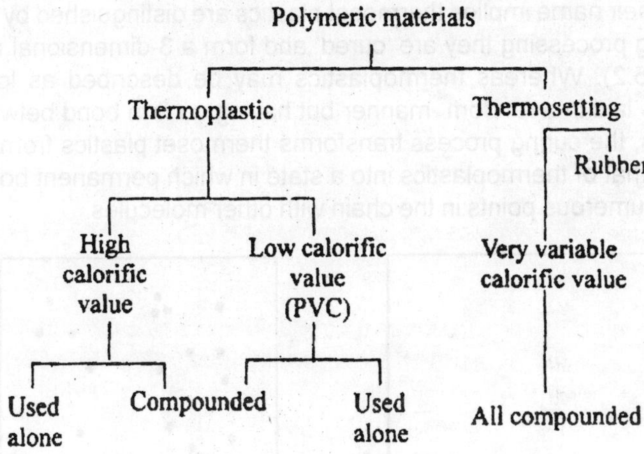

Fig. 15.1 Thermosets and thermoplastics

This very simplified arrangement in no way illustrates the wide variety but serves to meet the fundamental differences.

Of the two main families - thermoset and thermoplastics - the difference is in the molecular structure. Molecular weight in polymers is relatively very large and the description chain molecule is often used. Side chains exist in various forms and in thermoset polymers the side chains join during processing to form a rigid 3-dimensional network. No such network forms in thermoplastics so, when they are heated and softened, the molecules are free to take up new shapes and positions. Hence, thermoplastics may be recycled easily whilst thermosets are much more of a problem.

Thermoplastic Polymers

A further broad classification into those which are used in conjunction with other polymers and chemicals and those which are used in a relatively pure state gives a further guide to recycling.

Polymers which are used on their own, i.e., polyethylene, polypropylene, polystyrene, etc., are relatively easy to recycle and recycling may be repeated a number of times without undue deterioration.

Blended and compounded polymers are less stable and more liable to deterioration during recycling, i.e., PVC and ABS. Additions may be made to polymer to improve their stability but are expensive and hence are used very sparingly.

Thermoset Polymers

As their name implies thermoset plastics are distinguished by the fact that during processing they are 'cured' and form a 3-dimensional network (Figure 15.2). Whereas thermoplastics may be described as long thin molecules laid in a random manner but having no firm bond between the molecules, the curing process transforms thermoset plastics from a state similar to that of thermoplastics into a state in which permanent bonds are made at numerous points in the chain with other molecules.

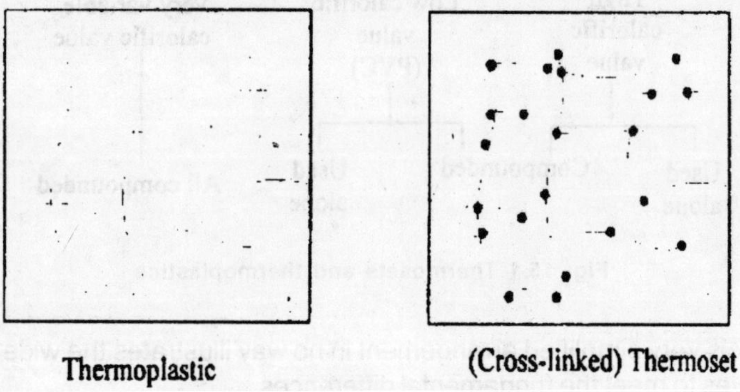

Fig. 15.2: Molecular network

Rubbers

These are regarded as a particular class of thermosets in many respects. Until they are vulcanised, the material is largely thermoplastic in that it may be physically reshaped without major loss of properties. Vulcanising is similarly explained as a molecular cross-linking but the process of de-vulcanisation has not yet been devised.

Because of the particular peculiarities of the rubber indsutry, considerable attention has been given to the problem of recycling. Two forms of product are marketed - crumb and reclaim. Nevertheless, the problem of de-vulcanisation remains unsolved.

Natural Rubber

This material is obtained from trees and thus is to some extent, a regenerating raw material.

Synthetic Rubber

These are obtained from oils in various forms and are dependent upon reserves of oil. They are 'tailored' to provide particular properties such as oil resistance, flexibility at extremes of temperature, resistance to ozone, etc., and therefore cannot be regarded as capable of replacement by natural rubbers although in some respects, synthetics can be used in place of natural.

Compounding Ingredients

Particular optimum properties of many polymers are only obtained by compounding both with other polymers and with mineral fillers. A very wide range of properties are thus obtained by the incorporation of a large variety of compounding ingredients. This is particularly true of thermoset plastics, including rubbers and of thermoplastics such as PVC.

It is thus possible to make PVC, either as flexible sheet for clothing and packaging or, as a rigid material for building applications such as drainage piping, guttering, etc.

Thermosets are often compounded with paper, mica, clays, marble flour, etc. The quantity of polymer is then changed to meet the service conditions. Often it is reduced to a level which is just adequate to act as a binder. The price is greatly affected since most of the fillers are also cheaper than the polymer.

Rubber compounds are even more complex. In addition to the polymer and filler, there are added small percentages of chemicals, often expensive ones, designed to assists or control the vulcanisation process and to provide resistance from attack (i.e., ozone).

With all these materials, visual identification of the compounded ingredients in a product is impossible and difficult even with the aid of analytical techniques.

PROCESSING

Polymers are converted to products by a variety of techniques but all are subjected to the operations in the same general sequence. Ingredients are blended, then shaped and finally stabilised. Importance is attached to the blending operation and in some applications, the material is supplied to the converter in a blended state. Heat is usually both applied and generated during the blending and shaping operations and must be extracted during or after the stabilising stage.

Compounding

Having selected the ingredients, they must be converted to a homogeneous blend so that physical properties are constant throughout the product. In all cases the compounding renders the ingredients inseparable but it is still possible to rectify any omissions of faults in dispersion.

Fabricating

For thermoplastics the fabrication represents the final processing operation. Processes such as blow moulding would be very expensive were it not possible to re-process the trimmings. It is the normal custom and practice to recover process scrap from thermoplastics.

Thermoset manufacture combines the fasbrication and cure process within the one mould. All waste from fabrication is, therefore, cured waste and by definition, difficult to recover. Rubber fabrication processes are sometimes separate from the vulcanisation stage. In these instances it is theoretically possible to recover fabricated scrap. In practice there are usually so many different formulations that it makes segregation and re-use in the original compounds an administrative impossibility.

As with thermoset, so it is that rubber mouldings are fabricated and cured within the mould. Waste trimmings, etc., are therefore, cured and unable to be re-shaped.

Finishing

It follows that only finishing scrap from thermoplastics manufacture is uncured and hence suitable for immediate recycling.

SOURCES OF WASTE

From previous comments it may already be apparent that it is necessary to distinguish between the waste which arises within the manufacturing industry and that which comprises the waste used to make plastic articles or containers.

Industrial scrap is usually classified and segregated. Consumer scrap is rarely fully identifiable. Value is very much dependent upon classification cleanliness and non-contamination, hence whilst industrial scrap can find a market with relative ease, this is not so with consumer scrap.

Industrial waste

Contractors exist who will collect from, re-process and return thermoplastics to the processor. They will also make additions to make up for processing losses of additives. This type of operation is particularly useful for materials such as PVC which are more susceptible to degradation during processing.

Used Products

Waste used to make products of both plastic and rubber have in recent years become potentially emotive topics for discussion, often unnecessarily and unwisely. Usually the factor which determines the value as a recyclable material has little to do with the material. It is determined by the cost of collection, segregation and decontamination.

Generally, plastic containers are light and have a high volume/weight ratio. They can be baled but still they are expensive to transport. Segregation is visually possible into containers of similar types and often this also provides a separation of different polymers but this is made more difficult where closures made from dissimilar materials are fitted. Labelling and the adhesive used can also provide a very significant contaminant where very thin-walled containers are concerned.

Types are also in the problem area; not because they cannot be recycled but because they are re-used and are collected for this purpose. The most simple way is by applying a new layer of tread rubber to the tyre's periphery. A retreaded tyre has virtually a new tyre life and hence, is a very economical technique. In preparing the tyre to receive the new tread rubber, the periphery is buffed, removing some of the old tread. The powdered rubber is termed 'crumb' and it is sold as a processing ingredient for use in small quantities in a fresh compound.

Another use for old tyres is found by manufacturing a material, known as 'reclaim' To make 'reclaim', the whole tyre is shredded and the rubber compound part is separated from the fabric and steel reinforcements. The rubber powder is then treated by a combination of heat, mechanical work and chemicals. The resulting softened rubber crumb is finally refined by passing it through a very closely set two-roll mill and refined into sheets approximately 0.02 mm thick. These filmy layers are wound on a drum until enough layers are there to cut off as sheet approximately 3/4 inch thick.

Again this material is used to impact particular properties to fresh compound as well as to make cheaper compounds.

QUALITY AND NATURE OF WASTE

From the above discussion, it is concluded that polymers are compatible with each other in varying amounts. Some are compatible with others; most have a deleterious effect whilst others are almost completely incomparable. It is good practice to mix 'like with like' but save for industrial waste, this is almost impossible. Compromise is therefore necessary.

Rubbers

Whilst it is advantgeous to separate the polymers, many products are designed using blends of two or more synthetic rubbers with material. Most tyres are blended in this way - truck tyres contain more natural rubber than passenger-tyres. The best that can be achieved with re-using tyre waste is to use truck scrap in truck and passenger waste in passenger tyres. However, addition of vulcanised waste above 10-15% reduces the product quality below the acceptable level.

With specialist rubber polymers, such as silicone and viton, recovery is more simple but the product is more critical so it is important that careful tests should be applied.

Thermoset Plastics

Thermoset Plastics waste is usually cured or part cured. It is in lumps and flash and since it has little use it is usually discounted as rubbish. Some processors grind it to a powder and incorporate a small percentage as filler.

Thermoplastics

Thermoplastics industrial waste is usually in the from of sprues and runners or misformed products. Granulating machinery is available to deal with this form of waste. Additionally, waste is caused when colours or polymers are changed, i.e., when producing the same product in a colour range or when changing from one product to another. It is then necessary to 'purge' the injection barrel of the machine. The usual result is a lump of polymer which is both difficult to granulate and of varying colour/polymer and of very little value. It is possible to purge into a water tank but few, if any, factories use the technique.

Consumer waste can vary from highly contaminated to clean and it is this aspect which most affects its re-use. Some contaminants may be driven off during recovery processing but others may prove dangerous not only to the processing plant but in the future use of the product.

OPPORTUNITIES FOR RE-USE

Rubbers

From what has preceded it may be rightly concluded that to recycle rubbers is not easy. By examining the list of various industrial classification of recycled rubber or rubber products inevitable conclusion is that, whilst there are opportunities for use, few if any, depend entirely on waste rubber and the use of waste rubber will not result in exceptional economy. Nevertheless, it would be entirely wrong to convey the impression that only marginal savings are possible. There are a number of companies which make good business based on recycling rubber. What is true is that at the head of each company is person who regards the additional profit as important and has the desire to use waste material.

Tyres

Brief mention has already been made of retreading. To the layman conservationist, it is a process that is full or opportunity but when the conservationist is also a motorist many pitfalls become apparent and he purchases new tyres. There are a number of pros and cons of retreading and in general situation may be summarised by saying that with normal careful use, a tyre casing should outlast two treads. But, it may only require one unfortunate occasion with a brick or sharp kerb to create the beginning of a casing weakness which, with continued normal use, will get worse and possible render the tyre unfit for retreading. It is this hidden factor which makes many road users to become cautious. It must be accepted that some slightly weakened cases cannot be identified visually from the exterior or interior of the tyre. By the same token, if a tyre is driven over or against an object early in its first 'life' and does not immediately puncture, it will have a potential weakness. Yet there are few who would in those circumstances remove the tyre for examination. There is, in all or us, a degree of illogicality.

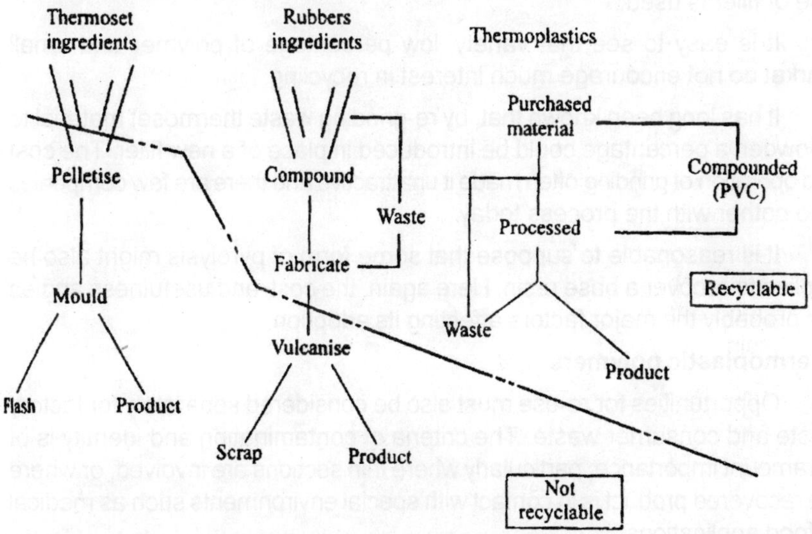

Fig. 15.3: Recycling opportunities for rubber, thermoplastic and thermosetting ingredients

The retread industry is very aware of the problem of casing inspection and discussions are in progress towards instrumenting a more positive method of examination for ply failure and ply separation.

It has always been a target for researchers to manufacture a better from of recyclable rubber. Recent years have presented a number of new patents which are being carefully examined but as yet no breakthrough has been achieved at commercial level. Such a breakthrough would help the rubber industry but would be unlikely to affect the natural problems of tyre disposal or re-use.

General Rubber Goods

There is currently very little use made of any used product of the general rubber goods sector. Diversity of compound, costs of collection and segregation are technically reasons for lack of industrial interest but practically, it must also be acknowledged that there is lack of a necessity. In its formative years, the main products were shoe soling and cycle tyres. They were collected as tyres are today. If necessary, they could doubtless be collected, and re-used.

Thermoset

A similar result it conceivable from thermoset plastics as is obtained with rubber. However, the market is very much smaller and the need is negligible. Thermoset polymers are usually compounded with 40-60% filler and the fillers are relatively cheap materials. Furthermore, more than one type of filler is used.

It is easy to see that variety, low percentage of polymer and small market do not encourage much interest in recycling.

It has long been known that, by re-grinding waste thermoset material to a powder, a percentage could be introduced in place of a new filler. The cost and operation of grinding often made it unattractive and there are few companies who bother with the process today.

It is reasonable to suppose that some form of pyrolysis might also be applied to recover a base resin. Here again, the cost and usefulness angles are probably the major factors affecting its adoption.

Thermoplastic polymers

Opportunities for re-use must also be considered separately for factory waste and consumer waste. The criteria of contamination and identity is of paramount importance, particularly where thin sections are involved, or where the recovered product is in contact with special environments such as medical or food applications.

Factory waste

Most factories have considered recycling their own waste and have adopted one of a number of courses of action.

For critical products virgin material is used. For non-critical products, sprues and runners are re-introduced after simple re-granulation. Additionally, sprue and runners from critical applications may be used in down-graded products. Careful segregation of polymers, grades of polymers and colours is practised. Degraded scrap (e.g., PVC) and contaminated mixtures such as occur when colour or material is changed on a machine are discarded as rubbish.

Usually colour is found to deteriorate before physical properties are grossly affected and this is the guide which determines whether material is discarded. A particular example of this is shown in the photographs of low-density polystyrene. The material was beginning to show signs of brittleness after the sixth pass but it is apparent that some loss of clarity had occurred much earlier. It is, however, important to appreciate that every unit of work which is applied to a plastic cause a change in physical properties which, although not grossly affecting the product quality, will require some slight alteration in processing conditions. Table 15.1 shows the effects on a material which has simply been re-ground after one extrusion. Not only has the characteristic quality of the material been changed but it has been found necessary to change the output rate of the machine.

Table 15.1: Properties of virgin and re-ground powder

	Virgin	Re-ground
Bulk density	682 g.1	613 g/1
Output rate	226 g/min	183 g/min
Fusion started	12 turns	12 turns
Fusion complete	80% at die	50% at die
Melt pressure at die	1875 psi	1800 at die
Melt temperature at die	210°C	197°C
Appearance	Brittle in places, glossay, smooth some porosity	Tough ripples on one side, no porosity
Motor current (amps)	7.0 - 7.5	6.0
Hopper flow	Good	Poor
Brabender fusion time	25 min	24 min
Brabender melt torque	3150 Mg	3150 Mg
Brabender melt temperature	185°C	198°C

Decisions whether to recycle should, therefore, be both technical and economic ones. Plastics generally involve a low labour content, hence material cost and production rate are the main ways of economising. It is not sufficient to say that because a material is capable of recycling it should be recycled within that particular factory nor indeed within any factory.

Consumer Waste

Conversion of consumer waste incurs the additional hazards of -

i. Product and general contamination
ii. Identity.

Losses and changes, caused by the actual recycling of the material, are multiplied out of all proportion when the product as well as dirt have to be considered. To promote the re-use of consumer waste it is necessary to revise many of the concepts which are at the foundation of plastics processing. The most important of these are -

i. Thin-wall section
ii. Minimum material content.

At the extreme, a lump of grit can easily be larger than the thickness of the plastic sheet on which it resides. Re-extrusion must inevitably give rise to a faulty product with holes or grit protruding from both faces.

Material cost is relatively high for virgin polymers. Consumer scrap should be much less although it will attract costs of collection, separation and washing. Hence, more material can be afforded. This fact creates problems elsewhere because more energy will be required to heat and cool the material, most of which are good heat insulators, and processing time will be increased.

A number of companies in Europe, Japan and America have attacked this problem, some suçcessfully, but it is largely a market development exercise, not a problem of plastics technology.

ULTIMATE DISPOSAL

Limitations on re-use currently make it a necessity to find a satisfactory method of disposal, but even with good techniques and markets for recycled polymers, there will come a time when no further re-use is possible and disposal is the only course of action.

Traditional methods of disposal have received criticism from many quarters but cheaper alternatives are very elusive and, until such time as new techniques are evolved and adopted, landfill is likely to remain the most frequently used technique.

The first task is, therefore, to make the best use of existing methods. Having ensured this, it will become important to attack the problem of resource utilisation. This is the second, but infinitely more important task.

Landfill

The Department of the Environment report "Refuse Disposal" quoted the figures given in Table 15.2.

Table 15.2: Disposal of waste

Disposal technique	%
Direct tipping on land	90.4
Pre-treatment by separation/incineration	7.6
Direct incineration	0.7
Pulverisaiton	1.0
Composting	0.3

Direct incineration and pulverising are being adopted increasingly but direct tipping will remain the major method for a number of years.

In landfill, plastics and rubbers represent relatively inert materials which take many years to decay longer than metals but less than ceramics. Large articles can thus form pockets in a tip into which concentrations of other materials may collect. Otherwise, however, they will not, by themselves cause pollution by leaching.

Degradation, whether natural or accelerated, can be a different matter, and acceleration may be caused by spontaneous combustion. Hence it is important that plastics and rubbers, like many other materials, should be carefully deposited in landfill. It is generally accepted that pulverisation of the refuse will greatly assist in the creation of a homogeneous tip, unlikely to cause trouble to water-courses or to those who wish to make use of the reclaimed lands.

Reversion to base materials

Ultimate disposal may come close to being a complete recycling process, if the polymer is reverted to its base ingredients i.e., oils and gases. Polymers are hydrocarbons and hence may be treated in this way. With most materials the route is not easy and many small fractions result which are not readily reverted into the polymer from which they originated. A notable exception is methyl methacrylate from which acrylic sheet is made, and back into which acrylic sheet may be turned. For the remainder, the best that can be done is to use the distillate as a feedstock in companies which make a wide range of chemical hydrocarbons, solvents, gases, etc.

Conversion to Heat

It is but another step to convert the hydrocarbon to heat energy. The polymers from which plastics are manufactured are currently derivatives from fuel oils, generally destined to be burned. Manufacture into plastics may be regarded as an interlude which makes an additional use of the oil before its eventual incineration. Calorific values (save for PVC) are high, sulphur content is low and, plastics burn easily (Table 15.3).

Table 15.3: Calorific values of polymers

Polymer	Calorific value Btu/lb
Polyethylene	1.89×10^4
Polyisoprene	1.84×10^4
Nitrile rubber	1.70×10^4
Polyisobutylene	1.89×10^4
Polystyrene	1.67×10^4
Polyvinyl chloride	0.67×10^4
SBR rubber	1.77×10^4
(House coal)	1.2×10^4

Furthermore, incineration results in the maximum percentage volume reduction. Tyres have been reduced to around 5% of the original weight and volume.

THE FUTURE

It was popular to forecast a civilisation engulfed by plastics waste. We believe, we have learned the fallacy of this argument although there is still in many quarters a reluctance to face the impending facts and plan for disposal and re-use. The days of cheap fuel have ended suddenly and we have been told that a saving in energy use has been achieved. To sum up, recycled and carefully discarded rubbers and plastics can make their contribution so that the advantages which they have given society in their prime uses may be converted into still more advantages when they are discarded.

16

Useful Information

ABBREVIATION

AC	azodicarbonamide
ADS	air-dried sheet
AHEM	Association of Hydraulic Equipment Manufacturers
APF	all purpose furnace (black)
ACM	polyacrylic rubber
ASTM	American Society for Testing and Materials
AU	polyurethane (ester) rubber
AZDN	azoisobutyronitrile
BASRM	British Association of Synthetic Rubber Manufacturers
BR	polybutadiene rubber
BS	British Standard
BSH	benzene sulphonyl hydrazide
BSI	British Standards Institution
CBS	cyclohexyl benzthiazyl sulphenamide
CCV	catenary continuous vulcanisation
CF	conductive furnace (black)
CHR	chlorinated butyl rubber
COD	cyclooctadiene
CR	polychloroprene rubber
CSM	chlorosulphonated polyethyiene
CV	continuous vulcanisation
CVNR	constant viscosity natural rubber
DBP	dibutyl phthalate

DCPD	dicyclopentadiene
DIN	Deutsches Institute fiir Normung
DNPT	dinitrosopentamethylene tetramine
DOTG	di-*o*-tolylguanidine
DPG	diphenyl guanidine
DPTS	dipentamethylene thiuram tetrasulphide
EDTA	ethylene diamine tetraacetic acid
ENB	ethylidene-norbornene
EP	ethylene propylene rubber
EPC	easy processing channel (black)
EPDM	ethylene propylene terpolymer rubber
EPM	ethylene propylene copolymer rubber
ETU	ethylene thiourea mercaptoimidazoline
EU	polyurethane (ether) rubber
EV	efficient vulcanisation
EVA	ethylene vinyl acetate
FEF	fast extrusion furnace (black)
FF	fine furnace (black)
FPM*	fluorocarbon rubber
FSI*	fluorosilicone rubber
FT	fine thermal (black)
FVSI*	fluorosilicone rubber
GMF	quinone dioxime
GPF	general purpose furnace (black)
GR-S	Government rubber-styrene (SBR)
HAF	high abrasion furnace (black)
HBS	cyclohexyl benzthiaxyl sulphenamide
HCV	horizontal continuous vulcanisation
HMDA	hexamethylene diamine
HMF	high modulus furnace (black)
HMT	hexamethylene tetramine
HOFR	heat resisting, oil resisting and flame retardant
HPC	hard processing channel (black)

HS	high structure (black)
HSMB	hydrosolution masterbatch
IEC	International Eectrotechnical Committee
IIR	isobutylene isoprene (butyl) rubber
IISRP	International Institute of Synthetic Rubber Producers
IR	polyisoprene rubber (synthetic)
IRHD	internal rubber hardness degree
IRI	Institution of the Rubber Industry
ISAF	intermediate super abrasion furnace (black)
ISO	International Organisation for Standardisation
LM	low modulus (black)
LS	low structure (black)
LVN	limiting viscosity number
LVNR	low-viscosity natural rubber
MB	masterbatch
MBI	mercaptobenzimidazole
MBT	mercaptobenzthiazole
MBTS	dibenzthiazyl disulphide
MDI	diphenylmethane-4, 4-diisocyanate
MOCA	4, 4-methyl-bis-2-chloroaniline
MPC	medium processing channel (black)
MPF	medium processing furnace (black)
MRPRA	Malaysian Rubber Producers Research Association
MRRDB	Malaysian Rubber Research and Development Board
MT	medium thermal (black)
NBR	acrylonitrile butadiene copolymer (nitrile) rubber
NDI	naphthalene-1,5-diisocyanate
NR	natural rubber
NS	non-staining (black)
OB	*pp'-oxy-bis*-benzene sulphonylhydrazide
OENR	oil-extended natural rubber
OEP	oil-extended polymer

OESBR	oil-extended styrene butadiene rubber
PAUS	pale amber unsmoked sheet
PBN	phenyl-β-naphthylamine
PMMA	polymerthylmethacrylate
PP	partially purified
pphr	parts per hundred of rubber
ppm	parts per million
PRI	plasticity retention index
PSI*	phenyl methyl silicone rubber
PTFE	polytetrafluorethylene
PVA	polyvinyl alcohol
PVC	polyvinyl chloride
PVSI*	phenyl vinyl methyl silicone rubber
RAPRA	Rubber and Plastics Research Association
RFL	resorcinol formaldehyde latex
r.h.	relative humidity
RRIM	Rubber Research Institute of Malaysia
RSS	ribbed smoked sheets
SAF	super abrasion furnace (black)
SATRA	Shoe and Allied Trades Research Association
SBR	Styrene butadiene rubber
SC	slow-curing (black)
SCF	super conductive furnace (black)
SCI	seal compatibility index
SI*	dimethyl silicone rubber
SMR	standard Malaysian rubber
SP	superior processing (NR)
SPF	super processing furnace (black)
SRF	semi-reinforcing furnace (black)
TCR	technically classified rubber
TDI	toluene diisocyanate
TDM	tertiary dodecyl mercaptan
TETD	tetraethyl thiuram disulphide

TMTD	tetramethyl thiuram disulphide
TMTM	tetramethyl thiuram monosulphide
TR	polysulphide rubbers
VCV	vertical continuous vulcanisation
VGC	viscosity gravity constant
VP	vinyl pyridine
VSI*	vinyl methyl silicone rubber
WLF	Williams Landel Ferry (equation)
XCF	extra conductive furnace (black)
ZDC	zinc diethyl dithiocarbamate
ZDMDC	zinc dimethyl dithiocarbamate

SYMBOLS

A	area
Å	angstroms = 10^{-8} cm or 10^{-4} μ
B	bulkiness (of black)
C	driving torque, rate of creep length of crack electrical conductivity
c	volume fraction of filler
D	diffusion coefficient
D	diameter
E	young's moludus, extrusion shrinkage
esu	electrostatic units
H	effective plume height (H' + ΔH), metres
F	force
f	shape factor
G'	elastic shear modulus
G"	viscous shear modulus
H	hysteresis
ΔH	latent heat of vaporisation
h	height of uniformly mixed inversion layer, metres
k	Boltzmann's constant

L	length; torque
DL	maximum change in torque during vulcanisation
M	molecular weight
M	average molecular weight of phase
M_c	number average molecular weight between cross-links
m	metre or mass
N	number of chains per unit volume
n	flow index
n	sum of numerical values (frequency); or a number
P	penetration rate
	anisometry (of black)
P	total pressure
p	partial pressure
Q	anisometry (of black); permeation coefficient
*	ASTM D1418 now uses the symbols FMQ FVMQ, PMQ, PVMQ and MQ in place of FSL, FVSI, PSI, PVSI and SI respectively: and FKM in place of FPM.
Q_s	differential heat of adsorption
R	rate of recovery, ideal gas constant
r	radius
S	rate of stress relaxation, solubility
STP	standard temperature and pressure, 32°F and 1 atmosphere
T	absolute temperature, structure factor (of black)
T_g	glass transition temperature
t	time
n_t	volume fraction of rubber in swollen gel
V_s	molecular volume of the solvent
V	volume adsorbed

V_m	volume adsorbed to form monolayer
v	velocity
W	stored energy density work per unit volume
g	strain surface energy rate of strain
d	phase angle, solubility parameter strain (tension)
e	rate of strain (tension)
h	viscosity
å	extension ratio
v	number of cross-links (per cubic centimetre)
r	density
s	stress
F	characteristic energy (per unit area of crack)
t	relaxtion time
c	interaction constant (Flory Rehner equation)
W	Angular velocity

CONVERSION FACTORS

To convert	Multiply by
Millimetres (mm) to inches	0.039
Metres (m) to feet	3.28
Metres (m) to yards	1.09
Square centimetres (cm^2) to square inches	0.155
Cubic centimetres (cm^3) to cubic inches	0.061
Cubic centimetres (cm^3) to pints	0.0018
Grams (g) to ounces	0.035
Kilograms (kg) to pounds	2.205
Kilograms-force per square centimetre (kgf/cm^2) to pounds-force per square inch	14.3

Degress Centigrade (C) to degress Fahrenheit 1.8 and add 32

1 megagram (Mg) = 1 ton approx.

1 gigagram (jg) = 1000 tons approx.

Multiples and Sub-multiples of Metric Units

Multiple	Prefix	Symbol
10^{12}	tera	T
10^{9}	giga	G
10^{6}	mega	M
10^{3}	kilo	k
10^{2}	hecto	h
10	deca	da
10^{-1}	deci	d
10^{-2}	centi	c
10^{-3}	milli	m
10^{-6}	micro	m
10^{-9}	nano	n
10^{-12}	pico	p
10^{-15}	femto	f
10^{-18}	atto	a

17

Quality Control in Rubber Industry

INTRODUCTION

The last 3-4 decades have witnessed a remarkable transformation of quality function in the rubber industry. From a minor obscure activity visually relegated to the lowest level, it has emerged as a major industrial function which has attracted the attention of senior management. Front page news can be due to negligence of quality and can form the basis of law suits running in millions.

Before going on to quality control, let us analyse what is quality. Of all concepts in the quality function none is more important than the principle of 'Fitness for Use'. Fitness for use is determined by all the features of a product which the consumer considers as beneficial and necessary to him. The user is exacting and carefully scrutinises the product which means that the more the features are beneficial to the consumer, the better the quality.

FACTORS RESPONSIBLE FOR QUALITY CONTROL

The major parameters which are responsible for 'Fitness for Use' are -

i. Quality of design

ii. Quality of performance

iii. The abilities

iv. Field service.

The above parameters are converted into standards and when we say quality control, we mean controlling the standards.

Quality Control

Quality control is the regulatory process through which we measure actual quality performance, compare it with the standards and act on the difference. The other common meaning which is associated with quality control is function or duty which must be carried out to achieve the quality of the product.

According to Japanese Industrial Standards, quality control is "a system of methods which ensures the economical manufacture of products combined with quality to satisfy users' needs".

There are enormous topics which are related to 'total quality control' which involves quality planning, quality cost and quality improvement. Vendor classifications are based on quality and so many other factors. Here, we shall be restricting ourselves mainly to statistical quality control. Is statistical quality cotntrol, most of the decision-making in the quality functions rest on the base of statistics, i.e., the collection, analysis and interpretation of data. Some of the items or problems for which the statistical tool kit helps are -

i. Predicting future results
ii. Predicting the performance or failure rate
iii. Determination of sample size to estimate true value, tolerance limits, etc.

Important tools of statistical quality control

i. Frequency distribution
ii. Control charts
iii. Acceptance sampling.

Results of statistical quality control

i. Improvement in quality and reliability
ii. Reduction in scrap and rework, leading to economy in raw materials used
iii. Location and removal of production bottlenecks
iv. Scientific evaluation of standards for quality and production
v. Decreased inspection costs
vi. Improved level of customer satisfaction and the company's image.

Quality characteristics

The quality control characteristics can be divided in two categories -

i. Measurable
ii. Non-measurable.

The data obtained by measurement are called cariables and that which are non-measurable and obtained by classification are termed as attributes. Examples of measurables are - diameter of shafts, length, weight and width of parts, etc. Examples of non-measurable characteristics are finish defects like blisters, scratches, etc.

DATA COLLECTION AND SUMMARISATION

Most of the decision-making in quality control tests is based on the collection of data and summarising it. Sometimes one method provides a useful and complete summarisation. In other cases, two or more methods are necessary to have complete clarity.

Frequency Distribution

Frequency distribution is a simple statistical tool in which large data are presented in such a way that the central tendency and dispersion are made very clear. The Table 17.1 shows the raw data representing the tube weight of 100 tubes.

Table 17.1: Weight (kg) of 100 tubes

3.37	3.34	3.38	3.32	3.33	3.28	3.34	3.31	3.33	3.34
3.29	3.36	3.30	3.31	3.33	3.34	3.34	3.36	3.39	3.34
3.35	3.36	3.30	3.32	3.33	3.35	3.35	3.34	3.32	3.38
3.32	3.37	3.34	3.38	3.36	3.37	3.36	3.31	3.33	3.30
3.35	3.33	3.38	3.37	3.44	3.32	3.36	3.32	3.29	3.25
3.38	3.39	3.34	3.32	3.30	3.39	3.36	3.40	3.32	3.33
3.29	3.41	3.27	3.36	3.41	3.37	3.36	3.37	3.33	3.36
3.31	3.33	3.35	3.34	3.35	3.34	3.31	3.36	3.37	3.35
3.40	3.35	3.37	3.32	3.35	3.36	3.38	3.35	3.31	3.34
3.35	3.36	3.39	3.31	3.30	3.35	3.33	3.35	3.31	3.31

It may be noted that the weights of tubes vary from 3.25 to 3.44. The same data is shown in Table 17.2 after tabulation. Here, we have arranged the values in decreasing order, showing the number of times, or frequency of the occurrences of each value.

The Table exhibits a range of values from 3.25 to 3.44 or 17 intervals of 10 grams each. When it is desired to reduce the number of such intervals, the data are grouped into cells. The above data is grouped into a frequency distribution of only six cells, each of 30 grams (Table 17.3).

Graphical Representation of Frequency Distribution

The characteristics of a frequency distribution are revealed even more clearly when represented graphically. There are several methods of showing a frequency distribution in graphical form. The most important is the frequency histogram. Here the horizontal axis is divided into segments to represent the different class intervals and the heights are proportional to the frequencies.

Frequency Curve

If the middle points of the rectangular bars are joined by straight lines the resulting curve is known as the frequency curve. For a smooth curve, the groups of the class intervals are made narrower.

Table 17.2: Tally of Weight (kg) of 100 tubes

Weight (kg.)	Tabulation	Frequency	Cumulative frequency
3.45	-	-	-
3.44	I ,	1	1
3.43	-	-	-
3.42	-	-	-
3.41	I	2	3
3.40	I	2	5
3.39	III	4	9
3.38	I	6	15
3.37	III	8	23
3.36	III	13	36
3.35	IIII	14	50
3.34	I	12	62
3.33		10	72
3.32	IIII	9	81
3.31	IIII	9	90
3.30	-	5	95
3.29	III	3	98
3.28	I	1	99
3.27	I	1	100
3.26	-	-	-
3.25	-	-	-
Total		100	

Table 17.3: Frequency distribution of tube weight

Boundaries	Midpoints	Frequencies	Cumulative frequency
3.415 - 3.445	3.43	1	1
3.385 - 3.415	3.40	8	9
3.355 - 3.385	3.37	27	36
3.325 - 3.555	3.34	36	72
3.295 - 3.325	3.31	23	95
3.265 - 3.295	3.28	5	100

Measures of Central Tendency

In a frequency distribution curve, it will be observed that most of the values will be concentrated within a region which is somewhere between the two extremes. This is the region where the process is set. It is known as the central tendency and is one of the two most fundamental measures in statistical analysis.

The three principal measures of central tendency are -

i. Arithmetic mean, which is calculated by adding the observation and dividing by the number of observations

ii. Median, the middle value when the figures are arranged according to size

iii. Mode-value, which occurs most often in data.

The arithmetic mean is the value which is commonly used measure.

Measure of Dispersion

Data is always scattered around the central tendency and the extent to which this data is scattered is called dispersion. The measure of dispersion is the second of the two most fundamental measures.

Commonly used measures of dispersion are range and standard deviation. Range is defined as the difference between the maximum and minimum value of a set of observations. As the range is based on only two values, it is useful when the number of observations is small (maximum 10).

The most important measure of dispersion is the standard deviation which is best defined in the form of a formula -

$$S = \sqrt{\frac{(X - \bar{X})^2}{n-1}}$$

where, S = Standard deviation

X = Observed values

$\bar{X}$ = Arithmetic mean

n = No. of observations.

Example - The weight of 15 samples of an item were - 6, 9, 12, 8, 8, 9, 10, 6, 5, 7, 5, 9, 11, 8, 7.

$$\bar{X} = \frac{6+9+12 --- +11+8+7}{15} = 8$$

$$S = \sqrt{\frac{1(x_1 - \bar{x})^2 = +(x_2 - \bar{x})^2}{n-1} + ...} = \sqrt{\frac{(6-8)^2 + (9-8)^2 + ...}{14}}$$

$$= \sqrt{\frac{60}{14}} = \sqrt{4.29} = 2.1$$

Procedure for Setting Control Charts for $\overline{X}$-R Chart

1. Select a sample of convenient size (usually 3 to 5 successive items) and measure the important quality characteristics of each of the items.
2. Record all these measurements on a suitable data sheet.
3. Compute the mean and range of these measurements and record them on the data sheet.
4. Repeat (1) to (3) until about 25 such samples have been collected, maintaining a uniform sample size throughout.
5. Accept the final value of $\overline{R}$ as being the standard range for the process.
6. Read off the value of A from the Table A corresponding to the sample size of n.
7. Compute $A\overline{R}$.
8. Compute $(\mu + A\overline{R})$ - this is the upper control limit for sample means.
9. Compute $(\mu - A\overline{R})$ - this is the lower control limit for sample means.
10. Read off the value of D from Table-A corresponding to the sample size of n.
11. Computer $D\overline{R}$ - this is the upper control limit for sample ranges.
12. Prepare charts for sample means and ranges on a squared background with the range chart situated exactly below the mean charts on the same piece of paper. The charts will show the values of the means and the ranges on a vertical scale at the left with a horizontal scale indicating the time and date of sampling.
13. Continue selection and examination of samples and record the mean and range of each sample on their respective charts against the time and date of sampling. Mark on the chart the point at which any technical change in the process occurred.
14. Accept the process as producing a quality conforming to the standard as long as every plotted point falls within the control limits on both the mean and range charts.
15. If any plotted point falls on or above the control limit on the range chart, it indicates an increase in the process variability, which must be remedied immediately by appropriate technical action.

16. If any plotted point fails on or beyond the control limit on the mean chart, it indicates a shift in the process level which should be remedied by a setting change.

The values of A and D for sample size 3 to 5 are shown as under -

Sample size	A	D
3.	1.023	2.574
4.	0.729	2.282
5.	0.577	2.114

Interpretation of $\overline{X}$ and $\overline{R}$ Charts

The possible interpretations are as follows -

a. Average chart goes out of limits.

This indicates that the average setting of our process has changed. The explanation is as follows -

b. Sudden change - possibilities are -

i. A new batch of material with different characteristics has been started.

ii. A chemical batch has suddenly picked up an impurity, perhaps because contaminated work has been inserted into it.

iii. Unauthorised adjustment, for example, of curing temperature.

c. Gradual change - the following are examples of how a drift might be caused -

i. Chemical batches are becoming gradually spent.

ii. There has been a gradual build-up of impurity in a chemical batch.

iii. A gradual drift in a process setting.

iv. Range chart goes out of limits -

The range going out of limits indicates that the process variability has increased.

d. Possible reasons for a increase in variability are -

i. A batch of much more variable material has been started.

ii. Ingredients have not been properly mixed.

iii. Temperature distribution within a furnace is uneven, perhaps because a heater has failed or a vent has become blocked.

iv. There may be operator variations, for example, in timing a cycle.

CONTROL CHARTS FOR NON-MEASURABLE CHARACTERISTICS

Control charts for $\overline{X}$ and R require actual measurements to be made, e.g., lengtrh control charts. For non-measurable characteristics, normallycalled attributes, only a count of observations of characteristics is required. As in the case of the chart for $\overline{X}$ and R, samples are taken from production at regular intervals and number of defects, recorded. The chart enables us to take corrective action when the proportion of defects is abnormally high. Attribute charts must be designed to suit the process concerned and based on the study of past performance.

The two main control charts of attributes are as follows -

i. Erection of per cent defective chart (p chart)

ii. Number of defects per unit chart. (c chart)

Fraction Defective Chart (p chart)

This is a single chart showing the number of defective items observed in a sample of n items or the fraction defective in a sample. The fraction defective may be used with respect to a single quality characteristic or with respect to two or more characteristics considered collectively. The control chart line for samples of sizes n are -

$$\text{Control line for} = \overline{p} = \overline{p} \pm 3 - \sqrt{\frac{\overline{p}(1-p)}{n}}$$

where $\overline{p}$ is the total of defectives in all samples divided by the total units in all samples and "n" is the number of units in any sub-group. The control chart for $\overline{p}$ is most effective when sample size is greater than 50 or when the number of defective units per sample is 4 or more. Data for calculation of the p chart is given in the Table 17.4.

Calculation for p Chart

The total number of tyres tested was 14163. The total number found to be defective was 1010. The average sample size was -

$$\overline{n} = \frac{14163}{19} - 745.42$$

The average fraction defective was

$$\overline{p} = \frac{1010}{14163} = 0.071$$

Table 17.4: Calculation of p chart

Week no.	No. tyres inspected	No. of defective tyres	Fraction defective p
1.	724	48	0.067
2.	763	83	0.109
3.	748	70	0.094
4.	748	85	0.114
5.	724	45	0.062
6.	727	56	0.077
7.	726	48	0.055
8.	719	67	0.093
9.	759	37	0.049
10.	745	52	0.070
11.	736	47	0.064
12	739	50	0.068
13	723	47	0.065
14	748	57	0.076
15.	770	51	0.066
16.	770	51	0.066
17.	719	53	0.074
18.	757	34	0.045
19.	760	29	0.038
Total	14163	1010	1.352
Average	745.42	53.16	0.071

Control limits for the chart = $\overline{p} \pm 3 - \sqrt{\overline{p}(1-\overline{p})} = 0.071 \pm$ .....

$$3\sqrt{\frac{0.071(1-0.071)}{745.42}} = 0.071 \pm 0.023 = 0.043 \text{ and } 0.10$$

Thus the upper control limit for $\overline{p}$ = 0.10 and the lower limit for $\overline{p}$ = 0.043

Number of Defects per Unit Charges

This chart makes direct use of the count of defects. This chart is effective when the number of defects in a unit is large but the percentage of any defect is small. Examples are defects on a metre of yarn, breakdown on a machine per shift. As an example, the defects per unit of yarn are given in Table 17.5.

Table 17.5: Defects per unit of yarn

Sample no.	Total defects	Defects per unit
1.	17	1.7
2.	14	1.4
3.	6	0.6
4.	23	2.3
5.	5	0.5
6.	7	0.7
7.	10	1.0
8.	19	1.9
9.	29	2.9
10.	18	1.8
11.	25	2.5
12.	5	0.5
13.	8	0.8
14.	11	1.1
15.	18	1.8
16.	13	1.3
17.	22	2.2
18.	6	0.6
19.	23	2.3
20.	22	2.2
21.	9	0.9
22.	15	1.5
23.	20	2.0
24.	6	0.6
25.	24	2.4
Total	375	37.5

Calculation

Formula for control chart lines are

Control limit for c chart = $= \overline{c} = \overline{c} \pm 3\sqrt{\overline{c}}$

where c is the total number of defects in all samples divided by the number of samples.

Number from the table central line $= \bar{c} = \frac{375}{25} = 15.0$

Control limits $= \bar{c} \pm 3\sqrt{\bar{c}} = 15.0 \pm 3\sqrt{15.0}$

$= 15.0 \pm 11.6189$

Thus upper control limits for $\overline{C}$ chart = 26.6189

Lower control limits for c chart = 3.381

INTERPRETATION OF p AND c CHART

A point above the upper control limit in a p or c chart indicates a deterioration in the quality level and hence corrective action is needed. A point below the lower control limit indicates "too good' a quality to be a standard performance. Just as an assignable cause is suspected to have influenced a point outside the upper control limit, it is reasonable to suspect that another assignable cause would have created that "too good" performance. The corrective action in such a case naturally, is to identify that assignable cause and perpetuate it in the process so that the standard performance is improved.

18

Suppliers of Plant and Equipments

RUBBER MANUFACTURING MACHINERY

Kelachandra Iron & Steel Works Chingavanam
Kottayam, Kerala-686531
TEL : +91 (0) 481 430596
FAX : +91 (0) 481 430406
E-mail: kelachandra@vsnl.com

Intermix Machinery Manufacturing Pvt. Ltd.
K-57, Opp. Peeragarhi
Udyog Ngr.
New Delhi-110041.
TEL : +91 (0) 11 25472655
FAX : +91 (0) 11 25472654

Ravi Engineering Works Pvt. Ltd.
Prop. Janak Industries Pvt. Ltd.
18/34. St. No.5, (Rly. Line Side)
Anand Parbat Indl. Area
New Delhi, NCT of Delhi-110005
TEL : +91 (0) 11 25725517
FAX : +91 (0) 11 25764369
E-mail: ravieng@nda.vsnl.net.in

Sandhu Enterprises
BE-192A, St. No. 5
Hari Nagar,
New Delhi-110064.
TEL : +91 (0) 11 25408719
FAX : +91 (0) 11 25132357
E-mail:
sandhuent@mantraonline.com

Santec Hydrofluid Engineers
GD-96, 'Santec House'
Vishakha Enclave
Pitampura
Delhi, NCT of Delhi-110088
TEL : +91 (0) 11 27311039
FAX : +91 (0) 11 27315473
E-mail: santec@bol.net.in

Slach Engg. Works Pvt. Ltd.
15, Najafgarh Rd.
New Delhi, NCT of Delhi-110015
TEL : +91 (0) 11 25441916

Uttam Singh & Sons
B-6, Phase-I, Indl. Area
Mayapuri
New Delhi, NCT of Delhi-110064
TEL : +91 (0) 11 25400757
FAX : +91 (0) 11 25457099
E-mail: uttamsingh@hotmail.com

MP George & Sons
Ahipuram
P.O. Udyogmandal
Kochi, Kerala-683504
TEL : +91 (0) 484 555307
E-mail: mpgfoundry@hotmail.com

Larsen & Toubro Ltd. Heavy Engineering Divn.
Powai Works
Saki Vihar Rd., Powai
Mumbai, Maharashtra-400072
TEL : +91 (0) 22 8581401
FAX : +91 (0) 22 8581594
E-mail: 3870-sra@ve-dak.ltindia.com

Malik Engineers
Unit 1, Shailesh Indl. Est. NO. 1
Navghar,
Vasai Rd. (E)
Pune,
Maharashtra-401210
TEL : +91 (0) 20 8839751
FAX : +91 (0) 20 8830751
E-mail: malik@malikengg.com

Manav Rubber Machinery Pvt. Ltd.
Plot No. 24-B, "Param Sukhshanti"
2/10, S V Rd.,
Jawahar Ngr.
Goregaon (W)
Mumbai, Maharashtra-400062
TEL : +91 (0) 22 8723166
FAX : +91 (0) 22 8725164

Janatha Rubber Industries
154-W
Kalarampatty Rd.
Salem, Tamil Nadu-636015
TEL : +91 (0) 427 469139
FAX : +91 (0) 427 465531
E-mail: somanc@vsnl.com

Larsen & Toubro Limited Heavy Engg. Division Rubber Processing Machinery
L & T Chennai House
Post Bag 5247, 10
Club House Rd.
Anna Salai
Chennai, Tamil Nadu-600002
TEL : +91 (0) 44 8460141
FAX : +91 (0) 44 8460069

Asian Power Cyclopes
Rochipura
Majra
Dehradun,
Uttaranchal-248171
TEL : +91 (0) 135 620488
FAX : +91 (0) 135 620961
E-mail: asian@nde.vsnl.net.in

RUBBER MIXERS

Machinkraft Equipment
337, 3rd Rd.,
Sindh Hsg. Soc. Aundh
Pune, Maharashtra-411007
TEL : +91 (0) 20 5887464
FAX : +91 (0) 20 5880353
E-mail:
info@machinkraftequipment.com

Enfab Industries Pvt. Ltd.
C-2, Shanthi Niwas
Mettuguda Secunderabad,
Andhra Pradesh-500017
TEL : +91 (0) 40 7824343
FAX : +91 (0) 40 7830010
E-mail: enfabs@hd1.vsnl.net.in

Surya Industrial Equipments
D-109, Phase-I, IDA
Jeedimetla
Hyderabad, Andhra Pradesh-500055
TEL : +91 (0) 40 3096355
FAX : +91 (0) 40 3098163

Base Industries
Plot No. 138-B
IDA, Mallapur
Hyderabad, Andhra Pradesh-501507
TEL : +91 (0) 40 7823073
FAX : +91 (0) 40 7823073
E-mail: enfabs@hd1.vsnl.net.in

Avtar Singh & Sons
C-129, Phase-II
Mayapuri
New Delhi-110064.
TEL : +91 (0) 11 25130861
FAX : +91 (0) 11 25160752

Industrial Machinery Co.
205, Kanchan House
Karampura Cmplx.
New Delhi-110015.
TEL : +91 (0) 11 25116159
FAX : +91 (0) 11 25431706

Ravi Engineering Works Pvt. Ltd.
Prop. Janak Industries Pvt. Ltd.
18/34, St. No.5, (Rly. Line Side)
Anand Parbat Indl. Area
New Delhi, NCT of Delhi-110005
TEL : +91 (0) 11 25725517
FAX : +91 (0) 11 25764369
E-mail: ravieng@nda.vsnl.net.in

Slach Hydratecs Equipment Pvt. Ltd.
15, Najafgarh Rd.
New Delhi, NCT of Delhi-110015
TEL : +91 (0) 11 25441917
FAX : +91 (0) 11 25441916
E-mail: slach@del2.vsnl.net.in

Indian Expeller Works Pvt. Ltd.
A-4, Naroda Indl. Est.
Naroda
Ahmedabad, Gujarat-382330
TEL : +91 (0) 79 2821855
FAX : +91 (0) 79 2830194
E-mail: dinesh@indexpell.com

Kelachandra Iron & Steel Works
Chingavanam
Kottayam, Kerala-686531
TEL : +91 (0) 481 430596
FAX : +91 (0) 481 430406
E-mail: kelachandra@vsnl.com

Frigmaires Engineers
Janta Indl. Est.
Gala No. 8, Opp. Phoenix Mill
Senapati Bapat Marg
Lower Parel
Mumbai, Maharashtra-400013
TEL : +91 (0) 22 4945624
FAX : +91 (0) 22 2187750
E-mail: fe@vsnl.com

Bainite Machines
C-10
Nand Dham Indl. Est.
Agnishaman Dal Marg, Marol
Andheri (E)
Mumbai, Maharashtra-400059
TEL : +91 (0) 22 8505910
FAX : +91 (0) 22 8500465
E-mail: bainite@bom8.vsnl.net.in

Durga Industries
Saksalia Indl. Est.
Chincholi Bunder Rd.
Malad (W)
Mumbai, Maharashtra-400064
TEL : +91 (0) 22 8726466

Malik Engineers
Unit 1, Shailesh Indl. Est. NO. 1
Navghar
Vasai Rd. (E)
Pune, Maharashtra-401210
TEL : +91 (0) 20 8839751
FAX : +91 (0) 20 8830751
E-mail: malik@malikengg.com

Manav Rubber Machinery Pvt. Ltd.
Plot No. 24-B, "Param Sukhshanti"
2/10, S V Rd., Jawahar Ngr.
Goregaon (W)
Mumbai, Maharashtra-400062
TEL : +91 (0) 22 8723166
FAX : +91 (0) 22 8725164

PMS Great Floorings Pvt. Ltd.
E-13 Block, MIDC
Bhosari
Pune, Maharashtra-411026
TEL : +91 (0) 20 7122989
FAX : +91 (0) 20 7122332
E-mail: moti@pn2.vsnl.net.in

Richardson & Cruddas (1972) Ltd.
A Government of India Undertaking
Sir J J Rd.
Byculla Iron Works
Mumbai, Maharashtra-400008
TEL : +91 (0) 22 3776832
FAX : +91 (0) 22 3731491

Anant Corp.
P.O. Box 14
Bassi Rd.
Sirhind, Punjab-140406
TEL : +91 (0) 1763 22187

FAX : +91 (0) 1763 20187
E-mail: anant_corp@vsnl.com

Anant Engg. Works
Bassi Rd.
Sirhind,
Punjab-140406
TEL : +91 (0) 1763 22037
FAX : +91 (0) 1763 22037

Anant Enterprises
P.O. Box 5,
Bassi Rd.
Sirhind, Punjab-140406
TEL : +91 (0) 1763 22452
FAX : +91 (0) 1763 20452

Sant Rubber Machines Pvt. Ltd.
P.O. Box 3, Sirhind,
Punjab-140406.
TEL : +91 (0) 1763 20439
FAX : +91 (0) 1763 41360
E-mail:
santrubber@santmachines.com

HP Singh & Co.
75, Ganesh Chandra Avenue
Kolkata,
West Bengal-700013
TEL : +91 (0) 33 2371680
FAX : +91 (0) 33 2255457
E-mail: hpscocal@vsnl.com

GN Engg. Works
388/H/13, Tangra Rd.
Kolkata,
West Bengal-700015
TEL : +91 (0) 33 3297189
FAX : +91 (0) 33 3295550

RUBBER MOULDING MACHINERY

Amrut Brothers
24, Manorath Est.
Nr. Milan Cinema
Saraspur
Ahmedabad, Gujarat-380018
TEL : +91 (0) 79 2168163
FAX : +91 (0) 79 2168163
E-mail: exports@amrutbrothers.com

Kloeckner Desma Machinery Pvt. Ltd.
Plot No. 5120
Phase-IV
GIDC Estt., Vatva, Ahmedabad,
Gujarat-382445
TEL : +91 (0) 79 5840200
FAX : +91 (0) 79 5830384
E-mail: klockner@satyam.net.in

Emdet Jamshedpur Pvt. Ltd.
B-7 & 8, Indl. Est.
Adityapur
Jamshedpur,
Jharkhand-832109
TEL : +91 (0) 657 407968
FAX : +91 (0) 657 407968
E-mail: emdet@netkracker.com

Durga Industries
Saksalia Indl. Est.
Chincholi Bunder Rd., Malad (W)
Mumbai,
Maharashtra-400064
TEL : +91 (0) 22 8726466

Larsen & Toubro Ltd. Heavy Engineering Divn.
Powai Works
Saki Vihar Rd., Powai
Mumbai,
Maharashtra-400072
TEL : +91 (0) 22 8581401
FAX : +91 (0) 22 8581594
E-mail: 3870-sra@ve-dak.ltindia.com

Manav Rubber Machinery Pvt. Ltd.
Plot No. 24-B, "Param Sukhshanti"
2/10, S V Rd., Jawahar Ngr.
Goregaon (W), Mumbai,
Maharashtra-400062
TEL : +91 (0) 22 8723166
FAX : +91 (0) 22 8725164

Northern Machineries Pvt. Ltd.
C-29, Phase-II
Focal Point,
Ludhiana,
Punjab-141010
TEL : +91 (0) 161 671509
FAX : +91 (0) 161 675066
E-mail: ralson@satyam.net.in

Pal Machine Tools (Regd.)
11390, St. No. 2
Partap Ngr.
Indl. Area-B, Ludhiana,
Punjab-141003
TEL : +91 (0) 161 534854
E-mail: pathydron@indya.com

Braga Industries
63-B, Northern Phase
Ambattur Indl. Est.
Chennai,
Tamil Nadu-600098
TEL : +91 (0) 44 6254103
FAX : +91 (0) 44 6257032

Hydro Craft
11-B, Vijayalakshmi Layout
1st St., Ganpathy
Coimbatore,
Tamil Nadu-641006
TEL : +91 (0) 422 532704
FAX : +91 (0) 422 532704
E-mail: ganesh_hy@rediffmail.com

Larsen & Toubro Limited Heavy Engg.
Division Rubber Processing Machinery
L & T Chennai House
Post Bag 5247, 10
Club House Rd.
Anna Salai
Chennai,
Tamil Nadu-600002
TEL : +91 (0) 44 8460141
FAX : +91 (0) 44 8460069

Modern Plastics Equipments
35, Perumal Kovil Thottam
P N Palayam Rd., Nr. Rly. Level Cross
Ganapathy PO
Coimbatore,
Tamil Nadu-641006
TEL : +91 (0) 422 530836

Sky Hydraulics
13-A, Kalaivanar St.
Athipet, Chennai,
Tamil Nadu-600058.
TEL : +91 (0) 44 6566468
FAX : +91 (0) 44 6259352

Texwin Hydraulics & Engineering
207, P.O. Box 2121
Bharathiar Rd.
Ganapathy, Coimbatore,
Tamil Nadu-641006.
TEL : +91 (0) 422 533599
FAX : +91 (0) 422 533599
E-mail: tex_hyd@yahoo.com

Industrial Machinery Co.
205, Kanchan House
Karampura Cmplx.
New Delhi-110015.
TEL : +91 (0) 11 25116159
FAX : +91 (0) 11 25431706

JRD Rubber & Plastic Tech Pvt. Ltd.
K-49, Model Town
Delhi-110009.
TEL : +91 (0) 11 27234947
FAX : +91 (0) 11 27416295
E-mail: jrdrp@ndf.vsnl.net.in

Karamson Engincoring Corporation
3/24, Kirti Ngr. Indl. Area
New Delhi-110015.
TEL : +91 (0) 11 25417621
FAX : +91 (0) 11 25433577
E-mail: kencor@sify.com

Manoj Engg. & Scientific Industries
Plot No. 3, Gali No. 1
Anand Parbat Indl. Area
New Rohtak Rd.
New Delhi-110005.
TEL : +91 (0) 11 25714314

Mishra Hydraulic Pneumatic (India)
48/25/18
Hastal Village
Nr. Central School
Uttam Ngr.
New Delhi-110059.
TEL : +91 (0) 11 25648196
FAX : +91 (0) 11 25635927
E-mail:
mishrahydraulic@mantraonline.com

Santec Hydrofluid Engineers
GD-96, 'Santec House'
Vishakha Enclave, Pitampura
Delhi, NCT of Delhi-110088
TEL : +91 (0) 11 27311039
FAX : +91 (0) 11 27315473
E-mail: santec@bol.net.in

Slach Hydratecs Equipment Pvt. Ltd.
15, Najafgarh Rd.
New Delhi, NCT of Delhi-110015
TEL : +91 (0) 11 25441917
FAX : +91 (0) 11 25441916
E-mail: slach@del2.vsnl.net.in

RUBBER MOULDS

AV Engineers
Plot No. 89, Sec. 3,
IMT Manesar, Gurgaon,
Haryana-122050
TEL : +91 (0) 11
FAX : +91 (0) 11 4622520
E-mail: avengg@bol.net.in

Dheeru Tools
FCA-326, SGM Ngr.
Faridabad,
Haryana-121001
TEL : +91 (0) 129 5429310

Indo-Danish Tool Room
M-4 (Part), Phase-VI
Tata Kandra Rd., Gamharia
Jamshedpur,
Jharkhand-832108
TEL : +91 (0) 657 408061
FAX : +91 (0) 657 407723
E-mail: idtr@dte.vsnl.net.in

Durga Precision Tools & Dies
16, 2nd Cross
MSR College Rd.
Bangalore,
Karnataka-560054
TEL : +91 (0) 80 3446115
FAX : +91 (0) 80 3365105
E-mail: dptd@mantraonline.com

Edizi Gauge & Tools
C-4, 1st Main,
Kalappa Block, R C Puram
Bangalore,
Karnataka-560021
TEL : +91 (0) 80 3123025
FAX : +91 (0) 80 3120602
E-mail: edizi@vsnl.com

RNR Techno Services
No. 33, 13th Main Rd.
Mahalakshmi Puram
Bangalore,
Karnataka-560086
TEL : +91 (0) 80 3496848
FAX : +91 (0) 80 3496848

Sanmuga Tools
72, Rajeshwari Layout
Begapalli Post, Hosur,
Karnataka-635126
TEL : +91 (0) 8337 79638

Shankar Die Works
New No. 3/107
Rajeswari Layout
Govinda Agraharam
Begapalli Post, Hosur,
Karnataka-635109
TEL : +91 (0) 8337 78701

Spark Engineers
N-4, Phase-III
SIDCO Indl. Est., Hosur,
Karnataka-635126
TEL : +91 (0) 4344 77736

Triyami Tools
MPLUN, 21, Sect. F
Sanwer Rd., Indore,
Madhya Pradesh-452015
TEL : +91 (0) 731 722762
FAX : +91 (0) 731 722762

Ashna Enterprises
C-10G, Malad Indl. Est.
Ramchandra Extn. Lane,
Kachpada, Malad
Mumbai,
Maharashtra-400064
TEL : +91 (0) 22 8885317
FAX : +91 (0) 22 8885317
E-mail:
ashnaenterprise@hotmail.com

Lekshmi Dies & Tools
Room No.B 218
Bhagat Singh Ngr. 2
No.2 Rajaram Gallery
Goregaon (W), Mumbai,
Maharashtra-400104
TEL : +91 (0) 22 8769057

National Standard Duncan Ltd.
Plot No. F-4, Rd. No. 22 & U-2
Wagle Est., Thane,
Maharashtra-400604
TEL : +91 (0) 22 5820158
FAX : +91 (0) 22 5320952
E-mail:
nasdun.thane@gems.vsnl.net.in

Vishal Moulds Manufacturing Pvt. Ltd.
S-158, MIDC
Bhosari, Pune,
Maharashtra-411026
TEL : +91 (0) 20 7122423
FAX : +91 (0) 20 7122422

SS Engg. Works
1569, St. No. 11
Dashmseh Ngr.
Ludhiana,
Punjab-141003
TEL : +91 (0) 161 536895
FAX : +91 (0) 161 531377

Electro Dies & Tools
Plot No. 5, Rd. No. 4
22, Godam Extn.
Indl. Est., Jaipur,
Rajasthan-302006
TEL : +91 (0) 141 2215239
FAX : +91 (0) 141 2212492
E-mail: joharihari@satyam.net.in

ARR Precision Tools
1418, Sathy Rd.
Ganapathy, Coimbatore,
Tamil Nadu-641006
TEL : +91 (0) 422 531984
FAX : +91 (0) 422 532028

Classic Moulds & Dies
K-20, Ambattur Indl. Est.
Chennai,
Tamil Nadu-600058
TEL : +91 (0) 44 6254488
FAX : +91 (0) 44 6244083
E-mail: classic_dies@hotmail.com

Sri Devi Engg. Works
46, Kambar St., TMP Ngr.
Padi, Chennai,
Tamil Nadu-600050.
TEL : +91 (0) 44 6259708

Tooling Center
9/40B, Onapalayan Rd.
Auto Ngr.
Edayarpalayam P.O
Coimbatore,
Tamil Nadu-641025
TEL : +91 (0) 422 402811
E-mail: v_b_pratap@yahoo.com

Gulshan Engg. Works
CB-7, Ring Rd., Naraina,
New Delhi, NCT of Delhi-110028
TEL : +91 (0) 11 25799130

Manik Industries
F-142, Phase-II
Mayapuri
New Delhi - 110064.
TEL : +91 (0) 11 25406738
FAX : +91 (0) 11 25406738
E-mail: manikindustriesmp@delhi-industry.com

Nirmal Engg. Works
4/34B, Gali No. 4-5
Anand Parbat Indl. Area
New Delhi-110005.
TEL : +91 (0) 11 25731034

RUBBER MOULDING PRESSES

Crane-Bel International Pvt. Ltd.
E-7, Sect. 17, Kavi Ngr. Indl. Area
Ghaziabad, Uttar Pradesh-201002
TEL : +91 (0) 120 4702107
FAX : +91 (0) 120 4700339
E-mail:
machinetools@crane-bel.com

CM Hydro Systems Pvt. Ltd.
3-6-286/617, RKS Apts.
Hyderguda, Hyderabad,
Andhra Pradesh-500029
TEL : +91 (0) 40 3222287
FAX : +91 (0) 40 3220195
E-mail: cmgroup@hd2.vsnl.net.in

Dynamic Hydrofab
B-195, Plot Piyarelal
Libaspur Rd.
Samaipur
Delhi, NCT of Delhi-110042
TEL : +91 (0) 11 27890388
E-mail: dynamichf@vsnl.net

Alpha Industrial Systems
B-97, Phase-I
Mayapuri Indl. Area
New Delhi, NCT of Delhi-110064
TEL : +91 (0) 11 25132584
FAX : +91 (0) 11 25682241
E-mail: teena_khanna@hotmail.com

Flowmech Engineers Pvt. Ltd.
G-Extn. 1, Kirti Ngr.
New Delhi, NCT of Delhi-110015
TEL : +91 (0) 11 25435415
FAX : +91 (0) 11 25191255
E-mail: flowmech@del3.vsnl.net.in

Hydromech Automation Pvt. Ltd.
1-6, DSIDC Cmplx.
Nangloi
Delhi, NCT of Delhi-110041
TEL : +91 (0) 11 25474563
FAX : +91 (0) 11 25477179
E-mail:
hydromech@chequemail.com

Hydromech Pneumatics & Hydraulics
WH-84, Phase-I
Mayapuri Indl. Area
New Delhi, NCT of Delhi-110064
TEL : +91 (0) 11 25131926
FAX : +91 (0) 11 25142554

Jain Hydraulics Pvt. Ltd.
1st Flr., 10066
Multani Dhanda
Pahar Ganj
New Delhi, NCT of Delhi-110055
TEL : +91 (0) 11 27529689
FAX : +91 (0) 11 25504343
E-mail: hewjhpl@ndf.vsnl.net.in

Osaka Hydraulic Industries
36/3, Opp. Mehrauli Rd. Turning
Badarpur
New Delhi, NCT of Delhi-110044
TEL : +91 (0) 11 26946226
FAX : +91 (0) 11 26464556

Slach Hydratecs Equipment Pvt. Ltd.
15, Najafgarh Rd.
New Delhi, NCT of Delhi-110015
TEL : +91 (0) 11 25441917
FAX : +91 (0) 11 25441916
E-mail: slach@del2.vsnl.net.in

Nihaal Industries
41, Gopinath Est.
Nr. Simla Ghar Ghanti
Soni's Chawl Char Rasta
Odhav
Ahmedabad, Gujarat-382415
TEL : +91 (0) 79 2890787
E-mail: nihalind@yahoo.com

Presswel Industries
Plot No. 152, Sect. 24
Faridabad,
Haryana-121005
TEL : +91 (0) 129 5233665
FAX : +91 (0) 129 5234788
E-mail: presswel@vsnl.com

Hind Hydraulics & Engineers
Plot No. 13, Sect. 24
Faridabad,
Haryana-121005
TEL : +91 (0) 129 5233308
FAX : +91 (0) 129 5234294
E-mail: hindhydr@nda.vsnl.net.in

KB Hydraulic Engg. Works (Regd.)
284, Sect.-24
Faridabad,
Haryana-121005
TEL : +91 (0) 129 5234997
FAX : +91 (0) 129 5234998
E-mail: press@kbeera.com

Bemco Hydraulics Ltd.
Udyambag
Belgaum,
Karnataka-590008
TEL : +91 (0) 831 441980
FAX : +91 (0) 831 441263
E-mail: bemco@belgaum.com

Jaak Hydro-Pneumatic Co.
No. 1, Visweswariah Indl. Est.
Mahadevapura
Bangalore,
Karnataka-560040
TEL : +91 (0) 80 8524460
FAX : +91 (0) 80 8524090
E-mail: jaak_hydro@sify.com

Plus-One Machinefabrik
Survey No. 323, Plot No. 25-26
Udyambag, Belgaum,
Karnataka-590008.
TEL : +91 (0) 831 441845
FAX : +91 (0) 831 441106
E-mail: plusone@blr.vsnl.net.in

Ramph (India)
E-1253/4, 12th Main Ward,
No. 2, Kammagondanahalli
Jalahalli (W)
Bangalore,
Karnataka-560015
TEL : +91 (0) 80 8389366
E-mail: ramphind@vsnl.net

Standard Hydraulik (I) Equipment Belgaum Pvt. Ltd.
B6/1, Plot No. 10
Udyogbag
Belgaum,
Karnataka-590008
TEL : +91 (0) 831 480566
FAX : +91 (0) 831 482033
E-mail: gopalchitnis@satyam.net.in

Marco Hydraulics
B/1, M N D'Souza Compound
Nr. Bora Transport Company
Opp. Kherani Cross Lane, Sakinaka
Andheri (E)
Mumbai,
Maharashtra-400072
TEL : +91 (0) 22 8591391
FAX : +91 (0) 22 8522584
E-mail: marcohyd@vsnl.com

Damania & Sons
B-22, Rd. No. 16
Wagle Indl. Est.
Thane,
Maharashtra-400604
TEL : +91 (0) 22 5820457
FAX : +91 (0) 22 5801989
E-mail: damania@bom4.vsnl.net.in

Larsen & Toubro Ltd.
Heavy Engineering Divn,
Powai Works, Saki Vihar Rd.
Powai, Mumbai,
Maharashtra-400072.
TEL : +91 (0) 22 8581401
FAX : +91 (0) 22 8581594
E-mail: 3870-sra@ve-dak.ltindia.com

Mitesh Associates
P.O. Box 2766
Kalbadevi P.O
Mumbai,
Maharashtra-400002
TEL : +91 (0) 22 8981319

Hydraulics Machine Tools
Old-21
Arumuga Gounder St.
Rathinapuri
Coimbatore,
Tamil Nadu-641027
TEL : +91 (0) 422 482083
E-mail:
hydraulicsmachinetools@yahoo.co.in

Hydro Craft
11-B, Vijayalakshmi Layout
1st St., Ganpathy
Coimbatore,
Tamil Nadu-641006
TEL : +91 (0) 422 532704
FAX : +91 (0) 422 532704
E-mail: ganesh_hy@rediffmail.com

Larsen & Toubro Limited Heavy
Engg. Division Rubber Processing Machinery
L & T Chennai House
Post Bag 5247, 10
Club House Rd.
Anna Salai
Chennai,
Tamil Nadu-600002
TEL : +91 (0) 44 8460141
FAX : +91 (0) 44 8460069

Pressform Industries
19-B, Yadavaliar St.,
Pattravakkam, Chennai,
Tamil Nadu-600098
TEL : +91 (0) 44 6359299
FAX : +91 (0) 44 6250736
E-mail: pressform@md3.vsnl.net.in

Janta Engg. Works
Rajendra Ngr.
Indl. Area, P.O. Mohan Ngr.
G T Rd., Ghaziabad,
Uttar Pradesh-201007
TEL : +91 (0) 120 4623455

Max Hydromech Engineers Pvt. Ltd.
Balitikuri, CTI Rd.
Naskarpara
Howrah,
West Bengal-711402
TEL : +91 (0) 33 6531686
FAX : +91 (0) 33 6531688

TYRE MACHINERY

Hind Hydraulics & Engineers
Plot No. 13, Sect. 24
Faridabad,
Haryana-121005
TEL : +91 (0) 129 5233308
FAX : +91 (0) 129 5234294
E-mail: hindhydr@nda.vsnl.net.in

Maan Machine Tools
119, Nr. Bus Stand
Nawlu Cly.
Krishna Vihar
Ballabhgarh,
Haryana-121004
TEL : +91 (0) 129 5240923
FAX : +91 (0) 129 5240123

ACC Machinery Co. Ltd.
Cement House, 121
M K Rd.
Mumbai,
Maharashtra-400020
TEL : +91 (0) 22 2039122
FAX : +91 (0) 22 2051065

Associated Tyre Machinery Company Ltd.
Cement House, 121
Maharshi Karve Rd.
Mumbai,
Maharashtra-400020
TEL : +91 (0) 22 2039122
FAX : +91 (0) 22 2080076

Larsen & Toubro Ltd. Heavy
Engineering Divn.
Powai Works
Saki Vihar Rd.
Powai
Mumbai,
Maharashtra-400072
TEL : +91 (0) 22 8581401
FAX : +91 (0) 22 8581594
E-mail: 3870-sra@ve-dak.ltindia.com

Laxmi Engg. Works
W/10, Panchal Udyog Ngr.
Goddeo Rd.
Bhayander (E)
Thane,
Maharashtra-401105
TEL : +91 (0) 22 8195976
FAX : +91 (0) 22 8195545
E-mail: lew@bol.net.in

Mohan Engineering Works
4/7, Piramal Indl. Est.
S V Rd.
Goregaon (W)
Mumbai,
Maharashtra-400062
TEL : +91 (0) 22 8743223
FAX : +91 (0) 22 8742591
E-mail: mohanengg@vsnl.net

Premier Engineers
Opp. Rly. Microwave Tower
Sirhind,
Punjab-140406
TEL : +91 (0) 1763 22260
FAX : +91 (0) 1763 22560
E-mail:
premierengg@santmachines.com

Braga Industries
63-B, Northern Phase
Ambattur Indl. Est.
Chennai,
Tamil Nadu-600098
TEL : +91 (0) 44 6254103
FAX : +91 (0) 44 6257032

Devon Machines Pvt. Ltd.
63-B, Northern Phase, Indl. Est.
Ambattur
Chennai,
Tamil Nadu-600098
TEL : +91 (0) 44 6253036
FAX : +91 (0) 44 6257032
E-mail: devon@md3.vsnl.net.in

Engineering Equipment Works
D-4, Ambattur Indl. Est.
Chennai,
Tamil Nadu-600058
TEL : +91 (0) 44 6357466
FAX : +91 (0) 44 6357466
E-mail: eew@vsnl.net

Intek Engineers
8, SIDCO Indl. Est.
Ambattur
Chennai,
Tamil Nadu-600098
TEL : +91 (0) 44 6255067
FAX : +91 (0) 44 6255067

Larsen & Toubro Limited Heavy
Engg. Division Rubber Processing Machinery
L & T Chennai House
Post Bag 5247, 10
Club House Rd.

Anna Salai
Chennai,
Tamil Nadu-600002
TEL : +91 (0) 44 8460141
FAX : +91 (0) 44 8460069

Product Engg. Industry
93-A, Indl. Est., Phase (N)
Ambattur
Chennai,
Tamil Nadu-600098
TEL : +91 (0) 44 6257932
FAX : +91 (0) 44 6257932
E-mail:
proden@giasmd01.vsnl.net.in

Bharat Electric Works
Opp. Peera Garhi, K-49
Udyog Ngr.
New Delhi, NCT of Delhi-110041
TEL : +91 (0) 11 25472654
FAX : +91 (0) 11 25471019

Industrial Machinery Co.
205, Kanchan House
Karampura Cmplx.
New Delhi, NCT of Delhi-110015
TEL : +91 (0) 11 25116159
FAX : +91 (0) 11 25431706

Mitsubishi Heavy Industries Ltd.
New Delhi Liaison Office
Dr. Gopaldas Bhawan, 1st Flr., 28
Barakhamba Rd.
New Delhi, NCT of Delhi-110001
TEL : +91 (0) 11 23354465
FAX : +91 (0) 11 23350280

RUBBER MACHINERY

Bal Krishna Tyres
418/422
Creative Indl. Est.
72, N M Joshi Marg
Mumbai,
Maharashtra-400011
TEL : +91 (0) 22 3080917
FAX : +91 (0) 22 3080909
E-mail: localsales@bkt-tires.com

Jayalakshmi Engineering Works
10/27-B, Sengaliappan Ngr.,
Ranganatha Puram
Sulur
Coimbatore,
Tamil Nadu-641402
TEL : +91 (0) 422 689286
FAX : +91 (0) 422 688175
E-mail: jew_eng_works@yahoo.com

Ramson Engineering Industries
C-1, 178/2
GIDC Est., Mehsana,
Gujarat-384002
TEL : +91 (0) 2762 56077
FAX : +91 (0) 2762 51335

Acu-Rites
105, Selvam Indl. Est.
Magadi Main Rd.
Bangalore,
Karnataka-560079
TEL : +91 (0) 80 3285077
FAX : +91 (0) 80 3357181
E-mail: acurites@sify.com

Northern Machineries Pvt. Ltd.
C-29, Phase-II
Focal Point
Ludhiana,
Punjab-141010
TEL : +91 (0) 161 671509
FAX : +91 (0) 161 675066
E-mail: ralson@satyam.net.in

Elgitread (I) Ltd.
Elgi House
1789, Trichy Rd., Coimbatore,
Tamil Nadu-641045
TEL : +91 (0) 422 319909
FAX : +91 (0) 422 574178
E-mail: info@elgitread.co.in

JJM Tyre Equipments
116, Periyar Ngr., Ramanathapuram,
Coimbatore,
Tamil Nadu-641045
TEL : +91 (0) 422 316455
E-mail: ganes@vsnl.com

Raj Tire Technologists
61, JJM House,
Periyar Ngr.
Ramanathapuram,
Coimbatore,
Tamil Nadu-641045
TEL : +91 (0) 422 316455
E-mail: rajtire@usa.net

Target Tools
49A, Nava India Rd
K R Puram Post,
Coimbatore,
Tamil Nadu-641006,
TEL : +91 (0) 422 560049
FAX : +91 (0) 422 562094

LATEX DIPPING MACHINERY

Vipraj Machine Tools Pvt. Ltd.
S. No. 745/1/2
Mumbai-Pune Rd.
Telgaon-Dhabade
Pune,
Maharashtra-410506
TEL : +91 (0) 20 5812955

Delta Rubber & Plastic Products
C1A/1, GIDC Indl. Township
Odhav,
Ahmedabad,
Gujarat-382415,
TEL : +91 (0) 79 2872334
FAX : +91 (0) 79 2870835
E-mail: deltarub_dayal@hotmail.com

VULCANISING MACHINES

Dipesh Engineering Works
3, Sheroo Villa, 87, P Rd.
Andheri (W),
Mumbai,
Maharashtra-400053.
TEL : +91 (0) 22 6336729
FAX : +91 (0) 22 6315507
E-mail: kjpatel_71@hotmail.com

Amis Engg. Works
60, SV Co-op. Indl. Est.
Balanagar
Hyderabad,
Andhra Pradesh-500037
TEL : +91 (0) 40 3776884
FAX : +91 (0) 40 7534617
E-mail: amisengr@hdl.vsnl.net.in

Delta Rubber & Plastic Products
C1A/1, GIDC Indl. Township
Odhav
Ahmedabad,
Gujarat-382415
TEL : +91 (0) 79 2872334
FAX : +91 (0) 79 2870835
E-mail: deltarub_dayal@hotmail.com

Plants (I) Agro Machineries Pvt. Ltd.
No. 80, Major Indl. Est.
Kalamassery Devp. Plot P.O.
Kalamassery,
Kerala-683109
TEL : +91 (0) 48455 344971
FAX : +91 (0) 48455 336214
E-mail: plants@md4.vsnl.net.in

Manav Rubber Machinery Pvt. Ltd.
Plot No. 24-B, "Param Sukhshanti"
2/10, S V Rd.,
Jawahar Ngr.
Goregaon (W)
Mumbai,
Maharashtra-400062
TEL : +91 (0) 22 8723166
FAX : +91 (0) 22 8725164

Nilos India Pvt. Ltd.
Hardevi Chmbrs.
91, Panthcon Rd.
Egmore,
Chennai
Tamil Nadu-600008.
TEL : +91 (0) 44 8262633
FAX : +91 (0) 44 8233295
E-mail: nilosindia@vsnl.com

RUBER KNEADING MACHINES

Machinkraft Equipment
337, 3rd Rd., Sindh Hsg. Soc.
Aundh
Pune,
Maharashtra-411007
TEL : +91 (0) 20 5887464
FAX : +91 (0) 20 5880353
E-mail:
info@machinkraftequipment.com

Enfab Industries Pvt. Ltd.
C-2, Shanthi Niwas
Mettuguda
Secunderabad,
Andhra Pradesh-500017.
TEL : +91 (0) 40 7824343
FAX : +91 (0) 40 7830010
E-mail: enfabs@hd1.vsnl.net.in

Surya Industrial Equipments
D-109, Phase-I
IDA, Jeedimetla
Hyderabad,
Andhra Pradesh-500055
TEL : +91 (0) 40 3096355
FAX : +91 (0) 40 3098163

Base Industries
Plot No. 138-B
IDA, Mallapur
Hyderabad,
Andhra Pradesh-501507
TEL : +91 (0) 40 7823073
FAX : +91 (0) 40 7823073
E-mail: enfabs@hd1.vsnl.net.in

Avtar Singh & Sons
C-129, Phase-II
Mayapuri
New Delhi,
NCT of Delhi-110064
TEL : +91 (0) 11 25130861
FAX : +91 (0) 11 25160752

Industrial Machinery Co.
205, Kanchan House
Karampura Cmplx.
New Delhi, NCT of Delhi-110015
TEL : +91 (0) 11 25116159
FAX : +91 (0) 11 25431706

Ravi Engineering Works Pvt. Ltd.
Prop. Janak Industries Pvt. Ltd.
18/34
St. No.5, (Rly. Line Side)
Anand Parbat Indl. Area
New Delhi, NCT of Delhi-110005
TEL : +91 (0) 11 25725517
FAX : +91 (0) 11 25764369
E-mail: ravieng@nda.vsnl.net.in

Slach Hydratecs Equipment Pvt. Ltd.
15, Najafgarh Rd.
New Delhi, NCT of Delhi-110015
TEL : +91 (0) 11 25441917
FAX : +91 (0) 11 25441916
E-mail: slach@del2.vsnl.net.in

Indian Expeller Works Pvt. Ltd.
A-4, Naroda Indl. Est.
Naroda
Ahmedabad,
Gujarat-382330
TEL : +91 (0) 79 2821855
FAX : +91 (0) 79 2830194
E-mail: dinesh@indexpell.com

Kelachandra Iron & Steel Works
Chingavanam
Kottayam,
Kerala-686531
TEL : +91 (0) 481 430596
FAX : +91 (0) 481 430406
E-mail: kelachandra@vsnl.com

Frigmaires Engineers
Janta Indl. Est.
Gala No. 8, Opp. Phoenix Mill
Senapati Bapat Marg
Lower Parel
Mumbai,
Maharashtra-400013

TEL : +91 (0) 22 4945624
FAX : +91 (0) 22 2187750
E-mail: fe@vsnl.com

Bainite Machines
C-10, Nand Dham Indl. Est.
Agnishaman Dal Marg, Marol
Andheri (E),
Mumbai,
Maharashtra-400059
TEL : +91 (0) 22 8505910
FAX : +91 (0) 22 8500465
E-mail: bainite@bom8.vsnl.net.in

Durga Industries
Saksalia Indl. Est.
Chincholi Bunder Rd.
Malad (W), Mumbai,
Maharashtra-400064
TEL : +91 (0) 22 8726466

Malik Engineers
Unit 1, Shailesh Indl. Est. NO. 1
Navghar, Vasai Rd. (E)
Pune,
Maharashtra-401210
TEL : +91 (0) 20 8839751
FAX : +91 (0) 20 8830751
E-mail: malik@malikengg.com

Manav Rubber Machinery Pvt. Ltd.
Plot No. 24-B, "Param Sukhshanti"
2/10, S V Rd.,
Jawahar Ngr.
Goregaon (W),
Mumbai,
Maharashtra-400062.
TEL : +91 (0) 22 8723166
FAX : +91 (0) 22 8725164

PMS Great Floorings Pvt. Ltd.
E-13 Block, MIDC
Bhosari, Pune,
Maharashtra-411026
TEL : +91 (0) 20 7122989
FAX : +91 (0) 20 7122332
E-mail: moti@pn2.vsnl.net.in

Richardson & Cruddas (1972) Ltd. A Government of India Undertaking
Sir J J Rd.
Byculla Iron Works
Mumbai,
Maharashtra-400008
TEL : +91 (0) 22 3776832
FAX : +91 (0) 22 3731491

Anant Corp.
P.O. Box 14, Bassi Rd.
Sirhind,
Punjab-140406
TEL : +91 (0) 1763 22187
FAX : +91 (0) 1763 20187
E-mail: anant_corp@vsnl.com

Anant Engg. Works
Bassi Rd.
Sirhind,
Punjab-140406
TEL : +91 (0) 1763 22037
FAX : +91 (0) 1763 22037

Anant Enterprises
P.O. Box 5, Bassi Rd.
Sirhind,
Punjab-140406
TEL : +91 (0) 1763 22452
FAX : +91 (0) 1763 20452

Sant Rubber Machines Pvt. Ltd.
P.O. Box 31, Sirhind,
Punjab-140406.
TEL : +91 (0) 1763 20439
FAX : +91 (0) 1763 41360
E-mail:
santrubber@santmachines.com

HP Singh & Co.
75, Ganesh Chandra Avenue
Kolkata,
West Bengal-700013
TEL : +91 (0) 33 2371680
FAX : +91 (0) 33 2255457
E-mail: hpscocal@vsnl.com

GN Engg. Works
388/H/13
Tangra Rd.
Kolkata,
West Bengal-700015
TEL : +91 (0) 33 3297189
FAX : +91 (0) 33 3295550

RUBBER EXTRUDING MACHINES

Associated Tyre Machinery Co. Ltd.
Cement House, 121
Maharshi Karve Rd.
Mumbai,
Maharashtra-400020
TEL : +91 (0) 22 2039122
FAX : +91 (0) 22 2080076

Bainite Machines
C-10, Nand Dham Indl. Est.
Agnishaman Dal Marg, Marol
Andheri (E)
Mumbai,
Maharashtra-400059
TEL : +91 (0) 22 8505910
FAX : +91 (0) 22 8500465
E-mail: bainite@bom8.vsnl.net.in

Kemtech International Ltd.
A-125, Shivalik
Malviya Ngr. P.O.
New Delhi, NCT of Delhi-110017
TEL : +91 (0) 11 26688343
FAX : +91 (0) 11 26680899
E-mail:
info@kemtechinternational.com

Avtar Singh & Sons
C-129, Phase-II
Mayapuri
New Delhi,
NCT of Delhi-110064
TEL : +91 (0) 11 25130861
FAX : +91 (0) 11 25160752

Industrial Machinery Co.
205, Kanchan House
Karampura Complex.
New Delhi, NCT of Delhi-110015
TEL : +91 (0) 11 25116159
FAX : +91 (0) 11 25431706

Ravi Engineering Works Pvt. Ltd.
18/34, St. No.5,
(Rly. Line Side)
Anand Parbat Indl. Area
New Delhi, NCT of Delhi-110005
TEL : +91 (0) 11 25725517
FAX : +91 (0) 11 25764369
E-mail: ravieng@nda.vsnl.net.in

Indian Expeller Works Pvt. Ltd.
A-4, Naroda Indl. Est.
Naroda, Ahmedabad,
Gujarat-382330
TEL : +91 (0) 79 2821855
FAX : +91 (0) 79 2830194
E-mail: dinesh@indexpell.com

Ramani Automation Systems Pvt. Ltd.
140, Phase-II, Indl. Area
Panchkula,
Haryana-134113
TEL : +91 (0) 172 592105
FAX : +91 (0) 172 591971
E-mail: ramani_engg@hotmail.com

Plus-One Machinefabrik
Survey No. 323, Plot No. 25-26
Udyambag, Belgaum,
Karnataka-590008
TEL : +91 (0) 831 441845
FAX : +91 (0) 831 441106
E-mail: plusone@blr.vsnl.net.in

Kelachandra Iron & Steel Works
Chingavanam, Kottayam,
Kerala-686531
TEL : +91 (0) 481 430596
FAX : +91 (0) 481 430406
E-mail: kelachandra@vsnl.com

19

Suppliers of Raw Materials

RUBBER MANUFACTURING CHEMICALS

Auto Steel & Rubber Industries Pvt. Ltd.
C-2-1, Technicians' Block
Bhosari Indl. Est.
Pune,
Maharashtra-411026
TEL : +91 (0) 20 7127701
FAX : +91 (0) 20 7127720
E-mail: asri@vsnl.com

Aerotech India Pvt. Ltd.
202, Shivam House
Karampura Comml. Cmplx.
New Delhi, NCT of Delhi-110015
TEL : +91 (0) 11 25433375
FAX : +91 (0) 11 25459768
E-mail:
headoffice@aerotech.wipro.net.in

Bhabani Pigments Pvt. Ltd.
7, E-Block, 2nd Flr.
Local Shopping Centre
Masjid Moth
Greater Kailash-II
New Delhi, NCT of Delhi-110048
TEL : +91 (0) 11 26211922
FAX : +91 (0) 11 26466908
E-mail: bppl@ndf.vsnl.net.in

Chowdhry Rubber & Chemical Co.
1403, Pan Mandi
Sadar Bazar
Delhi110006.
TEL : +91 (0) 11 23673373
FAX : +91 (0) 11 27534153
E-mail: anshdeep@del3.vsnl.net.in

Demaco Polymers Ltd.
B-1/G-3, MCIE,
Mathura Rd.
New Delhi,-110044.
TEL : +91 (0) 11 26959424
FAX : +91 (0) 11 26959112
E-mail: demaco@ndf.vsnl.net.in

High Polymer Labs Ltd.
803, Vishal Bhavan, 95
Nehru Place
New Delhi-110019.
TEL : +91 (0) 11 26431522
FAX : +91 (0) 11 26474350
E-mail: hpll@hpl-group.com

KLJ Polymers & Chemicals Ltd.
KLJ House, 63
Rama Marg
Najafgarh Rd.
New Delhi, NCT of Delhi-110015
TEL : +91 (0) 11 25459706
FAX : +91 (0) 11 25459709
E-mail: klj/
delhi@dartmail.dartnet.com

Orgo Products
E-1
Opp. Rana Partap Bagh
C C Cly.
Delhi, NCT of Delhi-110007
TEL : +91 (0) 11 27231050
FAX : +91 (0) 11 27231050

Rubber-Chem Corp.
9, Rehman Mkt.
Sadar Bazar
Delhi, NCT of Delhi-110006
TEL : +91 (0) 11 27771174
FAX : +91 (0) 11 23552019
E-mail: rubber@ndf.vsnl.net.in

Sachin Chemical Udyog
1414/2, Gali Chulewali
Sadar Bazar
Delhi, NCT of Delhi-110006
TEL : +91 (0) 11 23672453
FAX : +91 (0) 11 23558887

Shakti Minerals & Chemicals
1/2222, Ram Ngr.
Mandoli Rd.
Shahdara
Delhi, NCT of Delhi-110032
TEL : +91 (0) 11 22283065
FAX : +91 (0) 11 22297381

Yin Enterprises
B-14, Inder Puri
New Delhi, NCT of Delhi-110012
TEL : +91 (0) 11 25695576
E-mail: vinchem@rediffmail.com

Cosmos Chemicals
760, GIDC Est.
Makarpura
Vadodara,
Gujarat-390010
TEL : +91 (0) 265 642064
FAX : +91 (0) 265 31160
E-mail: cosmoschem@icenet.net

Gujarat Silicon Pvt. Ltd.
Amarnath House
Mitha Galli
Nr. Teen Darwaja
Grain Mkt., Jamnagar,
Gujarat-361001.
TEL : +91 (0) 288 676702
FAX : +91 (0) 288 755086
E-mail: gujsil@vsnl.com

Gujauxi-Chem
5, Hill Darshan
Opp. T V Tower
Drive-In Rd., Ahmedabad,
Gujarat-380054.
TEL : +91 (0) 79 6431379
E-mail: pranil1812@yahoo.com

Kairav Chemicals Ltd.
901, Parshwa Towers
Sarkhej
Gandhinagar Highway
Ahmedabad,
Gujarat-380054
TEL : +91 (0) 79 6751320
FAX : +91 (0) 79 6752214
E-mail: kairav@satyam.net.in

Sterling Chemicals
103-104
"Opel Square", B/h Express Hotel
R C Dutt Rd., Alkapuri,
Vadodara,
Gujarat-390007
TEL : +91 (0) 265 311664
FAX : +91 (0) 265 350557
E-mail: sterlchem@satyam.net.in

Universal Corporation
A-3/122
Associated Soc.
Old Padra Rd., Akota Garden Rd.
Akota
Vadodara,
Gujarat-390020
TEL : +91 (0) 265 310827
FAX : +91 (0) 265 310428
E-mail: unicorp@icenet.net

ICI India Ltd.
10th Flr., DLF Plaza
DLF Qutub Enclave 1
Gurgaon,
Haryana-122001
TEL : +91 (0) 124 6358400
FAX : +91 (0) 124 6359849

ICI Rubber Chemicals
6th Flr., Tower-B
Global Business Park, Gurgaon,
Haryana-122002
TEL : +91 (0) 124 6359836
FAX : +91 (0) 124 6359839
E-mail: sameer_sachdeva@ici.com

Mikasu Metreat
B-1, Phase-I, Indl. Area
Adityapur, Jamshedpur,
Jharkhand-832109
TEL : +91 (0) 657 408281
FAX : +91 (0) 657 407224
E-mail:
mikasu_metreat@rediffmail.com

Ava Chemicals Pvt. Ltd.
1/20 B, Narayan Plaza
26-A, Chandivli Rd.
Mumbai, Maharashtra-400072
TEL : +91 (0) 22 8523955
FAX : +91 (0) 22 8525790
E-mail: ava@bom2.vsnl.net.in

Multi Organics Pvt. Ltd.
503, Keshava
Bandra-Kurla Cmplx.
Bandra (E), Mumbai,
Maharashtra-400051
TEL : +91 (0) 22 6590118
FAX : +91 (0) 22 6590358
E-mail: mumbai@multiorganics.com

Aaamu-Urai Impex
53, Apollo Indl. Est.
Off Mahakali Caves Rd.
Andheri (E), Mumbai,
Maharashtra-400093
TEL : +91 (0) 22 8217930
FAX : +91 (0) 22 8217929
E-mail: aaamu@bom4.vsnl.net.in

Ace Chemie (I)
Office No. 5, Ground Flr.
Diamond Centre, LBS Marg
Vikhroli (W), Mumbai,
Maharashtra-400083
TEL : +91 (0) 22 5775143

All Chemical Pvt. Ltd.
78, V V Chandan St.
Vadgadi
Mumbai,
Maharashtra-400003
TEL : +91 (0) 22 3444794
FAX : +91 (0) 22 6425327
E-mail: kirang@satyam.net.in

Baerlocher India Additives Pvt. Ltd.
Godrej Soaps Cmplx.
Pirojshanagar
Vikhroli (E)
Mumbai,
Maharashtra-400079
TEL : +91 (0) 22 5188701
FAX : +91 (0) 22 5188703
E-mail: barindia@vsnl.com

Balaji Amines Ltd.
"Balaji Bhavan"
165-A, Railway Lines, Solapur,
Maharashtra-413001
TEL : +91 (0) 217 310823
FAX : +91 (0) 217 310821
E-mail: amines@pn2.vsnl.net.in

Deep Dop Niraj Chemicals Pvt. Ltd.
E-26, MIDC, Indl. Area, Nagpur,
Maharashtra-440028
TEL : +91 (0) 712 32657
E-mail: depdop@nagpur.dot.net.in

Demosha Chemicals Ltd.
105-A, Mittal Tower
Nariman Point, Mumbai,
Maharashtra-400021
TEL : +91 (0) 22 2872218
FAX : +91 (0) 22 2045997
E-mail: ndr@bom5.vsnl.net.in

Fine Organics
Fine House
Anandji St., Off M G Rd., Ghatkopar
(E), Mumbai,
Maharashtra-400077
TEL : +91 (0) 22 5093400
FAX : +91 (0) 22 5153215
E-mail: fine@vsnl.com

Finoric Chemicals (I) Pvt. Ltd.
5/16, Odina, 10
Central Avenue
Santacruz (W)
Mumbai,
Maharashtra-400054
TEL : +91 (0) 22 6049594
FAX : +91 (0) 22 6040021
E-mail: finornic@vsnl.com

Gomati Chemicals Pvt. Ltd.
Bhagwat, 1st Flr.
N S Rd., 2, Vile Parle (W)
Mumbai,
Maharashtra-400056
TEL : +91 (0) 22 6183623
FAX : +91 (0) 22 6147720

Hindustan Organic Chemicals Ltd. A Govt. Of India Enterprise
Harchandrai House
81, Maharshi Karve Marg
Mumbai,
Maharashtra-400002
TEL : +91 (0) 22 2014118
FAX : +91 (0) 22 2059533
E-mail: hoclras@bom3.vsnl.net.in

Jigna Organics
41, Abhisek, 303/307
Samuel St.
Mumbai,
Maharashtra-400003
TEL : +91 (0) 22 3420907
FAX : +91 (0) 22 3424493
E-mail: jigna.organics@bol.net.in

National Organic Chemical Industries Ltd. Rubber Chemicals Divn.
Mafatlal Chmbrs.
N M Joshi Marg
Lower Parel (E)
Mumbai,
Maharashtra-400013
TEL : +91 (0) 22 6558372
FAX : +91 (0) 22 3081717

Pukhraj Engg. & Chemicals Pvt. Ltd.
122-AB
Government Indl. Est.
Charkop, Kandivali (W),
Mumbai,
Maharashtra-400067
TEL : +91 (0) 22 8684972
FAX : +91 (0) 22 8682451
E-mail: mayohara@bom3.vsnl.net.in

Sarang Chemicals Pvt. Ltd.
2nd Flr., Mhatre Pen Bldg.
Dadar (W), Mumbai,
Maharashtra-400028, India.
TEL : +91 (0) 22 4376971

Shri Hap Chemical Enterprises Pvt. Ltd.
D-1, Sindhu House,3/5
Nanabhai Lane, Mumbai,
Maharashtra-400023, India.
TEL : +91 (0) 22 2041542
FAX : +91 (0) 22 2875618
E-mail: shrihap@bom3.vsnl.net.in

Solar Chemferts Pvt. Ltd.
Nr. New Empire Cinema, 3rd Flr., 15
A K Nayak Marg, Mumbai,
Maharashtra-400001, India.
TEL : +91 (0) 22 2078850
FAX : +91 (0) 22 2074228

Sunshield Chemicals Ltd.
Janki Niwas
N C Kelkar Rd.
Dadar, Mumbai,
Maharashtra-400028, India.
TEL : +91 (0) 22 4313265
FAX : +91 (0) 22 4307094
E-mail: sunshild@bom4.vsnl.net.in

Ventron Chemicals Ltd.
5, Onlooker Bldg., 14
Sir P M Rd.
Fort, Mumbai,
Maharashtra-400001, India.
TEL : +91 (0) 22 2665828
FAX : +91 (0) 22 2664150

Mittal Udyog
F-474, Phase-II
Indraprastha Indl. Area, Kota,
Rajasthan-324005
TEL : +91 (0) 744 424397
FAX : +91 (0) 744 500748
E-mail: info@metalsoaps.com

Shrihari Laboratories Pvt. Ltd.
E-81, Indraprashta Indl. Area, Kota,
Rajasthan-324005, India
TEL : +91 (0) 744 425973
FAX : +91 (0) 744 428748
E-mail: info@metalsoaps.com

Senka Carbon Pvt. Ltd.
T-29/A, Seventh Avenue
Besant Ngr., Chennai,
Tamil Nadu-600090, India.
TEL : +91 (0) 44 4910244
FAX : +91 (0) 44 4918722
E-mail: senka@vsnl.com

Northern Polymers & Chemicals
14/123-A, Gopala Chmbrs., 1st Flr.
The Mall, Kanpur,
Uttar Pradesh-208001,
TEL : +91 (0) 512 319606
FAX : +91 (0) 512 354054
E-mail: northexp@sancharnet.in

SR Chemicals
120-B, Udyog Ngr.
Dada Ngr.
Kanpur,
Uttar Pradesh-208022
TEL : +91 (0) 512 296092

Acmechem Pvt. Ltd.
Jabakusum House,
2nd Flr., Unit 34
Chittaranjan Avenue
Kolkata,
West Bengal-700012
TEL : +91 (0) 33 2369631
FAX : +91 (0) 33 2369631
E-mail: abcd@cal3.vsnl.net.in

Golchha Pigments Pvt. Ltd.
Suite No. 406, 6
Brabourne Rd.
Kolkata,
West Bengal-700001
TEL : +91 (0) 33 2254690
FAX : +91 (0) 33 2250072
E-mail: gp@golchhapigments.com

Kolmak Chemicals Ltd.
21-A, Shakespeare Sarani
Kolkata,
West Bengal-700017
TEL : +91 (0) 33 2477512
FAX : +91 (0) 33 2406476
E-mail: tioxide@cal2.vsnl.net.in

Petrochem India
12A, Lord Sinha Rd.
Kolkata,
West Bengal-700071
TEL : +91 (0) 33 2826775
FAX : +91 (0) 33 2826838
E-mail:
pcp.cal@gncal.globalnet.ems.vsnl.net.in

117. MANUFACTURE OF TIN CONTAINERS
118. MANUFACTURE OF STORAGE TANKS, PRESSURE VESSELS, HEAT EXCHANGERS
119. MARK II HAND PUMPS
120. MARUTI WORKSHOP CUM - SERVICE STATION
121. MECHANICAL JACKS
122. METAL CUTTING DIE DESIGN
123. METAL CUTTING OF AND GRINDING WHEELS (ABBRASIVE CUTTING WHEELS)
124. METAL HOOKS & CLIPS
125. METAL SEPARATION (COPPER, TIN, LEAD) FROM SPENT WASH ACID
126. METALLIC RING JOINTS
127. METALLIC GASKET (SPIRAL WOUND)
128. MICROVEE & ABSOLUTE FILTER
129. MICROWAVE OVEN
130. MILD STEEL INGOTS
131. MINI STEEL PLANT
132. MODERN VEHICLE WORKSHOP
133. MOPED
134. M.S.HINGES
135. M.S.INGOT AND HR. STEEL STRUCTURALS
136. M.S.INGOT BY INDUCTION FURNACES
137. M.S.PIPES
138. M.S. WELDING ELECTRODE
139. MUFFLERS & SILENCERS FOR THREE WHEELERS
140. NAIL CUTTER WITH FILER & MANICURE
141. NICHROME WIRE
142. NICKEL LINED SCREENS
143. NON-FERROUS ALLOY ROLLING
144. NON-FERROUS FORGING
145. NON-FERROUS FOUNDRY
146. NON PRESSURE
147. INCANDESCENT LAMP
148. NUMBER COMBINATION LOCKS FOR LUGGAGES
149. NUTS & BOLTS
150. PAPER COATED ALUMINIUM AND COPPER WIRE
151. PETROMAX CONTAINER
152. PHOTO ETCHING OF STAINLESS STEEL PLATES
153. PIPE GALVANIZING PLANT
154. PISTON RING-AUTOMOBILE
155. PLANT PROTECTION EQUIPMENTS
156. PLATINUM LABORATORY APPARATUS
157. PRESSURE COOKER & ALUMINIUM UTENSILS
158. PRESSURE COOKER (ALUMINIUM)
159. PRESSURE DIE CASTING
160. PRINTED ALUMINIUM COLLAPSIBLE TUBES
161. PRINTED TIN CONTAINERS
162. PRINTING PRESS (CYLINDER MACHINE)
163. PUMPS FOR CHEMICAL INDUSTRY (SPECIAL)
164. RAILWAY SLEEPERS (M.S.)
165. RAZOR TWIN BLADE
166. R.C.C SPUN PIPES
167. RECONDITIONING OF M.S. DRUMS/BARRELS
168. RE-ROLLING COPPER AND BRASS SHEET AND RODS
169. RE-ROLLING MILLS
170. RESIN COATED SAND
171. RESIN CORED SOFT SOLDER WIRES
172. ROLLING MILL (BY INDUCTION FURNACE) & MANUFACTURE OF BARS, ANGLES, SQUARES, TUBES AND OTHERS
173. ROLLER BEARING & FORGING
174. ROLLING OF STAINLESS STEEL PATTA
175. RUBBER INSULATED PLIERS (HAND TOOLS)
176. RUBBING COMPOUND FOR AUTOMOBILES
177. SCIENTIFIC LABORATORY EQUIPMENTS
178. SCOOTER ASSEMBLING
179. SECONDARY LEAD EXTRAC -TION BY SCRAP BATTERY PLATES,PIPES & SHEET
180. SEAMLESS M.S. TUBES & PIPES
181. SELF TAPPING STEEL SCREW
182. SEWING NEEDLES
183. S.G. IRON & ALLOY STEEL
184. SHEET METAL PRODUCTS, (FERROUS/NON-FERROUS)
185. SHIP/MARINE CONTAINER
186. SHOCK ABSORBERS
187. SHOE EYELETS
188. SHOT AND GRITS BY AUTOMIZATION PROCESS
189. SHOVELS
190. SILICO MANGANESE ALLOYS
191. SILENCERS (MUFFLERS) EXHAUST & TAIL PIPE FOR ALL TYPES OF VEHICLES
192. SINTERED BEARING
193. SINTERED BUSHES
194. SINTERED METAL PRODUCTS
195. SOFT AND HARD FERRITES
196. SPANNERS
197. SPARK PLUGS
198. STEEL PLANT (ELECTRIC ARC FURNACE BASED- EAF)
199. SPHERIODAL GRAPHITE CAST IRON
200. SPRAY DRYER
201. STAINLESS STEEL HINGES
202. STAINLESS STEEL SHEET ROLLING TO PRODUCE STAINLESS STEEL UTENSILS
203. STAINLESS STEEL UTENSILS
204. STAPLE PINS,PAPER PIN, GEM CLIPS ETC.
205. STEEL CASTINGS
206. STEEL CHAIN
207. STEEL FOUNDRY
208. STEEL FURNITURES AND ELECTRICAL APPLIANCES
209. STEEL PLANT (MINI)
210. STEEL RODS AND COILS FROM SCRAPS
211. STEEL ROLLING MILL
212. STEEL STRIPS (COLD ROLLED) SILICON WITH GRAIN RIENTED FOR ELECTRIC USE
213. STEEL TRANSMISSION LINE TOWERS & ROLLING MILL TO PRODUCE STEEL SECTION
214. STEEL FURNITURES AND ELECTRICAL APPLIANCES
215. STEEL WIRE DRAWING AND GALVANIZING
216. STEEL WOOL
217. SUBMERGED ARC WELDED PIPES
218. SUBMERSIBLE PUMP MANUFACTURING
219. SUPER ENAMELLED COPPER WIRE
220. THREE WHEELERS
221. TIE-ROD ENDS
222. TIN CONTAINERS
223. TOOLROOM AND SHEET METAL PRODUCTS
224. TRACTOR TRAILERS
225. TRANSMISSION POWER FITTING
226. TUBULAR POLES
227. SUPER ENAMELLED COPPER WIRES
228. TUBULAR POLES FOR ELECTRICAL TRANSMISSION (BY FABRICATION PROCESS)
229. TUBULAR POLES OF M.S. & HIGH TENSILE STEEL
230. VACUUM CLEANERS
231. VACUUM FLASK (STAINLESS STEEL)
232. VALVES FOR REFRIGERA TION AND AIR-CONDITION
233. VEHICLE WELDING & PAINTING
234. VENETION BLIND
235. WASHING MACHINES (AUTOMATIC & COMPUTERISED)
236. WATER CONTROLLER (AUTOMATIC)
237. WATCH STRAPS/CHAINS/ BRACELETS/BELT BRASS & STAINLESS STEEL
238. WATER COOLERS
239. WELDED WIRE MESH
240. WELDING ELECTRODES
241. WICK STOVES
242. WIND MILL WINDOW FRAME (FERROUS & NON-FERROUS)
243. WRIST WATCH

359. DI ETHYL OXALATE
360. DI METHYL ORTHOPHTHALATE
361. DI-METHYL PHTHALATE
362. DICLOFENAC GEL
363. DIOCTYL PHTHALATE (DOP)
364. DI PHENYL GLYCERINE
365. DI PHENYL OXIDE
366. DINITRO-CHLORO BENZENE
367. DISTILLED WATER
368. DODECYL BENZENE SULPHONATE
369. DUSTLESS CHALK
370. EDTA & ITS SALTS
371. ELECTROLESS NICKEL PLATING ON PLASTICS
372. ENDOSULFAN
373. EPOXY RESIN BASED COMPOUND
374. ETHYL ACETATE
375. EHTYL ETHER
376. ETHYL ALCOHOL (POTABLE LIQUOR)
377. ETHYL HEXANOL
378. EXTRACTION OF ESSENTIAL OILS BY SUGAR CRITICAL FLUID (CARBON DIOXIDE) METHOD FROM FLOWERS, HERBAL & SPICES
379. FERRIC ALUM
380. FERRO CHROME LIGNO SULPHONATE
381. FERRO MANGANESE
382. FERRO SILICONE
383. FERRO VANADIUM FROM VANADIUM SLUDGE
384. FERROUS SILICATE
385. FERROUS SULPHATE
386. FERTILIZER FROM ANIMAL BLOOD & LEATHER WASTE
387. FLUORESCENT TUBE LIGHT POWDER
388. FOAMED PVC COMPOUNDING & ITS PRODUCTS
389. FORMALDEHYDE
390. FRACTIONAL DISTILLATION OF D.M.O (DEMENTHOLIZED OIL)
391. FRACTIONAL DISTILLATION OF ESSENTIAL OIL & MEDICINAL PLANT EXTRACT
392. FRICTION DUST (LIQUID & POWDER) FROM CNSL
393. FRUIT FLAVOURS
394. FURFURAL FROM RICE HUSK
395. GARLIC ACID
396. GASKET SHELLAC COMPOUND
397. GEAR OIL
398. GIBBERELLIC ACID
399. GLASS PUTTY
400. GLYCERINE
401. GOSSYPOL (POLY PHENOL) FROM COTTON SEED OIL
402. GUAR GUM POWDER
403. HAIR FIXER (HAIR GEL TYPE)
404. H - ACID
405. HENNA PASTE MAKING
406. HEPTAL DEHYDE
407. HIGH CARBON FERRO CHROME
408. HYDRATED CALCIUM SILICATE BRICK
409. HYDRATED LIME FROM SEA SHELL
410. HYDROCHLORIC ACID
411. HYDRO FLUORIC ACID
412. HYDROGEN PEROXIDE (BY AUTO-OXIDATION PROCESS)
413. ICE PACKS (SOLUTIONS TYPE, WHITE GEL TYPE, VIOLET SEMI SOLID POLYMER TYPE)
414. IMPROVING DROP POINT PARAFFIN WAX FROM 45-50ºC TO 75-80ºC
415. INDUSTRIAL ALCOHOL
416. INTEGERATED COMPLEX OF EASTER & ALLIED PRODUCTS (D.O.P, D.B.P, ETHYL ACETATE WIRE ENAMEL & CABLE JELLY)
417. IMFL (WHISKY) & COUNTRY LIQUOR
418. IRON OXIDE FOR MAKING FERITTE
419. IRON SULPHIDE
420. JUTE BATCHING OIL
421. KESH KALA TEL (HAIR DYE LOTION) (VASMOL 33, BLACK NITE TYPE)
422. L-LYSINE MONOHYDROCHLORIDE
423. LACTIC ACID FROM WHITE SUGAR BY FERMENTATION PROCESS
424. LDPE GRANULES FROM VIRGIN (LDPE RESIN)
425. LEAD EXTRACTION FROM BATTERY SCRAP
426. LEAD OXIDE (A) LEAD MONOXIDE (B) LEAD TETRA OXIDE (C) GREYLEAD OXIDE
427. LIQUID GLUCOSE & ITS BY PRODUCTS
428. LIQUID OXYGEN BOTTLING PLANT
429. LIQUID SHOE POLISH
430. LIQUID FLOOR POLISH
431. LUBE OIL VISCOSITY IMPROVED FOR P.P.G/P.E.G.
432. LUBRICANTS ASHLESS 100% COMBUSTION
433. MAGNESIUM CARBONATE AND MAGNESIUM BICARMONATE
434. MAGNESIUM HYDROXIDE POWDER
435. MAGNESIUM SILICATE
436. MAGNESIUM SULPHATE
437. MALACHITE GREEN
438. MALEIC ANHYDRIDE
439. MANGANESE SULPHATE
440. MANUFACTURING OF CARBON MONO-OXIDE WATER GAS
441. MENTHOL BOLD CRYSTALS FROM FLAKES
442. MENTHOL CRYSTAL & MENTHA OIL
443. MERCURIC OXIDE
444. METAL PRE-TREATMENT CHEMICALS
445. METHANE GAS BY SODIUM ACETATE & SODA LIME
446. METHYL ACETYL RICINOLATE
447. METOL
448. METOL FROM HYDROQUINONE & METHYLAMINE
449. MICANITE
450. MICRO NUTRIENT MIXTURE
451. MINERAL WATER
452. MINERAL WATER AND PET BOTTILNG PLANT
453. MINERAL WATER IN BOTTLES, GLASS AND POUCHES
454. MINI CEMENT PLANT (BY ROTARY KILN PROCESS)
455. MIXED FERTILIZER
456. MOSQUITO & FLIES REPELLENT AGARBATTI (INCENSE STICKS)
457. MONO CHLORO ACETIC ACID
458. MONOCROTOPHOS (TECHNICAL)
459. MOSQUITO COIL
460. MOSQUITO COIL & MAT
461. MOSQUITO MAT
462. MOTHER TINCTURE & BIO CHEMIC MEDICINES
463. NAPHTHALENE & PHENYL (INTEGRATED UNIT)
464. NATURAL MINERAL WATER BY REVERSE OSMOSIS PROCESS
465. NICKEL PLATING BRIGHTNER (PRIMARY OR CARRIER BRIGHTNER & SECONDARY BRIGHTNER)
466. NICKEL SULPHATE
467. NICOTINE FROM TOBACCO WASTE
468. NICOTINE SULPHATE FROM TOBACCO WASTE
469. NITRO BENZENE
470. NITRO CELLULOSE SANDING SEALER/LACQUER
471. NITRO MUSK
472. NITROGEN & OXYGEN GAS PLANT
473. NON-IONIC SURFACTANT (WETTING AGENT)
474. NO-CARB PASTE
475. OCTANOL
476. ORTHO NITRO PHENOL
477. OXALIC ACID FROM MOLASSES
478. OXALIC ACID FROMRICE HUSK
479. OXALIC ACID FROM TREE BARK
470. OXALIC ACID FROM WASTE VEGETABLES
471. OXYGEN GAS PLANT
472. OXYGEN GAS PLANT (AIR SEPERATION METHOD)
473. PARA-AMINO BENZOIC ACID
474. PARA-AMINO PHENOL
475. PARA TOLUENE SULPHONIC ACID
476. PECTIN FROM RAW PAPAYA
477. PERFUME (LEMON & OTHERS)

Pay Rs. 8,000/- Only

for Tailor made Report
We (EIRI) are fully capable to prepare any report as per your requirements

478. PESTICIDE PREPARATION USING NEEM FRUIT & SEEDS (MARGOSA)
479. PET BOTTLES FROM PRE-FORM
480. PET PREFORM FROM RESIN FOR PET BOTTLES
481. PETROLEUM JELLY
482. PHENOL
483. PHENYL
484. PHENYL (BLACK) IN LIQUID FORM
485. PHTHALIC ANHYDRIDE
486. PHOSPHORIC ACID FROM ROCK PHOSPHATE
487. PHOSPHORUS BY CHEMICAL PROCESS
488. PHOTO EMULSION FOR ROTARY SCREEN PRINTING
489. PHTHALOCYANINE BLUE
480. PIGMENT EMULSION FOR TEXTILE
481. PIGMENT GUM
482. PLANT GROWTH REAGEN BASED CHLOROTHYL TRIMETHYL AMMONIUM CHLORIDE
483. PLANT HARMONES BASED ON 2,4-DICHLORPHENOXY ACENTIC ACID & NAPHTHALENE
484. PLASTICINE (MODELLING CLAY)
485. PLASTIC WASTE REPROCESSING
486. PLASTER OF PARIS BANDAGES
487. POLYESTER RESIN (G.P. GRADE LAMINATE GRADE, ELECTRICAL GRADE)
488. POLY VINYL ACETATE
489. POLYVINYL ACETATE EMULSION
490. POLYURETHENE FOAM
491. POTASSIUM DICHROMATE/ BICHROMATE
492. POTASSIUM IODATE
493. POTASSIUM NITRATE
494. POTASSIUM PERMAGNATE
495. POTASSIUM PER SULPHATE
496. POTASSIUM SULPHATE (FERTILIZER GRADE)
497. POTASSIUM PER OXY DI-SULPHIDE
498. POTASSIUM SILICATE
499. POTASSIUM STEARATE
500. POWER ALCOHOL
501. PVC RESIN FROM ETHYL ALCOHOL
502. PYRIDINE & ITS DERIVATIVES
503. RAPID FAST DYES (ONLY PROCESS)
504. REACTOR (CHEMICAL)
505. RECLAMATION OF USED ENGINE OIL (BY CLAY & VACUUM DISTILLATION PROCESS)
506. RECLAMATION OF SPENT BLEACHING EARTH
507. RECLAMATION OF NICKEL SPENT CATALYST FROM VANASPATI INDUSTRY
508. RECTIFIED SPIRIT FROM MOLASSES & MAHUA FLOWERS
509. RECTIFIED SPIRIT FROM RICE STRAW
510. RED OXIDE PAINT/PRIMER (ANTI CORROSIVE) BASED ORGANIC RED PIGMENTS
511. REMOVAL OF ANTIMONY FROM LEAD SCRAP
512. RESORCINOL
513. ROSIN SIZING AGENT
514. RESORCINOL
515. SALINE AND INJECTION WATER
516. SALICYLIC ACID
517. SANTONIN
518. SENNOSIDES FROM SENNO LEAF
519. SHOE POLISH
520. SILICA GEL (BLUE SELF INDICATING PROCESS)
521. SILICONE EMULSION
522. SILICONE FROM RICE HUSK
523. SILICON FROM SILICA (SEMI CONDUCTOR GRADE)
524. SILICONE RESINS
525. SILICONE SPRAYSILVER BRAZING FOIL
526. SILVER EXTRACTION FROM WASTE HYPO SOLUTION
527. SILVER NITRATE
528. SILVER PARTS FOR CERAMIC CAPACITOR SINGLE SUPER PHOSPHATE & MIXED FERTILIZER (NPK)
529. SINGLE SUPER PHOSPHATE (S.S.P) & SULPHURIC ACID
530. SODA ASH
531. SODA ASH FROM NATRON
532. SODA WATER BOTTLING PLANT (CARBONATED BEVERAGE)
533. SODIUM ALUMINATE
534. SODIUM BI-CARBONATE (BAKING SODA) FROM SODA ASH
535. SODIUM CHLORITE
536. SODIUM CHROMATE SODIUM CYCLAMATE
537. SODIUM DI-CHROMATE
538. SODIUM DI-CHROMATE & SODIUM SULPHATE AS BYE PRODUCTS
539. SODIUM HEXA META PHOSPHATE
540. SODIUM HYDROSULFITE
541. SODIUM HYPO CHLORIDE (BLEACH LIQUOR)
542. SODIUM ISO-PROPYL XANTHATE
543. SODIUM LAURYL SULPHATE
544. SODIUM LAURYL SULPHATE & SODIUM LAURYL ETHER SULPHATE
545. SODIUM NITRATE
546. SODIUM PETROLEUM SULPHONATE (EMULSIFIER)
547. SODIUM SILICATE FROM SILICA & SODA ASH
548. SODIUM SILICATE FROM (1) PADDY SILK HUSK 2) & SILICA
549. SODIUM CARBONATE & SILICA
550. SODIUM SULPHATE
551. SODIUM SULPHIDE BY BARIUM SULPHATE PROCESS
552. SODIUM SULPHIDE FROM AMMONIA & SODIUM CHLORIDE
553. SODIUM SULPHITE
554. SODIUM TRI-POLY PHOSPHATE
555. SOFTENER (CATIONIC ANIONIC & NON-IONIC)
556. SPIRIT FROM PINE APPLE
557. STANNOUS CHLORIDE
558. STEARIC ACID
559. STEARATES MANUFACTURE (CALCIUM, ZINC, ALUMINIUM, MAGNESIUM STEARATES)
560. SULPHUR FROM PYRITES & SLAG
561. SULPHUR CRYSTALS/LUMPS
562. SULPHURIC ACID
563. SULPHURIC ACID FROM DCDA PROCESS
564. SUPER PHOSPHATE (S.S.P)
565. SYNTHETIC IRON OXIDE (YELLOW)
566. SYNTHETIC RED & WELLOW IRON OXIDE FROM IRON FILLING & PICKLE LIQUOR
567. TARTARIC ACID
568. TOILET CLEANER
569. TOLUENE AND SBP FROM

Above all the Detailed Project Reports are available at *"ENGINEERS INDIA RESEARCH INSTITUTE"*. 4449, Nai Sarak (D), Main Road Delhi - 110 006

● Ph : 91-11-23918117, 2391 6431, 23840361, 31082370 ● Fax : 91-11-2391 6431

● E-Mail : eirisidi@bol.net.in

CRUDE NAPHTHA
570. TRIMETHYL AMMONIUM CHLORIDE
571. TRIPHENYL PHOSPHITE (T.P.P)
572. ULTRAMARINE BLUE (LIQUID)
573. UREA FORMALDEHYDE & MELAMINE FORMALDEHYDE POWDER
574. UNDECYLINIC ACID
575. VINYL ACETATE MONOMER
576. VITAMIN C
577. VITAMIN E
578. WASTE WATER TREATMENT PLANT FOR INDUSTRIAL SECTOR IN INDIA (ONLY MARKER SURVEY)
579. WIRE DRAWING LUBRICANT
580. WIRE ENAMEL
581. XANTHATES
582. YELLOW DEXTRIN
583. ZINC CHLORIDE
584. ZINC OXIDE
585. ZINC PHOSPHATING BY COLD PROCESS
586. ZINC SILICATE
587. ZINC STEARATE
588. ZINC SULPHATE
589. ZINC SULPHATE MONOHYDRATE
590. ACID BLACK
591. AURAMINE'O'
592. AZO DYES STUFF
593. DYE & DYE INTERMEDIATE
594. DYE INTERMEDIATES
595. MALACHITE GREEN
596. METHYLENE BLUE
597. PHTHALOCYANINE BLUE
598. PHTHALOCYANINE BLUE & GREEN
599. REACTIVE DYES
600. SULPHUR BLACK DYE
601. VAT DYES
602. WATER CHILLING PLANT
603. WADDING OIL (100%) FOR WADDING OF COTTON HOSIERY CLOTH IN THE DYEING PROCESS
604. WHITE OIL
605. WAX FLOOR POLISH

ELECTRICAL, ELECTONICS, COMPUTERS AND INFOTECH/IT PROJECTS

606. AIR CONDITIONING
607. ALUMINIUM ALLOY CONDUCTOR
608. ALUMINIUM CABLE
609. ALUMINIUM ELECTROYTIC CAPACITORS
610. AUDIO CASSETTE ASSEMBLING & RECORDING
611. AUDIO CASSETTES DUPLICATING RECORDING
612. AUDIO CASSETTES & AUDIO STUDIO
613. AUDIO CASSETTES PLANE & RECORDED
614. AUDIO MAGNETIC HEADS
615. AUDIO MAGNETIC TAPE
616. AUDIO/VIDEO CASSETTES
617. AUTO BULB/LAMPS
618. AUTOMATIC VOLTAGE STABILIZER
619. BATTERY PLATES
620. BACK OFFICE (Rs. 5000/-)
621. B/W TV & COMPUTER MONITOR PICTURE TUBE
622. BREAD BOARDS
623. CALL CENTRE
624. CAMERA (35 MM)
625. CAPACITORS
626. CARBON ELECTRODE USED FOR BATTERY CELL
627. CARBON POTETIOMETERS
628. CEILING FAN
629. CERAMIC INSULATOR
630. CHILDREN INFOTECH TRAINING INSTITUTE (Rs. 5000/-)
631. CHOKE AND PATTI
632. CHOKE AND STARTER
633. CHOKE USED FOR FLUORESCENT LAMPS
634. COLOUR TELEVISION
635. COLOUR AND BLACK & WHITE TELEVISION
636. COMPACT DISC
637. COMPACT DISC PLAYER (AUDIO/VIDEO)
638. COMPUTER EDUCATION INSTITUTE
639. COMPUTER ASSEMBLY
640. COMPUTER HARDWARE
641. COMPUTER KEYBOARD
642. COMPUTER PERIPHERALS
643. COMPUTER PRINTERS
644. COMPUTER RIBBON
645. COMPUTER RIBBON REINKING OR REFILLING
646. COMPUTER STATIONERY
647. COMPUTER STATIONERY &

IMPORTED HARDWARE PARTS
648. COMPUTER TERMINALS
649. COMPUTERISED WASHING MACHINE (AUTOMATIC)
650. COMPUTER SOFTWARE
651. CONDENSER FOR MOTOR USING MPP FILM
652. CONTENT DEVELOPMENT CENTRE (EOU) (Rs. 5000/-)
653. CONTROL PANEL BOARD
654. COOLING COIL FOR AIR CONDITIONERS
655. COPPER STRIP COIL FROM SCRAP
656. CORDLESS TELEPHONES
657. CYBER CAFE
658. CYBERKIOSK (Rs. 5000/-)
659. DATA PROCESSING CENTRE (Rs. 5000/-)
660. D.C. MICRO MOTORS
661. D.G.SETS
662. DISH ANTENNA AND CABLE T.V. NETWORK EQUIPMENT
663. DISTRIBUTION TRANSFORMERS & REPAIRS
664. DOMESTIC ELECTRICAL APPLIANCES- ROOM COOLER, WASHING MACHINE, WATER HEATER, ELECTRIC ROOM HEATER
665. E-SCHOOL
666. E-COMMERCE/BUSINESS
667. ELECTRIC ENERGY METER
668. ELECTRIC FANS
669. ELECTRIC HORN FOR AUTOMOBILE
670. ELECTRIC LAMP/GLS (INCANDESCENT LAMP)
671. ELECTRIC MIXER
672. ELECTRIC MOTORS UP TO 10 HP. REWINDING OF ALL TYPES OF MOTORS WATER PUMPS
673. ELECTRIC MOTOR WINDING (FOR FAN, MIXIES, ETC.)
674. ELECTRIC STEAM IRON
675. ELECTRICAL APPLIANCES
676. ELECTRICAL FIXTURES
677. ELECTRICAL STAMPING
678. ELECTROLYTIC CAPACITORS
679. ELECTROMAGNETIC RELAY
680. ELECTRONIC BALAST/CHOK
681. ELECTRICAL CHOKE
682. ELECTRONIC DIGITAL WATCHES
683. ELECTRONIC DIGITAL WEIGHING MACHINE
684. ELECTRONIC FIRE ALARM
685. ELECTRONIC GAS STOVE LIGHTERS
686. ELECTRONIC PRESSURE INDICATORS, ELECTRICALS, ELECTRONIC LIQUID LEVEL INDICATORS, ELECTRONIC TEMPERATURE INDICATOR, DIGITAL TACHOMETER
687. ELECTRONIC TELEPHONE INSTRUMENTS
688. ELECTRONIC TOYS
689. ELECTRONIC WATCHES & CLOCKS
690. FAX MACHINES
691. F.H.P MOTORS
692. FLOPPY DISKETTES
693. FLUORESCENT LAMP STARTER
694. FLUORESCENT TUBULAR

Above all the Detailed Project Reports are available at *"ENGINEERS INDIA RESEARCH INSTITUTE"*. 4449, Nai Sarak (D), Main Road Delhi - 110 006

● Ph : 91-11- 23918117, 2391 6431, 23840361, 31082370 ●Fax : 91-11- 2391 6431

●E-Mail : eirisidi@bol.net.in

LAMPS WITH INTRODUCTION TO MERCURY VAPOUR LAMP
695. FRANCHISEE COMPUTER EDUCATION CENTRE (Rs. 5000)
696. GAS DETECTOR (L.P.G)
697. GENERATOR SET & PUMP SETS
698. GENERATOR (BATTERY OPERATED)
699. GIS SERVICE CENTRE (GEOGRAPHICAL INFORMATION SYSTEMS)
700. HARDWARE FITTING FOR TRANSMISSION LINE OVERHEAD LINE MATERIAL
701. HEADERS FOR TRANSISTOR ICS SEMI CONDUCTOR
702. H.T & L.T INSULATORS
703. H.T & M.V INDUSTRIAL CUBICAL SWITCH BOARD
704. INFORMATION MOVING DISPLAY (L.E.D TYPE)
705. INSURANCE CLAIM PROCESSING CENTRE (EOU) (Rs. 5000/-)
706. INTEGRATED CIRCUITS
707. INTERNET BASED STOCK TRADING (Rs. 5000/-)
708. INTERNET SERVICE PROVIDER (I.S.P.)
709. JELLY FILLED TELEPHONE CABLES
710. LAP TOP COMPUTERS
711. LEAD ACID BATTERIES
712. LEAD ACID BATTERY PLATES AND ASSEMBLING OF BATTERY
713. LEGAL TRANSCRIPTION & SECRETARIAL SERVICES CENTER (EOU)(Rs. 5000/-)
714. LIGHT EMITTING DIODES (L.E.D)
715. LINEAR ICS TRAINER KIT
716. LOUD SPEAKER
717. L.T TRANSFORMER REPAIRING
718. MEDICAL TRANSCRIPTION CENTRE
719. METAL FILM RESISTORS
720. METALLISED POLYPROPYLENE, POLYESTER FILM CAPACITOR
721. MICA BASE ELECTRONIC COMPONENTS
722. MICA PAPER WASTE PAPER FROM MICA WASTE
723. MICRO PROCESSORS TRAINER KITS BASED ON MICRO PROCESSORS
724. MINI COMPUTER (PERSONAL COMPUTER)
725. MINIATURE CIRCUIT BREAKER (M.C.B)
726. MINIATURE WATCH BATTERIES (BUTTON CELL)
727. MIXER/GRINDER (MIXI)
728. MONO CHROME COMPUTER MONITOR
729. MOTOR START ELECTROLYTIC CAPACITOR
730. MULTI LAYER P.C.B
731. MULTIPLE RELAY FOR LOW VOLTAGE
732. NEON INDICATOR
733. NEON SIGN MANUFACTURE
734. OPTICAL FIBRE CABLES
735. ON LINE SHOPPING MALL (Rs. 5000/-)
736. OPTO MECHANICAL & ELECTRICAL EQUIPMENTS
737. PHOTO COLOUR LAB
738. PICTURE TUBE (B/W)
739. PLAIN PAPER COPIER
740. PLASTIC FILM CAPACITORS
741. POLYESTER CAPACITORS
742. PORTABLE GENERATOR SET
743. PORTAL
744. PORTABLE TELEVISION(TV)
745. POWER CAPACITORS
746. POWER INVERTERS
747. POWER PLANT
748. POWER TRANSFORMERS UP TO 600 KVA
749. PRINTED CIRCUIT BOARD
750. PVC WIRES & CABLES
751. RE-CONDITIONING OF PICTURE TUBE
752. RESIN CAST CT & PT (1 KV)
753. SEMI CONDUCTOR DEVICE
754. SEMI CONDUCTORS FOR TRANSISTORS & DIODES
755. SETTING UP OF A VIDEO STUDIO
756. SMOKE DETECTORS
757. SOLAR CELLS
758. SOLAR MODULES
759. SOLAR PHOTO VOLTAIC SYSTEM
760. SOLDER FLUXES
761. SOLAR WATER HEATING PANELS
762. STEEL FURNITURE & ELECTRICAL APPLIANCES
763. STEREO AMPLIFIERS
764. STEREO CASSETTE RECORDERS/PLAYERS
765. STREET LIGHT FITTINGS SURGE SUPPRESSOR
766. TANTALUM CAPACITORS
767. TEFLON COATED ELECTRIC CABLE
768. TELEMEDICINE (DISTANCE HEALTH CARE) (Rs. 5000/-)
769. TELEPHONE CORD/CABLE
770. TELEPHONE (PUSH BUTTON TYPE)
771. TELEPHONE (PUSH BUTTON & CORDLESS)
772. TELEVISION (CTV & B/W)
773. TELEVISION (3-D)
774. TELEVISION DEFLECTION COMPONENTS
775. TELEVISION SIGNAL BOOSTERS
776. TELEVISION TUNERS
777. TRACTION BATTERIES
778. TRAINING INSTITUTE OF MEDICAL TRANSCRIPTION
779. TRANSFORMER FOR B/W TV
780. TRANSFORMER FOR VOLTAGE STABILIZER & E.H.T
781. TRANSMISSION POWER LINE FITTING
782. TRANSMISSION TOWER FITTING
783. TV AUDIO EQUIPMENT CABINETS & THEIR ASSEMBLING UNIT
784. UN-INTERRUPTED POWER SUPPLY (U.P.S)
785. VARIABLE FREQUENCY
786. VARIABLE VOLTAGE A.C. DRIVE
787. VIDEO CASSETTES (COMPLETE MANUFACTURING & ASSEMBLING)
788. VIDEO CASSETTES RECORDER (V.C.R)
789. VIDEO FILM STUDIO
790. VOLTAGE REGULATOR FOR AUTOMOBILES
791. VOLTAGE STABILIZERS
792. VOLTAGE STABLIZER & T.V. GAIN BOOSTER
793. WAX AND CHEMICAL COATED, BRAIDED TINSEL WIRE
794. WEBSITE DESIGN & E-MAIL REGISTERING
795. WELDING ELECTRODES
796. WIND ENERGY POWER PROJECT (10 MW)
796A WIRES (METAL)

FOOD, AGRO FOOD, PROCESSED FOOD, AGRO PLANTATION, CULTIVATION, FARMING, DAIRY/MILK, TOBACCO/PAN MASALA, BREWERY & DISTILLERY, EDIBLE OILS, EOU FOOD PRODUCTS AND ALLIED PRODUCTS

797. ALCOHOLIC BEVERAGES & VENEGAR FROM COCONUT WATER
798. ALCOHOL DRINKS FROM ETHYL ALCOHOL BY MIXING OF VARIOUS FLAVOURS
799. ANTI SCALE COMPOUND FOR ADDING INTO SUGAR JUICE BOILING
800. APPLE JUICE CONCENTRATED & DEHYDRATED FRUIT & VEGETABLES
801. ARTIFICIAL FISH MEAL FOR POULTRY FEED
802. AUTOMATIC BISCUIT PLANT
803. BABY CEREAL FOOD AND MILK POWDER
804. BACTERIA FOR CANE JUICE
805. BAKER'S YEAST
806. BAKERY INDUSTRY
807. BANANA PUREE
808. BEER & WINE
809. BEER PLANT (BREWERY)
810. BIDI
811. BIDI & CIGARETTE
812. BISCUIT PLANT

813. BREAD (AUTOMATIC PLANT)
814. BLACK PEPPER (SPICES)
815. BREAD AND BISCUITS
816. BREEDING FARM
817. BROILER CHICKEN
819. BUTTON MUSHROOM CULTIVATION & PROCESSING
820. CANNING OF RASAGULLAS IN METAL CANS
821. CAFFEIN FROM TEA WASTE
822. CANNING OF FRUITS & VEGETABLES
823. CASEIN AND BY-PRODUCTS
824. CASHEW FRUIT JUICE FROM CASHEW FRUIT APPLE
825. CASHEWNUT KERNEL EXTRACTION FROM CASHEWNUT FRUIT
826. CASHEWNUT SHELL LIQUID & KERNEL PROCESSING
827. CASHEW FENI
828. CATECHEU (BY CHEMICAL PROCESS)
829. CATTLE FEED FROM TAPIOCA
830. CHEWING & BUBBLE GUM
831. CHICKEN/SHEEP MEAT PROCESSING
832. CHOCOLATE (MILK)
833. CIGARETTE AND BEEDIES
834. COCOA BUTTER FROM COCOA MASS
835. COCONUT PRODUCTS & BY PRODUCTS PROCESS COMPLEX
836. COLD/SOFT DRINKS
837. COLLECTION OF MILK AND MILK MAKING POWDER
838. COLLECTION OF MILK AND PACKING IN POLYTHENE POUCH (1/2 KG.1 KG. & 2 KG.)
839. CONDENSED MILK (SWEETNED)
840. CONFECTIONERY INDUSTRY (TOFFEE & CANDY, SEMI-AUTOMATIC PLANT)
841. COUNTRY LIQUOR FROM MOLASSES
842. CIGARETTE
843. DAIRY FARM AND DAIRY (MILK) PRODUCTS (PASTEURISED MILK, BUTTER, GHEE, PANEER)
844. DAIRY FARM TO PRODUCE MILK & PACKING IN POUCHES (50%) & CAN(50%)
845. DAIRY FOR MILK PROCESSING
846. DAIRY FARM (BUFALO)
847. DAL (PULSE) MILL UNIT
848. DEHYDRATION OF CARROT & GARLIC
849. DEHYDRATION & CANNING OF FRUITS & VEGETABLES
850. DEHYDRATION OF FIGS
851. DEHYDRATION OF FRUITS AND VEGETABLES
852. DEHYDRATED ONIONS AND ONION POWDER
853. DRY ICE BY BREAKING OF AIR
854. DRYING OF RED CHILLIES, HALDI, DHANIA, AND GREEN PEAS
855. EGG POWDER (40,000 EGGS PROCESSING PER DAY)
856. EXPORT OF PROCESSED FOODS AND MARINE PRODUCTS
857. FISH CANNING & POUCHING
859. FISH FARMING (PRAWN & OTHER MARINE PRODUCTS)
860. FISH MEAL
861. FLOUR MILL AND MUSTARD OIL
862. FOOD COLOUR & ORASTED GROUNDNUT GRAM PEAS, ETC IN POUCHES
863. FROG LEGS PROCESSING
864. FROZEN MEATS PROCESSING
865. FOOD FLAVOURS (WHISKY) VODKA, GRAPE, BUTTER SCOTCH)
866. FOOD PRODUCTS COMPLEX (DEHYDRATED ONIONS, GARLIC POWDER & FLAKES, CATTLE FEED, TOMATO POWDER, TOMATO PRODUCTS, CANNED FRUITS & VEGETABLES, TOMATO PURE, GROUN NUT OIL, REFIND OIL, DEHYDRATED GRAPES, BANANA POWDER & WAFFERS)
867. FRUIT JUICE, JAM, JELLIES & ALLIED PRODUCTS
868. FRUIT JUICE, PICKLES PROCESSING AND CANNING
869. FRUIT JUICE MAKING & PACKING IN PLASTIC CONTAINER/POUCHES
870. FRUIT PROCESSING (JAM & JELLIES)
871. FRUIT PULP & JUICE CONCENTRATES
872. FRUIT & VEGETABLE DRYING (FREEZE DRYING METHOD)
873. GOAT & SHEEP FARMING
874. GRAM DALL/PULSE MILL
875. GRAPE DEHYDRATION
876. HARD BOILED CANDY (TOFFEE & CANDY)
877. HERBAL CIGARETTES
878. HONEY PROCESSING & PACKAGING
879. ICE CREAM OF DIFFERENT FLAVOURS
880. ICE CREAM STABILIZER
881. ICE MAKING PLANT
882. INDIAN MADE FOREIGN LIQUOR (I.M.F.L)
883. INSTANT FOOD (IDLI MIX, DOSA MIX, GULAB JAMUN MIX)
884. INSTANT FOOD (INSTANT FOOD & FAST FOOD PARLOUR)
885. INSTANT NOODLES
886. INSTANT TEA
887. INSTANT TEA FROM BLACK TEA
888. INTEGERATED STARCH BAKING POWDER/YEAST INDUSTRY
889. IODIZED SALT
890. IODIZED SALT (ORDINARY MOISTURE-LESS/FREE FLOWING IN PLASTIC BAGS AND CONTAINERS)
891. JAM, JELLIES, FRUIT JUICE & ALLIED PRODUCTS
892. KATHA AND CUTCH
893. KHANDSARI SUGAR
894. KHANDSARI SUGAR & IMFL
895. LACTIC ACID FROM WHITE SUGAR BY FERMENTATION PROCESS
896. LACTOSE & BY PRODUCTS PROCESSING FROM MILK
897. LIQUID GLUCOSE AND ITS BYE PRODUCTS
898. MACRONI AND VERMICILLI
899. MALT EXTRACTION FROM BARLEY
900. MANGO PROCESSING (MANGO PULP, JUICE & SLICES)
901. MAYUR BRAND TYPE CHEWING TOBACCO
902. MINERAL WATER
903. MILK PRESERVATION & MARKETING TO WHOLE SELLERS (INPOUCH PACKING BY UHT TECHNOLOGY)
904. MILK PROCESSING AND PACKAGING OF MILK PRODUCTS
905. MILK PRODUCTS (CASEIN, LACTOSE, GHEE & WHEY POWDER)
906. MILK TOFFEE
907. MINI FLOUR MILL
908. MINI SUGAR PLANT
909. MISRI (PEARL SUGAR CANDIES)
910. MODERN RICE MILL
911. MURABBA
912. MUSTARD OIL EXTRACTION & REFINING
913. MUTTON TALLOW
914. NAMKEEN INDUSTRY (BHUJIA, CHANA CHUR ETC.)
915. NAMKEEN & SWEETS
916. NON-BASMATI RICE FROM PADDY
917. OLEORESIN, ESSENTIAL OIL, DYES & POWDER OF SPICES
918. OLEORESIN EXTRACTION FROM DIPTERO-CARPUT TURMINATUS AND PINUS KHASYANA
919. OLEORESIN EXTRACTION FROM CHILLI
920. PAN MASALA AND POUCH

Apart from the above mentioned reports EIRI is also having other most lucrative projects (as many as 30,000). You just name it and we have that report.

MAKING
921. PAN MASALA, TOBACCO, ZARDA & KIMAM
922. PANEER FROM MILK
923. PAPPAD PLANT
924. PAPAIN FROM PAPAYA (PAPAYA LATEX)
925. PECTIN FROM MANGO PEEL PECTIN FROM APPLE POMACE
926. PHYTO TEA (HERBAL TEA)
927. PICKLES AND SAUCES
928. PICKLES MURABBA ETC. (VEG. & NON. VEG.PICKLES)
929. PIGGERY MEAT PROCESS
930. PINE-APPLE JUICE PREPARATION & PACKAGING
931. POTATO CHIPS/WAFFERS
932. POTATO POWDER
933. POUCH FILLING & PACKAGING OF EDIBLE OIL & GHEE
934. POULTRY FEED
935. PROCESSED FOODS & SPICES (EOU)
936. PROCESSED READYMADE FOOD
937. PROCESSING OF FRUITS & VEGETABLES
938. RABBIT FARMING
939. RASGULLAS MAKING & CANNING IN METAL CANS
940. READY TO EAT PROCESSED COOKED FOOD
941. READY TO EAT SNACK FOOD (CRAX, ROLL & BALL TYPE)
942. RICE & CORN FLAKES
943. ROASTED/SALTED/ MASALA, CASHEW NUTS, ALMONDS & PEANUTS
944. ROLLER FLOUR MILL
945. SALT LICKS FOR CATTLE
946. SAUSAGES FOOD CASING
947. SOFT DRINKS
948. SOFT DRINKS ESSENCES
949. SOFT DRINKS (NON CARBONATED) MANGO, LICCHI, PINEAPPLE FLAVOURS FROOTI TYPE IN TETRAPACK)
950. SOFTY ICE CREAM CONES (FULLY AUTOMATIC)
951. SOFT/COLD DRINKS (COLA, ORANGE, LEMON ETC. FLAVOURS)
952. SOYABEAN PRODUCTS
953. SOYA MILK & PANEER
954. STARCH & ALLIED PROPDUCT FROM BROKEN RICE
955. STRAWBERRY CULTIVATION & PROCESSING
956. SUGARCANE JUICE PRESERVATION
957. SUGAR CUBES FROM CANE SUGAR
988. SUGAR PLANT
989. SWEET AROMA BETEL NUT
990. SYNTHETIC TALLOW
991. TAMARIND JUICE POWDER
992. TEA & COFFEE PROCESSING & PACKAGING
993. TOFFEES, GOLIES, CANDY (HARD BOILED)
994. TOMATO PRODUCTS
994. TRADING BUSINESS OF SPICES & PAN MASALA
995. TUITY FRUITY
996. VODKA FROM POTATOES
997. WINE, BRANDY, WHISKY & CHAMPAGNE
997. WINE FROM DATES
998. YEAST FROM MOLASSES
999. ZARDA, KIMAM NO. 60,90,120,160,240,300 & 400 (TOBACCO)
1000. ZARDA-ZAFRANI (BABACHHAP TYPE)

GUMS & ADHESIVE

1001. ACRYLIC ADHESIVE
1002. ADHESIVE (FEVICOL TYPE)
1003. ADHESIVE BASED ON POLYURETHANE
1004. ADHESIVE FOR BAND AID (JOHNSON & JOHNSON TYPE)
1005. ADHESIVE INDUSTRIES (LAMINATED, STICKER, DDL & OTHER TYPES)
1006. ADHESIVE FOR GASKET (LIQUID/PASTE)
1007. GUAR GUM
1008. GUM BOTTLE (PVC)
1009. GUM FOR PASTING LABELS
1010. OFFICE PASTE
1011. RUBBER ADHESIVE
1012. SURGICAL ADHESIVE PLASTER

LEATHER & LEATHER PRODUCTS

1013. HANDMADE LEATHER
1014. LEATHER AUXILLARIES & CHEMICALS
1015. LEATHER DYES
1016. LEATHER WASHERS
1017. LEATHER BOARD FROM LEATHER WASTE
1018. LEATHER FOR UPHOLSTRY (SOFA)
1019. LEATHER GARMENTS
1020. LEATHER GOODS
1021. LEATHER SHOES
1022. LEATHER SHOE & CHAPPAL
1023. LEATHER SUITCASES, BRIEFCASES & TRAVELLING BAGS
1024. LEATHER GOODS AND GARMENTS
1025. LEATHER GARMENTS, SHOE & CHAPPAL
1026. LEATHER TANNING
1027. LEATHER TANNING & GARMENTS (EOU)
1028. SHEEP SKIN PICKLING PLANT
1029. SHOE UPPER
1030. SPORT SHOES (PLASTIC)

MISCELLANEOUS PRODUCTS

1031. AGARBATTI (INSENCE STICK)
1032. AGARBATTI (Mosquito Repellent)
1033. AGARBATI BAMBOO STICK
1034. AGARBATTI SYNTHETIC PERFUMERY COMPOUND
1035. AIR FRESHNER (ODONIL TYPE)
1036. AIR TAXI
1037. AMUSEMENT PARK
1038. ANODIC ALUMINIUM LABEL
1039. AQUACULTURE PRAWN FARMING (100% EOU)
1040. AQUA CULTURE SHRIMP FARMING (100% EOU)
1041. ARTIFICIAL FLOWERS
1042. ARTIFICIAL JEWELLERY
1043. ASBESTOS YARN
1044. ASH TRAYS FOR MARUTI VEHICLE
1045. AIR BUBBLE PACKAGING
1046. ASPHALTIC ROOFING SHEET (METAL COMPONENTS)
1047. AUTOMATIC BOOK BINDING
1048. ALKYD RESIN
1049. APPLE JUICE CONCENTRATE
1050. BALL POINT PEN FEFILLS (JOTTER TYPE)
1051. BANK BRANCH BUILDING
1052. BANQUET HALL
1053. BIO-COAL BRIQUETTES FROM AGRICULTURAL CELLULOSE WASTE
1054. BOOT CREAM/POLISH
1055. BUFFING & POLISHING COMPOUND
1056. BRASS BADGES BY ETCHING
1057. BRIQUETTED FUEL FROM AGRO WASTE
1058. BRIQUETTING OF LIGNITE COAL

Above all the Detailed Project Reports are available at *"ENGINEERS INDIA RESEARCH INSTITUTE"*. 4449, Nai Sarak (D), Main Road Delhi - 110 006

● Ph : 91-11-23918117, 2391 6431, 23840361, 31082370 ●Fax : 91-11-2391 6431

●E-Mail : eirisidi@bol.net.in

1193. CANDLES (SEMI-AUTOMATIC)
1194. CORN OIL (MAIZE OIL)
1195. DEHYDRATED CASTOR OIL
1196. EUGENOL FROM CINNAMON LEAF OIL
1197. EXTRACTION OF ESSENTIAL OIL (CARDAMON, JEERA, AJOWAN, GINGER OILS ETC. & PACKAGING OF GROUND SPICES)
1198. EXTRACTION OF JASMINE ESSENCE
1199. EXTRACTION OF ESSENTIAL OILS BY SUPER CRITICAL FLUID METHOD FROM FLOWERS, HERBS & SPICES
1200. EUCALYPTUS OIL
1201. EXTRACTION OF OIL FROM OIL SEED EXPANDEREXTRUSION TECHNOLOGY)
1202. FAT LIQUOR SULPHATED OIL
1203. FLAVOURS FOR FOOD
1204. GARLIC OIL & POWDER
1205. GINGER OIL, SANDALWOOD OIL AND NAGARMOTHA OIL
1206. GINGER OIL
1207. GINGER OIL & GINGER DUST
1208. INTEGERATED WAX COMPLEX
1209. IONONE FROM LEMON GRASS OIL
1210. JASMINE & LILLY FLOWER OIL
1211. LEMON GRASS OIL
1212. LIQUID PARAFFIN
1213. LUBE OIL & GREASE
1214. LUBRICATING OIL
1215. MENTHOL CRYSTALS
1216. MENTHOL OIL & CRYSTAL
1217. MICRO CRYSTALLINE WAX
1218. MUSTARD OIL (EDIBLE OIL)
1219. OIL FROM ARTEMISIA HERBS
1220. PALM OIL CRUSHING UNIT
1221. PAN MASALA
1222. PARAFFIN WAX
1223. PARAFFIN WAX FROM SLACK WAX
1224. REFINED OIL-SUN FLOWER OIL, GROUNDNUT OIL, STAFF FLOWER OIL & COTTON SEED OIL
1225. REFINED VEGETABLE OIL
1226. RECLAMATION OF USED ENGINE OIL
1227. RICE BRAN OIL (R.B.O)
1228. ROSE OIL EXTRACTION
1229. SMOKE LESS CANDLE
1230. SPICE OIL & OLEORESINS
1231. SOLVENT EXTRACTION PLANT (OIL CAKE BASED)
1232. SYNTHETIC ALMOND OIL
1233. SYNTHETIC TALLOW
1234. SYNTHETIC GHEE
1235. VEGETABLE OIL EXTRACTION & REFINING
1236. WADDING OIL (100%) FOR WADDING OF COTTON HOSIERY CLOTH IN DYEING PROCESS
1237. WAX EMULSION FOR TEXTILE
1238. WAX FLOOR POLISH

PAINT, ENAMEL, SOLVENTS, THINNERS, INKS & VARNISH

1239. ACRYLIC EMULSION PAINTS
1240. ALUMINIUM PAINT
1241. AUTOMOBILE PAINTS
1242. BALL POINT PEN REFILL INK
1243. BITUMINIOUS ROAD EMULSION
1244. BITUMEN
1245. BITUMINIOUS FELTS FOR WATER & DAMP PROOFING
1246. BITUMINIOUS ROAD EMULSION RAPID MEDIUM & SLOW SETTING
1247. BUFFING & POLISHING
1248. CEMENT PAINT FOR WHITE & GREY CEMENT

1249. DISPERSANT
1250. DRY DISTEMPER
1251. DRY DISTEMPER & CEMENT PAINT
1252. DUPLICATING INK BLACK FOR GESTNER DUPLICATOR
1255. EMULSION PAINTS (WATER BASED)
1256. HAMMERTONE PAINT
1257. INSULATING VARNISH & WIRE ENAMEL
1258. IRON OXIDE PIGMENTS
1259. INSULATING VARNISH (POLY VINYL BUTYRAL BASED, FFC GRADE)
1260. LIME COLOUR (CEMENT COLOUR)
1261. SYNTHETIC RED OXIDE FOR FLOORINGS
1262. SOLVENT & THINNERS
1263. MARKING INKS (WATER PROOF)
1264. METAL NAPHTHANATE (AS DRIER FOR PAINTS)
1265. N.C.PUTTY
1266. OFFSET PRINTING INK
1267. OIL BOUND DISTEMPER PAINT
1268. PAINT BRUSHES
1269. PAINT REMOVERS
1270. PAINT INDUSTRY
1271. PAINT & VARNISH
1272. PICTURE VARNISH
1273. POWDER COATING PAINT
1274. PRINTING INKS (OFFSET, FLEXO & ROTO GRAVURE)
1275. PRIMER PAINT & ENAMEL PAINT
1276. PUTTY & WATER PROOFING PAINT
1277. PRINTING INKS (FLEXO-GRAPHIC INK)
1278. PUTTY (METAL CASEMENT)
1279. RED OXIDE PRIMER (ANTI CORROSIVE)
1280. REFRECTORY PAINT (GRAPHITE BASED)
1281. SCREEN PRINTING INKS
1282. SILK SCREEN PRINTING INK FORMULATION FOR PLASTIC, PAPER, CLOTH
1283. STAMP & PAD INK
1284. STOVING PAINT
1285. SPIRIT SOLUBLE MALEIC RESIN
1286. TEXTURE PAINT
1287. THINNERS AND ITS ALLIED PRODUCTS
1288. TONER INK
1289. VARNISH THINNER (SOLVENT)
1290. VACUUM METALLIZING LACQUERS
1291. WOOD PRIMER

PHARMACEUTICAL, DRUGS, AYURVEDIC/HERBAL COSMETICS & MEDICINES, HOMOEOPATHIC MEDICINES, DISPOSABLE SYRINGE, DENTAL COLLEGE & FINE CHEMICALS ETC.

1292. AROMATIC PILLS
1293. ASPIRIN
1294. AYURVEDIC PAIN BALM OINTMENTS
1295. AYURVEDIC CHURAN AND TABLETS
1296. AYURVEDIC TABLETS (HAJMOLA TYPE)
1297. AYURVEDIC/HERBAL PHARMACY
1298. AYURVEDIC SHERBATS
1299. AYURVEDIC PRODUCTS
1300. BULK DRUGS (E.O.U)
1301. BLOOD BAGS
1302. CALCIUM GLUCONATE
1303. CAPSULE, TABLET & INJECTION WITH MODERN INSTRUMENTS
1304. CASHEW FENI
1305. CHLOROQUINONE PHOSPHATE (BULK DRUGS)
1306. CLINICAL THERMOMETER
1307. DENTAL CLINIC

1308. DENTAL COLLEGE
1309. DENTAL GRADE EUGENOL
1310. DEXTROSE MONOHYDRATE, LIQUID GLUCOSE
1311. DEHYDRATED ONION & ONION POWDER
1312. DEXTROSE POWDER (ANHYDROUS FROM STARCH)
1314. DEXTROSE SALINE SOLUTION
1315. DISTILLERY (I.M.F.L)
1316. DISPOSABLE NEEDLES FOR SYRINGES
1317. DISPRIN
1318. DISTILLED WATER
1319. EMPTY HARD GELATINE CAPSULES
1320. FILLING & PACKING OF CAPSULES
1321. GLUCOSE - D - POWDER
1322. GLYCERINE
1323. HERBAL COSMETICS
1324. HERBAL SHAMPOO
1325. HERBAL HAIR OILS (AYURVEDIC)
1326. HOMOE & BIO-MEDICINES WITH MOTHER TINCTURE
1327. HOMOEPATHIC MEDICINES
1328. HYPODERMIC NEEDLES
1329. I.V. FLUIDS
1330. IBUPROFEN
1331. INFUSION & TRANSFUSION SETS (I.V. SET)
1332. INJECTABLE FOR PHARMACEUTICALS
1333. INJECTION AMPOULES PACKAGING BOX
1334. INTEGERATED SURGICAL COTTON
1335. ICE MAKING PLANT
1336. ICE & COLD STORAGE
1337. LACTOSE & BY PRODUCTS PROCESSING FROM MILK
1338. LICHEN (JATAMANSI CHARILA)
1339. LIQUID GLUCOSE AND ITS BY-PRODUCTS
1340. L-LYSINE MONOHYDRO CHLORIDE
1341. LIQUID GLUCOSE FROM POTATOES
1342. MEDICAL COLLEGE
1343. NICOTINE FROM TOBACCO WASTE
1344. OINTMENT-AYURVEDIC (YELLOW & WHITE)
1345. PHARMACEUTICAL AND FOOD GRADE GELATINE
1346. PHARMACEUTICAL INDUSTRY (TABLETS, CAPSULES, LIQUID, GEL, OINTMENT POWDER INJECTABLE)
1347. PHARMACEUTICAL UNIT (EOU) WITH FORMULA TIONS, INJECTABLES, ETC. PYRIDINE & DERIVATIVES
1348. SALT (IODIZED SALT)
1349. SALINE & INJECTION WATER
1350. SALINE WATER & DEXTROSE SOLUTION (I.V.FLUID IN PLASTIC BOTTLES)
1351. SORBITOL
1352. STARCH (MAIZE)
1353. SURGICAL ADHESIVE PLASTER
1354. SURGICAL BANDAGES
1355. SURGICAL GLOVES
1357. SURGICAL COTTON
1358. SURGICAL COTTON AND BANDAGE
1359. SYNTHETIC CAMPHOR POWDER
1360. TABLETS & CAPSULES
1361. TISSUE CULTURE
1362. TINCTURE FROM RECTIFIED SPIRIT
1363. TRIMETHOPIME
1364. VETERENARY MEDICINES (ONLY FORMULATIONS)
1365. VITAMIN 'C', SORBITOL' ANHYDROUS DEXTROSE, STARCH

PULP, PAPER, STRAW/GREY BOARD, KRAFT PAPER, PACKAGING, PAPER CARRY BAGE, PAPER FROM AGRO WASTE & STATIONERY ETC.

1366. AMMONIA PAPER
1367. AUTOMATIC BOOK BINDING
1368. ADHESIVE (FEVICOL TYPE)
1369. ALL PIN & GEM CLIPS
1370. CARBON PAPER
1371. CARD BOARD
1372. CARBON LESS PAPER
1373. CELLPHANE PAPER
1374. COMPUTER FORMS & SECURITY PRINTING PRESS
1375. CORRUGATED BOARD & BOX (PRINTED & LAMINATED)
1376. CORRUGATED BOARD AND BOXES FROM FROM CARD BOARDS
1377. CORRUGATED CARTONS FROM PLAIN PAPERS
1378. CORRUGATRED PACKING & MATERIAL (BULB & TUBES PACKING)
1379. DESK TOP PUBLISHING
1380. DEFOAMING AGENT FOR PAPER PLANT
1381. DRINKING STRAW PAPER
1382. D.T.P CUM OFFSET PRESS
1383. EGG TRAYS
1384. EXERCISE NOTE BOOK, REGISTER AND PAD
1385. FLEXOGRAPHIC INK
1386. GREETING CARD BY OFFSET PRESS
1387. HAND MADE PAPER FILTER PAPER
1388. HARD BOARD
1389. INJECTION AMPOULES PACKAGING BOXES
1390. INSULATIING PAPER
1391. KRAFT PAPER
1392. KRAFT PAPER FROM BAGASSE
1393. LAMINATED PACKAGING PAPER WITH PRINTING
1394. LAMINATION & COATING ON PAPER
1395. M.G. PAPER FROM WASTE PAPER
1396. MILL PAPER FROM WASTE PAPER
1397. MILL BOARD FROM RICE & WHEAT STRAWS
1398. MILL BOARD FROM WASTE PAPER
1399. MINI PAPER PLANT FROM SISAL
1400. MINI PAPER PLANT
1401. MULTI WALL PAPER SACKS
1402. NEWS PAPER FOR CHILDREN
1403. NEWS PRINT PAPER FROM RICE STRAW BAGASSE
1404. NEWS PAPER CHILDRENS
1405. NEWS PRINT PAPER
1406. OFFSET AND TREADLE TYPE PRINTING PRESS
1407. MILL BOARD BASED ON RICE STRAW
1408. PAPER AND BOARD FROM STRAW
1409. PAPER & PAPER PRODUCTS
1410. PAPER ENVELOPES
1411. PAPER CARRY BAGS
1412. PAPER BOARD CARTON
1413. PAPER CONES FOR LOUD SPEAKERS
1414. PAPER FROM AKRA
1415. PAPER FROM BAGASSE WITH CORRUGATED BOARD & BOXES
1416. PAPER FROM BAMBOO
1417. PAPER GLASSES FOR BEVERAGES
1418. PAPER FROM RICE HUSK & WHEAT HUSK
1419. PAPER FROM TREE BARK, EUCALYPRUS WOOD
1420. PAPER PRODUCTS
1421. PAPER PLANT (WHITE WRITING & NEWS PAPER FOR PULP & WASTE PAPER)
1422. PAPER PLATES, PAPER GLASS
1423. PAPER CONES & TUBES
1425. PAPER PLANT WITH DTP & PRINTING & PUBLISHING UNIT
1426. PAPER BASED PHENOLIC SHEET
1427. PAPER CUP FOR ICE CREAM
1428. PAPER TUBES SPIRAL WINDING COMPOSIT CONTAINER
1429. PAPER LABLE FOR BEER BOTTLES
1430. PARTICLE BOARD & BLACK BOARD WITH SANDING & LAMINATION OF PARTICLE BOARD
1431. PARTICLE BOARD FROM RICE HUSK
1432. POUCH FILLING & MAKING FOR TOMATO SAUCE
1433. POUCH MAKING &

GRAVURE PRINTING
1434. PROCESSING OF PAPER FOR FEEDING IN COMPUTER
1435. PULP FROM BAMBOO & WOOD
1436. PAPER FILES
1437. PLAYING CARDS
1438. ROSIN SIZING AGENT (FOR PAPER PLANT)
1439. SAND PAPER
1440. SANITRY NAPKINS
1441. SILICON COATED PAPER
1442. STENCIL PAPER
1443. STRAW BOARD AND GREY BOARD
1444. STRAW BOARD & MILL BOARD
1445. STRAW BOARD AND PAPER BOARD
1446. TISSUE PAPER FACIAL
1447. TISSUE MOIST TOILETERY CLEANSING TISSUE AND RELATED PRODUCTS
1448. TISSUE PAPER ROLLS
1449. TETRA PACK FOR MILK PACKAGING, GHEE & OTHER LIQUIDS
1450. TOILET PAPER ROLLS
1451. TOILET PAPER & NAPKINS
1452. WAX COATED PRINTED PAPER
1453. WET FACE FRESHNER TISSUE
1454. WHITE WRITING & PRINTING PAPER
1455. WRITING & PRINTING PAPER (PAPER MILLS)

PLASTIC, B.O.P.P, ACRYLIC, DISPOSABLE PLASTIC PRODUCTS, PET PRODUCTS, P.V.C, H.D.P.E, P.P, L.D.P.E., P.U, A.B.S, THERMOFOARMING, MASTER BATCHES, & POLYMER AND RUBBER PRODUCTS, TYRE, TUBE, ADHESIVE, SHEET, COIR & MANY OTHERS

1456. ABS GRANULES FROM ABS SCRAPS FROM OLD T.V. CABINETS, WHITE GOODS ETC.
1457. ACRYLIC BEADS
1458. ACRYLIC COPOLYMER EMULSION
1459. ACRYLIC LATEX
1460. ACRYLIC SHEET
1461. ACRYLIC SHEET & MOULDED PRODUCTS
1462. ACRYLIC TEETH
1463. AUTO TUBES
1464. AUTO FLAPS FOR TRUCKS & BUSES
1465. AUTO TYRES & TUBES
1466. BABY BOTTLES (PLASTIC) WITH WHITESILICON RUBBER NIPPLES
1467. B.O.P.P. FILM
1468. B.O.P.P. PRESSURE SENSITIVE SELF ADHESIVE TAPE
1469. BABY NIPPLE (SILICON)
1470. BABY NIPPLE (BIG SIZE)
1471. BALLOON PLASTIC ADVERTISING
1472. BLISTER FILM PVC
1473. BLISTER PACKAGING & POUCH PAKAGING
1474. BLOW MOULDING PLASTIC CONTAINER
1475. COATING ON METALIZED POLYESTER FILM/METALISED PAPER/ ALIMINIUM FOIL
1476. COATING ON PLASTIC (ELECTROLYSIS) & GLASS
1477. COIR FOAM (RUBBERISED)
1478. COLOUR COATING ON PLASTICS
1479. COLOUR MASTER BATCHES FOR VARIOUS PLASTICS
1480. CYCLE TYRES AND TUBES
1481. DISPOSABLE PLASTIC CUPS GLASSES, ETC.
1482. DISPOSABLE PLASTIC SYRINGES & NEEDLES
1483. DISPOSABLE PLASTIC SYRINGES
1484. DOUGH MOULDING COMPOUND (D.M.C)
1485. EPOXY RESIN
1486. EXPANDED POLYESTRENE MOULDING (THERMOCOLE)
1487. F.R.P AUTO,SCOOTER ROOFS & CEILINGS
1488. F.R.P PRODUCTS (HELMET, WASHBASIN SHEETS, ROOFING SHEETS)
1489. FIBRE REINFORCED PLASTIC (HIGH PRESSURE MOULDING WITH SMC BMC AND DMC)
1490. FIELD RUBBER CONVERTED TO THE 60% LATEX RUBBER
1491. FLEXIBLE P.U. FOAM
1492. FORMALDEHYDE CROCKERY & OTHER ITEMS
1493. FORMALDEHYDE RESIN (UREA, PHENOL,MELEMINE)
1494. GASKET SHEET
1495. GUM BOTTLE (PVC)
1496. GLASS BEADS
1497. HDPE COATED PAPER SACK
1498. H.D.P.E. BAGS
1499. H.D.P.E. CONTAINERS (BLOW MOULDING)
1500. H.D.P.E. CONTAINER, POLY JARS BY INJECTION MOULDING (FOOD GRADE)
1501. H.D.P.E. JERRY CANS
1502. HDPE MANUFACTURING FROM ETHYLALCOHOL
1503. H.D.P.E PIPE AND FITTINGS
1504. H.D.P.E. PIPES
1505. H.D.P.E PRINTED BAGS
1506. H.D.P.E TWINES AND ROPES
1507. H.D.P.E. & L.D.P.E PIPES AND FITTINGS
1508. H.D.P.E/PP BOX STRAPPING
1509. H.D.P.E/PP WOVEN SACKS
USING PLAIN LOOMS
1510. HOLOGRAM STICKERS-3D
1511. H.M BAG PLANT WITH PRINTING UNIT
1512. HAWAI CHAPPALS (RUBBER)
1513. I.V PLASTIC BOTTLE
1514. ICE CREAM CUP (PLASTIC)
1515. INJECTION MOULDED AUTO COMPONENTS
1516. INJECTION & BLOW MOULDED PLASTIC PRODUCTS
1517. INJECTION MOULDED PLASTIC PRODUCTS
1518. INTEGERATED COMPLEX ESTER'S & ALLIED PRODUCTS (D.O.P,D.B.P, & ETHYL ACETATE, BUYTL ACETATE, WIRE ENAMELS, JELLY CABLE COMPOUND)
1519. L.D.P.E. (LOW DENSITY POLY ETHYLENE) GRANULES FROM VIRGIN (L.D.P.E. RESIN)
1520. INTEGERATED SURGICAL RUBBER GOODS INDUSTRY
1521. INJECTION MOULDED PLASTIC BALLS
1522. L.D.P.E FROM ETHYL ALCOHOL
1523. LDPE MOULDED PRODUCTS
1524. LAMINATION OF COEXTRUSION MULTILAYER FILM IN ROLL FORM
1525. LATEX RUBBER
1526. LATEX RUBBER CONDOM
1527. MASTER BATCHES (COLOURED, P.V.C, L.D.P.E, H.D.P.E, ETC.)
1528. MELAMINE FORMALHYDE RESIN
1529. MOULDED LUGGAGE
1530. MULTI-LAYER (3 LAYER BAGS)
1531. MULTI-LAYER (3 LAYER) FILM WITH LAMINATION & PRINTING
1532. OIL SEAL
1533. PET BOTTLE/CONTAINERS
1534. PET BOTTLES FROM PRE FORM
1535. PET BOTTLE & MINERAL WATER
1536. PET PRE-FORM FROM PET RESIN
1537. PET PRE-FORM CUM PET BOTTLES
1538. PET PRE-FORM PET BOTTLES CUM MINERAL WATERS
1539. POLY CARBONATE RESIN
1540. PTFE COMPONENTS
1541. PU/PVC SOLE FOR SPORT SHOE BY IMPORTED M/C.
1542. PVC BATTERY SEPARATOR
1543. P.V.C COMPOUNDS (FRESH)
1544. P.V.C COMPOUNDS (SCRAP)
1545. P.V.C ELECTRICAL INSULATING TAPE
1546. P.V.C. EXTRUSION PROFILES
1547. P.V.C FITTINGS
1548. P.V.C FLEXIBLE FUSIBLE POWDER HEAT FUSIBLE POWDER
1549. P.V.C GRANULES (FOR

INSULATION & SHEETS GRADES)
1550. P.V.C GRANULES FROM PVC SCRAPS (WITH POLLUTION CONTROL)
1551. P.V.C HOSES
1552. P.V.C LEATHER CLOTH
1553. P.V.C FLEXIBLE PIPES
1554. P.V.C PIPES AND FITTINGS
1555. POLYTHENE BAGS (PRINTED)
1556. PVC PLASTICS FILM SHEET SOFT/RIGID
1557. PVC RESIN AND COMPOUND
1558. PVC RULAR
1559. PVC STABLIZERS (SINGLE PACK SYSTEM)
1560. PVC WIRE AND CABLES
1561. PAPER BASED PHENOLIC SHEET FOR ELECTRICAL
1562. PHENOL FORMALDEHYDE RESIN
1563. PHENOLIC RESIN
1564. PLASTIC BEADS FROM PLASTIC SCRAPS
1565. PLASTIC BUTTONS
1566. PLASTIC CANS
1567. PLASTIC COLLAPSIBLE TUBE
1568. PLASTIC CORRUGATED SHEET & BOXES
1569. PLASTIC FILM AND SHEETS WITH PRINTING FLEXO & ROTO/LDPE/HDPE/PP/HM/PVC
1570. PLASTIC FILTER MASTER BATCH & OTHER MASTER BATCHES FOR VARIOUS PLASTICS
1571. PLASTIC JERRY CANS
1572. PLASTIC GRANULES OR POWDER FROM PLASTIC SCRAP
1573. PLASTIC INJECTION MOULDED T.V. CABINETS
1574. PLASTIC ITEMS MANUFAC TURE FROM POWDER MELAMINE
1575. PLASTIC GOODS
1576. PLASTIC PIPES & TARPAULINES
1577. PLASTIC SHEET FROM SCRAP
1578. PLASTIC PLANT (BLOW MOULDING & INJECTION MOULDING)
1579. PLASTIC PRODUCTS (GOLD, SILVER, NICKEL)
1580. PLASTIC TOYS
1581. POLYESTER BEADING
1582. POLYESTER FILM
1583. POLYTHENE BAGS & AUTOMATIC PRINTING
1584. POLYTHENE PRINTED BAGS
1585. POLYURETHANE FOAM AND ITS PRODUCTS
1586. PROPYLENE FILM (PRINTED) & BAG MANUFACTURING
1587. PLASTIC MATS
1588. RAINBOW COLOUR ON PVC FILM & SHEET
1589. RED MUD PVC PIPES AND FITTINGS
1590. RE-RUBBERISED OF SOLID TYPE
1591. RESIN COATED SAND REXINE
1592. REXINE CLOTH & ALLIED PRODUCTS
1593. RUBBER ADHESIVE
1594. RUBBER AUTO PARTS
1595. RUBBER BELTING
1596. RUBBER MOULDING UNIT INCLUDING LINING RUBBER SHEETING
1597. RUBBER RECLAIMING
1598. RUBBER ROLLERS FOR TEXTILE MILLS & PAPER INDUSTRIES
1599. RUBBER & PLASTIC SHEETS. MATS & FLAPS
1600. RUBBER SHEET AND ALLIED HOSPITAL RUBBER GOODS
1601. RUBBERIZED PVC GASKET
1602. RUBBERISED COIR
1603. RUBBER COMPOUND FOR AUTOMOBILES
1604. SAFETY BELTS
1605. SILVER AND GOLD PLATING ON PVC AND NYLON-6
1606. SILICONE RUBBER NIPPLES/ TEATS
1607. SPECTACLE FRAMES (PLASTIC)
1608. SPUNGE RUBBER
1609. SURGICAL EXAMINATION GLOVES
1610. SYNTHETIC PEARL COATING ON POLYSTYRENE BEADS
1611. SYNTHETIC RUBBER ADHESIVE
1612. TEFLON MANUFACTURING
1613. TEFLON TAPE
1614. TEFLON TAPES & CABLES
1615. THERMOCOLE SHEET AND MOULDED PRODUCTS EXPANDED POLYESTERENE EXTRUSION PROFILES
1616. THERMOFORMED PACKAGING (BLISTER PACKAGING & POUCH PACKAGING)
1617. THERMOPLASTIC POLYURETHANE
1618. THERMOFORMED CUPS, PLATES & GLASS WITH HIPS SHEET
1619. THERMOCOLE
1620. THERMOCOLE BASED DISPOSABLE GLASS, CUPS & PLATES
1621. TOOTH BRUSHES
1622. TOY BALLOON, DECORA TIVE & INDUSTRIAL BALLOONS
1623. TREAD RUBBER
1624. TYRE RETREADING (HOT)
1625. TYRE RETREADING BY COLD PROCESS
1626. TYRE TUBES & FLAPS
1627. TYRE & TUBES
1628. UNSATURATED POLYESTER FOR REXINE
1629. V-BELT AND FAN BELT
1630. VINYL ASBESTOS AND PVC WALL PAPER
1631. VITON (FLUORO ELASTOMER)

SOAP, COSMETICS & PERFUMS

1632. ACID SLURRY, SYNTHETIC DETERGENT POWDER
1632. ACID SLURRY
1633. AGARBATTI SYNTHETIC, PERFUMERY COMPOUND
1634. AFTER SHAVE LOTION
1635. ANTISEPTIC CREAM
1636. BETA IONONE
1637. BLEACHING POWDER
1638. BLUE DETERGENT POWDER
1639. CLEANING POWDER (VIMTYPE)
1640. COLD CREAM
1641. COLOURED FLAME & PERFUMED CANDLES (RED, BLUE, GREEN FLAME)
1642. COSMETIC INDUSTRY (MODERN)
1643. COSMETIC INDUSTRY (SHAMPOO, SPRAY PERFUME, TALCUM POWDER
1644. DETERGENT POWDER (ARIEL TYPE)
1645. DETERGENT POWDER (NIRMA TYPE) FULLY AUTOMATIC PLANT
1646. DETERGENT WASHING POWDER
1647. FISH OIL SOAP
1648. GLYCERINE TRANSPARENT SOAP
1649. HAIR REMOVING CREAM
1650. HERBAL COSMETICS
1651. HERBAL SHAMPO & CREAM
1652. HERBAL/AYURVEDIC COSMETICS
1653. INCENSE POWDER, INCENSE STICKS & INCENSE CAKE
1654. OPTICAL WHITENERS
1655. ROSE OIL EXTRACTION
1656. SHAMPOOS (COCONUT OIL BASED COLD PROCESS)
1657. SHAVING CREAM
1658. SINDUR (KUMKUM)
1659. SOAP COATED PAPER
1660. SPRAY DRIED DETERGENT POWDER
1661. STAIN REMOVER
1662. TALCUM POWDER (FACE & TOILET POWDER)
1663. TOILET AND HERBAL SOAP
1664. TOOTH PASTE & POWDER
1665. WASHING DETERGENT POWDER AND WASHING SOAP
1666. WASHING POWDER LIQUID DETERGENTS, LOTION & SHAMPOO

TEXTILE INDUSTRIES, READYMADE GARMENTS, COTTON, DYEING, BLEACHING, CLOTH, HOSIERY, POWER LOOM, HAND LOOM, WOOLLEN, SILK, SOCKS, SURGICAL COTTON & MANY OTHERS

1667. ANGORA RABBIT WOOL
1668. BUCKRAM
1669. CANVAS SHOES, JUNGLE BOOT, BOOT RUBBER KNEES & BOOT COMBAT
1670. CARPET FROM COTTON WASTE
1671. CERAMIC THREAD GUIDE
1672. COTTON BUDS/SWABS
1673. COTTON FROM WASTE YARN
1674. COTTON ROLLS
1675. COTTON SPIDERS FOR LOUD SPEAKERS
1676. DENIM CLOTH
1677. DENIM CLOTH (INTEGERATED UNIT WITH BLEACHING, DYEING AND PRINTING)
1678. DISPERSENT FOR TEXTILE
1679. DYEING & BLEACHING
1680. DYEING OF HANK YARN
1681. EMULSIFIER FOR WOOL BATCHING OIL
1682. EMBROIDERY ON FABRICS
1683. GARMENT DYEING, WASHING & STITCHING (JEANS, JACKETS, SKIRTS & SHIRTS)
1684. GOVES KNITTING
1685. GUNNY BAGS
1687. HDPE WOVEN SACKS
1688. HDPE TARPAULINS USING PLAIN LOOM WITH LAMINATION
1689. HDPE/PP WOVEN SACKS USING CIRCULAR LOOMS
1690. HOSIERY CLOTH (COTTON) PROCESSING (BLEACHING, DYEING, FINISHING OF CLOTH)
1691. HOSIERY INDUSTRY
1692. HOSIERY MERCERISING
1693. HOSIERY PRODUCTS LIKE VEST, BRIEF, T-SHIRTS & SOCKS
1694. JACQUARD FABRICS
1695. JUTE COIR, GRASS ROPE/ SUTLI MAKING
1696. JUTE FELT
1697. JUTE TWINES
1698. KNITTED FABRICS
1699. LAMINATED JUTE BAGS
1700. LAMINATION OF HDPE WOVEN CLOTH (JUTE,COTTON, PAPER)
1701. NYLON YARN CRIMPING, DOUBLING AND BLEACHING
1702. PIGMENT BINDER FOR TEXTILE PRINTING
1704. POLYESTER RESIN FOR WIRE ENAMEL
1705. POLYESTER RESIN
1706. POLYESTER YARN FROM WASTE POLYESTER ZIP FASTENERS
1707. POWER LOOM
1708. READYMADE GARMENTS & HOSIERY
1709. READYMADE GARMENTS MERCHANDISE
1710. READYMADE GARMENTS & COVERS
1711. READYMADE GARMENTS & EMBROIDERY OF GOWNS, SHIRTS, BLOUSES, T-SHIRTS ETC. (ONLY LADIES)
1712. READYMADE SALWAR SUIT
1713. RECOVERY OF NYLON FROM NYLON WASTE
1714. ROTARY PRINTING AND DYEING ON COTTON, SYNTHETIC TEXTILE
1715. SANITARY NAPKINS
1716. SCREEN PRINTING ON COTTON CLOTH
1717. SEWING THREAD REELS & BALLS MAKING INDUSTRIES
1718. SCREEN PRINTING ON COTTON, POLYESTER & ACRYLIC
1719. SHAWLS (WOOLLEN)
1720. SHOE LACES
1721. SILK FABRICS ON HANDLOOM
1722. SOCKS KNITTING
1723. SPINNING, DOUBLING DYEING MERCERISING & BLEACHING OF COTTON YARN
1724. SPINNING & CARDING OF WOOL INTO YARNS
1725. STARCH BOOK BINDING CLOTH
1726. SURAT JARI
1727. SURGICAL COTTON & BANDAGE
1728. SYNTHETIC TEXTILE INDUSTRY(SUITING, SHIRTING, SAREES) TERRY CLOTH
1729. T-SHIRTS
1730. TOWELS, BED SHEET COVERS
1731. TERRY TOWEL
1732. TERRY FABRICS WEAVING UNIT
1733. TEXTILE AUXILLIARIES & CHEMICALS
1734. TEXTILE BLEACHING, DYEING & FINISHING & PRINTING OF COTTON FABRICS
1735. TEXTILE (HOSIERY)
1736. TEXTILE MILL
1737. TEXTILE DYEING & PRINTING
1738. TEXTILE PRINTING (JOB WORK)
1739. TEXTILE PIGMENT PRINTING BINDER
1740. TOWEL (TERRY)
1741. VELVET CLOTH BY FLOCKING PROCESS
1742. VISCOSE STAPLE FIBRE
1743. WADDING OIL (100%) FOR WADDING OF COTTON HOSIERY CLOTH IN THE DYEING PROCESS
1744. WEAVING OF DASUTI CLOTH WITH PRINTING, DYEING, EMBROIDERY & FINISHING
1745. WASHING OF JEANS & OTHER GARMENTS
1746. WORSTED WOOLLEN YARN CLOTH
1747. ZARI GLITTER SALMA SITARA OF PLASTIC FILM

INFOTECH/IT, HOSPITALITY, HOSPITAL, COLLEGE, SCHOOL, MEDICAL, ENTERTAINMENT CLUB, WARE HOUSING & REAL ESTATE, PROJECTS

1748. AMUSEMENT PARK
1749. AMUSEMENT PARK CUM WATER PARK
1750. BANQUET HALL
1751. CALL CENTER (DOMESTIC)
1752. CALL CENTER (INTERNATIONAL)
1753. CHILDREN RECREATION CENTRE
1754. COLD STORAGE
1755. COMMUNITY HALL
1756. COMPUTER EDUCATION INSTITUTE
1757. COMPUTER SOFTWARE
1758. COLLEGE
1759. CYBER CAFE
1760. DENTAL CLINIC
1761. DENTAL COLLEGE
1762. DIAGONOSTIC CENTRE
1763. E-COMMERCE/BUSINESS
1764. E-SCHOOL (Rs. 5000/-)
1765. ENGINEERING COLLEGE
1766. ENTERTAINMENT CLUB
1767. ENTERTAINMENT CLUB, HOLIDAY RESORT, 4 STAR HOTEL, AMUSEMENT PARK CUM WATER PARK, MUSHROOM & ITS PRODUCTS, FISH FARMING, LAKE FOR BOATING, DEER PARK
1768. FASHION TECHNOLOGY INSTITUTE
1769. FAST FOOD PARLOUR
1770. FIVE STAR HOTEL
1771. FOOD PARLOUR
1772. FRANCHISE TRAINING PROGRAMME FOR IIT & ENGINEERING ENTRANCE EXAMS.
1773. GOLF COURSE
1774. HEALTH CLUB, BEAUTY PARLOUR
1775. HEALTH CLUB AND FITNESS CENTER
1776. HEALTH RESORTS
1777. HOLIDAY RESORTS
1778. HOLIDAY RESORT CUM

ENTERTAINMENT CLUB WITH 4 STAR HOTEL
1779. HOSPITALS
1780. ICE CREAM PARLOUR
1781. INTERNET SERVICE PROVIDER (I.S.P.)
1782. MEDICAL COLLEGE
1783. MEDICAL COLLEGE, HOSPITAL & RESEARCH INSTITUTE
1784. MEDICAL TRANSCRIPTION CENTRE
1785. MENTAL RETARDATION HOSPITAL & CEREBRAL PALSY
1786. MOTEL/SMALL HOTEL
1787. MULTISTOREY COMMERCIAL COMPLEX
1788. MULTISTOREY RESIDENTIAL COMPLEX
1789. NURSERY SCHOOL
1790. NATURE CARE CENTRE
1791. NURSING HOME
1792. ONLINE SHOPPING MALL (RS. 5000/- REPORT)
1793. PORTAL
1794. REHABILITATION CENTRE FOR AGED & NEEDY PERSONS
1795. RESIDENTIAL CUM COMMERCIAL COMPLEX
1796. RESTAURANT
1797. RESTAURANT WITH PUB
1798. SCHOOL (PRIMARY)
1799. SCHOOL (HIGHER SECONDARY)
1800. THREE STAR HOTEL
1801. TOURIST CLUB
1802. TRAINING INSTITUTE FOR MEDICAL TRANSCRIPTION
1803. VIDEO FILM STUDIO
1804. WARE HOUSE
1805. WEBSITE DESIGN & E-MAIL REGISTERING

AGRO BASED INDUSTRIES

1806. COAL BRIQUETTES FROM AGROWASTE
1807. FURFURALFROM RICEHULL
1808. MUSHROOM CULTIVATION & PROCESSING (BUTTON)
1809. MUSHROOM GROWING & PROCESSING WITH AIR CONDITIONING
1810. MUSHROOM CULTIVATION & PROCESSING UNIT DEHYDRATION & PACKAGING OF OYSTER & PADDY STRAW MUSHROOMS
1811. ORGANIC MANURE
1812. PAPAYA CULTIVATION
1813. PAPAYA & TOMATO CULTIVATION
1814. PROCESSING & UTILISATION OF COCONUT
1815. PROCESSING OF SHEEP HAIR TO PRODUCE WOOL

BAKERY, CONFECTIONERY & FOOD PRODUCTS

1816. AGROLACTOR SOYA MILK
1817. APPLE FRUIT JUICE WITH CANNING BOTTLING
1818. AYURVEDIC SHARBAT
1819. BAKERY UNIT (PASTRIES, BREAD, BUNS, CAKE, TOFFEE ETC.)
1820. BAKING POWDER
1821. BANANA & ITS BY PRODUCTS
1822. BANANA POWDER
1823. BANANA WAFERS
1824. BANANA CULTIVATION
1825. BEER INDUSTRY
1826. DEHULLING OF JAUN FOR BEER
1827. BEER & WINE
1828. BEER, ALCOHOL, IMFL
1829. BESEN PLANT
1830. BISCUIT PLANT
1831. BREAD & BISCUIT PLANT
1832. BOTTLING PLANT COUNTRY LIQUOR FROM RECTIFIED SPIRIT
1833. BRANDY
1834. BREAD RUSKS
1835. CANNED FRUITS & VEGETABLES
1836. CANNING & PRESERVATION OF MEAT
1837. CANNING & PRESERVATION OF VEGETABLES
1838. CANNING OF MANGO PULP & MANGO SLICES
1839. CARBONATED BEVERAGS
1840. CASHEW FENI
1841. CASHEW NUT (DRIED & FRIED)
1842. CATTLE BREEDING
1843. CATTLE BREEDING & DAIRY FARM TO PRODUCE MILK
1844. CATTLE FEED FROM TAPIOCA
1845. CHEWING GINGER & AMLOKI
1846. CHEWING GUM
1847. CHILLI SAUCE
1848. CHILLI POWDER
1849. CHOCOLATE
1850. CIDER PLANT
1851. COCOA POWDER
1852. COCOA BUTTER & COCOA POWDER
1853. COCONUT SHELL POWDER
1854. COCONUT WATER
1855. COCONUT SWEET (WATERY)
1856. COCONUT MILK POWDER (DEHYDRATED)
1857. COCONUT PRODUCTS & BY PRODUCTS (INTEGRATED PLANT)
1858. COLD DRINK
1859. CURRY POWDER
1860. DAIRY FOR MILK PROCESSING (GHEE, BUTTER & PANEER)
1861. DAIRY PRODUCTS
1862. DAIRY PRODUCTS MILK PACKAGING IN POUCH (GHEE, BUTTER, ETC.
1863. DAIRY FARM TO PRDUCE MILK WITH PACKAGING (COW)
1864. DAIRY FARM TO PRDUCE MILK WITH PACKAGING (BUFALLOE)
1865. DAIRY FARM & MILK PRODUCTS
1866. DAL MOTH, CHANACHUR & BHUJIYA
1867. DEHYDRATION OF FRUITS & VEGETABLE
1868. DESICCATED COCONUT POWDER FROM COCONUTS
1869. DEHYDRATION & CANNING OF FRUITS & VEGETABLES
1870. DRY FRUIT ROASTING & PACKAGING
1871. DRYING OF RED CHILLIES, HALDI, DHANIYA, PEAS & GROUND NUT
1872. EGG POWDER
1873. FISH CANNING IN TIN & POUCHES
1874. FISH DEHYRATION (DRYING OF FISH)
1875. FISH MEAL
1876. FISH PROCESSING (BEAST FREEZING PROCESSES)
1877. FLAVOURS FOR FOOD INDUSTRIES
1878. FLOUR MILL (ROLLER)
1879. FROZEN MEAT
1880. FOOD DEHYDRATION (FRUITS & VEGETABLES)
1881. FRIED & ROASTED GROUND NUT, GRAMS, PEAR ETC.
1882. FRUIT JUICE MAKING & PACKAGING IN PLASTIC CONTAINER
1883. FRUIT JUICE IN TETRA PACK (DRINKS)
1884. FRUIT JUICE, SQUASHES, SAUCE & KETCHUP, JAM, JELLY, VINEGAR ETC.
1885. GARLIC FLAKES
1886. GARLIC POWDER
1887. GHEE & BUTTER
1888. GINGER (PULVERISED)
1889. GINGER GLAZING & PRESERVATION
1890. GINGER STORAGE
1891. GINGER PROCESSING
1892. GINGER OIL & GINGER DUST
1893. GINGER POWDER (DRY) & OLEORESIN
1894. GRAPE DEHYDRATION
1895. GRAPE CULTIVATION
1896. GRAPE JUICE
1897. HONEY PROCESSING & PACKAGING
1898. ICE CREAM & ICE CANDY
1899. ICE CUBE
1900. INVERT SUGAR
1901. IDLI MIX, DOSA MIX SAMBHAR MIX, VADA MIX, GULAB JAMUN MIX
1902. INSTANT COFFEE & INSTANT TEA

1903. INSTANT NOODLES
1904. INSTANT SOUPS
1905. IODIZED SALT FROM CRUDE SALT
1906. JAM CHUTNEY PICKLES & SQUASHES
1907. KATHA MANUFACTURING
1908. LECITHIN (SOYA BASED)
1909. LEMON & ITS PRODUCTS
1910. MACARONI MANUFACTURING
1911. MACARONI, SPAGHETTI, VERMICELLI & NOODLES
1912. MAIZE & ITS BY PRODUCTS MALTING PLANT
1913. MANGO PAPPAD (AAM PAPPAD)
1914. MANGO POWDER RIPE
1915. MANGO POWDER
1916. MANGO PROCESSING & CANNING (MANGO PULP)
1917. MEAT PROCESSING (CHICKEN MUTTON)
1918. MEAT PROCESSING (BUFFALO)
1919. MENTHOL BOLD FROM MENTHOL FLAKES
1020. MILK POWDER
1921. MILK POWDER & GHEE
1922. MILK POWDER, GHEE & SPICES
1923. MILK PRESERVATION & MARKETING TO WHOLE SELLERS
1924. MILK PRESERVATION & MARKETING TO WHOLE SELLERS (IN POUCHES)
1925. MILK TOFFEE MANUFACTURES
1926. MINERAL WATER
1927. MINERAL WATER IN POUCHES
1928. MINI FLOUR MILL ATTA MAIDA, SUJI & WHEAT BRAN
1929. MITHAI/HALWAI (SWEET & NAMKEEN)
1930. MUTTON PROCESSING
1931. PAN MASALA (MEETHA, SADA, ZARDA) MAKING & PACKING
1932. PAN MASALA AND POUCH MAKING
1933. PANEER (CHEESE)
1934. PAPAD & BARIYAN
1935. PAPAD PLANT
1936. PEPSICOLA IN POLYTUBES
1937. PETHA PACKAGING
1938. PICKLES
1939. PIGGERY/MEAT/CHICKEN PROCESSING
1940. PINE APPLE JUICE CANNING
1941. POTATO & ONION POWDER
1942. POTATO & ONION FLAKES
1943. POTATO CHIPS
1944. POTATO GRANULES
1945. POUCH FILLING FOR SAUNF SUPARI ILAICHI ETC.
1946. PRESERVATION OF RAWS MANGO JUICE
1947. PROCESSED CHEESE & MARINE PDTS.
1948. PULP FROM TARMARIND
1949. READYMATE PROCESSED FOOD
1950. RICE & CORN FLAKES
1951. RICE BASMATI (TRADING)
1952. RICE POLISHING & PACKAGING IN POUCH
1953. ROASTED/SALTED/MASALA/ CASHEW NUTS ALMONDS & PEA NUT
1954. ROLLER FLOUR MILL

INFOTECH/IT PROJECTS

1955. MEDICAL TRANSCRIPTION
1956. E-COMMERCE
1957. CYBERCAFE
1958. INTERNET SERVICE PROVIDER (ISP)
1959. COMPUTER EDUCATION CENTRE
1960. PORTAL (WEBSITE DESIGN)
1961. CALL CENTRE

TERMS AND CONDITIONS

FOR INDIA

1. Please ask for Quotations of Each ***Market Survey Cum Detailed Techno Economic Feasibility Report.*** Payable in advance through Draft/M.O./Cash in favour of 'ENGINEERS INDIA RESEARCH INSTITUTE', Delhi. Delivery by Regd.post within 2 Days. (Postage Free)

2. Ask for the Hi-Tech Projects Monthly magazine. Each Magazine covers many Project Profiles for selection of Industry.

FOR OVERSEAS

1. Please ask for Quotations in US $ of Each ***Market Survey Cum Detailed Techno Economic Feasibility Report.*** Payable in advance through Draft/M.O./Cash in favour of 'ENGINEERS INDIA RESEARCH INSTITUTE', Delhi. (Payable in India) Delivery by Regd.post within 4 Days.

2. Ask for the Hi-Tech Projects Monthly magazine. Each Magazine covers many Project Profiles for selection of Industry.

ENGINEERS INDIA RESEARCH INSTITUTE

4449, Nai Sarak (D), Main Road, Delhi - 110 006 (India)
Ph:. 91-11-23918117, 23916431, 23840361, 31082370
Fax: 91-11-23916431 E-Mail : eirisidi@bol.net.in
Website:www.startindustry.com
Also at : 4/27, Roop Nagar, Near Roop Nagar No. 1 School, Delhi - 110 007 (India) Ph:. 23840361